So you want to write a paper?

A HANDBOOK FOR WRITING ACADEMIC PAPERS & JOURNAL ARTICLES IN TODAY'S UNIVERSITY ENVIRONMENT

Kendall Hunt
publishing company

Christopher W. Smithmyer
Penn State University • University of South Florida—St. Petersburg

Kendall Hunt
publishing company

www.kendallhunt.com
Send all inquiries to:
4050 Westmark Drive
Dubuque, IA 52004-1840

contents

These are basic guidelines that can help you when you move on to later steps of writing a paper. This part of the process is so important that it is included in the introduction. Your reader is your purpose for writing; do not alienate your reader before you even start your paper.

Graduate students have a completely different way to approach their readership. They still have an initial readership of one; however, every graduate paper should be written in a way that it can be applied to your thesis, your dissertation, or can be published on its own (with a little work after the class). Whereas undergraduate papers will likely sit in a chest or a drawer for the rest of your life, graduate papers should be a demonstration of your talent to your field. When you are looking for a job, employers will look to see if you have published anything, especially in academia. Your publications will follow you for the rest of your life, so even a paper that you write in a elective class can come back to haunt you if you do not take it seriously. Therefore, when writing a paper as a graduate student, your initial readership is one person (your professor) but if you pass the class you should extend that readership to your thesis or dissertation committee, or a journal editor and the readership of that journal at large.

As this book is a handbook, some of you may be using this in your professional careers to write for a trade book or an academic journal. You have a broader readership. Where undergraduates and to a lesser extent graduate students should not present strong new arguments in their writing, if you are publishing in a journal or a trade book, then there is no point in publishing it if you are not presenting a new argument or new material. Above all, you need to write professionally and keep it technical enough that it is relevant in your field, but keep it interesting enough that people actually read it. This can be a narrow path to walk, but the more your practice the better you will be at it. Professionals and academics are at the forefront of developing new ideas (despite what the media tells us); do not shy away from controversial topics, but also do not put your career in jeopardy by taking on a topic that will get you fired.

People writing grants also need to write strong papers. Your goal as a grant writer is to convince a small group of people that you deserve money more than other people doing research in the same area as you. This means that you have to present your case more effectively as to why you deserve the funds more than others. You also have to make sure that you do not come across as pompous or unlikable. This means that you should know your readers. If you know who is on the committee, read any of the work they have done. People are naturally inclined to be supportive of people who share their passions. If you find that your project disagrees with one of the committee members, gloss over that section as much as possible while maintaining the integrity of the proposal. When writing a grant, be honest and do not make the committee mad.

Those of you who want to write for a paper rather than write a paper can still use this book to develop your skills. When writing for a newspaper or a magazine, your readership is very broad (unless it is a very narrow readership magazine). In this case you need to remember to keep your topic simple enough for the "everyman" to understand. While you can have some elements that a person may have to look up, if readers find themselves looking away from your article to Google every few sentences, you will lose their attention. This means that you should use short, concise sentences that keep the readers' attention. Further, when writing for a mass spectrum publication like a magazine or a newspaper, you will offend some people. Nothing is all lollypops and puppy dogs, as long as 51% of the people respect (not necessarily like) your writing, then you are doing a good job.

The last main type of writing that people find themselves doing is personal journals. In this case the readership is you, perhaps the hardest critic a person can have. When you write a personal journal, you do not have to write it to impress anyone. One page can be about your research of the day, the next can be about your love life or your pet. A personal journal is for you to keep a record of your thoughts so that you can use them in the future. Do not give in to convention and force yourself to write someone else's journal; write for yourself and write the best journal you can write.

Your readership gives you a very small amount of time to catch their attention. If your paper catches the attention of the readership, whether it be a professor, an editor, an employer, a committee, or yourself, then you have a better chance of succeeding in your paper. In the next section, we look at why you are writing your paper. Now that we know who you are writing to, the next part of the process is to determine why you are writing it.

WHY ARE YOU WRITING A PAPER?

No matter how much you like writing, it is still work. This means that you will always be writing a paper for a reason. No one writes simply to write, they are writing to practice, to achieve something, to remember something, or to produce something. Poets convert their dreams to pleasant words drifting in a pattern that inspires others to dream; professors write to improve the knowledge of future generations; professionals write to keep their jobs or to get their raise; students write to pass the class; and some people write journals so they do not forget parts of their life stories. Why you are writing a paper is important to what method you use in writing. Few professional trade books will accept papers written in poetic pentameter, and few professors want a paper that looks like your dream journal. Likewise, those who are looking for poetry or sweet prose do not want to read technical diagnostics. While writing, always keep in mind the reason you are writing.

The purpose of most writing styles is simple and this book will address four key areas that are common for people to write in. These areas are:

1. Courses;
2. Research;
3. Business/legal reports; and
4. Newspaper or magazine articles.

There are stylistic differences in how you begin your process for writing in each of these venues, but all of them start with who you are writing for and why you are writing. If you keep these questions at the forefront of your mind, you can succeed in writing any type of paper.

Students who are writing a paper have the most straightforward goal—they are writing to get the grade. The course is for learning, the term paper is to get the best grade possible. If you keep this at the front of your mind, then you have a better chance of winning the rat race that is college. When you start to write your paper, follow the guidelines that a professor has set forth for you. If you do not understand the guidelines, then do not be afraid to ask your teacher. Teachers are there to ensure that you have the best chance of learning the material set out in the class. Take advantage of their knowledge. If you are writing a paper for college, then you should always remember that the grade is the primary purpose for that paper, and anything else is ancillary.

Those who are writing research papers for journals or edited volumes have a different set of purposes when they write. Those engaged in this type of writing are looking to educate and convince their readers of a specific set of facts. Every paragraph, every sentence, even every word should be dedicated to this purpose. When researching, you know how boring a poorly writing meandering article is to read. Save your readership the suffering of a poorly written article and keep it focused on educating and convincing your readers of your point. You will find that a laser-focused article, interlaced with anecdotes, will keep the attention of a reader much more effectively than an article that tries to do everything at once, but accomplishes nothing.

Finally, if you are writing a newspaper or magazine article, you need to ask yourself why. This dying format is so complex because there are a variety of purposes for submitting an article to a paper. Are you writing to inform? Perhaps you are writing to convince someone of something? Maybe you are writing to champion a cause or defend a political position. With the current state of the nation's print media, you may even be writing to construct a reality other than the truth for the historic record. Before you write your article for a local paper (or a national paper), ask yourself why you are writing this article. If you cannot find a reason, then you will find it harder as you write to have an anchor for your piece, something that keeps you from drifting off topic.

Why we write is the reason that we leave for our personal journey through writing a paper. Not knowing why we are writing is like going on a trip, but not knowing where. While this can be an interesting exercise in broadening the mind (i.e., a reason), it is not something that you want to do in a professional or academic paper. Good professional writing is laser focused and does not leave the topic often. This means that wherever you write, you should have a note card, a post-it note, or some other reminder of what your purpose for writing is. This will keep you focused and make you a better writer.

HOW THIS BOOK SHOULD BE USED

This book is designed to be a handbook—to that end, the table of contents is as comprehensive as possible. If this is your first paper, then you should read most of the book to learn the tricks of the trade and the effective ways to get your message across. If you have written before, then you can simply look to the section that deals with the type of paper you are writing and use that information to reinforce the knowledge you already have. If you are writing a new type of paper for the first time, then you can read though the basics again and follow the process in this book. This book should be a tool for you, it should not be the be all and end all of your writing style. Like any good tool, it should be there when you need it but not be in the way when you do not.

Reading the book straight through once is always a good idea. Reading through the book allows you to familiarize yourself with the format so that when you are using the handbook to write a paper you know where the parts of the book are. At this point you may find it useful to tab the pages that are most relevant to you. This will allow you faster access to them when you are working on papers. That being said, books about writing are some of the hardest books to keep interesting, and oftentimes they are repetitive. Therefore, I have tried to note where the repetitive sections of the chapters are so you can skim over them. The difficulty in covering so many different methodologies in a concise package like this is the quality to quantity ratio. The goal is to maintain all of the essential elements of the methodologies we discuss while keeping the book short enough that it can be a manageable tool on your bookshelf.

When returning to use the book, after your initial read through, you can fully use the book as the tool that it is intended to be. Walk yourself through the checklists, making sure that you follow a workable flow of operations. A common flow of operations, one that can be easily followed, makes your audit trail that much easier to follow by anyone who seeks to replicate and validate your research. While patterns may seem boring, following the same pattern in your writing process will allow you to develop your skill set and become more comfortable as a writer.

This book can also be a quick reference guide for people who have been writing for years. Sometimes you become so used to your pattern of writing that some parts slip through the cracks. Following the checklists in this book can help you find elements that you missed, such as triangulation in a qualitative meta-synthesis paper. Using this book as a quick reference can also inspire you to try new methods when you hit a block, either writer's block or a theoretical block. This can help you push through a problem area and move your paper to the next level. Further, you may concentrate on case studies but find that the data you have lends itself more to a phenomenology or even a grounded theory. When you step out of your comfort zone it is always comforting to have a book handy that can walk you through the steps of your new endeavor. To that end, I hope that this book is helpful to you in all your writing projects.

THE FORMAT OF THIS BOOK

In any good paper, or book for that matter, you begin by telling people what you are going to tell them. This is your introduction. Then you tell them what you are telling them, in detail. This is the body of your book. Finally, you tell people what you have told them, by way of a summary. This is the conclusion of your book. Therefore, in this section we are going to look at the overall outline of the book and discuss what each part of the book is designed to do and how you can use each part. Any time that you are having trouble deciding which part of the book will help you the most in your project, simply return to this section and read through it again and it should direct you on your path again.

This book is broken down into seven parts (not including this introduction and the conclusion). Each part is designed to help you with a specific element of a specific writing process. The books begins with a part on the basics of writing, the things that you need to think about before you even choose the topic of the paper you are writing. This is the primordial soup of paper writing, where your paper can go in an infinite set of directions. In this section, we try to help you select the best direction out of that soup so your paper is most useful for your class/research/career. Part II begins the methodological section of this book (of which there are three arch-methodologies). Part II focuses on quantitative research or for most of us statistical research. This is the first set of methodologies that we look at for two reasons. First it is the most common methodology taught in colleges in the United States today.[5] Second, quantitative research tends to scare beginning writers, so we want to take away some of the mystique that surrounds one of the simplest maths out there. Part III focuses on the qualitative methodologies, specifically ethnography, case studies, phenomenology, and qualitative meta-synthesis. These are the core qualitative methodologies that most people will face in their academic or professional careers. Part IV ends the main section of methodological systems with theoretical research papers. This is often the most mysterious of the research methodologies, because undergraduate and even graduate students are not expected to develop new theory. We want to challenge that position as any time a paper has a hypothesis (which all good academic and professional papers have), there is an element of theory. Without the theoretical element of education, students are regulated to writing sixth-grade social studies/history papers that are simply regurgitations of other people's work.

Moving on from the methodology section, Part V is a catch-all section for papers that are not "research" papers. Research is in "air-quotes" because these methodologies still require significant research, but they will not be exposed to a large audience. In Part V we look at the ways to write a good term paper, a et of white pages, general business reports, legal briefs (not court briefs), gists, and hybrid methodological papers. Part VI dedicates itself to the finer points of data collection. While each chapter on specific methodologies will discuss the most common data collection methods for that methodology, Part VI will discuss the different methods of data collection in their own regards. For instance, while discourse analysis is not a common way to create a statistical dataset, the quantitative methodologies do not exclude this method of data collection by any means. Even though discourse analysis is thought to be qualitative/theoretical in nature, it can be used (quite effectively) for quantitative research. In Part VII we look at the style of your paper. Style is an important issue when you are sending a paper somewhere to be published/graded/examined.

CONCLUSION

Writing can become one of your most effective tools; whether it is for your career, your academic life, or even your personal life, writing creates a record of what you thought and the mark you made on the world during your life. People will judge you not only by the content of your work, but also by the format, the grammar, and the "feel." Writing, perhaps more than any other medium, can provide a flowing analysis of "who" you really are. The journey that we take each time we undertake

---

5. Nearly every major has some kind of college math requirement or statistics requirement. This goes doubly for graduate schools. Often students are left to fend for themselves when it comes to qualitative research or theoretical research.

writing a new paper is not so much a journey of learning what is outside in the world; rather, it is a journey looking at who we are inside as a researcher, businessperson, student, scholar, and even as a person.

CHECKLIST

These are the elements of writing a paper covered in the introduction:

- Ask yourself who is going to read this paper.
  - Your paper should cater to your reader.
  - Your paper should be within your reader's reading level.
  - Your paper should be in a style that your reader can understand.
  - The formality of the language will be dictated by your reader.
  - The acceptability of certain topics will be dictated by your reader.
- Ask yourself why you are writing this paper.
  - Your reason for writing can dictate your goal.
  - If you are writing for a grade, write for the grade.
  - If you are writing for research, make it the best research possible.
  - If you are writing for a promotion, make yourself look as good as actual.
  - If you are writing to convince, write the best argument possible.
  - If you are writing to yourself, be honest.
- This book should be used to:
  - Keep you focused, as tangents weaken writing;
  - Keep you within your methodology;
  - Help you keep an audit trail; and
  - Help you build a skill set that can be used for the rest of your life.

Part 1
THE BASICS OF ACADEMIC/ PROFESSIONAL WRITING

chapter 1
Introduction to Part I

Part I of this book focuses on the basics of building a good paper. Now by basics, we are not going to engage in a rapid fourth-grade English class to bring you up to speed. We are entering into this believing that you have acquired the basic grammatical skills to build a good paper. If you are worried about your skill set in this area, then you should pick up a copy of William A. Sabin's *Gregg Reference Manual*.[1] These types of grammatical manuals focus in on the minutia of comma usage, sentence structure, and a variety of other elements that some people are nervous about. Further, the style manual for whatever discipline you are in will also have instructions on how to present a good paper within that style. We will look at this area in sections 2 through 5 of Chapter 4.

The basics of academic/professional writing are akin to the foundation of your paper. As you read through the basics section, you are finding a logical site to build your paper, clearing the underbrush, establishing ownership of the idea, ensuring that others do not own the idea, and setting the methodological foundation that you will be using for the paper. If you do not do this, it is like you are building the proverbial "house on sand" and you will run the risk of all your hard work being for naught if someone already owns the idea, you do not lay claim to it, you make your paper too cluttered, or you do not select a logical topic.[2] Although walking through the basics will seem tedious for every paper you write, following these steps will help ensure that your papers are of appropriate academic/professional quality for your chosen endeavor(s).

---

1. William A. Sabin. (2005). *The Gregg Reference Manual* (10th ed.). New York: McGraw-Hill Irwin.
2. Matthew 7:24-27.

Going through the basics also means that you focus on the foundation of your paper(s) early and often. Oftentimes people enter into the paper writing process and do not think about their endgame. They want to get the paper written, then turn it in or publish it and be done with it. At each step of writing a paper you should think about how it can help your career. A term paper can be presented to a local Rotary or Kiwanis club to help increase your exposure to the community. A graduate paper can be presented at a conference or modified to be published in a journal. Professional papers can be presented as continuing education for a local company or even a large firm. Small papers can submit articles to larger newspapers and the Associated Press (AP). Every paper has the potential to be something special, but only if you focus on making sure that it is the best paper it can be. Always take the time to think about how this paper can be of use to you after the primary use is done. This will help you focus your foundation to meet both your long- and short-term needs.

Any writer, whether just starting or one who has written for 80 years, should always keep in mind the old adage "a penny of prevention is worth a pound of the cure."[3] Preparation helps prevent problems in the future. If you cite while you write, then you will not have to go back and remember where you found everything. If you proofread chapter by chapter, or section by section, then you will not have the monumental task of doing the first read-through after you have completed the paper. Each step of preparation that you take during the writing process will increase your ability to get the paper to market faster. This is why the basics are important, not because they are rules that every writer has to follow, but because they are tools that every writer can use to make the job easier. If you were going to pound in a nail, wouldn't you use a tool to do it? Then why when you have another simple task that has tools, like writing, would you resist using them that make your life easier? Do you want writing to be painless?

WHAT ARE THE BASICS?

The basics are a set of guidelines that help writers build a strong foundation for any paper that they are going to write. For the purpose of this book, we are going to look at eight foundational issues that every writer should know. These issues are concept, paper type, hypothesis/theory, format, approach, epoche, value to reader, and the methodological discipline that works for you. Although each of these is covered in depth in its own chapter, this section will give you an overview of each foundational issue so you can select the ones that you are going to use and skip over the ones that do not apply to you. Some are useful for everyone; some are less useful for certain writers. It is your job as a writer to determine which of these foundational issues are relevant to your paper.

---

3. Benjamin Franklin.

The first foundational issue that you should look at is the concept. Some people write whole pre-papers looking at concepts and some white papers are designed to be concept papers.[4] Within the writing style advocated by this book, that approach may be a little excessive; however, you still need to look at what type of concept you will approach in your paper. To use an analogy, the concept is the forest; it is the broadest possible vision of the topic that you are going to discuss in your paper. Where the concept is the forest, you are going to be writing about a single branch on a single tree. Before you start looking for this branch, you have to find the forest. Many people gloss over this step by saying, for example, "I am going to write a paper about racism in America…" or "I am going to write about history." Both of these are topics, but they are topics for a lifetime of study, not for a single paper. These are concepts that you are looking at, the genus of your paper. Through our process we will narrow down this massive concept into a workable paper topic that will help you achieve your goals.

Before you engage in writing, you should also look at what type of paper you are going to write. If we are writing in the concept area of sociology, then we need to know what kinds of papers are acceptable for sociological research. The same can be said for legal research; if we are writing in the concept area of a legal paper, then we should not chose ethnography as our methodology because the research elements in ethnography would not be useful in a court of law.[5] While we do not pick the specific methodology, or even the genre of methodology at this point, we do exclude those methodologies that are not acceptable for our current paper. Once we have established what research methods we cannot use, it is time to look at a topic. Selecting a topic is the process of looking at your concept, breaking it down into parts (the trees), breaking those parts down into elements (branches), breaking those elements down into ideas (twigs), and breaking those ideas down into topics (leaves). Each step of this process narrows your concept into more and more manageable pieces. While a book can be written at the branch or even the tree level, a paper should be as focused as possible to ensure that it covers the topic completely.

Once we have a topic, we can then look to develop a hypothesis or a theory. The hypothesis or theory is the framework of the question that the paper asks. If a paper does not ask a question, then what is it the answer to? A hypothesis is a statement of fact that you believe to be true, which you will try to prove or disprove through your research methodology. A theory is a set of statements (a group of hypotheses) that you try to prove or disprove both individually and as a group. Since nothing can be proven in the modern academic paradigm as true, researchers should attempt to prove the opposite of the hypothesis false; thus we must find the negative hypothesis (null hypothesis). With theories you create a null hypothesis for all of the hypotheses in the theory. Ensuring

---

4. In some disciplines these are called annotated bibliographies.
5. Some would argue that ethnographic research would make the court system more personable to people; however, this argument is beyond the scope of this paper and we will simply look at the majority argument.

that your hypothesis is strong and not a generalization will make your paper much easier to defend, whether in a class presentation or in a conference.

Format can be just as important to writing your paper as the paper type. Individual journals require a specific format for their articles, bosses require specific formats for reports, the courts and partners require specific formats for briefs, and professors require specific formats for papers. Selecting your format should not be something that you have to do on your own; most of the time your format will be selected for you. This book looks at four of the most popular formats in Chapter 5, and an additional method in Chapter 34, which specifically deals with legal writing. The four main formats we will look at are:

1. American Psychological Association style;
2. Chicago Manual of Style;
3. Modern Language Association style; and
4. American Bar Association/Yale Blue Book.

The format in Chapter 34 is actually a series of different styles that can be used in writing legal briefs. In all likelihood, you will only have to learn to write in one of these styles; however, knowing that other styles exist can enable you to write in a variety of journals.

In Chapter 6 we look at the approach that you will take toward writing your paper. Although the "write everything that comes to mind" approach that worked in high school can be effective at getting C papers and passing the course, if you are writing a professional or academic paper using that methodology then you will likely find it being returned as a failure, it not being graded, or with a pink slip. As your writing style evolves, you will find that you work best within a given approach. Three that we will cover in this book are:

1. Narrow → Broad;
2. Broad → Narrow; and
3. Chronological.

Each of these approaches has its benefits and drawbacks for the writer and for the reader. There is also no rule that once you choose one of these for a paper or project you are locked in for life.[6] Different writing methodologies lend themselves better to different approaches; therefore, you should take the time to choose your approach each time. This chapter will also look at how to write an effective outline.

---

6. If you are reading this as a college student (especially one of my students) take the time to write a paper in each of these approaches during your college career. This will help you develop your style and let you find out what you like.

Chapter 7 is the reprise to looking at readership. Now that you have chosen your concept, your paper type, your topic, and your approach, you may want to look at your readership again. If this is going to be a massive project, maybe you should talk to your boss or professor to see if you are able to write the paper with the intent of getting it published. If it is narrowly defined, maybe you should look at getting a grant for a broader study. While you should reexamine your readership each time you write a paper, you will not need to change each time you write unless your readership changes; most of the time the original readership will be the readership you keep for the entire project.

The next section looks at the concept of epoche. Epoche is a process of self-analysis to eliminate the bias from your writing. The bias that you cannot eliminate, you let your readers know about. This will make readers more comfortable and let them know that you are not trying to bamboozle them. Epoche can be a valuable process when just learning to write as it helps you define yourself. If you are in college, then your paradigm is changing. Likely different professors are going to try to bring you into their paradigm. If you are comfortable with that, feel free to go with it. However, if you want to truly make the best of your college tenure, then you should take the time to look at different paradigms and see what fits the best with your personal views and history. Epoche is a great way to do this as it makes you look at your self in detail.[7]

Chapter 9 is a gatekeeper chapter where we look at the value your paper holds for your reader. If you find that your paper will not be something that is valuable to you or your reader, then why are you writing it? Chapter 9 should be your reality check—the chapter that makes you take a look at whether or not your paper really needs to be written. This can also be the chapter of good sense. Even though writing a paper defending something that you believe in may make you feel better, if it is something that will get you ostracized, or even something that will lead to you failing a class, is the paper really worth writing? You should always take the time to anticipate the effect of your paper. This book is written to help you build a career, not to enable you to destroy it.

Finally, the last foundational element is what methodological set you should use to develop your paper. This is where you decide whether you should use a quantitative, qualitative, or theoretical approach to your research. This is an important step as it dictates where you can publish your paper (if it is being published), what data collection techniques you can use, how long it is going to take, and even what may cause you to reexamine your style and approach. Chapter 10 is the gateway to the second section of this book, the section that looks at individual methodological disciplines.

---

7. Epoche is also good for experienced writers, as sometimes we find our paradigms changing as we learn new things. Stagnation can be as damaging in a career as it can be in writing; therefore, you should always take the time to do epoche before you write a paper—even if you do not use it in the paper.

HOW LONG SHOULD I SPEND ON THE BASICS?

The basics are the most boring part of any paper. Beyond the exploration of the concept, topic, and epoche, most of it is simply doing the work to make sure that your paper is done properly. Like editing, most people wish that they could skip this step in paper writing. I highly recommend against it. Each paper you write you should go through the basics, and each time you do you will internalize the process more and more so that it becomes second nature to you. If you will permit me a brief story, I was always told that outlines were an important part of paper writing, but as a teen who "knew everything," I always skipped that step. Later in college, I just came to the conclusion that I could not write, and turned in papers that were just good enough to get me through my writing classes. It was not until I earned my first law degree that I found a professor who took the time to teach me to write. He taught me the reason why I should do an outline rather than just telling me that I needed to do an outline. Since then I have written dozens of articles and book reviews, two published books, two books that are being published, two books that are in the queue to be published, and of course this book on writing. Following the steps will make life much easier for you, which is why I have attempted to explain the necessity—not just the methodology—of each chapter in this book.

The question remains, however, of how long you should spend on the basics of each paper. The answer is simply, long enough. You should make sure that you do not blow through the steps of the basic writing process so quickly that you do not allow them to serve their purpose. What good is a small amount of saved time if you have to go back and rewrite the paper because the format is wrong or because your topic is too broad? Take your time in setting the foundation for your paper. Very little of what you do in the foundational steps of your paper will be wasted time. Even if you do not see it, your preparation will pay off as you get deeper into the writing process.

On the other hand, this does not mean that you should exceed your deadline because you are spending time on foundational issues. You need to go through the basic steps quickly. In college you will be given time to learn these steps; however, if you wait until you are in the workforce to learn how to write this way, then you may be pinched for time. The foundational steps should take about 10% of your total time (it varies by paper type) when you are a beginning writer and, as you become more apt at writing, it should take less and less time. For instance, breaking down the concept five times may seem overwhelming when you first begin doing it, but as you proceed through the process more and more times, you see that the branches that you ignore in the process become possible future paper topics. (This also lessens the time spent on foundation.) Keep notes on your process, you never know when ideas that you reject will become the cornerstone of a new paper or dissertation.

CHECKLIST

Each chapter of the book will have its own checklist. The following list is specific for Part I. Once you have mastered each section, check it off on the list.

- ❑ Concept (What is your forest?)
- ❑ Paper Type (What type of paper am I writing?)
- ❑ Topic (Have I narrowed my topic enough [or too much]?)
- ❑ Hypothesis/Theory (What am I trying to prove/disprove?)
- ❑ Format (What does my teacher want?) or (What does the journal/my boss require?)
- ❑ Approach (What approach should I use?)
- ❑ Outline
- ❑ Readership (What is my readership? Has my readership changed?)
- ❑ Epoche (Who am I?)
- ❑ Value to Reader (Why are people going to read this?)
- ❑ Methodological Discipline (Is my method qualitative, quantitative, theoretical, or a combination of these?)
- ❑ Keep notes on the process (both for audit trail and for future ideas)

chapter 2
Concept

INTRODUCTION

The first part of our journey begins before we ever step foot through the door to our mind. Before we can leave we must pack our tool bag and prepare for the journey. This means we must realize that as we are writing our papers, we will be taking a journey, and like any journey the process will be much easier if we prepare properly. To this end, we have to develop the basic concept for our paper. Doubtless, you have already begun formulating a concept for your paper, or have even moved farther down the planning track as you read the introduction and Chapter 1; that is good. However, if we are going to start the writing process at the beginning, then we should start making our writing notes as early as possible. This means that we should start at the very beginning with the concept.

So, the first question that we must address is, "What is a concept?" A concept is the broadest possible area of writing that you have interest in. This is something as grand as a discipline or a macro-level idea—for example, "Sociology of the Human Mind" is a concept; "History of Russia" is a concept; "The Biology of Swamps" is a concept; and "Particle Theory" is a concept. Concepts are ideas that are so large and so grand that a single paper cannot cover their topic even in the minutia. The concept becomes the forest through which you will explore to discover the topic of your paper. You are an explorer and the one who makes discovery because all knowledge is already out there just waiting for those of us who research to discover it.

Once you have established your macro-level concept, you need to ask the question of why this topic is important to you. Some of you who are students have a very simple answer to this—"because my teacher/professor told me to write on this topic." Even when you are being told to write on a specific topic, however, you should find some reason why the topic interests you. Interested writers write more interesting papers. Uninterested authors tend to have flat and listless prose that does not keep the attention of the reader or result in good grades. What is your interest in your subject? If you cannot find anything that interests you, can you connect this subject to one you *are* interested in? For instance, your professor or your boss tells you that she wants a 20-page paper on the anthropological history of the Aztecs. Assume for a moment that you have no interest in Meso-America culture. How can you link this topic to your passion, which we will say is business? The link I would make is looking at the social conventions that dictated social norms related to individual purchases. Much more simply, what were the fads in Aztec life? In this way you can look at how the culture developed to fulfill the topic of the paper while still working in an area in which you are comfortable.

This chapter is going to take us deep into the first step of writing a good paper. We will look at how to select the area about which you are going to write in more detail. Even at the macro level, slight changes in the way that we develop our research areas can dictate problems or the lack thereof that we will have later in the writing process. Next, we will focus on your discipline. Staying within our area of expertise is important, but just because a topic is just out of your area of expertise does not mean that you cannot write about it. Following that, in the third section, we look at why you are writing in this area. Much like the questions of whether this topic is valid in your discipline, the question of why you are writing this paper can dictate how the paper will be received.

In the final three sections of the chapter we begin to look at how your paper begins to develop. In these final three sections we distill the concept down to the level where it is ready to become a topic. In the fourth section we look at narrowing the focus of your concept down to an idea, then to an element of that idea. This will prepare you to choose a topic in the next chapter. However, before you choose a topic we want to look at two very important questions that will dictate how easy or how difficult it will be to write your paper. In the fifth section we look at whether the research has been done, whether in your discipline or in another discipline. Even if the research has been done, this does not mean that you cannot write on your area. Research needs to be confirmed as to the point that it makes to be valid. In the sixth section we look at whether there is data you can use for your topic and how difficult it will be to collect this data. All of these things should be considered before you enter into the paper writing process and commit your time and your reputation to a research goal.

This chapter will help you develop your concept to the point that you are ready to select a paper type and a topic. As was indicated in the introduction, this is the "packing your bag" and "finding your forest" for your journey to writing your paper. If you follow each of the steps listed in this chapter, then you will have a strong basis for your paper. Always keep notes during this part of the process, not just for your audit trail but also for your future research. In this process you may create more than one idea, the additional ideas that you create but do not use for this paper should be kept and preserved so that you can use them in a future paper, book, or dissertation. As you build up good notes on subjects, and keep abreast of subjects you have already written on, future papers will be much easier to research as you will have most of the research done. Your journeys in writing will become less like visiting new unexplored regions and more like returning home to the comfort of what you know.

AREA OF WRITING

Slightly less daunting of a task than writing about a concept is the idea of writing about an area. An area is a part of a concept, the trees to our forest. Now that you have chosen a broad concept, it is time for us to start whittling down the concept to a manageable topic. If your concept is "The History of Russia" then your area can be "The History of the Russian Tsars" or "The History of Russian Military Operations." These areas are still impossibly immense; however, they are a step closer to a manageable topic. Now we need to take a look at your concept, which is _____, and break it down into four areas of writing that you are interested in. Do not write down topics, these will come later, but look for big areas within your concept that you can use for later:

1. _____
2. _____
3. _____
4. _____

Breaking a concept down can be difficult, so some techniques that are useful are:

1. Breaking it down by region;
2. Breaking it down by timeframe;
3. Breaking it down by group of people;

4. Breaking it down by smaller group within main concept;
5. Breaking it down by subdiscipline within concept; and
6. Breaking it down by effect.

Each time you fill out this chart, it should be easier to break down a concept into more manageable areas. Practice makes perfect and do not expect to be perfect on the first try.[1]

These macro areas are the trees in our journey through the forest analogy, meaning that there will likely be many more areas of the concept that you do not see in your initial analysis of the concept. This is fine. You are looking for a specific topic within the concept, and are still several steps away. Do not force the process to be something that it is not. Although spending all night working to find every possible subject area within a concept may be a useful exercise for developing your writing skill, it does not get you any closer to your goal of having a completed paper. Your brain will tend to focus on things that you are interested in, so let your brain do its job. Writing a paper about something that you enjoy will be easier than writing about something that you force yourself to write about, and the paper will be better. As long as the areas of writing that you find meet the requirements of the paper that you are working on, then use the area that you believe you will enjoy writing about the most. Even if it is assigned, writing a paper is your journey, so have fun with it.

The reason that we start with the concept, then walk through the area, then later walk through the elements and ideas until we finally get to the topic is because focus is vitally important at this phase of writing a paper. If you get too spread out in your topical analysis at this point, the paper will be unwieldy and broad. Overly broad papers tend to cause the reader to lose interest rather quickly. Therefore, the purpose of walking through this process is to develop a disciplined approach to writing a paper. A focused paper will generally be given an A by a professor, be chosen for publication by an editor, and be accepted by an employer before an unfocused paper. If you are still in the process of developing your writing style, try to keep your newly developing style disciplined.

So, my newly found writing companions, we are ready to start our journey of writing an academic/professional paper. We have packed our bags by finding a concept that we want to write about and have begun the distilling process of breaking that concept down into different areas. With the concept we have chosen the forest that we are going to be exploring in this paper, with the writing area we have discovered the tree that we are going to analyze. As we get closer toward our goal for this chapter of finding a workable idea, which we will then break down into a paper topic in the next chapter, we are leaving behind huge chunks of research-worthy subjects. When you think of

1. Note that you can break a concept down into more than four areas. Some concepts will lend themselves to multiple break downs while others will stay fairly focused. Use your judgment in these area.

them, write them down and save them for a later date. They will also be useful as a repository of tangential ideas that do not fit in your current paper but you do not want to throw away. Your notes will eventually become a research journal, which you will be able to use in the future to write new papers and perhaps even become an expert in a specific subject area.

DISCIPLINE OF WRITING

You will notice at several points in this book that we will jump back and forth between looking at the paper you are writing and looking at you, the author. While this may come across as disjointed, it is an important part of the process. You are just as important as the topic of the paper you are writing. You, more than anyone else in the world, dictate what is written on your subject. You, more than anyone else, will dictate whether the paper is worth reading. As you write, therefore, it is important that you keep in mind who you are, but as a scholar and as a person, so that your paper represents what you want it to represent and is something that other people are going to want to read. This means that your paper must be valid and reliable. In this case for your paper to be valid, it must be a topic that you feel you are capable of writing about. You must be honest with yourself whether you believe that you are able to undertake writing on the level you have chosen. For the paper to be reliable, your readership needs to believe that you are capable of writing on this subject and other authors should be able to respect your research methodology if not your arguments as well. They need to be able to believe that you are writing in what you assert. This generally means that you should write within your academic or professional discipline, which is where you have the most credence.

This brings us to the question, "What is your discipline?" If you are a professional, a professor, a grant writer, or a lawyer you should know what your discipline is, so this should be a very easy question; however, if you are a student, your discipline may not be fully established yet. Readers who know their discipline can skim over this section, because it is likely something that you already know. Students, however, should take careful note on this section. Professors are likely to penalize students severely for writing outside their discipline; therefore, it is important for a student to be ready to write in the discipline that the professor expects.

Most students have entered formally into a major before professors begin to require them to write papers. Although this delays the process of students learning how to write papers, it does make a professor's life easier. If this is the case, and you have already declared a major before you are required to write your first college paper, then the question is answered for you—the school of your major is likely your discipline. If you have a good professor who starts you writing papers as soon as possible, then you may have to look at what you want to do before you can identify your discipline. This is a question of who you want to be. (If you are in college you should be asking yourself this question.) If you have not answered it yet, the simplest thing is to write the paper from a perspective of the discipline in which you are taking the class.

Now those of you who tuned out can start reading again. Our next step is to look at whether the area of writing you selected lends itself to your discipline. In most cases, the answer will be yes. Almost any topic can be written through the theoretical lens of any discipline. In some cases this will be harder than others, which is why we look at this early in the process. Biology can look at the "History of the Tsars of Russia" or "History of the Russian Military" by comparing the genetics of the royal house or the medical treatments of military doctors. Statisticians can look at these topics by the numbers; sociologists can look at social structures; medical professionals can look at diseases that affect either group; and the fine arts can look at art and literature that arose during this period. Areas are generally all inclusive, but knowing how your area fits into your discipline is important as you further refine your area into an element.

Next, we need to look at whether this topic is established in your discipline. To answer this question there are three possible answers:

1. No, this area has not been breached in my discipline.
2. Yes, there is some research on this area in my discipline.
3. Yes, this area is saturated with research in my discipline.

The most reassuring answer to this question is the second answer. If there is some, but not a lot, of research on an area in your discipline, then it is already established as reliable for someone from your school of thought to be writing on the subject, but there should also still be many topics within the area that can be used for original research. If you find that your area of research has been researched over and over again in your discipline, then you must ask the question if you can contribute anything new to the field. This means that you must do more "book research" to find parts of the area that have not been researched.

is the topic over researched in my field of study?

If you find that there is no research on this area in your discipline, then you should ask why this has not been covered. This answer to the question should be the most alarming. The why is often because people do not see your field as being sufficiently related to the area of research for your research to be valid, or because the cost is too high to use one of the methodologies that is normative to your discipline. Note, this is a death sentence to your idea. If you can find the reason that others

no research on your topic = a death sentence to your idea

have not walked this journey, then you can find a way to research your topic. If there is no connection between your field and the area of research (you should have noted this earlier in the chapter), you need to find a bridge between your discipline and the area that you want to research. If the cost is prohibitive, you should look to see if the information that the research will show is worth the expense (then look into grants and other ways to raise the money for the project). The final possibility is that you may have stumbled on something that has not been researched before because it is a new idea. This is shaky ground. You should make sure that you use a credible publisher or professor when you write this paper so the peer review process can help you evolve your idea. If you do have a genuinely new idea, then you need to be sure that you get credit for it. In this case you should only use people you trust to proofread your paper and to help you get it to publication.

WHY DO YOU WANT TO WRITE ON THIS AREA?

Returning the focus from the paper to you, any good writer should be willing to ask "Why do I want to write on this area?" A good answer to this question can make the writing process much easier, as knowing the reason you are writing will allow you more focus in the writing process. You will be your first critic, thus you have to get through your criticism before your paper will go anywhere. To answer this question, you need to ask yourself what your connection is to this topic. The best answer is that you have personal experience with the area and are interested, thus you can give a perspective that others may not be able to give. The next best answer is that you are interested in the topic, which means that you should be driven to do a good job writing. A personal connection without interest can still make the paper valid, but if it is not something that you are interested in, how can you hope to convey interest to the reader. Finally, if the answer is because you were told to write in this specific area, then you need to find a way to get yourself interested in the topic so you can turn in the best paper in a bad situation. There are many other possible answers to your connection to the topic; however, these are the ones most of you will find in normal writing experiences.

[handwritten margin notes: Connection to your topic / 1) experience / 2) intrest / 3) find intrest]

Before we move on, we should take a moment to look at personal connections to an area. Personal connections can be valuable to increase how reliable a paper is in the eyes of the readership; however, sometimes a personal connection can make a paper much harder to write. If your topic area covers something traumatic in your life, and you are not ready to write about your experience, then don't. Unless a doctor believes that it will be cathartic, there is no reason to force yourself to open old wounds for the sake of any paper. You can still write on the topic, but you do not have to make yourself vulnerable during the process by entering into an area where you are not comfortable.

On a happier note, you should also look at your qualifications in relation to the topic. As a general rule, anyone can write a term paper on any topic applicable to a class. Beyond this general rule, just because you are capable of writing on a topic, does not mean that you are qualified to write on an area. For instance, I have many degrees, but I have no business writing on the mechanics of cancer treatment outside the conflicts and emotions that arise. The cellular biology and the mechanical tools that are needed to treat the disease are beyond my sphere of knowledge, thus my writing on the subject could cause more harm than good. Always ask yourself whether you believe that you are qualified to provide usable research on an area. This should be the key question you ask yourself before you move on with the writing process. Whether the world thinks you are capable of writing on the topic is a question for another time, but if you do not believe that you are capable of providing usable research on a given topic, then you should take a step back and reconsider your area of writing. If you feel you are unqualified now, you will only be getting more specific as the process goes on.

Sometimes while doing this mini epoche, you will realize that others may not accept your qualifications. This can be quite normal. Some areas of writing are rabidly defended by the discipline that normally writes in them. If this is the case, then you may have to defend why you are capable of writing in this area. At this point this is a personal reflection to determine whether you are capable of writing on this point; later you may have to defend your right to write to others, but at this point you are defending it to yourself. You may use these defenses at a conference, or in a cover letter, or never at all, but having them prepared allows you to be ready for challenges from others to your qualification to write in any given area. Like in the other parts of this book, good preparation can save you many headaches down the road.

SPECIFIC IDEA

Now that we have done all of the analysis of the area of writing that we are going to do, we can move on to distilling the area down to something closer to the topic that we will actually write about. Continuing with the analogy that we have been using of a journey through a forest—the concept is the forest, the area of writing is the tree—now we move to the branches of the tree to close in on a workable topic. By way of example, we continue with our "History of Russia" concept, which is now "History of the Russian Military." This will give you an example as a point of reference as you break down your own concept to smaller and smaller pieces. Remember, the more focused we stay in the preparation to write the paper, the easier it will be to stay focused in the actual writing process.

So what is an element within an area of writing? An element is a smaller area of writing that allows the writer to draw closer to the topic that he or she is going to write about. Elements are a transitional step between concept and topic; however, elements are a key step as you continue your career. If you want to be an expert on a topic, you can keep strong notes of the different elements of your area of writing. These elements will give you a good starting point for new ideas and future papers. If you stay within the elemental level, you will keep your general research focused enough that people will be able to link the different topics of your papers with a field of expertise. So let us assume that our discipline is history; therefore, we need to break down our area of writing "History of the Russian Military" into elements. Some possible examples are:

1. Russian Military History
2. History of the Russian Military, 1900–2000
3. History of the Russian Military, 1800–1900
4. History of the Russian Military, pre-1800s

Now as you can see, I used two different techniques to break down the area of writing. For the first part, "Russian Military History," I reversed the meaning of the term, thus instead of looking at the logistics and hardware of the military, this topic looks at the history of engagements during the history of Russia's military. The second technique I used was breaking the area of writing down by time. The whole history of a region's military from the beginning of time is a difficult subject; however, if you break it down into 100-year pieces you can find specific ideas that you want to look at. For our selection process, we are going to chose the second element, "History of the Russian Military, 1900–2000."

Now it is your turn. You do not have to use reversal or time-based elements to break down your topic. You could use groups, ideas, theories, or anything that relates to your topic. All you have to do is break your area of writing down into a more manageable element that you can then work from. Try to get at least four:

Chosen Area of Writing: _____

    1. _____

    2. _____

    3. _____

    4. _____

How did you break down your area of writing to elements? Generally, you will not want to use the same technique in the next section where we break the elements down into ideas (this is not a hard rule, but it does keep the process more dynamic).

Now that you have an element of the area of writing within the concept that you chose at the beginning of your journey, it is time to refine the concept even further. In this process you are going to take your element and turn it into several ideas. Most people skip over the phases before this step; however, there are many processes that you have already done that if you skip over may lead to your paper being broad and unwieldy. If you take the 10 to 20 minutes to properly refine your concept to an idea, rather than just starting with an idea, you will have the ability to move up and down your idea tree if you find that your idea has already been taken in the next step. If you start here with the idea, then you will have to start from scratch if your idea is already taken. In the case of our Russian military paper, we have an element—"History of the Russian Military, 1900–2000"—which would be a great topic for a book, but is still too broad for a research paper. To resolve this and move to the idea phase, where things become more complex and we do our first research, we need to break the element into ideas. You should try to get at least five ideas:

1. History of the Russian Cavalry, 1900–1930
2. Russian Nuclear Development in the 20th Century
3. Russian Naval Forces, 1950–2000
4. Russian Ground Forces, 1950–2000
5. Russian Air Forces, 1950–2000

As you can see, we broke the main topic into ideas within the topic. We also reduced the timestamp of the research. This narrows the research to ideas that would make good ideas for a book or book chapter, but ideas that are still too broad for a research paper. However, rather than immediately reducing them to the topic level, we are going to research these topics a bit to see if they have already been covered and if there is valid data that we can use in our research. Before we move on to the next section, it is time for you to break your chosen element down into ideas:

Chosen Element: _____

    1. _____

    2. _____

    3. _____

    4. _____

Now that you have your ideas, it is time to do some brief research to find if these ideas are going to provide you with a good topic.

RESEARCH IDEA: HAS IT BEEN DONE?

Now that you have an idea, you are at the phase where you need to vet the idea to be sure that you can work on it as a research topic. This means that first you need to ensure that you idea has not been researched to the point that it is not feasible to do new research. Even if you are going to "prove" someone else's research was valid, you want to check and make sure that this area has not been done to the point that no one will read new research on the area. For your research to be taken seriously, you need to ensure that it has a sense of "newness" that will make it something your readership wants to read.

The reason that this process is engaged at the idea level rather than at the topic level is because even if an idea has been researched (most people do not go the whole way through the writing process), there still may be topical areas within your idea that can still be researched. If "The History of Russian Cavalry, 1900–1930" has already been researched by several people, this does not mean that you cannot find a specific topic within the idea that has not yet been researched. Some researchers make a career writing critical pieces finding the minutia of what other researchers have missed and attacking the whole of the researcher's body of work. This is lazy research and writing, but some people make a career out of it. If you find that your idea has been researched before, follow the steps in Chapter 3 that either complement or condemn the research that already exists through finding a focused, specific topic.

Another thing that you should look at when researching ideas is whether the idea has been done in your discipline. Many times one discipline will research a topic through the theoretical lens or lenses of that discipline, but ignore the lenses of other disciplines. This can be a way for you to break into the subject for your discipline and to look as if you are multidisciplinary and take the time to research journals from other disciplines. Twenty years ago this would have been a time-consuming and difficult process; however, with the plethora of journals that a student or researcher can access within minutes at a university library, this process can take a mere few hours. When doing this process, however, make sure that you do abstract searches as well as full articles, because some databases do not hold the full articles so you could miss previous research by skipping over abstracts.

[handwritten margin note: – has there been research done in another disapline]

Note: Keep notes of the research you search through in this process, writing down articles that are similar or supportive of your idea. You can use these articles when you are doing research for your paper.

Next, even if the idea that you want to research has been done, you should discover if there have been new occurrences in the field since the time of the previous writing. Just because a topic has been written about does not mean that you cannot look deeper into it. If you are writing on civil rights, for example, and your topic is "Brutality against Homosexual Hispanic Males of Columbian Decent in Los Angeles," and someone has already written on this topic, but there have been three new cases of brutality since the paper was written, you can write a paper that is complimentary to the original paper by reviewing the original and augmenting it with the three new cases. This allows you to expand the sphere of understanding about this topic **and** your article (if published) will show up in searches with the original article. Further, you can link two papers on the same topic by reviewing them through the lens of your discipline.

As with our analysis of the area of research, you should also take a moment to see if anyone has discussed your idea. When an idea is totally without research, you should always ask why. If it is so new that no one has picked up on it yet, then you may have found a new idea; however, if it is an idea that has been around for a while and no one has looked at it, then there may be underlying reasons. Always look to see if it is dangerous, whether researching that idea is taboo (and why), whether someone powerful in the field is suppressing research on that idea, whether the government is suppressing research on that idea, whether it has been discovered and patented but the information is being withheld by a private company or person, and whether there is too little data or the data that is available is too expensive to recover. We will discuss if there is too little data or if the data is too expensive to recover in the next section.

RESEARCH IDEA: IS THERE DATA?

When you are doing your initial review to see if someone else has researched your idea, you should also be looking to see if there is any data on your idea. Even in the dumbest bullion searches you should be able to find research articles that are tangential to your idea. If tangential articles are all that you find, then you should take the time to review these articles to see what information is available on your idea. In many cases, the reason that there is not direct information on your idea is because there simply isn't any or the information is too expensive to recover. The eating habits of jellyfish in the Proterozoic period may be interesting (to someone); however, if there is no fossil record, nor a written record of what those ravenous jellyfish ate, then there is no way to do the research.

If you are set on writing a paper on this topic, then you would be constrained to writing a theoretical paper on the topic. This means that you would have to theorize what the jellyfish ate. This does not mean that you can write a completely speculative paper; your theory needs to be grounded in some sort of fact. Micro-barbules in the fossilized skin of a specific fish that are similar to the barbules in jellyfish stingers today can be the basis for theory. Too often in the modern academy, pseudo-scholars take areas where there is no evidence and speculate on what happened. This can lead to "research" papers (or mainly television shows) that teach people "facts" that have no factual basis. Unless you want to be associated with fields that chase Bigfoot, you should always stick to ideas where you can find at least one instance of something supporting your theory.

Next, ask yourself where you are going to find data. Sometimes data is in your local college library, just waiting to be accessed. Other times data may be on a volcanic island populated by deadly snakes. You need to use your good judgment whether data is in a place you will be able to access it. You also need to look to your university Institutional Review Board (IRB) as to whether your topic is ethical to research. Releasing bunnies onto the snake island to see if they can breed faster than the snakes eat them may have a valid research point; however, is it ethical and is it humane? A good general rule is, when in doubt check with the IRB (or your company's HR or ethics department). Additionally, you should look at what kind of data you will have access to. While it is unimportant in this part of the process, when we move on to Chapter 3 it can help determine what type of paper you are going to write.

The final question we ask in this chapter is the question of money. First, how much will the data cost you to acquire; and second, do you have the money to pay for it? While we live in a dark age of institutional research, we are in a golden age of research funding. If there is a marketable prospect for your research, then there is a good chance that you will be able to find a company that will give you some money to fund it. If there is not a marketable prospect, non-profits and government agencies are giving money away like it is Viagra. As long as there is a good reason for doing your research, you should be able to get some help in funding it. This should make you ask, "Is my research worth the cost?" If it is, then look for funding. If not, then keep thinking about your research until you find a use. Never forget that there are human costs in research as well as money costs; do not spend too much of yourself on a project that is not worth it.

CONCLUSION

Moving from concept to idea, and in the process discovering a little bit about yourself, is a valuable step in developing a high-quality research paper. As we have noted, many people simply start at the idea phase and jump right into the paper without the information and research that the preoperational stages give them. This means that when they reach a difficult point in the paper, and there is one in every paper, they will not have the foundational work that we have established in this chapter to fall back on. Here is where most papers crumble, because they have no foundation.

Following the steps in this chapter does not guarantee you a good paper, but it does give you a fighting chance. If one in five people in the United States writes an original paper in college, then you are competing with 60,000 people every time you write a paper. The more specific your topic, the more you can reduce the number of people you are competing with. This means that every time you narrow your topic—from concept to area, from area to elements, from elements to idea, then finally from ideas to topic (discussed in the next chapter)—you are shedding off some of your competition. Being a big fish in a small pond is ideal for writing. How much effort you put into picking your topic in the next chapter will determine just how small of a pond you are in.

CHECKLIST

- ☐ Concept (Write your concept as broadly as possible.)
- ☐ Area of Writing (Try to find at least four areas within your concept.)
- ☐ What is your discipline?
- ☐ Why do you want to write in this area?
- ☐ Elements (Try to find four elements of your area.)
- ☐ Ideas (Try to find four ideas within your element.)
- ☐ Research whether the idea has been done.
  - If not, why?
  - If so, can you pick a specific topic in the idea that has not been done?
  - If not, then can you use new information to complement existing articles?
  - If not, then can you redo the research subject to support the existing articles?
- ☐ Research whether there is data.
  - Is there data on the subject?
    - Where is it available?
    - What is the cost?
    - Who controls it?
    - Is it worth the expense?
  - If not, how will you get data?
    - Tangential sources
    - Research expedition
  - Is it ethical?

chapter 3
Paper Type

INTRODUCTION: PAPER TYPE AND TOPIC

The reason you are writing your paper can have a profound effect on how you go about your writing process. It can also have an effect on your chosen topic. Certain paper styles are more useful for certain types of papers, while other paper styles are more suited for other types. Defining your paper's purpose is one of the key processes that needs to take place before you settle in on a topic for your paper. Your topic should always meet the needs of your purpose; this will allow you to design the best paper possible.

To begin this process, we need to define the purpose of your paper. For some types of papers this is very simple, such as with an undergraduate student term paper. In this type of paper your purpose is to get the best grade possible. Epic discoveries and promotions are nice, but with a school paper you should always be focused on making the grade. Having good grades will open doors for you down the road that will allow you to make those epic discoveries and to get those promotions. Each time you sit down to write a paper, you should look at what you are writing the paper for. This is a repetitive part of the process, because you do it when you choose your concept, you do it when you look at your readership, and here you do it again when you select your paper type and topic. We recommend that you make a note card with the purpose of your paper written on it and post it somewhere near your workstation. If ever you feel that you are drifting from your main purpose, use the note card as a reminder of the reason you are writing this paper.

The purpose of your paper can also dictate the effort that you should be willing to put into your paper. A term paper should not warrant the amount of effort that a dissertation warrants, which in turn should not warrant as much time as a white page that determines whether you get promoted to CFO of a company. Generally, as you move through your academic and business career, papers will become more important. However, the amount of time you have remaining in your life will become less and less. This means that you should always determine whether the amount of effort required to create a paper, at any given time in your life, is worth the time that you will have to invest to complete the paper. A research paper that takes you away from your family and life for two years while your children are in their developmental stages may be demanding too much from a young researcher. Do not let research be something that destroys you.

Goals are also an important part of paper writing. Your goals should determine how you go about writing a paper. Every person should have several goals in life. For instance, a student who is writing a paper may have several goals:

1. To get a good grade on this paper;
2. To pass the class;
3. To graduate;
4. To get a good job;
5. To be able to support a family; and
6. To have a family.

The likelihood of a paper having a demonstrative effect on all of these goals is unlikely; but remember, "But for a nail the shoe was lost, but for the shoe the horse was lost, but for the horse the rider was lost, but for the rider the message was lost, but for the message the battle was lost, but for the battle the war was lost, but for the war the nation was lost, all for the wont of a nail."[1] For the goals listed above, passing the paper depends on the effort put into the paper. A bad grade on the paper could cause the student to fail the class. Failing the class could delay graduation and prevent the student from getting a good job. The lack of a job could cause the student to forgo having a family. Thus all the goals could be affected by not putting the effort into a single paper. Will this happen with every paper? Not likely; however, we should always put the effort befitting a project into the project to ensure that we are as successful in life as we possibly can be. If a project can have major effects on our goals, then we should redouble our efforts.

---

1. Chinese proverb.

Some projects will have secondary goals. Many times a paper that is submitted as a graduate term paper or a white page will have the potential to be something more. If you think your area of research has the potential to be something more than what you set out for it to be in the beginning, then plan for that as you write it. If you want to publish your paper in an academic journal or a trade book, plan for that as you write the paper. Go above and beyond the basic requirements and look to meet the requirements of the publication you wish to use. Taking an extra day to write a paper as a graduate student can get that paper published, which can lead to scholarships, conferences, and good jobs. Taking an extra day to write a paper as an employee can allow you to put that paper in trade books and increase your personal brand in your field. If a little extra time can turn your paper into something that is much more valuable to you than a paper that will just sit in a drawer collecting dust, then try and take the time to make it a tool that will work for your future.

At the end of this chapter we will go through the process of choosing a topic for your paper. This means that we refine the idea that you distilled last chapter into a workable topic, which we can then use in the next chapter to create a hypothesis or a theory. Your topic will be your lifeline when you are writing this paper; when we edit the paper you will look over each sentence and determine whether it builds up your topic or is tangential to your topic. Your topic will be your guiding star on your journey of writing this paper, which will keep you focused when you start to wonder off track. Your topic will become a compass, letting you know whether the literary turns you chose to take in your project are working toward your final goal.

This chapter is set up to read like a handbook, which means that the sections of the chapter are going to look at each paper type in turn and discuss their parameters. You do not have to read each section to get the maximum effect out of this chapter. If you know you are writing a term paper, then you know that it will not be a legal document read by the courts or a gist given to a CEO; therefore, you can read just the section on school papers. Each section will be broken into six parts (each a paragraph long). These parts are:

1. Purpose of the paper;
2. Requirements of the paper;
3. Citation in the paper;
4. Readership of the paper;
5. Whether or not the paper will be published; and
6. Length that is recommended for the paper.

In the final section of this chapter we look at refining your idea into a set of topics and then choosing one of those topics.

SCHOOL PAPERS

Most people who are reading this book are likely writing a paper for either graduate or undergraduate work. Congratulations, you are in college. When you have completed your college years you will be in the top 10% of the world in relation to education. You college education will provide you with the tools that you need to be successful in life. Realistically, it is you that determines whether or not you are successful in life. Getting into college gave you access to being a member of a club, the club of college graduates and alumni. Being a part of this club will open doors for you, but it is your job to walk through those doors. Having a good GPA could get you into a decent graduate school, and having a good portfolio of work should get you a good job. This means that you have to take each and every college paper as seriously as it warrants. Your underwater basket weaving class may not garner much attention when you apply for a mid-level management job after your MBA, but your "Iconography and the Failed Marketing Strategies of Corp X: A Case Study of Offensive Icon in Marketing Strategy" will likely get some attention.

The primary purpose of any undergraduate paper or graduate paper is to get the best grade that you can get on that paper so that you have the best chance of graduating near the top of your class. This is universal throughout the college experience. The question of purpose in a college paper is regulated to the secondary purpose of a college paper, and that is determined by you. Are you going to try to publish the paper? Both graduates and undergraduates have the opportunity to publish papers and notes in the modern academic landscape. If you want to publish your paper, or if you want to present it at a conference (easier for undergraduates), you need to keep that in mind as you choose your topic and write your paper. Your goals should be on that note card, right under the topic you have chosen.

Following is a quick list that reviews what you need for your college paper.

- Paper Requirements: These are the requirements for form and function of the paper. While you may be capable of writing an excellent ethnographies study on criminality within the public school system of your town, if the professor wants a simple research/term paper based on criminality in general, then that is what your professor should receive from you.
  - Undergraduate: Requirements are set by professor.
  - Graduate: Requirements are set by professor.

- Citation Style: This is the format of your citations. For the most part, college professors are going to require you to cite in either APA (American Psychological Association) or MLA (Modern Language Association) format. Some professors will opt for the Chicago Manual of Style format; and if you are in law school they will want you to use the ABA (American Bar Association)/Yale Blue Book format.
  - Undergraduate: Set by professor.
  - Graduate: Set by professor or by journal you want to publish in (with professor's approval).
- Readership: The readership for most college papers will be the professor who assigned it. In some cases where you are trying to publish, a secondary readership will be the editor of the journal and the tertiary readership will be the readership of the journal.
- Publishing: Undergraduate papers are hard to publish, but not impossible. Any graduate paper that you are able to publish should be published if you can find a journal in which to publish.
- Length of Paper
  - Undergraduate: 5–10 pages (or set by professor).
  - Graduate: 10–25 pages (or set by professor).

WORK PAPERS

Work papers are papers that are related to the job you have. By and large those of a nonlegal variety will be white pages. If you are in the legal field see the legal section of this chapter. Work papers differ from college papers in that you cannot simply "retake" the class in which you are writing work papers. If you do poorly in a work paper you could miss out on a raise, or a promotion, or even worse be fired. Work papers require you to be extremely focused on the topic of the paper and how your management wants the paper to be done. Getting cute with a work paper can get you fired, so stick to the demands of those who are giving you the assignment.

The primary purpose of a work paper is to advance your career (in some cases it may be to keep your job). Work papers are a difficult type of paper to write because often you are competing with coworkers. As a general rule, write the best paper that you can write without being labeled a jerk. If you put the black hat on, people higher up will begin to notice and if you are always the good guy, they will also notice that. Even as cutthroat as the business world has become over the last 30 years, people still want to have good people around at their companies. Publication is likely a secondary purpose for any paper written at work. This can also advance your career, but do not become so obsessed with publication that you allow your paper not to meet the requirements set out by your superiors.

Following is a quick review of what you need for your work paper.

- Requirements: These will be set out by the person who tells you to write the paper. If you are writing a paper for publication, make sure that it fits in with the company's guidelines and that you are within your contracted requirements for disclosing any publications to the company.
- Citation: Most fields have their preferred citation style. Unless instructed otherwise, use the chosen citation style for your field.
- Readership: This can fluctuate to extremes in a business environment. The readership can be as small as the person who assigned you the project, or as large as a major publication. When writing for work always keep a professional tone and focus on the goals you have set or that have been set for you.
- Publishing: This must be allowed by your company, then according to the guidelines of the trade journal/book.
- Length: Work papers can be anything from a one-page gist to an entire manual. This depends on what you are working on and who will be reading it. If your boss asks you for a white page briefing on project X, she generally will not want a 2,000-page treatise on the history of business in the Western world. Keep focused and only write about what you are required to write.

RESEARCH PAPERS

Research papers are what this book was written for. Whether you are a college student writing a thesis or a dissertation, or a faculty member or professional trying to further your career by writing an academic paper, research papers are the most common kind of papers that you will be dealing with. As a researcher, you want to have your paper be as focused and defendable as possible. There are very few subjects where people will not attack your work for their own gain. If you write a strong paper that gains widespread acceptance, you will be exposed to more attacks. About the only way that you will not have to defend your paper is if no one reads it. If no one reads it, then what is the point of writing it?

The main purpose of a research paper is to inform members of the academy of something. You may want to let them know about a new theory. You may want to let them know that an accepted theory is wrong. You may want to educate them about the habits of a village of people who moved to the Amazon in the 1960s and are still living as an uncomplicated commune. Regardless of what you are teaching people about, you are teaching them something that they did not know before. If you make this the primary goal of your research paper and do it well, then the publication of that paper will be easier once the paper is done. Journals are always looking for well-written papers.

Following is a quick review of what you need for your research paper.

- Requirements: These will be set out by the journal (or your faculty if writing a thesis or journal).
- Citations: The style will be determined by the field that you are in. When in doubt, ask.
- Readership: Your first readership is the editor of the journal you are submitting the paper to, then your readership is the readership of that journal. If you are writing a thesis or a dissertation, then you are submitting to your committee.
- Publishing: Yes
- Length: 20 pages (journal article), 100 pages (thesis), 100–1,000 pages (dissertation)

LEGAL PAPERS

Legal papers, or briefs, are written in the legal field. They are short explanations of legal opinion that can be easily assimilated by the reader. The two main kinds of briefs are those written for personal use/members of your firm, or those that are submitted to the court. This form of paper is highly stylized and will be covered in detail in Chapter 34. While these types of papers are basically restricted to the legal field, they can be a useful method of taking notes in any field. The ability to reduce an entire chapter down to one page can help you study for exams in short order. The ability to reduce entire reports down to one page can make your filing system at work much more accessible.

The purpose of a legal brief is to convey your assessment of a case or document to yourself or another person in a short one- or two-page document. These documents are then used to quickly access information for other uses. The goal in a brief is to be as succinct, yet as detailed as possible. When you write a brief, you should write it so that it makes your position known to the reader. These documents have a specific set of formats that will depend on who your readership is. Always cater to your readership in these instances.

Following is a quick review of what you need for your legal paper.

- Requirements: Either set by yourself, the firm you work for, or the courts. Papers for yourself can be any format you can use, papers for your firm should follow the firm's guidelines, papers for the court should follow the rules of court. The general formats are:
  - IRAC: Issue, Rule(s), Analysis, Conclusion
  - FIRAC: Facts, Issue, Rule(s), Analysis, Conclusion
  - CRIAC: Conclusion, Rule(s), Issue, Analysis, Conclusion
- Citation: ABA/Yale Bluebook style
- Readership: Yourself, your firm, or the court
- Publishing: Briefs are not usually published; however, legal papers tend to follow the IRAC form when they are sent to a legal publisher. Therefore, a brief can be expanded into a publishable paper, but this is a project that we will cover in Chapter 34.
- Length: 1 page (personal/firm briefs); length for court briefs will be set by the court.

GRANTS

The purpose of writing a grant is to get someone or some entity to give you money for a research project. Therefore a grant is different from other writing styles. With a grant, you already have a topic for a research project you want to pursue. This means that when writing a grant, your job is to make your topic look as important as possible and make your methodology for researching the topic as effective as possible. Writing grants should be done after you have decided on a topic and after you have chosen a methodology to use for your research paper. Attempting to write a grant too early will limit your knowledge of your own project and put you at a disadvantage when compared to people who have already completed the preliminary work for their project. Grants will be covered in detail in Chapter 35.

Following is a quick review of what you need for your grant request.

- Requirements: The requirements of any grant will be set out in the application guidelines. These guidelines will tell you what kind of projects the agency is writing grants for at this time. Always follow the guidelines for the best chance of getting a grant.
- Citations: Generally the agency does not care what citation style you use, as long as you use a consistent style and do not plagiarize. Plagiarism can have you blackballed for the grant agency that you are applying to and other agencies that they deal with.

- Readership: The grant writing committee. Some sites will tell you who they are, some will not. If you can find out who they are, try to cater to them as much as possible without diluting the spirit of your research.
- Publishing: No, for grant; yes, for publishing.
- Length: 1–3 pages, unless other lengths are specified by the grant writing agency.

GISTS

Gists are similar to briefs, but rather than being for yourself, people at your firm, or the courts, they are for a person in a position of power. Gists allow a company or government offices a way of making vast amounts of information available to persons in leadership positions without overwhelming them with paperwork. Therefore, the purpose of a gist is to make as much information as possible available to a leader using the smallest amount of space possible. This means that in one or two pages you must condense dozens of pages into a single readable document. This is not a form of academic writing, but is a form of writing you may be required to have in a business or government job.

Following is a quick review of what you need for your gist.

- Requirements: Set by company or agency, generally as much information as possible in a two-page bullet pointed document.
- Citations: None, unless they are relevant to the information contained.
- Readership: One person in a leadership position.
- Publishing: No
- Length: 1–2 pages, longer reports can be requested.

NEWSPAPERS/MAGAZINES

Newspaper articles are the most current event–based type of writing we will cover in this book. Newspapers are the public's first line of information about the world that they live in. While the format is increasingly changing from print media to digital media, newspapers are still a major source of information for people. The purpose of a good newspaper is to convey information in a timely manner to people who need it. The purpose of a bad newspaper is to spin the news to protect itself or help protect wealthy patrons. Magazines follow the same purpose as newspapers; however, they tend to be monthly or biweekly rather than daily. This means that the articles are longer and generally only hit the high points of the month's news. Magazines also tend to have a theme, which is the information that they present within their paradigm.

Following is a quick review of what you need for your newspaper or magazine.

- Requirements
  - Newspaper: Set by paper.
  - Magazine: Set by publication.
- Citations: Generally citations are avoided in either a newspaper or a magazine. If they are included they are generally done in line with no formal reference style.
- Readership
  - Newspaper: The community at large, for large newspapers the nation. Specific papers may cater to a specific demographic.
  - Magazines: Broad readership, determined by content of magazine.
- Publishing: Yes, very little point in writing a newspaper or magazine article if it is not going to be published.
- Length
  - Newspaper: quarter to half page.
  - Magazine: 1–3 pages, more if publisher allows.

Now that you are more informed about the types of papers you can write, select a style and be prepared to write in that style for the duration of the project. From this point on, you will formulate your paper with the paper type in mind. Though the steps for papers are the same, from this point on you will be focused on the goals and precepts laid out by your specific paper type. The more purely you stay within your chosen paper type, the more focused your paper will be and the better you will be able to stay on track. As you pick your paper style, remember that this choice will decide many of the elements in your paper. If you change it later, you will have to go back through your ground work and refocus it to your new goal.

NARROWING YOUR IDEA TO A TOPIC

The next step in your paper writing process is to narrow your idea into a topic. Your topic is simply another step in the refinement of your concept; however, your topic is the penultimate step to deciding the direction of your paper. Now that you know what type of paper you are writing, thus having identified the purpose, you are able to select a topic that will maximize the effectiveness of your writing so that you can achieve your goals. Your topic, more than any other foundational element, is a crossroads of the creative process. Once you know your topic, you can begin your journey into the writing process.

This section is necessarily brief as it repeats a process that you have already done three times; however, special care should be taken in this step to ensure that you have a specific topic that you are able to ask a question about, thus introducing the next step of the hypothesis. For the purpose of our reduction, we are going to select an idea from our Russian history example presented in the last chapter. Our ideas related to Russian history were:

1. History of the Russian Cavalry, 1900–1930
2. Russian Nuclear Development in the 20th Century
3. Russian Naval Forces, 1950–2000
4. Russian Ground Forces, 1950–2000
5. Russian Air Forces, 1950–2000

These five ideas house dozens of possible paper topics; however, we should be careful in how we select which idea we want to work with for this specific paper. In our example, we are writing a graduate research paper for a social-history class. This leaves us with quite a few options for paper topics as this style of class is very broad.

For this example, we are going to look at "Russian Nuclear Development in the 20th Century," because it fits the needs of the class and because our previous steps have shown that there is significant information on the subject and current events may change the relationship between the United States and Russia, thus making our choice to write more interesting and relevant to the academic world and the general population. This means that our graduate research paper can be converted from a course paper to a paper that can be published. Before we get ahead of ourselves, however, we should reduce our idea down to at least four possible topics:

1. Russian Nuclear Power Development from 1990–2010
2. Russian Nuclear Disarmament: A History
3. Russian Nuclear Submarines: Threat Assessment
4. Russian Rocketry and New Weapon Delivery Systems

Each of these topics is related to the idea that we were already working with. The first one was developed from our original idea, though an extra 10 years were added in the new millennium to cover more modern elements. For each of these topics, we need to look and see whether we are able to develop a question for them. For the second topic we can ask the question, "Did Russia meet its nuclear disarmament obligations to the extent that the United States and United Nations believed they did in the 1990s?" As long as you can ask at least one valid academic question about your topic, the topic should be workable.

Now we turn our attention to your paper. You must break your general idea down into a specific topic. You simply follow the same pattern that allowed you to reduce your concept to an area, your area to an element, and your element to an idea. Try to get at least four topics from your idea:

Chosen Idea: _____

    1. _____

    2. _____

    3. _____

    4. _____

Now take each one of these ideas and see if you can generate a valid academic question (the question does not have to be perfect, we will refine questions when we get to hypotheses and theories in the next chapter):

Question 1: _____

Question 2: _____

Question 3: _____

Question 4: _____

If you cannot form a question for each one, do not worry. As long as one of the topics you have created is valid you still have the ability to work with that topic. Sometimes if you leave the process and take 5 or 10 minutes to think about the process you can come up with a valid research question for you topic. If all of your topics have a valid academic question attached to them, then you now can chose the topic for your paper.

Now that we have completed the processes in this chapter, you are looking at your topic for your paper. Write it on your note card and hang it somewhere in your workspace. At the end of every paragraph, at the end of every page, and at the end of every day you spend working on your paper, ask yourself whether your actions in that paragraph, page, or day worked toward your topic. The more focused you stay on your topic, the easier your paper will be to understand and the more likely that your paper will reach the goal that you have set for yourself or that has been set for you. Your topic is now your compass on your journey to write your paper.

CHECKLIST

- ❏ Identify the type of paper you are writing.
- ❏ Identify which idea from your idea list you are going to use.
- ❏ Break that idea down into topics.
- ❏ Check to see if a valid academic question can be asked about each topic.
- ❏ Choose your topic.
- ❏ Write your chosen topic down on your note card.

chapter 4
Hypotheses and Theories

INTRODUCTION

As a professor, one of the most frustrating things I see when I assign a research paper is the way that students are trained in high school to write a paper. Most students enter into college thinking that simply looking up a set amount of data on any given topic is a research paper. This is simply not true. Without a **research question** you do not have a research paper. Now there are research questions that do not involve hypotheses, some camps would argue that several of the methodologies covered in this book do not have a hypothesis; however, any good research paper should have some basic kind of research question.[1] Using this method, all papers we write will have a hypothesis (except the papers from the miscellaneous section).[2] The miscellaneous paper types will each have their individual research questions that must be answered in the absence of a hypothesis.

The sooner we can train students that an academic paper must have a question to answer, the sooner we will have a nation that is actively engaged in answering those questions. Research in the United States today has become a milieu of information that has no purpose, broken sporadically

---

1. From my experience phenomenologists tend to argue adamantly that their methodology does not require a hypothesis. Although it is true that their method does not require a hypothesis, it is also true that a phenomenology with a hypothesis is more focused than one without. Even those without a hypothesis still need to have a research question to lend context to the research.
2. Some Miscellaneous papers will have hypotheses, but not all.

with valuable data and research.[3] This manifestation of academia is upside down. The vast majority of research papers should be of extensive use to those who are working in those fields. The exception to the rule should be the useless research paper that manages to make it through journal editorial boards. By focusing on a research question, whether it be a hypothesis or a theory, you can demonstrate the rigor of your research. Therefore even if your topic is not of use to me, those who will find it useful will be able to realize that it is useful to them by the hypotheses in the methodology section or abstract.

When stating your research question, one of your first propositions is to identify it in a way that people will want to read it. "Are the people of the island of Fiji experiencing an economic revival?" is a valid research question; however, I am guessing that your mind either drifted to an idealistic beach of what you envision Fiji to be or shut off entirely when you read this question. While it may be a valid question, it is phrased in a way that is very broad and quite boring. A better question for a research paper may be, "Has the economic revival, sparked by the ingress of international trade, positively affected the lower class citizens of Fiji?" This question is much more specific, looking at a specific cause of economic growth in relation to a specific group of people. By way of another example, our topic "Did Russia meet its nuclear disarmament obligations to the extent that the United States and United Nations believed they did in the 1990s?" is a question, but it is not a good research question. We can make it a better question by changing it to "Did the *government* of Russia meet its nuclear disarmament goals *stated under UN Resolution 3472B* to the extend that *experts* in the United States and within the United Nations believed they did in the 1990s?"[4] As you can see, we have made some minor changes to the text, but they create major changes in the meaning. First, we are looking at the actions of the government of Russia, while it can be assumed that any dealings with a sovereign nation will be with its government, Russia is a special circumstance as it used to be the USSR. Now there are multiple nations within that region that had nuclear weapons at their borders. Next, we look at United Nations Resolution 3472B, which is one of the UN resolutions establishing nuclear weapon-free zones in specific areas. This further refines the data that we will be looking at. Finally, we are looking at the opinions of experts. Young researchers tend to chase red herrings down rabbit holes, and nuclear weapons are one area where people can find themselves immersed in crackpot theories by conspiracy theorists. The small change to experts allows the researcher to eliminate all non-mainstream theories and look only at the work of experts. This research question is not a hypothesis, but the hypothesis will be built from this research question.

---

3. *See Generally* Claire Howell-Major & Maggi Savin-Baden (2010). AN INTRODUCTION TO QUALITATIVE RESEARCH SYNTHESIS: MANAGING THE INFORMATION EXPLOSION IN SOCIAL SCIENCE RESEARCH. New York: Routledge. (Note I am Using a version of ABA/Yale Blue Book Citation in this book, I chose this because it reduce the reference footprint and is simple to cite the same sources throughout the book.)

4. UNODA (2015). "Nuclear-Weapon-Free Areas." United Nations Office of Disarmament Affairs, available at http://www.un.org/disarmament/WMD/Nuclear/NWFZ.shtml (January 4, 2015).

Your research question should merge your skills with the topic that you are researching. If you are a novice researcher, then your skill set is very broad; generally it is the discipline in which your major lies. If you have been writing for years, your research skill set will hopefully be more specialized and will be something that you are known for in the field (or something tangential to the area for which you are known). So take your topic from the last chapter and create your research question, as specifically as practical, so you are prepared to create a hypothesis or a theory:

Topic: _____

Research Question: _____

_____

_____

_____

This research question will help you build your hypothesis and null hypothesis as we go through the chapter (or theory if you are writing theoretical paper).

Now that your research question has been formulated, you can move on to the more rigorous task of turning that research question into a hypothesis (or in more complex cases, your theory). In the first section of this chapter we look at what a hypothesis is and how a hypothesis is used in research. Since this book is designed to be used by many different disciplines there are different variations on how hypotheses are used. In the second section we look at theories and define what they are. There are two competing levels of theory, basic theory and established theory, that need to be discussed as to how they can be used in papers. Following that section, we look at how theories are to be used in academic papers. Here you will choose between a hypothesis and theory for your writing. We can also make a basic rule that unless you are established and have several papers penned under your name, the general assumption is that you will write a paper based on a hypothesis.

In the fifth section we discuss one of the more philosophical parts of writing a paper. Academia has established that nothing can be proven outright, as you do not know if there is a situation in the multi-verse where what you are asserting is different under a different set of circumstances; therefore, nothing can be proven as absolutely true. However, you can prove something wrong, as a statement only needs to be false part of the time for the statement to be false. Therefore the academic system in the United States uses a system of disproving the opposite to support the original hypothesis. This process is called the use of a null hypothesis. Lastly, in the sixth section, we look at the proper way to frame a hypothesis or a theory. How you word your hypothesis or your theory will determine whether either one can be easily defended from critics in other papers or at conferences.

By the time you complete this chapter, you should have a hypothesis or theory that you can use in the formulation of your paper. This enables you to move on to the next two steps of the writing process, choosing a citation style (Chapter 5) and selecting your research approach (Chapter 6). These are two parts of the writing process where it will take you longer to read the chapters than it will for you to do the actual processes that they recommend. The hypothesis becomes the first step that you take in your journey of writing a paper. The concept and the steps that you took to distill it down to a topic/research question were foundational, now you are actually engaged in the creative process and can begin to discover something that other people have not written about.

WHAT IS A HYPOTHESIS?

Google defines a hypothesis as "a supposition or proposed explanation made on the basis of limited evidence as a starting point for further investigation."[5] This definition is technical and meets all the needs of a person who wants to get the definition of a hypothesis correct on a test. But what does it really mean? Dictionary.com likewise has the definition of hypothesis as "a proposition, or set of propositions, set forth as an explanation for the occurrence of some specified group of phenomena, either asserted merely as a provisional conjuncture to guide investigation (working hypothesis) or accepted as highly probable in light of established facts."[6] Wow! This definition is even more complex than the definition from Google. In some disciplines, complexity of definitions is a requirement, but our goal in this book is to make the writing process as simple as possible; therefore, we will work from the definition that a hypothesis is "the believed answer to the research question based on preliminary research." Short, sweet, and to the point. If you have followed the process in this book to this point, you have looked up several articles on your topic, so you know something about your research topic. Once you have a research question, your hypothesis becomes the assumed answer of that question. This does not mean that it is correct, it just means that you have built this hypothesis based on preliminary research. This is where you have the advantage if you have done all the processes laid out in this book. You will have a basic knowledge of your subject

---

5. Google (2015). Available at https://www.google.com/?gws_rd=ssl#q=definition+hypothesis (January 4, 2015).
6. Dictionary.com (2015). "Hypothesis." Available at http://dictionary.reference.com/browse/hypothesis (January 4, 2015)

area so you can make an educated decision and avoid your hypothesis being the other definition on Dictionary.com: "a mere guess or assumption."[7]

Another theoretical construct that you may find yourself working with during the writing of your paper is a working hypothesis. A working hypothesis is one that you establish at the beginning, but you find something early in the research process that forces you to change your hypothesis (i.e., you discover that someone else has researched the exact same hypothesis and you are completely wrong, thus you have no new material to write about). If this is the case then your hypothesis becomes a first working hypothesis and you should create a new hypothesis that will become your active hypothesis and continue the research process from that point. Do not look at the discarding of the working hypothesis as a failure on your part, as the elimination of something that has already been done allows you to move on into areas of new research without encroaching on already established positions.

There are two schools of thought on how a hypothesis should be worded. Some academics believe that a hypothesis should be an affirmative statement; others feel that a hypothesis should be an affirmative question. Either will work with this process; however, we are going to cover the process of writing your hypothesis as an affirmative statement. If your discipline requires you to write your hypothesis as an affirmative question, then basically you will follow the same steps then convert the statement into a question. The reason that we are selecting the statement school over the question school is because the statement school is more common and the question school tends to be a more complex way of formulating a hypothesis, thus is more confusing. The end product is basically the same and the hypothetical statement is simply a cleaner methodology.

Now, it is time to form a hypothesis. We could wait until after you have decided whether you are using a hypothesis or a theory, but in this case the practice is good and it will show you how to do it for future papers. If you do not agree with me, then skip it and come back to do it when you decide whether you are using a hypothesis or a theory. It is your book, so use it how you like. For those of you who are still working through the process:

Research Question: _____

_____

_____

---

7. *Id*. (Note: Id is an abbreviation for Ibid, which means to look at the citation above this one. For the purpose of this footnote, I am citing the same webpage that I had cited in the last footnote.)

Hypothesis:

_____

_____

_____

Having a clean hypothesis will enable you to have a focused approach as you work your way further through the process. As a bonus precaution, and to get in the habit of doing it, compare your hypothesis to your topic statement; if they do not relate you are already off track, so either rewrite your hypothesis or tweak your topic statement to come in line with your hypothesis.[8]

WHAT IS A THEORY?

A theory is the other option when writing your paper. Theoretical papers are covered in Part IV of this book. Theoretical papers are more complex than hypothetical papers because a theory has more issues to support than a single hypothesis. Google defines a theory as "a supposition or system of ideas intended to explain something, especially one based on general principles independent of the thing being explained."[9] Dictionary.com's definition is also quite complex: "A coherent group of tested general propositions commonly regarded as correct, that can be used as principles of explanation and prediction for a class of phenomena" or "a proposed explanation whose status is still conjectural and subject to experimentation, in contrast to well established propositions that are regarded as reporting matters of actual fact."[10] Once again these definitions are proper, but are overly complex for our purposes. Therefore, we are going to establish a **general theory** as "a set of hypotheses that support one another when combined for a proposed explanation for an event or phenomenon."

General theories can be broken down into two types of theory for our purposes. **Basic theories** are ones "that are yet unproven and the current researcher is establishing support for component hypotheses that support the explanation of the theory." These are theories that are being created by

---

8. This should be the last time that you tweak your topic statement. From this point out, you should change your working hypothesis rather than change your topic.

9. Google (2015). Available at https://www.google.com/?gws_rd=ssl#q=definition+theory (January 4, 2015).

10. *See* Dictionary.com, *Supra* at http://dictionary.reference.com/browse/theory [Note: in this citation, we are looking at dictionary.com, which is the same source as the above footnote; however, since there is another footnote in between we cannot use "*Id.*" Supra means as seen above.

the researcher as they are writing their research paper. **Established theories** are ones "that have already been shown to be factual by research." Some of you may be writing papers in support or critical of established theories (one that is common to attack is radical feminist theory). Just because a theory is widely accepted does not mean that it has not been proven to be wrong; for example, the flat earth theory, the earth as the center of the universe, and the theory that Keynesian economics is a stable system have all been proven wrong for years (some even centuries) yet people still cling to them. Luckily, with the exception of the followers of Keynesian economics, most theories that have been proven wrong are regulated to a group of followers who simply do not want to accept reality.

For a theory to be valid the component hypotheses must be shown to be likely and they must be shown to support the general premise of the theory. Simply putting a general theory out there, with no support, and expecting people to believe it is not academic research.[11] If you are going to write a theoretical paper, you must:

1. Create a theory;
2. Establish hypotheses that support the theory;
3. Show the hypotheses to be valid; and
4. Show how the hypotheses relate to the theory.

This means that a theoretical research paper should prove at least two, likely more, hypotheses for it to validate a theory. Further, the theory should be validated by several people at different institutions for the theory to be vetted. So, a theoretical research paper is sufficiently more work than a hypothetical research paper and should generally only be attempted by someone who has already published hypothetical papers on the subject.[12]

The more data you can show to support a theoretical position, the stronger the position will be. This is one of the reasons that theoretical papers should be limited to experienced authors. Even the most strongly supported new theory will come under attack from people who oppose the change. For instance, several research articles have shown that marijuana damages the interaction between hemispheres of the brain and can cause problems with both long- and short-term memory in the general population. This has been established for nearly 20 years. However, those who support the legalization of marijuana tend to find outliers in the general population that do not suffer the negative effects of marijuana and hold them up to be the "normal" person. This results in there

---

11. It is good marketing.
12. For instance, my Dissertation *Quadralectics* focused on the conflict created at the confluence of different socio-economic systems. Previous to writing *Quadralectics* I had written on conflict and international relations. I simply took the next logical step to combine the two.

being confusion about a subject that should be completely established. Thus, those who support the realistic research on marijuana and the damage it does need to keep piling on data to show that their research is valid. When you are writing a theoretical research paper, realize that others will challenge your research if it challenges the status quo. The more support you can garner through validated hypotheses, the better you will be able to defend against these assaults on your research.

Before you engage in a theoretical research paper, make sure that you ask yourself if you are willing to put yourself through the time and pressure that a theoretical research paper requires. Where a simple hypothetical research paper can be completed in the space of a few weeks, a theoretical paper can take months or even years to write (this is not including the time that it will take you to gather the data and test the theory). Theoretical research papers are the result of years of work, not simple term papers you can turn in on short notice. If you truly believe that you have a valid theory that you can prove, then prove individual hypotheses in individual papers and then combine the research into a theoretical paper citing your original research. This will allow you to establish yourself as a writer and build a catalog of publications after your name.

HOW DO I CHOOSE BETWEEN A HYPOTHESIS AND A THEORY?

When choosing whether you want to write a hypothetical research paper or a theoretical research paper, you need to take into consideration the practical elements of each type of paper. As a general rule, hypothetical research papers are easier to write, easier to prove, and easier to publish. On the other hand, a single theoretical research paper has been known to cement an academics career at a prestigious institution. Ultimately, the choice is yours as to whether you write a hypothetical research paper or a theoretical research paper. Here are some general guidelines to help you decide.

1. Amount of Work: A theoretical paper will generally be more work than a hypothetical paper. This is because to show support for a theory you need to show several valid hypotheses. Each of these hypotheses needs to be supported by disproving the null hypothesis. An additional danger with writing a theoretical paper is that if one of your foundational hypotheses is proven to be wrong, it can unravel the whole theory.

2. Amount of Credit: Writers tend to get more credit and acclaim for writing theoretical papers. The Academy knows that good theory papers take more time than good hypothetical research papers; therefore, professionals are willing to give credit where credit is due. That being said, an important hypothesis can bring a writer a lot of credit if the presentation is well done.

3. Time: Time is a fluid factor. Some theoretical papers can be researched and written within the course of a year; other hypothetical papers can take decades. As a general rule, however, theoretical papers take a longer time to research and write than hypothetical papers.

4. Cost: Generally, theoretical papers cost more to prepare than hypothetical papers. Each theory will have several hypotheses that need to be proven, which means you will do the work that you do for a hypothetical paper many times over in a theoretical paper. This can greatly increase the cost.

5. Point in Your Career: As a general rule, hypothetical papers are generally more suited to younger writers where elder authors can summarize their life's work into theoretical papers. This rule is by no means hard and fast. Young authors can and have written theoretical papers and veteran writers have made careers out of writing hypothetical papers.

These guidelines are just here for your consideration and are generalities. There is no rule that says a high school student or first-year college student will not write a theoretical paper that will shake the foundations of academia. There is also no rule that states a person who has been writing for 50 years cannot make a career out of writing hypothetical research papers. Writing comes from the person who is putting pen to ink, or in the modern age fingers to keys. What type of paper you write is ultimately up to you.

THE NULL HYPOTHESIS

As we noted earlier, the null hypothesis is the result of philosophical and factual forces within the academic system. It is asserted that with the diversity of the universe no positive statement can be proven to be true, including this one. Therefore, we need a way to show a statement is valid without proving it to be true. This is established by proving that the opposite of the statement is false. In this way we use logic to determine that if the true opposite of something is not true, then the original is more likely to be true. While this does not prove that the hypothesis is true, it proves that the hypothesis is more likely to be true.[13] In this way we establish support for our hypothesis.

prove opposite is false

Disproving something is simple. For instance, if the null hypothesis is "this book is red" and this book is clearly not red, then we have disproved the null hypothesis. The more complex the idea, the more difficult it is to show that the idea is not true. Further, articles that are written in the negative are difficult to read, so the way that we disprove a null hypothesis is by showing that the

---

13. Jerry W. Willis (2007). FOUNDATIONS OF QUALITATIVE RESEARCH: INTERPRETIVE AND CRITICAL APPROACHES. Thousand Oaks: Sage. At 127.

hypothesis is more likely to be true than the null hypothesis. In most qualitative research papers the null hypothesis is not even mentioned, though a good author should still do the work to develop a null hypothesis. Even in statistical or theoretical papers, the work with the null hypothesis is generally done outside of the writing as to not confuse the reader. Let us return to our example of the Russian military. Our hypothesis is, "The Russian government did not fulfill its duties under the UN resolution relating to nuclear weapon-free zones to the expectations of U.S. and UN experts." We can then say that the null hypothesis is, "The Russian government did fulfill its duties under the UN resolution relating to nuclear weapon-free zones to the expectations of U.S. and UN experts." Now if we can prove this statement to be false through the work of our research and writing, then the converse must be true and we have "proven" our hypothesis.

Now let's look at your hypothesis. First of all, what is your hypothesis? Write it on the lines here:

Hypothesis: _____

_____

_____

Now when writing your null hypothesis, you need to ensure that it is a question that has a yes or no answer. This means that you may need to adjust your hypothesis so that it can be inverted into a yes or no question. If your hypothesis is "This book is blue" then you need to be very specific in your null hypothesis. The statement "This book is red" could be seen as the opposite of "This book is blue." Proving this book is not red does not do much to support the idea that this book is blue. However, the statement "This book is not blue" is a direct opposite statement to "This book is blue" thus proving that the statement "This book is not blue" is false and supports "This book is blue." (It does not prove that the book is blue, because the book could be blue and red, which would make the statement "This book is blue" a half truth.) So now it is your turn. What is the null hypothesis to your hypothesis?

Null Hypothesis:

_____

_____

_____

FRAMING YOUR HYPOTHESIS/THEORY

How you word your hypothesis or theory can determine how your paper is received. As with anything in this politically correct society that we live in, if others cannot attack your hypothesis or theory directly, they will then turn their attention to you. In a course paper, you have little worry that the professor will develop an innate hatred to your theory; if the professor does, you may have to pick another theory. However, in the real world, you may find that others want to attack your theory but they are unable or are too incompetent to find flaws with your work. Then their attention will turn to you. This creates an added layer of pressure for researchers in the new millennia. As critical academia becomes more accepted, more and more people follow this lazy format of academic discourse. If they can find a misworded sentence in your hypothesis, then they will use that to devalue all of your research.

The first thing that you should look for is whether your hypothesis is too broad.[14] If your hypothesis is too broad, there will doubtless be areas of the hypothesis that you did not research to the saturation point. If this occurs, all that it takes is one datum of evidence that supports your null hypothesis or disproves your hypothesis and your work will have been for naught. Therefore, when you are crafting your hypothesis and your null hypothesis, you should make sure that they are as narrow as practical for a research paper. This will help protect you from critical academics.

Another problem that faces some writers is that they take the advice from the previous paragraph too far and make their hypothesis and null hypothesis too narrow. This can lead to two major problems. First, you may eliminate too much of your readership. If your topic and hypothesis are too narrow, it will not pique the interest of enough people to make writing your paper worthwhile. The number of people who read your article that are needed to make your work a success varies by field. In sociology, for your paper to be groundbreaking hundreds of thousands of people will have to read your paper. If your area of writing is gluton physics, then your successful readership is much smaller. However, in each field you still have to get a segment of the field to acknowledge your work for it to be truly successful.

Another problem that some people may face is words with different meanings in different disciplines. Sometimes if your paper crosses disciplines or is a multidisciplinary paper and the lexicons of the different fields do not match up, then you will face problems. Personally, I wrote a paper rectifying the Big Bang theory and an eternal God and had a physics professor at an Israeli university review the paper. He stated that the paper was excellent, but many of the terms I used in the paper

---

14. The same rules apply for theories, it would just be monotonous to write hypothesis/theory 20 times over the next several paragraphs.

had different meanings in the field of physics than they did in the field of sociology, so there were problems in translation that made the paper convoluted. Always be careful that your words mean what you want them to mean, and always be careful not to tick off the political correctness police unless you want to fight with them (which can be fun).

CHECKLIST

- ❑ Write a good research question.
- ❑ Decide between a hypothesis and a theory.
- ❑ Write a good hypothesis or theory.
- ❑ If you choose a theory, break it down into multiple hypotheses that can establish each point of the theory.
- ❑ Write a null hypothesis for your hypothesis/hypotheses (for theory).
- ❑ Check to make sure your null hypothesis is actually the opposite of your hypothesis.
- ❑ Check the wording to make sure that it is not:
  - Too broad;
  - Too narrow;
  - Politically incorrect; and
  - Offensive/racist.[15]

---

15. There is a difference between being politically incorrect and being actually offensive. Politically incorrect work offends people with thin skin and people who cannot have their point challenged. After you get a few papers published, feel free to tick off these people. Offensive or racist writing materials, on the other hand, have no place in academic writing. Always make sure to use the proper terms when referring to specific groups of people. When in doubt, ask an expert how to define a group.

chapter 5
Format

INTRODUCTION

Aside from the actual content of the material you are writing, the format may be the most important factor in deciding whether your paper will be published. The format of your paper is the font style, the parts of the paper you choose to use, the way you cite sources, and the overall appearance of your paper. The different combinations of how words and paragraphs go together can determine whether your article gets published in a top-tier journal or gets sent back to you with a "Dear Author, We do not believe that your article fits our needs at this time" letter. The central theme of this chapter is that no matter what type of paper you are writing, you should always strive to make the format match up with the expectations of the person/people who are going to be reading it.

One of the first places that you should look to find advice on what format you should use is in your own discipline. Most academic disciplines have one format or another that the majority of writers in that format use regularly. This format is generally one of the big four citation styles with some slight changes. This is not always the case, however, as some disciplines (such as sociology) have their own formatting and citation that is recommended by the discipline, but not by the journals in that field. This is an area where, if in doubt, you should ask what format to use in your preparation. Starting in the recommended format will make it easier to get your paper published and will show the people reading your paper that you are "one of them" and part of the club of writers in your discipline. Fighting against the establishment may have impressed liberal professors in your college classes, but it is a surefire ticket to getting your paper discarded when it hits an editor's desk.

The four main formats for writing an academic or professional paper make up the vast majority of guidelines for writing in a journal or a trade journal. While it is true that some journals modify the requirements slightly to fit their own needs, the vast majority of the rules that you should be following will be found in one of these four citation styles. Once you find out what style your discipline requires, buy a copy of the sourcebook for writing in that format. Having that reference alongside this book will help you stay focused and within the format you need to get your article its best chance at being published. The main texts for each book are:

1. American Psychological Association (2009). *Publication Manual of the American Psychological Association*, 6th ed. New York: APA. (ISBN 13: 978-1433805618)
2. Modern Language Association (2009). *MLA Handbook for Writers of Research Papers*, 7th ed. New York: MLA. (ISBN 13: 860-1200663914)
3. Kate L. Turabian &Wayne C. Booth (2013). *A Manual for Writers of Research Papers, Theses, and Dissertations*, 8th ed. Chicago: University of Chicago Press. (ISBN 13: 978-0226816388)
4. Columbia Law Review & Harvard Law Review (2010). *The Blue Book: Uniform System of Citation*, 19th spiral edition. Cambridge, MA: Harvard Law Review Association. (ISBN 13: 978-0615361161)

Now as you can see, all of these book are in later editions; so, if you want to have the most current copy of any of these styles, you need to keep up with them as they print new copies. With the exception of the *Chicago Manual of Style*, all of them are due for an update, so if you buy them now, you will probably have to buy a new copy in the next year or two. An option for those of you who wish to save money (at least on APA and MLA) is to buy an older edition of the book and use resources like Owl Purdue to bring your material up to date.[1]

This chapter is going to follow a rather simple format. In the first section we will look at the question of what a publisher wants from a paper. Not all publishers have the same standard; the better publishers are going to be more specific about what they want, because their status allows them to be more demanding. In the next four sections, we will look at the basic formats of the APA, MLA, Chicago Manual, and ABA Blue Book, respectively. In each of these sections we will look at the history of the writing style, the basic formatting rules of each style, the basic citation rules of each style, and most important who uses each style. These sections of the chapter will not make you experts in each of the citation styles, but should be useful as a handbook for checking the basic cita-

---

1. The Purdue online writing lab is an excellent resource for all types of writers. You should take a moment when you get the opportunity to pursue the information on the site. Available at https://owl.english.purdue.edu/ (last visited January 5, 2015).

tion and formatting elements as you write a paper. In the final section of this chapter we will look at how journals change the citation styles slightly and some of the pitfalls that you should look out for when writing papers for specific journals.

The goal of this chapter is to give you a basic understanding of the differences between citation and formatting styles. Too often, college professors will teach students the professor's favorite citation style and exclude all others. This provides students with only a one-sided view of a diverse system of writing styles in the United States. As boring as it is, I have actually seen students arguing in hallways which style of citation is better. If you are going to become a professional writer, you should familiarize yourself with all of the styles, then choose the one that will be used in the journals that you want to publish in. As a multidisciplinary writer, I have had to learn the basics of APA, Chicago, and ABA Blue Book for my writing. You will eventually find your formatting and citation style that is used predominantly in your discipline, then you can master it and it will be second nature to you as your write your future papers.

WHAT DOES THE READER/PUBLISHER WANT?

All publishers want what they ask for. Although this seems like a simple statement, many beginning writers believe that they know what the publisher needs (or the professor needs) more than the publisher (or professor). This results in some people writing brilliant papers that are rejected because they are not what the reviewing person asked for. This is one of the easiest mistakes in writing to avoid. If you give the reviewer what he or she asks for, then you have a much better chance of your paper achieving the goal. Though it is your journey that you are taking while writing a paper, always be accepting of things along the way that make your trip legitimately easier.[2] Think of it this way, if you are on a hike and you see one path through briars and thorns and the other through a grassy meadow, which path makes more sense? You build your own briar patch when you elect to ignore the reviewer's guidelines and set your own format.

Another reason that you always follow the reviewer's guidelines is because you are making a product for them. They are your customer at this moment in time. Even if they are an idiot, the customer is always right (especially if you are just starting out). Each time you write a paper, whether for college, for research, or for your career, you are building a brand for yourself. This brand is going to be how people see you at college, in the research community, or at your place of business. While

---

2. Only use legitimate means to make your project easier, do not plagiarize or use already written works. You will be wasting your time and with the new systems in place electronically you will likely get caught.

being seen as a rebel seems cool in high school, in college, academia, or in business being a rebel can mean that your work does not get seen at all. Professors will return your paper ungraded. Journals will reject your manuscript and bosses will tell you to do the project again or fire you. When you are writing, your reviewer is your customer; and customers have the choice whether to take your product or to look for someone else.

If you start your project from the beginning following the format set out by the reviewer, then you will also find that it makes the editorial process easier. We cover the editorial process in Chapter 53, but it is important to note here that you are the first editor of your paper. The format is important because you want your writing to fit in to the journal by appearance. Having flashy fonts, oddly laid out paragraphs, or some other gimmick to make your paper stand out on the page will only grab the reader's attention for a few seconds at the most. The articles that people are going to pay attention to are the ones that are formatted properly and that stand out because of their content. Anyone can change their formatting to make their article look different, but if you want your article to be truly different you need to become a true wordsmith.

AMERICAN PSYCHOLOGICAL ASSOCIATION

The format and citation style of the American Psychological Association (APA) dominates the requirements for most academic journals in the social sciences and the "hard" sciences. APA format was an effort begun by James McKeen Cattel in 1904, when he attempted to create a uniform system of citation for several journals that he reviewed, *Science*, *Scientific Monthly*, and *Psychological Review*.[3] This was challenged by Edward B. Titchener, who was head of Cornell University's psychology program at the time.[4] Titchener stated, "Science and I think Universities, must be heterogeneous if they are to be at their best."[5] He continued, "This bashing of spelling and punctuation takes the joy out of writing as aesthetics."[6] This led Titchener to call Cattel's process a "Machine made product."[7] However, standardization won out over creativity and the APA citation style was born. Critics accuse APA of being without creativity and character as metaphors, analogies, and most creative language is discouraged in this overly formal writing style.[8] Regardless of the criti-

3. Pedro Almeida (2012). "The Origins of APA Style (and why there are so many Rules)." JEPS Bulletin, Official Blog of the Journal of European Psychology Students. Available at http://blog.efpsa.org/2012/07/10/the-origins-of-apa-style-and-why-there-are-so-many-rules/ (January 5, 2015).
4. *Id.*
5. E.B. Titchener (1904). "Letters," Letter to J.M. Cattel, JMC.
6. Almeida, *Supra.*
7. *Id.*
8. American Psychological Association (2009). *Publication Manual of the American Psychological Association*, 6th ed. New York: APA.

cisms, APA is used by hundreds of journals and other publications and reigns supreme over much of the academic landscape in the United States and abroad.

Some of the areas that you will commonly use in academic papers can be slightly confusing, especially if you write your first paper in APA format. Some common formatting issues are:

1. Running Header: A running header is a shortened title that appears on each page.[9] Additionally, you should have the words "Running Head" preceding the actual running header on the title page of your paper.[10]
2. Page Numbers: These numbers should appear on all pages of your paper/article. The page number should appear in the upper righthand corner of the page.[11]
3. Margins: APA margins should be 1 to 1.5 inches from each side of the page.[12]
4. Section Headings: These are titled parts of your paper that you use to break your paper down into more manageable parts. The way that these are broken down depends on the complexity of your paper and you should check either the APA publication manual or OWL Purdue for your specific needs.[13]
5. Labels: These are common parts of all APA papers. They should be demarcated as a label in the normal size and font of the text.[14]

These are the nuances that you are most likely to come in contact with while writing an academic or professional paper; however, other areas where there are specific rules are lists, tables, figures, and of course the sections of the paper and the citations, which we will cover in the next few paragraphs.

The main parts of an APA paper—that is, the parts that all papers should have—are the Title Page, the Abstract, the Main Body, and the Reference page.[15] The Title Page should present the title of your paper, your name, your institution, and show your reader what the running header should be. The Abstract is a 250-page preview of what your paper is about and the methodologies that you will use in your paper. The main body of an APA style paper can vary depending on the content of the paper, but the basic elements of the body are:

---

9. APAStyle.org at http://www.apastyle.org/learn/quick-guide-on-formatting.aspx (January 5, 2015).
10. *Id.*
11. University of Wisconsin-Madison (2015). The Writers Handbook: APA Documentation Guide. At http://writing.wisc.edu/Handbook/DocAPAFormat_PageNumber.html (January 5, 2015).
12. *Id.* at http://writing.wisc.edu/Handbook/DocAPAFormat_Margins.html (January 5, 2015).
13. *See* APA, *Supra;* OWL Purdue, *Supra.*
14. APAStyle.org *Supra* at http://www.apastyle.org/learn/quick-guide-on-formatting.aspx (January 5, 2015).
15. The Writing Commons (2015). At http://writingcommons.org/format/apa/668-order-of-major-sections-apa (January 5, 2015).

1. Introduction;
2. Methodology;
3. Data;
4. Analysis; and
5. Discussion.

In a dissertation, you may have a literature review section interspersed between the introduction, methodology, and data sections to show that you have researched whether this material has already been covered by other authors. The final section, the Works Cited page, should include the quotes you referenced in your paper, formatted to APA style.

The part of APA format that gives people the most problems is the citation style. Much of this stems from having three main places for citations: those in text, those secondary in text, and those on the works cited page. In addition, the citation process differs between journal articles, books, newspapers, conferences, and websites. While we will provide examples of each of these problem areas, the best way that I have ever heard APA citation explained (at least the Works Cited citations) is that there are three sentences in all citations. The first sentence is made up of the author and the data. The second sentence is made up of the title and the edition. The third sentence is made up of the publication the work cited appears in and the publisher. If you have all of these sentences in your citation, even if your APA format is still incorrect, you will have all the information to give credit to the person you are citing.

In-Text Citation

When referencing an author in the text of your paper (whole book), you need to have the author's name and the year. If you are making a direct quote or material from a specific page (or range of pages), then you need the author's name, the year, and a page number.

EXAMPLES

Whole Book Citation: In *Wealth of Nations*, it is established that the incentive for a person to work is the gains realized from his work (Smith, 1776).

Whole Book if Author's Name Is Mentioned: In *Wealth of Nations*, Smith (1776) establishes that the incentive for a person to work is the gains realized from his work.

Quote: In *City of God*, the Sage of Hippo states "neither ought eternal life be sought from Juventas." (St. Augustine, 442, p. 185)

As a general rule place the parenthetical as close to the author's name as possible. If there is a long quotation (more than 40 words) then look to the guide for formatting of large block quotations. Remember, only quote an author when necessary, use your own words whenever possible.

Reference Citation

PERIODICALS

Smithmyer, Christopher W. (2010). "A Synopsis of Synthesis: A Review of Major and Savin-Badin's *An Introduction to Qualitative Research Synthesis.*" *The Qualitative Report* 15:5 at http://www.nova.edu/ssss/QR/QR15-5/major.pdf.

BOOKS

Smithmyer, Christopher W. (2013). *The Seven Swords of Strategic Business Facilitation: A Handbook for Business in the 21st Century.* Dubuque, IA: Kendall-Hunt.

NEWSPAPERS

Smiley, Joe (2014, December 23). Business as Usual. *Altoona Mirror*, p. 2A.[16]

ONLINE SOURCE

Smiley, Joe (2015). "Business as Usual," *Business Online* (←title of online periodical) (volume number, if available). Retrieved from www.madeupwebsite.com.[17]

These are the basic requirements for citation under this style. If you are writing a complex paper in this area that you intend to publish, look to the APA Manual or OWL Purdue to find specific citation guidelines for other sources not listed here.

MODERN LANGUAGE ASSOCIATION

The Modern Language Association has been around since 1883. It was formed to allow members to discuss changes in the research system of the United States and the world. The Modern Lan-

---

16. This is a made-up newspaper article.
17. Also a made-up website.

guage Association is not limited to English language journals; it incorporates programs in many languages that are considered modern. The MLA produces four major periodicals: ADE Bulletin, ADFL Bulletin, Profession, and PLMA.[18] This format of citation and writing is the main format used in the humanities and the arts and thus this is the second most popular citation format in academia.

MLA, like all major writing styles, has its own quirks that are conventions you should adhere to if you are writing in this style. Some of the more pressing conventions are:

1. Leave only one space after a period. Most word processors automatically adjust to two spaces after a period so you will have to watch this one;
2. The page numbers should be in the upper righthand corner of each page;
3. Use italics sparingly, generally only for the titles of longer works;
4. Put endnotes on a separate page prior to works cited page, do not use footnotes;
5. Generally no title page;
6. Section headings should be numbered (Arabic), then a period, then space, then section name.[19]

MLA's conventions are simpler than those of APA, which sometimes lets people believe that they are less important. Citation format and style tend to be a major sticking point for editors, so always try to conform as much as possible when writing your paper.

In-text Citations

MLA requires that the author's name and the page number appear in the text, which differs from APA because the year of the work is not printed in the text.

EXAMPLES

Smith stated that the development of individual control of the industrial machine granted the nation to move forward during the industrial revolution (167).

Much of the success during the industrial revolution was caused by individual control of the industrial machine and the non-interventionist policies of the government (Smith, 167).

---

18. MLA Website (2015). At https://www.mla.org/about (January 6, 2015).
19. OWL Purdue, *Supra*.

Direct quotes function much the same as they do in an APA paper with the small quotes appearing in text and the larger quotes being blocked off:

Example

> The premise "What does he mean by *fate*?" denotes the folly in the Roman system of religion as related to their gods (Augustine, 143).
>
> St. Augustine denotes the folly of the Roman system of gods in the question "What does he mean by *fate*?" (143).
>
> St. Augustine states:
>> "And if any one attributes their existence to fate, because he calls the will or the power of God itself by the name of fate, let him keep his opinion, but correct his language. For why does he not say at first what he will say afterwards, when some one shall put the question to him, 'What he means by *Fate*?' For when men hear that words, according to the ordinary use of language, they simply understand by it the virtue of one particular position of the stars which may exist at the time when any one is born or conceived, which some separate altogether from the will of God, whilst others affirm that this also is dependant on that will"
>
> defining the difference between general fate and the will of God (143).[20]

As you can see the text is indented from both sides so that it stands out from the rest of the text. This helps distinguish the works of another author from your own words.

Reference Citations

All sources should be organized in alphabetical order by the last name of the authors. Use the title for sources without authors.

Periodicals

Smithmyer, Christopher. "A Synopsis of Synthesis: A Review of Major and Savin-Badin's *An Introduction to Qualitative Research*." *The Qualitative Report* 15.5 (2010). Print.

Books

Smithmyer, Christopher. *The Realistic Republican*. New York: Amazon. (2012). Book.

---

20. St. Augustine (1993 ed). *City of God*. New York: Modern Library at 143.

NEWSPAPER

Smiley, Joe. "The Newspaper Article." *Blackrock Herald* Dec. 17 2014, English edition. Print.

ONLINE SOURCE

Penn State University, "Faculty Handbook." The Pennsylvania State University, 2010. Web ← note that the URL is no longer required for MLA.

CHICAGO MANUAL OF STYLE

The Chicago Manual of Style (CMS) is the primary writing and citation style for the American Anthropological Association and the Organization of American Historians. While these are two niche fields, there are a large number of journals that ascribe to the CMS methodology. Started in 1906, the CMS was originally developed as a set of rules for students attending the University of Chicago. The CMS was published on line alongside the hardcover edition for the first time in 2010 and is now in its 16th edition. Many colleges have this style, in addition to APA and MLA, on file at their libraries for those disciplines that use it. The CMS has two variations of citations, one in text and one in notes (NB).

We recommend using the footnote system. The first time you use a source on a page you should reference all the pertinent information about the source. This means that you should put the author's name, the title of the sources, the elements of the publication, and the date. If you cite the source later on the same page you can use the last name of the author, a shortened title, and the page number. If you cite the same source twice in succession you can use the word *Ibid* to denote that you are referencing the above line. Some other rules that may differ from other styles are:

1. You will use block quotations for quotes longer than five lines;
2. Notes and bibliographies should be single spaced;
3. Page numbers belong at the top of the page;
4. Subheadings can be used in most papers; and
5. Title pages are used in CMS.

Reference Citation

PERIODICALS

Smithmyer, Christopher. "A Synopsis of Synthesis: A Review of Major and Savin-Badin's *An Introduction to Qualitative Research.*" *The Qualitative Report 15* no. 5 (2010): xx-xx. ←Page numbers.

BOOKS

Smithmyer, Christopher. *The Realistic Republican.* New York: Amazon (2012).

NEWSPAPERS

Same as other periodicals.

ONLINE SOURCES

Smiley, Joe. "My Webpage." Joe Smiley's WebPages (publishing organization, if any). (Publication date/last visited date). URL.

As with other styles, look into the manual for more complex citations (multiple authors, odd sources, historical speeches). These citations outlined are the basic citations that most people will use when working with this style.

AMERICAN BAR ASSOCIATION/BLUE BOOK

In the field of legal writing there is currently a war going on between citation styles, which is likely why the legal citation style system does not drive the other systems out of use. The key style system for legal writing is the Blue Book (ABA Blue Book, Yale Blue Book, Harvard Blue Book, among others). This system has been in use since the turn of the last century, but due to the contentious nature of workers in the legal field (both on the editing staff and off) there have been several challenges to the Blue Book. The first major challenge came in 1989 when the Chicago Law Review attempted to counter the Blue Book with a Maroon Book. Although the project failed, it did point out some of the flaws in the Blue Book that needed attention. In the 1990s, however, activist editors made additional changes to the Blue Book (which have partially been rectified) that led to the

ALWD manual. The *ALWD* movement has somewhat petered out, so the Blue Book is used by most attorneys in most court systems today.

Legal writing style is highly formalized, as it is needed to be used by the courts. This means that it will follow the format given to you by the professor, the journal, or the court. If you have any questions, please contact the group who you are writing the paper for. Legal writing has many purposes—it can be academic or professional. For the purposes of this chapter, we look at the academic side of the writing. For more information on writing legal briefs please see Chapter 34.

Citations

One of the more pleasant elements of the Blue Book format is that in-text citations are generally the same as citations in the reference section. This is how a book would appear in the text:

> Adam Smith, WEALTH OF NATIONS (page number) (Editor [if available]), (publisher) (year of publication) (original publication date).

In the reference section it would appear:

> Smith, Adam, WEALTH OF NATIONS (Editor [if available]), (publisher) (year of publication) (original publication date).

Notice that the only changes are the last name comes first and the page number is removed. These are the changes that are made with all citations in this style, so generally you can cut and paste your footnote to the reference section (which only appears in academic papers; briefs use tables of sources and tables of cases).

PERIODICALS

> Christopher Smithmyer, *A Synopsis of Synthesis: A Review of Major and Savin-Badin's AN INTRODUCTION TO QUALITATIVE RESEARCH.* The Qual Rept (page number where article begins), (pages where cited material is) (2010).

NEWSPAPERS

> Joe Smiley, The Newspaper Article. *Blackrock Herald* Dec. 17 2014, at (page number).

Joe Smiley, *My Webpage*. Joe Smiley's WebPages (publishing organization, if any). (Publication date/last visited date). Available at (URL).

INDIVIDUAL JOURNAL RULES

When writing a paper, whether for class or for research, always cater to the needs and wants of the person who is going to be the gatekeeper for your paper. If the paper is going to be submitted for a class, then make sure your paper is what the professor wants it to be. If your paper is being written for a business paper, make sure that you are making it what the person reading it wants. If the paper is going to a journal, make sure you fulfill the guidelines. Successful writing is 50% doing a good job, and 50% making sure that the material gets read. It does not matter how brilliant your writing style is, if your **gatekeeper** does not read your paper then it is just words on a page that are never read.[21] If you are working your way through this process to write a paper, then you are putting a lot of hard work into this project. Do not let it all be for naught, take the time to learn what your gatekeeper wants; this will make your life a lot easier.

When you are writing for publication, especially in academic journals, the writing style and citation that the journal uses is very important. The writing style and citation are not simply some quirk of the editor or the owners, but the style and citation that they require are key to the journal's identity. If the style or citation is sloppy, then who will want to read the journal? If there are several different modes of citation, then tracking the sources becomes confusing for the reader, which also hurts the journal. The journal's goal is always to put out a good product that will keep the journal in business. If you help them reach this goal then you have a much better chance of your paper being published. Make it easy for the gatekeeper to say yes to your paper.

---

21. A gatekeeper is an editor, professor, judge, or other person that dictates whether the document you are submitting gets reviewed.

CHECKLIST

❑ Find out what citation style your discipline uses.
❑ Familiarize yourself with that style.
❑ Find out what citation and style you are expected to use for your paper.
❑ Check to see that there are no modifications of that style.[22]
❑ Follow the style to make it easy for the gatekeeper to say yes to your paper.

---

22. Some journals use their own style, which is one of the big four with slight modifications. Always check to see if there are modifications. Most editors will not trashcan your paper if you do not meet all the minor modifications; however, if you take the extra time to do the modifications it is likely that the editor will notice.

chapter 6
Approach

INTRODUCTION

Now that you have distilled your concept down to a topic and a hypothesis, identified the goal of your project, and selected the citation style that you are going to use, it is time to look at funding your project. If you are an undergraduate student working on a term paper, you probably do not need this chapter. If you are a professional, even if you do not believe that your project will cost you anything, you may still want to read this chapter. There may be some hidden costs that you did not consider. Either way, knowing the process for developing funds for a project is a valuable knowledge set to have.

This chapter is a primer chapter; the research approaches introduced in this chapter will each receive their own chapter later in this book. At this point you need to *consider* the type of data collection process you plan on using. We are not setting the process in stone at this point, rather we are building the definition of your project so you can propose your project to your university/company/grant agency to receive funding and have the wherewithal to complete the project. A focused project proposal is just as important as a focused paper. If you do your proposal correctly, then you should be able to get the approval/funding you need to complete your process at no expense to yourself.

How you collect the data is going to determine the "feel" of your paper. A paper where the author was in the bush dealing with the problems of the people she is studying feels different than a paper where a researcher uses the analytical tools of the lab or book research setting to answer a question on a theoretical level. Both approaches are common in the modern academic setting; however, where you are planning to publish/work/get money from may have a specific approach that they want you to follow. Just like you want your paper to appeal to the gatekeeper, you want your proposal to appeal to the **pursekeeper**. What data collection technique you are going to use is vital to ensuring you meet their expectations.

In this chapter, we will look at the reasons why you are examining your approach before you even select a research design—that is, approval and funding. In the first section of this chapter we look at the sources of funding that are available to most researchers in any field. Wherever you are doing your research, there is generally an agency or a private company that wants the research done; however, different types of research funding come with different strings attached, so be wary. In the second section we address your project design and what it will take to get approved. The approval mechanism that most people will face during their research is an Institutional Review Board (IRB). Next, you learn of the different macro-techniques of data collection that you have at your disposal for your research. This list is not all inclusive and is further augmented by Chapters 39 through 48 later in this book. The key areas that we will look at are:

1. Book Research (Section 3);
2. Observation (Section 4);
3. Surveys (Section 5); and
4. Participation (Section 6).

Each of these sections will give you the basic idea how the macro-research strategy works. This will allow you to prepare proposals to your management/supervisor/IRB.

SOURCES OF FUNDING

While research is a vital part of the educational process, money makes the world go round. If you do not have the money to eat, then you are not going to be spending your days looking through old books trying to find the literary impetus to Hamlet's tragedy in *Hamlet*, you are going to be looking for a way to afford to feed yourself. Funding opens all kinds of doors for people in most professions. Universities are always broke, companies always want someone else to pay the bill for their research, and the court system is always looking for a way to eliminate the charges in its budget. If you are a person who can, legally and morally, bring money into your institution then you will be treated well (at least as long as the money flows). This section is going to look at some of the ways authors generate funding for a project.

The most common way that researchers generate funding for a project is by means of their university. Generally to secure this means of funding a researcher goes to the department or division head with a proposal for a project, explains why it will benefit the university, then hopes that the department or division head will help them find a grant writer or tell them to write a grant proposal themselves for the project. The grant writing process can often be skipped if the university already has an endowment or a trust that focuses on that area or research. The strings attached to a research project funded by a college are generally not too constricting; the project must protect the public image of the university, the findings must be credited as the researcher being attached to the university, and the research may be used by future researchers to promote study in this area at the university. If your university (or another university) will fund your research, this is generally the best source of research funding. The application process is generally simple, the timeframes are generally lax, and no one is "buying" your research for a specific interest.

Governments are another great source of funding for research projects. If there is one thing that governments are good at, it is giving away other people's money. For a project to gain the interest of our domestic government (or the domestic government of any developed nation) it needs to be politically correct, novel enough to catch someone's attention, and safe enough that it passes an IRB. Governments tend to have more money to give away than universities, but the drawback is your research will probably become public as a condition of your project. The only situation worse than your research becoming public as a condition of your project is if the government censors your research and classifies it (not a problem for most of us as our research is not interesting enough to get classified). Foreign governments can also be a source of research funding, if the subject has a direct interest to that government. This is a situation where you have to allow your personal ethics to tell you whether you should be doing research for another government. Doing research on the migration patterns of geese for the Canadian government is probably a pretty safe project; however, doing nuclear weapon delivery systems for the North Korean government is probably something that will get your passport yanked.

Non-profit or not-for-profit companies in the United States generally have a small portion of their yearly budget set aside for outside research that supports their cause. If you are researching something that has non-profits set up to research it, always utilize them as a way to secure funding. This is another area where ethics should guide you as to whether you should accept the money. The United States is very liberal about who it allows to be a non-profit. While accepting money from

Easter Seals to research childhood diseases will probably increase the reliability of your research project, accepting money from the Ku Klux Klan or the New Black Panthers to research diversity will probably ensure that the only publication you can get your research in is *Mad Magazine*.[1]

The next step down the ladder is endowments. Endowments are piles of money that people have donated to secure research in specific subjects. Logic would dictate that if your research project was in an area where there was an endowment that the endowment should be the first place that you look for money; however, logic could be in error. Endowments are generally known by people in the field that they support, which means that most people doing research in that area will be asking the endowment for money. Endowments are a great place to get funding, but you will be competing against many other people. You should seek out the endowment as a means of funding, but it should not be the source of funding that you hinge your project on.

The final area of funding that we are going to look at is private companies. Whether you go to a private company for funding comes down to two things:

1. Whether your research will be taken seriously if it is funded by a company that has interests in the area that you are researching; and
2. Whether your research is interesting enough that a company would want to fund your research.

Private companies do not generally just give money to researchers without some private interest and that does not make them evil, because the purpose of a company is to make money. As a researcher, your job becomes showing the company why your research will make them money. As long as this does not affect the quality of your research there is no problem seeking funding from private companies. Once again, however, this is an area where your own personal ethics should come into play. Researching the best way to reduce carbon dioxide emissions from coal plants for greener power would be an excellent topic that plants would likely want to help you with; however, researching marketing techniques to get 18-year-olds with no history of smoking to start buying cigarettes for a major tobacco company may be morally shaky ground.

Getting funding often comes down to how important your research is and how bad you want to do the research. It also comes down to what you want your reputation to be within your field. Corporations, endowments, and some non-profits have a stigma that follows them around in certain segments of academia. When in doubt whether you should accept funding from a given group, ask your mentor what that group's standing in relation to the field is. If they are a group that is accepted

---

1. This is asserting that the research would then be a joke, not that *Mad Magazine* is racist—it makes fun of everyone equally.

wholeheartedly by your field, then they are likely a good group to try to get funding from; however, if they are mistrusted by your field or those who take research monies from them are pariahs, then you may want to seek other funding for your project. Remember, it is your journey and who funds it is up to you.

PROJECT DESIGN

Having a clear vision of your project will help you secure funding. As a rule, academics are not the best administrators in the world. They tend to see the specific point that they are working on and ignore the broader concept. This is one of the reasons that we started the paper writing journey at the concept level, because a good researcher should be able to relate his or her topic in the broadest possible sense to draw in the interest of as many people as possible. If you focus your sales pitch to your college or funding agency too narrowly, then they may not see the general appeal of your research, which can be devastating as you try to secure funding. As a result, we recommend that you build your sales pitch the same way you build your paper.

1. First identify the general concept area of your paper (we will stick with our Russian history example). Relate to the college or agency why this conceptual area is important. For instance, with the invasion of Chechnya, American interest in Russia is quickly growing as Putin seems to be set on rebuilding the USSR.

2. Next, discuss the area that you want to work in, explaining that Russian history is a huge topic and you want to make your paper as focused as possible, so you are breaking it down by steps. In the case of our example, since this was an invasion people are interested in the military prowess of Russia.

3. The third step is to select why you broke your area of research down into topics. You simply explain that the process you are using will focus your research as much as possible. In our case we selected the Russian nuclear threat.

4. The final area you discuss with your funding source before the research question is the topic area, which was the "Compliance/Noncompliance with United Nations Rulings on Nuclear Weapon–Free Zones."

5. If they want your research question, tell them your research question the way that it appears on our note card. You want this to be as formal as possible and as narrow as possible. Ours is "Did the *government* of Russia meet its nuclear disarmament goals *stated under UN Resolution 3472B* to the extend that *experts* in the United States and within the United Nations believed they did in the 1990s?"

6. This shows the people you are asking for money that you have selected a topic that people care about and that you have focused your research so that the project is doable (funding and danger not withstanding) and you have made the topic broad enough that if someone asks what you are researching you can give a simple reply: "Russian military actions."

By explaining the scope of your project in a way that others can understand, they can see why it is important, and when you can relate it to others quite simply, you get the funding agency to buy in with the project before it even starts.

Some research agencies will want to know what your hypothesis is before they will consider giving you funding. If you are going to prove that a company committed fraud in its banking practices, then that bank will not be in much of a hurry to see your research come out. However, if you are trying to prove that they have an exemplary record and follow all regulations, they will likely be more supportive of your cause. This is not to say that you should cater to your funding group to that extent; however, how you word your hypothesis can make the difference between getting funding and not getting funding. Remember, if you disprove your hypothesis you are still contributing to the field. The truth is the goal, not to prove yourself correct.

The main thrust of this chapter is looking at the basics of planning your data collection technique. While there is a whole part of this book dedicated to planning your data collection technique, this section is focused on explaining your data collection technique to a funding agency so that you can get money. If you do not include any technique, the agency will likely not fund you as your project is not fully developed. If you go into the meeting with 300 pages of surveys, an observational flowchart, and 2,000 books and journals that you need to review, the agency may believe that you have bit off more than you can chew and deny your project or that your project is already complete. The key is to go into the meeting/application process with a basic overview of your data collection technique with which you can then build on as the project goes on.

Finally, before you start asking for money, you should check with your institution's IRB (or with a private company's) ethics group. When you are asking for money, the funding agency is going to want to know if the entity that you are affiliated with is going to support you or disown you. A paper published by "former X University professor, Blankity Blank" does not look as impressive as "currently employed University X professor Blankity Blank." IRBs are challenging but they are the voice on our shoulder that keeps us from getting so caught up in our research that we allow our morals to slide. We all have a civic duty to ensure that our research is not hurting innocent people, and funding sources are going to look to see if we have upheld that duty as we design our research projects.

BOOK RESEARCH

The main type of research that most people are going to do in their lives is book research. This does not mean that you are only going to look at books—far from it. Generally book research includes books, journals, newspapers, magazines, online sources, microfiche, microfilm, and any other static sources that you can access at a library, archive, or private collection. Book research is the most common form of research because in college many schools do not teach their undergraduate students how to do formal research. So the students go to the library, find their minimum number of sources, and turn in a paper that is simply regurgitated data from other authors (if you are lucky and they did not plagiarize). Properly done book research follows a format such as phenomenology, descriptive statistics, or QMS. This means you have a research question and a hypothesis.

When doing book research, find the seminal work on the subject you are researching and read the whole thing. This will point you in the right direction and give you most of the sources that you need. The bibliography will give you the sources that the authors used in creating the work and if you search databases for books and journal articles that cited the seminal work you will find the newest research on the subject. Your research should spread out like a spider web from that central source. Always make optimal use of journals—even if you are doing historical research you can find anthologies of journal articles on the subject with more data. Books are like computers, in growing fields they are out of date before they are published; however, journal articles come out monthly thus are on the cutting edge of the subject. Other sources may be more current still, such as newspapers. However, the fresher the source the less criticism that the source must endure. Books are reliable because you can go back and read journal articles citing them to see if they were properly researched. To an extent, journal articles go through the same vetting process, just in an abbreviated nature. Newspapers come out daily, so their fact checkers have a hard job to do. Remember the Benghazi report that said the embassy staff was killed because of a video, and it was later found to be false, but it was still published in the papers? Other sources will have different levels of reliability and different uses in different types of papers. Personal letters are not academically vested, but they can show how a person felt at a specific time.

Book research is a valuable tool in any research project, and should generally be your first step before even a field project. If you take the time to establish a research plan in the books before you even go ask for funding, you will show the funding agency that you are committed to the project and that your are not simply following a whim that you will later forget. When doing book research, always consider the source. Just as books can be great repositories of knowledge, they can also lead you down the wrong path. There have been historical books that have been written intentionally to deceive and others that have deceived because of poor research. Never let one source be your guide in any research project.

OBSERVATION

While book research is the most common form of research in the modern world, observation may be the most common form of research throughout history. Observation is how you see the world; each and every one of us goes through life observing things. Observation is not limited to what you see; however, it can also include what you taste, smell, hear, touch, and "feel" about a situation. Observation gave us the great Greek dialogues, Newton's theories, and even some of the great artistic projects in the world throughout history. Observation is not without its own difficulties as what we see can be deceptive, whether by cause of those who are being observed or because of our own presuppositions deceiving ourselves.

One of the key advantages of observation research is that you get to see your project firsthand; this means that there is no filter. Unfortunately most college research at the observational level is limited to observing a local place (which is what I have students do) or having students "observe" a documentary. Either process is a great way to *introduce* someone to observation; however, when people do not leave their comfort zone they are less likely to "feel" the environment that they are in. Observation is a great tool for research at any level, and should be part of any college experience.

The key drawback to observation as a research methodology is that most of the easy observations have been done. Looking at Mexican heritage and life in Mexico City, done. Watching the evolutionary process of fruit flies, done by every science class in the 1990s. There are reasons why observational studies on certain areas are not done. Here are a few of the reasons:

1. Danger: Sometimes observational studies are dangerous. The secret lives of terrorist wives is not the safest thing for anyone to be researching. Always be aware of situational danger when entering into an observational research project. Watching lions mate is also a dangerous proposition.
2. Difficulty: Some things just do not happen when you want them to. The movie *Twister* from the 1990s was a great example of how researchers could chase tornadoes, but nature does not always cooperate. Take the lion example above. You never know when lions are going to mate, but when they do they generally are not going to invite researchers. This means that you, or your camera, has to be at the right place at the right time.

3. Cost: I would love to research the conflict resolution techniques of Sherpas in the foothills of Mt. Everest, but I do not have the wherewithal to go on my own and I do not think that I can secure the funding to observe this at this point in my life. We always have to look at the cost, both in money and in time, that a research project entails. While a multigenerational study about the effects of drinking Red Bull on childbirth may be interesting, possibly even useful, a person who just reached her 82nd birthday is not going to see too many more generations.

4. Status: Some observational studies have a stigma that goes with them that some people are not willing to accept. Do you really want to be the guy who watches monkeys defecate or the woman who watches swingers at adult clubs? While both of these could be valid research topics (note for the purpose of any of my classes these are not valid research topics), some people do not want to be associated with these kinds of research. Remember, you will be known by your research, so what you do becomes you.

Observation is a valuable tool, but take the reason why it has not been done into consideration when you are setting up your project.

SURVEYS

Surveys are one of the more popular methods for collecting information for research. Surveys allow access to people and allow people other than the researcher to pass collect information. These endearing qualities make surveys one of the most attractive methodologies for collecting data for those in graduate school. With the advent of the internet, we see even more people using surveys as there are providers who allow you to post surveys online for people to take and help you with your research. Some of these are fairly mainstream (which I would not recommend) such as Facebook; others are more suited to individual academic disciplines. Regardless, surveys are possibly the easiest way to collect data for your project.

One of the big problems with surveys (that you face to a lesser extent with other methodologies) is that everybody lies. This is a universal rule that researchers have to deal with. While you will find the occasional person who tells the truth—Buddhist monks, the pope, saints—most people will instinctively tell you what you want to hear. This means that you need to ensure your questions are not leading. Most of the time when you seek funding and you are using a survey to collect data, the funding agency will want to see the survey questions. To ensure the best chance of your project getting funded, always make sure that the questions are not leading and that they allow people to give honest answers without them trying to guess what you want them to say.

Saving the biggest advantage for last, surveys make it easy for you to keep the identities of your participants anonymous. Protecting your participants is vital in some research and ethical in all research. While the occasional participants will want their name in the document, most people want to live in the shadows unknown. To this end the anonymity of the survey is second to none. As long as people do not sign their names, the survey paper or online survey (assuming it is sent from a public computer) will make it almost impossible to trace who your sources are. This can make your life much easier when you are dealing with a topic where people could get fired or worse.

PARTICIPATION

Participation is a methodology that is generally limited to the social sciences or the humanities, though it is gaining more acceptance in the physical sciences. The reason that participation has been taboo for so long is because there is the danger that the researcher will taint the evidence by his or her participation. If you are looking at the agricultural traditions of a tribe in the Amazon, and you are using a hoe you bought at Home Depot, you will skew your data. Obvious mistakes like that are easy to see; however, learned mannerisms and habits are often harder to pinpoint. Epoche becomes vital in cases where you are participating in your research.

The advantage of participation is that you can understand the lived experiences of the people involved. While you will not be totally immersed (e.g., you will not know the fear of the harvest not producing enough grain because you can always leave), you still are closer to the research than most other people. This makes auto-phenomenology, grounded theories, and auto-ethnographies very useful for other researchers in the field. The key question you must answer when you are participating is why your participation makes the research more valid rather than less valid.

As an avid *Star Trek* fan, those of us who research social sciences have a strong duty to ensure that we do not destroy a society by our research.[2] If we research a tribe of people who are interesting, who live quaint lives on the edge of the rainforest where they are accessible to tourists, then we may destroy their way of life by pointing them out. When people go to see the Seminoles in southern Florida, it is a come-for-the-culture but stay-for-the-casinos mentality. Much of their culture has been lost, because people are interested in them. If you create interest about a group, a place of beauty, or even a set of documents, remember that your research can destroy these things just as much as it can preserve them. Sometimes you should make locations anonymous and preserve the culture by leaving out unnecessary facts.

---

2. I'm referring to the prime directive here for you Trekies.

PRIMING THE PUMP

This chapter is just an overview of some of the methodologies that we will cover in the later chapters of this book. The purpose is to make you aware of these methods before you start to apply for aid. Ideally, everyone would read the book from cover to cover before they start their project. Truthfully, most of you are working as you read; which is fine, too. This chapter is to make sure you know some of the macro-methods for collecting data and know how they will be used. Hopefully, this will help you get funded for your project.

CHECKLIST

- ❏ Are you going to require funding?
- ❏ Do some book research before you apply for funding.
- ❏ Identify a source of funding that you are targeting.
- ❏ Prepare a prospectus for them (concept, method, purpose).
- ❏ If you want to be safe, apply to multiple funding sources, write a customized prospectus for each.
- ❏ Will observation help your project?
- ❏ Will surveys help your project?
- ❏ Will participation help your project?
- ❏ Pick the method that will work best for you, does not put unnecessary strain on you, and will allow you to provide the best research possible.
- ❏ Do not forget to mail funding letters, because sometimes they're forgotten on computers when emailed at attachments.

chapter 7
Readership

INTRODUCTION

Ah, our triumphant return to the topic of readership. As annoying and boring as this topic can seem, it is a topic that many people gloss over in their attempt to rush the writing process. Understanding your readership is vital if you want to be a successful writer. This book, for instance, targets several different groups that I hope read it in the future. On one hand, we have you, the person who is reading this book right now. I hope that the different levels of the writing process are helpful in your journey to write whatever paper you are working on. On another hand, we have people who are seeking to write term papers, students who are seeking the inside track in the rat race that is academia. To these people the art is just as important as the science of writing. Beyond them we have the researcher, the person who is trying to leave a mark on the world by helping solve an unsolved problem. To you we wish the best of luck. Then we have the business professional, who is looking for a handbook to help boost a career. Also, we have the legal writer who is seeking to learn how to win arguments, and the grant writer who is seeking money. All of these people, as well as you my dear reader, are looking for ways to write better papers I have written what I have written to be as useful to all groups as possible while not trying to exclude any group.

The question of "why is the reader important?" is more important in modern academia than it has ever been. In the time before the Dark Ages, academics believed that the common people were illiterate fools—the illiterate part was correct, but the people were not fools. In the Middle Ages the academics believed the same thing, that the common people were illiterate fools. They were less correct than their ancestors, because the people were learning how to read. Now in our time some academics still believe that regular (nonacademic) people are illiterate fools, but they have never been more wrong. People today have more access to information and data than at any point in the history of human-kind (even if they spend most of it looking at porn and cats with odd facial expressions). When there is a reason that they need data, they can go to the internet and get it. The world has changed and academia must change with it. This means that we need to learn to write to the needs of the reader, whether that reader be a teacher, an editor, an employer, a judge, general academia, or the general pub-lic, we have an obligation to write for the world to understand. The reader has become our customer, and if they cannot understand your writing then they will not buy it (or use it). The academy can no longer be an isolated alcove of bigoted authors who believe they are the only ones in the world who have or need knowledge; no, for humanity to get out of this dark age of government interventionism, radical Islamic terror attacks, and politicians being corrected by 4-year-olds we need to accept that humanity must be able to access what we write, for better or worse.[1]

Beyond the moral implications of making sure that our research is accessible, we also have the prac-tical implication of making our writing accessible. Namely, if we do not make our writing accessible to our reader(s) then they will likely not read what we have written. If this is the case, then what is the point of writing? While this is being written, we are writing this from the viewpoint that you want your material to be read by someone. One of the benefits of taking into consideration who will be reading your materials is that you can write, during the writing process, in a way that makes the person you are trying to get to read your work to actually want to read your work. This means you must envision your readership as your customers. The customer is always right, remember that. If you have a broad readership, like general academia or the general public, then your writing should be more general and you should avoid using lingo or industrial terms, and you should keep it to a length that your audience will want to read. If your audience is very specific, say an editor, a boss, or a professor, then you can make your paper or article very specific to cater to that person's needs. This is something that you should think about as you write your paper; therefore, below your topic and your research question (the one on your note card you made in Chapter 3) write down who you expect your reader to be.

One point of caution, do not let your quest to appease your reader ruin your paper. If you know that your reader will not accept your paper, then perhaps you should wait to write the paper. For instance, if your professor is a radical feminist who believes that men are at fault for everything, then turning in a paper about why the world was better when we were in the age of kings would not be an idea; or if you have a professor who believes that sports are a waste of time and money, a term

---

1. Unless of course you are researching something dangerous, because if you publish that openly someone will be on YouTube hurting themselves.

paper on why college football programs should be given a larger percentage of the school budget may be ill advised. Do not write something that you know your reader will hate. If you need to write a paper on a topic that your reader will hate, then pick a different reader (i.e., a different class, a different journal, a different job). Also do not let your reader corrupt your data—just because your reader wants something, do not let yourself lie in your paper. Always tell the truth, that way it is easier to keep your stories straight.

In this chapter, we are going to look at seven different readers whom most of you are going to be writing for. This list is not exhaustive, it only covers those readers who are likely to be used by most writers. In each section of this chapter we will look at three elements:

1. Position of the reader;
2. Your goal for this reader; and
3. the method you use to reach your goal.

The position of the reader is why your reader is reading your paper. Unfortunately, most people in society do not simply pick up academic papers to read; therefore, you will generally have a reason why your reader is reading your paper. Second, you should identify your goal in relation to this reader. This will typically be in line with your general goal for your paper. Finally, we will cover some methods used to reach your goal. While every paper is a unique little snowflake, the successful approach is a hard worn path. If you follow this path then your journey to write a paper will be that much easier.

TEACHER

Perhaps the easiest person in the world to write for is your teacher or professor. This person's job is to make sure that you succeed in your class. Whether they are good at this job is an entirely different matter, but if they required you to buy this book at least they have good taste in books. Professors need to know that you have assimilated the data for the class. This is not to say that you memorized it, because anyone can memorize data. Assimilation means that you have adapted the data into what you know and are capable of using that data. This is the key difference between a high school paper and a college paper; high school papers show that you have the data, college papers show that you can use the data.

When it comes to writing for a teacher your goal is quite simple, you need to prove to the professor/ teacher that you have learned the data that he/she taught you. This means that texts of focus for your paper should be texts that he/she assigned you to read for the class. While most professors love when students have the ambition to go out and research documents other than what they have been assigned, we also want you to read the material that we have given you. Even if you cite each book you are assigned once or twice it lets us know that you took the time to read the books that we spent hours looking for in relation to the class. That being said, simply citing the books that are assigned for the class is not enough for you to reach your goal of getting the best grade possible on your paper.

The methodology to get a good grade on a college paper is still pretty simple. First, you want to stay within the bounds of the class. Your job in college is not to show your teacher that you are the smartest person in the classroom, because this generally agitates the professor who is part of an arrogant breed that likes to think that since you are paying the college for us to teach you that we actually do have something to teach you. Your goal has to be to show the professor that you have assimilated the material— believe me this is a much easier goal. The next thing that you should look at is the requirements of the assignment. Follow them completely. It doesn't matter how good your paper is, if you are supposed to write on biology and you write on marketing for cattle companies, you will be lucky to get a D on the paper. Then when you are doing your pre-research, keep in mind the theories that are being taught in the class. Stick to those theories. You may be a constructive anarchist in your personal life, but if the class is on Bentham and Utilitarianism you should probably pick that theory for your theoretical lens. Finally, keep the paper within the scope of the class; if there are topics you covered in class, relate the paper to them. Do not work harder than you have to on a college paper. In college the professor is on your side, so the greatest obstacle between you and that 4.0 average is you when you do not follow the instructions.

EDITOR OF JOURNAL

Editors are a different animal than college professors. While college professors know that they are going to be the only people to read this manifestation of your paper, journal editors know that whatever articles they put in their journal will affect the reputation of the journal. This means the position of the journal editor is to be a gatekeeper that keeps out materials that are not going to improve the reputation of the journal. Unlike a professor, these editors are not there to coddle you or lead you by the hand. Their job is to protect the reputation of the journal, so if you facilitate this for them then you will make it easier for them to say yes to you.

Your goal when you are writing to a journal is to get your article published and increase the recognition of your personal brand. For this to happen, you need to get your article published. This means that your goal should be to meet the requirements of the journal as closely as possibly. As such, you should always take a little time to familiarize yourself with the requirements and readership of any journal in which you want to publish. Remember, your goal in journal writing is to make it as easy as possible for the journal editor to pass your article on to review rather than pass on your article.

To help an editor say yes, you need to follow the journal's rules as closely as possible. Make sure to follow all the submission guidelines, citation guidelines, and formatting guidelines. I know several editors and all of them have told me that if authors do not follow the submission guidelines, then how can they be sure that they followed the methodological guidelines for doing their research? Your ability to follow the rules is your first impression with the editor, so always make sure to make a good first impression. Next, read the journal before you submit to it. Just reading the web page is not enough, because different journals cater to different parts of the field. Just because a journal is in the social sciences does not mean that it is a one-size-fits-all field. I like *Alternative Perspectives in the Social Sciences* for sociological papers and *The Qualitative Report* for writing projects. APSS is laid back in its writing style and allows the author large freedom in writing, TQR is very structured, which facilitates how-to papers quite well. If you want to be a professional writer, take the time to look into the journal (this also works for publishers of books) that you want to publish with. Try to get your material to fill a gap in the knowledge of the field, but still conform to the feel of the journal.

EMPLOYER

Employers are a more diverse group of gatekeepers. Different employers have different goals when it comes to the writing by their employees. But there is one thing that all employers have in common: they have a budget that they have to stick to. If your writing helps them with that budget (whether as marketing, brand recognition, name recognition, or even undermining the competition) they are more likely to be happy about your writing. An employer is likely to be more friendly to you than a journal editor, so do not be afraid to ask questions; however, do not take advantage of this and overwhelm your boss with questions. They have other jobs to do also. Further, while a journal editor can only reject your paper if they do not like it, an employer can fire you or demote you if your paper becomes a problem.

Your goal for writing a paper for your job is to keep the gatekeeper happy. As long as the paper is factual and keeps your employer happy, it should be good for your career. Try not to burn bridges, because today's competitor could be tomorrow's employer. This is where it pays to be an actual researcher rather than a critical writer. Critical writers tick people off, a lot. However with researchers, if people do not like your material or are not interested then they generally do not read it. No harm no foul. Those who do like your topic will seek it out. Business writing is one of the safest ways to get started writing—just remember to not tick off the boss.

The method for keeping the boss happy is simple. Ask enough questions to stroke the ego of the person reading your submission, but do not go overboard so that they feel like they are writing the article for you. Good rule of thumb, if a person sighs when you ask them a question then you have gone too far. Make sure that your topic is helpful to your business; and do not publish things that will hurt your company and expect a raise for them. If your report is damaging to your company, then you should keep it internal and attempt to fix the problem that you discovered.

JUDGE/ADVOCATE

Most people think judges and advocates represent a strong shift away from other types of readership, so they enter into a brief or legal paper with the idea that they have to convince the judge or other advocate that their position is correct. This can be a problem as the judge or advocate realizes that this is the goal of the writer. Generally, a judge or a lawyer is going to be highly educated, which means that they do not like to be led around by the nose. Therefore, a different approach may be required than the traditional legal writing approach. The position of a judge is that they want justice to be served (most judges at least—we will not cover dealing with activist judges in this book). Other advocates want their side of the story heard. Both groups do not want to be argued to, they want to make up their own mind. For that purpose, it can be best to write the brief as an informational argument rather than a persuasive argument.

Your goal when writing a legal paper is to convince the person that you are writing to that your position is correct. In the United States, years of depreciation in the primary and secondary education system have created a pool of jurists that believe the way to show you are correct is to show that the other side is incorrect. While this can be effective (and very effective in marketing), it is not always the best way to win an argument. The best way to show that your position is correct is to actually show that your position is correct. This means that you need to educate your reader as to your position, why it is correct, and why the reader should believe it is correct.

This process is simpler than it sounds. The first step is identifying your argument, which is why the brief chapter of this book is so much different from the other chapters. Once you have established your argument, you need to develop evidence that shows why your argument is correct. A small portion of the brief should be dedicated to errors in the other side's argument (or even acknowledging their strengths). The goal is to provide evidence to support your argument so that your reader reaches the conclusion on their own (technically with your help) that you are correct and that your argument is better. This will allow them to feel as if they have "bought in to your argument."

GRANT/SCHOLARSHIP AGENCY

The goal of a grant or scholarship agency is to give money to the most qualified researcher who is researching a topic that is related to the goals and mission of the agency. The secondary goal of a grant writing committee is to ensure that the endowment supporting the grant writer's ability to write grants stays functional. This means that grant writers are looking for paper proposals that are on the cutting edge of the field that they represent and proposals that are marketable to donors so that money will keep flowing into the accounts of the endowment. Grant writers know that they have to give out money and to do that mission they need to take in money, so your goal needs to enable them in their efforts.

As a general goal for any paper, you want your paper to be the best that it can be. This means that you need to maximize the efficiency of your research while maintaining enough time to keep your life going. Many researchers do not realize that the secondary goal of a grant writing agency is to keep the agency solvent. This can give you an advantage. Is your research marketable to donors as something that makes them want to give money to the agency? Research topics such as "Increasing the viability of the United States economy through Central Pacific regional manufacturing: A case study on bringing jobs to the Los Angeles area" is much more marketable than "The drug lord's side of the story: An ethnography of power, corruption, and human trafficking through the eyes of those who sell the drugs." Patriotism sells, no one wants to donate for the sympathy of drug dealers. If your topic is not a marketing gem, do not try to make it one; however, if it is a marketable idea then let the committee know how your idea can be marketed to their donors. The more of their work you do for them, the easier it will be for them to say yes.[2]

GENERAL ACADEMIA

General academia is not a primary readership; rather it is a secondary readership when you publish in an academic journal. The goal of the academy in general is to have as much information as possi-

---

2. This has to be done within reason. Coming out and telling the grant agency that they would be silly not to fund your article will likely make more people mad and decrease your chance of getting funding.

ble on a given subject in an easily readable database. When you are focusing on appeasing the editor of a journal, some writers forget this. The difference between great writers and good writers is that they write to appease the editor and to help the academy in general. This means that great writers focus on both goals while writing their papers. The goals are not mutually exclusive so writing to be readerships is not difficult, it just requires that you focus on both groups as you write the paper.

Your goal as a writer should be to meet the requirements of the journal while making the article as easy to assimilate by the academy as possible. There are no hard and fast rules for accomplishing this, but there are a few guidelines that can help you. If the article is for a specific discipline, then use the language that is used in that discipline to refer to jargon elements. The readership will feel more comfortable if the language is in their own lexicon. If the article is to be presented to a larger audience, then stay away from jargon and use common language, explaining the more difficult concepts so that the average academic can understand them. Also, graphs and charts can help readers understand what you are trying to present, but do not force them into your paper. An unnecessary graph or chart adds to the length of the paper and sometimes reduces the chance that the article will even be read. This brings us to the final point, length. Shorter articles are thought to be easier to read, whether this is true or not depends on the article. Look at your own research habits, unless an article is vital to your research you probably (like everyone else) read the short articles first to get them out of the way. Brevity is a great tool to ensure that your material will be read, so always try to keep the article as short as practical without cutting out any important information.

GENERAL PUBLIC

Writing for the general public, as you would do for a newspaper or magazine, is similar to writing for general academia, as there are two levels of readership you are trying to reach, with the exception that the second group, the public, is generally not as highly educated as in the academy. Now there are two clear dangers here:

1. Writing over the heads of the general public so that no one can understand your work and you appear arrogant and an "ivory tower" academic; and
2. "Bushing" it, which is trying to speak down to your audience and treating them like simpletons or actually making yourself come across as simple.[3]

---

3. Former president of the United States, Bush II, was intelligent but tried to speak down to his audience and came across as if he was not intelligent.

Either of these dangers can sideline an article and get you massive blowback from the community in which you publish. Therefore, the best advice is to treat the general public as if they are intelligent but do not use the same lexicon as in your academic papers. This should allow you to treat them with respect and to convey all the information that you need.

Your goal when writing to the general public depends on what the purpose of your paper is. If you are trying to convince the public that something is the right idea, then you would approach your piece like you would a legal article, give them enough information that the only decision that they can logically make is the decision that you are leading them to. Do not insult their intelligence by using trickery or smear tactics, but simply give them the reasons that they should choose your side. If you are writing simply to inform, treat your readers with respect. High-in-the-sky articles alienate people, it is a fact of writing. If you try to convince people that you are smarter than them, they will likely hate you for it (whether or not you are right). Any group that you are writing to you should treat as peers (unless you are writing to a boss or a judge, then give them the respect they deserve). This simple statement will serve you well in any writing situation.

CONCLUSION READERSHIP

Your reader is your customer; if you do not put forth a good product that they want, then they will not accept your work. Despite the claims of the liberal left side of academia, the academy is a free market of ideas; good ideas are rushed to the top and hold places of reverence for a long time. This is not to say that bad ideas and fads do not rise to the top from time to time, but they are often quickly proven wrong as the market reestablishes itself. The advice for writers is the same as the advice for businesspeople—if you can provide a better product at a lower price you will do well. The price of your product is generally fixed to the amount of time and money that you put into your research; therefore, the element that you have control over is the quality of the product. If you take the time to examine your readership, then you can cater the product to them. You may not have the best idea on the market or be the best writer in any given area, but you can ensure that for your readers you have the product that best meets their needs. If you do this then in your own little niche you can become a force to be reckoned with.

CHECKLIST

- ❏ Identify your primary reader.
- ❏ Define what your primary reader wants.
- ❏ Look at how you can cater your paper to your primary reader without diluting the content of your paper.
- ❏ Identify your secondary reader.
- ❏ Define what your secondary reader wants.
- ❏ Look at how you can cater your paper to your secondary reader without diluting the content of your paper.
- ❏ Deliver the best product you can for your customer.

chapter 8
Epoche

INTRODUCTION

When writing a paper, you must realize that you are putting a lot of yourself into the paper. Ten different authors could have the same data but you would still see 10 different papers. To be a great author, you must be willing to look at yourself and realize what parts of yourself are going to go into the people. Ignoring this is like having a black blot of ink on each page of your paper that takes your reader's attention away from what you are trying to tell them. Epoche is one of the ways that you can control the personal elements that you put into your paper. By working your way through the process of epoche, you can identify personal areas that you may/may not interject into your paper. This greater understanding will allow you greater control over the quality of your paper.

So let us begin by looking at what epoche is. Merriam Webster defines *epoche* as "the methodological attitude of phenomenology in which one refrains from judging whether anything exists or can exist as the first step in the phenomenological recognition, and description of sense appearances: Transcendental reduction."[1] This definition is correct, though it is quite complex and only refers to epoche in relation to phenomenology. Moustakas, author of the preeminent work on phenomenology, explains it better by noting, "The researcher following a transcendental phenomenological approach engages in a disciplined and systematic [plan] to set aside pre-judgments regarding the phenomenon being investigated."[2] This definition is more direct and easier to understand but still

1. Merriam-Webster (2015) at http://www.merriam-webster.com/dictionary/epoche (January 10, 2015).
2. Clark Moustakas (1995). *PHENOMENOLOGICAL RESEARCH METHODS*. Thousand Oaks: Sage. At 22.

restricts epoche to phenomenology when it is a procedure that can help in other disciplines. For the purpose of this book epoche is "the process of identifying pre-judgments that can affect research and guarding against negative effects throughout the writing process."

While the epoche process dominates transcendental phenomenology, it is useful in other methodological approaches as well. However, in other methodologies there is less call to include the results of your phenomenological self-assessment in your actual research paper. While phenomenologists "need" the epoche to separate them from their research project, other disciplines allow or even expect some of the author to be in the paper. In these disciplines, the epoche is a personal self-assessment that allows you to understand what parts of yourself will be vying to be a part of your paper. To that end, knowing what parts you're trying to get into your paper will allow you to make an educated decision about which parts to let in and which parts to keep out.

In this chapter we take a brief tour of this writing process's version of epoche. For phenomenological purists, we recommend that you review the phenomenological process in Moustakas's *Phenomenological Research Methods* and review Chapter 21. This chapter will be an introduction, a survey of epoche if you will, that allows you to do self-assessments when you write a paper. This chapter begins by looking at who you are. Knowing yourself is one of the key elements of being a good writer (or rather the continued discovery of self is an important element). Second, we look at your biases. Your biases are the general factors that skew your opinion of one or more things. Only the ones that relate to the paper you are writing matter, but knowing your biases is always good. Next, we begin looking at factors that can heavily affect your paper. In the third section we look at the biases that your discipline trains you to believe; and in section four we look at the biases that you have trained yourself to believe through your ideological paradigm. When looking at these biases, it is important to know that not all bias is bad. If you hate people who abuse children, that is a good bias for they are bad people. Do not let yourself epoche all morality and common sense out of your paper. Parts five and six look at your job and religion specifically. While there are other areas of a person's life that we do not cover, I have noticed that these two elements guide a person's reasoning more than any other elements. By understanding how you view things through these lenses you will be able to understand yourself more fully. This chapter concludes by looking at what types of papers you want to include your epoche in, and what kind of papers you write where your epoche will be self-assessment. This is important as epoche can show people who are reading your work where the paradigm of the work came from. All in all, epoche will allow you to write a better paper whether you include it in the text or not.

WHO ARE YOU?

In all of classic literature, one of my favorite lines is when the Caterpillar asks Alice "Who are you?" in *Alice's Adventures in Wonderland*.[3] This question resonates with many people because of the clarity that the question brings. Whenever you answer the question, "Who are you?" then you have already changed because before you answered the question you were, in fact, a different person. Thus the question itself becomes cylindrical. Knowing who you are is a constant conversation that you must have with yourself. Those who feel that they have discovered themselves at a young age have only discovered themselves at that point in time. This is why beatniks are so sad, they are locked in a moment of their own life. For those who strive to be as vibrant as possible, they should always be asking "Who am I?"

By constantly being involved in a self-assessment conversation with yourself you can understand how it affects your writing. Look at how different writers react after a great tragedy—Charlie Hebdo, for instance.[4] Some authors condemned the acts of the Islamic terrorists who perpetrated the act against the people of France. These authors were living in the real world and looked at the act of terror as it was, simply an act of barbarism from a sociopolitical group straight out of the Dark Ages. Others tried to find justification for the attack to absolve the terrorist, a relativist approach, that we must understand why they did it and that since they are not part of the mainstream culture they cannot be wrong. This position is and was ludicrous that people died and relativists argued that it was justified because of an offensive cartoon. Others still wrote that even though it is known that the terrorists were radical Islamists that they were not at fault and society will just use this as a reason to further oppress the privileges that this group claims over other groups. This is probably the most disturbing because it is a hate group turning the victims of a crime that they perpetrated into the criminals so that the true criminals can play the role of the victim. As you read over these positions, you can see how a person's worldview can skew the research that they do on a given subject. This is why epoche is so important. People, in some cases, want to know where the author is coming from in their assessment of the situation.

Now, this chapter is not about condemning the work of other authors. If you want to do that, read a book on critical analysis and meta summary. This chapter is about knowing the weaknesses and strengths of your writing based on who you are. Remember, just because you have a strong opinion on something does not mean that you cannot do research on it. There are cancer researchers who hate cancer but are doing some of the best work they can against it. Are they biased? Of course

---

3. Lewis Carrol (1865). *Alice's Adventures in Wonderland*. New York: Dover Thrift Editions.
4. This was the mass murder in France by Muslim extremists.

they are; however, their bias does not eliminate them from doing the research; in fact it makes them passionate about what they are doing. Know what your passions are, and then you are the judge of whether they affect your writing in a positive or a negative manner.

BIASES

Everybody is biased. If others tell you that they are not biased, then they are lying to you and lying to themselves. You may not like dogs, you may not like people who do not like dogs, but within your psyche there is something in this world that you are biased against. You know what, live with it. Everyone in the world is biased against something. Those people who are successful do not let their biases run their lives; the writers who are successful do not let their biases rule their writing.[5] As we have stated not all biases are bad—if you hate child abusers good for you. However, you need to know that you hate child abusers if you are working on a project that relates to a child abuser. Doctors, for instance, have to treat their patients even if they hate everything the patients stand for.

There are some biases that are socially acceptable (e.g., to dislike criminals), and there are some biases that are not acceptable (e.g., racism). When doing epoche and looking at your bias, you need to determine whether the things that you are biased against are socially acceptable and are acceptable to people who are researching the topic you are researching. If you are strongly against illegal immigration then you may not be the best person to write an argument for the funding of new welfare programs for illegal immigrant mothers in the United States. You have a conflict of interest. Conversely, if you are against abortion and are a doctor, then you may be the perfect person to write a pro-life paper describing when a child can feel pain in the womb. It is your job, however, to look at your bias and determine whether your bias is acceptable.

In this section, we look at some of the most common biases that people face in their everyday lives. If you are in college, the most common bias you are going to face is liberal or conservative bias. Good professors do not let this interfere with their teaching. I am a conservative, and if I have a student turn in a liberal paper with well-thought-out positions that is well researched, then they receive an A for their efforts. I have turned in papers (which were later published) with mildly conservative viewpoints, and had professors give me low marks for them because of the position, not the content. When you are writing your paper or article, know what your slant on the liberal/conservative argument is and also know your readers' slant on the argument. If you have a conservative professor that is known for being harsh to liberals, do not write a liberal manifesto for the class. If

---

5. There are some fields where you can write to your biases. These are not covered since this is not academic writing (except in grant writing and legal writing).

you know you want your article to appear in *Rolling Stone*, then do not write a conservative piece for a liberal magazine. Pick your battles. Professors have the pens, editors have the say of whether something is printed or not. Don't tick off your readers. Know your bias and know their bias.[6]

Race is another area that people are unfortunately biased against. This is still a fact of life. Rule #1: do not be a racist in your writing; Rule #2: do not be a racist in your life. Bias against something that a person has no control over is evil. However, this does not mean that your research should be skewed away from FACTS that appear to be racist. If you will pardon me an anecdote. I have a friend who hates the standard bell-shaped curve. He learned in an anthropology class that the bell-shaped curve in education is biased against black students because of socioeconomic pressures from the past. Now most of this statement is true. Education has been underserving the black community worldwide because of racist positions held by some races in the past. Statistics have shown that on a nationwide level more blacks fail our schools than whites or Asians of the same category. However, this does not mean that the bell-shaped curve is biased. This means that there are still social problems in the United States that few people are willing to talk about seriously that are causing problems in the education system. This does not mean that the data are biased; it means that the system that produced the data has a problem. People are racist (not all people), but data are either true or false. If the data are true then they can show a general problem or a systematic problem. Just because you do not like what the data say does not mean that the facts are wrong or biased, it just means that someone needs to do something to correct the situation.

Ethnicity is much like race in the regard that people will hate based on ethnicity. It is also much like race in that it is bigoted to be against an ethnicity based on stereotypes or old wives tales. Ethnocentrism is natural in writing; however, everyone centers their opinion based on the way they were conditioned in their own ethnic/sociocultural group. You are the center of your world. Now, how you treat people is a completely different story. You can compare mores, traditions, even opinions based on facts and data about another ethnicity (or your own ethnicity in an auto-ethnographic study). However, you need to ensure that you use real facts and give the other culture a chance. That being said, it is perfectly all right to speak out against a society that allows rape, slavery, or torture. You do not have to accept things that are evil or wrong just because somebody is different, just do not accuse someone of being evil or wrong just because they are different.

There are thousands of things that people can be biased about. This section covers just a few of them. When doing your own epoche, take the time to look at the things in this world that you are

---

6. If you are writing for a political science class or writing a political piece for some reason, feel free to ignore this advice. Do not self-censor when you are publishing something. Do self-censor if you have a professor who is known for playing to his or her own bias.

against and see whether they are as bad as you believe they are. Some will be and some will not be. There are things that are bad because of their very nature and there are other things whose good or evil varies based on the nature of how they are used. Know what you like and what you dislike, then defend your position using facts. If you can do this, then you should be on a solid position to defend yourself (even if you are wrong).

DISCIPLINARY VIEWS

Your academic discipline will have a major effect on who you are and what you see as right and wrong in the world. Different disciplines have differing world philosophies, some even have other disciplines as rivals. Political scientists tend to believe that law and the social sciences are part of their discipline, where the other two disciplines see political science as an extreme subset of general sociology. Either position can get you in trouble if you are working in the other field. As a writer, you should know the common views of your discipline and also know your personal views. Very few of us that write are cookie cutter soldiers in our own discipline, as we have our own ideas and thus we write to express them. After identifying your biases, you should take the time to identify the biases of your discipline. This will help you be a better author.

Identifying the belief system of your discipline can be difficult. Take, for example, my chosen discipline, conflict studies. As a conflict professional there are several viewpoints that people acknowledge for practitioners to hold:

1. First wave: The people who broke away from the legal field to find another way to deal with legal/social problems in society.
2. Second wave: People who stated that the field should be separate from the legal field completely because the legal field stifled the creativity of the conflict professionals.
3. Third wave: A group that pushed back supporting the position that the field should be highly professionalized and that the legal industry already had the patterns for the movement.
4. Fourth wave: The cooperative element, which stated that both the legal side and the anti-legal side could be combined with a synergy bringing fourth a new model.
5. Fifth wave: Believe that legalism has its place; however, the conflict processes in alternative dispute resolution should be the primary source of conflict resolution, not an alternative. The legal system should be regulated to the alternative status.

These so-called waves are generally accepted by pure conflict scientists. However, even this no-menclature can be a problem as it sounds like anthropological terminology for feminism. To understand the biases of your discipline, you may have to look at the biases of the specific subset of your discipline to which you adhere. To make matters more complex, if you fall in between two subsets, you may have to identify the biases of both sets.[7] Taking the time to know your disciplinary bias will allow you to strengthen your understanding of yourself and will help to make you a better academic writer.

To make matters more complicated, many professors train their students that their disciplinary worldview is the only valid worldview out there. This sends thousands of college graduates out into the world with a quarter of the disciplinary picture. If you are a writer, then you must take the time to look at the other worldviews within your discipline, even if you are just going to argue or disprove them. One of the best ways to win a debate with a "purist" is to bring out arguments from a subset of their discipline; when they dismiss those arguments as problematic, then they are undermining their position or the position of the discipline. This can be very effective in legal arguments or in grant writing where you know the position of those with who you are competing.

Regardless of what discipline you are in, or where your discipline stands on a given topic, the question remains about how it will affect your writing. The answer should be that your discipline is simply another lens through which you view your subject matter. The lens is not the observation, it simply determines what you will see in the world and what is blocked out. If you believe in your discipline, then there is no problem with sticking to your disciplinary views. Just do not be arrogant and believe that there are no other views out there. You may have to defend your research from someone in another field that looks at the situation another way. Know that the other views are out there and be prepared to deal with them if the need arises.[8]

THEORETICAL VIEWS

Whereas your disciplinary views are mostly thrust upon you from your education and training, your theoretical views can be developed by your own relationship with the world. For my theoretical viewpoint when writing in the social science, I am a positivist utilitarian conservative (PUC). This paradigm covers most of the situations that I have come up against during my time as an academic

---

7. In some cases this is easier because it allows you to distinguish yourself from the "herd" by knowing which biases of each subset you agree or disagree with.

8. One thing that you should avoid is creating your own problems. Generally if you are speculating on problems that may come up, save them for a rebuttal paper. If you try to go too far in identifying problems with your own work, you can give people what seems that they would not have otherwise found. Keep it simple.

and student. Your personal theoretical paradigm is something that you will develop over the course of your career. Will I always be a PUC? Perhaps or perhaps not. We are always learning so our theoretical views can change. This is where your views differ from your disciplinary views. It takes years for a discipline to change, but individuals can change in the matter of hours when they learn something new.

When you look at your theoretical paradigm, look at what theories you have learned that seem to make the most sense to you. If a theory makes sense and you can defend it easily, then do not fight it. If you want to have a specific theoretical premise, like radical feminism, but the major tenants of the belief system seem silly to you, then maybe you are not actually a radical feminist but another type of feminist. I know many people who want to be part of a theoretical paradigm because it is cool (liberalism is a common cool one) but they are unable to rectify what they believe with what the paradigm teaches. Do not fight logic just to be part of a clique. Cool paradigms change every 10 to 15 years. If you have a set of beliefs then stick to them. Stand for what you believe in.

In regard to paradigms it is easier to find contrasting paradigms to the position you hold. For me, I love to mess with relativist, socialist liberals. Their paradigm is the opposite of what mine is. Their relativism believes that no answer is correct, while I believe there is an answer to every question. Their socialism believes that everyone should have everything given to them, where I believe that people should be given what they need and work for what they want. Their liberal philosophy and my conservative philosophy is what drove me into politics and may drive me into politics again. I am biased against relativism, socialism, and liberalism, and I am fine with it. You need to find if there are theoretical paradigms that you are against. If you know what you stand against then you will have an easier time identifying it in your writing and keeping it out where it needs to be.[9]

YOUR JOB

Getting away from theory and into the real world, you also need to look at what kind of work you do, day to day to make a living. This can have a profound effect on your writing when it comes to a specific topic. I know this very intelligent young woman who used to be a diehard liberal and had been given awards based on her service to the political party she belonged to. She was a state congressman's assistant and was fed a constant meal of the party line while she was at work, prior to that she had been a teacher and the union had reinforced her positions. After leaving the congressman's employ she began working as a supervisor at a non-profit that dealt with homeless children

---

9. If you are biased, then do not take it out on your students or classmates. They should have the privilege of developing their own personal paradigm; guide them, do not force them.

and their parents. This had a major effect on her worldview. Within a year she was attending libertarian meetings and arguing against her former leaders. Getting your hands into the real world can change your views on what you believe. It is easy to be a relativist while you are in college (I can make fun of them now because I revealed that I was a positivist in my epoche), but when you get into the real world you find out very quickly that there may be a clear right and a clear wrong.

Another part of your job, other than just the environment, that can affect your worldview is the training that your job provides. Each trainer is going to have a worldview. Each boss is going to have a worldview. They will, whether intentionally or inadvertently, start to push their worldview on you. If you are in a career, you may want to at least look at the new worldview. If it is a stepping stone job, then you may want to act like you accept it but keep true to your disciplinary view or your theoretical paradigm. However, realizing that your training could change your worldview is one of the reasons why you should take 20 minutes or more to do epoche for every paper that you write.

There are also special instances when you should know what your position is based on your job. If you work at an abortion clinic, then if you publish a paper showing the vast volumes of research that unborn children still feel pain and are considered persons under homicide law but not medical law, you may lose your job. Do not shoot yourself in the foot with your research. If your research is going to cost you your job, then you should at least make sure that you have another job lined up before you publish the research. This means you have to be aware of the environment in your field. Do not destroy yourself for the purpose of a single minor publication.

The final area that you may want to look at while doing your epoche about your job is whether any of the topics that you normally think everyone knows, regular people actually do not know. If you are an electrical engineer and are writing an op-ed piece for the local newspaper, everyone may not know what level of amps will kill a person. If you are saying that 2 amps is dangerous for some household appliance, then you may have to explain why it is dangerous. When in doubt, explain. This will allow your research to reach more people and thus be more useful to everyone.

RELIGION

I debated including this topic in the chapter because it is such a highly controversial topic; however, I eventually realized that because it is such a highly controversial topic is the exact reason that it should be included. If you are religious, then your religion is a part of you. Do not let yourself be discriminated against because you are one of 99% of people who believe in something. You also must be aware of your religion in that you cannot discriminate against others (unless it is a compare and contrast paper). Knowing who you are includes all parts of your personality; you should not deny who you are simply for convention. That being said, do not force your beliefs down another person's throat where it does not matter. Did any of you get offended by my characterization of liberals, socialists, or relativists earlier in the chapter? While I really do not care, normally I would not have put those things in a book of this type. When you are writing, make an educated decision whether your religion, your theory, your discipline, or your job's positions should appear in your work. Just because something is part of you does not mean that it should be shown in inappropriate places—social modesty has its place even in academic writing.

TO WRITE OR NOT TO WRITE

In this final section we look at whether you should write about your epoche in your article/paper, or whether your epoche should just be for your own self-assessment. Either way, walking through the steps in the checklist at the end of the chapter will allow you to have a better understanding of yourself and can make you a better writer. However, just because you took the time to do something does not mean that the whole world needs to know. Further, there are parts of your epoche that you should not include in your writing even if you do discover they are relevant. For instance, if you find that you are biased against X, then putting that in your paper will likely kill any chance you have of getting published (it may even get you blackballed by journals in certain fields). You should acknowledge your problem/bias, and in the case of racism try to seek out some help to get over it.

In qualitative research, you should mention any relevant conflicts of interest that you have in your methodology section. The key element here is relevant. Your job and religion may be relevant, they may not. Your discipline (which should be evident from your bio) and your theoretical paradigm are more likely to be relevant, but do not force them to be relevant. As a general rule, only add epoche to your paper if it will help the reader trust you, if it lets them see that you have a bias but are willing to deal with your bias to make sure your research is top quality. If a journal tells you to take out the epoche, do it. This is something that makes you easier to sell; if the consumer does not want it, then do not include it.

In quantitative research epoche is very rare, and there is a reason for that. In statistics you allow the numbers to do the talking. The only people who would be skewing data are the ones who do not want to get caught, so they are not going to reveal their bias. Only in extremely rare circumstances would I recommend trying to include epoche in your statistical work. Most likely the journal will either ask you to take it out or reject the article wholesale. When dealing with hard objective data, there is not ethical reason that your personal viewpoints should skew the data. If you find that your paper reports something that you feel that strongly about, generally you just do not publish the paper as an academic paper.

In theoretical papers epoche is not the norm, but perhaps it should be. Theoretical papers, more than any other type of paper, are subject to the opinions and positions of the theories. This means that your personal beliefs could have a major effect on your research. For this type of paper, do the epoche then contact the journal or reader and ask if they would like epoche included in the work. If they do not know what epoche is, then you should probably exclude it. If they want it, then supply it. If they do not want it, then do not supply it. Either way, do the epoche first so that you know if there is a valid reason for you to ask the question. If they say they want epoche and you have no relevant biases, you will be in the undesirable position of either placing an irrelevant epoche or making up bad things about yourself.

Epoche is an old idea that is having a resurgence. If you learn to do epoche, then you will always have the skill available should you need it (or if you simply want to use it). Do not force epoche on people. Some authors want people to know about their views so bad that they force epoche into their writing. Your reader cares about your research, but they may not care about who you are. Epoche should be used when there is a bias that you are overcoming to write your paper/article, but do not let it become the obstacle that you are trying to overcome in your writing.

CHECKLIST

- ❑ Do your epoche.
- ❑ Is epoche normally written in this type of paper?
- ❑ If yes, then write it as normal.
- ❑ If no, ask journal/readers if they would like epoche (state reason).
- ❑ Ensure that it is well written.
- ❑ Do not force epoche into your paper. It is a tool to help you, not hurt you.[10]

---

10. I look at epoche like a chainsaw. It can be useful sometimes, and sometimes it is just dead weight. The only thing you know is that if you try to force it somewhere it does not fit that it will hurt you.

chapter 9
Value to Readers

INTRODUCTION

Though this is one of the later chapters of Part I, the value of your article to the reader should not be an afterthought. Now that you have developed your concept from its broadest possible format, down through the area of research, breaking off individual elements, reducing it to a topic, a research question, and then a hypothesis, you are familiar enough with your topic to ask the big question, "Why should people read this?" Why your paper should be read is a big part of your journey of writing. If no one wants to follow you on your journey to where you lead them, then your writing is simply an academic exercise. In this chapter, we will review why someone would want to read your paper, written by you, so that you will be able to convince a teacher or a publisher that you have reached your goal and can help them reach theirs.

First, we need to ask the question, "What is my paper for?" Do not worry; we are not going to rehash the questions that we asked in the first few chapters. We do, however, need to look at what people are going to use your paper for once it is complete. Will it be a reference for academics on the cutting edge of the field? Will it be required reading for an undergraduate or graduate class? Will your paper be an obscure novelty that few people read or will it be a stack of papers someone uses to keep a coffee ring off of a favorite end table? What you want your paper to be used for will define how you write it. The general answer is that your paper should be used for research or for required reading, and if you are writing for these two purposes then you should try to write the best paper that you possibly can.

Next, you need to look at why a person would want to read a paper by someone like you. If you are established in the field, then the answer is easy. However, if you are just getting your start then you need to be more forceful in why your research is worth reading. When making your argument as to why your article is worth publishing/reading, do not try to disparage other authors. If you disparage others then the best case scenario is the publisher thinks you are just a hot head; worst case scenario the established writers blackball you and you cannot get a job or get articles published. I have always been a fan of the "kill them with kindness" approach. In writing this means explaining why your theory/hypothesis deserves to be published and why it is relevant. If you cannot convince yourself that your research is worth reading, then it will be hard to convince someone else.

Is your research better than your competition? The answer to this question is something that you keep to yourself; you do not need to shout from the rooftops that your work is better than others. If your work is truly better than others, the people in your field will take note of it and your work will make its rounds in all the right places. Self-promoters are generally the only ones who hear their self-promotion. If someone else supports you, then you will get noticed by the field. This chapter will look at some of the ways that you can make sure your article is worth reading. It is a short chapter, but nonetheless important. We will look at whether your paper expands knowledge, makes someone's job easier, or makes a choice easier. All three of these reasons can help your paper get read, and thus help you realize your goal of being a published author.

EXPAND KNOWLEDGE

Most academic writing is to expand the knowledge of the reader. Thus the goal of papers that expand the reader's knowledge is to convince them, in the abstract, that your paper will expand their knowledge. How you do this is up to you, but an effective way that I recommend is to commit one sentence in your abstract to each part of your paper. In this way your potential reader can see your topic (intro), your method, where you procured your data, your conclusion, and where you see your data being used. As with the editor of the journal, if you make it easy for the reader to say yes to reading your paper, there is a better chance that you will have a readership. A second tip in this area is to keep the language simple in the abstract. If you confuse a reader, you have lost that reader. The only jargon you should use are buzz words that draw readers in.

A key factor in getting people to read informational papers is to keep the paper succinct. Long papers take time to read, and a person is going to try to get as much information as possible in a short amount of time (most people reading papers are college students or college professors on a time line). This means that you should make your article long enough to relay the information you need to relay, but not allow yourself to go off in tangents that unduly lengthen the paper. This can be a fine line to walk as everyone thinks that all of their research is important. Words of wisdom that you should live by are that all of your research does not have to be forced into one paper.

Another way that you can increase the number of readers who are interested in your paper is to target a specific niche. While it may seem counterintuitive to limit your research by a narrow topic, the reality is that the more narrow your topic the better job you can do researching the topic. It is better to have a laser focused paper on a small subject than an unwieldy behemoth that poorly covers a huge topic. By sticking to a niche you can also develop a reputation for yourself as an expert. Experts are read more often than nonexperts, so take the time to get your name known in your area or expertise.

Informational papers can also be compellation papers that take a cross section of the research in the field and synthesize it (or if you want to take the easy approach summarize it). Most fields are expanding so quickly that people cannot keep up with all of the research. It's better to pick a specific niche of the field and build a compellation that synthesizes all the current work on that topic. People will read your paper to bring themselves up to date on the topic. As long as you synthesize the data that you find into common trends or phenomenon, you have a new paper that brings together the current material in your field.

One thing that most fields require is that your research be new. Old research is of little use unless you can put a new spin on it. While there are fields where rehashing old theories is the vogue (economics, for example), most fields are always looking for something new. If you cannot find something new in your topic area, either pick a new topic area or find something that is new to your field. You can take something from another field and apply it to your field using the lenses of your theoretical paradigms. Fisher did it when he converted Maslow's hierarchy of needs to the field of conflict resolution. If you do this, however, be sure to give the original author credit and explain how it fits differently into your field than into other fields.

MAKE SOMEONE'S JOB EASIER

People are generally lazy. This is a fact about humanity that we have not been able to change for millennia. However, one of the areas where humans seem to be willing to do the most work is in getting out of work. If you write a paper that can make someone's life easier, then there is a good chance that someone will read your work. I assume that you are reading this book because it will help you write a paper without going through all the pitfalls that I had to go through. Good for you. If you can write a paper that makes others' lives easier, then they will likely read your paper just to get that advantage in the field.

Writing a paper about what you do for a living can be helpful. I write a lot to keep my job in academia. While I am not a professional writer, I am a writer who needs to write as part of my profession. This is why this book is targeted to three main groups—academic writers, legal writers, and students. Other experts can help people who are writing in other areas (such as fiction where I have no experience). Papers that are related to your trade, with simple instructions on one specific thing, are a good way to get started in writing. If you do something in a way that other people have not yet seemed to catch onto, then you can write on that subject and make other people's lives easier. If it is something truly novel, then patent it so you can make money before you publish it.

If you want to write about a series of things that are in the same category, then you may want to write a "handbook" style paper. Handbook papers are longer because they cover two or three things from the same subject area. These can be useful if there are a variety of different situations when a skill is useful, when there are multiple environments where your idea can be used, or when there are different tools that can be used to do the same job in different situations. Writing a handbook is a stepping stone between writing a paper and writing a book. If your handbook is going to be over 70 to 80 pages, then you may want to look at fortifying it to make it into a book.

In lieu of epoche in a trade book, you may want to look at explaining why you are qualified to write on this subject. Do not begin, "I am qualified to write on this subject because... ." This type of beginning will make you look arrogant and turn off your reader; to define your qualifications pick the two or three most relevant aspects of your career and include them by way of introduction. Your biography line in the footnotes should cover the rest of why you are qualified. If you want an example of a biography there should be one on the back cover of this book or the dust jacket if you bought the hardback edition. Between your biography and your introduction, you should be able to qualify yourself to write on your topic.

MAKE SOMEONE'S CHOICE EASIER

The final reason someone would be reading your work is because you are trying to convince them of something. For most people, this means that you are writing a legal paper or a gist or applying for a grant/scholarship. These are the two main situations in academic writing where you should be actively trying to convince someone of something where there is more than one acceptable answer. This section of the chapter has two subsections, because the method for making someone want to read your legal work is worlds away from making someone want to read your grant application. The first subsection deals with legal papers; the second subsection deals with grants/scholarships. For more information on these topics, look to Chapters 34 and 35, respectively.

Making Someone Want to Read Your Legal Paper

When people read a legal source it is likely for one of two reasons. Most commonly, people read legal sources in relation to a case or an appeal. In this instance, the reader of your material will likely be a judge or another lawyer who is helping/contesting you on the case. The other instance where people read legal materials is when they are doing research for a case. In this instance, an academic/legal article is a secondary source. In either case, there needs to be a reason your reader chooses to read your work. Let's look at a few of them.

The first and most likely reason people read a legal paper or brief is because they are looking for somewhere that all the data on one topic has already been brought together as one source. The vast majority of legal writing is meta-synthesis or meta-summary, thus the legal sections in this book should be read alongside Chapter 22: QMS. Since the reason most people will be reading your legal work is that they want all the relevant data in one place, it is in your best interests to make sure that all the data is as current as possible and as comprehensive as possible. This means that for your legal research to be of any use to your reader it must be as exhaustive as possible.

Another use of legal research is based on the citations. In many cases, the person reading your work will be more interested in the sources than they will be in the content. Legal writing involves a process called shepherdizing, In this process, a lawyer or researcher back tracks all cases from the time they were decided to the present to ensure that the law has not been changed by a new law or by a new ruling. This process is very long and tedious (if you pay for it the computer can do it for you); however, it is essential to ensure that the legal research is valid. This means some readers will read your work exclusively to see if there have been any new developments in the field they are researching. This means that your citations need to be correct and as current as possible.

Finally, readers in the legal field expect that a legal article/brief will be formatted to support one position or another. This is because the legal field tends to be an all or nothing prospect. In that light, you are presenting an argument why one position or another is correct in a legal paper you write. Some will be as simple as writing a brief saying that a conclusion is right because that is the conclusion that the court reached. Some will be complex, arguing multiple court cases with a combined end result that is different from any of the cases read alone. Whether complex or simple, your writing journey as you write a legal piece helps take readers from where they are to where you want them to be.

Making Someone Want to Read Your Grant Application

When writing a grant you must take a slightly different approach than you take when you are writing a legal brief. Where you "tell" the reader that you are correct in a legal brief, you need to "show" the grant or scholarship agency that your project is the best project for them to devote their attentions to. As a result, your argument in a grant application is highly informative. First of all, you want to define the parameters of the project. Some authors tend to simply rewrite their project proposal in the grant application and end it at that. Successful writers look for language in the mission statement or project statement of the grant writing agency that can be mirrored in the project description. This does not mean that you should change what your project is, but you should change your description to meet the language of the agency you are applying to.

For grants and scholarships, you should pre-research the project that you are planning on doing. This means your grant application should not be sent in until you are, at least, to the element phase of your concept breakdown. If you were a grant writer you would choose, "I would like to do a general study on the sociology of primates" or "I would like to do an ethnographic study of Spider Monkeys during their migration from Green Valley to the Foothills of Red Mountain looking as social hierarchies as they develop and/or decay." Knowing what you are writing about shows that you have taken at least some time to research your topic before applying for your grant. Library research generally only takes the writers a short time to complete. This means that you can have this part done before you apply to ensure the grant agency sees you as a self-starter and a go-getter.

Additionally, grant agencies will expect to see why you need the money for your project and why they should give it to you. This means that you should have a framework of project expenses already designed before you even begin looking for your grant agency. Further, you need to use this section to once again explain how your project fits within the agencies mission and helps them fulfill your goals. As magnanimous as grant agencies are, they still do not generally give money to people just because the people want it. There needs to be a good reason. Your application is the place to explain to them why you are a good cause to spend money on.

Finally, it never hurts to explain to the reader how your project helps people, not just the people at the agency but people in general. Some academics will disagree with this, because they believe research for research sake is a valid expenditure of money (which it is when the nation has fed all its people, educated its children, and secured its borders); however, the "good" that a project does for the world cannot be understated. The more people a project is going to help, the more likely your project will be seen as valid. While this should be a short section of your paper, it is a section that can mean the difference between getting a grant and getting rejected.

The value to readers of any paper lies in how it makes their lives easier. Whether it is giving them knowledge, making their job easier, or making their choices easier, a paper must have purpose to have value. Your personal crusade or manifesto will enjoy a much smaller readership than a paper that teaches people how to farm properly in arid regions or explains gravity in a way that helps the space program. Academic papers are not the place for crusades, they are the place to help others in their careers. To ensure that your journey of writing has a good end, make sure that you lay down a path that others can follow. The easier your path is to follow (assuming it goes to the right place) the more likely you are to have a strong readership.

CHECKLIST

- ❑ What is the purpose of your paper?
- ❑ Why should others want to read it?
- ❑ Will it expand their knowledge?
- ❑ Will it make their job easier?
- ❑ Will it make some choice in their life easier?

chapter 10
Research Methodology

INTRODUCTION

Now we are prepared for our journey through writing a paper. We have set our destination (research question), we have drawn our map (concept → topic), and we have checked to see who we are taking along with us and whether we are fit to make the journey. Now all that we have left to do to prepare is select the vehicle that will carry us to our destination. This vehicle is our research methodology. This is how we get from where we are now to where we want to be at the end of the paper. Choosing the correct research methodology can have a major effect in what grade you will get for a paper or in which journals you can publish. Further, what you want to study will have a major effect on what methodology you choose.

The choice of methodology is your first big step from preparation to actual process. While you can change your research design pretty much at will during the planning phases, once you begin to collect data your methodology is difficult to change without going back and recollecting data in the proper form. Small shifts, like the type of ethnography, you are doing can still be made, but once a methodology is chosen you should try very hard not to change it. This choice will determine the type of paper you are writing; however, before you go through the trouble of choosing a methodology take the time to make sure your methodology has not already been chosen for you. Some journals have a specific style that they require their writers to use for their articles, this often includes methodologies. Most professors want their students to do some form of synthesis, so they have their methodology chosen for them also. Do not put yourself though the headache of choosing a method if it is already chosen for you.

For the purpose of this book, there are three macro-methodologies for researching and writing a paper. These are quantitative research, qualitative research, and theoretical research. These three types of research papers will cover most of the academic writing that people will do doing their lives. To this end, each of these macro-methodologies will be covered in their own part of this book. Part V covers the miscellaneous papers that you may have to write during your lives. These paper types will cover most papers you will write as a result of your trade or in your early college career. The major chapter in Part V that may be of great interest to anyone who is writing an academic paper is Chapter 37: Hybrid Methodology Papers, which details how to combine methodologies from the four previous parts.

Some people ask why choosing a methodology now is more efficient than choosing a methodology once data has been collected. While this process works excellent for a basic freshman term paper in college, it can assure failure for an advanced research paper. The methodology you choose dictates the method that you will use to collect data. If you go into the Australian bush collecting samples of deadly snake venom, then you have completely excluded most of the qualitative methodologies (except case study) and some of the theoretical methodologies. If you do the research first, you are loosing control of your project as you are letting the research choose your methodology, and if your research chooses your methodology, then it can also choose your question and dilute your hypothesis. Allowing your research to choose your methodology is more akin to journalism than academic writing. In journalism you investigate a subject in detail, in academic writing you prove or disprove a hypothesis through data and research. Both are effective, but only one is academic writing.

Now that we have laid the macro-methodologies at your feet, it is time to choose one. In this chapter we are going to look at each of these methodological families by way of an overview to help give you the information to enable you to choose a methodology. The sections in this chapter give a brief description of the different methodologies that we will cover in this book. Each section will correspond with a part of the book, and each subsection will correspond with a chapter. Once you find a methodology that you feel will work for the type of research that you want to do, you can read the part or chapter on the methodology that you chose. That way this book can be used as an effective handbook and you do not have to reread this book every time that you want to write a paper.

QUANTITATIVE RESEARCH

Quantitative research is the study of statistics, whether base statistics or anomalies, to allow the research a better understanding of the current situation within a given population or to allow the research to predict the likelihood of a phenomenon within like populations. Quantitative esearch is often called statistics, but statistics are simply a part of quantitative research. The macro-methodology is broken down into three distinct methodologies that can be effective in a variety of different fields. The three methodologies are General Statistics, Descriptive Statistics, and Predictive (Inferential) Statistics. Each of these processes serves a general purpose.

So when should you use a statistical methodology for your research paper? Statistics are effective when the research materials can be objectively quantified, thus allowing the numbers (i.e., the raw data) to be analyzed through algorithms to create a descriptive or predictive model of a population. Or in more colloquial terms, statistics are used when the data are numbers that can be put into statistical formulas to answer specific questions. Many people are afraid of statistics, but all statistics is comprised of is a series of basic math problems. To make statistics even easier, most disciplines have a discipline specific computer program that will do the math for you. All you have to do is get the data and plug the numbers into a spreadsheet. So if your data lends itself to being a quantifiable set of numbers, it may then be in your best interest to look into a quantitative methodology.

General statistics is a term that is not often used in the field—in fact, if you are taking a statistics class you will probably not hear the term much. General statistics is the basic step of a statistics process; however, it is used to ensure random sampling. Random sampling is the process of ensuring that your statistical sample is random, thus indicative of the population that you are sampling. Without a random population your study will be skewed toward whatever de-randomized your study and thus the validity will be questionable. Whether you are doing a predictive or a descriptive statistical study, taking the time to randomize your sample will help ensure that your study is valid and reliable.

Descriptive statistics use the numbers gained from a random sample to describe a population at large. The larger your sample the more reliability you have in relation to the population that you are studying. This type of statistics is often seen in the form of a poll, though polls are not the most common method for gaining statistical data in an academic setting (polls are bodies of participants who want to take part in the poll thus are actively engaged, surveys and other data collection techniques require you to go out and find people who may or may not be interested in your subject but are still members of the population). Descriptive statistics will have a margin of error, even if the whole population is surveyed because of human error. While your subject may not be human (i.e., a geological survey of geological periods within rock structures), your research subjects doubtless will be human. This type of statistical study is used when you want to describe the makeup of a given population.

Predictive statistics attempts to predict the actions within a population by looking at the previous actions of a similar population. The basic logic behind predictive statistics is that if something has happened 100 times in a row there is a likelihood that it will happen again if the same circumstances are applied during the experiment. Further, predictive statistics incorporates probability. For example, a standard American roulette wheel has a 1 in 38 (approximate) chance of landing on any given number. We know this because if the wheel is balanced it has an equal chance of falling into any of the slots and there are 38 slots.[1] Predictive statistics takes the probability and/or previous actions of a population and uses that information to determine what may happen next. For instance, if one of the spokes in the roulette wheel is bent, there may be a statistically higher chance that the ball may fall in one slot rather than another. If this chance exceeds the odds that the table is paying, then there is a chance to make money by betting on the more likely number. This form of statistics is useful for making an educated guess of what is going to happen in the future.

Statistics is often considered to be one of the most difficult classes in a college atmosphere. This fierce reputation is mostly myth and legend and wholly ill deserved. Statistics is a very basic form of math, with a smattering of algebra scattered in. The difficulty most people have is with the Greek letters that indicate an equation. If you want to do statistics, but do not always remember what the Greek letters mean you are more than welcome to make a chart and hang it on your workspace wall. Once you get out of college no one is going to hassle you to memorize the equations. Once you have the equations you can simply plug in the numbers (or better yet plug the numbers into a software package) and then you will have the data you want to use for your study. The advent of the computer age has made statistics easier, so help stop the fear and tell people that statistics is as easy as 1 + 1.

QUALITATIVE RESEARCH

Qualitative research also has a nasty myth about it. Some people (especially in the hard science) feel that qualitative research is less valid because it is based on subjective observations made by the researcher or other researchers. This misconception has largely been added to by the modern

---

1. The approximation is because there are scenarios (statistically insignificant) where the ball will hit a spoke and fly out of the bowl.

relativism movement which tells researchers that everything that they believe is wrong.[2] The truth about qualitative research is that by and large it has more rules than statistics and those rules are more complicated. The big difference is that quantitative research is done in the language of mathematics and qualitative research is done in the researcher's spoke language. This eliminates one of the major steps that people have problems with in quantitative research. Both qualitative research and quantitative research are highly structured so that they will help prove or disprove a hypothesis that answers a research question. If you stick to any of the qualitative methodologies your research can have the same validity and reliability as any statistical paper has. It all relies on you following the rules, no matter how complex, and delivering an honest interpretation of the data.

Qualitative data is most often associated with projects that have highly subjective data. This is where qualitative studies really shine. The problem with statistics is that it is difficult to categorize how happy a person is, or how much pain a patient is in, or which location for vacations is most beautiful. These questions are all subjective. True you could rate them on a scale of 1 to 10, but what if my definition of happiness is different from yours, or you can handle more pain than I can, or even you like rainforests and I like beaches? Our ratings of 1 to 10 may have completely different meanings, thus the validity of the statistics would be off. Thus enter qualitative methods. Qualitative methods allow you to look at happiness on a case-by-case basis, relate the amount of pain that someone is in to the painful events that a person has experienced in their lives, and put the most beautiful location in the context of what the observer sees as beautiful. Qualitative research allows you to give context to answers that would in statistics just be wrought numbers. This allows qualitative methods to be descriptive enough that subjective data is still valid in a study.

A drawback of qualitative methodological approaches is that the results of a study cannot be used as a predictor of a society. Qualitative studies look specifically at what their subject is doing in that time frame. Just because there was a study overviewing sexual assault cases in Chicago that happened between 2012 and 2013, it does not mean that there will be similar occurrences in 2014-2015. Qualitative methods create a timestamp for data that are occurring and that may never occur again. As a side note, this is one of the reasons that grounded theory is not included in the qualitative methodologies. Grounded theory seeks to be applied to other situations so it fits more into theoretical methodologies than into qualitative methodologies.

The four major methodologies that are currently being used in qualitative research are ethnographies, case studies, phenomenology, and qualitative meta-synthesis. While there are other types of qualitative studies, these are the most common forms that you will be exposed to. Each of these methodologies has a specific pattern of actions that a researcher must take to ensure that they main-

2. Very broad interpretation of relativism, actually closer to postmodernism.

tain the validity of the process and maintain validity and reliability in their research. As you look over these types of methodology, if you feel you are going to do a qualitative study then think about what kind of data you are planning on gathering for your project.

The first type of qualitative research project we will look at is ethnography. Ethnography is the scientific study and descriptions of the society, culture, practices, and actions of individual people, groups of people, or societies of people. This style of research is primarily done through observation, though it can be done through synthesis if the person, group, or society is unable to be observed physically or temporally. An example of an ethnography would be "The Cultural Practices of Hopi Indians Today: A comparison of social practices within the Hopi Indian Community of X and the Practices of the Hopi people throughout history." In a study such as this, the researcher would observe the practices of the Hopi people in their society today, then do book research and interviews to see how those practices have changed over the last however many years. This type of study is an excellent exploratory study into the methods and practices of a society and requires a good mix of book research and actual field research.

The second group of qualitative research papers that we are going to look is case studies. A case study is a process of research and analysis of a specific person, group, or event over a period of time. Case studies are more focused than ethnographies, in that they target specific people, groups, or events rather than looking at persons, groups, and societies as they interact in daily life. For instance, while an ethnography may look at John Doe in a paper called "The Life of John Doe: An Ethnography of a Regular Person Living in Brooklyn, New York" a case study would be looking at John Doe as a specific person, "The Life of John Doe: A Case Study of a Man from Brooklyn New York Who Did/Does X." As you can see, a case study has a theme, where an ethnography is more exploratory. Case studies tend to rely heavier on book and interview research as the target event has generally passed before someone knows that it will be academically significant. That being said a researcher with great foresight can do a case study of a scheduled event, or even begin recording data as an event that they are present at is occurring and then build a case study around that data.

As the third qualitative research methodology that we will cover, phenomenology is the study of the lived experiences of a person, group, or society. Phenomenology has a broad range of different styles that can be implemented; we are going to look mainly at general phenomenology in this book as phenomenology is a multidisciplinary approach to research. Phenomenologists tend to use their own version of phenomenology that they develop through their working practice; however, one element of phenomenology that is always present is examining the lived experiences of people who lived through or were affected by or are talking about a specific phenomenon. An example of a phenomenological paper title is, "A Study of the Lived Experiences of Sex Slaves in Saudi Arabia: A phenomenology of the abuse, torture, and assault of young men ages 16-18." In this study, the phenomenologist would discuss with the victims what happened to them, by whom, and how it happened. Phenomenology research focuses on interviews, surveys, and a smattering of focus groups to build up a data set.

The final area of qualitative research that we will cover is qualitative meta-synthesis (QMS). QMS is the practice of gathering work on a specific subject, through book research, until a point of data saturation is reached, then analyzing the research of other researchers to prove a hypothesis of your creation with data they did not directly use in their work. QMS done poorly looks like a first semester term paper. QMS properly done can create new theoretical inroads or compress data to make it more accessible for researchers. QMS is a rigorous process that is almost completely book and journal research that requires detailed coding, design, and analysis elements and a strong research trail. This type of research is effective in disciplines where data are changing quickly and the most up-to-date data are needed by practitioners and researchers.

Qualitative methods are especially useful in the social sciences where researcher bias can taint data. With the process of epoche, qualitative methodologies can do exploratory, specific case, general phenomenon, and synthesis research and allow the reader to know what type of perspective the researcher is coming from. Qualitative research is also excellent in creating an academic historical record that can be used in the future to build hybrid data sets for predictive models or theories. If you are going to select a qualitative research methodology, just be sure to follow the rules to the detail. With quantitative research if you miss a detail your equation is completely wrong, if you miss a detail in a qualitative study your reliability may be completely wrong, too.

THEORETICAL RESEARCH

Theoretical research is the grandfather of all research methodologies. With elements of both qualitative and quantitative research styles there is always some question as to what theoretical research actually is. For the purpose of this book, theoretical research is the unified approach to analyzing and proving/disproving a set of interrelated hypotheses within one theoretical or disciplinary paradigm. Whereas good qualitative or quantitative research studies focus on problems at the research level or the hypothetical level, theoretical research tends to look at a problem at the topical level. Macro-level theory may approach the elemental level or even the area level. The more general the theory, the more research is required and the more data needed to support a theory. Theories are also philosophical on the level that once a theory is proven to be true (or almost proven to be true) it becomes an academic law. For instance, the laws of thermodynamics were originally theories of thermodynamics but repeated testing showed that they were always true within our limited understanding of the universe; therefore, we call them laws. Theoretical research begins a process that may take hundreds of years to move a theory from a law.

The big questions that are approached in theoretical research are the who, what, why, when, and how of the academic world. The theoretical questions avoid becoming too specific for fear of leaving out a valuable piece of what the researcher is looking for. In our other two macro-methodologies, we saw how being hyper-specific was an advantage. In theoretical research being that specific may invalidate the research as something that disproves the theory may be overlooked because the focus of the research is too small. Questions like, "How does gravity work?" or "What created the Universe?" are questions that theorist have battled over for hundreds of years. Even something that we can see happening like evolution is still argued in some segments. (BTW, Darwin did get the evolutionary function backwards.)

We will briefly cover how to do who, what, where, when, and how research in later chapters. The key area of theoretical research that we will cover will be grounded theory research in Chapter 24. Grounded theory is generally considered a qualitative process, or in some schools it is considered a hybrid process, but we will look at it as a theoretical process with hybrid traits. Grounded theory uses the theoretical processes of observation and research to show that the elements of a proposed theory are not false. In reality it is a microcosm of the entire theoretical process, distilling the entire who, what, where, when, and why process into one functional system.

Theory tends to be looked at as an academic end game. Researchers work their entire careers to put together hypotheses in fragile matrixes that can be called a theory. The danger in this pattern is that while the research is valid and proven, the interrelationship of the research can be attached, as the hypothesis seems to be cobbled together from a lifetime of research. This method only works if you start with a vision of what you want to show and it becomes your life's work. We recommend that you build a theory from the other end, beginning with a theory that allows that theory to evolve as you prove and disprove elements during the course of your career. This allows the theory to be fluid until you lock it into place, likely after most of your career. This will allow future researchers to see the evolution of your theory and your thoughts on the subject so they do not have to spend time following blind alleys that you have already followed.

HYBRID METHODOLOGIES

While hybrid methodologies are grouped together in Part V: Miscellaneous Methodologies, they are of special note here. Some research does not lend itself to being looked at through one methodological lens. Some matters in our world are broad enough that if you look at them through a simple descriptive statistical lens or an ethnographic lens you would not have enough of the picture to properly address your hypothesis. In this case, you may have to draw techniques from multiple methodologies. This is generally an advanced technique, but depending on your research you may have to learn how to do this process to move forward with a specific project that you are working on.

When dealing with hybrid methodologies, the important thing to note is that you do not have to pioneer the methodology on your own. There are many journal articles about hybridizations of the major research methods in qualitative, quantitative, and theoretical research. If there is already an article written on the hybridization that you want, do not try to reinvent the wheel (though you can modify it to make it better and possibly get a second paper out of it). If you find that you are using a hybridization that there is no research or methodological papers on how to do it, first ask why not, then create your own methodological design using elements from the "donor" methodologies. As you design remember not to force elements that do not seem to fit together in the same process. Let your process come together easily because the less you force things, the less you are going to have to force things as you apply your research to your method.

MISCELLANEOUS METHODOLOGIES

There are times when you are going to have to write a paper that does not fit into one of the above categories. We have grouped these other methodologies into a catch-all category we call Miscellaneous Methodologies. These methods are generally unrelated and should be read independently if you are using them for a specific process. These methods are:

1. Term Papers
2. Business Papers
   a. White Papers
   b. Reports
   c. Trade Journals
3. Legal Papers
   a. Briefs
   b. Academic Papers

4. Gists
5. Grants

As you can see, some of these categories have their own subcategories that you may be required to use in a paper.

Term papers are the most common papers that people are going to write in their lifetime. Either in college or in high school, someone is going to require a person to write a term paper. Most papers should be written within a QMS format; however, because some professors and high school teachers have not been taught proper QMS format, we are going to include a method that will satisfy the requirements for a "regurgitation paper." Chapter 31: Term Papers will walk you through the process of creating a meta-summary of data on a specific subject. As you read it you will notice that this method is a hybridization between meta-synthesis and a case study. Even in a paper as simple as a term paper it is good to maintain a rigorous model of research.

Businesses require a number of different types of papers from employees. Chapter 32: White Papers will cover the process for writing each of these types of papers. It is important to remember, however, that each corporate culture may have its own format for writing papers that will be submitted to the company or for the company. The first type of business papers that will be discussed is the chapter's namesake, white papers. A white paper is an authoritative paper, written with little citation and based on the knowledge of the author, on a given topic. The author may augment his or her knowledge with citations, but mostly this form of paper is designed to relay the knowledge of a company's "expert in a specific area" to the rest of the people at the company. The second type of paper is a report. A report is just what is sounds like, a paper that reports the functions or results of a practice or even within or outside of the company. The third area of business papers that we look at is trade journals. Trade journals are similar to academic journals with the exception that they have fewer rules and are specifically related to a given trade rather than an academic discipline.

Legal papers are the next section in Chapter 34. Outside the macro-methodologies and possibly trade journals, briefs will likely be the most common type of nonstandard paper that readers of this book will be writing. There are two types of briefs. The first (the one we cover in depth) is a note to yourself or someone else at a firm that tells the reader the details, data, and result of a case in a one-page document so that the reader can internalize and synthesize the data quickly into another document. The second type of brief (the one we will briefly talk about) is a court brief, which is an argument submitted to the court outlining your argument and the weaknesses in the argument(s) of your opponent(s). The second main type of legal paper is a legal journal article (or note written by a law school student). A journal article in the legal academy follows many of the same rules as in the normal academy except the format is closely akin to Issue, Rule, Analysis, Conclusion, since that is the general business model. It is also common in legal journals to submit your article to multiple journals at once.[3] A note is a legal article written by a student that was once looked upon as less authoritative, but as the requirements have grown so has the acceptance of student notes.

Gists are like briefs except that they are designed to be used by CEOs, leaders, and presidents. These are short documents from department heads so that the leader of a company can stay up to date on the operations of their organizations. While these documents are heavily researched, they are not heavily cited as they are for internal use only. They also do not conform to any requirements as to the format—basically the format is whatever the boss likes. Some gists may even be in bullet point format. The main goal for these papers is to allow the reader quick access to whatever information he/she needs to keep things running smoothly.

Grants are the final section of the oddball category. A grant is a proposal and request for money. The proposal side of a grant is a detailed description of a proposed project for the information of a grant writing agency. The request side of the grant is telling the grant agency why you believe they should give money to you for your project. Grant agencies are inundated with requests for money each day; when you write a grant it should be short, informative, and to the point. The more time you take to ensure that you write your grant properly, the better chance you have at receiving the grant money that you so desperately need.

CONCLUSION

Choosing your macro-methodology (and of course your methodology) is an important part of the writing process. To relate it to our journey analogy, it is like choosing whether you are going to use a bike, a car, walk, or even use a helicopter. Each vehicle has benefits and drawbacks that will heavily affect where you go, where you can go, and how you will get there. Take the time to choose your methodology and seriously consider multiple options rather than just looking at one option and choosing it because it is easy. Your writing becomes your portfolio, thus it becomes part of your brand. If you choose the wrong methodology, then it can look bad for your personal brand. Take a few extra minutes to ask, "How could I use this hypothesis for a phenomenology, and how would that compare to using it in an ethnography?"

---

3. University of Washington School of Law (2014). *Writing for & Publishing in Law Reviews: Submitting Manuscripts*. Available at https://lib.law.washington.edu/content/guides/lawrevs-sub (January 13, 2015).

This is another area where this book can be an excellent tool for you to decide what type of paper you are going to write. Take the time to read or even skim a few methodological chapters and let your mind find connections between the methodologies described herein and your personal research goals. You may find that you are approaching your project from the wrong direction or even that you are overlooking an important opportunity that you could have with one methodology that is not available in another methodology. The more you learn how to do research, the more you will be able to do with research.

CHECKLIST

- ❑ What type of macro-methodology are you using?
- ❑ Why?
- ❑ Will a quantitative study work bBetter?
- ❑ Will a qualitative study work better?
- ❑ Should I be doing a theoretical study?
- ❑ Why is my chosen methodology the best methodology for me?

CONCLUSION PART I

As we embark on this journey to write a strong academic paper, you have completed your preparation (if you have followed the advice of this book). Each time you go through this process, you will have to read less of the guidelines as the process becomes internalized and the process itself will seem to be shorter. The preparation phase of a paper is vitally important if you want to write a strong academic paper. Take the time to outline your ideas, as these outlines can be invaluable when you come back to write another paper or when you want to bring out an updated version of your paper. When I first learned to write academically, I thought these processes were just busy work and that I could skip over them and still have a good paper. I was wrong, so do not make my mistake. Take the extra 20 minutes to develop your concept and process and it will save you hours on the back end.

Your writing journey begins with an idea, and that idea is part of you. As you work your way through the process of writing a paper you will find yourself in a place different from where you started. Whether you end up in a place where you want to be or you end up in a place where you do not want to be, it will be because of your preparation. You would not start a journey through a jungle without a map and a plan of where you want to go, would you? Writing a paper is the same thing. There are mazes of data out there that can get you lost. There are forests of published papers that can direct you toward your goals or away from them. There are poorly written articles that can lead you to dead ends or other perils; and there are critics out there who are looking for the slightest mistake in your research so that they can grab a hold of and ruin you with it. It truly is a jungle out there, but through good preparation you will have the ability to ensure that you write the best paper you can write.

Part II
QUANTITATIVE RESEARCH

chapter 11
Introduction to Quantitative Research

INTRODUCTION

Of all the research methodologies out there, quantitative research may have the most undeserved reputation for being the most difficult of all. In many fields, people do not like math because of the way that the United States teaches mathematics in our school systems. Quantitative methods, or statistics, tend to be the most feared branch of mathematics because they are a "gatekeeper" class in many disciplines. Another reason why statistics has an undeserved reputation for being hard is, some people have apoplexy when someone referees to a mathematical function in common language rather than by its statistical name or by the Greek letter assigned to that function. In all reality, statistics is a system of basic mathematics with fancy nomenclature. Here is the inside secret on statistics: if you properly design your research study, then the computer does most of the hard mathematics.

College students and professors in my fields, the social sciences and law, tend to avoid statistics like the plague, but in all reality statistics are the easiest of the macro-level research methodologies to do correctly. While bad theory and bad qualitative practices can be done fairly quickly, statistics tend to take less time if you are using the proper methodology. Once the mystique of "scary math" is taken away (because the computer does most of it for you), you will find that if you want to do a relatively speedy academic paper, statistics is the method that you should use. Statistics has a simple set of rules—get data, analyze data, and write about findings through a theoretical lens. These are the only three steps in a statistics paper. Some qualitative methodologies have as many as 10 steps and theoretical papers up to 25 steps. Once you get past the "scary math" that chases most people away from statistics, you will find that it is a friendly style in most disciplines.

Statistics does have its niche market in the academic field. Quantitative research methodologies should be used on projects that have finite objective variables that you want to test in relation to one another, or finite objective variables that you want to predict through inferential statistics. Statistics may not be the right methodology for you if you are going to be working with a large volume of subjective data, or if the spectrum of your data cannot be easily placed within a numeric system. Just like the other two macro-level methodological families, statistics is a tool and if used properly it can make your life much easier.

Statistics may be the methodology for you if you are person who does not tend to focus on the details of a situation. If you are more concerned with the numbers and the ability to repeat your report and get the exact same results (or similar results within a margin of error) then you may be more inclined to use a statistical method than a subjective one such as ethnography. Personality styles can play a large part in selecting the proper methodological style for you, and you may want to try out a few styles and methodologies over the course of your career to see what is the right fit for you at any given time of your life.

Another consideration that you should take into account is that some data lends itself to quantitative studies. If you enjoy reading over government or corporate reports where there are more numbers than words, then you may find that quantitative research piques your interest. Data-heavy research with few details and large volumes of numbers fit into the quantitative family of methodologies quite well; whereas studies that look at the context and nonnumeric details of a situation are more suited for qualitative or theoretical research. Trying to force a qualitative research project into a quantitative framework will be just as difficult as the reverse. Take the time as you prepare your study to be sure that you have selected the correct macro-methodology. This will help you select the right tool for the job at hand.

WHAT FIELDS USE QUANTITATIVE RESEARCH?

Different fields look at the various types of research differently. That being said, quantitative research is definitely an industry standard in academia. Almost every academic field that does research has some element of the field doing quantities research at any given time. From legitimate traditional fields such as mathematics and biology to fields that draw in the people academics do not like to talk about, such as futurists and crypto-zoologists, all fields have some way that they use statistics to further the research of their field. (Honestly the only people that I can think of who do not use statistics are in the field of "pure" philosophy.)

The fact that statistics is used in almost every field in academia is not a free license to use statistics for all of your projects. Besides the considerations we listed above about qualitative research, there are two varieties of statistical research that are accepted as usable in some fields but not in others. Descriptive statistics are generally acceptable in most fields, because they are simply reports on what is happening in society with a random sample; but there are fields, such as education, where descriptive statistics can be criticized. Inferential or predictive statistics are also accepted in most fields, but some fields have too many variables for an accurate prediction to be made. In these highly dynamic fields, it can be safer to stick to descriptive statistics or even look at qualitative or theoretical methodologies.

There will be numeric data in all fields. It just lies in the hands of researchers to identify how it should be used and what type of statistical method they should engage in. If you take the time to look at your data, or the area where you believe you are going to get your data from, you will find that most of the time the data will tell you what kind of methodology you should be using. If the data you are looking at describes what society looks like, then you should use descriptive statistics. If you are looking at the future, then you probably want predictive statistics.

LIMITS OF QUANTITATIVE RESEARCH

Like any other tool, quantitative research has its limitations. If you attempt to exceed these limitations, then you may find that you are trying to drive down a narrow hiking trail with a 4x4. Using the correct writing tools on your journey to write this paper will make your life easier. All too often academics try to force a methodology that they "like" to be something that it is not. Humanity has spent millennia designing and augmenting research methodologies to be efficient for specific actions. Quantitative research has its niche, and that niche is numerical and mathematical data. When you begin to step outside of these types of data, quantitative research can do more damage than good.

One of the key limitations of quantitative data is that it does not do well with rich, high context data. Rich data is data that has so many details that it cannot really be boiled down to numbers efficiently. A situation such as "The tall woman in her early 40s had deeply tanned skin, her hazel eyes seemed to dance beneath the wisps of hair dangling from her head, likely braided by the local village girls during the day. She smiled as if she were having fun, even though it appeared that she did not know the dance that the villagers were doing, though the villages, for their part, did not seem to notice her apparent lack of knowledge as they continued. The drum beat rose high into the sky and the harvest festival moved into its second day." While some of the data could be translated into mathematical data, most of the data are contextual, so a rich data qualitative or theoretical approach may be better to gather the data. Highly contextual data is data that has meaning within the culture or subculture you are looking at, but not within the larger culture in general. Something as simple as a revealed ankle on a woman could have deep meaning as an adulteress or a harlot in some primitive cultures but in society in general most people would see it as meaningless. Researchers using statistical methods have a difficult time differentiating between the meaning in the context, but they can use it to show the relative difference between items in high context and low context cultures.

In the same vein, some topic areas are just not conducive to numerological analysis. How happy someone is, or how blue a picture is (though this can be measured with highly scientific instruments) are generally not topics that you can say, "That is a five or that is a two." Some scales are so relative to the person who is experiencing them that placing the observation on a numeric scale would be meaningless beyond that person. The common question "How effective was this professor on a scale of 1 to 10?" is an effective question if the students all have the same relative experience with the same professors, but when people come from diverse background, one student's opinion of what a good professor is compared to what another student's opinion of what a good professor is may be worlds apart.

One constant truth that limits most data collection methods is the axiom that everybody lies. Whether to ourselves or to others, each person lies to improve his or her situation in some way. This can be troublesome in research collection because even if people believe they are being honest on surveys or in interviews, they can still be lying to themselves, especially if you ask subjective questions. Some people would argue that observational data are more secure as researchers make a conscious effort not to lie to themselves, but the outward appearance of others may be part of their lies. Further, researchers' senses can lie to them during their observations. The fact that human beings lie in some way or another does not change the validity of statistical data. On the aggregate in a properly done study you should get enough truth to offset the lies, but you should be aware that not all data are as truthful as they are purported to be; sometimes, you as the writer need to dig deeper and ensure the validity of your incoming data.

The final problem that some researchers face is not with the methodology, but with themselves. Some people are just not able to work the numbers needed for statistics research. Now generally this is a result of a physical handicap or a disease. "I do not like math" is not sufficient reason to say you cannot do statistics, it is a reason that you do not want to do statistics. Severe dyslexia, blindness, and other maladies can prevent researchers from being able to properly see the numbers that are needed to do statistical work. This does not exclude them from the field, as many people see these problems as challenges to overcome, to become leaders in the field. Others need researchers to work with them to develop the ideas that are in their heads. If you have a disability, challenge it and use it as fuel to drive you forward.

QUANTITATIVE PRINCIPLES

Like all other methodologies quantitative research is defined by several core principles. These principles separate quantitative research from the other macro-level families based on the nature of the methodology. Quantitative data collection is similar to the other two in that it requires the data to be accurate, but it facilitates this accuracy through mathematical formulas rather than through epoche and triangulation. Accuracy is the cornerstone of good research and when developing a quantitative research design, you should always be careful to ensure that you have the data to ensure proper accuracy in your work.

By and large (though there are some exceptions) quantitative data collection methods require some sort of objective numerical data to be examined. While "How much pain you feel" is a subjective issue, "how much pain the patient reported feeling on a survey" is objective. Statistical surveying allows data to be converted from subjective to objective data (though the researcher needs to inform the readership that this was the method of conversion through the methodology section). By relying on objective data, a researcher allows other researchers to use the same data source to repeat their experiment or research. This should allow the second researcher to procure a similar answer to the research question within the studies margin of error.

The penultimate trait of a qualitative study that gives practitioners of this methodology some bragging rights is that their data, if done properly, should be able to be transferred to the entire population that they are examining. Qualitative methodologies, by and large, are limited in the transferability of their findings beyond the specific group that they are studying. Quantitative methods allow the researcher to transfer the data to the whole population as their sample is expected to be a representative group. The larger the random sample size, the greater likelihood that it will be representative of the general population.

The ultimate expression of statistical prowess is the accurate forecasting of future events within a population or subject based on inferential statistics. Accuracy is the holy grail in this area as the more accurate a forecaster can be, the better they can anticipate changes in market, developments in the population, or even geological formations that may yet remain undiscovered. The key to proper forecasting is ensuring that there is an established pattern, that the pattern relies on variables, and that observation of these variables can allow the researcher to "predict" future manifestations of the pattern. Some fields are better at it than others, but forecasting definitely differentiates statistics from other research methodologies.

FORMAT

Chapter 12 begins this part of the book by looking at the differences in descriptive and predictive statistics. One of the key problems in higher academia in the United States today is that descriptive statistics and predictive statistics are both taught in the same class as if they are part of the same process, when in all actuality they are both standalone methodologies. In the qualitative sphere, each method is taught as its own distinct entity, but this is not the case for quantitative methods. Descriptive statistics is taught as if it simply flows into predictive statistics. If the academy separated these two methodologies into two separate classes, then perhaps students would not get the two methods confused.

Chapter 13 looks at the process of descriptive statistics. At its heart, descriptive statistics wants to tell people a story through numbers. If you are afraid of math and want to do a descriptive statistical project, look at this statistical methodology as a storytelling process. Rather than descriptive verbs and adjectives, you use specific numbers to tell people where the story begins, where its middle is, and where the story ends. This approach can help many people scale the wall of fear that surrounds mathematics as a whole in the United States. Grade school and high school teachers who were bad at math teach it as if it should be challenging, where nothing is more natural than the story of 1 + 1. In this chapter we break down the elements of the process to tell the story of descriptive statistics so that you no longer have to be afraid of the "boogie man" of mathematics.

Chapter 14 looks at predictive statistics, which are also feared in the world of academics. It is believed forecasters, being the wizards of the statistical world, generally cast auguries of numbers to predict the future, but realistically predictive statistics are just as rational and finite as any other research method. Once the mystique is lifted from the field, anyone can do statistics, just like anyone can do theory or qualitative methods or anyone can use a hammer or a screwdriver—it just comes down to being taught to do it. Chapter 14 breaks away the mystique of predictive statistics and shows you how it can be used in your next research project (where applicable).

Chapter 15 takes a moment to look at the process of statistical sampling. Having a good sample is a necessity for a good research project, but it is vitally important for a statistics paper. The validity of your sample sets the validity of your paper, if you have a bad sample then your data will be off and you will have a bad paper. In this chapter we look at some of the things you can do to help randomize your sample, or if randomization is not possible how you can properly describe your sample so that the population comes in line with your sampling methodology.

Chapter 16 briefly looks at some of the helping tools that are out there in the field of statistics today. Twenty years ago, statistics was a field for people with minds that could bring all the numbers together quickly, or those who could spend the years looking at data in a race against time to make their findings before their data became outdated. This is not the case anymore. Anyone with a laptop or personal computer can buy a statistics program that will do all the calculations. If you learn the statistical program, then you can simply enter the data and tell it what to do. This changes the field of statistics from being able to do the math to being able to design studies. If you learn to use the tools that are at your disposal, then you can make your life much easier as a researcher.

This part on statistics is not a full statistics class; I am not going to give you 200 math problems, send you off to do them, then critique your answers. This part is designed to help you walk through the process of designing a statistical study. Programs such as SPSS will do the math for you, so I am not going to scare you with the math. We are going to talk about the elements that make a good statistical study and how you can make sure that they are included in your research project. Statistics is just another tool, you would not be afraid of a hammer or a screwdriver (unless a serial killer is wielding them), so why would you be afraid of statistics (even if a serial killer is wielding them).

CHECKLIST

- Breathe, it is only math.
- Have you done the steps in Part I to select a macro-level methodological family?
- How does your field use statistics?
- Which statistical method do you feel you should use?
- Why?
- Can you supply:
    - Accuracy?
    - Objective data?
    - Either a population where the data can be transferred;
    - Or a population where the data can be forecasted?

chapter 12
Writing in the Qualitative Methods

INTRODUCTION

Quantitative research is not an overly diverse field, as there are two basic approaches that you can take to giving people data based on numeric information. The first brand of statistics is descriptive statistics, which is just what it purports to be: Researchers use the statistical information to describe to their readers what is going on in their report. The second brand of statistics is inferential statistics. This style is a bit more complex. As its name implies, you are able to *infer* information based on what the statistics are; however, most people use this form of statistics to *predict* what is going to happen. As this is the most common use of inferential statistics we are going to describe them as they are being used and will call the predictive statistics in the course of this chapter (and later chapters).

As researchers, we must acknowledge that each type of statistics is a separate methodology. While the two can be used together, they are unique and separate. If they are used together, then you are using a hybrid quantitative methodology, and you should refer to Chapter 37: Hybrid Methodology Papers for information on combining two methodologies. Looking at statistics as a tool can help you put your statistical methods in the right place; if you look at descriptive statistics as a sledge hammer and predictive statistics as a claw hammer (carpenter's hammer), then you can sometimes see more clearly how they are going to be used. A sledge hammer is used to break down something, whether it be concrete, dry wall, or some other construction element that needs to be dismantled, this tool will do the job with ease. This is what descriptive statistics are for, breaking down information so your reader can understand it. Conversely, a claw hammer is used for building something new, which is the purpose of predictive statistics. With your claw hammer you build up a house and with your predictive statistics you build up a theory. You can try to use the wrong tool for the job if you like, if you try to tear down a building with a claw hammer it will take you a long time and if you try to pound in nails with a sledge hammer you will end up with sore fingers. Using the right tool at the right time will make your life much easier, and the same thing is true about literary tools.

In this chapter we cover the differences between descriptive and predictive statistics in detail. This will allow you to select your methodology, review your methodology (Chapters 13 and 14), then select a sampling technique (Chapter 15). In most statistics classes, you do these things in the opposite order—you review your sampling technique, then you review your methodologies, then you select a methodology. The reason that we reverse the order is because this is not a statistics book, this is a writing book. First you need to know the types of quantitative research you have available, then you need to know which type of quantitative research you are going to do, then you need to know how you are going to sample for that research. Hopefully, this will make understanding statistics much easier on you and take away some of the fear that surrounds the simplest data collection method. The last chapter of this part will look at the software that can make your life easier. However, understanding the quantitative methodology that you are going to be using is vital, but learning both at the same time can be confusing and add to the fear; therefore, in this chapter we will discuss each type of statistical method briefly, then help you choose one of the methodologies to use for your project.

USES OF DESCRIPTIVE STATISTICS

Descriptive statistics are statistics that allow for the analysis of data by describing, showing, or summarizing data in ways that show meaningful patterns or the lack thereof. Descriptive statistics are the first level of statistics; they are the tool for breaking down data so that it can be built back up in other forms (predictive statistics or meta-summary). However, sometimes your project will just need you to break down the data, and when this is the case descriptive statistics are a methodology in themselves. They allow you to summarize data in a way that allows you to show patterns, or the lack of patterns, thus showing your hypothesis to be true or false. Like any tool, when used properly descriptive statistics can allow you to complete your project efficiently and with excellent workmanship.

- Summary
- Show patterns or lack of
    - shows if hypothesis if true or not

The most common use that you will find yourself using statistics for is to describe a population or a site. Descriptive statistics allow you the objective numerical methodologies to walk your readership through their journey to understand what is going on within a population. While descriptive statistics lack the rich, detailed description that is the hallmark of qualitative research methodologies, it has its own form of rich description that makes it one of the primary research methodologies used in the world today. Numbers allow a statistician to compress amazingly large volumes of data into a short, quantitative statement. This means that you can understand the grain production of the United States by type and state in a simple chart, the ethnic origin of a Tunisian enclave with a simple sentence, or even the aggregate average of some vast population with a single number. Descriptive statistics are one of the most efficient ways to describe large volumes of data.

Another productive use of descriptive statistics is to show different elements of the same population. Not all populations are homogeneous, where the variable or variables that you are studying are the same throughout the population, except for outliers. For instance, in most of human society people have four fingers and a thumb on each hand. An outlier would be a person who has lost a finger or who has a birth defect. With most statistics you will find that your populations are heterogeneous. A heterogeneous society is a society in which the variable or variables that you are studying are not constant throughout the society. In these cases descriptive statistics can break the heterogeneous group into homogeneous subgroups, which can then be catalogued and the data analyzed.

Descriptive statistics also give you the opportunity to show correlations within populations. If person X has Y then person X probably does Z. These types of correlations can allow you to understand how elements within society interact. This is not a predictive methodology. Predictive methodologies try to find the solution to a question about the future, whereas describing things as they are presently situated is a descriptive method. A descriptive methodology attempts to find the answer to a question that is going on in the present. For instance, if you do a study that shows 98% of babies born into domestic families within a population have received their vaccinations, then if you take an individual from that population who has lived within that population for a lifetime, you can assume with a high level of certainty that the person has been vaccinated. This method is not perfect, but it is effective (the converse would be predictive, in that if you took a pregnant woman from the population you could say with a high probability that her child would receive vaccinations after birth).

Descriptive statistics also allow us to have percentiles. A percentile is a notation of how one individual ranks in relation to other members of the population. It would be unwieldy in large populations to rank each individual by specific rank, for that would require a survey of the whole population; rather, we find a cross section of the population to establish the mean and quartiles, then we can rank individuals within those percentiles allowing people to know where they stand. Oftentimes this is used as a method for ranking schools in a state or ranking students within their age group. Percentiles can also give individuals or organizations information on what elements of their performance they need to improve. If a sporting goods company is in the 98th percentile of effectiveness with hockey sticks and in the 13th percentile with baseball bats, then company officials know they need to improve upon their baseball bats (though there is room for improvement in the hockey stick market, too).

The final use we will discuss regarding descriptive statistics in this chapter is for loss prevention. If you know how many of your products are flawed, then you can prepare for problems that you are going to face in the future. If your study shows that one in every million units has a defect that is dangerous, then you can use a hybrid methodology (attaching descriptive to predictive) to find out how many lawsuits you can expect for your product's failure. The descriptive statistics creates data that can then be used in the predictive process. The descriptive data does not give the loss prevention personnel enough information for an inference—other variables such as number sold, the litigiousness of the population buying the product, and the amount of flawed units that can be recalled from the market before the problem manifests are all variables that will need to be taken into account for proper predictive statistics.

USES OF PREDICTIVE STATISTICS

Predictive statistics is another brand of quantitative methodology entirely. Whereas descriptive statistics attempt to describe what is, predictive statistics attempt to describe what will be. Descriptive statistics are generally thought of as boring and commonplace, while predictive statistics have the aura of prediction that ancient augers and fortunetellers had about them; however, predictive statistics are based on science and if used correctly can give us an astounding view of what specific variables are going to do in the future. The danger of predictive statistics is that sometimes people believe that they can do more than they are designed to do, which can lead people to publish fallacious studies and make claims about predicting reminiscent of these self-same augers and fortunetellers. In your journey to write a paper, ensure that you stay with the methodologies that are proven and avoid overreaching the limitations of your methodology.

One of the most basic functions of predictive statistics is probability, the likelihood that an event will happen to a specific variable. If you have the ability to isolate a specific variable and have a way to control/know the other variables that are affecting the target variable, then you have a good chance at identifying the probability of an event. Simple probability is the chance of your event happening within a given set of possible occurrences. A simple example is the flip of a coin. There are two possibilities—heads or tails. Thus the probability, all things being equal, of the flip coming up heads is 50% or 1:2 (i.e., there is one chance of the desired event coming up within two possible outcomes). Probability can be a useful tool on its own in many cases, but it can also help you do more complex predictive statistics.

Once you know the chance of something happening, then the next step is to be able to predict what will happen. This is where many students get themselves in trouble when using predictive statistics. Just because a probability states that something has a chance of happening does not mean that it is going to happen in a given time frame. For instance, there are six sides on a normal dice; if we roll the dice six times then there is a high probability that the number 6 will come up once; however, there is still a chance that it will not come up at all or may come up multiple times. Using probability and stating that this number will "eventually" come up is a poor use of predictive statistics and has cost people millions of dollars at the craps table. Predictive statistics is separate from probability in that you are looking at what has happened and looking at what will happen because of a pattern. (If 3 comes up 51 times out of 100 rolls on a dice, then you may be able to assume that it will come up again because you can assume there is a flaw in the dice. If 3 comes up 20% of the time then it is close enough to the average estimated occurrence that you could just be seeing a slight outlier.)

Forecasting goes beyond simple prediction by looking almost exclusively at patterns based on probability, to look beyond the next occurrence well into the future. Forecasting is an excellent tool for business modeling that allows the forecaster to find patterns looking at historic data (years of data, not just the last few dozen dice rolls) and then take the variables that affected the occurrences in the historic data and look for similar variables that may affect future data. When done properly, forecasting can give a statistician the ability to find complex patterns in finite systems; however, like prediction, if forecasting is used beyond the way that it is intended to be used it can cause people to rely on faulty forecasts, getting a hurricane when they were set for a nice sunny day.

Estimation is another tool that predictive statisticians put in their researcher's toolbox. By using a combination of descriptive and predictive statistics a researcher can make an educated guess as to what is going to happen in the future. This is not as strong of a finding as a forecast, because the systems are often not finite, but it can still be effective within simple infinite systems. Estimation allows you to use a restricted form of forecasting, acknowledging the flaws in the methodology, to predict within a system that would otherwise be unpredictable. You can estimate that a pair of dice is going to come up 7 before you roll 4. Most of the time you will be correct, but the data are based on the probability and your ability to predict based on that probability (this is different from prediction because you are not selecting an occurrence, you are stating an occurrence is more likely than not based on a probability). The difference is a fine line to be sure; however, the distinction can help you understand the variance in statistics a little better.

To apply predictive statistics to a collegiate field, we can see how it can be used in quality control. If you know the amount of bar stock you have for making a metal part is 5 feet and the machine punches a hole every 7 inches to separate pieces of stock, you know that after every nine punches there is going to be a short piece going into the system. Knowing that this is going to occur, you can take precautions to ensure that this "mini" piece of stock does not get sent to the manufacturing floor (or make sure it is recycled). This prediction ensures that these mini-pieces are not sent to your customers who are expecting full 7-inch pieces. By using predictive statistics in your research, you can look for patterns in descriptive statistics; combine them with probability of variables changing to look at the likelihood of specific events happening in the future.

CHOOSING DICTATES FORMAT OF PAPER AND MATH

One of the biggest differences between descriptive and predictive statistical methods is how the paper is written. When you are writing for a descriptive paper, you are telling your reader the way the world is now; when you are writing in a predictive fashion you are telling them how the world may be at some time in the future. This changes the tone, the purpose, and the goals of your writing. To be a good writer in the qualitative methods, you need to know what systems you are going to use and what tone you will take with your readers.

Descriptive papers should be written in an informative tone, much like a qualitative paper. In a statistical paper you want to limit your use of adjectives. Quantitative methods, especially descriptive statistics, are expected to be as objective as possible. If you begin using adjectives in your writing, you are introducing subjective and imprecise terms into your work. While "red" seems to be a simple concept, is it red red or is it scarlet, crimson, or blood red? These types of questions can cause you to loose credibility in a quantitative paper.

Predictive papers often have a stronger tone to them, sometimes even argumentative, because you are convincing your readers that your method for forecasting what is going to happen is accurate. The more aggressive the prediction, the more aggressive your tone should be. You do not have to make strong arguments for a probability—most people can do that math themselves when you give them the numbers. Predictions often draw more questions; forecasting more questions still. If you are bold enough to make an estimation in an academic paper, then you should have the facts and arguments to state why that estimate is proper.

If you treat descriptive and predictive statistics like the two separate tools they are, then you will find that your time working with statistics will go much more smoothly than if you try to force descriptive statistics into a predictive problem or vice versa. All methodologies are tools, and the more specialized you get in a methodology the more specialized of a tool that it is going to be. On your journey to write your paper, make sure that you choose the correct tools for your project. If not you could find yourself sitting there with a sledge hammer and sore fingers when all you needed was a screwdriver.

CHECKLIST

- ❑ Did you go through Part I and look at the methodologies?
- ❑ Why did you select the quantitative macro-methodological family?
- ❑ Are you describing what is in the world now? (Descriptive)
- ❑ Are you describing what the world is going to be? (Predictive)

RECOMMENDED READING

Anderson, Sweeny, & Williams (1999). STATISTICS FOR BUSINESS AND ECONOMICS, 17TH ED. New York: International Thompson.

Weiss, Neil (2002). INTRODUCTORY STATISTICS, 6TH ED. Boston: Addison-Wesley.

chapter 13
Descriptive Statistics

Note this is not a statistics chapter; it is a chapter on how to write on predictive statistics.

INTRODUCTION

In my personal opinion, descriptive statistics is one of the easiest forms of data collection and analysis in the pantheon of recognized methodological approaches. Descriptive statistics looks at what is going on the world, so you do not have the burden of predicting what is going to happen, you just have to state what the current state of things is. Next, as long as you can identify the cross section that you are collecting from, you can identify the population that the data describes. Once you collect your data, there is a plethora of software out there to help you manage and analyze your statistics, every thing from Microsoft Excel to SPSS and other high-end software. Descriptive statistics has a bad rap as being a difficult methodology to perform, but truth be told it is one of the easiest methodologies out there, which is why we have chosen to describe it first in this book.

If you are thinking about choosing descriptive statistics, look at your hypothesis. Is your hypothesis discussing what is currently going on or something that has already happened? These are the two areas where descriptive statistics can shine for you. If you are looking at what is going to happen in the future, then you should be using another methodology for your study. Next, are you looking at objective values or subjective values that can be given a numerical place holder? If you are dealing with finite variables that lend themselves to clear identification by numerical placeholder, then you have probably selected the correct methodological approach. However, if your variables are based on emotion or on spectrums that defy objective categorization and numbering, then you may want to look at one of the qualitative methodologies.

If your study meets the requirements above, then there are two purposes that descriptive statistics serve quite well. First, statistics is capable of compressing the infinite world into a set of finite numbers that people can easily understand. If you are going to research the grain production of the Midwest states from 1950 to 1980, divided by state, type of grain, and year, then you would like to have the numbers broken down into a system where after you do the analysis you can see the data categorized so if you wish to look deeper into one of the categories (such as sorghum production in 1967) you will be able to find that data within the study and not have to do the data collection phase all over again. Good descriptive statistics not only help you answer your hypothesis but also help other people answer theirs by organizing data into a compressed, readable view of the world.

The second major use of descriptive statistics is to tell people where they stand among a group or population. It seems to be human nature to compare oneself to other people using numbers that are of our own creation. How much do I weigh and how does that relate to other people who are my sex and my height? How smart am I and how do I relate to other people around the world. What is my country's oil production and where does it rank among other world oil producers? These types of questions seem to pique the curiosity of people across the spectrum of race, gender, economic status, and any of the other categories that we have created for ourselves so that we can compare ourselves against "like" people. Descriptive statistics allows us to answer these questions so we can know how our weight compares to other people of the same sex and height, how our intelligence compares to other people around the world, and how the United States or any other country compares to the world in relation to oil production.

This chapter is a primer to teach you how to use statistics in your writing. This chapter is not a substitute for a good statistics book or a statistics class, this is a writing chapter to help you take the numbers you create using your statistical methods and convert them into a paper that anyone can understand. In the first section we look at the ability of descriptive statistics to summarize data in a way that other people can understand and use for research, business, or any other area where statistics are valuable. We also discuss the use of frequency in descriptive statistics and how it differs from using frequency as a tool to predict something under a predictive statistics model. In the second section we look at some of the common measurement terms associated with descriptive statistics. Sometimes mathematics, particularly statistics, can seem like another language. If you take the time to learn the language and learn what all the words mean, then the world of mathematics is actually a quite simple place to do your research. In the third section we look at the bell-shaped curve, even as I am writing this I can feel many of you shudder. The bell-shaped curve is actually a simple set of mathematical formulas that let a researcher discover where an individual, group, or society falls within a given population. The curve is simply a visual representation of what your data already say. In the fourth section we look at the process of developing correlations between differing variables. This requires us to look at the ideas of independent variables, dependent variables, dependence, and the problem of spurious correlations.

This chapter, hopefully, will take away some of the fear you may have about statistics. We approach statistics in academia as a problem that must be solved when really all statistics are is another set of tools that we can use to solve other problems. Fearing statistics is like looking at your tool bench, seeing a hammer setting there and then wondering how you are going to get rid of the hammer so you can pound in the nail. The hammer is the tool that you need to pound in the nail, whereas statistics is the tool that you can use to analyze your data and support your hypothesis.

SUMMARIZING DATA

Our world is covered with data, everything we see, hear, smell, taste, or feel can be seen as one type of data or another. This means that we have so much data in this world that it is difficult to create a proper research spectrum to cover it all. Think about this, when the Romans were a world power humanity did not even know about the existence of germs. That is a whole discipline of research and knowledge that we did not know about. Fast forward to the 1920s, and if you asked someone where you could buy a computer they would look at you like you were crazy; computer sciences were unknown to our species. In a world with so much data we do know about, we have to question what's out there we do not know about. We cannot even manage the meager portion of the universe we do know with qualitative data, that is where statistics come in.

Descriptive statistics allow us to take the immense volumes of data that humanity has collected from the beginning of written history and compile it into more manageable "chunks" of data. The "chunks" are then areas that people can deconstruct and study in more detail. Imagine statistics as the card catalogue of an immense library—without the catalogue how would you find the book that you need? Sure, you may know where a few books you normally deal with are, but most of the books would appear to be randomly placed. Statistics give order to the randomness of the data in the world. By looking at statistical studies you can find specific points that you are looking for. If you are creating a statistical study, then you are the person putting order to the chaos.

One way that you can summarize data is by using charts and graphs. While we will cover the specifics of charts and graphs in Part V, it is important to know their general purpose in summary as we go through this chapter. The old saying "A picture is worth a thousand words" is in no area more true than in statistics. If you can create a logical graph that displays large volumes of data in an efficient way, then you can categorize an entire field quickly so that others can follow your research. Graphs and charts are often easier for readers to consume because where it may take 500 pages to describe the grain example from above, it may simply take two or three pages of charts or graphs. This visual data makes the transition from your research to the minds of the reader that much easier.

Descriptive statistics are also the method of choice when dealing with something where the details may distract the reader. While a qualitative report on the chaos that ensued after the 9/11 radical islamic terror attacks may inform the viewer, it may also skew the viewpoint of the reader. Too many details can create an emotional state that draws the reader away from the research that you are trying to present. If your research paper was on the temperature and stress ratings of building grade steel and how they failed under the conditions of the 9/11 events, then getting your reader emotional about the tragedy would only cause him or her to reflect on what happened that day rather than reading your material. Descriptive statistics can give you the "sterile" feel of a paper that allows the reader to keep focused on the topic. This can also be a limitation, because if you want to convey the pain and hardship of the families that lost loved ones when the World Trade Center fell, then you may have a hard time conveying the depth of that data with numbers. In a case such as this you may want to use a hybrid method or a qualitative method.

Descriptive statistics also allow you to demonstrate the frequency of events in the past. This idea of frequency should be kept separate from the use of frequency as a pattern in predictive statistics. To continue the tool analogy, frequency is like a claw hammer. On one hand it can be used to pull out a nail and take apart something—just like descriptive statistics deconstruct massive amounts of data to make them more accessible to the reader—and on the other hand, the hammer can be used to pound in a nail thus building something, just like predictive statistics build a model for the future. Frequency has two purposes as it is partially in the area of descriptive statistics and partly in the area of predicative statistics.

Summarized data opens the reality of the world to your reader in a brief overview. Some people fail to see the advantage that this can be in an academic setting. While it may take years to teach a criminal justice student every theory that is relevant to the field in detail, a chart of what theories are out in the world and which ones are still in use can limit the amount of time that is spent of theories that are no longer valid. Charts can allow you to compress detailed analysis of a government into a single report, giving your readers a graph that shows the growth in some areas of the economy while other areas are slowly deteriorating; a dot plot can show you the seeming random feeding patterns of black bears in cornfields. Truth be told there are very few areas where summarizing data using quantitative methods is not at least part of the field. The question then becomes whether summarizing the data is the answer to the question, or whether summarizing the data will lead you to new and unanswered questions. This is where descriptive statistics become even more interesting. When you go beyond categorizing and step into measuring, a whole new world of data is at your fingertips.

MEASUREMENT TERMS

As you walk through your journey of writing a quantitative paper, one of the first things that you need to do is learn the language of the landscape you are walking through. Terminology tends to have simple meanings but because of years of departmental and philosophical isolation the terminology of a specific methodology differs from the language of the general public. This can often be confusing to people who are newly entering the field; therefore, we take a moment in this section to help clarify the words that are commonly used in quantitative methods. This is not an exhaustive list of all the terms you may find when you are working your way through a quantitative paper (for a longer list see the site in the footnote as a good reference).[1]

The first basic term that everyone who is learning about statistical mathematics should learn is the word "average." One reason that you should learn about it is because average has different manifestations depending on the way that it is being used in a system. The common use for average is the same as the meaning of the word "mean"; however, some people also use it to indicate the mode or the median within a data set. Right off the bat this confuses many would-be mathematicians, causing them to think that mathematics is difficult and beyond their grasp. I choose to look at average as being like the word "apple"—that is, there are many varieties of apple (Granny Smith, Macintosh, Red Delicious, etc.) but they are all apples. The same goes for the mean, the mode, and the median—they all are differing terms meaning a specific thing, but they are all still types of averages. If you push this confusion out of the way, then statistics begins to look more logical and much easier to understand.

The first type of average that we are going to look at is the mean. The mean is what people are commonly talking about when they speak of an average. The mean is the amount you get when you add up a set of numbers then divide by the number of numbers in the set. For instance, if you have

---

1. A good source is the glossary of the math department at the University of Berkley at http://www.stat.berkeley.edu/~stark/SticiGui/Text/gloss.htm.

[3,4,5,5,4,3,] the mean would be 4 because the sum of the numbers is 24 and there are 6 numbers in the set. Then you do the simple math, 24/6 and you have your mean. When some one asks you for the average of a set of numbers this is what most people are asking for; however, as you learn more about the field you should take the time to ask whether they are looking for the mean, the median, or the mode in any academic setting.

The second type of average is the median. The median is the number that you end up with when you take a set of numbers, order them by value, then select the number that occurs at the midway point. For instance take our original set [3,4,5,5,4,3]. If you order them in ascending order they become [3,3,4,4,5,5]. To find the median number you select the number that is in the middle, which in this case there would be a tie between the 4s. If there is not a number in the exact middle (i.e., you have an even number of numbers in the set) then the median number is the lesser of the two middle numbers (thus the smallest number that at least half the numbers in the list are no greater than including itself).[2] In the example of [3,4,5,6,7,8] the median number would be 5. So, 5 and 6 are the two middle numbers, but 5 is the lesser of the two thus it is the smallest number that no more than half of the numbers in the series are greater than. Using the median lets you find another type of average that can help you in your calculations, especially by helping to identify outliers in your data set.

The third type of average that is important to doing basic descriptive statistics is the mode. The mode is the most commonly appearing number in a series of numbers. For a simple example in the series [3,4,5,5,6,7] the number 5 appears more often than any other number in the series; therefore, the number 5 is the mode of the series. In our original example [3,4,5,5,4,3] all three numbers 3, 4, and 5 are equal in their frequency, thus they are all modes of this number. The mode is useful for quality control. Outliers can drastically affect the validity and accuracy of a study. For instance, in the sequence [2,3,3,3,4,5,127] the average of the group is 21; however, 21 is not an accurate representation of the group because the 127 is much larger than the rest of the numbers. This is where the median and the mode are useful. The mode for this data set is 3 and the median is also 3. Since the mode and the median are both one third of the mean, it indicates that as a researcher you should look to see if there is an outlier that is skewing your data. Skewed data are data that are not symmetrical in relation to the average.

Just because you have skewed data does not mean that there is a problem in your math or in your sample. If I have a class of 40 students, the population is 40. When I administer a test, the data set is 10 students with a score in the 90s, 15 students with 80s, 5 students with 70s, 3 students with

---

2. UC Berkley (2015). "Glossary of Statistical Terms. University of California" Berkley, Berkley at http://www.stat.berkeley.edu/~stark/SticiGui/Text/gloss.htm.

100s, and 7 students with 0s. This means that the mean of the equation is 52.5%, that the "average" grade in the class is failing (0). However, the mode of the test is 80, and the median is also 80; therefore, most students passed the class. All three of these numbers are correct; however, because we are examining the whole population of the class, even the outliers represent the reality of this situation in this naturally skewed data set.

Percentiles are also a statistical term that you will come across from time to time when you are writing. Simply put, a percentile is the smallest percentage number ($p\%$) where the number of numbers below it does not exceed the percentage. For example, if we have a data set of [1,2,3,4,5,6,7,8,9,10] the number 1 would be in the 10th percentile. The reason for this is, 90% of the numbers appear above the number we are looking at, so the percentage of numbers below the target number (including itself) is 10% (100% – 90% = 10%). The number 8 is in the 80th percentile, only 20% appear above it; therefore, 8 and itself are below 80%. Percentiles are useful to measure where you stand in relation to other persons within a designated population (e.g., Jimmy has an IQ of 113 so he is in the 95th percentile).

Quartiles are like percentiles, but they limit the measurement to a broader assessment of a group. Quartiles can be useful when your data are not specific enough to allow you to place a person/group/object in a specific percentile or when you are trying to protect a person. Those who have a score in the 1st percentile may take it better if they are told they are in the 1st quartile. Quartiles are not as accurate as percentiles, but this is not always a bad thing. Quartiles can allow you to broadly talk about a large cross section of the study population without committing to specific percentiles that can be challenged. When writing, quartiles can also allow you to address a large group without specifying the exact percentile of the group under study. If the median of the group is modal then the 2nd and 3rd quartiles may be similar, thus the percentile may be irrelevant but the quartiles may still hold some relevance.

This vocabulary lesson ends with a discussion of correlations. A correlation is the measure of association between two variables. Correlations are an assessment of whether two variables are related, but always be careful to ensure that you are not making spurious correlations (see the correlation section of this chapter). Generally, if one variable goes up another variable with a positive correlation will rise with it, while a variable with a negative correlation will decline as the original variable increases. If this relationship is causal, then the variable that has control over the situation is the independent variable and the variable that changes due to the movement of the independent variable is the dependant variable. Correlation between variables is one element of descriptive statistics that translates very well into predicative statistics.

These are some of the most common words that you will find in the statistical lexicon that may not appear in your day-to-day usage of the English language. If you are having trouble with the language of statistics, do not be afraid to find a statistical glossary to help you through it. You would not be embarrassed to get an English → French dictionary if you were learning French, would you? Of course not. Learning statistics, or any type of math, is simply learning a new language in which you can work. The more time you spend practicing it, the more fluent you will become in it. Some people have an aptitude and will pick up the mathematical language when they first hear it, but the rest of us have to work to master this new language. Once you learn the lexicon of statistics, however, you have another excellent tool that you can use for your research projects.

THE BELL-SHAPED CURVE

Many people see the bell-shaped curve as the epitome of all that makes statistics scary in the world. Countless hours are spent by high school math teachers "introducing" students to the bell-shaped curve as an analytical tool of a "new" kind of math called statistics. This is part of the problem. First, many high school teachers are not statisticians, which means that they may be teaching students the wrong way to use the bell-shaped curve. (Note this chapter is on writing in statistics, not on using statistics directly, so if you want more on how to do the basic functions of statistics look at the recommended reading at the end of the chapter.) Next, teachers drill into students' heads the specifics of the bell-shaped curve to the point that when many of these students get to college and have a mathematician teach them, they are so bored with the topic that they do not even listen. But the biggest problem with the way that we teach students about the bell-shaped curve in this country is that this curve is not a tool in itself, but a result. Learning the functions that go into the bell-shaped curve is the key to using it effectively.

A bell-shaped curve is a graph, and as with any other type of graph it represents where numbers fall during the course of a study. A bell-shaped curve is a very specific type of line graph where the averages and the quartiles line up with very specific requirements, but it is still nothing more than a graph. Since graphs are a result or a study and a writing tool, the bell-shaped curve should not be treated like a mathematical function or a formula; those things were already done to create the curve. Once you start to look at a bell curve as an end product rather than a tool to get to an end product, it is no more scary than a picture of a hammer or a picture of a screwdriver.

When writing, a bell curve can be a very useful tool indeed. It can allow you to convey that the group you are studying has a set of averages that fit into the curve. Each percentile on a perfect bell-shaped curve has a value that can be determined by doing simple equations in relation to the curve. Once again the functions related to the bell-shaped curve are not part of the curve; the curve itself is the data set that someone is doing analysis on. When you are writing, you can use the common knowledge of a bell-shaped curve as a tool to convey where someone or something falls within a given set of percentiles. If you use the bell-shaped curve for this purpose, it will get you through most papers where such a curve is the center of attention.

If you are an education major, by this point you may already be complaining. If you are not, you need to be introduced to one of the reasons the bell-shaped curve is taught so poorly in many disciplines. The bell-shaped curve enthusiasts do not care about being PC, not at all. In the 1980s it was discovered that the bell-shaped curve in education presented "racist" findings about the educational level of inner-city black students. Rather than accept that there was a problem in the educational system the way that it stood at the time, the primary and secondary educators of the United States, along with a fair number of anthropologists, decided that it was not their fault, but there was a problem in society and the bell-shaped curve led to racist results. This argument is idiotic. The bell-shaped curve can no more lead to racist results than a hammer, a screwdriver, or a cup of tea. However, the debate began that it was unfair to use a standardized system of assessment on diverse populations because the assessment did not represent the cultural values of all the groups being represented. In some cases this may have been true; however, the assessments they were complaining about were reading, writing, and arithmetic. While individuals may have specific aptitudes, math is not racist, nor are the skills of writing or reading. The boondoggle about the bell-shaped curve being racist was simply a distraction to keep the academy from looking at the problem of underqualified teachers in primary and secondary schools in the 1980s and 1990s. The system is slowly righting itself now, but with 20 years of bad educational data because the bell-shaped curve was thought to be racist allowed the United States to go from first in the world in education to sixteenth. If we restore standardized assessment across the country, we can look and find the areas where we need improvement. Hence, the bell-shaped curve was not "racist," it is hated because it pointed out flaws that no one was ready to face at the time.

It is also important to note that the bell-shaped curve is not the only curve that is used for analysis. Curves can be skewed to the right or skewed to the left. Curves that are skewed to the right lean toward what would be higher percentiles on a bell-shaped curve (they are not higher percentiles on a skewed curve because the percentiles are the parts of the curve that are skewed). On a left skewed curve the percentiles are skewed to what would be the lower percentiles on a normal bell-shaped curve. Skewed curves can show success or failure on specific variables within a given system. On a grading curve if the scores are right skewed, you know that your students are doing well on the assessment. If your grades are left skewed, then your students are doing poorly on their assessments. This means that there is a problem in the course. The curve cannot tell you specifically what the problem is, just that there is a problem. Further studies need to be conducted to find out what the problems are.

Bell curves can be an efficient graphical representation of a population; however, they can only be efficient if they are properly supplied with good data. Like any mathematical system, if bad data is entered into the equation then you will get the wrong answer. This has been another problem that we have seen in education, schools cheating on standardized tests to get more money for their school. This of course skews the curve and makes poor schools look like good schools; however, union protections for teachers have kept teachers from getting fired for cheating scandals.[3] We cannot repair the system unless we deal with the problem and cheating is never a way to deal with a problem.

In your own writing, you have to be careful not to allow your opinions to affect your presentation of the statistics, the numbers represent what is really going on in society. While it may be tempting to mess with the numbers so that they fit your personal belief system, it is not ethical and you will likely get caught. Academics used to "fudge" the numbers so that they would meet the requirements of their specific paradigm, but now there are dozens of people who read journal articles and news articles to find where researchers changed the numbers or made a mistake. Odds are if you are unethical or do not check your numbers, your work quality may end up in the lower percentiles of the bell-shaped curve.

CORRELATIONS

Other than the bell-shaped curve, correlations are one of the main uses of descriptive statistics. A correlation is an assessment of the relationship between two variables. There are four main types of correlations that we look at in this section. The first type of correlation is a positive correlation. In a positive correlation when the independent variable rises or falls a dependant variable with a relationship will rise and fall with it. The increase and decrease in the independent variable does not have to be the same as the increase or decrease in the dependent variable, but the direction of movement should be the same. For instance, if the independent variable moves one unit to increase in value and the dependent variable moves three units to increase in value, and this happens every

3. Rich Motoko & John Hurdle (2014). "Philadelphia Principals Fired in Cheating Scandal," *New York Times* (Jan 22, 2014) at http://www.nytimes.com/2014/01/23/us/philadelphia-principals-fired-over-cheating.html?_r=0. Notice that the principals were fired but not the teachers.

time that the independent variable increases (or decreases) then there could be a positive correlation between the variable even though the dependent variable moves three times as far as the independent variable.

The second type of correlation is a negative correlation. In a negative correlation when the independent variable (A) moves in an increasing direction the dependent variable (B) moves in a decreasing direction. The amount of movement does not matter, only the reliability of the fact that if A moves up then B moves down. Negative correlations can be useful in showing that depleting one resource can cause another reference to grow or that destroying something can cause increasing problems in another area. Negative correlations can also show that when improvements are made to a specific area, then the crime rate in that area tends to fall (i.e., better education can decrease the crime rate over time).

The third type of correlation is a null correlation. A null correlation occurs when the movement of the independent variable has no effect on the movement of the dependent variable. Thus if A moves in an increasing direction, B may increase, decrease, or stay the same. Null correlations may seem like a failure, especially if your hypothesis was that a correlation existed; however, a null correlation can disprove a null hypothesis, thus advancing a hypothesis or a theory. Therefore, it is important to record both when there is a correlation and when there is not a correlation in any experiment.

The final type of correlation that we are going to talk about is the spurious correlation. A spurious correlation is an apparent correlation between two variables, but when tested over a period of time you find that they actually have no relationship at all (or are related to another variable). The extreme danger of this is that an unknown independent variable can make two dependent variables look like they are related over a period of time. This is why hypothesis testing must be done multiple times on similar subjects. The classic example of a spurious correlation is that the ice cream sales on the New Jersey Boardwalk increase the incidence of sexual assault.[4] Obviously we do not have a case of rape inducing ice cream, what we have here is a third hidden variable, the weather. Ice cream sales on the Boardwalk increase in the summer, as does the number of people at the beach. The increased number of people allows for an increased prevalence of sexual assault in the area, thus the weather is the independent variable not the ice cream.

Another type of spurious relationship is when the variables are completely unrelated, but give the appearance of being related. The example for this is my anti-lion rock. I have a rock in my pocket, which is the independent variable and it keeps lions away (lions are the dependent variable). The

---

4. Unknown source.

(bad) logic behind this is that since I have the rock and I see no lions, that the rock must keep lions away. This logic is completely false, but the data would support that as long as I do not go to a place where there are lions, the zoo or Africa. If I do go somewhere that there are lions, the rock will fail and I will get eaten. The worst part of this type of spurious relationships is that some statistics would say that my getting eaten is an outlier and would still claim the validity of the anti-lion rock. When you are looking at variables, take a step back and use common sense to see if a correlation makes sense. If there is no logical way that my anti-lion rock could keep lions away, then maybe it is not an anti-lion rock.

When you are using correlations in your writing take the time to test them multiple times if you can. Each time you test your hypothesis and correlation, you will create more data that can prove or disprove your hypothesis. Even if you find that your hypothesis is incorrect, it is better that you find it out while testing rather than after you publish. You can always show that the hypothesis was wrong and contribute to the academy on the subject; however, once you publish your findings it is difficult to pull them back if you realize that you made a mistake. Correlations are an excellent tool to use in a statistical study, just ensure you are using them correctly.

CHARTS AND GRAPHS

One of the most user-friendly features of descriptive statistics is the ability to convert numerical data into visual data. Visual data is any data that is conveyed to your reader through a graph, chart, histogram, dot plot, or any method other than raw numbers or prose. Visual data can be quite useful in conveying large amounts of data to your reader in a short space. Whereas appendixes of spreadsheets can convey the raw data that you used to discover your findings and to create your project, the readers are more likely going to be interested in your direct findings as they read through your work. This is why large volumes of data should be either put in the appendix or annexed so other researchers can look at them later, but the compiled data that is directly related to your project should be included as visual data.

In this section we look at some of the main methods that people use to convey visual data when writing a descriptive statistics report. We are not going to cover every method that is in use, only the ones that are commonly used by most people. The first common type of visual data is a chart. A chart is a system of rows and columns that allow a reader to find data based on the content matter of that data. For instance:

Year	Average Temperature	Average Rainfall	Average Birthrate
1980	70	51"	-3%
1985	72	57"	1%
1990	71	40"	2.5%
1995	70	45"	6%
2000	69	62"	4%

As you can see, you can find the (made up) rainfall for 1995 by simply finding the 1995 year on the chart and following the chart to that year's rainfall. These types of charts can make data easily accessible to your reader, and they are easy to integrate into your paper.

Sometimes you want to show relationships between different elements of your data during the course of your project. While a chart will show relationships, it requires that your reader find each line that they are expected to read and analyze them against another line of your chart. Graphs are an effective way to visualize comparative data so your reader can easily find it. One of the simplest forms of graph is a dot plot. A dot plot is a graph where each marked point expresses the meeting of two data lines (streams). Another way that you can show the relationship between two dependent variables and an independent variable is with a bar graph. A bar graph uses colored bars to represent the data rather than individual dots on a graph. For instance:

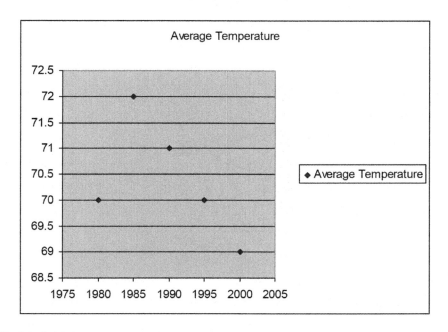

In this chart you can see the average temperature based on the year. It provides your reader with an easily accessible demonstration of the data in a quick access visual form. Lines can be added to a dot plot to make it a line graph. A bar graph also gives you the opportunity to demonstrate multiple streams of data in a single graph. For instance:

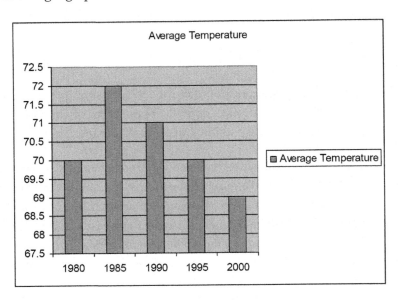

Spider graphs can also be effective, because they can give you a relationship between spikes in your data.

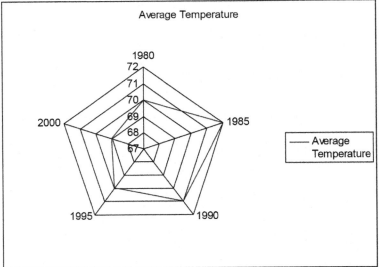

This lets you see that the highest year for data is 1985 and relative to the other years the data had a much higher temperature (+2 degrees from the median). Graphs can also be used in predictive statistics; forms of the bar graph such as the histogram are very useful in determining probability.

Writing in statistics is one of the most basic forms of research writing, where you collect data, you run the data through the proper equations, then you analyze the findings to see if they support or disprove your hypothesis. The key to writing in statistics is to keep your data honest, valid, and interesting; of the three the later is the hardest one to do. Statistics are generally a sterile and safe form of academic writing, where you do not have to get involved with the emotional or subjective details of the study but are focusing on the wrought facts that can be measured, remeasured, and measured yet again with the same results. Using descriptive statistics is an excellent way for you to tell your readers about the world in a way that is difficult to criticize or argue with, but this all relies on you ensuring that your data is good. Good statistic writing is a staple in any field, and the better the descriptive statistics are in a field the better other researchers in the field who use predictive statistics, qualitative methods, or theoretical methods will be able to do their jobs. Descriptive statistics involves a fields foundational way to know "what is out there" and if you are doing a descriptive statistics project you are contributing to the future of your field.

CHECKLIST

- ❑ Have you collected objective data?
- ❑ If you have collected nonnumerical data have you converted it to numerical data?
- ❑ Have you learned how to use your conversion software?
- ❑ Will visual data help you convey your message?
- ❑ Are you using the proper terms and being as specific as possible?

RECOMMENDED READING

Anderson, Sweeny, & Williams (1999). STATISTICS FOR BUSINESS AND ECONOMICS, 17TH ED. New York: International Thompson.

Banks, Marcus (2007). USING VISUAL DATA IN QUALITATIVE RESEARCH. Thousand Oaks, CA: Sage.

Weiss, Neil (2002). INTRODUCTORY STATISTICS, 6TH ED. Boston: Addison-Wesley.

chapter 14
Predictive Statistics

Note this is not a statistics chapter; it is a chapter on how to write on predictive statistics.

INTRODUCTION

The holy grail of academic writing is to create a study that is effective enough that your hypothesis is correct enough that it looks as if your work predicted the future. This is a strategy that many have desired and few have achieved; however, when you are using predictive statistics (also known as inferential statistics) you are expected to be correct within a given margin of error. This means that if you fail, and many do, you will lose credibility in the field and can be ostracized. Fear not, because failure in predictive statistics is caused by three easily solvable reasons: (1) bad design, (2) bad math, and (3) bad writing. As most modern quantitative researchers rely on computers to do the math for their statistics, bad mathematics is becoming less and less of a problem in the field (though bad proofreading of spreadsheets is growing as a problem). Therefore, this chapter looks at the way that you can lead a better designed or statistical study and how you can write properly so that your findings are not overreached by your claims.

Before we even begin we must acknowledge the cardinal challenge of predictive statistics, that it is an imperfect method and there will always be a margin of error. Even if you have a complete population rather than a sample and millions of years of data, a single choice or an evolutionary change could throw your prediction off by the smallest margin. This means that no prediction will ever be full proof. To that end, the first lesson that we teach in this chapter is an important one: YOU WILL ALWAYS HAVE A MARGIN OF ERROR IN A PREDICTIVE RESEARCH PAPER. Sorry about the "text yelling" but this is an important fact that all researchers in the quantitative field must understand and accept. If you ever read a paper written that states it does not have a margin of error, then it was either written by a fool or a wizard and we do not see many wizards running around in the real world (fools we have plenty of though).

As we enter into our study about how to write in the predictive quantitative methods, we want to look at three very important factors in any study, but all the more important in studies where you are trying to predict something: (1) variables, (2) accuracy, and (3) reliability. Finding the correct variables is the first step in designing a good quantitative study. We do not want you scouring the world for the classic "Rape–Ice Cream" example.[1] Always take the time to identify your dependent and independent variables, and then use common sense to see if the relation between them is real or spurious. Next, attempt to take all measures to ensure the accuracy of your study. First, this involves accurately identifying your population. Do not claim to be analyzing a larger population than your study is actually looking at, always be clear and accurate on who or what you are studying. Simple problems like taking a convenient sample rather than a representative sample are all it takes to ensure that your study will predict the wrong thing. While collecting a representative sample may be time consuming, it is worth the effort when your study is accepted by the academy rather than being lampooned. Finally, strive for reliability. If you have worked hard on the first two factors, then the third factor should fall into place. Identifying the correct variables and their relation to one another and ensuring that your data collection strategy uses a representative sample from a properly identified population will allow others to replicate your research and if they follow the guidelines that you have set out, then they should procure similar results. If you ensure the variables, the accuracy, and the reliability of your study, then you should produce a reasonably valid study within an acceptable margin of error.

This chapter walks you through some of the ways that you can use predictive statistics to write an academic paper. A single dataset of statistics can have a multitude of uses, but too often statisticians write the paper on the subject the data was collected for, then forget about the data and start col-

---

1. The Rape–Ice Cream example is a common teaching tool in the social sciences. Urban legend has it that a graduate student in sociology did a study on the increase of rapes on the New Jersey Boardwalk in relation to the increase in the amount of ice cream that was being sold in the same period of time. In a social science class the professor then goes on to explain that even if the facts say that there is a relationship, you need to use common sense to see that there is a spurious relationship and both of these variables are dependent variables based on the independent variable of weather (i.e., there are more people on the boardwalk during hot months; therefore, more people are buying ice cream and there are more potential victims for any crime).

lecting data for a new product. There are vast sets of statistical data sitting in university labs, offices, and libraries that have been harvested for one goal but contain so much information on other areas. A good statistician with a good data set should be able to put out three or four papers easily from any given dataset. In this chapter we look at some of those uses for statistical data. In the first section we look at probability and how it is used. This is one of the most common uses of statistics and one that acts as a gatekeeper to the field; too many people believe that all predictive statistics are probability and the concept of probability confuses them so they do not use this tool set. This is similar to not using your ratchet set because you are missing one of your sockets. In the second section we look at the ability of predictive statistics to be used as an estimation tool. There are vast fields in business, science, and politics where you do not need to predict something accurately to be successful, you just have to get close most of the time (meteorology). Estimation based on quantitative data can be an effective niche for many of you budding statisticians. In the third section we look at one of the more hands-on uses of statistics, hypothesis testing. While this may seem like a dull area, many of the greatest discoveries in the world have involved mathematical hypothesis testing. In the fourth section we look at another common use of inferential statistics, inferences between similar populations. If the Democrats in Connecticut (which have a similar makeup to the Democrats in Oregon) vote in a specific way, then we may be able to make an inference on how they will vote in Oregon, but only if the data are collected properly. The fifth section begins looking at the technical workings of predictive statistics and the idea of variance. While variance may sound complicated, it is simply how far numbers tend to spread out in a data set or study. In the sixth section we discuss regression. Regression is a method of estimating the relationship between variables, and in the seventh seven we look at one of the more practical uses of predictive statistics, forecasting. The use of statistics for forecasting often involves a hybridization of quantitative and qualitative statistics. The chapter concludes with a look at quality control. Quality control is a possible use of statistics where one looks at how often a problem arises and what efforts need to be conducted to prevent damage in regard to those problems. This should be able to alleviate many of your concerns about writing a predictive statistics paper.

PROBABILITY

Probability is the most basic tool in a predictive statistician's tool bag, but it is also one of the most often misunderstood tools. Probabilities are not an exercise in the statistician predicting the future, rather when you write about probability, you are giving your reader the opportunity to predict the future. This means as long as your mathematics and research design are correct, the burden of proper prediction lies on the person who wishes to use your probabilities. Therefore, the first lesson of probability is that you should place the burden of doing the prediction on your reader—that is, to simply give the proper ratios and probabilities so that your reader can make the correct predictions.

Modern mathematicians often see statistics and probability as two separate fields. Probability is a tool that is used in predictive (and sometimes descriptive) statistics, but involves different formulas so is often categorized separately by those who are hardcore mathematics professionals. In most research fields and undergraduate programs, statistics and probabilities are both taught in the same course (which can add to the confusion). This is why they are included as a tool in the inferential statistics chapter of this book rather than a statistical method of their own accord. Probability is the likelihood that an event will occur within a given parameter as classified as a percentile number between 0 and 1. In laypersons' terms, probability is the chance that an event will happen, written as a percentage.

The question that many writers ask about probability is how they can use probabilities in their papers. A probability tells the reader the likelihood that something will happen. This is not predicting that the event will happen in a given time frame (unless the probability is 100% which is rare at best), it is simply indicating the number of possibilities that the event will happen out of the total number of possibilities that could happen. Probabilities work best when you are explaining a finite situation, such as a dice roll. When a six-sided die is rolled there are seven possibilities, six on a flat surface where a cocked die is not a possibility. The possible outcomes on a flat surface are the numbers 1 through 6. Assuming the dice is properly made, the probability of each number coming up is 1 in 6 or 17%. This does not tell you what the next roll will be, just what the odds are of a specific number coming up.

Probability is a useful tool for writers who wish to show the likelihood of something happening within a given framework. To continue the dice example, some people could say that the likelihood that a 6 will come up if the die is rolled four times is 68%. This does not tell your reader that the die will come up with a 6, rather it tells them that the more times you roll the more the likelihood of a 6 coming up increases. Where many people get in trouble with probability is when they assume that the above example is proper mathematics. However, while the likelihood that a number will come up over the course of time does increase, probability does not guarantee that the number will come up in any given time frame. The fallacy appears when the number of options matches the number of times the event occurs. Under the above example, the odds of a 6 coming up in six rolls would be 100%, which is not true. Thus when writing about probability do not let simple probability lead you down a simple path to simply the wrong answer.

Another danger that non-mathematician authors face when writing about probability is not taking into account all the variables. Take, for instance, we do not have a flat surface and a cocked die is a possibility, then this changes the number of possibilities and thus the probability. Further, if the dice is not well made, we can see other problems arising as one number may be more likely than another. When using probability, make sure that you have accounted for all of the variables. Do not let yourself fall into the simple probability trap that challenges many writers in the quantitative methods.

Probability is a tricky proposition in a paper, and authors of most academic papers want someone to come up with answers about a question, not a likelihood. Although probability can be a useful tool in other statistical methods, we do not recommend that you base an entire paper around probability itself. Forecasting and population inferences are much more effective ways to mathematically predict the results of a chain of variables. Properly doing these methods is more complex than simple probability, but can give you much more concrete answers and allow you to protect your reputation if you go into the business of predicting the future.

ESTIMATION

A much safer use of predictive statistics is estimation. Wrought prediction suggests that you are going predict the exact outcome of a specific event, whereas estimation allows you to "get in the ball park" and still be right. Estimates are useful for writers in the social sciences, the hard sciences, the humanities, and business fields because if you do estimates about repeat events and your estimates are reasonable, then the aggregate of the events will balance out the variance in the estimates. Whereas readers are likely to be interested in probability in a one-time event, most scholars, businesspersons, among other fields prefer accurate estimations over longitudinal phenomena.

An estimation is a rough calculation of a number, value, quantity, or outcome of an event. It is an educated guess on what is going to happen based on what has happened before and the probability of something happening again. As with probability, the greater the number of variables involved the more difficult it is to make a good estimation; however, estimations are generally more forgiving as they should be used for repeated like events. If you have a good estimation and it is off by 1 the first time, and 2 the second time, then –2 the third time, and –1 the fourth time, over the aggregate you have a good estimate. Now how close you need to be in your estimate depends on what you are estimating. The number of grains of wheat in a bushel gives you much more latitude for variance than the estimated maximum height of a rollercoaster rider for the purposes of safety.

As a writer, you should only use estimations when they are absolutely called for, and then only if you have enough information. If you are writing about the dietary habits of a small Amazon village and you see that each family eats one melon a night and there are five family units in the village, then you can estimate that there are five melons consumed during that meal. However, if you see two families in New York City eating a melon and know that there are 5 million families living there, then the estimate that 5 million melons are eaten each night would be a bad estimate. Your sample needs to be representative and the more repetition that you see in your data collection the better able you are to make an estimate.

Estimation gives you more control over the predictive process, because you are using more data to make your estimate; however, basic estimation is still very inexact. As with any inexact method, you must make an effort to ensure that the margin of error is acceptable and that the estimation is valid in the aggregate over the long run. Always keep an open mind about estimation in your tool box as a methodology, but also remember that it has its purpose and prediction of a single event will be only reliable as the limits of the variance among the supportive data.

HYPOTHESIS TESTING

Predictive statistics do not do well as a method for testing hypotheses. Predictive statistics look at an event that is going to happen in the future and infer what the results of that event are, thus the answer tends to be a hypothesis rather than something that can be used to test a hypothesis. This does not prevent predictive statistics from being useful as a method to create a hypothesis and/or a theory about what is going to happen in the future related to a specific event or phenomenon. Predictive statistics give you the tools to create a new theory and support the theory through the use of equations and statistics, even if the hypothesis is untestable due to temporal circumstances.

When using predictive statistics to theorize about something that is going to happen in the future, be sure to support your theory with as much data from the present and the past as possible. If, for instance, you are attempting to show that the world water supply will only support 10 billion people at the maximum, then you would show the water usage related to one person, the aggregate water usage by a small group of people, and the aggregate water usage by a large group of people, then determine how much fresh water there is and determine how many people it would support. The method requires you to use multiple variables in your equations (e.g., the amount of water one person needs is not limited to what that person can drink and use personally, but also the water used for food and products that they use).

The more detailed your model, the more data that you will need to support it. Some newspapers will do a report on how many people the world's water supply can support and simply divide the world's known supply by the amount of water two or three of their workers use in a day. This is bad modeling because it only looks at one variable that by itself has a huge potential for variance in the amount of water used from person to person. As a writer, you need to look beyond simply hypotheses based on "vogue" ideas and look to find as much relevant data as possible to support your claim. Always take the time to brainstorm for as many variables as possible. The more variables you look at (whether you keep them or discard them) the better you are able to create a hypothesis and a theory supported by historical and current fact.

As a final note on hypothesis testing, a good way to establish your model as effective is to build a model that can be tested during the course of its longitudinal operation. If your model looks at the water usage by humanity over the next 50 years, then create a hypothesis for 10 years, 20 years, 30 years, and 40 years. If the same factors are at play over that time frame, then you should be able to forecast those numbers from your dataset. If your hypothesis is correct, then each milestone that you are correct on will add credibility to your model. If your model is longitudinal over a long period of time, be careful to note that major changes in the area you are researching could affect the numbers (such as the discovery of a new source of water under the earth's crust in the above example or a leap forward in desalination).

INFERENCE BETWEEN TWO POPULATIONS

Another area where predictive statistics shows its merits is when two similar populations have the same event going on at different times. For instance, we have one group of 100 pigs (same breed, sexual heterogeneity, group weight, and health) that is going to be used for food at one time period, and another 100 pigs (same as first group) that is going to be used at a different time. It can be inferred that if the first group of pigs feeds 3,000 people, then the second group of pigs would feed a like amount. If the second group of pigs lost 4 pigs that were of the average weight and type of the group, then we can infer that the second group of pigs will feed 120 less people. This inference is an estimation, because the people eating may take more or less meat; however, over the aggregate if 100 groups of 100 pigs feeds an average of 3,000 people, then we can assume that a similar group of 100 pigs will be sufficient to feed a group of 2,700 people at another event.

Inferring between populations is a tricky use of predictive statistics, but is a tool that when used effectively can be very efficient. For a writer to infer data between two similar groups, the groups must be similar (at the aggregate) to one another on most of the major variables. One cannot assume if

100 pigs feeds the crowd of 3,000 bacon lovers that the same number of pigs will be needed for a convention of vegans. (One group eats meat and the other group does not.) The burden falls on the researcher to justify not only his or her hypothesis, but also the similarity of the group.

Oftentimes we see mainstream writers attempt to use statistical inference between two populations that are not similar. For instance Connecticut Republicans and Texas Republicans; Connecticut Republicans tend to be more liberal on the social issues than Texas Republicans. Therefore, if a newspaper makes the assumption (not the inference) that Texas Republicans will vote the same way as Connecticut Republicans on a socially liberal but economically conservative candidate, then their assumption is nothing more that a guess based on bad facts. The onerous to show that the two populations are similar falls on the researcher so that they do not mislead their readers.

Any time you are considering writing a paper or journal article using predictive statistics between two similar populations, be careful. The two populations are generally dissimilar in some way, whether you see it or not requires you to have a strong knowledge of both populations. If you are working to use inferential statistics between two groups, then take the time to research the groups in great detail, for it is the details that make them different. Even groups such as Pennsylvania Mennonites and Southern California Mennonites have their differences, just be sure you know what they are and whether they will affect your research.

VARIANCE

To begin to understand variance, one must first understand variables. Rather than being a specific number, a variable is a place holder in an equation whose value can be changed depending on the needs of the equation. If you are looking at the number of people that it takes to use up 100 gallons of gasoline in one day, then the variable (n) would be the number of people. It may take more people to use up 100 gallons in Fiji than it does in the United States because of the shorter distances that people have to drive in Fiji. In research parlance, a variable is any element of the study that can be changed and whose change may or may not affect the other variables in the study.

The two main types of variables that are used in research projects are independent and dependent variables. An independent variable is the catalyst in an experiment. The independent variable is not expected to react to a change in the dependent variable. The dependent variable is the variable that the researcher is going to watch. The general theory behind the system is that when the independent variable is changed by the researcher, the dependent variable will change (or will not change depending on the hypothesis). The interrelationship between the independent variables and the dependent variables forms the core of many basic statistical studies.

Two other types of variables that you may come across in your research writing are continuous random variables and discrete random variables. A continuous random variable is a variable where the value may fall anywhere within an infinite spectrum. A discrete random variable is a variable that has a finite number of values, which can be given specific probabilities of occurring. Both types of variables are common in major statistical studies and should be used in the situations that they are designed for. For instance, a continuous random variable could be the weight of a grain of sand between 0 and 1 milligram. While the parameters of the spectrum are finite, the potential number of values is infinite depending on the precision of the measuring tool. Conversely, the number of possibilities for a dice roll is seven with each having a probability of 1 in 6 on a balanced die. This is an example of a discrete random variable.

Once you understand what a variable is (there are more types of variables but these are the common ones that you will likely see in your statistical papers), it can be easy to see the meaning of variance. The variance is simply how far numbers tend to spread out in a dataset or study. In our first example of a continuous random variable, the variance was 1, since there was a maximum possible difference in the highest value to the lowest value of 1. In the second example the variance was 6 since there were possible outcomes. With small datasets you can count the difference between the low number and the high number (if all numbers are the same then the variance is 0). In larger datasets you will need to follow a simple formula that can be found in any statistics book ($s^2 = \text{sum}[(x_i - \text{avg})^2]/n - 1$) where s^2 is the variance, x_i represents every term in the set individually, avg is the mean of the set, and n is the sample size. (Sum and avg were used because the mathematical symbols for sum and avg affect the formatting of the page.)

The two tests of variance that you should be aware of are the chi-squared test and the F-test. Both of these tests are useful in their own way and will be used by specific fields for variance testing. If you are unsure which test your field commonly uses or you are not sure when your field commonly uses either of these tests, then consult with an expert in your field. Generally, a chi-squared test is useful when the variance of a population is equal to a specific value.[2] The F-test can be used if the variance within two populations are equal.[3] Writers use chi-squared tests to show relationships within the variance of two variables and the F-test when dealing with normally distributed populations. How these two methods work is beyond the scope of this chapter, but if you are doing a

2. NIST.GOV (2015). ENGINEERING STATISTICS HANDBOOK at http://www.itl.nist.gov/div898/handbook/eda/section3/eda358.htm
3. *Id.* at http://www.itl.nist.gov/div898/handbook/eda/section3/eda359.htm.

quantitative study then you must learn which test is the proper test for you and the proper way to perform the test.

As a writer who is not a mathematician, variance can seem like a difficult term to deal with and is often left out of papers (or worse, used improperly in papers). Variance is simply the maximum difference in values that a data set has or can have. If you use variance in your writing in this way, then you can be safe in knowing that you are doing the right thing. The more complicated analysis such as the chi-squared and the F-test should be reserved for those who (1) need them, and (2) are willing to learn the proper way to do them. Most statistics research (at least at the basic level) will not need the researcher to go into that much detail; however, if you are required to have detail at that level, take the time to learn the proper methods for doing each test (or get the software for the tests). If you take the fear out of the terminology by understanding it, you will find why quantitative papers are some of the easiest papers to write.

REGRESSION

Regression, the second boogeyman of predictive statistics, is a method of estimating the relationship between two variables. Once you understand this as the key concept of regression, then the more complex terms seem much simpler. One of these terms that seem to give statistics students fits is regression models. Regression models are charts that allow a researcher to make a prediction based on historic data that has been measured for regression.[4] These models are generally based on models with linear regression. Linear regression is a regression where there is a relationship between two variables that follows a straight line. (Nonlinear regression is a relationship that does not follow a straight line, but follows some other shape.) In a linear regression, the relationship will be either positive or negative. In a positive relationship if the independent variable rises, so does the dependent variable; if the independent variable falls, then so does the dependent variable. In a negative relationship if the independent variable rises, the dependent variable falls and vice versa.

When writing a predictive statistical paper, using linear regression can be a good way to support your argument that your model is valid. Most people can follow linear models easily. Nonlinear models can be more difficult to write about as the explanation of why there is a change in the shape of the model can be difficult for some people to grasp. Regression is one area where good writing calls for good graphs. Good graphs are a visual representation of your model. If a person can see

---

4. Stockburger, David (n/a). Introductory Statistics: Concepts Models and Applications "Regression Models." At http://www.psychstat.missouristate.edu/introbook/sbk16.htm.

a regression model, whether linear or nonlinear, then they can better understand the relationship between the variables. This can make your statistical paper much easier for the layperson to process.

FORECASTING

One of the main goals of predictive statistics is to be able to accurately forecast future occurrences based on past data. Forecasting incorporates probability, estimation, variance, and regression into one useful tool. As with all statistics, the better your data the better you will be able to forecast. This process begins by collecting all the proper data you need for your dataset to the point of saturation. The more data you collect the better chance that the aggregate of the collected data will eliminate the problems caused by outliers. An outlier is a test result that falls outside the normal pattern of all test results. Generally these are circled on the graph to indicate that they were taken out of the equation.

Once you have collected the data, you should then go through the process of finding the probability (if you have a discrete continuous variable), the variance, and then map the regression. If there is a correlation between the two variables, then your regression model should give you the formula that you need to determine the value of the dependent variable if you enter the independent variable into your spreadsheet. While learning the equation is important for a greater understanding of the statistical process, most writing can be done with the results of the equation from your statistical software. If you have a good regression model, then you can estimate what the result will be with any given independent variable that falls within the model.

If you are doing good academic research, you will always couch your forecast as an estimate. The more narrowly you focus your estimate, the more useful it will be to your reader but the higher the chance that your estimate will be off. Conversely, if you estimate the outcome within the totality of the variance, you will correct all of the time (unless you have an outlier), but the data will have limited usefulness to the reader. As a researcher, you need to determine how reliable you want your estimate to be. Generally if you are correct 95% of the time you have a good model. However, the more important the work (chances of a heart being accepted by a recipient) the greater the need for highly focused accuracy.

QUALITY CONTROL

Our journey through predictive statistics ends where it began, with its direct link to descriptive statistics. Quality control is one of the most common uses of statistics because companies want to know if they are going to have problems with their product or services. If you can collect the descriptive statistics for a product that has been out for any period of time, and then use the descriptive statistics to find the variance of product quality and build a regression model, you should be able to predict fairly accurately the likelihood of a problem arising within known parameters.

One way that companies like to control the quality of their products is by knowing how many flawed units (or flawed service jobs) are going to be produced. If a company can estimate the number of flawed products, then they can take measure to protect their profits from these problems. For instance, if a company knows that 1 of every 100 products will have a flaw, then they are able to build the cost of that flawed product into the cost of the good products. Then, when there is a problem, they can give the consumer a new product to replace the flawed product at no cost. Likewise, when there is a problem with a service job, the company can fix the problem if the cost of the flawed jobs is built into the cost of the properly done jobs. Knowing the number of flawed products allows a company to protect its profit line and maintain good customer service.

Knowing the number of flawed units also gives the company the ability to sort out the flawed units to prevent them from ever getting to a consumer. If a tire company knows that 1 of every 1,000 tires has a bubble in it that can allow the tire to blow out, then they can have their workers (or a machine) look for that flawed product. Knowing that 1 of every 1,000 should be flawed, if a company makes 6,000 tires in a day, they need to have their workers find 6 flawed tires to have a good chance that no dangerous products will make it to the consumer. When combined with the first method of quality control, companies can protect themselves from lawsuits quite readily.

The third use of predictive statistics in quality control is damage prevention. Occasionally a product is going to make it into the market that is flawed. Many of these flaws will never be realized by the consumer, so there will be no loss to the company. Other flaws will be realized quickly by the consumer and the company will be able to replace the flawed unit with a properly functioning unit. If the costs of the flawed units are built in, then there is also no cost to the company in this instance. However, in a small percentage of cases, a dangerous flaw will make it past both the company's inspectors and the customer's inspection of their product and someone will get hurt. Predictive statistics can help a company prepare for the lawsuits that may arise from these types of problems.

Predictive statistics is a useful method for creating basic studies on general populations and in-depth studies in areas where there are large volumes of numbers. The highly profitable areas of predictive statistics are in quality control and forecasting. These are the tools and the jobs in statistics that are highest in demand. Any time you do statistics, remember to follow the equations, proofread your data entry, and ensure that your data collection is reliable and within industry standards.

CHECKLIST

- ❏ Have you defined your population properly?
- ❏ Is your sample representative?
- ❏ Is your sample large enough?
- ❏ Is your population too large?
- ❏ What statistical method are you going to use?
  - Probability
  - Estimation
  - Hypothesis testing
  - Forecasting
  - Quality control
- ❏ Have you proofread your data entry?

RECOMMENDED READING

Anderson, Sweeny, & Williams (1999). STATISTICS FOR BUSINESS AND ECONOMICS, 17TH ED. New York: International Thompson.

Banks, Marcus (2007). USING VISUAL DATA IN QUALITATIVE RESEARCH. Thousand Oaks, CA: Sage.

NIST.GOV (2015). ENGINEERING STATISTICS HANDBOOK at http://www.itl.nist.gov/div898/handbook/eda/section3/eda358.htm

Stockburger, David (n/a). INTRODUCTORY STATISTICS: CONCEPTS MODELS AND APPLICATIONS "Regression Models." At http://www.psychstat.missouristate.edu/introbook/sbk16.htm

Weiss, Neil (2002). INTRODUCTORY STATISTICS, 6TH ED. Boston: Addison-Wesley.

chapter 15
Sampling

INTRODUCTION

If you are preparing to do a quantitative study, then one of the first questions that you must ask yourself is whether you can procure a workable sample for your project. A sample is any group within a population that is less than the entire group, of which you want to use the portion of the group to support or disprove your hypothesis. If this was all that was required for a quantitative project to be workable, then quantitative methods would be the method of choice for nearly every project; however, to have a truly successful quantitative project, you need to have a representative sample. A representative sample is a portion of the population that accurately represents the larger population. No matter how well you do the math in a quantitative study, if you do not have a representative sample then your data cannot be ascribed to the population at large.

So what makes a good sample for a quantitative study? A good sample contains subjects or objects that, when viewed as an aggregate, represent the changes related to your variable in society. If you have a society where 50% of the people are White, 10% Hispanic, 10% Black, 10% Asian, 10% mixed descent, and 10% indigenous, then a sample of 100 people should be approximately 50 White, 10 Hispanic, 10 Black, 10 Asian, 10 mixed descent, and 10 indigenous individuals. You could be one or two off in any category, but for a sample to be representative it needs to represent society accurately. Assuming that your study is related to genetics of racial descent, this sample would not be representative if you were looking at highest grade achieved by males and females with no regard to race. The representation should be based on your variables.

If you are embarking on a statistics study, and you have a good sample, then you should make it known in the paper how you achieved your sample. In academia too few people check the statistics of other people's work. If your work is being checked by someone, either it is a popular study or you have a person who is trying to undermine you by attacking your work. A common question is, "Who checks these things?" The answer is generally no one, but if you do not have a good sample and someone does check your work, then your career could be over before it really gets started. Therefore, always take the time to do good research and check your statistics. If you follow a given methodology honestly, then you do not have to worry about others looking over your shoulder because all they will find is correctly done work.

In this chapter we look at the process for collecting a good representative sample for a statistics project. We start with an overview of how you get a sample, whether it be representative or not. Statistics generally come from databases, but someone has to create that database before it can be used. If you are researching something new, then you will likely be the person creating the database. Next, we look at the usefulness of the internet. There are dozens of excellent academic and government databases online where you can harvest your datasets. Following that, we go to some more traditional methods, like standing in the mall or positing information for people to volunteer. These methods require more work but can provide you access to more obscure data. Finally, we look at the procedures for accessing government records. While many of the government records that you will be looking for may be available online, some of them may require a freedom of information request. The more effort you put into collecting a good sample, the better your final project will be.

GETTING A SAMPLE

The first thing that you have to look for when you get a sample is whether the data that you acquire is valid. Validity is determined by the relationship between the methodologies used by the researcher and the scientific or research method used in the collection and analysis of data. For instance, if you are attempting to discern the type of clothing being shopped for by mall-goers at the local mall for a statistical presentation on a new marketing campaign, going to a mall to survey people about their interest could be an effective way to procure data. On the other hand, if you are looking to discern the national opinion of whether Americans support or oppose abortion, going to a local mall will not give you a valid representative sample of the entire United States. This is the real tricky part of a qualitative study, making sure that your data that you collect is representative enough to make your study valid.

The better your sample is, the better the validity of your study will be. The three areas that we look at in this section to improve validity are:

1. What is the population you are talking about?
2. Does your sample represent that population, or should you change your population?
3. What is your margin of error?

If you take the time to answer these three questions each time that you are doing a quantitative study, then you are well on your way to ensuring some measure of validity. A good rule of thumb in a quantitative study is you should not try to do a study that is too large for your resources, because that is a surefire way to guarantee low validity. Rather approach the question in regard to a population you can accurately sample.

The first issue is, "What is your population?" A population is a group of subjects, whether human, animal, or inanimate, that you are trying to discern information about through a representative sample. A population could be the people who live in the town of Dysart, Pennsylvania; the turtles that return to the beaches of Ft. Lauderdale to bread each year; or even the cereal boxes produced by Company X on any given day. All that is required for something to be a population is a set of boundaries, both physical and temporal, for you to identify within the bounds of your study. While you may enter into your study looking at a population you want to sample, you may find that it is easier to allow your project to define the population and the sample size.

An effective method for conducting a well-designed quantitative study is to break an unwieldy population into smaller segments. The sports team preferences of the greater Lake Michigan area are much easier to collect data on than the sports team preferences of the entire United States. The data are still valid and if done correctly, reliable. It may take a bit of control, but sometimes a researcher with a budget must forego the massive project and focus on performing little pieces of the grand project that they want to do. If you look at the greater Lake Michigan area one year, then the Midwest the next, then the Northeast the next year, you can build toward your massive project and get multiple publications along the way. The best research is often a compilation of syntheses of smaller research projects, so do not be devastated if you learn that your project is a little too big for you right now. Take your time and build up your research ability to allow you to do the larger projects. Grant agencies look at your record of success when determining who to give money to, so if you show them that you are addressing reasonable sized projects and you deliver what you say you will, then you may be the one that gets the grant.

Knowing your margin of error is vital for any statistical study, and it is often based on your sample dynamic. You do this by taking the percentage of the population that you are sampling, multiplying it by itself subtracted from one, then dividing that by the number of subjects in the sample that have the trait you are looking for in your research. Now we have to get the calculators out, because you want to find the square root of the number you just came up with, then multiply that times your Z number for the percentage of confidence that you want to have. Now, you will find your Z-value on a chart (one can be downloaded from the internet or there are often Z charts in most statistics books). Here is a sample Z chart:

Percentage of Confidence	Z-value
80	1.28
90	1.65
95	1.96
98	2.33
99	2.58

Do the simple math and you have your margin of error in a +/− number. If you do not put a margin of error in your study, then you will automatically look as if you forgot a major step in any quantitative study. (Margins of error can also be used in qualitative studies but are often omitted because the study is not transferable.)

Getting a good sample is the first major issue that you will face in creating a quantitative study that will weather the storm of public scrutiny. If you follow the steps here of looking at what your sample is, then looking at whether you can reduce the population dynamics by reducing the population size to see if you have an acceptable margin of error, you will increase the validity of your study in the eyes of your peers. A reliable study is important when you are embarking to create a system of statistics to support or disprove your hypothesis.

THE INTERNET

Fifteen years ago when I was an undergraduate student, the internet was just beginning to be a tool that could be used by everyone to find statistical datasets where they could harvest data. Some mathematicians were clinging to their random number tables, fearing Isaac Asimov's ghosts in the machine would take away their livelihood. My first statistics teacher, who was a statistician for a business, told us that his job was going away, and he had accepted that but we still needed to learn statistics. He was right on both counts. There are fewer and fewer companies that use statisticians to do the statistics work for their companies, most of them have been replaced by machines and data entry personnel. And he was also correct that we needed to understand statistics, because as fewer people were involved in creating the massive amount of statistics that society operates on, there would be more and more corruption.

The internet is a playground for researchers. If you know where you are looking you can research most topics in the world without ever going out into the field. True, it takes away some of the fun of being a researcher, but if you can stay out of the sewers of Paris or out of a plague zone, you may have more of a life to do research. When you are researching on the internet, you need to ask some ★ very important questions of any site that you use:

1. Is the site from a recognized source?
2. Is there an author listed or is it a compilation by a university, knowledgeable business, or government entity?
3. Is it a joke site?
4. Is it a site that is respected by the community? (Avoid wikis or 50/50 news sites.)
5. Is the data current? (Outdated sites are bad.)
6. Has this information been debunked?

If you have an answer to any of these questions that you feel uncomfortable about, then talk to someone before you use the information on the page. If you are in college, ask a professor. If you are in the business or academic world, then ask a peer. Do not risk spending months on bad data, always check your sources if you are working with the internet.

Once you have found reliable data on the interest, hopefully it is from multiple sources. You can take this data and form it into a dataset. Find the data that applies to your population, harvest as large of a dataset as you reasonably can, then enter it into whatever software program you are using (or into your spreadsheet if you are not using modern software). Collecting data off the internet is very easy, just be sure to cite your source. Even if you are collecting raw data from a website, you are still using someone else's work, so give the source credit. Surveys online are also very simple, and can give you a modicum of control if you use sites with already formatted survey programs. Just be careful, the anonymity that allows people online to tell the truth also allows them to lie with impunity. Be sure to limit your scope enough that you can set control measures to keep your data honest.

"STANDING IN THE MALL"

Standing in the mall is the first of the old-school methods that we look at for collecting statistical data. Standing in the mall is not limited to physically standing in the mall, but is a catch-all term for research where you go to a location and pass out surveys for people to fill out. Standing in the mall means that you are going to a location and giving surveys to random people as they walk past, hoping that enough people will fill out your survey to give you a decent sample size. Locations where you can "stand in the mall" include but are not limited to malls, universities, conference centers, businesses, hospitals, or sporting events. (Always remember to get permission before collecting data at a private location.)

Standing in the mall is an excellent way to get data easily with minimum expense. The only costs of this method are your time, the cost of getting to the location, the cost of printing out your surveys, and often the cost of buying a few small items so you are not thrown out of the location (even if you ask permission and are given permission at a store, you should still buy something to show appreciation, although use reason if you are doing a survey at Tiffany's because no one expects you to buy anything). Standing in the mall also allows for natural randomization of your survey sample, if you ask as many people as you can as they walk past, you are getting a sample of the population that is passing through; whether this population is representative of the general population you are surveying depends on how well you did designing your population parameters.

There are some drawbacks to using the standing in the mall method to collect data for your project. First of all, not all places will allow you to stand around questioning their customers. Business owners, rightfully so, often feel that the intrusion on their customers' privacy may drive customers away. Further, not everyone that you approach will actually fill out a survey for you. Young people are more likely to respond to a survey, but other demographics have an abysmal response rate.[1] When you are standing in the mall you can expect many people to tell you "no." This can skew your sample toward the people who are willing to actually answer your questions. Another danger that you should be aware of is that people will often lie on surveys, especially the young people who are more likely to answer your questions. This means that when you review your surveys, you need to look for answers that indicate your respondents were just messing with you. Consider this example: If the question asks "where do you live?" and they put "the moon," then you can tell they may not be taking the survey seriously.

---

1. Pew Research Center (2012). Assessing the Representativeness of Public Opinion Surveys. At http://www.people-press.org/2012/05/15/assessing-the-representativeness-of-public-opinion-surveys/ (February 9, 2015).

Standing in the mall is an effective, albeit simple, approach. It is an inexpensive way to collect large amounts of data quite easily. With ease, however, comes the difficulty of dealing with naturally randomized data rather than mathematically randomized data. This can lead your study to being heavily skewed toward one element of the population or another. This should not discourage you from doing the "mall" surveys; however, you should be aware that when you do this you will have to spend extra time checking the reliability of your data. The ease you experience in collecting the data will be subverted by the difficulty you experience when you have to enter and analyze the data.

INFORMATION POSTING

Have you ever walked across a college campus and seen those pieces of paper with the tassels cut into the bottom with phone numbers. There are many reasons that people post them—for room-mates, to sell a car, because they want guitar lessons—but you also see pieces of paper asking people if they want to participate in a research study. These posters are often vague (double-blind studies require them to be vague), and they often promise some token of appreciation ($20, a free pizza, or a movie ticket). This is another way that research subjects can be collected for a study, the simple method of information posting.

The main question that I hear people ask about information posting is, "How do I post my study so that I get good data from a sample that I can use?" This can be tricky in the qualitative realm, but here in the quantitative realm it can be downright disheartening. A post should have the information that the potential subject needs to determine if they can be in your study. If you are studying the effects of Alzheimer disease in grandparents upon their grandchildren in their early to late 20s, then you would want to ensure that the participants:

1. Are in their early to late 20s;
2. Have grandparents; and
3. Have grandparents who have been diagnosed with Alzheimer disease.

If they do not meet any one of these categories, then they should not be in the main study. Howev-er, you may want to have people who do not meet one or more of these categories to act as a control group for your study so you have something to compare with your collected data.

The second most common question is, "Where should I post my request?" This question is based heavily on what you are studying. If you are studying grain intake by purebred horse breeders, then posting your information request at the local gas station will likely not gain you many responses. In this instance you would look for someplace where large numbers of people in this category meet, such as a racing event. Colleges, malls, churches, and hospitals (once again ask for permission) are good places to collect data. In the modern era, the internet can be a valuable tool for this type of data collection. By going to a few topic-specific chat rooms, having your Twitter or Facebook followers post a request, and sending requests out to a college listserve, you can greatly increase your number of respondents. If you are using the internet, keep your survey short to increase responses, because people are generally willing to do a 3- to 5-minute survey but not respond to 500 questions. Also, be very clear in who you want to respond. Many online programs will allow you to create "check-boxes" where you can ask the key questions to your survey, so if a person does not meet the requirements then his or her survey is stored in a separate file.

The reason many people use the information posting method is because it shifts some of the burden to the population to respond. In the mall method, you are doing all the work in asking people to participate and about 75% of people are going to say no. However, with the information posting method, the people who respond are by and large going to be eager to participate. You still have to do the legwork of filtering out the people who do not qualify for your study (if money is involved you are going to find people who want to slip into the study), but by and large this method is easier than the standing in the mall method. That being said, once you send out your requests you have no way of encouraging people to participate. If you change the enticement, then the people who did it early will be disappointed, so you are regulated to simply reposting your request in topic-specific chat rooms. There is also the danger that you will get too many responses, but if you are using software that is easily accommodated it will actually help your margin of error.

Information posting is a useful technique to collect data for small to mid-level studies. It can be effectively used for larger studies as well, but this requires much more work on the part of the research team. Generally, the larger the sample size the better the results, so large studies are effective; however, if you go to all the work of doing a large study you should write a book on your findings so that you can promote all the details that are relevant to your topic. In small to mid-level studies, information posting shines as a good way to get participants that fit into your study demographic.

GOVERNMENT/BUSINESS RECORDS AND RANDOM NUMBERS

Before you go out into the world to collect data for your project, it behooves you to see if the data that you need is already collected and available for analysis. Certain businesses and government agencies do nothing but collect vast amounts of data. These entities use the data for a single analytical purpose, then generally archive it. This is a horrible system for the American taxpayer (British, Australian, French, German, and Canadian taxpayers as well), but it is incredibly beneficial for researchers in any of these countries who can gain access to the data. To a researcher, these vast reserves of data are an excellent starting point for any topic that matches up with the population from which the data was collected.

Business data can be more difficult to acquire than government data; however, if there is a benefit for the business you are requesting the data from (and the data is not damaging to the business) then many businesses will provide you with data as long as it is inexpensive for them to do so. When you are asking a business for data, be careful not to shoot yourself in the foot. Proprietary data, private data of employees and customers, data on illegal actions, and information that can be damaging to a company's image will generally gain you a "no" response when you ask a company for data. Further, if you have previously bashed the company in your work and they know that, they are not going to help you undermine them. Therefore, when asking for data from a company, make sure that you form your request in a way that makes it seem like you are doing the research to benefit the company or the industry that they are in. Even the best corporate goodwill only goes so far.

With the government, collecting data can be a chore. Some data are freely available online from individual agencies (the Central Intelligence Agency, World Fact Book, Department of Agriculture Statistics). These data sources are a treasure trove of facts that can be easily collected, cited, and analyzed into a workable project. The only problem with this data is that everyone with a computer has access to it and it can be difficult to find a "new" topic to address. The less available data that the government has is generally less available, because it is classified or because of general governmental incompetence. If the data are withheld simply because of incompetence, then a Freedom of Information Act request can compel the government to give you the data (though generally you do not have to go that far, you can generally just ask the proper department). If the data are classified and you believe that the classification is illegal, you can also make a Freedom of Information Act request and see where it takes you. However, if you compel an agency to give you information (even if you win) do not expect them to be friendly the next time you ask for data.

The final part of this chapter looks at random numbers and random number tables. While this does not fit directly into the section, it is an important part of quantitative research that should not be overlooked. As a social scientist, I tend to overlook the importance of random numbers in the "hard science." When you are creating a sample of inanimate objects (or people or animals from a large population), random numbers can allow you to pick a truly random sample of the population. This can increase the accuracy of your study and decrease your margin of error (the real margin of error, not the calculated margin) if done properly. Most statistics books have a random number chart somewhere in the book, and if you select every seventh (or any) number from the chart you can randomize your results each time you use your chart. This helps you find a random sample that better represents the population you are studying.

CONCLUSION

Sampling is a skill that everyone doing quantitative research should work on improving each time they do a study. We can never be an expert at being random, but we can eliminate more and more bias each time we do a study. The methods listed in this chapter are only a few of the methods that you can use to sample a population for a quantitative study; however, these are the main methods that most people are going to use to collect data. If you are serious about becoming a quantitative researcher, purchase a good book on statistics. As this is a general academic writing text, we do not have the space to go into a detailed analysis of every statistical method for sampling available.

CHECKLIST

- ❑ What is your population?
- ❑ Why did you choose this population?
- ❑ Is this the population that best fits your study?
- ❑ Can you sample this population accurately?
- ❑ Where will you sample this population?
- ❑ What technique will you use to sample this population?
- ❑ Is this a type of data that the government or a specific business field collects?
- ❑ Do you need to randomize your sample with a random number chart?

RECOMMENDED READING

Anderson, Sweeny, & Williams (1999). STATISTICS FOR BUSINESS AND ECONOMICS, 17TH ED. New York: International Thompson.

Weiss, Neil (2002). INTRODUCTORY STATISTICS, 6TH ED. Boston: Addison-Wesley.

chapter 16
Software, Calculations, and Conclusion
Part II

INTRODUCTION

Welcome to the new millennia, it is not 1922; therefore, the days of doing exhausting calculations by hand without the benefit of computers should be over. The current wave (it is not a new wave as it has been going on for 25 years now) in statistics is to use the software that is available effectively to perform calculations. Unfortunately, there are two schools of thought on how to train people to do statistics in the modern academy, either teach the students the time-tested and outdated method of learning the equations by hand, even though no students are going to do them by hand in their job, or professors throw students in the deep end by telling them to use software that they have no training in. The field of statistics is slowly merging with the field of computer applications and operations. The sooner we begin training future researchers in the new methodologies the sooner quantitative research can lose its shadow of fear and become a class that students actually enjoy.

While students and researchers should still learn the basic elements of statistical research methods, the years of the equations being drilled into the heads of undergraduate students are over. All this antiquated methodology does is create a system of fear that drives talented students away from becoming quantitative researchers. When I speak of Statistics 200 in my classes, which is the gateway statistics class at my current institute, you would think that I was telling children about the boogeyman. Eyes glaze over, students look into their books, breaking all eye contact as if I was going to ask them to do a chi-squared test by hand on a dataset with 1,000 datums. The academy needs to move into the modern era and treat quantitative research as the digital science that it is.

Modernizing the teaching methodology for quantitative research can bring a whole new generation of quantitative researchers into the field. Qualitative research does not move forward without quantitative research and quantitative research does not move forward without qualitative research. One is the ying to the other is the yang. Modernized teaching methods where we teach the basic equations so that the students understand them and know where to find them (similar to how we teach students about binary code but do not require them to memorize binary code) frees up a large portion of the semester to teach students how to use the data they collect. Of all the students who take statistics, 99% of them will likely never do another statistics problem by hand (unless they take another statistics class). Is it not a better method to teach them the idea, teach them how to use the data once collected, then train them in the proper use of the software rather than forcing them to learn it on the fly on their own?

This brief chapter will look at some of the benefits of using software to do the calculations for statistics and also how we can use the time that we save to teach students how to use their data, rather than just how to collect it. Of the six statistics classes that I took during my time in college, only one ever taught the use of the statistical data. That class spent one week covering it. Meanwhile I had four semesters in my Ph.D. program teaching the use of qualitative research methodology and how to write in that field. Why is there such a disparity? In the first section we look at the software that is available for use in the quantitative field. As there is a software package for each field out there, I will only look at the packages that I am familiar with—SPSS (they are all very similar) and Microsoft Excel. In the second section we discuss the spreadsheet and how it is your friend. Like a guard dog or a large horse, a spreadsheet can be scary when you first approach it; however, once you see how useful it is that fear goes away and it becomes a valuable part of your life. In the third section we discuss human error facilitated by the old statistical methodologies, and the way that treating statistics as a computer applications class can get rid of some of that human error. In the final section of the chapter (and end of Part II of this book) we discuss the need to be vigilant in editing your spreadsheet.

SOFTWARE

As you may be able to tell from the introduction, I am a firm supporter of teaching statistics as a computer applications class rather than as a pure math class—it makes sense. Statistics has always been a bastard child of multiple departments; each group trying to push off the duty of training statistics to another set of faculty. Like any research methodology, statistics is a tool; thus there is no reason to fear it. All you need to know to work the major software packages is your data and your goal. Once you have these two main components, the software package will walk you through your process just like when you check your email.

The software that I am most comfortable using is SPSS, by IBM. IBM states, "With SPSS predictive analytics software, you can predict with confidence what will happen next so that you can make smarter decisions, solve problems and improve outcomes."[1] Since I learned how to use it, SPSS has evolved into a complete statistical tool, but at universities many professors are only teaching it as augmentation of handwritten statistics rather than a method on its own. With SPSS (and any other discipline's software) you have the ability to design your spreadsheet from the ground up, eliminate human error (which we talk about later), and even allow the system to create your regression models, all with a software package that can be learned in a few weeks (if taught properly).

The key to moving from where we are now, in an age where students are afraid of statistics because it is confusing, to an age where students are accepting of statistics and treat it as something as simple as checking their email requires three steps:

1. Teach students the meanings of terms as a vocabulary system (preferably in high school). Students do not need to memorize all the equations for statistics unless they are going to become professional statisticians, rather they need to know the meaning of the terminology so that they are able to find the equations that they need and populate them (remember Einstein said that the smartest person in the world does not know everything, but knows where to find everything). We do not force students to learn the electromechanics of a cordless drill before we let them use one in shop class, so why should this tool be any different?
2. Properly teach students what equations are used in what situations (preferably in undergraduate studies). Half of the difficulty of statistics is understanding that the language for statistics is different from the language of regular math (much like accounting). If we teach students the language that is being used (or change the language to bring it in line with regular math) we can make the study of statistics a relatively easy class.
3. Properly train students to use SPSS, Excel, or whatever spreadsheet/database program their major requires (preferably in undergraduate studies). Statistics is a tool, but we barely train students to use it before we send them out into the world with it. With the amount of training that goes into training students to use a bar break or a rotary saw, we should be able to spare the time to teach them to use a spreadsheet that they probably understand better than the person teaching them. True, there are safety concerns with physical tools (which is why we require training in them) but there are also safety concerns when we allow thousands of people who have just enough training in statistics out into the research world, the public and private sectors, and give them control over statistical operations that affect the lives of millions of people.

---

1. IBM Web Solutions (2015). "SPSS" at http://www-01.ibm.com/software/analytics/spss/.

If we follow these three easy steps, a student can be fully trained in statistical analysis and research in a semester or two. All it requires is that we treat statistics like the burgeoning field of computer science that it is.

FEAR AND SPREADSHEETS

Spreadsheets are another thing that some college students fear. This can be a problem when a spreadsheet is an excellent organizational tool for many different types of research projects. Therefore, you just need to change how you look at spreadsheets as a tool. A spreadsheet is a mini database with a built-in calculator. If you are using a spreadsheet with formattable cells (pretty much anything from 1995 on) then you have the ability to store both quantitative and qualitative data in your spreadsheet. This can be an excellent tool for you to keep your notes organized and help you move your projects forward.

The only major drawback of using a generic spreadsheet (like Excel) is that some of the tools that are available in the more specialized systems (such as SPSS) are not available. It is a common "you get what you pay for" scenario. However, many of the common statistical functions can be performed on regular spreadsheets, you just have to be willing to take the time to program in the equations. This can be a little more time consuming but it can save you money in the end.

ELIMINATING (SOME OF) THE HUMAN ERROR

One reason that software makes the lives of statistical researchers so much easier is that it reduces some of the human error. Even the best of us screw up our handwritten equations from time to time. This is doubly true with students who are under deadlines, trying to accomplish social as well as academic lives, and who may be running short on sleep (these problems are also true for professional researchers, too). Computer-based software packages allow researchers to eliminate one of the areas where common human errors occur, the calculations. While you still have to design a good project and collect good data, the peace of mind that you can gain from a software system that will do your calculations for you can be priceless.

Software also enables people who are bad at mathematics to do statistical research. Some people do not have the aptitude for mathematics. Academia discriminated against these people for hundreds of years by insisting that statistics was the dominant means of research in most fields. Now many universities are understanding that theoretical research and qualitative research are coequal methodologies for different research areas. Now with good software packages that are user friendly, any researcher has the ability to do statistical research, regardless of math aptitude.

Software also enables researchers to do calculations in a few seconds versus weeks. Some statistical calculations, especially on large datasets, take forever by hand. Software eliminates this problem. Now as long as you take the time to enter data into a spreadsheet (or have a TA enter the data into a spreadsheet), you can have the results of complicated tests very quickly. This enables you to concentrate on collecting as much data as possible, even if you are up against a deadline. The hard math that precluded studies from being done by individuals in the past are now opened up because of the ease of new software packages.

CONCLUSION: RECHECK YOUR RECHECKED DATA

Statistics are many people's idea of torture in academic writing, by the mythos that surrounds statistics is mostly rumor created by outdated methods. Quantitative methods are among the easiest research methodologies for anyone who has the least bit of competence with a computer. If you can enter data into a spreadsheet, then you can do statistical research. All it takes is patience. If you have patience, then you can study anything that can be converted to a number and that you have the funding to explore.

The key thing that hangs up a modern statistician is the impatience that society breeds into us. We live in an on-demand society, so we want answers right away. Oftentimes this means that we skip one of the most important steps in any research process—that is, editing your dataset. With all research, making sure that you enter your dataset into your note-taking system is important, but with statistics it is vital. One missed space, one extra number, one flipped function, and you could ruin your whole project. Therefore it is vital that you check your data, then recheck your data, then recheck your rechecked data. Just like in good writing you tell them what you are going to tell them, you tell them, then you tell them what you told them, in good statistics you check your data entry thrice.

Fear of math is instilled in students in the United States for some reason that I cannot fathom. Mathematics should be taught to students as early as possible by qualified teachers. Math teachers must understand proper teaching methodology, so students gain the most knowledge during instruction. The new model of making math egalitarian and "as long as you tried you get points" is a recipe for failure. There are few black and white topics in the world, and math is one of them. If you do the math right you will get the right answer, and if you enter the data into the computer properly and select the right function you can have the right statistics.

CHECKLIST

- ❏ Did you find a program that works with your discipline?
- ❏ Did you take a training (online or physical) on that software?
- ❏ Did you learn the meanings of terms and their uses?
- ❏ Did you check your data entry?
- ❏ Did you recheck your data entry?
- ❏ Did you recheck your rechecked data?

RECOMMENDED SPREADSHEETS

General: Microsoft Excel
Social Sciences and Humanities: IBM SPSS
Business: NCSS Statistics Software
Law: Learn R (Yale Library)
Medicine: R or SAS
Physical Sciences: SAS/STAT

All recommendations are based on reviews. I am only proficient in SPSS. I recommend that you research the common software used in your field.

Part III

QUALITATIVE RESEARCH

chapter 17
Introduction to Qualitative Research

INTRODUCTION

Qualitative research is a research methodology that focuses on developing a greater understanding of the rationale, opinions, motivations, traditions, and cultural elements related to a hypothesis or related to a group that is the focus of a hypothesis. Qualitative research goes beyond the methodologies of quantitative research, which are limited by the numerical values and objective requirements and explores deeper into the substrata of the research topic. Qualitative data can take a researcher deeper into a subject matter than most quantitative methodologies, but researchers must remember that when they are taking these extra steps to explore deeper into a subject matter there are more rigorous controls that help protect the integrity of the research due to its subjective nature.

A question that many authors ask themselves is why they should take the time to do a qualitative research study. Qualitative research requires more work, generally more time, and has more constraints on what you can and cannot do to ensure validity of your study. That being said, qualitative research does give you more freedom in designing a study because qualitative research can allow you to study elements of a subject matter that are statistically inaccessible or statistically insignificant. Qualitative research allows you to go beyond the numbers and delve into the actual fabric of your subject matter, feelings, traditions, cultural mores; even colors, scents, and sounds all become relevant data that can be examined using a qualitative methodology. Where quantitative data merely tells the reader about a subject matter, qualitative data (when done correctly) can actually take your reader there.

When beginning a study, you should always take the time to choose between macro-methodologies. Qualitative and quantitative research methodologies both have their place in academic study. Qualitative research methods provide a more exploratory option than the quantitative methods. This means that when you have a broader question, or your hypothesis is less sure, you can use a qualitative methodology to explore the subject matter you are looking into without hampering it with biases necessary to convert observations to statistics. For instance, if you are studying the happiness of parents who live at home with their children rather than working while the other spouse is the sole breadwinner, a qualitative study would allow you to do in-depth interviews, gauge the feelings of a broad spectrum of subjects, and compare and contrast them based on their contextual response. In a statistical study you would be regulated to having your subjects boil their feelings down to a number on a scale or even comparing divorce and suicide rates of working parent/stay at home parent pairs against dual working parent pairs. Qualitative research methods give you more versatility in how you can study a problem and do not limit your study to what can be numerically and objectively observed.

When comparing methodologies you should also look at the differences between qualitative research and theoretical research. Where qualitative research methodologies are exploratory on one specific issue or a small collection of issues, theoretical research can expand to a much broader topic. Generally, a theoretical research project will be comprised of several smaller qualitative or quantitative research projects. If you find that your project is getting too unwieldy, then possibly you should look at it as a theoretical project and boil your topic area down another level so that you can begin doing singular research projects. Multiple qualitative studies (or quantitative studies) can sometimes be interlinked to allow you to create a theoretical study on the topic.

This chapter is an overview of qualitative methodology as a standalone group of methodologies. In the first section we look at what fields commonly use qualitative research. You will find that as you write more and more research papers, some fields are more accepting of specific methodologies. In the second section we look at the limitations of qualitative research. Like any research methodology, qualitative research is a tool. If you attempt to use a tool for a purpose other than what it was designed for, then you may find yourself with an inefficient tool, or worse a broken tool. In the third section we look at the principles of qualitative research, the elements that separate qualitative research from the other research methodologies. In the last section we review the format of the chapter and the individual methodologies that will be covered.

WHAT FIELDS USE QUALITATIVE RESEARCH?

Can you imagine a lawyer using a hammer in daily activities? Think about it, the normal tools of a lawyer are pens, papers, and interns, but what if a lawyer tried to use a hammer to get all the elements of the job done? The lawyer would be inefficient, right? This is because a specific tool should be used for a specific job, so when you try to use the wrong tool for the job you can do more damage than good. This is a problem many people often face when they begin trying to use the wrong research methodology. Qualitative research methodologies are excellent when they are used for what they are meant to be used for; however, when someone tries to force them into a project that they are not designed for they can become a hindrance and even corrupt the project. In this section we look across major disciplines to see whether qualitative research methodologies are useful in each discipline and how they can be used.

Qualitative research methodologies seem to be tailormade for the arts and humanities, which tend to deal more in existential data than in actual numerical data. It is difficult to measure the feeling inspired by a poem or how much a specific scene frightens you in a play; thus, the rich contextual data of the qualitative methods can be useful. This is not to say that there are no uses for quantitative data in the humanities—language studies and individual languages can use statistics to track the progress of students, theaters can use statistics to show whether a show may do well in a certain area, and of course anything can be compared based on use value. Qualitative research is a useful tool in the humanities but should be weighed against what you are actually researching in the study.

The social sciences also have a strong attachment to the qualitative research methodologies, but the social sciences also are strongly affiliated with the quantitative methodologies as well. Different areas of the discipline ascribe to different methodologies to the point that faculty members can have arguments. The simple truth is that it depends on the research you are doing which macro-methodology will work best. The social sciences have some of the broadest research areas in all of academia, neither qualitative nor quantitative research can lay claim to the whole field. Hybrid methodologies should abound in the social sciences, and in some cases they do. This means within the social sciences you should make sure of what your research goals are and then choose the methodology that is best suited to you.

The hard sciences have a tenuous relationship with the qualitative research methodologies, but the qualitative research methodologies are starting to make inroads into these fields. The hard sciences are dominated by quantitative and theoretical research methods because of the nature of the science. A very specific scientific method is used, repeatedly, to determine whether a hypothesis is valid or not. These repeated tests lend themselves to statistics, which in turn can be combined with other statistics to support or disprove a theory. However, at the very basic single test level, qualitative research is beginning to make a resurgence. More detailed descriptions can lead to more statistics, which in turn can lead to better data for statistical comparison. Thus, qualitative research has its place, albeit limited, in the hard sciences.

Qualitative data in business is regulated primarily to marketing and customer support, though it is used in limited fashion in other areas. Business is dominated by numbers, but the consumer side of businesses eventually boils down to people. Across a nation or a region, the aggregation of specific numbers can allow wrought statistics to be used as a method with an acceptable margin of error. Modern business is learning, however, that when hybrid (quant/qual) methodologies are used to collect research data, the individual desires can be tracked more readily across the spectrum of the customer base, thus allowing a better response to customer need and increasing the aggregate success rate. Outside of marketing and customer service "pure" qualitative research methods are having difficulty making inroads, but as hybrid methodologies link with quantitative methodologies they are helping companies be more successful.

The medical field has always had a strong relationship with the qualitative methods. Some of the ways that are needed to describe medical procedures and disease just cannot be put completely into numbers. This means that the qualitative data in the medical field is at least, if not more, important than the quantitative data. That being said, the medical field is becoming more and more of a business each year (especially with government interference), thus the qualitative data that has made the U.S. medical system one of the best in the world is slowly being replaced by numbers that bureaucrats with limited education can understand. This necrotizing of medical research is beginning to severely damage the field.

The legal field is basically a methodological free-for-all. Quantitative data are commonly used in mortuary tables so that values can be placed on even the most basic elements of human life. However, the pleas that an attorney makes to a jury are based on the anticipated response to a qualitative description, which is thus based on a hybrid methodology. Affidavits and depositions are generally completely made up of qualitative data; therefore, if you are writing a legal paper, any methodology that makes sense will help you build a strong argument for your project; you just have to take the time to pick the right methodology.

The only field that seems to avoid qualitative data like the plague is the field of mathematics. In a field that is dominated by numbers, qualitative data has little or no place. There may be some odd exceptions to the rule that allow for singular qualitative methodologies to be used from time to time in the field of mathematics, but by and large mathematical studies will be quantitative data. Math journals tend to exclusively want theoretical or statistical data—how numbers "feel" is of little interest to them. So unless you have a problem that absolutely needs qualitative data to support your hypothesis, you should use quantitative data in mathematical studies.

LIMITS OF QUALITATIVE RESEARCH

As we have noted, qualitative research is not a be-all catch-all, easy methodology that people can just substitute in whenever they are too lazy to find the proper methodology. It is a set of specific methodologies designed to be used in a specific way. Qualitative research does have limitations that can eliminate qualitative research methodologies from contention when beginning a project. Understanding these limitations can allow you to have more control over your research. In this section we look at the general limits of the qualitative research methodologies, because if you know your limits then you can select the right processes to overcome them.

First of all, qualitative research projects by and large are not able to be generalized. The reason for this is that you are studying a specific area of subject matter and that area is so specific that it may not translate to other areas. This does not mean that no qualitative research is able to be generalized; however, most of the time the only way that you can generalize a qualitative study is when you have two or three other similar groups that you can compare it to. For instance, if you are studying a tribe in the central Amazon and believe that your study shows primitive communities have stronger familial ties, which in turn allow society to grow and prosper, you may not be able to generalize this to other primitive communities on its own merits. However, if your study shows this data and you can find several other studies that come to the same conclusion studying other primitive communities, then you can use a hybrid methodology to show a correlation (quant/qual).

The second limitation that can cause qualitative researchers headaches is that in some fields qualitative research methodologies are seen as "loose" methodologies. What this means is that a portion of the field, whether correctly or incorrectly, believes that the structure of the methodology is amorphous enough that anyone can do anything and still claim to be within this methodology. This misconception has been fueled by people using "general qualitative methodology" as a research method and not linking their research to an identifiable hybrid qualitative methodology. If you are planning on doing qualitative research and wish to combat this misconception, always have a strong methodology section in your paper. This will allow your reader to see the steps that you have taken to collect valid and reliable data on your subject matter.

Critics will also claim that qualitative research is based on subjective observations and conjuncture. This argument is in two parts and must be addressed as such. As for the later part, that qualitative research is based on conjuncture, this argument is false in regard to properly done qualitative research. Qualitative researchers should always be conscious that they are not going to make assumptions or conjunctures in the course of their research. If the odd event occurs that requires an assumption to be made, the researcher should clearly denote this in his or her work. As for the first point, that qualitative research is predominantly subjective, this statement is false. It is the inference that is incorrect. Critics argue that subjective data are less useful than objective data, which is also false, because 90% of your life is made up of subjective data that you are screening from the world around you. There are even philosophical arguments that we will not get into that mathematics is a subjective field objectified by the agreement of generations of mathematicians. There is no problem with subjective data as long as you provide rigorous controls to ensure quality.

A practical criticism of qualitative data is that there is less protection for subjects within a qualitative research study than there is within a quantitative research study. This statement is true, but there are safeguards that one can take to improve the safety of subjects. Quantitative researchers boil their subjects down to numbers, which become harder to trace (unless you really know what you are doing). This keeps their subjects anonymous, thus helping shield their identities. Qualitative researchers have to take extra steps to protect the identities of their subjects. A person can be identified by the rich data a research gives in his or her report. This means that researchers should work hand in hand with their Institutional Review Board to ensure that all participants are protected.

QUALITATIVE PRINCIPLES

Qualitative research has some core principles that anyone who wants to do a qualitative study should be aware of. The first of these is that a qualitative research study should provide rich, detailed data. The more detailed your data is, the better you will be able to analyze your data using one of the following methodologies. Qualitative researchers cannot simply be happy with knowing the number of participants or the number of times that the participants took a specific action; qualitative researchers must go beyond that, delving into the how, the what, the why, and the where. Detailed data is the hallmark of a good qualitative research study, thus the researcher must show exceptional focus in recording the data.

Qualitative data should also focus on one key concept of a given subject area. By focusing on a specific concept the researcher can collect even more rich data for his or her study. When you are observing, interviewing, or even giving a survey you will never be able to get every datum on every aspect of your subject. Even if your spend a hundred years observing, interviewing, and surveying there will still be data that slips through your web. This means that for you to complete an exceptional study, you must limit what you are looking for to as focused a topic as possible. This will allow you to concentrate on a specific feature and observe as much data about it as humanly possible.

Finally, qualitative data goes beyond the numbers. If you find that your qualitative study is beginning to read like a statistical manuscript, then you may have selected the wrong methodology for your project. Qualitative methodologies look at the who, the what, the when, and the where in the most focused way possible. Numbers can give you an explanation of a situation, but it takes detailed descriptions of the data to actually take your reader to your research site in their mind. This is the goal of qualitative research, to break the bounds of three-dimensional space and transport the mind of your reader to a place they want to read about.

FORMAT OF PART III

Part III looks at the specific methodologies that you may choose to use in your qualitative research study. Part III provides you with an introduction to each of these methodologies but should not be considered the be-all and end-all of research on the topic. Part III is a primer; it is designed to give you enough information that you can do a basic paper within the given methodology. If you want to do advanced methodological research please look into the recommended reading at the end of each of the substantive chapters.

In Chapter 19 we review the practices that you will use to do a proper ethnographic study. Ethnographies allow you to explore a situation that you are not familiar with and gain as much raw data as possible on the subject. The data collection methodologies for ethnography mostly focus on observation, but interviews, surveys, and book research can also help create more rich data for your analysis. Ethnographies analyze data by taking the rich data gathered in the data collection phase of your project and comparing it through a theoretical lens either emic or etic. This allows the researcher to generalize within the specific group that is being observed, but does not let the researcher generalize findings to the broader population.

In Chapter 20 we review the practices that you will use to do a proper case study. Case studies allow you to take a detailed look at a specific instance, whether a person, a phenomenon, or an event, and give a detailed explanation of it through a specific theoretical lens. Data collection for case studies focuses on interviews and surveys, but book research and observations can be used depending on the time of the study. The analysis will be the application of a specific theoretical lens from a discipline relevant to the case study. Depending on the nature of the case study, a researcher may or may not be able to generalize the findings to a broad population.

In Chapter 21 we review the practices that you will use to do a proper phenomenology. Phenomenological studies allow the researcher to build a dataset based on the lived experiences of persons involved in a specific phenomenon. Surveys and interviews are the main tools to gain data on lived experiences; book research can be used in limited circumstances (when the lived experiences are in the previous research), and observations can be used in auto-phenomenological studies. The analysis should use a specific theoretical lens to compare the lived experiences to what happened in the phenomenon on a broader scope. Phenomenologies can generally not be generalized to a broader population.

In Chapter 22 we review the practices that you will use to do a proper qualitative meta-synthesis (QMS). QMS studies allow a researcher to garner data from previous studies to build new hypotheses or theories. Data collection in QMS is predominantly book research, though surveys and interviews can be taken of the researchers who completed the source studies. The analysis within a QMS study is focused on allowing the researcher to build support for a new hypothesis or theory based on data already in circulation in the field. QMS is designed to broaden the scope of older research so that it can be moved into new areas; however, whether the research can be generalized to a broader field depends on the subject material.

Part III of this book should provide you with the tools to do a basic study within one of the described methodologies. It should also give you the information to research more advanced methodologies if your specific situation calls for an advanced research methodology. Qualitative research methodologies have a reputation for being easy, but the more you learn about them, the more you find out that they are more rigorous than most of the statistical methodologies and some of the theoretical methodologies. If you want to have a good qualitative research study, take the time to follow all the steps and ensure that your data are both valid and reliable.

CHECKLIST

- ❏ Have you completed the steps from Part I?
- ❏ Why is a qualitative research method right for you?
- ❏ Which method do you think will be of the most use for you?
- ❏ Why did you choose qualitative research at the exclusion of the other macro-methodologies?
- ❏ Why did you choose your methodology at the exclusion of the other qualitative methodologies?

chapter 18
Choosing a Qualitative Methodology

INTRODUCTION

Some authors claim that their normal methodology is qualitative, as if qualitative research was a single methodology with its own set of rules and requirements. This becomes a difficult problem because if you are trying to use "qualitative" research in general, the different rules for actual qualitative methodologies sometimes conflict. The qualitative general approach is workable for term papers (though most people who claim they are doing this are doing some sort of QMS hybrid), but when you are doing an actual academic research paper you need a more specific methodology to ensure that you have to tools to secure your data's validity and reliability.

In qualitative research, as in any other research, your method defines your process. Your method also determines your terminology, your data gathering techniques, and in some cases even defines where you can get your work published. Just putting down "qualitative methodology" is like hitting a home run and stopping at third base. There are four steps to identifying which research methodology you are going to use:

1. Identify the topic that you will be working with.
2. Create a research question and hypothesis for your project.
3. Find the macro-methodological family that will best help you deal with your question/ hypothesis.

4. Select a methodology from the macro-methodological family that best suits your needs as a researcher.

Those who say they are doing "qualitative research" are stopping at the third stage, thus they have not completed their research development process.

Your methodology also can have a major effect on your funding. Different universities and different grant writing agencies have specific ways that they want research proposals to look if they are going to give out money. One of the key elements in any research proposal is that the research methodology is clearly defined. If you place yourself in the position of a committee member looking over dozens of proposals, knowing that the committee can only give funding to one organization, how would you treat proposals where the methodology was not clearly defined, or worse poorly defined? You would likely give the money to the people who have done their due diligence and prepared a document that meets all the requirements of your proposal policy. Methodology is a key element in your funding proposal so make sure that you complete all of the methodological steps before you start looking for funding.

The earlier you identify your research methodology, the earlier that you will be able to plan to effectively use your methodology in relation to your topic. Different qualitative methodologies have different data collection procedures, different analytical procedures, and different readerships. If you move halfway through the process with plans to do an ethnography then change your mind and decide to do a phenomenological research paper instead, there are elements that you are going to have to go back and change, not the least of which being your research question. When you change your research question you are changing your whole project; therefore, you should make every effort to select the correct research methodology before you begin researching or writing your paper. As with all things when you write academically, proper preparation can save you hours of revision time. Clearly identify your methodology before you put pen to paper.

This chapter is going to look at some of the questions that you should ask yourself when choosing between the different qualitative research methodologies. This chapter assumes that you have completed Part I of the book looking at how you select macro-methodological families, thus you have a valid reason for selecting a qualitative methodology as your method of choice. If you have not, I suggest that you return to read through Chapter 10 so you have an idea what you are getting into (unless a professor has assigned you a specific methodology).

In the first section of this chapter we look at what the goal of your research is. Knowing the goal of your research is essential to identifying what type of research methodology you are going to use.

In the second section we look at the type of research you are going to be performing. Whether you are exploring, arguing, or even supporting the research of another person, knowing the type of research that you are getting into will enable you to make a better choice when you select a research methodology. In the third section we look at the anticipated methods that you may use to collect data. Having a good data collection plan before you select a research methodology can be helpful; however, some people wait until they have selected a research methodology before they select a data collection method. This is a chicken–egg question and heavily depends on the researcher. Finally, in the fourth section we look at the different types of methodologies and how you will structure your approach to researching them. This section acts as a primer for later sections of the book so that you know what you are getting into before you start reading about the step-by-step pattern of researching within a qualitative format. Having these primers as an introduction can help you see the whole picture while we are describing the individual pieces that make up the methodology; this is done for your benefit so you can see the method in context.

GOAL OF RESEARCH

When you are looking at your research goal you have to ask yourself the main question that comes to anyone else's mind when beginning a research project: "Why are you doing this?" Research is hard work and you need to have a reason why you are subjecting yourself to the rigors, committing the time, and opening yourself up to criticism in the way that a research paper does. If you cannot answer this question to yourself, then how are you going to answer it to other people when they ask you why you are researching your topic. Here are a few stock answers than can be of help when you are asked this question:

1. Because my teacher/boss said I had to (This is the easiest answer if you are assigned a project and simply need to get it done and do it well.)
2. Because this question needs to be answered (Some questions just need to be answered. They can be questions that have bothered you for some time, questions that have plagued mankind for all time, or even something you heard last week that you cannot get out of your mind.)
3. Because I have the ability to answer a longstanding question (Sometimes a question will find you. Your experience may be unique in a way that allows you to see the answer to a question in a way that few other people are able to do.)
4. Because if I do not then someone else will (Maybe you want to make sure that the question receives the time and attention it warrants. It may be a popular issue that you do not want

some network talking-head to answer so you decided to answer the question using a real academic methodology.)

5. To help other people (Helping others is the best reason—for example, cancer needs a cure, crime needs prevention, or we need a potion or machine that keeps politicians from lying. If you can discover the solution to one of these problems, that is a noble reason to do research.)

6. For fortune and glory (Indiana Jones put it best, "Fortune and glory kid, fortune and glory."[1] Some people write for the fame, some people write for the money. If this is enough to drive you to write, then hopefully it is enough to sustain you when you hit your breaking point.)

Each of these answers has its own pros and cons that make it a good or bad reason for doing research, but the matter comes down to when you are reaching your breaking point for time, money and relationships will you be able to justify why you are doing your research project to yourself in the same way that you justify it to other people. This is a question that only you will be able to answer and you will only be able to answer it when you reach one of those breaking points. Therefore you should consider it well when you start, ask yourself why you are doing this research.

Another thing that you should look at when you are looking at the goal of your research is your research question. Now you will have your main research question, which is:

_____

_____

_____

But you should also have a "cocktail party" research question that you can tell anyone and they will be able to understand it. You can write that here:

_____

_____

_____

When I was writing my dissertation, I was studying what occurs when socioeconomic groups move from one state of socioeconomic evolution to another state and examining the conflict that arose at the confluence of those two socioeconomic states with the theory that it would be like across

---

1. *Indiana Jones*, 1981.

multiple examples, which it was. No one knew what I was talking about when I told them this so I began to tell people, "I study conflict during socioeconomic change." Nice, short, and to the point. No, it does not have the detail that the full disclosure has, but it was enough to get me through a conversation. By having a "cocktail party" answer to the question "what are you researching?" you can make it easier to explain yourself to your friends and family.

Some people in academic circles may take the time to ask you what your hypothesis is. All in all they expect you to be one of those armchair academics who do not have a hypothesis, you are just in it to write a paper. By having a simplified version of your hypothesis you can show that you are actually doing the work to do your research properly, without looking smug like the person who asked you the question. Your "cocktail hypothesis" should be complicated enough to explain what you are doing but not so complicated that a person should have to be an expert to understand what you are saying. It should be something that any competent researcher in your field should be able to understand.

Knowing these three elements of your research project will make defining how you are doing your research easier. Like children exploring the world for the first time, the follow-up question to any of the above questions from your colleagues, friends, and family members will be "why?" You can then proceed to regale them with why you selected your specific methodology and sub-methodology, why others in the field have done it differently, and why your research will be useful to others until their eyes glaze over and they wish that they had not asked you the question. Always keep your answers short and to the point so that you do not drive people away by bragging about your research.

WHAT KIND OF RESEARCH ARE YOU DOING?

A more technical aspect of this area of questioning is finding what type of research you are doing. By this point you have decided that you are using a qualitative methodology, and some of you even have a methodology in mind, but the purpose of your research can also help you narrow down a specific methodology that will suit you the best. For our purposes, there are three kinds of research that you should be choosing qualitative research for:

1. Exploratory research;
2. Argumentative research; and
3. Supportive research.

Each of these research methods can be useful for a specific purpose and each can lend itself well to a specific type of methodology. In this section we look at each of these types of research and link them to the methodology that generally works best for their purpose.

The vast majority of qualitative research papers will be exploratory in nature. In an exploratory research paper the author tries to find new knowledge in a subject area because of the belief that something exists. Authors of some exploratory papers try to prove a very specific point, "that culture X does activity Y when circumstances are Z." Others are more broad in their approach: "There is a difference in the way that Culture X acts when Z happens." Both of these questions are valid, both are exploratory, but both lend themselves to different types of research methodologies. The first example seems to be a good research question for a phenomenological research study. The researcher has a theory that a specific phenomenon (act) happens when specific circumstances are met and looks at the "does," which is a lived experience. This would lend itself quite well to a study of the lived experiences that cause the act in those specific circumstances. The second question seems to be a good question for an ethnography. The researcher is sure that something will happen, but does not know what is going to happen. The observational methodologies for an ethnography seem almost customer made for this situation.[2] Researchers are not regulated to one specific methodology; however, the first example could also be done as a case study, while the second example could be done as a QMS project. Researchers will have to identify what they want to do along with how they want to do it.

In an argumentative paper, an author wants to prove that something happens against the arguments of someone else. Different from exploratory papers where you have a hypothesis, in an argumentative paper you are telling people what is going to happen then seeking to support it. While the difference in thought is mostly contextual, the difference in appearance is quite substantial. Authors of argumentative papers very clearly tell readers what they are supposed to think, then support that command with facts and research that support the position. Case studies and QMS papers are very strong candidates for this type of writing as their ability to have laser focus can pinpoint the argument to the point it is difficult to disagree with. Ethnography and phenomenology are not as effective for argumentative papers as they tend to follow the flow of the research at a more organic level than CS and QMS.

Supportive research papers support the work of another. This is also called disciple work. Supportive research finds a position that the researcher believes is written by another author and does a similar experiment to show that the research is valid. While this is predominantly done in the hard sciences, there are instances of it in the humanities and the social sciences (Marx, Hegel, Keynes). Any form of qualitative research can be used to support the work of another author, but if you are repeating an ex-

---

2. Fetterman, *Infra*.

periment you do need to use the same methodology that the original author used. In these cases you follow in the first author's footsteps to prove that his or her work is more efficient than a rival's work.

Different authors tend to select different types of papers based on their own personal brand. Some people envision themselves as the consummate explorer; others see themselves as the defender of this position or that position. Still others see themselves as contrarians who will always be opposing the mainstream views, or followers who wish that the academy would accept the work of someone they admire. Whatever the case, knowing which of these styles you are going to write in can allow you to choose or eliminate different methodologies from contention. This can make your selection process easier, and help you keep your focus on getting your project done.

ANTICIPATED TYPE OF DATA

Some questions are so specific that only one type of data is available for them. When this is the case, you should allow your choice of methodology to be decided by the type of data that is available. Each type of data has at least one specific methodology that will prove to be effective, so it is important to consider the type of data collection that you are going to use for your project. Some methods of collection are:

1. Observation—The bread and butter of ethnography (though it can be used in other methodologies). Observation allows you to see and interpret what is going on with a group and to record as much detail as possible.
2. Book research—While all qualitative research methodologies require book research to some extent, QMS is dominated by book research. In book research you find the data of other authors and either support, decry, or synthesize what they have discovered.
3. Surveys—Although useful in both case study and in phenomenology, they can also be used in any qualitative methodology. Surveys let you ask specific questions and allow your participants to answer them on their own time.
4. Interviews—Although used in almost all qualitative research in some fashion, they are mainly used in case studies and phenomenology. Interviews give the researcher the freedom to ask focused questions to follow up on previous answers.
5. Mixed methods—These bring in data collection methods from all of the above categories to allow the researcher to get the maximum quantity of rich data possible. Sometimes the cost can be prohibitive, but if you can use mixed methods your data will provide you more to analyze.

This list is not exhaustive, but it can give you an idea of the main methods that will be used to collect data in your project. For a more robust list, look to Part VI: Data Collection. The rules of which collection strategies work best for which research methodologies are not hard and fast; however, when you step outside of what your tools are to be used for you will find that you are making more work for yourself.

METHOD AND STRUCTURE

Each type of qualitative research methodology is going to require you to approach that methodology in a different manner because, despite the insistence of quantitative researchers, all qualitative research methodologies are not the same. Each methodology requires a specific approach. In this primer section we look at some of the intricacies that differentiate between the four main types of qualitative research. For the purpose of brevity, qualitative meta-summary follows all but the last step of the qualitative meta-synthesis section.

An ethnography focuses the attention of the researchers on the details of the situation they are observing.[3] This allows the researchers to create their own set of richly detailed data that can then be used for analysis. The preferred research methodology for an ethnography is undoubtedly field research; however, this research should be augmented with book research.[4] If the possibility presents itself, then researchers should attempt to get surveys and interviews with the subjects (if relevant). Each additional data collection methodology will increase the depth of the data, thus allowing for more detailed analysis. In the analysis, researchers should choose a theoretical lens through which to examine the data, either emic or etic, in relation to the subject matter being viewed. This will allow researchers to present a detailed paper to the readership explaining the circumstances that answer the research question, thus supporting or disproving the hypothesis.

A case study focuses the attention of the researchers on the details of a specific case, either present or in the past.[5] This allows researchers to create a rich data set with information about all aspects of the case they are studying. A case study is more broad than an ethnography, as the ethnography looks at specific pieces within a case or phenomenon, while the case study looks at the entire case. The data collection for a case study should be interviews (if available) and surveys (if available), augmented by book research.[6] Observation can be an excellent tertiary data collection method, but

---

3. Emerson, *Infra.*
4. Id.
5. Stake, *Infra.*
6. George, *Infra.*

may not be practical in some cases. Analysis should be conducted by applying the data relevant to the research question through a theoretical lens, thus supporting or disproving the hypothesis.

A phenomenology looks at an even broader event than a case study. Phenomenologies look at the live experience of the participants or observers of a phenomenon.[7] The key data collection methods for a phenomenology are interviews and surveys, which should be augmented with book research on the phenomenon. Observations can be useful, but generally will only be available if the researcher observes the phenomenon as it happens. This can require planning by the researcher for a known future event. The data should be analyzed by looking at it nonjudgmentally through a theoretical lens. The goal of a researcher in a phenomenology is to not allow any of their own bias to cloud their interpretation of the events, thus giving the reader as pure as possible the participants' lived experience on the subject.[8] This data should then be used to answer the research question, thus supporting or disproving the hypothesis.

QMS looks that the data within a given field for similarities that can be brought together to form a synthesis. QMS allows the researcher to build new theory based upon what already exists in the field. This method allows for distillation of multiple studies into one concrete format. The data collection method of QMS is book research, which should be augmented by interviews and surveys to the authors being used when available.[9] Observation is impractical in QMS because the events generally have already occurred in the past. Long-term events can be viewed but the timestamp will be off so this is generally not recommended. QMS can be used either to answer a research question, thus supporting or disproving a hypothesis, or as part of the theoretical approach to build new theory on current data.

---

7. Moutakas, *Infra*.
8. *Id*.
9. Major, Claire Howell & Savin-Baden, Maggi (2010). *An Introduction to Qualitative Research Synthesis: Managing the Information Explosion in Social Science Research*. New York: Routledge.

CHECKLIST

- ❑ Why did you select qualitative methods?
- ❑ What is the goal of your research?
- ❑ What kind of research are you doing?
- ❑ What type of data do you anticipate?
- ❑ Will ethnography work for you?
- ❑ Will a case study work for you?
- ❑ Will phenomenology work for you?
- ❑ Will QMS work for you?

RECOMMENDED READING

Block, Gertrude (1999). Effective Legal Writing: For Law Students and Lawyers, 5th ed. New York: Foundation Press.

Druckman, Daniel (2005). Doing Research: Methods of Inquiry in Conflict Analysis. Thousand Oaks, CA: Sage.

Gibbs, Graham (2007). Analyzing Qualitative Data. Thousand Oaks, CA: Sage.

Riessman, Catherine Kohler (2008). Narrative Methods for the Human Sciences. Thousand Oaks, CA: Sage.

Willis, Jerry (2007). Foundations of Qualitative Research: Interpretive and Critical Approaches. Thousand Oaks, CA: Sage.

chapter 19
Ethnography

INTRODUCTION

Why should you select ethnography for your research methodology? What reason could you have to look into a culture, your own or another, compare and contrast that culture to your understandings, analyze the data you collect, then present it in a thick description that allows your research to be useful to the academy? Actually, there are many reasons to select ethnography. But first, let's look at what an ethnographic study entails and how you can use an ethnographic approach to fulfill the goals of your current project. Ethnographies have very specific uses in the academic world, and after you have completed this chapter you can make an educated decision whether ethnography fits your specific need.

First, an ethnography is the scientific study and description of the society, culture, practices, and actions of individual people, groups of people, or entire societies. This is a structured tool for the development of understanding of people in their native "habitat."[1] When you begin an ethnographic study, part of the process is leaving your comfort zone and entering into your subjects' world to see the differences and similarities from both your side and their side. As you build your ethnography, you will find that you are building a story of your subjects that goes beyond their understanding of their own culture and well beyond your preconceptions of their culture. Ethnographies attempt to describe sociological phenomenon as they actually are, avoiding the bias of one side or the other.

---

1. Ethnographies do not have to be in a native environment, they can look at developments that occur when people are outside their native environment.

This creates a scholarly record of the world as it was at a specific period of time, which can be a valuable addition to the historical and analytical record.

I like to look at ethnography as the process of exploring reality, beginning with as clear of a blank slate as possible. You should not enter into an ethnography with preconceptions of the subjects; the lens of an ethnography should be as pure and as basic as possible to ensure that you provide the least biased analysis of the subjects as possible. While many ethnographers do not subscribe to epoche as a tool to protect the validity of their writing, we highly recommend that you prepare yourself by looking at your biases before you enter into an ethnographic study. Your preconceptions, whether wrong or right, can taint your research and make it less valuable to the historic record.

Ethnography is a valuable tool in a qualitative researcher's tool belt. It is an exploratory methodology for discovering things about something that you know little about for the beginning research and a progressive method for experts to learn even more about a subject they have been studying for a lifetime. The key value of ethnography is that it can answer questions that you have not asked yet, or rather it can build datasets for hypotheses that themselves develop during the course of research. These are the answers we seek in doing an ethnography. Ethnography allows researchers to immerse themselves in a society, whether it is their own society or another society, and still remain methodologically "pure" in their analysis of reality as it stands.[2]

There are some drawbacks that a researcher should know before embarking on the process of writing an ethnographic paper. First of all, an ethnographic study cannot allow the researcher to speculate that the practices held within the observed group will be held by the society at large. Often beginning researchers attempt to make generalizations based on ethnographic research, but that is not the purpose of the data that you collect. A second problem is that researcher bias can be very dangerous to ethnographic studies. Misconceptions, whether preconceived or developed during the course of the project, can cause the researcher to miss information that may be relevant to the study. This can be countered by entering into the ethnographic study with as open a mind as possible, allowing yourself to develop data as broadly as possible to catch as many of the details of your situation as possible.

This chapter provides you an overview of the process for building an ethnographic research study. First, we are going to look at the landscape of the subject area, which includes the process of leaving your comfort zone and entering into a culture that may be alien to you. From this point we will then look at the process of taking field notes, the primary data collection method for an ethnography. Observations are not the only data collection methodology available to the ethnographer. We

---

2. The etic and emic relationships in an ethnography tend to mix but must be clearly defined in the paper.

SO YOU WANT TO WRITE A PAPER

will also look at how to do interviews and surveys in relation to an ethnographic study. In the fifth section we continue with a look at the analytical process that will be used during your ethnographic study. The analytics in this chapter are very simple and follow a hybrid QMS/ethnographic model. If you would like more details on purely ethnographic analytics, please look at the books in the recommended reading section at the end of the chapter. The final section of the chapter looks at the writing process for ethnography. The process is very simple and follows the writing process that has been covered in detail throughout this book. The fifth section of this chapter, therefore, is primarily to refresh your memory and stop you from forgetting any vital parts.

If you choose ethnography as your research methodology, then you have the ability to explore people, cultures, and societies at a depth that few other methodologies allow. Ethnography places you in the heart of your research subject group, going into their world to find out about them. Ethnography allows you to build or continue building a knowledge area in as specific or as broad of a paradigm as you choose. If your research question causes you to explore something, then ethnography may be the right methodology for you.

LANDSCAPE OF THE SUBJECT AREA

Before you enter into an ethnographic study, you need to realize that you are going to enter into a subject area that is alien to you (even in auto-ethnographies). You are putting away your reality, the safe and comfortable world that you have built for yourself and replacing it with a different reality, one that may not be as comfortable. This means that you have to first shed your reality and blend into the new reality to properly do your study. If you want to do an ethnographic study on the disposition of muslim communities in free Iraq toward Americans, wearing an "I Love New York" t-shirt where wearing cutoff jean-shorts and sitting on the front stoop of a mosque will likely get you noticed as an outsider rather than get you good data. To properly perform an ethnographic study you need to adopt the dress and mannerisms of the group you are studying as much as possible so your presence does not contaminate the research site and your appearance does not bias your subjects against you.[3]

This means that before you enter into an area that you must do some base research as to what the normal elements within the society are. If a society does not allow women to move around unac-

---

3. Some researchers argue that you cannot contaminate a site because a site is always fluctuating. This is a Eurocentric bias because the European derivative communities are among the most accepting of outside cultures (at least in the modern era); therefore, the speculation that all societies are like the European derivatives is a faulty realization. Sites can easily be contaminated by a researcher and a researcher should take all possible precautions not to contaminate their sites.

companied and you are a female researcher, then you should make an effort to find someone to go with you for the sake of appearance. Preparing for an ethnography can be a tricky endeavor as too little preparation risks you being exposed as a researcher and contaminating the data you collect, while too much research before you enter into the area can solidify biases and preconceptions about your research subjects to the point that you are simply there to "confirm" what you already "know." Find out the dress, the mannerisms, the sociocultural elements, and the daily habits of the group that you are trying to study, then use this information to blend into the group while still keeping an objective mind in relation to your research.

While doing an ethnographic study, realize that everything you record should be taken in context. (Because this is vitally important we will cover it again in the field notes section.) Without context, actions have no meaning. If you are not considering the environment in which your observations occur, then when you analyze your data you risk taking the actions of your subjects out of context and biasing the data. Therefore, all information that you record should be detailed in both contextual and temporal elements of the situation you are observing.

When performing your ethnography, you should decide quite early on whether you are performing your analysis from the emic or the etic perspective. An etic perspective looks at the research subject from the perspective of the researcher, both theoretical and social.[4] A majority of ethnographic studies in the social sciences end up being etic in nature because the predisposition to relate social and intellectual norms to your own personal frame of reference is difficult for many people to overcome. Emic studies view the collected data through the eyes of the people who are being observed.[5] Emic studies require the researcher to overcome their own personal bias and their own personal perspective to analyze the research subject(s) from their own viewpoint. Emic studies can also be difficult as you may be required to justify something of your research subjects that you find repugnant.

Another area of the contextual landscape that may be important is the significance of ritual within the society. Symbols and rituals in other societies can give meaning to actions that the uninitiated do not understand. One way to look at this phenomenon is akin to how we look at jargon within different fields in academia. In one field, the word "triangulation" may be rather meaningless. In most of the social sciences and humanities, triangulation is not commonly used in general research so it has no real significance. In mathematics and geography, triangulation has a very specific meaning, such as when you know the distance from two points to a common point you can identify the distance from the points of origin based on the relationship between the points of origin and the

---

4. *See* Fetterman, *Infra (See Recommended Reading).*
5. Emmerson, *Infra (See Recommended Reading).*

focal points (if math is not your strong point do not worry). In qualitative research, triangulation takes on another meaning entirely. Triangulation in qualitative research means that you confirm a premise by using multiple sources to confirm your finding. For instance, you find that a particular ritual within your research group seems to be a time of sadness for the participants. You can support this finding by identifying other instances of the ritual causing like effects. While this does not prove a finding it does confirm that it is valid within the given dataset.

Another part of the subject area landscape that should not be underestimated is the social diversity of the group that you are studying. Homogenous groups tend to lend themselves better to studies that relate to the cultural norms of a group, whereas heterogeneous studies lend themselves better to diversity and operational studies. Going into any research area and allowing the preconception that the group is either homogeneous or heterogeneous can be devastating to your research. Always allow your research (whether book or observation) to support your assumption that a group is homogeneous or heterogeneous before you allow that data to become part of your normative thought process.[6]

Beyond accepting the diversity, or lack thereof, within your research group, you should also withhold judgment on actions that are socially acceptable in the research group and/or ethically acceptable in your research discipline. Standing by while children are sold into slavery or suicide bombers are trained may be acceptable to your research group, but they are not ethically acceptable. If something that is a crime against humanity is observed during the course of your research, then you should report the incident to the proper authorities as soon as possible. While you have a duty to protect the identity of your subjects, you also have a duty to protect the people of the world in general against crimes against humanity.[7] You should always withhold your judgment whenever possible, but not at the expense of your ethics or morality.

The landscape of your subject area is going to be dominated by these things, so the goal of your ethnography is to navigate these landmarks so that your journey through the writing process will be as effective as possible. The goal is not to conquer these elements of the landscape, but to allow them to guide you through your ethnographic process. Each ritual, each exception to a seemingly untouchable cultural rule/taboo, each symbol that you find the meaning of becomes a datum of data within your dataset. The deeper you delve into your subject's sociocultural structure, the more you will be able to understand/compare their world to yours in your ethnographic paper.

---

6. Emmerson, *Infra*.
7. Leave the really dirty stuff to journalists, because their ethical codes are slightly more liberal.

FIELDNOTES (OBSERVATION)

Fieldnotes are the primary data collection method used in ethnographic research.[8] Fieldnotes are a systematic method of recording data while in the field for later use in research and analysis. The brilliant element of fieldnotes is that they can be adapted to the needs and skill sets of any researcher. As you develop your ethnographic style, your technique of collecting fieldnotes will also evolve. This allows you to become a more efficient researcher as you search for more and more data. The key, however, to taking good fieldnotes is that you follow the same pattern each time you make observations, thus allowing you to have comparable data when it comes time for the analysis.

An important factor to realize when you enter into the field to collect data is that you are never going to be able to collect every datum of data in every scenario. There are some things that you cannot see; there are some things that you will not understand; there are contextual elements that you will not have access to even if you spend years in the field. Good ethnographic fieldnotes consist of getting the most relevant data you can from an observational session and realizing that you will not be getting all of the possible data. For instance, you are observing the public dress of a group of people who are a cultural subset in the city of West Palm Beach, Florida. While you will be able to see the surface clothes that they are wearing, you will not be able to see the undergarments of the people (in most cases). As a researcher, you must realize this limitation of your research. The alternative is to go around asking people what undergarments they are wearing, which is a method covered in the interview/survey sections of this chapter. You can never get absolutely every datum of data out a situation by observation, because there are a number of things the human senses cannot detect and even more things that we cannot understand because of lack of context.

When you are in the field, you must realize that you are applying your reality onto subjects' lives. No matter how multicultural or educated in diversity you are, you are not the person you are observing; therefore, all your observations are going to be through your personal lens. This means that the more "raw" data you take down in comparison to subjective data, the better. Observations should be made on objective criteria as much as possible. If someone is picking up a glass and drinking, and you see all the movements and actions in this statement, then you can record that the person has picked up a glass and drank from it. However, if you do not see all the actions then you should say, "It appears as if subject X is picking up a glass and drinking from it." As you do not know everything that a person is doing or thinking, be very clear in your own notes to distinguish between what you know is happening and what appears to be happening.

---

8. *See* Fetterman, *Infra.*

Depending on your research question, your field notes should focus on the primary question type of your study. If you are researching "who" then concentrate your research on "who." If you are researching "what," then concentrate your research there. While it is true that the more details you collect in your research the more detailed your analysis can be, it is also true that if you are researching the patterns of garments and their meaning in the West Palm Beach community we talked about earlier, the tastes of the food will not be as relevant as other details you could be collecting. Always make your data collections as detailed as possible, but also make sure that you take the time to keep your data collection focused on the issue at hand. Without data on your specific topic, you will not have much of a paper.

When taking fieldnotes, all five senses and your "sixth" sense can come into play. For most of us, sight will be the primary sense that we use to collect data in a given situation. We are socially acclimatized to perceive our world through what we see—it is the nature of the way we are built both physically and mentally. During most field excursions, you will rely on your sight to be the primary carrier for data. Try to collect as much visual data in as much detail as possible. Rich data, which we cover in the next paragraph, will allow your reader to visualize what you are trying to present to them.

Hearing is the second sense that most people relate to research. While the sights may be the primary carrier of information to most people, sound will also play a major role in most ethnographic studies. Be careful to take detailed notes about the sounds that you hear that are relevant to your study. Oddly enough, the two senses that the human body seems to have the best ability to recall are taste and smell, so both should be included in your fieldnotes. Taste and smell can provide your reader with a mental stimulus that builds up recall for the data they are assimilating in your work. Touch is an interesting element in ethnographic studies. Touch can be a difficult bit of data to collect in a social sciences/humanities ethnography. If you go around groping your research subjects you will likely get expelled/fired. Touch can be useful when doing ethnographies of cultural items. "The cold granite rock face of the Slovakian Castle was rough to the touch but smooth enough that one could not climb it without the aid of significant climbing gear…" is a note that allows you to recall how the castle felt while you were observing it. This can be useful, especially when people may be using your research as a secondary source in similar cases for contrast and comparison (i.e., "The polished marble of the Roman Villa had a warm feeling even though the night air was chill, this stood in stark contrast to the coldness of the granite even in the warmest part of the day").

The final sense that you may use in ethnographic research is your "sixth" sense—that is, the feeling an area gives you. While this should be used sparingly in your writing, it can be quite useful in your fieldnotes. How the situation felt to you can inspire you to remember elements that created that feeling. "The small hut of the medicine man hung heavy with the smoke of an assortment of herbs that he kept adding to the fire, his skin glistened with sweat even though his face was covered with the white powder. The whole situation gave off the air that I was in a tribal village hundreds of years ago, even though the medicine man's shop was at the intersection of E 25th Avenue and 1st St." Later when you are going over your fieldnotes, the feeling of the situation may help inspire you to remember other features that added to the experience.

As you may have seen in the preceding paragraph, providing detailed descriptions from each of your senses helps you have better data for an ethnographic study. In ethnography this is called rich data. Rich data draws from all five senses to give the researcher, and later the reader, a more detailed experience of what the writer is trying to convey. For example, look at these sentences and ask yourself which one will be more useful in data compellation:

1. "The clerk at the gas station wore a black shirt and a company hat, he stood behind a glass partition." Or
2. "The clerk at the gas station, a Caucasian male who appeared to be in his 20s, wore a wrinkled black polo shirt with sweat stains, to **speculate** because he had been working a long shift, he also wore a brown ball cap with the red "Jiffy Gas" logo emblazoned on it, the "JG" easy to read against the brown background. He stood behind the partition, which was scratched and cracked from **apparent** abuse, in his smoky little cubical, which allowed the researcher to **speculate** that the "do not smoke sign" was more for the customers than the staff. The acrid smoke also **led me to believe** that it was not tobacco he was smoking."

Which note is better? I assume most of you selected the second note, because it has more detail and records relevant senses of the researcher (there is no taste here, or sound, and the feeling did not seem to be relevant). You also see that there are key words, put in bold for your convenience, to show the researcher when he/she was making a speculation and when he/she was making an observation. Detailed notes lead to detailed data, which in turn allows you to provide detailed analysis for your project.

The final recommendation for taking fieldnotes is to be as unobtrusive as possible. If you stand there writing in a notebook or speaking into a tape recorder, someone may speculate what you are doing and change his or her actions. In the modern world, taking notes on your cell phone can be effective; people will just assume you are texting. On the other hand, if you are in a developing country with primitive conditions surrounding you, writing with a pen and paper may be less obtrusive. Some ethnographers use other mediums to record their environments, including:

1. GPS navigation tools;
2. Computers;
3. Cameras;
4. Camcorders;
5. The Internet;[9] and
6. Hidden cameras (where legal).

The tools that you use will be dictated by the environment that you are in and the safety of using them. There are some areas of the world where you do not want to be using a brand new GoPro camera because you may get it stolen off of you. Use your judgment to balance the need to be unobtrusive and the need to collect as much data as possible.

Fieldnotes should be your primary data collection technique for an ethnographic study, but this does not mean that fieldnotes should stand alone as the only ethnographic data collection technique. Book research/journal research (Chapter 40), Interviews (Chapter 43, and later this chapter), and Surveys (Chapter 44, and later this chapter) are useful tools to triangulate the data you collect through observations. Rich data is vital to a good ethnography, but rich data alone cannot carry an academic research paper.[10] If you collect good fieldnotes, however, you will have an excellent starting point to develop your research plan and it will make your data analysis process much easier.

INTERVIEWS

Interviews are another tool that should be included in the tool bag of an ethnographer. An interview is a meeting where information is gathered. In an academic sense, an interview is a meeting where a researcher can gather information through asking a research subject(s) a series of questions or allow the research subject to tell a narrative story about the subject being researched. There are many types of interviews, many of which will be covered in Chapter 43: Interviews. However, in an ethnography there are specific elements that an interview should contain that are different from other interviews. In this chapter we are going to look at general interviewing and how to write questions for an ethnographic interview, narrative interviewing, and conducting group interviews. These are the primary interview types that most ethnographers will use (for a full list, check out the books in the recommended reading section at the end of the chapter).

---

9. Fetterman, David M. (2010). Ethnography: Step-by-Step, 3rd ed. Thousand Oaks, CA: Sage.
10. Emmerson, *Infra*.

In a general interview the researcher will ask questions to the subjects and the subjects will, if they are comfortable, respond to the questions. The difficulty in an ethnographic situation is that you are likely from a different culture than your research subject; therefore, your understanding of what is socially offensive and their understanding of socially offensive may differ. This offense may be something that goes both ways as their cultural norms may allow them to do things in the interview that you find offensive. Researchers must establish what their own tolerance for these situations is and have a contingency to remove themselves from an uncomfortable/unethical/dangerous situation. In a general interview, a researcher should ask open ended questions that leave the purview of the question open for the subject to interpret the question and answer it to the fullest extent possible. Such types of questions will allow the flow of information to be controlled by the subject, thus allowing for less researcher interference in the data stream. There are times when you may have to ask closed ended questions that require a yes/no (or other dyadic) answer. Such types of questions can allow you to bring a subject back on topic if the answers begin to wander.

Another type of question that researchers should familiarize themselves with are direct questions. Direct questions focus the attention of the research subject on a specific aspect of the topic being discussed. If, for instance, you are interviewing a survivor of a terrorist attack and the survivor is telling you about the moments before the bomb went off, but then glosses over the exact moment when the attacker walked into the room, you can then ask specific "who, what, where, and when" questions about the perpetrator. Direct questions allow you to garner more detailed data during the interview process to compare with your data from observations. Indirect questions are questions that allow your subjects to re-enter the answer that they had started to the open ended question before you asked the direct questions. These questions are mental placeholders: "What happened after the bomb went off" can bring a subject back to the same point in the story where the subject left off when you ask direct questions. One way to look at questioning is this: The open ended questions are a television show and the direct questions are the annoying actors who interrupt the show with story notes. The story notes are very informative but break up the flow of the answer. The indirect questions allow that flow to pick up where it was interrupted.

Leading questions are a type of questions that young and old researchers fall into the trap of using. A leading question is a question where the answer is suggested by the wording of the question. Some are actual questions: "Isn't it true that you were leaving the building when the terrorist entered the lobby?" Although this is phrased as a question the researcher has already determined the answer. This type of questioning can be very dangerous in high context cultures where people do not question authority, because it can cause a subject to agree with the researcher even if the researcher is not correct. Another type of leading question is where a researcher simply makes a statement and lets it hang as a question: "You did not know the terrorist?" These statements are even more likely to cause the subject to agree with the researcher rather than tell his or her own story.

Narrative interviewing is a form of interviewing that is based almost exclusively on the subject telling his or her story and the researcher only interrupting for directed questions when the subject approaches the research area. This form of interviewing is much broader than general interviews because the subject has control of where the interview goes, not the researcher. In narrative interviews the researcher is exploring the context in which the subject lives, sometimes not completely knowing where the story will go. People who research serial killers tend to use this format because once people begin to talk without interruption, and notice that a person is listening, they tend to go into more detail than if the researcher was asking wrought questions and jotting the answers down on a sheet of paper.[11] Researchers who use this style of interviewing tend to practice reflective listening, which is the practice of using follow-up questions to show the subject that you are listening. This format allows researchers to get very detailed and very deep data that may not otherwise be accessible due to a given situation.

Another type of interviews that can work well in an ethnographic situation is group interviews. A group interview, which is different from a focus group, is the same as a general interview, but instead of it being one on one the interview is with a group. Group interviews have the advantage of providing security for the subjects and allowing the memories of one group member to stimulate the memories of other group members. There are drawbacks to group interviews. Some people may be embarrassed to speak about the topic you are researching in a group setting. This can cause people to refrain from providing information that they would have otherwise provided. Additionally, a group can create "groupthink" false memories. If one person "remembers" a detail in a flawed way, the other members of the group can confirm that flaw to be part of the group. It is important for a researcher to weigh these benefits against the dangers when deciding whether to have a group interview or do interviews one on one.

Interviews may be a secondary tool in most ethnographic studies, but they are a valuable tool that can clarify or reinforce data that is gained through the observation process. When interviewing, always be careful to understand and appreciate the situation of your interviewee. In the serial killer example, if there are other bodies buried somewhere, bugging the subject about them will not likely get you anywhere. The criminal knows that the admission of more bodies will turn a sentence of life in prison into the death penalty. While some experts may disagree, beginning ethnographers should do their observations before the interviews so that the opinions of one person in the study group do not create preconceptions that taint the other data collection methodologies.[12]

---

11. Fetterman, *Infra.*
12. Emmerson, *Infra.*

SURVEYS

Surveys are another technique that can help solidify the data that you gather during your observations in an ethnography. A survey is a general examination of facts or opinions within a group of people by way of a survey medium. A survey medium is the method that you use to take a survey (see Chapter 44), such as paper surveys, digital surveys, or internet surveys. A survey can allow people, anonymously, to provide data to a researcher about a given subject. This can be useful in both high and low context societies as the anonymity prevents the subject from being singled out by either the researcher or the rest of the community.

Surveys are basically long-distance interviews; in the legal community they are generally called interrogatories. To create a survey, you create a list of questions that you want to ask your subjects, then provide them with the questionnaire, and when they are completed they can return the information to you. Surveys can be effective because they can be sent inexpensively over long distances and to multiple destinations, thus limiting the cost of your study. Additionally, surveys allow your subject to respond at their convenience, thus eliminating the problem of busy schedules preventing interviews. The problem that you may face with surveys in an ethnography, especially anonymous ones, is that you cannot do immediate follow-up questions with the subject.

The type of study you are doing dictates the type of questions that you use on a survey. Quantitative surveys tend to use questions that are either closed questions or questions where the subjects are required to answer on a scale. While these types of questions can be useful in an ethnographic study, they should also be supplemented by open questions that allow the participant to write as much detail as they desire. This will allow you to gather more rich data from your surveys for use in analysis. With surveys, as with interviews, be careful not to taint your data by using exceedingly leading questions. While you can suggest the direction you want the answer of the question to go towards, for example topic, you should be careful not to answer the question yourself in your question. With surveys neutral questions generally provide better answers. Neutral questions allow you to show your subjects that you care about what they believe and what they are talking about and that they are not just another number on a form.

ANALYSIS

Ethnographic analysis is similar to other qualitative analysis structures. You will gather your data, you will code your data, then you will use your thematic or theoretical lens to analyze the data in relation to your research question. There are, however, key terms that experts in the ethnographic field use, kind of the language that is required to get you into the club. In this section we are going to look at the processes in coding, how to triangulate your data, the use of cross referencing in relation to the literature on your subject, how to build graphics for your research (if necessary), and how to group your data into thematic clusters for the writing phase of the ethnography. By building this into your pattern of paper development you will be able to strengthen your research at each step of the writing process.

Coding is a simple procedure that is used across the spectrum of qualitative papers. Coding is the process of categorizing data to allow valid comparisons to be made between each individual datum. Without coding the data, the "analysis" would simply be a report on the data that the researcher collected during the course of the research. By coding and categorizing data, you allow like elements of the data to be compared to one another. My recommended method of coding is recursive frame analysis (RFA) based on the Chenail & Keeney work on the subject.[13] For a detailed listing of how to use RFA read Chapters 41 and 42, Recursive Frame Analysis and Legal Recursive Frame Analysis, respectively.

Triangulation is a process that you can use to ensure the reliability of your data. The process of triangulation is looking for complementary data from different sources that confirm (or sometimes deny) information gained in the primary research. For instance, if during your observation of a group of skateboarders in Berlin you notice that deference is given to the skateboarders who use long boards rather than normal skateboards, you could triangulate this data by looking at other research on skateboarders from other locations. This could show that the phenomenon that you are observing is unique to your research group in Berlin, or it could show that this is a common distinction between skateboarders. Another method you could use for triangulation is a secondary data collection method. After your observation, if you can secure an interview or interviews you could ask whether there is a hierarchy among different types of boards. Triangulation prevents the researcher from making assumptions based on one element of the study or a single research method and can give depth and reliability to the study.

During analysis of your collected data, and during secondary research in journals or books, make sure that you cross reference your data to similar information. Cross referencing is the process of denoting where similar information appears in another source. By cross referencing as you are doing your research, you will be able to find the data faster when you are writing about the subject,

---

13. Chenail, Ronald, Cynthia Somers & Joy Benjamin (2009). "A Recursive Frame Qualitative Analysis of MFT Progress Not Tipping Points." *Contemporary Family Therapy* 31:87-99; *See Also* Chenail, Ronald J. (1995). "Recursive Frame Analysis." *The Qualitative Report* 2:2.

and you will be able to cite additional sources that support the argument you are presenting. Cross referencing can be done through a process of writing sources on notecards with a categorical system for your project, or if you are tech savvy you can hyperlink different parts of your notes to websites or a document with the information in it.[14] Hyperlinking can also be done in the writing process, but check with your professor/publisher before complicating the document.

You can also begin to create charts when you are analyzing your data. As you compare the data you have acquired with currently held positions (if any) and theoretical lenses, you can have a chart that shows the comparison to your reader. Some writing formats encourage this, while others discourage it. This is another area where you should seek counsel with your professor/publisher before putting in the time it takes to create charts. If you are going to make charts, keep the following types in mind:

1. Flow charts allow the reader to follow a system of events from one point to another even if there are places where there are multiple options for the actor.
2. Simple charts are just data in chart form so that the information can be accessed quickly by the reader.
3. Graphs are visual representations of data that show differences by way of bars, lines, or colors of area.
4. Patterns, such as idea trees, can show readers how an idea developed. For instance, if the group you are studying has a tradition of wearing kilts, you could trace the development of the kilt through history and look at some of the other options that were not selected.

By displaying visual data you are breaking up the block text to give your reader something else to look at, but you are also breaking up the flow of the text for the prose of your report. The costs and benefits of visual data should be reviewed before the creation of a chart, graph, or pattern.

Once you have coded your data, built the reliability through triangulation, and have decided if you are using visual data or not, you can begin to organize your data into thematic clusters. While we will not go into the process here at the depth that it will be covered in Chapters 41 and 42, it is important to know what you are doing as you look at the writing process. A thematic cluster is a collection of datum that are related by theme whether or not they are temporally related. Something drawn from your observations could be related to something garnered from your interviews, which in turn could be related to something that you read in your pre-research. By clustering all

14. To insert a hyperlink in Word, simply right-click where you want the link, then select the source from the menu that you want to hyperlink to. You can also create a general documents with citations so you can track the sources that way, too.

of this information together, you have data that can be analyzed in a like fashion through your theoretical lens. How you do this will depend on the theory you choose and the discipline in which you are writing.

Analysis is what separates a common term paper from a valid academic paper. Term papers regurgitate data to show that you have learned the material; academic papers synthesize data to show that you have assimilated and can use the data. The latter is the greater goal for an academic. By doing a proper analysis, and outlining the analysis as you go, you will be able to build your paper much more efficiently. If you have to go back and forth between analyses and writing, you can often lose your flow and have the piece seem disjointed. Whereas a book can have a different "feel" in different areas because of the length, a paper should remain focused at all times so the prose should be similar the whole way through.

WRITING

When you are working your way through the specific writing processes in these books, by the time that you type your first words on the screen of the actual paper (or write them if you are doing it the traditional way) your paper should be pretty much finished. In this section we are going to look at the physical processes that are used to make writing as efficient and painless as possible for an author. We are going to start where we left off in the analysis section, grouping the data together into thematic clusters then categorizing those clusters by type. While this process is similar in other qualitative methodologies there are elements here that are specific to ethnography. Following the categorization we will look at outlining. Outlining will allow you to build your paper gradually, increasing the depth and character of the work. Further, a good outline allows you to keep your paper focused, if you find yourself drifting look over to the outline to bring yourself back to the topic. Finally, we will look at the final steps of your journey, the actual writing of the paper. Each chapter in this part (and Parts II and IV) offers the catharsis of writing your paper. Once the paper is written the only elements that remain are listed in Part VII: Style, which will help you put the bells and whistles on your paper that will get it noticed by professors and editors.

With ethnographies, two of the most important parts of your data are vivid descriptions and quotes. Vivid descriptions are the evolution of rich data into something usable in the writing process.[15] In a vivid description you take the rich data from your observations and interviews to combine them into a triangulated description of the ethnographic phenomenon that you are researching. Cluster-

---

15. Emerson, Fretz & Shaw (1995). Writing Ethnographic Fieldnotes, 2nd ed. Chicago: University of Chicago Press at 14.

ing data together this way allows you to turn it into the prose of your paper quickly and efficiently, all the while keeping the description as rich as possible. One of the goals of an ethnography is to transport the reader to the moment in time where you collected the data, so that they can learn about the discoveries you made during your journey to writer your paper.

Quotes are another excellent tool in ethnographic writing. Unlike quoting another source from a journal or a book, ethnographic quotes allow you to relay the data to the reader as it was given to you. This can have the effect of giving readers a sense of buy-in as they will be looking at the same data as you looked at when you were making your analysis. This takes the filter out of the process that can breed distrust between writer and reader. If readers have the same data as you have, then they will be able to analyze the data along with you as they read and if you did your job properly come to the same conclusion as you.

Once the clusters are categorized you can then move on to outlining. I cannot express enough how important outlining is if you are going to write an efficient paper. An outline is an organization of your thoughts in a way that allows you to integrate your data, thus allowing you to write your paper more efficiently. For most papers, you can start with a basic outline:

1. Introduction
2. Methodology
3. Data
4. Analysis
5. Conclusion/discussion

This should be the skeleton of your outline. Once this is built you can begin putting elements of what you are going to write about into your outline. For instance:

1. Introduction
   a. Hook
   b. What this paper is about
   c. Why it is important
   d. What your basic findings are
   e. Format of the paper

This is the basic level at which you should develop your outline, then go through each section of the paper (2, 3, 4, 5) and fill in the elements that you have used for an ethnography. The methodology section could look like this:

2. Methodology
    a. What methodology you are using and why
    b. What data collection methods you are using
    c. Description of data collection method 1
    d. Description of data collection method 2
    e. Description of data collection method 3
    f. Analytical method you used
    g. Any ethical considerations you have taken (subject protection, location protection)

Once you describe each of these elements you have a seven-paragraph methodology section that should satisfy any IRB or publisher as to how the study was conducted. Some of these categories can be broken down even further.

a. What methodology you are using and why
    1) Ethnography
    2) What is ethnography?
    3) Why are you selecting ethnography?
    4) What type of ethnography are you using (if using a specific type)?
    5) Why did you choose that specific type?

Each of these lines can be one sentence in your paragraph. If you go through each of your sections and outline them with this level of detail, then writing your paper will almost be an afterthought of the process where you fill in the prose with vivid descriptions of your subject and subject area.

Once you have outlined your project, the writing should be simple. All you need to do is take the fragmented ideas that are in the outline (all of which should be topically similar) and convert them into smooth reading prose. The goal when you reach the writing phase is not to build new information, because that should have been done in the analysis phase and in the outlining. In your writing phase you should be making the data that you are presenting as easy to understand for your readership as possible. This means that the sentences should be flowing, the transitions should be relevant, and the vivid descriptions should transport your readers to the location of your study in their mind. This is part of the process that takes practice, as writing has been deemphasized in our public school system in the United States; however, once you master this process (which is simple descriptive grammar), people in your field will want to read your writing.

If you have been reading this as you are going through your writing process, then your paper should be nearing completion. After the outline is done, writing becomes very simple. A 20-page paper should take no more than a few hours to write if you have gone through the outlining process for each chapter to the level of detail that we recommended. It may seem like the process is tedious, but when you practice it and get proficient at it, you will be able to write 10 to 20 pages very quickly (not including the research—a 10-year longitudinal study of adulthood rituals in sub-Saharan Africa will still take over 10 years). If you follow the process, you will have a paper. The next step is to review your paper, edit it, and look at the stylistic elements that are covered in Part VII.

CHECKLIST

- ❏ Have you done your pre-research?
- ❏ Have you selected your data collection method (observation, interviews, surveys, book research)?
- ❏ Have you selected a research subject/area?
- ❏ Have you examined the landscape of the subject area?
- ❏ What cultural considerations should you be aware of before entering this area?
- ❏ What tools should you use for your observation?
- ❏ When is the best time to start your observation?
- ❏ How long will your observation be?
- ❏ Will there be multiple sessions?
- ❏ Will you use interviews?
- ❏ Have you written your questions?
- ❏ Are the questions socially sensitive?
- ❏ Are your questions properly worded (open ended, direct, non-leading)?
- ❏ Are you using surveys?
- ❏ Are your surveys socially sensitive?
- ❏ Are you wording your questions properly?
- ❏ Have you coded your data?
- ❏ Have you triangulated your data?
- ❏ Will you be using visual data?
- ❏ Have you done your outline (vivid descriptions, quotes, thematic clusters)?
- ❏ Did you write your paper?

RECOMMENDED READING

Methodology

Atkinson, Paul, Coffey, Amanda, Delamont, Sara, Lofland, John, & Lofland, Lyn (Eds.) (2001). HANDBOOK OF ETHNOGRAPHY. Thousand Oaks, CA: Sage.

Banks, Marcus (2007). USING VISUAL DATA IN QUALITATIVE RESEARCH. Thousand Oaks, CA: Sage.

Chenail, Ronald J. (1995). "Recursive Frame Analysis." THE QUALITATIVE REPORT, Volume 2, Number 2 available at http://www.nova.edu/ssss/QR/QR2-2/rfa.html.

Druckman, Daniel (2005). DOING RESEARCH: METHODS OF INQUIRY FOR CONFLICT ANALYSIS. Thousand Oaks, CA: Sage.

Emerson, Robert M., Fretz, Rachel I., & Shaw, Linda L. (2011). Writing Ethnographic Fieldnotes, 2nd ed. Chicago: University of Chicago Press.

Fetterman, David M. (2010). ETHNOGRAPHY: STEP-BY-STEP, 3RD ED. Thousand Oaks, CA: Sage.

Keeney, Hillary & Keeney, Bradford (2012). "Recursive Frame Analysis: Reflections on the Development of a Qualitative Methodology." THE QUALITATIVE REPORT Volume 17 Number 2.

Rubin, Herbert J. & Rubin, Irene S. (2005). QUALITATIVE INTERVIEWING: THE ART OF HEARING DATA, 2ND ED. Thousand Oaks, CA: Sage.

chapter 20
Case Studies

INTRODUCTION

Case studies are a valuable tool in the tool kit of any writer. While case studies can be used in a quantitative sense, applying descriptive statistics to a specific case, the vast majority of case studies are focused in the qualitative methodologies. Generally, case studies are excluded as a means of establishing a theory, unless they are used in combination with other methodologies to support or demonstrate the validity of individual hypotheses of a theory. What matters at this particular moment is your case study and the reason that you chose case study as the methodology for your project. Case studies have a wide variety of uses and how you use the case study for your project will dictate a large part of the approach.

So what is a case study specifically? A case study is the process of recording or analyzing a specific person, group, situation, or phenomenon with an eye to present detailed records or histories of the actions and events related to the person, group, situation, or phenomenon. Long story short, you are attempting to take a specific incident and record and explain the actions that take place during the incident or that are related to the incident. Case studies are an excellent tool to do a detailed study of a specific incident. The more relevant details that you can provide for your case study, the more able you will be to show your reader the importance of your case. Like an ethnography, you may choose to transport your reader to the site of your incident (or person) with detailed analysis, or you may choose to approach your case as a person from a statistical background would and present a sterile and scientific explanation. The choice is yours and will largely be based on your discipline and who you are as a person.

To begin, we must define what a case is within this paradigm of case study writing. A case is a specific person, group, event, phenomenon, or occurrence that can be defined within a set of parameters that define the extent of the "case." Your case should have a beginning and an end, and while they may be influenced by eternal stimuli that occurred before the event began, or after the event ended, there are still temporal boundaries for the existence of the case. The ability to define the case specifically allows for the researcher to define the parameters of the study clearly and concisely for the project. If your case does not seem to have a defined set of parameters, then you may be looking at another type of study such as a phenomenology or even a grounded theory.

Once you have selected a case, you should take the time to define why your case is useful to your reader. This area of designing a case study allows for very broad interpretation of the use of the study. A study may be useful because the case that is being study has elements in common with other cases that have been occurring during a given time frame, thus the case studies can be compared to see if there is a trend. Case studies can also be useful because the case that is being studied is unique and only will occur once within a given time frame. The explanation of why the case is important is not as important as your ability to define some valid reason why the case is important.

Case studies are one of the most broadly used methodologies within the academic setting. After statistics, most disciplines in modern academia recognize case studies as a valuable methodology for building a greater understanding of the subject matter within a discipline. For instance, a biologist may study a specific case of leukemia to determine the progression of the disease, a study that can then later be used in conjunction with other case studies to show the difference between the way leukemia affects a variety of individuals. Case studies can also be used in the social sciences, to look at the specific group dynamics within a cult or other subcultural group. The versatility of case studies adds to the diversity of their uses, which makes case studies one of the primary research methodologies in academia today.

The first thing that you must do when you are contemplating a case study is select the topic that you are going to research. This involves the same process of distilling a concept down to a topic as that covered in Chapter 2: Break your concept into different areas of research, break those areas down into elements, and break those elements into topics. Once you have selected a topic for your research, then you are ready to start to look for a case related to your topic. This can be done easily by asking a research question, creating a hypothesis, and then finding a case that is related to your hypothesis. Very specific cases will be applicable to the hypothesis based on their nature; on the other hand, general cases will be useful because they can be applied generally across a larger cross section of the population. Where you want to publish and what you would like to publish about should guide your decision as to how specific of a case you should choose.

In this chapter we will walk you through the process of building a case study. In the first section we discuss how you can design a case study so that the procedure you will be using is working with you rather than working against you. Too often researchers enter into a case study without a proper plan and end up having the data collection process working against them. In the second section we look at methods to collect data for a case study. This collection practice follows along the same methods as other qualitative methodologies (specifically phenomenology), and will be augmented by the data collection chapters in Part VI. In the third section we look at data coding and how properly coded data will make your analysis easier. This leads into section four, analysis. The analysis of a case study focuses on applying a given theoretical lens (whether you create it or you find a relevant lens) to the data you have collected. In the fifth section we discuss how you can triangulate the data to build a stronger case for your findings; and in the final section we broaden the usefulness of case studies by looking at how similar case studies can be used to build a comparative model to look for trends within the topic area.

Case studies are a valuable tool that almost any researcher can use in the field. They have a simple analytical approach which is half hypothesis testing and half providing a historical explanation of the event. This diversity of method allows for a diversity of use that many other research methodologies cannot match. Novice researchers should be careful not to overextend their case study project. This can be done by trying to cover too large of a case; the more carefully you set your research boundaries the more focused you can be when you are doing your analysis. Doing a small case study extremely well is better than doing a large case study poorly.

DESIGNING YOUR CASE STUDY

Case study design is an oft underappreciated aspect of doing a successful academic case study. If you enter into a case study by simply gathering facts and reporting on them, then you are pursuing the case study from a journalistic approach rather than from an academic approach.[1] Case studies should have a hypothesis, even if you do not mention it in your final paper. It is the hypothesis that gives meaning to the case study, and the case that proves/disproves the hypothesis. By properly designing a case study, researchers can develop their study into a type of social experiment that they are using to build the knowledge of the discipline or field.

When you are designing a case study one of the first questions that you must ask is what type of case you have. Different cases need to be approached differently. While you can go into areas of Ferguson,

1. And end up with a case report.

Missouri, to interview victims of the recent violence in relative safety, a case study into the marital lives of a specific group of terrorists in Kashmir would not be a study that you should be doing by direct interviews (unless you can find some way to safely interview spouses of terrorists). The type of case that you choose will dictate a large part of how you have to approach the research for your project. Once you determine the main research methodology, then you will be able to integrate other data collection methodologies to augment your research and give your readers rich descriptions.

One of the main types of case studies that are done in most fields are historical case studies. In a historical case study you select a specific event that you will examine and attempt to bring new features to light or describe in a way that supports a selected theory. Historical case studies have a goal of expanding the knowledge of the academy and a specific field in relation to a specific event. If you are a botanist and you choose the Civil War as a topic for your discussion, you may elect to put forward a theory that the lack of demand for specific southern crops during the conflict reduced the grafting techniques used in evolution of specific species. This would use data that is collected to show that there was a decline in the evolutionary progress of your specific plant. Other projects could attempt to prove that a famous event happened at a location other than where it was thought to have happened, such as the shooting site of Bonnie and Clyde which could be over 100 yards to the north or south of where it is currently speculated to be.

Another type of case study takes the time to look at specific current events. This method is similar to looking at historical cases; however, in this format you can look at the developments currently occurring in a specific situation and relate those events to a theoretical perspective that explains the phenomenon in the event. This is not a phenomenology because you are not studying the lived experiences of the participants in the event. Current event case studies allow for the academy to have more direct understandings of the way things actually occurred, rather than the politicized descriptions presented by mainstream periodicals. They are also effective as a means of developing longitudinal studies looking at the developments within the aggregate of similar current event case studies.

Case studies that look at a specific element of a phenomenon are also common types of case studies, but sometimes these case studies are confused with phenomenologies. A phenomenology looks at the lived experiences of the people who lived through a phenomenon through an *emic* point of view; however, a case study will generally look at the factual developments of the phenomenon from an *etic* point of view. Sometimes it is even effective to do parallel studies of a case study and a phenomenology on a specific instance since you will be collecting data in the same area anyway. Case studies that deal with parts of a phenomenon should always take great care to remain ideologically "pure" to keep from having an ill thought-out hybrid methodology in an otherwise well-designed paper.

My favorite types of case studies to read are those designed to correct a misconception in history. The Travel Channel, at the time of this writing, has an excellent show called *Expedition Unknown* that does corrective case studies about some of history's greatest mysteries. The basic idea behind corrective case studies is that much of what you are taught in high school is false, either by mistake or by propaganda. This means that there are hundreds of topics that can be explored to find out if they are actually true. Did Columbus discover America? What about the Vikings or the Jewish people? How about the Native Americans, or the skeletons that were found that predate the Native American migration by hundreds of years? Who is right and who is wrong? Case studies can make arguments for each of these "discoverers" but corrective case studies look specifically for the truth.

Beyond the conceptual type of case study, there are "academic" types, which are simply clarifications of form. These styles of case study are:

1. Explanatory—This type of case study is used to answer a question between causal links. If, for instance, polar bears move south during the cooler months, you could use the actions of a polar bear or a small group of polar bears to explain the format of this migration.
2. Exploratory—This type of case study looks at what happens when specific stimuli are entered into a given situation. This is the common type of case study that is used in laboratory methods.
3. Multiple Case/Comparative—In this form, a researcher looks at multiple cases within the same genre and compares/contrasts them to look for differences in the cause/effect matrix.
4. Intrinsic—This is a simple study of a case, this does not build theory or build understanding of "abstract or generic" phenomenon.[2] This is the type of case study used if you want to understand a specific phenomenon from the perspective on an actor (similar to a phenomenology).
5. Collective—Similar to multiple case studies, but done by several actors over a course of time, then compiled by a researcher (using a method similar to QMS). [3]

When writing the methodology of your paper you should note which type of case study you are doing, and define the specific type for the convenience of the reader. This gives your writing more body and helps the reader better understand the method that you have used.

After you find a type of case study that you want to do for your project, you should take the time to look to see where the data is. While most of us would like to do an onsite study for six years in Hawaii, if we are studying the day-to-day experiences of survivors of the Rwandan genocide, Hawaii

2. Stake, Robert E. (1995). THE ART OF CASE STUDY RESEARCH. Thousand Oaks, CA: Sage.
3. *Id.*

may not be the place to do our research. To be a proper researcher, we oft have to acknowledge that the first source of research for any project will be in the library of our local university. University libraries may not have all the data we need to do a proper study, but they can help us find where we should look for data. Then once we have a location, we need to look at how were are going to access the data.

One of the biggest challenges academics find to their research projects is the search for research funding. Gone are the days where a university would allow a scholar to do research there, with room and board, if they teach a class a year. If you want to be a resident at a university and get paid enough to cover your basic living expenses (not to mention your research expenses) you will likely have to teach at least three (maybe four or five) classes a semester. Grants can be an effective way to find research funding, but you are competing with several hundred people for most grants. Endowments, trust funds, even private companies will sponsor researchers, but you have to take the time to find the ones who have money to give and you will also have to take the time to apply for the money. Accessing data is often much harder than simply knowing where it is; other than book research, most research is going to cost you dearly in both time and money.

Once you find a source for your data and a source of funding, you should also take the time to understand how much data you will need. With a quantitative study, you can do analysis of the population you are studying and find the right number of surveys or interviews to have a reasonable margin of error; however, with a case study you will need to reach a point of saturation. Saturation is the point where no new data within the set boundaries of your study appear to be new. This is why it is vitally important to set concrete boundaries for your case study, if you do not you may never reach the point of saturation where you can show your data's reliability.

Finally, you need to ask yourself the question of where and how you are going to write your study. You know you are going to write X type of case study, but what analytical tools are you going to use, where will you find office space for the time you need to collect your data, code your data, analyze your data, and then write and edit an academic quality paper? These are all questions that you need to ask yourself as you begin designing your study. Grant agencies will want to know this information, and so will universities. While you are always able to change your plans as the project develops, ensure that you have a plan at the beginning of the process. This will make you appear more professional and it will show others who are looking at the development of your work that you know what you are doing.

COLLECTING YOUR DATA

Where you accumulate your data can be just as important as what type of data you collect; therefore, your method, location, and recording methodologies are very important factors for a researcher designing a case study project. In this section we take a brief look at effective research tools that can be used in a case study. If you select any of the methods in this section, please look to Part VI for a more detailed explanation of how to collect data using a given technique.[4] This section also looks at recording tools that can make you a more effective researcher when working on a case study. How you record your data joins what data you record and where you record the data as the three key issues of data collection in a case study project.

As with any type of academic writing, the tools you use for your writing are a key element of how successfully you will capture the data you need for your project. That being said, there are several tools that any case study researchers need to have at the ready while they are planning their data collection. These tools are:

1. Pen and paper—Even in the digital age, having a pen and paper constantly available to write down findings or ideas is vital. By the time you pull out your cell phone or tablet and open *One Note* the idea may have slipped away. In any writing style you should always have a pen and paper handy.
2. Digital drop box—Since we are in the digital age, printing out dozens of journal articles that you may use one page of is not very conscientious of the environment; therefore, environmentally conservative authors can now use a digital drop box to store articles they intend to harvest data from, thus keeping printing costs down and helping the environment.
3. Tape recorder (hard tape or digital)—Case studies shine when the researcher can get interviews from people who were there for the event or interviews of people who have researched the topic for a long period of time. If your interview subject will allow it, always have a tape recorder available so you can have a full transcript of the interview.
4. Camera—A regular still camera is an effective tool for doing field research. You can photograph a page of a book that is in a reserve collection (though you should ask permission first) or you can take pictures of the site where the event happened. Pictures can then be incorporated into your article (especially if you are submitting to a digital journal) or they can be reserved to remind you of things that you saw on site. (If using digital, back up photos on digital drop box.)

---

4. Part VI: Data Collections includes Chapters 39 through 48.

5. Video camera—Using a video camera combines the benefits of a tape recorder and a camera into one. While the video will not likely make an appearance in your final project, it can be useful to have video of the site for presentations at conferences on your paper. (Remember, you should always try to get as much out of a paper as possible. If using a digital video camera, back up data on digital drop box.)

6. Extra surveys—If you believe that you are going to get 100 people who are willing to take your survey, then take 200 surveys. People will mess up and want new ones or there may be more people available than you expect. You save a lot of paper with a digital drop box, so print a few more sheets so you do not miss valuable data.

Researchers must have these basic tools in their collection. Even inexpensive versions of these tools can be lifesavers in the field.

Once you have your tools ready, it is time to begin your research. The first area where a case study researcher should start is in the library (or if you have access to university archives from your computer that will work, too). Book and journal research are the first tools that you should employ in your case study research. At this point in the process it is assumed that you have done your pre-research and know whether anyone else has researched the topic in relation to the theory that you are using. We also assume that you are doing new research. Now you take the time to use bullion searches to find as much data on your subject as plausible until you reach a point of saturation. If you are using a digital drop box and you find an article or book that has something related to your topic, then save it to your drop box and note the page number on your pad so you can find it easily. Also take time to note the searches that you used and what journals and books you found data in to preserve a valid research trail. Huge volumes of data are not necessary for a good case study; case studies are an area where quality far exceeds the value of quantity.

Site visits are the second most effective method for doing case study research. While visiting the site will give you a unique perspective on what happened at the event (hopefully), it also will put you at "ground zero" for your event. This will likely put you in a position where you can find people for interviews or surveys who actually lived through your event. If your event is historical, a site visit may give you access to a local historical society that keeps records on all the research done on the event. While this puts you into a secondary "book research mode" it generally gives you access to documents and artifacts that are not available anywhere else. A second type of site you may want to visit is any museum that houses artifacts from the event. The more well known the event, the larger a museum you may have to visit. If you do visit a museum, be sure to ask the curator about any other articles that are salient to the event you are researching, and if so whether you can see/photograph them for your research. Always be courteous to a curator, even if the answer is no.

If the event you are studying is an event in the future and you know when it is going to happen, then you may have the opportunity to observe the event as it unfolds. In this case you will want to take notes and record the data any way that you can—notepad, multiple cameras, multiple video angles, possible audio recordings (systematic, radiation, or other scientific measurement criteria). The more data you collect at the event, the more data you can archive and analyze. If you are doing research for the benefit of the academy, then you should try to record as much rich data as possible, even if it does not relate to your topic. The data you collect can then be archived for future research on the event, possibly even in another field so that the event can be better understood from multiple viewpoints.

Surveys and interviews are the two hallmark techniques for collecting data for a case study, but they are the techniques that should be implemented last in case study research. The final research tool status is not because they are less important but rather because they are more important. Before you form your questions for your interviews or surveys you want to have as much data as possible so that you can write intelligent questions. Your participants are giving up their time and sometimes their anonymities for your study; you owe it to them to have well thought out concise questions for them to answer. Further, the better your questions are the richer the data will be. Also remember that surveys and interviews are a privilege for you, not them, so respect your subjects.

DATA CODING

Data coding in a case study is vitally important. In this section we will look at three coding methodologies that can be used in relation to case study research. The first methodology is thematic coding, which is the standard coding methodology used in the field. The second coding methodology that we use is topical coding, which is similar to thematic coding but with a few marked differences. The third methodology, the method that we recommend for most case study papers, is recursive frame analysis (RFA), which will be looked at briefly here and in great detail in Chapter 41.[5] Using a standard coding method will allow you to create a robust research trail, thus allowing IRBs and other researchers to follow in your footsteps to validate your findings or to build upon your findings.

Generally, thematic coding is seen as "a form of qualitative analysis which involves recording or identifying passages of text or images that are linked to a common theme or idea allowing you to index the text into categories and therefore establish a framework of thematic ideas about it."[6] For

---

5. *See* Chapter 41.
6. Betterevaluation.com (2015). Thematic Coding. Available at http://betterevaluation.org/evaluation-options/thematiccoding (February 8, 2015).

this book we are going to go a step further in defining thematic coding as a coding methodology that allows researchers to identify elements of their research (text, interviews, surveys, photos, etc.) into thematic categories thus allowing the researcher to establish a framework into which additional ideas can be coded and categorized. The change between definitions is notably minimal; however, extending the ability to use thematic coding beyond text research is incredibly valuable for in-depth qualitative researchers. To organize an item by thematic coding, you look for similarities in ideas, then place those things that are similar together and those that are different apart. Then you take the things that are different and go through the process again, making ever smaller and smaller piles of different data until you have all of your data categorized into a theme. At this point any additional data can be placed in the category it is similar to, or if the data is wholly different it can be given its own category. Once all of your data is coded thematically, you are ready to analyze it based on your hypothesis or theory.

Topical coding is a more basic form of coding where you divide the data by topic rather than by theme. Topical coding allows the researcher more freedom in determining how broad or how narrow the topics will be.[7] During the course of the coding process the researcher also has the ability to change the parameters of a topic, thus entering more data or removing data from the category. This is a good method for beginning researchers as it gives them more control over the categorizations and prevents the data from becoming overwhelming. Once you have your data separated into distinct topics, you are then ready to analyze your data based on your theory or hypothesis.

The recommended method in this book for data coding is recursive frame analysis. RFA is the process of breaking data down into contextual elements, which is similar to thematic or topical coding; however, RFA has a structured framework that beginning researchers can follow to organize their coded data.[8] Though we cover this in detail in Chapter 49, the basic gist of RFA is that you take the contextual groups and sort them by galleries, then sort these thematic groups again by topic (wings). At this point you should have a very good structure for analysis, but RFA does leave you the option of sorting the topical groups again by theme (and this process can continue back and forth until you have reassembled the data into a structural framework you are ready to work with).[9] RFA tends to be easier for most first-time researchers, and even some longtime researchers, because it gives you a definite structure into which you can apply all of your data.

A dangerous mistake that many first-time researchers make is not coding their data. If you do not code your data, you are wondering through your journey to write a paper without knowing the lay

---

7. *See* Stake *Supra.*
8. Ronald Chenail (1997). Recursive Frame Analysis. The Qualitative Report.
9. *Id.*

of the land. Your coded data becomes a map that you can use in your analysis to know when the right time to apply the theory is, and when you have the luxury of adding more data to improve the reader's experience. Well-coded data is easy to write in your data section and therefore you will have a robust data section to analyze in your analysis section. Without coded data, the data can appear random and can be difficult to apply reasonable theories to. If you want to be a great writer, always take the time to code your data.

DATA ANALYSIS

The analysis is the bread and butter of any case study. Without the analysis your paper is simply a report on what happened in your event. BEWARE, some academic authors and some professors are willing to accept case reports as case studies, but they are simply reports. For a paper to be a true case study it has to have some analysis in relation to a hypothesis or a theory.[10] Because you are developing writers (or even established writers) do not get into the habit of writing reports and calling them case studies—this dilutes your field and makes it difficult for new students to understand the differences between case studies and case reports.

In your analysis section, you should state your hypothesis or your theory (even if you stated it elsewhere in your paper). Letting your readers know what your hypothesis is can give them the mental framework they need to understand how your data (which they likely just read) applies to your hypothesis or theory. You can either enter your theory as the first sentence of your analysis section, then have the topic sentence for the first paragraph follow it, building your data into your theory, or you can use the first paragraph of your analysis to state and explain your hypothesis. This is the preferred method of this book because it allows your position to be reaffirmed in your readers' mind before they begin to read the actual analysis.

If you are using a hypothesis, then you should explain to your reader what theory you are basing your hypothesis on. Some authors choose to ignore this phase, but that is lazy writing. If you are doing your first paragraph as an explanatory paragraph for your hypothesis, then you should take the time to explain how it applies under the theory you have chosen.[11] This is a point where some writers who are not following the pattern this book has laid out realize that they do not have a hy-

---

10. George, Alexander L. & Andrew Bennett (2005). Case Studies and Theory Development in the Social Sciences. London: BCSIA.

11. As you become a more accomplished writer, you will find that you fall more into specific paradigms, rather than just general theory. Too often, researchers try to make everyone happy by writing as a generalist; do not fall into this trap! If people do not like your theoretical paradigm that is not your problem, if you try to cater to them and write something that you do not believe in you will have a more difficult time defending your work.

pothesis or a theory. If this is the case, then you are writing a case report, not a case study. If you want to convert your case report into a case study, then you should take the time to find a theory that explains what you have recorded. You can also create a hypothesis if there is need for one in your case study (see Chapter 4).

The next step in data analysis is to take elements of your data and apply them to the theory that you are exposing, then use them to support or discredit your hypothesis. There are several ways to do this; however, one of the simplest ways is to take a contextual, thematic, or topical group and show how the data in that group supports the theory. If you are using a higher level group (thematic or topical), then you can use the component elements from the contextual coding as supporting elements of your group's structure. This allows your coded data to reinforce itself as it builds support for your chosen theory.

When you are doing your analysis, one area that is often overlooked by some researchers is that your data is not guaranteed to support your hypothesis. Some people try to force the data to be supportive (whether through legitimate or illegitimate ways). This is bad research methodology. Even if the data does not support the hypothesis, that does not mean that it is a bad project. A negative result can still contribute to the academic knowledge of the subject. If you find yourself in a situation where the data does not support the hypothesis, report on it honestly. This will gain you a reputation that you are more interested in good research methods than in personal pride.

TRIANGULATION

One of the hallmarks of a good qualitative study is triangulation of the data you collect and the use of triangulation to confirm the soundness of your analytical method. If you researched your data to the point of saturation, then triangulating the data should not be hard. Generally, you will want to have at least two instances of observation/interview/survey data that support an assertion you are making. Whereas in an ethnography, some events will only happen once during your observation period (although you can augment them with book research), in a case study you should try to find other grounded examples of what you are proposing. This is the process of triangulation.

The process of triangulation is looking for complementary data from different sources that confirms (or sometimes denies) information gained in the primary research source. Basically, this means that you want to confirm your observation or collected data with another source to increase the reliability of the data collected. If you see something happen, it can just be a fluke that it happened to happen while you happened to be there; however, if you can confirm the observation with several interviews and possibly even some historical book research, then it may be that your data was not a one-time occurrence. Triangulation of qualitative data is the mark of a developed researcher; novices see something happen once then write on it without confirming why it happened or what variables affected it. This type of "shoot from the hip" research gives qualitative research a bad name. Strong researchers will take the time to confirm their research through the process of triangulation.

The process is very simple. You have fact A. Fact A states, "When I saw the leader of the group (code name "el Hefe") step into the room I noticed that all the male members of the group took a step forward, almost like a stumble." Now this observation is interesting, and if you are doing a historical ethnography, then it is excellent rich data; however, if you are doing an exploratory case study, this observation proves nothing. To triangulate the data you may want to interview two or three members of the group who made the stumbling step forward, which can confirm or deny your observation that this is significant. You can also send surveys to other researchers who have observed this group to see if they saw the same effect. Finally, you can look to journal articles for book research on this group to see if past researchers have noticed the same effect. Ideally, all of the secondary research you do will confirm your observation. If two of the three confirm it, and none deny it, then you can still go forward with it. If only one of your secondary sources confirms your observation, or one of the secondary sources challenges your observation, you can still put your observation in your project, but should note to the reader that this was not triangulated or that there is some argument about the meaning of the observation. All main datum that you use for your project should be triangulated (if possible).

Triangulation is one of those monotonous elements of writing that many people try to skip over; however, this can leave research open to critique and other problems. If you are going to be a successful writer, you should take the few hours that are needed to triangulate your data. Each datum that you triangulate will strengthen the reliability of your paper and help you ensure that your research is as cutting edge as possible in regard to your subject matter. Further, good triangulation makes for good speeches at conferences, and most researchers tend to believe presenters who have several sources for each fact more so than those who rely on simple observation alone.

COMPARISONS

One of the major criticisms of qualitative research is that the data collected is not transferable due to the small sample sizes or the subject matter of the study. In most qualitative methodologies this is true that non-transferability is an issue; however, in case study (and to a greater extent QMS) there is the opportunity for the study to be transferable. The transferability of the study is highly dependant on how deep into the case you go and whether the information is something that is related to a larger population, another population, or another time period among the population you are studying. This is a decision that researchers must make as they are doing their study: "Does the data I have collected apply to any other group/time other than the one I am studying?" If it does, then you as the researcher have the added burden of showing how it is transferable.

If you decide that your study is transferable, then the first step that you should take is to see if other researchers have looked at similar topics. If you did your pre-research as recommended, then you should already have a good idea of whether this is the case. The reason that you want to know about other research in similar areas is because those research studies may be supporting/competing data for your study. Supporting data increases the likelihood that your study can be transferable, while competing data can show that the transferability is limited. The more similar studies you find the better choices you can make on whether your findings are transferable and if they are what the scope of that transferability may be.

The theoretical paradigm, or theoretical macro-paradigm, that you use and that the other authors use may also be an issue as to the transferability of your study to other groups/times. If your study is done through a positivist perspective and the complementary study is done through a relativist perspective, then the integration of the two studies may be very difficult. There is a silver lining to this situation; however, if you can show complementary elements from two competing theoretical macro-paradigms then you will have strong support that your study is transferable across a broad cross section of the group(s) that you are studying.

Another holy grail of case studies is if you can find a trend that has not been exploited throughout the similar case studies. If your research continues as an unnoticed trend, then you may have the opportunity to demonstrate the trend and build upon your personal brand. Even if the trend has been noticed before, you can use your research as a continuation of the trend to give your study added validity and credibility in the field. Trends are the ideas the transcend the limits of general qualitative research, to demonstrate the trend you may even drop into a hybrid format where you use limited statistics to show a descriptive analysis of your findings in relation to the findings of others in the field. If you find a trend between your research and other research in the field, then you may be starting to evolve your hypothesis into the beginnings of a strong academic theory.

CHECKLIST

- ❑ Is case study the right methodology for you?
- ❑ Why?
- ❑ What type of case do you have?
- ❑ Where is the data?
- ❑ Can you afford to get to the data?
- ❑ How much data do you need?
- ❑ What research methods will give you the richest data?
- ❑ How can you augment that data with other research methodologies?
- ❑ What coding method are you going to use?
- ❑ Why?
- ❑ What is your theory?
- ❑ What is your hypothesis?
- ❑ Have you compared elements of your data to your theory/hypothesis?
- ❑ Did you triangulate the data?
- ❑ How many times did you triangulate the data?
- ❑ Is your study transferable?
- ❑ Are their similar studies?
- ❑ Is there a known trend?
- ❑ Is there an unknown trend?
- ❑ Does your research support or discredit the trend?

RECOMMENDED READING

Flick, Uwe (2007). Managing Quality in Qualitative Research. Thousand Oaks, CA: Sage.

George, Alexander L. & Andrew Bennett (2005). Case Studies and Theory Development in the Social Sciences. Cambridge, MA: MIT Press.

Gibbs, Graham (2007). Analyzing Qualitative Data. Thousand Oaks, CA: Sage.

Stake, Robert E. (1995). The Art of Case Study Research. Thousand Oaks, CA: Sage.

Willis, Jerry W. (2007). Foundations of Qualitative Research: Interpretive and Critical Approaches. Thousand Oaks, CA: Sage.

chapter 21
Phenomenology

INTRODUCTION

Phenomenology is the reporting of the lived experiences of an individual or group who shared an experience or common experience of a phenomenon. Deriving from the Greek, meaning "logic of that which appears," phenomenologies are a researcher's way of finding the emic meaning ascribed to an event by a group of people from an etic standpoint. With very rare exceptions (genetic phenomenology) you will be an outsider from the group in relation to the event that you wish to study; therefore, the phenomenological family of methods provides you a way to surrogate the viewpoint of the individual or group that experiences an event to a larger audience. Phenomenology is an exercise in removing your meaning from the study and applying what the subjects believed and experienced to a theoretical or hypothetical framework. A good phenomenology not only takes the reader to the phenomenon that is being discussed, but also allows the reader to see the phenomenon through the eyes of those who lived it.

Phenomenology is one of the most complex groups of qualitative research methodologies if for no other reason than the number of phenomenological methodologies that are available for the researcher to choose from. In this chapter we discuss eight different methods of phenomenological inquiry beyond the basic "generic" phenomenology that we are covering in depth for use. Those of you who wish to make phenomenology your career's primary method of inquiry would do well to seek out a mentor who espouses a particular phenomenological type and learn a specific phenomenological method. This will focus you in a niche but it will help you gain notoriety in the field as well.

Realistic phenomenologies are phenomenologies that approach the research project looking for information that crosses cultural and sociological boundaries and is common within all human socioeconomic groups. Realistic phenomenologies look at matters that seem to be constant within all spheres of societal evolution, such as religion, traditions, ethics, philosophical norms, gender roles, and so on. Realistic phenomenology has the distinction of focusing the readers' view on the commonality of the human condition. Even when the topic of discussion is something alien to the reader, the author frames it in a macro-frame that makes it, in some way, relatable to the reader as common with something from his or her own life.

Constitutive phenomenology "suspends pregiven status of conscious life as something that exists in the world and is preformed in order to secure the ultimate intersubjective grounding for the world and the positive sciences…"[1] Based on Husserl's work from the 1910s, constitutive phenomenology deconstructs those truisms that we have accepted into our lives and reconstitutes them as axioms that transcend the bounds of disciplinary science. Almost a foundational sort of QMS procedure, constitutive phenomenology can be effective when dealing with macro-level ideas that are caught in interdisciplinary limbo. By deconstructing the "truths" that individual disciplines have constituted as "articles of faith," constitutive phenomenology can allow the researcher to create a universal language in the microcosm of his or her macro-level research.

Existential phenomenology strives to go beyond the physical realities of the world and examines the meta-physical and existential elements of culture and society. Based on authors such as Heidegger, Kyoshi, and Shuzou, existential phenomenology attempts to support and destroy hypotheses based on "why" rather than "who, what, where, when, and how."[2] As such, it is highly useful as a bridging tool between qualitative research and theoretical research that deals with the question of why. Addressing topics such as conflict, beliefs on death, beliefs on the meaning of life, and other questions that each individual generally answers for themselves, it can be said that existential phenomenology looks at those things beyond this life which permeate into the ether.

Hermeneutical phenomenology is the common form of phenomenology used in the academy today. Hermeneutical phenomenology is based on the idea that all elements of human existence are interpretive, thus placing this methodology firmly within the relativist macro-school of academic reasoning. Hermeneutical phenomenology looks at the world as you would if you were the reflection in the mirror; your reality is not important, only the reality of those on the other side of the looking glass. This approach is a double-edged blade. On one side, hermeneutical research can

1. Linsenmayer, Mark (2011). "Types and Scope of Phenomenology," THE PARTIALLY EXAMINED LIFE. At http://www.partiallyexaminedlife.com/2011/01/21/the-types-and-scope-of-phenomenology/.
2. *Id.*

allow the researcher to discard the bonds of preexisting bias and belief to focus completely on the meaning of what they are collecting from individuals who observed the phenomenon. On the other side, hermeneutical phenomenology can quickly discard reality for a farce perpetuated upon the researcher (who is an outsider) to improve the image of people being observed. Tyrants, dictators, and slave traders throughout history have preyed on the hermeneutical approach (before it was even named) for centuries, trusting the researcher to become enamored with the perspective presented by the subjects to a point where they ignore reality and write academic propaganda for some of the worst people in history. Examples can be seen in "Hitler will never attach the UK/Russia," "The Nazis are an effective society who could not be doing the human rights abuses claimed by displaced Jews," or even "Islamic terror is not their fault; it is the fault of the United States." All of these ridiculous positions are created through poor hermeneutical research. Always when you are conducting hermeneutical research, take a moment to step back from your research and ask yourself whether you are reporting on reality or on a reality created for you to report upon.[3]

Transcendental phenomenology is a philosophical type of phenomenology that looks at events in the world without the constricting influence of morality or reason. By removing the contextual elements outside of a specific phenomenon, transcendental phenomenology allows the phenomenologist to look at the phenomenon on its own merits. Too often we see researchers imputing meaning into a phenomenon from a source that has no relation to the phenomenon, sometimes a source that is unknown to the participant(s). Transcendental phenomenology allows the researcher to look at the phenomenon as if it were the only event occurring at that time, then build a spider web of relations to that event to expand the universe of the event. This is an excellent methodology for those who are writing their first phenomenology as the research starts at a given point then expands as far as the researcher wants to take it.

Naturalistic phenomenology looks at how natural events and phenomenon are perceived in nature, assuming that the phenomenon and the consciousness of the phenomenon are part of the natural setting. Naturalistic phenomenology is often used in the "hard" science, though it often is done without being named (there is still a prejudice against qualitative methods in the hard sciences). Naturalistic phenomenology allows the researcher to look at events that include beings other than humans. Animals and plants have experiences; however, they cannot relate them to us. Naturalistic phenomenology allows the researcher to interpret the events and apply them to subjects. This field of phenomenology can expand its realms as the natural setting is always changing. There are dangers to this methodology, as novice researchers are apt to place value on actions in the natural

---

3. My apologies if I offended any Hermeneutical researchers here, this is a valuable technique for research; however, it is a technique that can be perverted to direct the researcher away from the topic at hand and into a fantasy that perpetrates a fiction supported by the subjects.

setting without truly understanding them. With this model, the more experience a researcher has in the specific field, the more likely the data will be valid and reliable.

Generative phenomenology is cutting edge. It is not cutting edge because it is a new method, rather it is cutting edge because it is looking at new lines of thought that are developed during the course of a phenomenon. Generative phenomenology looks at the new developments within a given society based upon a specific event or phenomenon that changed the way the people lived or perceived the world around them. The life of Jesus Christ could be seen as a topic for a generative phenomenology because it changed the way that one third of the world's population sees the world today (actually how 99% of the world's population sees the world today because nearly everyone deals with people of Judeo Christian cultures or descent at some point).

Genetic phenomenology, or auto-phenomenology, is an autobiographical methodology for looking at something that has occurred in your life or something that has occurred in your culture that has changed the way that you view the world. This is a quasi-phenomenological form as you are acting as both the reflection in the looking glass and the thing that is reflected. This is another danger-ous methodology to use, especially for novices because you as new researchers tend to make one of two mistakes. The first mistake is when researchers ignore the reflective element of phenome-nology all together and simply writes what they think. This moves the study out of the realm of phenomenology and into the realm of an opinion-based case study. The second danger is at the other end of the spectrum, where researchers fall into the infinity complex and keep questioning the data they discover because they do not know if they are looking at it from the perspective of the subject or from the perspective of the reflection. When properly done, auto-phenomenologies are an excellent addition to the academic canon; however, they are one of the most often messed up methodologies and therefore should only be done under the supervision of an expert or if you have done them successfully before.

Phenomenology is a nontransferable methodology that looks at the microcosm of reality rather than the macro-level phenomenon in reality. This may be confusing because even though you are looking at a micro-level nontransferable opinion, you can still look at it in the context of the great-er society. Phenomenology gives the academic record unique insight into how people who lived through an experience saw the experience that they were living through. This removes one lens of research and gives people access to the raw experiences that people lived through. Good phenom-enologies remove the researcher as anything but an arbiter of information, allowing the actual lived experiences of the subject(s) to shine through as an example of what really was perceived.

Phenomenology is widely used across many fields because of the historical aspect of the phenomenological method. Phenomenologies provide insight into the lived experiences of people who have lived through phenomenon that may never happen again or phenomenon that may not happen again for a long time. This insight can be invaluable to understand why people reacted the way that they did during an event. Phenomenologies can also provide extremely rich data (rivaled only by observational ethnographies) for QMS projects to synthesize data from the field. The lived experience juxtaposed beside the "academic record" can show the differences in opinion about what happened. As the academy becomes more sterile in its relativistic approach to data collection and storage, the phenomenological histories that are available can show people that there is often an answer to questions of history that are simply covered up because they are inconvenient.

This chapter begins by looking at what lived experience is in context of phenomenological research. Phenomenologies that do not reach into the emic perspective from their etic perch and collect lived experiences tend to fall short of the phenomenological (and academic) standard and are simply opinion-based case studies. In the second section we look at the difference between meaning of thoughts and events; and we attempt to explain the difference between noema and noesis, which are two of the most highly contested words in all of science research. This leads us into the third section, where we look at the difference between intent and language in phenomenological research. In our researcher lives, the intended meaning of an act or a word may very well be different from the actual meaning when filtered through all of the relativistic or positivistic lenses that the academy places upon us. In the fourth and fifth sections we look at two concepts that become very important in phenomenological research, group identity and temporal identity. The concept of group identity involves the pitfalls that many researchers face when categorizing members of a given group; some of these pitfalls can be viewed from the concept of temporal identity. This chapter concludes with a discussion of how phenomenology is an emic perspective from an etic point of view. The synthesis of emic and etic studies can be beautiful in a phenomenological report if it is done correctly; however, it can become a disgusting chimera if the researcher does not follow the process correctly and perform an actual phenomenology.

LIVED EXPERIENCE

At the heart of any good phenomenology are the lived experiences of subject(s). Without the lived experience, a phenomenology is simply a case study. The genius and the complexity of a phenomenology come from the fact that you are providing the reader with an emic perspective from an etic point of view, blending the mental lenses of research in a way that no other research methodology does. This allows your reader to see into the culture that you are studying from an etic point of view, just as you did; but the integration of the lived experiences allow for the emic understanding of the events in context with society. The effectiveness of a properly done phenomenology is redoubled by the ability of the etic writing style to place the emic data in a context that they can relate to.

The first type of lived experience is individual lived experience (ILE). ILE is the experience of a given subject from his or her perspective without a contextual element beyond the individual's own rational. ILE derives from the personalized emic framework of a human being, in that we tend to be the centers of our own universes (or our familial group tends to be the center of our universe). From this perspective, persons see what is going on in the world as a system of events that affect them or their family group. This relationship between experience and effect can be collected and coded in relation to how individuals see the changes in the world as affecting them.

The second type of lived experience that we look at is group lived experiences (GLE). GLE is the experience of a subject within a group that he or she relates to and self-identifies with. GLEs provide researchers with data that extends beyond people who were at the flashpoint of a specific phenomenon. A flashpoint is the event or series of events that an outside person thinks of when a phenomenon is mentioned. For instance, when most people think of the 9/11 attacks on the United States, we think of the Twin Towers or the Pentagon (or some of us think of that field in Pennsylvania). These are the flashpoints. Because of group lived experiences, most Americans (or people worldwide) could identify where they were and what they felt as part of GLE. I was sitting in front of the old blue PennStan building on Pleasant Valley Boulevard in Altoona, Pennsylvania, in one of my father's work vans waiting for him to come out of the supply house. I remember Steve "The Frogman" Kelsey was just entering into one of his joke monologues. He started then he said, "A plane has just flown into the World Trade Center." I waited for what felt like hours for a punch line, expecting a priest and rabbi joke or something of that nature, but the punch line never came; a minute or two later he said, "A second plane has flown into the World Trade Center, we believe that the United States is under attack." Even though it is fifteen years from that day, I can still remember where I was when the phenomenon happened. This is part of the GLE of most Americans.

These lived experiences are very important for academics in the future to understand why humans did what they did after specific events. Due to relativism in academia, revisionist history seems to be the vogue; and then only revisionist history that makes the West out to be the "bad guy." ILE and GLE protect the integrity of the historical record because they let people know what people were thinking during specific events in the past. Phenomenologies have the duty and the privilege of exploring the ILE and GLE of people and groups to better understand the "why" of why society is the way it currently is. While history can change the "official facts" it cannot change the memories and feelings that are ingrained on the human soul from a major event.

Oral histories are an excellent source for data on events that have happened in the past but where you are unable to access the people who lived through them. Oral history projects, which are a collection of lived experiences related by those who lived them for the purpose of collecting a historical archive, are created by many non-profit and historical groups across the country. If you are unable to find one online that meets the needs of your study, you may be able to speak to a local historical society. Some of the smaller societies have collections of local oral histories but do not have the resources to house them online. While collecting firsthand accounts personally can be a more efficient and rewarding process, using oral histories as a primary source can open you up to more data, which can give your reader a richer experience when reading your work.

NOEMA AND NOESIS

"Noema" and "noesis" are the two complicated words of this chapter. Other than emic and etic, few words and concepts give researchers fits as often as this terrible twosome. Firstly, both words are similar in appearance; therefore, those of us who speak no Latin or only a smattering of Latin are often at a loss to distinguish between them. Next, they are among those terms that people use to feel good that they are a researcher and the reader is not (for the benefit of the researcher, if I use them I explain what they are then use them in normal speech). Finally, there is argument in the field as to what the specific meaning of the words are; however, in this chapter (and in this book) we are going with two simple definitions. The challenges of noema and noesis aside, they are important concepts to be aware of as you engage in phenomenological research; if you study both the noema and the noesis you will be able to give your reader a much more detailed assessment of the lived experiences of your subjects.

Noema is the physical object that is the focal point of a thought, judgment, or perception. Now the difficult part of noema is that it is the physical object as it relates to the thoughts that the subject is having about it, not the physical object as it stands in reality. While noema is generally only used in phenomenology, it can be related to the observations within ritual drawn from different types of ethnographic studies. In a proper ethnography, the object of a ritual often has symbolic meaning beyond the physical meaning of the object. The same can be said for the object that is the focal point of the noema, its meaning goes beyond what is seen to what it is seen as.

The reason that noema is relevant in a phenomenological study is to show the reader what the underlying meaning behind an object is. For non-Christians around the world, the cross is a symbol of Roman torture (though others have used it). For Christians, the cross is a representation of the love of Christ for all mankind. This makes the meaning of the symbol very different in a Christian church from what it would be in a pagan Roman temple. This is an extreme difference as one culture sees it as a representation of love, the other sees it as a representation of hatred and violence. If the reader was from the second culture, then the meanings of buildings adorned with a cross could be misconstrued as something completely different. Understanding the noema and the symbolism within a phenomenological study will allow your reader to have a greater understanding of what you are looking at.

Noesis is the exercise of reason as a function of the intellect. The noesis is the mental act that permeates through the understanding of an event in the eyes of those who lived through the event. While the symbolism of an event gradually develops over time, to continue the Christian example the cross was not adopted until well into Christianity's first few centuries; the noesis or mental reasoning of the event tends to be rationalized very quickly. Within minutes of the terror attacks on the World Trade Center, there was already speculation that the Chinese were attacking the United States. While this later was proven to be false, people rationalized that the only nation at the time with the power to even marginally challenge the United States was China, not a terrorist band of extremists from the Middle East led by a disenchanted sociopath. Noesis is an image of what the people believe happened, whether right or wrong. Whether the perception of the people is correct or incorrect, it is still valuable to know what they think and how they came to that conclusion.

The way I choose to remember the difference between noema and noesis is through a set of legal terms *actus rea* and *mens rea*. *Actus rea* is the guilty act that a person commits in a crime. While the meaning of the term is not identical to noema, it is similar enough that it helps me remember that noema is the act (noema ends with an A; *actus* starts with an A). *Mens rea* is the guilty mind, which matches up with noesis. Noeisis and *mens* both end with "s" so it is something similar that one can anchor the idea on. Each set of words functions within its discipline in basically the same fashion; in the phenomenological world noesis is the mental aspect, in the legal world *mens rea* is likewise. In the legal world *actus rea* is the physical component, in phenomenology noema is likewise. While it is not a technically sound comparison, the juxtaposition of the four terms can be a nice mnemonic tool to remember the difference.

Beyond the difficulty of remembering which is which and what their relevance is, capturing the physical and the mental aspects of phenomenology from the viewpoint of the subject will allow your project to relate more information to the reader. The goal is to collect each subject's ILE and GLE in a way that your reader can see into the inter-workings of the event and culture that you are looking into. The noema looks at the physicality of what happened in the phenomenon from the perspective of your subject and the noesis allows your reader to understand the thought process that led the subject(s) to act in the way that they did.

INTENT AND LANGUAGE

The next element that you should consider when looking at doing a phenomenology is the intent of meaning and the language. Intent of meaning is what we are trying to confer when we speak to another person. Language is the social consensus of what words mean as they are used. The language that the subject is using may not always convey the intent of meaning that they intend. Sometimes a phenomenological researcher must ask questions to clarify the meaning of statements made by the subjects. By ensuring that you get their intent of meaning rather than just the language that they are using, you can provide your reader with a much richer experience reading your work.

Socially, we must understand that language has meaning based on what our specific social group assesses it to mean. To this end, language has the ability to become symbolic in its nature. Take, for example, the phrase "phat" from the 1990s. With the rising obesity levels in the United States more and more people were realizing that they were overweight—that is, fat. One of the trends in the 1990s was owning a term that was being used against you, so fat became phat, meaning "pretty hot and tempting." Eventually the word left the overweight community and could be used by anyone to say someone was "pretty hot and tempting." If a researcher was speaking to someone using this word and did not know the intent within the language, then they could come to the false conclusion that being overweight in society was a good thing in the 1990s.

As a researcher and an author, you have a duty to your reader to explain the colloquial meanings of words as they are used by the subject. Even if you do not agree with the connotation that the subject places on the word, you still have a duty to explain to the reader what the subject means. This is part of delivering an emic study from an etic point of view—you introduce and explain the subject's sociocultural norms as you explain the data of your paper. This immerses your reader in the subject's world and even gives the reader insight into the subject's mind.

GROUP IDENTITY

Who are you? No really, who are you? Odds are if you tried to answer this question you first responded with your name, and then identified yourself with the group whom you most align yourself with. This is the natural way that we identify ourselves as members of a Western democratic society—first we are individuals then we are members of specific groups. Did the group you identified yourself with shock you (you can be honest since no one else will ever know; books are good at keeping secrets). Knowing who you are and who you see yourself related to will allow you to better understand whether you are going to perceive another person as being part of another group.

As a researcher, you must ask yourself who you are studying. Even if you are not going to impute any attributes upon your subjects, you need to come to terms with how you see your subjects in your own mind's eye. Is their culture better, worse, or equal with yours? Do you really understand them? Is there something that they can teach you and your reader that will make you and your reader's lives richer, easier, or more fulfilling? Acknowledging, if only to yourself, how you see your subject is an important part of honestly researching a group. If you find that you are biased against a group, then you should let your readers know your bias, or at least do all that you can to offset your bias as much as it is needed for your research topic.

Next, you must address your relationship to your subject. Do you have an emic relationship? Do you have an etic relationship? The type of relationship you have with your subject group will determine how you see them during the course of your study, but it will also determine how they see you as a researcher. You will often find that it is easier to collect and code data from your own culture, but where is the fun in that? It is the hours of looking through collected data for symbolism and meaning that truly helps us learn about the world around us. It is the adventure of exploring something that is unknown that causes many of us to write, which is the fun of the journey to write a paper.

A question that you should ask yourself is whether the subjects see themselves as part of the group to which you are assigning them. This does not mean that your assigning them to your classification is incorrect, because terrorists, for example, do not see themselves as terrorists but they are still terrorists, but you should question whether you are assigning the group or whether someone else is assigning the group. Group identifiers in a project come from three sources (if you identify all three then you will be well on your way to an exceptional phenomenology): (1) what Western society and academia impose on a group; (2) what the researcher imposes on the group; and (3) what the group itself assumes. Knowing how each of these groups sees the subject group can help your reader understand the context in which your study is presented.

Another structural element you may be interested in presenting to your readers is how the group came to be. Groups are generally formed three ways: (1) people are conquered and adopted into a specific group (external); (2) people form a group of mutual consensus (internal active); and (3) people become a group because of natural and social conditions (internal natural/internal inactive). The contextual in which the group was formed should give you some insight into what type of formation process it faced. This information can help your reader understand elements of how the group exists.

The group identity can provide a method for you to convey more information about your group to your reader. Knowing the "back-story" of a subject or group of subjects can make the subject more relatable to your reader. This in turn can help pull your reader deeper into understanding the phenomenon you are attempting to relate through lived experience. Who we are is much more than what group(s) we belong to, but what groups we belong to can have a major effect on how others see us. The same is true for your subjects, how they are seen by you, society, and themselves will shape how the reader will come to see them.

TEMPORAL IDENTITY

A subject's temporal identities are as important as the group identity. A person's temporal identity is where they see themselves in time. A group's temporal identity is how advanced they see themselves in relation to other societies and cultures. For instance, in the United States we tend to see ourselves as more advanced than the people who lived in 500 AD Germany. We have better tools, more rights, better food, better healthcare, and so on. Each culture tends to have another group that they see themselves as being ahead of, and want to stay that way. Phenomenology can use this temporal identity to give more depth to the group you are studying.

A key question when looking at temporal identity is, "How advanced is the society?" Advancement can rely on a plethora of variables, and some studies will combine multiple variables to create a scale. When conducting a study where temporal identify is relevant, identify the variables that you are going to use in your identification of the temporal identity. Multiple variables will give you multiple points or comparison, but for simplicity's sake we are going to look at the level of development of free speech rights. In the United States we have highly developed free speech, though it is being encroached upon by the federal government. In 500 AD Germany, free speech was limited to what your tribal leader allowed you to say or think (towards the end it depended on what the Huns allowed you to say).[4] This comparison could allow you to make a statement that in regard

---

4. http://www.timemaps.com/history/central-europe-500ad.

to free speech rights, we are more advanced than the region that is now Germany was in 500 AD. Identifying your variables can help you make your socioeconomic evolutionary claim between your subject group and your reader group. (The plight here would be that people from that region should have more rights.)

Being from a society that is considered advanced, most people reading this will have to shield themselves from temporal bigotry. We see this phenomenon in society, especially academia, all over. Temporal bigotry is assessing cultures from the past by the same moral standard that we use today, or assessing one group of people from the past by our modern moral standards but excusing another culture because they are not from the same subset. The crusaders were evil because they should have known better, but the first crusade was in response to Islamic aggression against the Judeo-Christian states in what is now Israel. American colonists were evil because they owned slaves (slavery is evil), but the African and Arab merchants and despots who sold their people into slavery were not, because slavery was "culturally acceptable" to them. Blaming the colonists (who were wrong) and the crusaders (who were right) under a modern interpretation of morality and giving their counterparts (slave merchants and Islamic radicals) as pass because they were not enlightened is temporal bigotry. Do not try to assess modern morality onto past cultures, even our ancestors, unless you are willing to assess all subjects within the same context.

On the other end of the spectrum is temporal nostalgia. Temporal nostalgia is remembering the past as the "good old days." You hear people talking about how great it was in the 1930s: "The greatest generation ever." While they did win the great wars and industrialize the United States in our second industrial revolution, we must also remember that Hitler, Stalin, Lenin, and Mao were members of this generation. We saw the Russian and Chinese death marches, the fall of Eastern Asia into chaos under their leadership. We should also remember that even in the United States and the West, Blacks, Hispanics, Asians, Italians, and multiple other races and ethnicities did not have the same rights as central European Whites, and the "greatest generation ever" fought against recognizing those rights. Temporal nostalgia results in revisionist history where the heroes and villains are both treated the same to preserve the myth of a golden age.

Finally, beyond looking at the identity (group and temporal) that you assess on your subjects you must look at the temporal identity that they assess on themselves. The older generations in Iran see their society as more developed than the decadent society of the United States; they are wrong but that is how they see themselves. The views of the subject should always be noted in a phenomenology because the views of the people are relevant to how they act within their society. Always look at relationships, national pride, and personal assessments when you are trying to determine how a subject or group of subjects sees their society in relation to other nations or societies.

AN EMIC REPORT WITH AN ETIC PERSPECTIVE

The heart of a good phenomenology is being able to immerse your reader in an emic world of your subject's lived experience of a phenomenon, but presenting it from an etic perspective so your reader is able to relate to the data. If you have a valid hypothesis and can achieve this synthesis of methodological imperatives you will be well on your way to an excellent phenomenological report. To achieve this level of proficiency, you must be willing to sacrifice the time to examine the data you collect from both an emic and an etic point of view, compare the noema and the noesis, then frame it in regard to a tri-lateral analysis of group dynamics (outside imposed images, researcher imposed images, and internal images in both group and temporal identity). While phenomenology has the reputation for being one of the easiest forms of research to master, once you get beyond a simple basic phenomenology it becomes very, very complex.

When producing a phenomenology, you are the mirror reflecting the views of your subject. As such you are neither an actor in their world nor an indicator of what happens; you are only an arbiter of what information you pass on to your readers. A good phenomenologist will be like a clear mirror, by looking into your work the reader will be transported into the world of your subject. This is done by providing the full emic experience of your subject(s) and the phenomenon they are experiencing. Poor phenomenologies are like a cloudy piece of polished brass. Your readers may be able to make out some vague shapes and colors, but the details of what your subject experiences and lived through will escape them. As a researcher, it is your duty to present a clear image of what the lived experiences of your subjects are, both for your reader and for the canon of academic history.

Phenomenology is a methodology that you either do wrong or you do correct. There is very little middle ground as you are conveying a person's experiences as they see them. If you elect to choose phenomenology as a methodology for your project, realize that your subjects (even if they are bad people or inanimate objects) are bearing their souls and their stories to you, which gives you an ethical responsibility to portray them as clearly as possible to your readers. Phenomenology is the ultimate synthesis of emic data and etic reporting. It gives you the ability to show your readers the inter-workings of a society that they may never see or have to this point not been able to understand. Phenomenology bears the extra burden of being a rich source of data for QMS projects, so a phenomenologist should be recording their data not just for the readers of this time, but any time in the future where the phenomenon they are studying once again becomes relevant.

CHECKLIST

- ❏ Who is/are your subject(s)?
- ❏ How many interviews/surveys/observations do you need?
- ❏ Are you getting lived experience or just simple answers?
- ❏ Have you delved into both the noema and the noesis?
- ❏ Are you recording the intent of meaning or the language?
- ❏ Have you looked at all three aspects of a group identity?
- ❏ Have you looked at all aspects of the temporal identity?
- ❏ Is your report giving emic data?
- ❏ Is your report analyzing it from an etic point of view?

RECOMMENDED READING

Moustakas, Clark (1994). PHENOMENOLOGICAL RESEARCH METHODS. Thousand Oaks, CA: Sage.

chapter 22
Qualitative Meta-Synthesis

INTRODUCTION

In the world of academia, the volume of research that is being done at any given time is immense. We have dozens of fields, hundreds of universities, and thousands of researcher labs in the United States alone. This volume of research is not catalogued, not organized, and in some cases never even published; this means that each time an article is forgotten another researcher may spend the time researching the topic again just to learn what we already know, or even worse this knowledge may be lost to humanity forever. This is where the process of qualitative meta-synthesis (QMS) comes into play. QMS is a tool for creating new research from old research and cross linking old research so that the data topics are not lost from the academic record.

QMS is the methodological approach of collecting rich data from published works to apply that data to a new hypothesis, but it can be so much more. The process of cataloguing and coding existing research creates a framework of applicable topics, usable by researchers in a given field. Each QMS paper contains within it a literature review that cross links dozens of papers, sometimes even multiple fields, into an easily consumed review that acts as the foundation for new theory or hypothesis testing. QMS papers constantly "stir the pot" of existing research bringing old research to the top so that it can be looked at by new eyes in different fields. This allows us, as a species, to build on existing research without committing the time to "rediscovering" something that is already done.

The process of QMS has one of two goals. The most basic goal is to use data from existing studies to create a synthesis of new data that will support a new hypothesis. Every study has data that can be applied to uses other than what it was used for when it was originally published. Researchers can conduct a "second harvest" of data from existing studies to provide a data set of rich data for a new study. Some researchers will be lucky enough to find data from multiple sources that create a synergy—that is, a conclusion supporting a hypothesis that is more than its component parts. While synergy in a synthesis project is rare, these types of papers can point to major accomplishments or shortcomings within a discipline.

There are very few fields where QMS is not a much needed remedy to the information explosion that is currently occurring.[1] If a field is established, QMS provides a constant comparative method for existing literature. If a field is just developing, QMS allows researchers in that field to establish theory by looking for synergy or synthesis from developed theories in other fields. QMS is an advanced methodology, but it is one that is ingrained in every American college student because it is the way that students are taught to write essays for class. While the methodology that is taught at most schools is highly informal, it does provide students with an exceptional introduction to the methodology of QMS.

This chapter is broken down into six sections. In the first section we discuss the basic elements of synthesis, explaining those elements by way of a dialectic model. This should provide you with the basic elements of synthesis so you can know what type of data you are in need of to synthesize. We build upon this in the next section by looking at the elements of research synthesis. This second section takes the philosophical elements of synthesis and brings them into the physical world. Section three begins the "how to" section of the chapter, where we look at how to glean rich data from already published sources in a way that does not violate copyright laws or plagiarism rules. In the fourth section we show you how to organize the data you collect by coding, which then allows you access to the topic of the fifth section, supporting a new hypothesis with already peer-reviewed data. This chapter concludes with the understanding that all QMS articles are from an etic perspective, because using external research doing an emic report would be difficult.[2]

---

1. Howell-Major, Claire & Savin-Baden, Maggi (2010). An Introduction to Qualitative Research Synthesis: Managing the Information Explosion in the Social Sciences. New York: Routledge.
2. One could do an emic QMS if they use data collected by an external author about a group in which the researcher was currently a part of.

DIALECTIC SYNTHESIS

Before you can truly understand research synthesis, you should understand the concept of synthesis as a whole. Synthesis is the process of taking a thesis and an antithesis, combining them (philosophically), then looking for the ideas arising from the combinations and declaring them as a synthesis. If thesis and the antithesis work together and do not annihilate, then you may find that you create a synergy. This concept was first discussed in detail by Hegel, but has been around since the earliest histories of mankind. Dialectic allow us to see the world in a way where two seemingly unconnected and uncomplimentary elements can be used together to create something new.

A thesis is the basic conceptual element of any idea or research question. Your thesis is your main idea, that element of your project that is at the core of everything. When you are writing, it is important to have a clear thesis, not simply because a good thesis with make your reading more accessible for your reader, but also because any paper that relies on the synthesis of data needs a good thesis for the process to take shape. Therefore, your thesis becomes the starting point of your paper—a conceptual island where you can then look for more information in a structured manner.

The antithesis, or more accurately, antitheses, are the raw data out in the world that does not support the thesis on its own. The antitheses need to be coerced by the thesis to a point somewhere in the middle so that they can be of use to the paper. This coercion pulls the antitheses toward the conceptual center of the thesis, but also can pull the thesis off center. When there is a single thesis and a single antithesis, you can find that your theses move quite a bit toward the antitheses, thus making the synthesis more of a synergy of your thesis and antithesis. However, if there are multiple antitheses then they can act to balance one another out, theoretically, and thus the original theses can be both the thesis and the synthesis.

When the thesis and the antitheses take on the guise of noncompeting forms you will find that their relationship becomes less competitive and more supportive. In these cases, you have the opportunity to have synergy. Synergy is a symbiotic relationship between a thesis and an antithesis (or antitheses) that can build toward a relationship that is para-supportive. If multiple theses and antitheses line up, they can form an array that supports itself based on the weight of the idea. This symbiotic form can allow someone to develop a new idea based on old ideas.

In philosophy, the goal of using a dialectic model is to allow the logical relationship between thesis and antithesis to develop to a point where it gives you insight above and beyond the insight that either the thesis or the antithesis could give you. If you build a thesis that has multiple antitheses, then you can effectively design the paradigm so that the mutual pull between the thesis and antitheses effectively balances out and your thesis holds the position of both the thesis and the synthesis.

RESEARCH SYNTHESIS

Research synthesis is modeled on the idea that data can be synthesized more easily when the thesis is at the center of a collection of antitheses, and the antitheses pull on the thesis which keeps it in the center of the philosophical paradigm created around the thesis. To simplify this, think of the thesis as the center of a snowflake, and each antithesis is a branch of the snowflake, pulling the center toward its end. If the snowflake is symmetrical along each axis then the center will hold its position. If the synthesis is out of balance then the snowflake will start to break apart under the pull of one side being stronger than another. When this happens data from one antithesis will pull your thesis away from the original concept and your project can begin to spin into another topic area entirely.

To do good research synthesis you need to ensure that the data you are collecting is balanced around your thesis. Having the data centered on your primary concept will allow you to keep the focus on your primary concept without the data pulling your research away from your main goal. You must understand that the data from without will have some control on your research; if you totally isolate your research from your actual data then your data will be skewed toward what you want. Thus when you build your research, focus on collecting complimentary research from multiple sources that allows the synthesis to remain focused on your main concept.

Sometimes research synthesis can be more complex than normal dialectic analysis. Even at the philosophical level the data can manifest itself a three-dimensional model. When looking at a three-dimensional model of data, you need to be assured that the balance is maintained across all three axes, which will allow you to maintain the primary concept of your project as the center of your research universe. Good planning can lead to an easier path when you are writing your paper.

One reason why research synthesis is so successful as a methodology is because it actively draws from multiple sources. Many normative styles of research draw only from their own discipline. Synthesis research can draw from multiple different fields. This increases the diversity of the data, thus increases its richness. As we have noted throughout this book, the richer that your data is the more you will be able to draw your reader into your work. Thus, the more fields that you can (reasonably) draw data from the better your paper will be in the eyes of the reader and the more disciplines your work will be relevant in.

To have good research synthesis, then you must research a topic until you have reached a point of saturation. Saturation is the point where each new source you use for your research turns up data that is similar to or the same as previous data. All good researchers approach a point of saturation within the bounds of the study, but when performing research synthesis it becomes essential. Saturation allows for each antithetical branch to have the same validity thus the same pull on your thesis. Saturation allows you to keep your research focused on the topic that you want.

The second element that builds up the credibility of good synthesis research is triangulation. Anything that increases the stability of any of your antitheses can increase the stability of the model in its entirety. The process of triangulation is looking for complementary data from different sources that confirms (or sometimes denies) information gained in the primary research source. Each additional source (within reason) that supports the data provided by an original source will increase the reliability and validity of the data, thus increasing the validity and reliability of the study. Note that this only works if you are using valid and reliable sources for your project.

RICH DATA FROM PRINT SOURCES

The genius of the QMS process is that it is the recycling of the academic world. To build a new theory or hypothesis, a researcher looks for elements of previous studies and repurposes them. This has a few advantages and a few disadvantages. The primary advantage that you will find when using secondary sources as primary sources in a QMS paper is that the data you are looking at has already gone through the IRB and the peer review processes. This means that (1) you do not have to do an IRB (or may just have to do a light IRB) as long as QMS is the only methodology in your paper, and (2) your data has been coded and critiqued by another professional so your coding process should be quite simple.

When you are working on a QMS paper, you must be discerning in the data that you use to create your dataset. Not all data that is published in the world is worthy of being in an academic paper. Some authors slip in opinions or data that has not been tested, other data may be outdated or have some other flaw. As a QMS researcher you have a duty to look at the reliability and validity of any data that you intend to use in your dataset. This should not prevent you from creating a rich dataset; rather it should strengthen your dataset as you triangulate your data collection process until you reach a point of acceptable saturation. The richer you allow your dataset to become, the richer your analysis can be, thus allowing your project to be more useful to your reader.

The main sources for QMS data are phenomenologies, ethnographies, case studies, and grounded theory papers. Other paper types, such as statistical papers, raw theory papers, and other QMS papers may be used but they are generally less useful as sources for rich data. When harvesting data from any of these sources, always make sure to look at all sections of the articles; the data sections may have the greatest abundance of data, but many authors contribute new data in other sections that may be useful for your study. Being a good QMS researcher requires you to look deeply into many articles to squeeze out every datum of rich data for your dataset.

QMS is a qualitative methodology, but this does not mean that it cannot select data from quantitative articles for the dataset. Quantitative data can provide an anchoring effect for the data in a qualitative study. Each source that is not a primary source moves a paper away from the primary topic of the original researcher. This can quickly destabilize the integrity of the research as it is moved outside of its context and procedure. Quantitative data can provide an anchoring effect to draw the data back toward its original use. To do this you should build a topic sentence around qualitative data and then use qualitative and quantitative data to support it; or build a topic sentence around qualitative and quantitative data then use primarily qualitative data to support it. This will allow you to keep the integrity of the qualitative part of the QMS study.

One danger that beginning QMS researchers often face is that they pull out more than data from another author's paper. QMS requires that you harvest data, but as you harvest the other author's opinions and analysis your paper becomes less and less your paper and more and more a collective case study of other papers. As a QMS researcher you need to practice discipline and limit your harvesting to the harvest of rich data from other sources. If you wish to use other authors' analyses in your paper, do so on a comparative level, separating your work from theirs. This distinguishing activity will help build credence in your work by showing (1) that it is original, and (2) that you have done your background research and looked at other authors' work.

The data harvest process can be one of the more difficult elements in a QMS study, but that can be said about any study's methodology. QMS requires a level of discipline that many other methodologies do not; it requires you to keep some things that you find as interesting on the outside of your study because they are not data, rather they are other authors' opinions and analyses. If your readers wanted to read another author's work, then they would read that author or at least read an annotated bibliography that contains that author. Your QMS paper should be your work, the data you collect should be treated as data from any other source; you should look for rich data, discard data that does not apply to your topic, and only keep opinions if your QMS paper is going to have a phenomenological slant.

CODING

Coding is the process of organizing your data so that you can analyze it easily and accurately. Coding is one element of any paper that gives a large amount of "poetic" license to the author. As a researcher you can choose to organize your data by way of thematic grouping, thematic clustering, topical grouping, topical clustering, or recursive frame analysis (RFA). Thematic grouping is putting all data that is within the same theme in the same group. Thematic clustering is similar, but you are giving each cluster a broader scope than you would a grouping. Topical grouping allows you to group together items based on whether or not they support individual topics. Topical clustering follows the same pattern as thematic clustering in that it allows for the clusters to have a broader base than the primary group.

RFA is the recommended methodology of this book. In RFA, the researcher breaks all the data down into contextual elements, then organizes those elements within a preset model based on a museum.[3] The contextual elements are arranged into galleries, which are data elements with the same theme. These thematic galleries are then arranged by topic, in areas called wings. The wings are then coded thematically again to organize them as museums. Finally, the museums can be once again organized into topical elements called districts. This system can be repeated as many times as needed until the data all has a common matrix. Because of this system we recommend RFA, since it allows researchers to build a matrix where they can put their hands on any data that they need at any time by following the thematic relationships between the data. These matrixes can be integrated so that they allow researchers to put their career of research into a categorized system.

PROVING A NEW HYPOTHESIS WITH OLD DATA

When looking at QMS as a methodology, many people ask why you would want to prove a new hypothesis with old data. To many of us, going out and doing the research is one of the key benefits of writing a research paper. Any time you can collect your own data for a project, feasibly, then you should make every effort to do so; however, if the data collection is too difficult or too expensive because of the specific type of data that you need, then you should look at QMS as a methodology that will allow you access to a topic that you otherwise would not be able to do. QMS harvests data just like any other system, but it puts all of your data literally in the palms of your hand (or on your computer screen).

---

3. Chenail Article (1995).

To keep your QMS project pristine and to fend off accusations of rehashing old data under a new title, you need to keep an active research trail for your QMS paper. This means that you note where you collected and harvested data for each contextual element. This is another area where the museum analogy works quite well: just as a museum would catalogue and organize where each exhibit came from, you too should organize and catalogue where each datum came from. If you can show this in your research trail you can build a model that shows you collected your data in a normal fashion as if you were collecting data for another project.

One reason that some researchers find QMS so frustrating is that they are discovering what is hidden in plain sight. When you are reading a collection of papers on a given topic and do not see something that seems obvious, sometimes that is why it has not been discovered. If your topic seems too good to be true, then make sure that you redouble your efforts in your literature review. As you search to see if your topic is new, think of every conceivable combination of search terms to see if someone has looked at your topic. Nothing is worse than doing a QMS project only to find that someone else has already researched the topic, except maybe if you cite their paper but miss their theme in your paper. Take the time, but realize many of the answers to the world's great mysteries are out there in plain sight just waiting to be discovered.

AN ETIC REPORT

You will find that 99.9% of QMS reports are etic reports. Since you are using data from secondary sources, it is almost a foregone conclusion that your perspective for the paper will be an etic perspective. There are limited cases where a person from within a social group may write a report on his or her own social group based on the interpretations of other authors, but this type of emic/etic report is quite rare albeit quite insightful. Many of you will not have this advantage so your reports will be firmly in the etic realm.

One of the reasons that QMS is so successful is that authors are twice removed from the research subject. While a bond can be built based on data and "familiarity" with the subjects from hundreds of man hours of reading about a topic, this still does not run the major risks that are involved with being on the ground with a subject. This can give QMS research a level of separation that allows researchers to protect their work from bias. On the other hand, you may find that this removal from your subjects can be a two-edged sword. It is difficult to ask a subject that is already dead his or her opinion on a subject or a follow-up question. Researching data through a secondary source limits the freedom of a researcher and can add challenges that other methodologies do not face.

Objectivity is another advantage of QMS research. The levels of separation from your subjects can remove the subjective bias that exists in other methods. If something is printed as data in an academic journal, it can be accepted as fact at least as long as you are working from a trusted article. This "objective" subjectivity gives QMS a greater reliability than many other qualitative methods. If you build your case around "objective" facts found in research articles, then anyone who wishes to follow your work can look at the same articles. While they may challenge the validity of your data, they are generally unable to challenge the reliability of your research trail.

As the most objective methodology of the qualitative family, you are not looking for subjective answers or conjuncture; you are looking for a developed hypothesis that is supported by data that other researchers can also find. If you build too many opinions into your QMS report, then it can fall victim to the problems that any other research methodology faces. A QMS researcher must be diligent in looking into the data sections of other authors to find what they have missed. This diligence can be exhausting, but can help you build a well thought out paper and help reference the information explosion in the social sciences.[4]

CHECKLIST

- ❑ Have you done a literature review?
- ❑ Is the data you collected pure data?
- ❑ Have you culled any opinions or external analysis from your dataset?
- ❑ Is your data coded so you can follow the dataset?
- ❑ Does your report present new data in a way that maintains the integrity of the rich data?

RECOMMENDED READING

Major, Claire Howell & Maggi Savin-Baden (2010). *An Introduction to Qualitative Research Synthesis: Managing the Information Explosion in Social Science Research.* New York: Routledge.

Sandelowski, Margarete & Julie Barroso (2002). "Finding the Findings in Qualitative Research." Journal of Nursing Scholarship 34:3.

Sandelowski, Margarete & Julie Barroso (2003). "Creating Metasummaries of Qualitative Findings." Nursing Research 52:4 at 4.

Sandelowski, Margarete & Julie Barroso (2007). *Handbook for Synthesizing Qualitative Research.* New York: Springer.

4. Major & Savin-Baden, *Supra.*

Part IV

THEORETICAL PAPER

chapter 23
Introduction to Theory

INTRODUCTION (WHAT IS THEORY?)

The final group of methodological approaches to writing an academic research paper is the theoretical family. This grouping is more complex than the quantitative or qualitative research because both of these methodological families are integrated into the theoretical family. Trying to create a theory that does not have its genesis in both qualitative and quantitative research is like trying to create a bridge with only one end, no matter how long you work on it you will find that your project is never finished. This part of the book opens your mind to the ying and the yang of writing theoretical papers, the quest to support your theory with both quantitative and qualitative data.

Theories are the mystical element of the academic religion; these are our axioms—though unprovable we accept them because they have not been proven false. Sectarian violence in this religion takes to the battlefield of academic journals, the bishops, rajas, and imams are the men and women who create new theory or find suitable changes to old theory. If you write a qualitative or quantitative paper, whether you know it or not, you are firing a shot in these wars. Your hypothesis will either support or undermine one of the plethora of theories out there. Your hypothesis may pass undetected, be lauded as a decisive victory, or be attacked by people who support another theory. The only way to rise above this morass is to create theory of your own, thus dictating a new paradigm within the academic canon.

Theoretical research is the politics behind the battles at the quantitative and theoretical levels. When you engage in theoretical research you are working at the super-macro level in the theoretical realm that you are dealing with (even if that realm itself is a micro-level theory). As a theorist, your research should be above supporting one basic theory or another; your job is to present a new theory that eliminates the problems of an old theory and moves the "society" of academia forward. Theoretical researchers are responsible for the "quantum leaps" of academic research. Science saw leaps when gravity and relativity were discovered. Each time a new language is translated or discovered English takes a theoretical bound forward. Social sciences have been blessed with many leaps in the last 200 years (utilitarianism, rational choice, strain theory, etc.). Even fast-paced fields like business and law have had their paradigms shaken when on-demand publishing and a one world system (respectively) were developed. Theory drives innovation, for the hypotheses that test new theories will not be written if the theories themselves are not presented.

Theories are the core tenants of the major disciplines. Some disciplines have multiple theories that are in constant battle with one another for recognition. This ordered chaos is the primordial ooze from which progress develops. Take physics for example, the battle between "big bang" and "string" theories have led people who were working in each of these fields to have major breakthroughs in their field. While we still do not know which of these fields is correct, we do know that the field is moving forward in leaps and bounds. On a more controversial topic, we see the debate between positivism and relativism played out in the Middle East where female genital mutilation (FGM) is becoming a more and more common practice. Relativism says that we cannot judge those who are committing this crime against humanity because it is part of their culture; positivism states that these young ladies have the right to go through life without being maimed. As one sided as this argument is, there are authors who support both positions.

The first major classification of theory that we will look at (your discipline may break theories down into different categories) is the macro-level theory. Macro-level theories affect an entire population. The size of the population does not matter, because a macro-level theory can affect a population as large as the biome of insects on the planet earth or as small as one person in a specific situation. Macro-level theories are the grand theories that encompass entire fields. Most physics theories fall into this category, as do the top-level theories in social sciences. These theories are fewer in number because just a few of these theories can cover most of what humanity currently knows. It is postulated that there could be a super-macro level theory that encompasses everything, but it is undiscovered as of yet.

The second major classification of theory is meso-level theories. These are theories that cover a large portion of a population or subject but do not cover the entire thing. Meso-level theories are designed to deal with specific events that occur within a given subject or population. For instance, broken window theory applies to a large portion of any nation; however, it is not applicable in natural settings where the chaos of nature removes the ability to determine whether something is being taken care of or not. Meso-level theories are excellent when the theorist is working in the area that the theory covers, but quickly become useless in areas outside of that scope.

The third type of theory, macro-level theory, is the most common. Micro-level theories deal with a specific event or subject, looking at why, where, when, and how it will happen (or any mix of these). Micro-level theories look at the microcosm of existence and explain why specific events happen. In some ways, micro-level theories are similar to hypotheses; however, even the micro-level theories are made up of several hypotheses, which make them more complex than their lesser brethren. Micro-level theories can be used in concert to support meso- or macro-level theories in their own right.

This chapter establishes the basics that you should know about theoretical research before you enter into reading the other chapters of this part. Theoretical research is on the cusp of being outside the scope of this book. Theoretical research can deal with anything and everything that is more complex than a single hypothesis; therefore, you should always consult specific texts from your discipline for theoretical research in unison with this text. In the first section of this chapter we look at the reasons that you may choose to create a theory. Theoretical research is not for everyone and generally not for beginners. The simplest approach is to find and correct the errors in an established theory; as you embark on creating your own theory the system gets infinitely more complex. In the second section we look at the people who create theory. Theoretical research is not limited to super-geniuses—anyone can discover a theory if the circumstances are right. In the final section we look at the format of Part IV of this book, as we walk through the next six chapters and how they relate to theoretical research.

WHY CREATE A THEORETICAL PAPER?

Of all of the different families of research papers, theoretical papers are the most difficult to write. This comes about for three reasons. First, a theoretical paper requires that you support several hypotheses before you can even assert a theory exists. This means that you either must do the research yourself to build up these hypotheses or you must find other authors who have already established support for the requisite hypotheses. Second, you must fit all of this information into one paper that a publisher will print. Anything over 80 pages tends to give journal editors pause as it will eat up nearly a quarter of any given edition. This means that you have to reduce multiple hypotheses into the length of one normal paper (some journals will work with you on this). The final reason that theoretical research is more difficult is because you will place yourself in the line of fire or anyone who supports a theory that you are surpassing or replacing. In some academic areas thousands of people will have worked their lives to support a false theory (like cultural relativism) only to have it proven wrong or supplanted, thus their livelihood is forever changed. Some of these researchers will change with the times; however, many of them will challenge the new theory vigorously to maintain their fiefdom.

So if writing theoretical papers is so difficult, then why do people write them? People write theoretical papers to advance the knowledge of the human race. If Galileo and Copernicus had accepted the old model of the universe, then where would our space program be today? If Columbus would have accepted that the world was flat, then where would we be today? The challenge of theoretical writing brings with it the reward of new discovery. To continue our jungle guide analogy, when you support a hypothesis you are showing your reader one branch of one tree or one rock on one hillside. When you write a theoretical paper you can show your readers the entire vista of the world and explain it in a way that is not overwhelming. Theoretical research establishes the world in which our hypotheses are developed.

The highest level of theory that a researcher can hope for is to discover a law of nature. A law is a theory that in no known way can be disproved. As precursors to laws, theories have the distinguished possibility of being immortalized by a research field. Once a law is established, it is unlikely that it will change anytime within generations. The only reason that a law can change is when something is discovered that allows it to be disproved, or when a mistake of the theorist is found. Either way, these laws are few and far between. The ultimate goal of many theorists is to discover a law that will immortalize them in the annals of history.

WHO CREATES THEORY?

When we think of a theorist we tend to think of a person in a lab coat looking at test tubes and beakers in a laboratory. Some of us think of an Indian Jones type of character blazing a trail through some long forgotten jungle in the Amazon or in Africa. This is the common vision of a theorist, someone who is smarter than us or better than us in some way that enables the person to find new things in the world that we will be able to use. Many people who do discover new theories are those who dedicate themselves to a lab, field, or library for the greater portion of their life. Most theories are developed by people who dedicate massive amounts of time to their research and build an amazing body of life's work that they can summarize into one cohesive theory. But they are not the only people who discover theories.

Many people discover theories, especially micro-level theories, in the course of their daily jobs. You do not have to be a genius to discover a theory, you simply have to be aware of what you are seeing in the world to the point that you understand you are seeing something new. Each year millions of inventors create things that make their lives easier; a much smaller portion of those people realize that if their invention makes their life easier then it could make the lives of others easier, too. These are the theorists whose theories never make it past their living room. These are the people who do not have the support system to send their theories to the masses. These are the neurons of the collective human conscious that we need to tap to expand the scope of human knowledge and allow our generation to be the next generation that creates a quantum leap forward for our species.

As authors, we have to be aware of academic bias and fight against it wherever we find it. Academic bias is the belief that only theories and hypotheses discovered or supported in an academic setting are of any use to a given field. When we allow this belief to permeate the academic landscape, we cut out millions (or billions) of people who may have valid ideas because they are not "educated." Most of the major discoveries of mankind have been made by men and women that would be considered uneducated by modern academia. We have to fight against this stigma and give anyone who has a valid idea a fair hearing, only then can we use the entirety of human consciousness to solve our problems.

FORMAT OF PART IV

Part IV covers one theoretical method, then looks at five different types of theoretical questions. The theoretical method covered in Chapter 24 is grounded theory. Grounded theory is a method of establishing a theoretical base using observation and other data collection techniques to build up support for a collection of hypothesis. When used as a qualitative method, researchers generally limit the grounded theory process to a single hypothesis. This is like having a 1969 Mustang and only taking it to church on the weekends. Grounded theory is one of the best research methodologies for building a new theory on the market (the empirical method being the other major research methodology in the STEM fields). Grounded theory is placed in the theoretical section because when it is used properly, it is the only theoretical method that a social scientist ever needs (if you are in the STEM fields then you should learn the empirical method also).

The next three chapter look at the three easy questions in the lexicon of theoretical research—the why, who, and where. The reason that these are called the "easy" questions is not because they are less difficult to research (there are why, who, and where questions that have never been answered and some that will never be answered), but because their concepts are more simple than the other two questions. In Chapter 25 we look at the most common theoretical question of "why." This is one of the first questions that humans learn to ask, and it is one of the most important questions for us to know how our world works. In Chapter 26 we move on to the question of "who." The "who" questions are generally historical in nature, looking at "who" has done something, although there are those "who" theorize about "who" is doing things in society, and "who" will do things in the future. Then in Chapter 27 we round out the easy questions by looking at "where" questions. These are often the most overlooked theoretical questions; however, the question of "where does the human race go from here?" may be one of the most important questions that anyone has ever asked.

Moving ahead to Chapter 28 we breach into one of the harder theoretical questions, the "what" questions, which are more complicated questions because the substance of the answers is not defined in the questions. "What makes us human?" is a question that has been asked millions of times and people have come up with millions of answers. Those who take on the "what" questions in their research are people who spend the time narrowing down the scope of their theoretical research question to a pinpoint, but often it is the pinpoint that bursts a dam of new questions when answered. Chapter 29 breaches the hardest question of the theoretical family, the question that has perplexed historians, philosophers, physicists, and even the common man: "when?" The "when" question is saved for last because it is the most complex of theoretical questions. We first must understand the existential question of "What is time?" Is time linear, radial, digital? The answer to this question is yes, and that is what makes "when" the most difficult of theoretical questions. Lastly, Part IV concludes with a summary of information covered in this part to help those of you who decide to go on the epic journey of writing a theoretical paper.

chapter 24
Grounded Theory

INTRODUCTION

The Grounded Theory Institute defines grounded theory as "a general method [that] is the systematic generation of theory from systematic research."[1] Grounded theory is the base method of theory generation and the method that most disciplines use to develop new theory (whether they know it or not). Grounded theory is often compared to the empirical or scientific method as a counterpoint; however, the empirical method is a hypothesis testing tool that can and should be used in the development of grounded theory. Thus grounded theory is the only real academic theory generation tool out there (there are variations of grounded theory, but all follow the same basic rules). Researchers who wish to move beyond hypothesis testing into theoretical development have little choice but to master the skills of grounded theory if their work is going to be taken seriously, even in fields that do not recognize grounded theory as their primary theoretical methodology.[2]

The Grounded Theory Institute's definition of grounded theory is broad and covers any systematic approach that one could use to develop theory. Nonetheless, their definition is a proper definition of grounded theory. However, this is a definition created by experts for experts; for those who are journeymen into the field of developing theory a simpler definition could be useful, so in this chapter we will look at grounded theory as "a systematic testing of multiple hypotheses for the purpose of showing an interwoven web of data and hypothesis that supports a perspective that is broader

---

1. GTI (2015). "What is Grounded Theory?" *Grounded Theory Institute at* www.**groundedtheory**.com/what-is-gt.aspx.
2. The other alternative is non-grounded theory, which is simple speculation.

than any single hypothesis can support on its own." Grounded theory, to continue our jungle guide analysis, takes the reader through the whole forest, stopping briefly to look at individual trees and plants but with a greater plan to allow the reader to understand the entire ecosystem and how it relates, both within itself and to the world around it. Theory is the tour of the entire jungle while hypothesis testing is a tour of a single tree.

As the goal of academia is to expand the knowledge of humanity, and it seems that expanding the knowledge of humanity in the broadest possible sense is what grounded theory tends to do, why do more people not attempt to create theory? The answer is quite simple: because it is not easy. Grounded theory is not a simple qualitative or quantitative methodology.[3] Though many claim that it is a qualitative method, it contains theoretical elements that remove it from the qualitative family.[4] This does not mean that qualitative elements cannot be used to support a theory (most of the time they are required) or that elements from grounded theory cannot be used in hypothesis testing, rather it means that grounded theory is a different type of method and it should be treated as such. Academics use grounded theory more than they know, for almost every theory that has been developed through human history has been developed from this systematic approach. As with many cross-disciplinary approaches grounded theory may be called one thing in one discipline and another thing in another discipline, but anywhere a systematic approach is used to demonstrate a systematic theory, grounded theory is likely the methodology being used.[5]

The other question that people sometimes ask (i.e., "Why should I use grounded theory when I can just come up with a theory on my own?") causes others to take pause at the all-inclusive nature of grounded theory. To answer this question, we must look at the systematic nature of grounded theory. Grounded theory provides a stable base for the theory, not simply by creating a system of three or more hypotheses that support the theory, but by interconnecting these hypotheses with complementary data. This creates an integrated network of theoretical pathways that support the system, so even if one of the datum in a single hypothesis proves to be false the remainder of the data is sufficient to support the theory. Some see this approach as overkill, but as we move into a society where relativist criticism is the key type of "research," the more support a new theory has built into its system, the more likely that theory will survive the initial barrage of criticisms and attacks.

---

3. GTI, *Supra.*
4. *Id.*
5. Some of the STEM fields use high-level mathematics to create theory, which is a variant of the GT approach; however, the absence of nonnumerical data and the similarity to a natural law often precludes the use of the term "grounded theory" in relation to the research. The same approaches can be used in these instances, and modifications should be made in accordance with your field's standard operating procedure.

SO YOU WANT TO WRITE A PAPER

In this chapter we walk you through the basic process of building a grounded theory paper. We begin by looking at the concept of hypotheses being combined to make up a theory. Before ever embarking on a journey to write a theoretical paper, you should have a series of hypotheses that you believe support the theory and a means to support the component hypotheses. In the next section we look at the process for gathering rich data for your complementary hypothesis, and then archiving it in a way that will allow you to use individual datum in multiple hypothesis proving exercises. Then we look at Glaser and Strauss's constant comparative model in relation to Chenail and Keeney's RFA model. These two models, when used in concert, allow you to create a data archive that lends itself directly to multiple forms of analysis in complementary hypotheses. The more complete your dataset, the more actively you will be able to compare individual datum. In the fourth section we discuss the idea of saturation and how it should be used in relation to your project. While reaching the point of data saturation can be labor intensive, the saturation process helps increase the likelihood that you do not miss any data in your theory. Following this, we look at the significance of symbols in theory generation, more from a social sciences and humanities perspective, although symbolism can have relevance in the STEM fields. Symbols can be anchors that help your reader relate to the issues in your theory. In the sixth section we look at triangulating data, which is the process of looking for complementary data from different sources that confirm (or sometimes deny) information gained in the primary research source. Triangulation, when used in concert with saturation, allows you to have reasonable confidence in the reliability and validity of your theory. In the concluding section we discuss how to write a theoretical paper so that it is defensible and so your readers can understand it. The who process is for naught if no one can understand your research!

THE HYPOTHESES THAT MAKE UP THEORY

As you embark on your journey to create a new theory, understanding the way that theories come together is vital to writing a good theory. Too often we see authors writing a theoretical statement without first identifying the underlying hypotheses that must be proven. This leads to having unsupported theories and thus is bad research methodology. In this section, we look at how hypotheses and theories interact as your theory begins to manifest. Without a good set of hypotheses, your theory will not have the support it needs to pass the test of academia. While the theory may still stand (like relativism) because people "feel good" about it even though it is an unsupported theory, it can create entire disciplines of research based on a false supposition, which can be incredibly damaging to the academic canon.

So the first understanding of this type of theoretical generation is that theories are a group of hypotheses that interact and support each other in such a fashion that they allow for a postulate to be built that later becomes a theory. A postulate is a suggestion or assumption about the existence of the truth, fact, or basis used as a framework for reasoning, discussion, or belief.[6] In effect, the postulate is a working theory, until you build the hypothetical underpinnings to support it. Much like a piece of clay is but a piece of clay until a potter's hands form it into a vase, a postulate is just a postulate until a researcher forms and supports it by building defensible hypotheses as a foundation. Good theory must have a series of hypotheses that have been supported as true for it to stand in the field of academia.

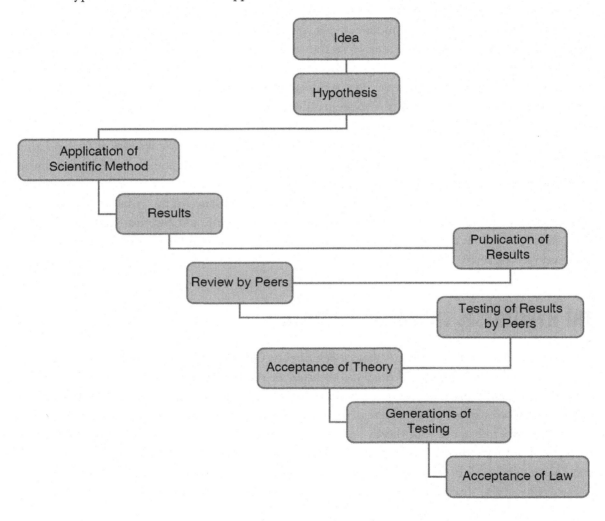

6. Definition based on Merriam-Webster definition.

An image that can be used when you are developing theory, as a reference for support, is the image of a stool. A three-legged stool is stable, and a four-legged stool is even more stable; however a stool with one leg or two legs is not stable at all and requires a balancing act for anyone to sit on it. Likewise a theory supported by only one or two hypotheses is more difficult to balance and keep upright in the tide of academic criticism. Each hypothesis that you add to your theoretical foundation can support the theory and make it more stable. Some theories are supported by who disciplines, which is akin to a stool being attached to a wall (some of the walls are more stable than others). As you build your theory, ask yourself whether you would be willing to stand on your theory alone and allow your career to depend on the hypotheses that you have put forward to support your theory. If you are uncomfortable with the stability of your theory, then you may need to find more hypothetical legs to put under it.

To continue the image of the stool, one bad leg can make a stool very unstable. If one leg is shorter, or weaker, or just there for aesthetics, then it is the weakness that can cause the stool to collapse. Likewise a theory with a bad hypothesis can be very unstable. As you are building your theory, only select hypotheses that you can support and that have been researched. Whether you did the research or whether it was done by another does not matter, just as long as the research into the hypotheses was done well. A good theory cannot afford to have a hypotheses that does not fully support it—this would be the weakness that your critics can use to undermine your whole theory. If a hypothesis does not pass muster, then you may have to leave it behind. A stool with two good legs that is difficult to sit upon is much better than a stool with three legs when one of the three is bad and will fail at any time.

The brilliance of a good theory is that the hypotheses that support it should create a synergy that makes the theory more than the sum of its parts. With our stool example, wicker is a fairly weak material. A single strand of wicker could not hold much together; however, when multiple strands of wicker act in concert they can create a system that holds a stool together for a human to sit on. The individual strands are important, but how they work together can be even more important. So, too, with hypotheses. The interweaving of hypotheses and data is the element of theoretical research that takes theorizing beyond being a simple scientific process to being an art form. As a theoretical researcher, you have to see how the individual hypotheses react with the data and react with one another. Each connection that hypotheses make across the underpinning of the theory is another support that can ensure your theory stands even the fiercest academic storm.

To build good hypotheses, you need to ensure they are supported by good research work; this where good theoretical research is supported by good quantitative and good qualitative research. Any time you venture into the forest of theory building, you need to be assured that any hypothesis that you use for support is valid, because these hypotheses are the paths that you follow on your journey to write a theoretical paper. Some hypotheses (hopefully) will have already been tested by others who have ventured into this area, just not as deeply as you hope to go. If you find good research discovered by others, then it can be used to help you in developing your theory. If this research is old, then you may have to "re-blaze" the trail started by someone before you. The newer research will be more accurate (hopefully) and it will be more relevant to your reader. At other times you may have to venture into your field on your own to support hypotheses that no one else has ever looked at. This can be a daunting task as each hypothesis that you seek to support will need to be supported by its own research methodology. Though you may use the same methodology to support multiple hypotheses, it is still important that you follow the process in detail for each step. This is where having a good data archive is a lifesaver.

Ensuring that your hypotheses are valid is one of the most important steps in developing new theory, for without good hypotheses there is no real theory. The more complex your theory, the more complex your network of hypotheses will be; if you want to have a large theory, then the hypotheses supporting it will need to be robust. As a theoretical researcher, do not make your theory any more complex than it needs to be. A simple theory can be supported by three or four simple hypotheses and can withstand the test of time. Larger, more complex theories will take more time to build because they need to answer more questions. As you build your theory, realize that some theories require other theories first, so in order to build your stool you must first build another stool on which it can sit.

RICH DATA AND STABILITY

There is nothing that can support a theory as well as rich data and good logic. These should be your two primary goals when writing a theoretical paper. Since this is not a text on logic, I will just say that you should go through your logic three times to ensure that you have thought through everything (most of us will go through our logic dozens of times). However, since this is a book on research methodology, the data collection is very relevant to what we are talking about. Since good theory is supported by good hypothetical methodology, and good hypothetical methodology is supported by rich data, then good theory must also be supported by rich data. As we have seen in the methodological sections, good data means having a rich description, an accurate description (numbers are included here), and multiple sources to confirm individual data points. If you can achieve all these things and have a good logical foundation, you are well on your way to developing good theory.

Theoretical research is unique in that you are supporting multiple hypotheses while building your theory. These hypotheses should be integrated in a way that the data used to support one hypothesis may be useful in supporting the other hypotheses. As such, you should be building an archival system of data as you research each hypothesis that makes up your theory. The unique interaction of the multipoint data that you collect in each hypothesis may establish concrete connections between the hypothesis that you are working on and other hypotheses in your theory. These data connections (we will call them strands) allow you to put cross supports in your theoretical foundation. This increases the stability of your theory's foundation and allows you to easily connect one hypothesis to another.

As you research each hypothesis in your theory, you will find that your data archive grows. This means that you have new data that may or may not be useful in a previously supported theory. This can be useful in many ways. First of all, if you are publishing your hypotheses as you establish them, you can build an excellent body of work and a reputation in the field if you augment previous papers with new data. Second, by introducing new hypotheses to the field, you may find others start to work in the same area as you, giving you other research to integrate into your greater theory. If you are the only one who is working on a theory, people may see you as a radical. If you are leading a field of researchers on a new theory, then entire disciplines may stand up and take notice of your work. As your data archive grows, always take the time to go back and look at previous hypotheses and see whether new data will make them even stronger.

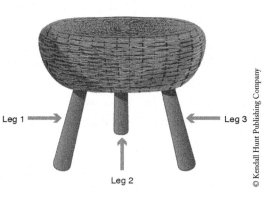

Leg 1

Leg 3

Leg 2

© Kendall Hunt Publishing Company

As you near the end of your hypothesis supporting stage, you should have a fairly robust data archive that is approaching saturation for the topic that you are working on (as you build the archive you should include anything related to the main theory in your dataset). This means that you may be able to support your hypotheses without new research. Though this is tempting, do not fall into the trap of resting on your research laurels. Support your hypothesis with the data from your archive, but always be combing the new literature in the field to see if new data is coming out. If you use the same sources for all of your work, your work will become stale for the reader. When you have a new project, do a few more interviews, take additional surveys, go to the site to observe the location again, and check out other researchers' work in the field. Part of the art form of theoretical research is always keeping your material fresh; it may take more work but it will also keep things more exciting for your readers.

Once you have created the archive (or as you are creating the archive) you need to have a good tool to navigate the data. Like an explorer wants to have a map, a good researcher wants to have a good coding and analysis tool. We highly suggest Chenail and Keeney's recursive frame analysis method (see Chapters 41 and 42). This coding and analytical methodology allows you to categorize your archives across projects so that when you need to look back into a specific area, you will have a map of all of your data. This methodology is also useful because it allows you to input new data into your matrix without changing the topical or thematic constraints of your research. While RFA is not the only analytical tool on the market, it is one of the better tools for this type of theoretical design.

As your strands of interconnected data begin to form in your research, the path to supporting your theory will become more apparent. The forest of research that you have delved into will begin to seem less like a jungle and more like a series of interconnected paths. Sometimes these paths will lead right to where you want them to go; other times these paths will lead you to new and undiscovered data. This is part of the adventure of research, theoretical research in particular. You must enter into a research project with an open mind; you can hope to find data that will prove your hypothesis right, but if you are willing to be proven wrong you can learn so much more.

GLASER AND STRAUSS'S CONSTANT COMPARATIVE MODEL

No discussion of grounded theory would be complete without a discussion of Glaser and Strauss, the progenitors of the field. Before they "discovered" grounded theory, Glaser and Strauss believed there were two forms of analytical method being used in academic:

> If he wishes to convert qualitative data into crudely quantifiable forms so that he can provisionally test a hypothesis, he codes the data first, and then analyzes it. He makes an effort to code "all relevant data [that] can be brought to bear on a point" and then systematically assembles, assesses and analyzes these data in a fashion that will "constitute proof for a given proposition."[7]

or

> If the analyst wishes only to generate theoretical ideas—new categories and their properties, hypotheses and interrelated hypotheses—he cannot be confined to the practice of coding first then analyzing the data since, in generating theory, he is constantly redesigning and reintegrating his theoretical notions as he reviews his material. Analysis after coding operation would not only necessarily delay and interfere with his process but the explicit coding often seems an unnecessary, burdensome task.[8]

---

7. Glaser, Barney & Strauss, Anselm (2008). *The Discovery of Grounded Theory: Strategies for Qualitative Research*. New Brunswick, NJ: Aldine Transactions.
8. *Id.*

They attest that their new method is superior because it "combines by analytic procedure of constant comparison, the explicit coding procedures of the first approach and the style of theory development of the second."[9] Thus by taking the coding mentality of the first approach and the comparative model of the second approach, Glaser and Strauss created a hybrid methodology that is one of the most commonly used in academia today.[10]

With the advent of the discovery of grounded theory, researchers now had a methodology to enter into theoretical research. Postulation as well as trial and error were still tools of methodology; however, as grounded theory developed the methodology was more formalized so it could be repeated, thus the reliability of theories grew exponentially. The discovery of grounded theory also limited the creation of new theories, as it creates a more labor-intensive process with greater controls placed upon it. Less "flimsy" theories stood up only because no one could disprove their multitude of elements. This brought the academy into a time where the innovations were less, but the quality of those innovations was extraordinary.

The coding and analytical method recommended in this book is recursive frame analysis (RFA), but in itself RFA is an evolution of the constant comparative method. It could in fact be called a constant comparative and cataloguing methodology. RFA maintains the spirit of Glaser and Strauss's constantly looking at how new data integrates into the theoretical matrix, but gives it the added benefit of cataloguing the data in a pattern that is easily identifiable. This enables the researcher to maintain the vigor of the constant comparative approach and still keep a workable archive of data.

One benefit (of many) that is mutually shared by the constant comparative method and RFA is that by the time the coding is complete, a portion of the analysis is already done for you. As you are constantly comparing and contrasting one datum to another, you find that the comparison and contrast part of the analysis is already done. This frees up the researcher to do in-depth interactive research on the way the data react with each other. While getting into the habit of doing the constant comparative method or RFA can be tedious, the amount of time that a skilled CC or RFA researcher can save in his or her analysis can be priceless over the course of a career.

SATURATION

Saturation is important for any type of research; however, saturation holds a very special place in the grounded theory methodology. Saturation is researching a subject until the data you are newly col-

---

9. *Id.*
10. *See* GTI, *Supra.*

lecting is redundant to the data you have already collected. In any of your research projects you should always be seeking a point of saturation as the saturation level of the material that you are researching indicates how reliably your research method can be replicated. If you search until there is no additional known elements of the subject that you are researching, and you find several new elements, then you can be assured that your theory will stand up to initial criticism against its validity and reliability.

The interesting caveat of grounded theory is that it relies on multipoint saturation. Multipoint saturation not only looks to see that you have reached a saturation point in your research on all relevant hypotheses, but also requires that you seek a level of saturation on the interconnected nature of the data. Each datum should be investigated for its relationship to other data. These interconnected relationships will build strands of data connectivity, which will make your data archive more integrated and stabilize the data within your hypotheses. Good grounded theory requires that you build upon these relationships as well as upon your base hypotheses.

Saturation and multipoint saturation are important in the grounded theory process because a single datum that violates one of the major hypotheses of your theory can prevent your theory from ever being a law. Further, if someone discovers data that is an exception to your theory, they can create a new theory (similar to yours) that simply compensates for the data that is contrary to your theory. This can remove your theory from the academic canon and replace it with theirs. This makes it imperative that you extensively research a given topic within your theory to the point that you are sure that all easily discoverable data currently in circulation supports (or at least does not discredit) your theory. Saturation is very time consuming and repetitive, but if you fail to seek a point of saturation you may find yourself working to support someone else's theory.

In any field there are multiple methods to reach a point of saturation; in fact, there are multiple paths to reach saturation in any given project. As a researcher, part of your job during the data collection (and analysis) phase is to determine whether you have reached the saturation point of your topic. Unfortunately, this point is different for every project and for every researcher. When working on projects of this nature (like quadralectics) I favored a multivaried approach to data collection. The majority of the work was a meta-synthesis based on primary sources and meta-summaries. Secondary data was collected through observations, both my own observations and historical records that included detailed observations. Secondhand oral history projects, interviews, and surveys rounded out the process. Once the collection process was completed, I catalogued the information according to a variant procedure of RFA. Each time I found a gap in the theory, I would return to the research phase using a constant comparative method to tighten up any weak links. By the time that it was complete, I was very familiar with the material and knew that the theory I was proposing was valid and reliable.

While another researcher may have chosen different names for the phenomenon within my theory, they would be hard pressed to find areas that are not covered by the quadralectic continuum.

When you take on a multiple methodology approach, you must realize that you are going to have to reach a point of saturation on all elements and on all connections between the elements. This means that you need to be dedicated to the process. If you choose to look at the process as a journey to write a paper, and see the labor that you are putting into the research process as looking to discover new knowledge or to rediscover lost knowledge, the process can be quite enjoyable. My research journey in quadralectics took me into parts of the linguistics field. This was a whole new area, at least for me. So it opened my eyes to relationships between socioeconomics and linguistics that I had never imagined (not to mention shattering my belief in high and low context cultures).

One word of warning as you enter into a process of seeking data saturation for a process, be careful to limit the parameters of your theory. While the adventure of discovering a macro-level theory can be intoxicating, it can take countless hours to do. Most of you thinking of writing a theoretical paper are looking at doing a thesis or a dissertation. My dissertation chair gave me good advice, advice that should be passed on to all students. If you try to prove everything, then you will end up proving nothing. Your current project is no more than a drop in the bucket, it does not have the fill the well of human knowledge. Doing this project well will open doors to allow you to begin other topics, so do not try to overdo this project and concentrate on it being the best work you can put forward. This advice got me through my dissertation; hopefully it will help get you through your theoretical paper.

SYMBOLIC SIGNIFICANCE

Symbolism is important in any research, but none so much as in theoretical research, especially grounded theory. Symbols within research (and the rituals that develop around them) are an anchor to the physical and meta-physical context of your study. Everyone has symbols in their life; therefore, everyone can relate to the concept of a symbol, even if they cannot relate to the symbol itself. Even in the STEM fields, symbols can be powerful anchors in the descriptive language that you use to describe your theory to your reader. If your goal as an author is to draw your reader into your paper, symbols may be the best portal through which you can draw them.

Symbols also can become a thematic or topical point of reference. People have an easier time assimilating data if they can associate it with something. Symbols are an excellent point of reference because at some basic level everyone can relate to the concept of a symbol. For instance, if you are writing a paper on government intervention within the field of the internet, then you may choose a pirate flag as a symbol. When the internet downloading craze became famous in the 1990s, the media dubbed the downloaders as pirates. This proved to be an error for the media and the recording industry as the term "pirate" was adopted by the downloaders and even used as a term of pride. Though the music and video industry spends billions attempting to enforce archaic laws from a time before the digital age (basically digital monopoly), the internet piracy movement still rallies around the symbol of the pirate flag. This symbol could be used as a topical point (as could the band Metallica as they were seen as the spearhead of the industry movement).

You can also build your analytical method around the use of symbols. Each logical argument needs a starting off point; you cannot know how to get from here to there if you do not know where here is. Giving readers a symbol as a focal point, then building your argument or analysis from that focal point gives them something to grasp onto while they are trying to understand complex ideas. Symbols act as signposts on your journey through the jungle of data to discover your theory. The better the symbols and the closer they are to the paths on which you are leading your readers, the more easily your readers will be able to consume the data and understand your reasoning.

Symbolism is one of those research tools that writers either love or hate. If you are a writer who hates symbolism, do not let me change your style. There are people reading this who absolutely hate that I use an analogy as a vehicle to carry the major theme of this text, but that is who I am and will not change. If you elect to eschew symbolism and lead your readers to your research in a different way, then always select some method to mark your path. While symbols may be signposts, you could leave breadcrumbs of data (constantly relating the new logical element to a single point of data) or even blaze an ever so wide trail (explain things to your readers on a grade school level). Whatever method you choose to keep your data relatable to your readers, make sure that you keep your path going the whole way through your research; there is nothing more frustrating for readers than to be halfway through understanding a theory and the author leaves them alone in the jungle of data with no way to find their way to the end of the trip.

TRIANGULATION

Triangulation is the process of looking for complementary data from different sources that confirms (or sometimes denies) information gained in the primary research source. Triangulation is a labor-intensive process in a normal hypothetical paper, but in a major theoretical paper it can be the work of years. Each element of primary data should be triangulated for confirmation or denial by at least two secondary sources of information (multiple source of primary data can also work). Each point of data that you present in the individual hypotheses should be confirmed by no less than two additional sources. Denials can be done with one, but it is better if you triangulate the source of the denial. Remember the data supports hypotheses and the hypotheses are the foundation of the theory.

Triangulation within theory is difficult, not so much on the finding the data level but on the authenticating the data level. By the time you reach a point of triangulation within your theory (after your analysis when you have already begun to support your primary hypotheses) you should have a fairly robust matrix of saturated data within your data archive. Thus the problem with triangulation in a theoretical paper is founded in figuring out which data best confirms your primary data source. There is no need to support a datum with more than ten data sources, because anything more than six or seven is oftentimes redundant (although ten sources may be useful on a contentious issue). As an author, it falls on you to select the best sources of triangulation from a jungle of saturated data.

As you weave your web of analysis in your theory, linking the individual hypotheses to one another through the individual and multivaried strands, you should also be innately triangulating individual data points. Strands that link different hypotheses often find their anchor points on different data; therefore, the linking data should be one of the sources that triangulate your main points. Using this "shortcut" can be an effective way of showing which data points are the best data points to triangulate important pieces of data. This format also repeats the individual data points that are important so that your reader assimilates them more quickly.

If your theory requires you to be critical of another theory (which is something that you should be very careful of because the disciples of that theory will defend it), then you need to ensure that you have triangulated the data that undermines the original theory. Triangulating denial data is done much the same way as triangulating regular data. If you are being critical of another theory, then it is recommended that you use several points to show that the original theory is wrong. Oftentimes this is not possible; therefore, you need to show the reader why the problems in the original theory are normative for that theory and not a simple fluke. This helps you establish trust in your own theory because you are detailed in your criticism of another theory. If you have a single element that disproves a theory, make sure to confirm that the element is valid.

Triangulation is also important because you should ensure that your critics do not find any dead ends, either in new material that you put forward or in criticisms that deny the validity of other theories. While not as damaging to your theory as someone finding evidence that your data is wrong, if someone can find a dead end in your research that was not explored it can cast questions on your ability as a theorist. Unless you are creating a micro-level theory, no one person (or one generation) can be fully expected to explore all of the physical, meta-physical, and philosophical questions revolving around a theory. No one expects you to. What is expected is that in your conclusion or discussion you talk about areas of the new theory that can be explored by other authors (or that you will explore in the future). This establishes that you understand that your theory is not a law and is not perfect…yet. Building good theory is a long-term project and having the humility to acknowledge that there are elements as yet undiscovered is an important part of being a good theorist.

Triangulation gives your reader multiple paths that allow them to get to the same point. To continue our jungle guide analogy, each new point that you put forward to triangulate an original point is another path that your reader can take to achieve a point that you are making in your paper. In the jungle one path may involve a steep grade, another a small rock climb, and yet another a swim across a stream, and all three paths lead to the same vista, but different people will go different ways. If you put forward a good theory, people from multiple disciplines will read your theory; this means that they may have different ways of approaching data. If you give them several ways that they can approach your theory, you will make it easier for them to assimilate your data and easier for them to accept your theory.

WRITING THEORY

While each different brand of theory will have its own section in its own chapter about how to write that particular theory, Chapter 24 concludes with a general approach to writing a theoretical paper. These general guidelines lack the specificity of the individualized approaches in the later chapters, but the general approach will give you a catch-all for when you have difficulty with a specific type. Further, the general approach is better for large macro-level theories. The first rule of good theoretical writing is that the hypotheses should be woven together in a way where if one data strand is damaged by a critic or a change in the environment, then the interwoven aspect of the theory keeps that one strand from unraveling the whole work. Each time you layer a new hypothesis into your theory, make sure that any data links that it has to other hypotheses are highlighted. This will establish a level of stability throughout your theory to ensure that one changing data point will not destroy years of work.

As you weave your hypotheses into your theory, be cognizant of holes in your theory. Holes in a theory do not necessarily make it a bad theory, just an incomplete theory. If you find that you have holes in your theory, there are two approaches you can take. The first is to go back and do more research to fill the hole and strengthen your theory. This is the safer of the two but is more time consuming. The other option is to acknowledge the hole in the theory and admit that new research needs to be done in this area. This is particularly useful in the social sciences when an *emic* point of view is needed and you will never be accepted as part of the group. Putting forth the theory with the hole does not mean that you are a bad researcher, it just shows that you are willing to ask for help. Though if the hole is easily fixed, then do it yourself.

When writing, always be aware of the length. People are less likely to read a voluminous theory; however, they are less likely to trust a short theory. As you develop your theoretical research, you will find a balance between proper length and getting your point across. As a rule of thumb, you should always go back and edit out 20% to 40% of a paper when you are a young writer, 10% to 30% of a paper as a journeyman writer, and 5% to 15% as a veteran writer. The longer you write the more the editing process will be internalized and the less time you have to spend cutting pieces and tangents out of your writing.

As you write, keep your message simple and clear. No one wants to read a convoluted theory. Leave those to the long-dead people from the 1800s and radicals who need their theories to be convoluted to brainwash freshmen. Good research should be as clear as possible. If you give your research to a peer and the peer cannot understand it, then you need to go back and simplify it. This does not mean that your theory needs to be gutted; rather, it means that your writing may need to be cleaned up. Stay away from complicated words unless they are absolutely necessary. Use the proper terms for your discipline, but if a word is a colloquialism or a trade term then explain it for those who are not in the field. As with anything, customer service is important in writing, so make your product what your readers want it to be.

Writing a theoretical paper is a labor of love, but it is rewarding when you finish your theory. However, just because you publish the paper (or book) on your theory does not mean that you are done with it. The publication is the beginning of your defense. Anything new will be challenged, as this is part of the academic vetting process. Do not be discouraged, if you did good research and followed the directions herein then your paper should be defensible. When you reply to critics, keep it short and professional. Be personal in your responses; do not put the black hat on yourself. Anything you write in reply to critics write as a teacher, as if you are educating them. Always write it at a level that is simpler than your original paper, so it will appear to other readers like your critic is too simple to understand your work. Do not be condescending, just stick to your guns and you can defend a paper written in this style. Theoretical papers are the most adventurous journey through writing many of us will ever make, so enjoy the experience and put forward the best theory you possibly can.

CHECKLIST

- ❏ Have you written out a clear theory?
- ❏ Have you identified the hypotheses that support your theory?
- ❏ Can you support the hypotheses?
- ❏ Have you researched to a point of saturation?
- ❏ Have you used the constant comparative model?
- ❏ Have you triangulated all your main points?
- ❏ Do the data points interlock between hypotheses?
- ❏ Have you identified any symbols and if so how are you using them?
- ❏ Did you weave your hypotheses together?
- ❏ Did you look for holes?
- ❏ Is your paper simple and clear?

RECOMMENDED READING

Charmaz, Kathy (2006). *Constructing Grounded Theory: A Practical Guide Through Qualitative Analysis.* Thousand Oaks, CA: Sage.

Chenail, Ronald J. (1995). "Recursive Frame Analysis." *The Qualitative Report* 2:2.

Chenail, Ronald, Cynthia Somers, & Joy Benjamin (2009). "A Recursive Frame Qualitative Analysis of MFT Progress Not Tipping Points." *Contemporary Family Therapy* 31:87-99.

Glaser, Barney & Anseim Strauss (2008). *The Discovery of Grounded Theory: Strategies for Qualitative Research.* New Brunswick, NJ: Adline Transactions.

chapter 25
"Why" Papers

INTRODUCTION

"Why" papers are the most basic type of theoretical papers to write, not because the question "why?" is easier to answer, but because it is generally the first question that human beings ask as children. Everyone knows a toddler who is going through the "why" phase and, even though we do not like to acknowledge it, human beings are still going through the "why" phase of our maturation as a species. Those theorists who choose to take on the "why" questions are advancing the most basic, foundational level of human understanding. If we do not take time, as a species, to answer the "why" questions, then all of the other theoretical and philosophical questions will be without context, simply answers in a structureless world.

A "why" paper is a paper that asks the question "Why?" Why does the sun come up in the east and set in the west? Why did Americans insist on voting for Bush II and Obama twice? Why are people fascinated with reality TV? Why does on-demand shipping work better in a direct supply chain company? Why should we have the right to remain silent in a criminal case when we are the defendant? Each field has its own "why" questions that need to be asked. The interesting thing is that "why" questions all have answers. The sun rises in the east and sets in the west because of the rotation of the earth around the sun. Our nation voted for Bush II and Obama twice because the corporate structure that controls both parties likes regularity, even at the expense of competent government. People watch reality TV because they want to see that other people have it worse than they do and that class is a myth perpetrated by society. On-demand shipping works better because it eliminates the need for storage space of large quantities of goods. And the right against self-incrimination protects people from the state forcing them to make their own case against themselves. If you come across a "why" question that you do not know the answer to and you are not able to find an answer for, then this may be a theoretical question that you should undertake researching.

The "why" question is one of the most common questions asked, not only in academia but in our species as a whole. Even lesser animals such as cats and dogs seem to have the "why are you doing that" look on their face when they see a human do something stupid. "Why?" seems to be the universal question. As academics we need to take the time to answer as many of the "why" questions as possible. No matter what field you are in, you will probably have access to researching a "why" question. If you do, always take the time to explain it as you would to a child. The better we understand the "whys" of the universe, the better we can address the other theoretical questions in academia.

Some people ask the question of why they should embark on seeking the answer to a "why" question, not realizing that they are asking one in their query. Some people see "why" questions as too basic, thinking that they are undignified for an advanced researcher to ask. Generally the people who hold these viewpoints probably should not be doing theoretical research because if they cannot see the value of "why" questions one has to doubt their judgment on the value of data within their research. The other groups that challenge the "why" questions are radicals on the extreme right or the extreme left who feel that humanity is as advanced as it will ever be. Both groups of radicals see our current humanity, in all its problems and debauchery, as the pinnacle of human evolution. The truth is humanity and society are both evolving (radicals are trying to slow it down but they cannot stop it). With each "why" question we answer, we are moving closer to a greater understanding of the universe. While humanity may never unlock all the secrets of the universe, the more "why" questions that we answer the better our understanding will be of what we know and do not know.

This chapter, along with the other four types of theory chapters, is quite short; therefore, they are an easy read. If you are considering taking on a theoretical paper, then I recommend that you read all five of the theory type chapters before you begin. While the chapters are divided by question, you will find that most structurally sound theories focus on one specific question, but have elements from the other questions present in an explanatory role. Thus, the theory types are like a set of sockets in your tool bag—having one will work sometimes, but if you have all of them ready you can take on almost any project.

WHY ASK WHY?

At the heart of any "why" paper is the questions of why something occurs or happens. Humans have an innate desire to control things in the world around them; I suppose it is because control gives us some measure of security. The first step to controlling an event around us is to understand what is going on within the event. This means that we must ask "why," because it seems to be the default question that human beings ask when a tragedy happens. (This needs to be answered first because it is the anchor, or the first major question.) The mindset here is, people need a reason for something bad or good to happen, even though in nature the reason often has nothing to do with bad or good.

"Why" questions are interesting because they nest. Nesting is the process of one question leading to another, which leads to another, which leads to another. Think of it as one of those Russian nesting dolls, and each time you open one up there is another inside. "Why" questions can draw a researcher into an infinite cycle of questions as any time you have an answer to a question you can pose another "why?" For instance:

Q: Why does the sun rise in the east?

A: Because the earth rotates around the sun in a fashion where it causes the illusion of the sun moving through the sky, whereas the sky is actually moving around the sun.

Q: Why?

A: Because the earth orbits the sun in a cycle that takes approximately 365 ¼ days.

Q: Why?

A: Because the sun's gravitational pull keeps the earth from going out into space and our momentum keeps us from crashing into the sun?

Q: Why?

As you can see, "why" can go on forever. Like a child exploring the world for the first time, humans are exploring our universe. Each "why" can lead to another "why" and then another. As researchers, we can only establish one level of theory at a time; then once that theory is established we can begin answering the next "why" question.

As we build our theoretical paradigm, we should create the focus on the building process of the theory, not the excavation of the theoretical foundation. If we establish, with multiple hypotheses, that our theory is correct, then the excavation of the foundational issues are not necessary for the support of the theory. When you build a house, once you find bedrock you do not dig up the bedrock to see how big it is before you build the house; once you establish that you have a foundation point you can then leave the philosophical questions about "how sturdy" it is until another time. Once you are sure that you have the requisite level of sturdiness you can move forward with building up, not tearing down. Future projects can look at the foundational issues; you are working on building the masterpiece that the world will see, not the technical details of "why" the foundation is secure (see a nested "why" question).

"Why" questions are also important philosophically. Without the "why," does anything really matter? Regardless of what we like to tell ourselves, we are a species that thrives on stability and habit. Even the dirty hippies that fight against the system do so because being a contrarian is a stable state for them. "Why" gives us the foundation that we need to explore other important questions. The "what/how," the "where," the "why," and the "when" questions all begin and end with "why" questions. "Why" is the theoretical anchor that makes us explore our world; therefore, understanding "why" can lead us to understanding other things.

HOW "WHY" PAPERS ARE FRAMED

In each of the following four chapters, we conclude with a section on framing the question. In this section, I look at the five major families of education (social sciences, physical sciences [including maths], business, law, and the humanities/philosophy). Each of these macro-disciplines has a particular way that it looks at each of the theoretical question types. These sections are to act as primers for your research but you should always look at the most current style in your field for questions of each type. The way that fields address these questions moves quickly with the fads, and if you want your researcher to be accepted then it should be in the format of how your field is working on that question type.

Social sciences are currently in a phase where they are semi-avoiding the "why" question. As you may have noticed, I do not like relativism. It is a broken theory, like a cult that has infected higher academia. Relativism is based on the postmodernist philosophy that all things known are wrong (generalizing a bit here), and that your perception is based on your experience but cannot understand the morality (right/wrong) of another person or group because their experience may be different. It takes the "judge not lest ye be judged" idea to an absurd level well beyond where it makes sense.[1] There is right in the world, there is wrong in the world, and there are many things that are in grey areas that need context to be understood, but all things fall into a category. Female genital mutilation is wrong, no matter what a particular culture feels about it. Rape is wrong, no matter the culture. Babies having babies is a symptom of a systemic problem in society, no matter the subculture. Giving people a free pass just because of their culture or personal experiences just allows others a free pass for "similar" circumstances. In social science the "why" question is central to the discipline's understanding of the world. "Why do conservative/radical Muslims practice female genital mutilation?" is an important question. Whether it offends people or not should not be an issue if women are being tortured (and some die from it). We need to understand the "why," so that we can correct the problem. You can be a realist without being a racist.[2]

In the physical sciences the "why" is the dominant question in the field. The number of "why" questions that the physical sciences take on each year shows just how far we have to go as a species to increase our understanding of our own world. Those in the physical sciences look at why ecosystems need specific parts. Why do chemicals interact the way they do? Why is energy transfer inefficient in so many of our products. Each time they answer one of these "why" questions, the wealth of human knowledge grows and we are a better species because of it.

The two central "why" questions to business are "Why are we making money?" and "Why are we not making money?" Both questions are central to the proper running of a business. Unlike the other fields, in business the "why" questions often lead to "how/what" questions rather than other "why" questions, because businesses want to maximize their profits and minimize their losses. Once you understand why you are making/losing money you can then look at how to maximize or minimize the situation, respectively. Asking the "why" question in business can be a very lucrative career and this (along with how) are the main questions that consultants are asked to answer.

Of the five macro-disciplines the legal community probably makes the least use of the "why" question, mainly because of the nesting problem. With the possible exception of motive, the legal community does not care why a person committed an action (unless there is a mens rea requirement or a negligence claim). If "why" can be made an issue in a case, then the case can be convoluted to the point of absurdity with nested "why" questions. This would break the legal system and people would not get justice; therefore, the system recognized early on that the "why' would only get in the way of investigating the "what."[3]

---

1. Mat 7:1-3.
2. This paragraph was written during the ISIS crisis in the Middle East, upon editing the idea of removing this paragraph was considered; however, it makes a salient point, FGM is a barbaric practice and academia should not be silenced on protecting women's rights.
3. Sometimes the legal community looks at why a judge rules a specific way or why Congress passed a given bill.

"Why" in the humanities tends to follow the same path as "why" in the social sciences; in fact, many schools are starting to assimilate the humanities and arts into the social sciences as they are a cultural artifact. This leads humanities to the same infection of relativism that the social sciences have. In philosophy, however, the "why" questions are a core concept to the field. Most philosophical questions revolve around asking "why?" This may be why philosophy is the foundational field for all non-professional doctorates (law, medicine, pharmacy, and psychology are professional doctorates). This is why we receive a philosophical doctorate, or Ph.D. The why is the foundation of academia; hence the last questions we answer in college are the first questions that we ask as a child.

"Why" questions are the core of research and theory. If you are beginning a theory and do not have a strong "why" question answered as your foundation, then you are not ready to move on to another type of question. You do not have to answer every "why" question, but you do have to find one that is answered to a sufficient level that it can stand on its own (people will still ask why, but they do not have to ask why). Do not make the mistake of discounting the "why" in your research, lest you find yourself grasping your head asking, "Why can I not get my paper published?"

CHECKLIST

- ❏ Is your "why" question a good foundation?
- ❏ Has your "why" question been answered?
- ❏ When you read your theory is the first thing that pops into your head another "why"?
- ❏ What is your field's position on "why" questions?

chapter 26
"Who" Papers

INTRODUCTION

Asking the question about who did something is an important part of who we are as human beings. When an event occurs, we want to know who were the participants, especially in English-language-speaking countries. If we look at the grammar of a good sentence and compare it to the grammar of a passive sentence, then we will see that the "good" sentence identifies the actor in the subject, while the passive sentence does not identify the actor until the predicate.[1] This is because when we visualize what is going on in the sentence, we expect to know who the actor is before we begin to understand the action. Sometimes as researchers, the question of "who" did it will be left unanswered by history, which can become a lifelong quest to answer such a simple question.

So what is a "who" theory? A "who" theory is any theory that answers a research question that starts with *who* (e.g., *who* built the pyramids, *who* invented soccer, *who* were the first people in the Americas). "Who" theoretical papers are often confused with "who" hypothetical papers because the answers are generally very simple. The key difference is that "who" theoretical papers tend to incorporate some of the elements from "how" theoretical papers to justify the theoretical position. The Egyptians built the Great Pyramids using basic mathematics developed by their philosophers. The English claim to have invented soccer (football) and named it such because it was played on foot not on horseback (like polo). There were likely people in the United States before the "Native"

---

1. Sabin, William A. (2005). THE GREGG REFERENCE MANUAL: A MANUAL OF STYLE, GRAMMAR, USAGE AND FORMATTING. Boston: McGraw-Hill Irwin.

Americans, who came across the land bridge and were forced down the West Coast by increasing numbers of people coming across the land bridge.[2] As you can see, "who" and "how" integrate well in answering the "who" questions.

Most fields use "who" questions, though they are used more rarely than other theoretical questions. People often overlook the "who" questions because they can often be answered as hypothetical questions, thus do not give the esteem that theories give a researcher. However, "who" questions can gain a researcher great fame if they discover something or someone that has been the topic of debate for many years. These type of "who" questions are generally the theoretical questions because many facets of "who" need to be answered and defended. Researchers who answer a "who" question quite well could in the future become the researcher subject of someone asking who discovered what they did.

This chapter looks at the question of "who" in detail, how it is to be used, where it can be used, and who is likely to ask "who?" In the first section of this chapter we look at our society's obsession with the question "who?" Some other societies in the world eschew the "who" question because they do not have the same status structure that has existed and is still developing in our country. In the next section we look at how "who" questions are famed in each of the big five macro-disciplines. Each discipline approaches the question of "who" differently, thus we see "who" being asked in a multitude of different ways. If you elect to do a "who" theoretical paper, be prepared for a long period of time exploring what others have forgotten. If the question of "who?" was easy to answer, then there would already be a theory on your topic.

WHO CARES ABOUT WHO?

Western society is build around "hero" worship. Our famous people throughout history are icons that we build our society around. People try to live their lives like Christ or Buddha. People try to be successful like singers and football players. Even though academia is pushing to discredit heroes and redeem villains, society seems to gravitate toward traits that we wish we could see in ourselves. While it may not be in vogue now, studying the "who" of society can be an interesting theoretical approach for someone who is breaking into theory. "Who" goes well beyond the simple question of "Who did something?" and can address the question of "Who is this person, really?" This dynamic between two questions keeps the "who" question active when looking at new people, whether they are famous or not.

---

2. There are many books out there on suppressed history. The censored history series is a good place to start.

There are countercultures around the world that do not iconize people. Australia, for example, does it less than the United States as upstarts in business can blackball themselves if they do not go through the proper channels. There are cultures around the world where fame and fortune are a curse rather than a boon.[3] In these cultures it is more difficult to find out who discovered what in that culture as they hide their names intentionally. If you are researching a subject like this for history, then it can be difficult to find information that does not want to be found.

Studying the "who" question can also get you attacked by the liberal left in academia if you do it properly. Currently diversity is vogue, which is good; however, the diversity that is in vogue now is diversity of classification not of individuals. Those of us who challenge the mold and do not fit into easily categorized boxes can be ostracized for being different. The position that people are different based on who they are as individuals is not popular as the easier approach is to identify them by their race, ethnicity, or creed. It is hypocrisy of the highest level and is a hypocrisy that you should avoid if you are to be a serious researcher.

Studying the question of "who" allows people to look at their roots and see where they come from, both as a person and as a society. "Who" we are comes from who we were, but "who" we were does not dictate who we are. Out ancestors and previous societies are an influence on our makeup, but they do not define us as a person. When researchers say "Blacks believe this" or "Whites believe that" it is racism to attribute one belief to a whole group of people based on race. This is not good research and not good theory. Human beings are not cogs in a machine that are all the same and all working for the same goal. We are individuals and the "who" questions point out that individuality.

The "who" questions also identify who we are as a species. "Who" we are is more than the sum of what every individual since the beginning of time has done. We have evolved as a species and we have evolved as individual societies. Looking at the achievements that we have made over the long history of humanity helps us see the goals that have been realized, but it also shows us that in the future our goals that seem impossible now may yet become reality. Think of the first cave person who watched a bird fly and wished that humans could take to the air, for them it was a pipe dream but now air travel is common. "Who" discovered these things, when combined with when, puts a timestamp on achievement that can allow us to see the progress of our species one step at a time.

---

3. While studying in Australia, I found that in the legal community those who were the best at their jobs kept a low profile, as "famous" lawyers became targets to be chopped down by the industry. This was called "big poppy theory" there, but has other names around the world.

HOW "WHO" QUESTIONS ARE FRAMED

In the social sciences, the "who" question has been largely regulated to "who a person really is." Criticism of cultural icons, especially Western cultural icons, is an easy way to get tenure at many schools around the country. While this would seem like a bad thing, it shows that all people are flawed and that we can achieve greatness despite our personal flaws. There is still limited exploratory research into who was the first to do certain acts, but this research has slowed likely because of fear that once a person is discovered his or her character will be attacked. It can be assumed that once the character assassination craze in the social sciences is done, real historical research can once again come out of the shadows.

In the physical sciences the stigma of being a flawed human being is more readily accepted than in my own field. If a scientist discovered something, then he or she got credit for it. It is their achievement that is lauded not their character. This may be a better approach to "who" research, but it will be a long time before the other macro-disciplines follow this path. Moving humanity forward should be a primary goal of researchers, but we should stay within the bounds of moral common sense.

In business the question of "who" generally focuses on who did what and how we can make it better. Business is profit driven, thus those who succeed and those who fail are the people of note in "who" type papers. As a researcher if you can show how a person was successful or what a person did that caused the failure, then your paper will be valuable in the field. Any time the capitalist machine can be moved forward, the business field will look at that research as golden.

In the legal field, the question of "who" revolves around who created specific arguments; however, it is mostly seen as a novelty. This is a stark contrast to the fields of humanities and philosophy where the "who" gives you claim to a discovery much like in the physical sciences. Many an artist or philosopher has rested on the laurels of their one great achievement; in some cases horrible theory and horrible art have been accepted because they came from the hands of a grandmaster.

CHECKLIST

- ❏ Has your question already been asked?
- ❏ Why is the person who did what you are looking at relevant?
- ❏ Is this person well known?
- ❏ Are they an icon in their culture?
- ❏ Is your paper a character assassination? If so, then you are better than that.

chapter 27
"Where" Papers

INTRODUCTION

"Where" questions are the explorer's papers; these are the papers that ask where something is, where something was, or where something will be and try to tell the world something lost about human knowledge or where we need to go as a species. "Where" papers are often overlooked as simplistic because they have such a simple questions; however, "where" questions are often the questions that take the longest to answer. As a researcher, looking to answered and unanswered "where" questions can be difficult, but also rewarding. "Where" questions answer the history of our world, the present of our world, and the future of our world, building theory that can eventually be proven as fact.

A "Where" paper is a paper that discusses the location of some event, relic, or person. The most common use of "where" theory (though it is generally not known) is in the criminal justice/policing field as they look for people who have committed crimes. Any time there is a question of where something is, a "where" paper can be written; the likelihood of that paper being read depends on how important the object of the search is to the world/academic community. "Where" theories tend to be much shorter times than other theories because they are subject to being proven; however, this does not mean that the theory itself is any less important. The question of "where" must be asked before the proof of "where" can be entered into the historical record.

"Where" papers can be done in any field; however, the most dramatic papers are done by archeologists or history authors. Anthropologists write a lot of "where" papers, but these are generally written as a precursor to a manifesto. "Where" papers are distinguished as an excellent way to build a historical record, but how they are used tells us how useful they are. Further, when you can establish something as fact, writing the "where" paper previous can risk someone stealing your project.

In this chapter we look at why "where" papers are relevant and how you can write an effective "where" paper. In the first section we break down the different elements that make a theoretical "where" paper relevant in the academic marketplace of ideas. "Where" papers build perspective and thus can be an effective tool in understanding our world. In the second section we look at the common format of a "where" paper. The simplistic nature of the "where" paper makes it one of the simplest types of theoretical papers to write. "Where" papers are good tools, but are not the type of theory that you can retire off of (unless you are an archeologist who discovers a very cool place). "Where" theories are merely stepping stones on the path to bigger and better theoretical realizations.

WHERE ARE THE WHERE PAPERS?

Knowledge of a location can be a very important element in many aspects of human life. It can also be a very important part of establishing a historical record for future generations. Before a location can be discovered, especially one that has been lost for a long time, there needs to be some discussion of where the item, person, or place that is being sought is located. Take, for instance, treasure hunters. They must have an idea where a ship sank to do a proper search for the treasure. This speculation of location can come from two sources, guessing and theory. If researchers are just going to guess where a location is, then they may end up wandering a jungle or ocean for years. The more professional way to approach the site of a specific location is to develop a theory about where the location is, then use that theory to discover what you are looking for. In this case your theory may be short lived, but if it is proven to be correct, then it is worth it.

"Where" papers are not limited to a single location. Social scientists and those in the natural sciences can use "where" papers to discuss the paths and the shapes of migrations. Knowing when and where one group (whether human or animal) moved from one location to another can be valuable not only for the human record but for current information as well. The knowledge of where herbivores moved in ancient times could indicate where large caches of vegetation are, and what was once vegetation can now be fossil fuels. This can make the understanding of migrations very important.

Another major use of "where" papers is to correct misconceptions of history. Since the 1960s, the United States has been the victim of "revisionist history" where persons with an agenda (both conservative and liberal) have rewritten history to suit their own needs. These false agendas have been built into government documents and college curriculums. Theories that tell the real "where" that events occurred and can correct the historical record can eliminate the work of these educational apostates and keep the academic canon a real record of human history.

"Where" papers allow us to understand where we are in the world. Knowing where problems are in our world allows us to solve them. Knowing where good things are happening in our world lets us emulate them. Knowing where historical sites are in the world allows us to study them. The knowledge of "where" is the simplest form of theoretical research, but it can still have an amazing impact on how we see the world that we are living in and studying. "Where" papers may be easy, but they are important.

"Where" papers can also allow us to see where we can go. The history of mankind is a history of movement. As we look at how movement evolved over the generations that have passed, we can also look at where we can move toward in the future. The earth has been highly explored and while it still houses secrets that we will discover in the future, we have the opportunity to explore more than just our little planet in this vast universe. "Where" papers may be simple but they can answer the most important question humans have: "Where do we go from here?"

HOW "WHERE" PAPERS ARE FRAMED

"Where" papers are more than just a researcher saying, "I think I know where X is." "Where" papers are based on the idea that your theory is supported by fact, just like any theory.[1] Just speculating does not make a set of typed words a research paper; "where" papers can be some of the most difficult papers to support with facts because if the facts were easy to understand then someone else would have found your item/location. No matter what your field, when you begin building a "where" paper you are going to be in for a long process. With "where" papers just follow the steps to prove your hypotheses and you will be able to support your theory with the facts you discover.

In the social sciences "where" theories are used to discuss where objects, people, and locations are throughout the societal record. This opens up "where" papers to have a multitude of topics depending on what area you are researching. "Where" theories should be published just as you are leaving on an expedition to find what you are looking for. If you publish any sooner, then you may find people waiting for you at the site you are trekking to. "Where" papers allow those of us in the social sciences to voyage to amazing new places to look at aspects of the world that people never knew or may have forgotten. This makes "where" papers a powerful tool in the social sciences.

---

1. The Travel Channel's *Expedition Unknown* tends to look for "where" theories.

In the physical sciences, "where" papers are very short lived. Generally, as soon as the theory is proposed, the person proposing the theory examines the theory to see if it is true. The exception to this rule is when people create theories that will take hundreds of years to prove (where there are habitable planets, for instance). "Where" theories are generally short-term theories in the physical sciences that allow a researcher to prove something then move on to another theory. The better the "where" theory is written, the better enabled the researcher will be to build another theory atop it.

In business, the theory comes down to where the profit is, where the loss is, where the supply is, and where the demand is. Generally, the latter is the most lucrative. Businesses are built around the concept of generating profits. If you can write a good "where" theory paper in the business field and establish a profit model that lasts, then you may open the door to personal success in the field. Where events happened can be an often underrepresented type of "where" paper in the business field, because people can have attachments to famous things, and building a model around local legends can be a lucrative model.

In the legal world, the humanities, and philosophy, "where" papers are not common. In the legal world, "where" theories are part of the case. In the humanities, "where" theories are part of the set. In philosophy, "where" theories quickly can become irrelevant. If you are involved in one of these area, then you may want to take a careful look at whether a "where" theory is the right choice for you. While they are not entirely excluded by these fields, "where" theories are quite rare and even more rarely well received.

It is simple to write a "where" paper, but do not let that simplicity fool you; it can take years or a lifetime to discover something that has been lost (or to discover something that has never been found). "Where" papers are built on the archeological tradition that spawned them; they are a foundational tool that once discovered are quickly covered up by other theories. Finding the base theory in a "where" situation may not be glorious, but it may open the doors you need to discover other types of theories that can build your career.

CHECKLIST

- ❏ Is your location/thing/person known by others?
- ❏ Is it something that Western academia has not discovered?
- ❏ Is your topic of interest to others?
- ❏ How will you find your topic?
- ❏ Are you allowing yourself enough time to find your topic before you publish so your idea is not taken?
- ❏ Will anyone fund you to find what you are looking for?

chapter 28
"What" and "How" Papers

INTRODUCTION

At first glance, "what" and "how" papers do not seem to fit together in the same chapter. "What" papers are the more reality/existential dynamic questions, while "how" questions are the mechanical/hands-on type of questions. This dynamic between the two seems to suggest anything but the idea that they should be housed in the same chapter. But when were really look at the "what" and the "how" of theory, they are similar in their nature beyond their location together in this chapter. Both "how" and "what" are technical questions about how the world is made. "What" is the progression of "how" in the theoretical sense, as "what" can be defined as "how" it is made and "how" it came to be. As these two theoretical macro-fields circle each other in a double helix of information, researchers can ride the connections between the two macro-forms to find new theoretical understandings of the world around them.

A "what" paper looks at what an object/person/place/theory/symbol/etc. is; it can look at anything in the world around us and try to explain the essence of that topic. As such, a "what" paper can be a useful tool in building theories about a specific topic. The difficulty is keeping "what" theoretical papers separate from simple descriptive papers. A "what" theory paper looks at something that has not or cannot be proven. It is not a paper that says "The sky is blue"; rather, it discusses the philosophical question of what the sky is. It is not a paper that looks at instances of racism, but asks the question of what racism is. In either of these cases a "what" paper can use examples, but the examples are not the answer to the theory, just supporting elements for your theoretical hypotheses.

A "how" paper, on the other hand, looks at the process for designing/building/changing/etc. an object. "How" papers are mechanical; they are not "how-to" guides based on a known process, but on hypotheses for a better system. The more hypotheses that you have to support your "how" paper, the more likely your "how" paper will be effective as a tool to increase efficiency in a given process or expand the understanding of how something was created in the world.

"What" and "how" papers are used in all fields, and quite often. They are often mistaken for descriptive or how-to papers, but there are real "what" and "how" papers circulating in the market today. Their use opens up new doors within a field for even deeper research into a given topic. "What" and "how" papers are explanatory in nature, thus they enable a discipline to explain something that is primary to a paradigm. This can be something as simple as a concrete item or as difficult as a concept. Either way, you need to have good hypotheses to support your claims of "what" and "how."

In this chapter we look at how to use "what" and "how" theoretical papers to expand your author's tool bag. In the first section we look at the existential elements of "what" as a theoretical question. Pure description is used for hypothesis testing; therefore something deeper is needed to test the theory. Next we look at the use of "how" questions. While "how" questions look at the construction of topics in the world, they are not simple how-to questions and should not be treated as such. In the third section we look at how these paper types can be used in the five macro-disciplines. As "how" and "what" are actually part of the same question, their use in the macro-disciplines is very similar.

"WHAT?"—THE EXISTENTIAL QUESTION

The question of what something is can be a very philosophical question. "What" is the stronghold of the relativists because "what" can really depend on the person who is observing. Each time a "what" question is answered, there can be a different answer; thus, the stronghold of the flawed theory of relativism is also its greatest weakness. Since all of the theory is logic based, the validity is very high; however, because of the observational nature of "what," the reliability is virtually nonexistent. "What" thus becomes the faith of relativism and the bane of many other types of research.

Relativism aside, "what" is still a very important member of the macro-theoretical questions. The most important item when designing a study is, "What is your research question?" Without defining the boundaries of your study, your study can quickly become unwieldy and useless. The same problem involves paradigms. If the question of "what" is not answered fairly early in the theoretical process, then the theoretical process stalls out as no boundaries have been defined. "What" therefore defines the boundaries of the paradigm and the concentration of any theoretical system.

"What" papers share many similarities with "why" papers. Both ask questions that are open for interpretation from multiple disciplines. The way to address these problems in these theoretical systems is to address the question from a multifaceted approach. If you come from a multidisciplinary background, then you can use that background to integrate hypotheses from different areas. If you are not from such a background, then you can bring peers in on your project to give it the multifaceted approach that a "what" question needs.

If you are writing theory and not philosophy, be careful not to delve too deeply into the existential nature of "what," because it is a deep subject that can distract the researcher from the primary goal. As you address the essence of the "what" you can lose direction in your study. Thus within the "what" you must define an additional set of existential boundaries to keep "what" manageable. If you allow "what" to remain amorphous, then you will be chasing unicorns while others in your field answer the question you sought to answer.

"HOW?"— THE MECHANICAL QUESTION

In the dichotomy of "how" and "what" there is a clear delineation between two types of researchers. Generally, if you are comfortable with "what" then "how" becomes mundane in your eyes. Likewise, if you are a "how" person then "what" tends to be too ivory tower and fluffy for your liking. "What" tends to do well with auditory learners and visual learners, while "how" tends to do well with people who learn through tactile and hands-on learning. Ironically, they establish many of the same things, thus are both quite useful. "How" is the question of how something became and how we can repeat the process to understand our universe (or how it will happen again without our help).

One way to look at "how" questions is to look at things not yet done. This is one of the key areas of the physical sciences. If something cannot be done now but is theoretically possible, then someone is (or should be) researching how it can be done. If it is a good thing, then humanity will prosper from this knowledge. If it is a bad thing, like chemical weapons, then knowing how will let us prevent others from doing the process to create them. "How" is the knowledge of creation, and creation can be a very powerful tool in the hands of people who want to help others (conversely it can be a powerful tool in the hands of bad people, like radical Muslims, too).[1]

"How" can also answer the question of how we build new things that are not yet here. Spaceships, the cure for cancer, or protections from genetic diseases are all things that we can ask "how" about. The "how" theories are an answer to a question just like any other theory. The more detailed we are

1. No Nukes for Iran.

when we ask questions, the simpler it will be to find the theoretical answers. Thus the "what" and the "how" are eternally intertwined for the betterment of humankind.

Finally, there is the industrial application of "how." This is the question of whether there is a better way to do things. This style of paper is very near to a hypothetical paper or a how-to paper. Generally these types of theories are only supported by two or three hypotheses. Although you might think that this would make them unstable, the quick turnaround from theory to proof usually prevents them from being destabilized. You should be careful with these types of papers, because the U.S. Patent Office is violating the Constitution and issuing procedural patents so your "new" idea may be encroaching on an idea that someone else is hoarding.

HOW "WHAT" AND "HOW" PAPERS ARE FRAMED

In the social sciences, "what" papers are king, or rather pseudo-king. Many of the new papers in the social sciences do not actually put forth a theory, rather they attempt to present a new facet to an old theory from a relativist point of view. These theoretical papers are not "what" papers, but simply observational reports offered in support of a favorite theory. "How" papers are more technically sound, but less popular. As they require a positivist perspective (way 1 is better than way 2), they are seen as dangerous to the relativist position and often attacked.

In the physical sciences, the question of "what" generally comes down to defining a specific topic. The "how" questions are the major moves forward in the physical sciences field, in fact they are the primary means of study in these fields. A good "how" paper (generally only five to seven pages) can be enough to establish someone in the physical sciences. However, it can take years to create the hypothetical and empirically tested system that will be entered into a physical sciences "how" paper.

In business and law, "what" and "how" are questions of convenience. Few theories are put forward on these two areas, but massive amounts of research are done in these areas because they open up more efficient means of operation. In the legal or business areas, rather than writing a theoretical "what" or "how" paper it may be more advantageous to write a brief or white page, respectively, to build your credibility within a field.[2] If you come up with something truly unique, then you can always patent your idea and make others pay you for it.

Finally, in the area of humanities and philosophy, "how" is a tool to get to "what." "What" and "how" are the central questions to the discipline, though few theories are created in these areas.

---

2. *See* Chapter 32: White Pages and Chapter 34: Briefs.

Philosophical meanderings can be heavily based in either question, so learning the process can be valuable. And in the humanities, either question can advance the field you are working in; however, publishing a theoretical paper in these fields is often seen as taboo as you are setting something in stone that is generally an interpretive matter. Always be the judge of whether a new paper will hurt or harm your career.

CHECKLIST

- ❑ How does your field see "what" and "how" questions?
- ❑ Can you support your theory with hypotheses or is your theory actually a hypothesis?
- ❑ How much support can you make for your theory?
- ❑ Can you patent it?

chapter 29
"When" Papers

INTRODUCTION

Time is the most complex topic of all theoretical papers. As human beings we do not understand time. Is it a constant stream moving in one direction with no starting point (or a point in the distant past)? Is time a digital apparatus where each moment is unique in time as the world passes around it? Some even speculate that time is a flow like a river that one can move back and forth through, just like any other dimension. Which of these ideas on time are correct? Perhaps they all are correct. Fortunately, when it comes to writing theoretical papers, all are accepted as paradigms in which a paper can be written. Choosing one of these paradigms is what separates a theorist who works in time from the theorists who are just wasting their time.

A "when" question is any question that deals with the time or timing of an event, person, place, society, concept, or topic (hereinafter topic for ease of reading). These questions want to anchor a topic somewhere in the timestream so that it can be compared to other events within the same range. For example, a social scientist could look at the development of a meso-American group in comparison to a sub-Saharan African group at a single point in time, 1850 for example, then compare the development from that point to another point in time, say 1900. This would allow the researcher to look at where each society evolved and where each society stagnated. "When" questions build context for other theoretical questions and thus are some of the more important questions that human beings have asked.

"When" questions are used in most fields, but "when" theories are much harder to find. The difference between a "when" question and a "when" theory is that the theory is supported by hypotheses,

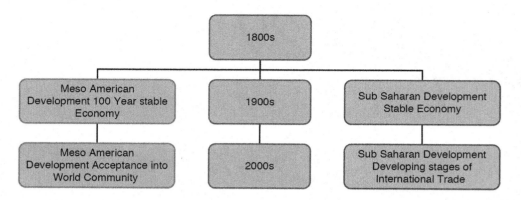

which are in turn supported by facts; the "when" question is simply answered by facts. Thus, "when" theories are much more complex and require that a researcher look much deeper at a topic than simply when the topic happened. A "when" theory should be multifaceted, looking at how individual elements of the topic are situation, both physically and developmentally, within the timeframe or timestamp that the study covers. Good "when" research is challenging but presents a broad scope of understanding when the research is complete.

This chapter is different from the format of the other chapters in certain ways: the conclusion to Part IV is included at the end, and the concept of time comes in three "families," which are each examined in respective sections. The first section looks at the concept of time as a constant. This is the family of theories that time is an immutable force that goes in one direction at a constant speed and cannot be changed or moved within. The second section looks at time as a flow or a stream. This family (which has heavy research going on now) believes that time is a dimension and like other dimensions can be moved through in a positive or negative direction. The third family does not get involved in the discussion of whether one can move through time or whether it is an immutable force, rather it looks at single movements (timestamps) or small groupings of time (timeframes) and the events that went on in the given designation. This is the topic of the third section.

TIME AS A CONSTANT

One of the ways in which time can be seen is as a constant, immovable force in the universe. Time is the great equalizer, for no matter the size be it a sun or a simple bacteria, time dismantles and reassembles all things. As an immutable force, the question of "when" begins to take on the specter of a "how" question as placing things within the timestream only links them to certain points in time. When approaching a theoretical paper on "when" as it pertains to time as a constant immutable force, an author is generally looking at how things were different before the progress of time marched on.

In this family of time theories, time is constantly building upon itself. Time itself is ethereal, only visible in the changes we see in the world around us. Our bodies age, houses sag, the world erodes and rebuilds itself. All of these things are brought on by the inevitable march of time. Looking at what was can be an interesting experiment, and theorizing about long forgotten things can be done by building up strong hypotheses to support your theory. If you choose to take this approach look at time not as a barrier that is shielding you from your research, but as a gateway that leads you to the path of what you want to know.

Those that ascribe to the belief that time is an immutable force understand that the progression of time is moving toward not the end of itself, for time is a concept; rather, time is moving toward the end of consciousness. Time exists because things realize it exists, not just humans but anything that is self-aware (maybe things on other planets, too). This means that the force of time is a psychic force, or rather a mental understanding of time as a force that we cannot see or fully understand at this point in our evolution. Our understanding of time then becomes a vessel in the timestream, something that we use for context as the raging river of time flows underneath. As we write papers, we are gauging the depth of the river as we journey toward our written paper.

Understanding time is akin to understanding life, and our understanding will always be complete because we do not know what is coming in the future. If we somehow do gain the ability to look into the future of the timestream, then this family of temporal logic will cease to exist because the stream becomes a dimension rather than a force. Thus, to write in this topic one must accept that we cannot know the future, but we can infer the future through proper methods. If you write a "when" paper using this family of time theories as your guide, then you will find that statistics (especially predictive stats) are one of your best hypothesis testing tools.

TIME AS A FLOW

There is an old Garth Brooks song that goes "Time is like a river, ever changing as it flows and a dreamer's just a vessel that must follow where it goes."[1] This is a good analogy for those who feel that time is a flow. As a researcher who believes that time is a dimension, thus it can be moved into in multiple directions, an author must be willing to look at how cause and effect can interfere with one another in the system. This system is much more complex than the constant flow approach, but since humanity has not found a way to mess with our own past (or future) we still have a very approachable system.

The concept that time is a dimension allows for the belief that you can move forward and backward in time. Now this is not a simple process. Just like it takes great effort to move off of the baseline in the dimension of height, so too does it take effort (energy) to move through time. To this point,

---

1. Brooks, Garth, *The River*.

humanity has not discovered that type of energy, so time travel is still impossible. Please note that this book does not take one position or the other. The first proposition that time is a constant force is easier to support because all the data we currently have leads us to believe that; however, the premise that time is a dimension that can be moved within opens up a much brighter (or darker) future/history for humanity. Both of these families of theory have their merits, but neither has been proven yet so we have the option of working in either.

In this version of time, the past is a frontier to be explored. Even if we cannot go there we can theorize how different events in the past, had they been changed, would affect the present and the future. Theorists in this area can then look for like sets of circumstances in the modern world and look at how we can affect the future by working in the present. Unfortunately, there are also those who call themselves "futurists" who "predict" the future based on shoddy theoretical work about the past (and often speculation about the present). This group of researchers has damaged the reputation of people who do time flow theory to the point that it is difficult to take seriously. If you elect to get into this field, make sure that you support your propositions with hypotheses so that your theory can wear the inevitable criticism.

For those who research in this area, time becomes a map for exploring the past. For those who write alternative histories and look for similarities in the present, minor divergence from the path of time can change major elements in society. These theories will always be theories (unless we time travel), so it is a "safe" area to do theoretical research. If your logic is sound, then the reliability of this type of research is very high; however, the validity is very low because we will never know if you are correct. The map of time always leads to now, changing the direction at one point leads to some other place we know nothing about.

The greatest challenge to doing time flow theory is that you cannot show that it is real. Most data that we currently have in our collective human knowledge shows that we cannot change the course of time; however, there are those exceptions that seem to empower time flow researchers. How you see time can determine how you research time. Either way, always make sure to have tested hypotheses to support your claims.

TIME AS DIGITAL

For most of us, the "when" in our "when" papers is not going to be dealing with the physics problem of how time is construed; rather, we are going to be looking at a specific time stamp or time frame. This is the most common format of time analysis in most of the academic world. In this situation you define a beginning time and an ending time for your theory and then theorize what happened between time A and time B. This is very useful in historical data across all fields. This approach looks at time as a series of moments, and as authors we have the ability to describe each one of these moments.

Of note there is another approach in this philosophy, the Cartesian approach. Under the approach founded by Descartes, he assumed that the world was created and destroyed every moment by a para-supremely powerful being. Then the being would create the world anew to deceive us, as Descartes speculated that this being was a deceiver. The reason why this is noteworthy is that this was a transitional theory within a logic problem that Descartes ultimately discarded. The ultimate proof that this was the construction of the universe ended in the often paraphrased, "I think therefore I am."[2] Understanding that this is a disproved understanding of the universe can help you immerse yourself into one of the other camps, if you want to deal with temporal physics.

Looking at time from a digital perspective, even when we do not accept this as the way that the universe "is" allows us to examine each moment in human history in the microcosm. By defining a clear set of boundaries for our study, both temporal and physical, we can accentuate the detail that we put into our research projects. The more narrowly we construe out project, the more focus we can give to each element; thus we can give readers a more interesting analysis of the data. Our boundaries, when properly done, allow us to immerse our readers into our research, helping them journey through the same path that led us to our final product.

HOW TO FRAME A "WHEN" PAPER

In the social sciences, "when" papers are fairly simple because we are looking for when a social event happened in the past. As long as we do not overreach when we are setting our studies boundaries, these types of papers can be very easy for sociologists, archeologists, anthropologists, and others in the social sciences fields. There are two ways for us to define time in the social sciences, either by asking help from the hard sciences and getting things carbon dated or by relying on oral histories. Oftentimes the later is easier but the former is more accurate. Your hypothesis, if you want it accepted, should be founded on both social science and hard science.

In the physical sciences the mechanism for defining the time of a sample is complex, but the papers are quite simple. You theorize what the data of a sample is from the carbon decay within the sample. Easy. This is still a theory because there are elements that can corrupt carbon sampling; however, the likelihood of these problems is quite low. Therefore, in the physical sciences the research takes a significant amount of time for a "when" paper, but the actual paper writing can be as simple as three to five pages.

---

2. Biffle, Christopher (1996). *A Guided Tour of Rene Descartes Meditations on the First Philosophy*, 2nd ed. London: Mayfield Publishing Company. (Loose interpretation).

In business and law, when can be the difference between winning and losing in a career. As a result, theories are not generally good enough for answering the question "when?" In either of these fields, "when" papers are very rare and should only be undertaken if you are doing historical work for an archive.[3] The "when" of a question generally does not have as much use in these fields. The same can be said for the humanities; however, there is a narrow gap of forensic data that is useful for dating pieces of art and collections. In these examples you may find "when" theories but they are linked to the hard sciences in the methods they use for this type of research.

CHECKLIST

- ❏ Which view of time are you using?
- ❏ Did you set parameters for your study?
- ❏ Have you supported your theory with valid hypotheses?

CONCLUSION PART IV

We should all ask the "who," "what," "where," "when," "why," and "how" questions in our daily lives. These six question types are the foundation of knowledge. While theoretical research is more complex than standard hypotheses testing, it is also foundational at the most basic level. Each time humanity discovers something new we establish a new baseline for future research. If you are a researcher who establishes a new theory and your theory proves to stand the test of time, then your theory will become the new starting point for future research. However, a theory is just a theory until it is proven to be a law or disproven as simply a thing to be tested and challenged.

The six question types (who, what, where, when, why, and how) are our tools to give us a better understanding of the world around us. Each time one of these questions is answered then we know more. Just because it is answered with a theory does not mean that the answer is any less relevant. For something to be proven, it must first be a theory, and to be a theory it must be some collection of hypotheses. Knowledge is a constant building process; just like a journey is one step in front of the other, the growth of human knowledge is one fact in front of the other. Until the question is asked the answer will not be sought; therefore, theories (and whether they are correct or not) shall always be one of the key areas for the growth of human knowledge.

---

3. When actions should be taken, for example when the death penalty should be used, can also be good topics for "when" papers.

Part V
BASIC AND PROFESSIONAL PAPERS

chapter 30
Introduction to Miscellaneous Methods

INTRODUCTION

While quantitative, qualitative, and theoretical methods are the main pantheon of academic writing methodologies that we face in the world today, there are also several lesser used methodologies that are useful to have as a tool in any writer's tool bag. Just because a methodology is neither commonly used nor commonly requested does not mean that it does not have a use in a specific circumstance. It is having the proper tools in these limited circumstances that will set you apart as an author in the academic setting. Each new tool in your tool bag is a new situation that you are prepared for.

As writing is a journey of discovery, sometimes you are going down paths that you do not normally travel. It is in these instances that you need tools that you do not normally use. It is similar to a guide exploring a new region of a forest, then realizing that he or she needs a carbineer to climb a rock face. While a carbineer is not a tool that is needed often, whenever the guide faces a situation where a carbineer is needed it is good to have one. The same can be said for writing, in that if a writer is facing a situation that is not the type of writing he or she does often, then it is good to have the tools necessary for the project. The goal of this part of the book is to give you those tools usable in rare situations.

A good writer, like a good guide, is a jack of all trades who chooses to master a few over the course of his or her career. This means that any time an opportunity arises in the course of normal business to expand one's skill set one should grasp the opportunity and become a more rounded writer. In this part of the book we look at some of the less common papers and how they can be integrated into your existing skill set. In the first section of this chapter we set the foundation by looking at some of the reasons that an author may choose to write in one of the miscellaneous styles. The reason for writing out of your normal style often dictates the type of writing that you may use in these circumstances. In the second section we look at how you can put good tools in your toolbox. Having a toolbox that is filled with worn or rusty tools does a craftsman no good, and this is also the case for writers. You should always be seeking to upgrade your skill set and further master your art. This introductory chapter concludes with a preview of the chapters contained in this part. Each type of miscellaneous paper has a specific task and a specific area of writing where it shines as a methodology. By the end of this part, you may not be an expert in all of these methodologies, but you will know the basics and have a good foundation for integrating these methodologies into your skill set.

WHY WRITE A MISCELLANEOUS PAPER?

Generally miscellaneous papers are a product of a requirements placed upon you by an outside source. The most commonly written type of miscellaneous paper is by far the term paper. Term papers are assigned by professors to examine whether a student has assimilated the data that has been presented in the class; thus each term paper is different in the nature of the need. You will find that this is the case for most types of miscellaneous papers; briefs are assigned by partners or judges, white pages are a result of industry or corporate need, reports are requested by a higher up, grants are required by the grant agencies. Newspapers (magazines) and hybrid papers are slightly different in that the need for these types of papers are dictated by the situation rather than by another person, but as with all miscellaneous papers these too are a product of requirement.

Sometimes minor papers are an author's way of stepping out of the shadows and into the spotlight for a brief amount of time. When your company needs a white page on the new product they are unveiling, a well-written paper can make or break a career. When a judge requires a case brief for a motion hearing, if it is your case brief that they use you could gain notoriety at your firm. If a grant company selects your grant, your university will take notice that you are bringing money into the school. Miscellaneous papers are often a gateway type of paper to introduce someone into a more permanent role as a writer, but this role will only open up for you if you do well and deliver the paper that is needed.

Some minor papers establish a writer as an expert within the general population. While many people are experts within their own field, few people gain notoriety among the public. Academic papers are just not read by everyday people. Some miscellaneous papers can provide a gateway to get your information out to the general public. It can be a difficult task for experts to transition their writing style from the trade papers that they normally write to a paper for the general public, but once they master this skill it can be a major boon for their career. Minor papers also allow for someone to make a minor point in the process of building a larger point. If you are building a large theory, minor papers can be a way to "test the waters" with the more controversial points to find the weaknesses in your theory before you subject it to peer review. The more careful you are in the release of your minor points the more effective the process can be to building a strong paper.

GOOD TOOLS IN A TOOL BOX

Ask any tradespersons if they have a tool in their toolbox that they rarely use and all will tell you yes. Having worked in the plumbing field for most of my teenage years, I can tell you that having a tool that you do not need is much better than not having a tool that you do not need. While this concept should not be carried to absurdity, it should be a conscious effort on your part to ensure you have the skills that you need to be the best writer you can be. Even if you never write a term paper after you get all the fancy letters after your name, it is still a good skill to have to teach others how to succeed.

The miscellaneous papers that are contained in this section are good tools to have in your tool bag. They are papers that are commonly written in the United States, though individual academics and professionals do not write them often (except reports). Having the ability to create one of these papers, even at the most basic level, can help you distinguish yourself from the pack in whatever field you are in. These are tools that can allow you to be more efficient and thus more useful to those who are above you in the chain of command. While these skills will not be practiced often, having them is much better than not having them.

From a holistic point of view, having these skills make you a more complete author. If you master all of the skills in this book (something few have done), then you are establishing yourself among the elite academic writers of history. Most of us, however, are going to learn one or two of the methodologies in this book then use the book as a reference for when the other types of papers become needed. This is alright, too. Knowing about these types of papers and knowing where you can find the pattern to write one is second only to mastering all the skills in the world. Everyone does not have to be a grand master writer, most of us can make it by being knowledgeable and proficient.

FORMAT OF SECTION

This part of the book walks you through eight different types of papers that you may be called upon to write in fairly short order. The individual chapters are designed as primers to get you to a basic level of proficiency so that you will be able to comply with a need if one should ever arise. If you augment the skills covered in this chapter with the skills covered in the other sections of this book, even the most novice paper you write in one of these styles will come across as if you are proficient in the methodology. All papers must be clear, they must speak to the audience, and reel the audience into the work. If you can build these three elements into your miscellaneous papers then you will be well ahead of your peers.

In Chapter 31 we look at the most commonly used miscellaneous paper, the term paper. A term paper is a writing requirement for a class to show the professor or lecturer that you know the material that was presented. Term papers are not a major research paper, rather they are a simple report on what was covered in class. In Chapter 32 we look at white pages. A white page is a business paper, published by a company or group of companies, that provides a semi-academic explanation of a new product, structure, or idea that is being introduced onto the market. Generally, white pages are produced during the patent/copyright process to establish ownership in the general market. In Chapter 33 we look at general reports and case reports. A report is a collection of data without a major synthesis that proves or disproves a hypothesis. A case report is a report the focuses on a specific case. Then in Chapter 34 we take the idea of a report one step further into the legal field to look at the existence of briefs. A brief is a concise document that explains the basic elements of a case, whether for general court or appeals court.

In Chapter 35 we look at how to write a grant. This topic was surveyed in the introductory part of the book, but will be covered in detail in Chapter 35. Next, in Chapter 36 we look at gists, which are the business world's version of a case brief. A gist is a concise document that informs someone in a leadership position of the details of a specific case in as brief of a document as possible. In Chapter 37 we look at the process for writing a hybrid paper. A hybrid paper is any paper that mixes two or more methodologies to meet the needs of a given project. As academic research evolves, we can expect to see more hybrid papers spanning both methodologies and research disciplines. We end with Chapter 38 by looking at how to write newspaper and magazine articles. While these are not strictly academic papers, they are still useful tools to have in one's tool bag.

Miscellaneous papers are tools like any other writing methodology. Just because they are used less commonly in the academic and professional world does not make them any less important when the need arises. If you have these tools ready in your tool belt when the need arises, then you may be able to advance your career with a single paper. Because of the rarity of their use, they are often overlooked, but if you are resigned to become a versatile author these tools should be part of who you are.

CHECKLIST

- ❏ Have you reviewed the major methodologies?
- ❏ Why does your project fall outside the realm of major papers?
- ❏ Which method do you believe you need to use?
- ❏ Review the chapter you believe you need.

chapter 31
Term Papers

INTRODUCTION

Term papers are the tourist's journey in our jungle exploration analogy. When you write a term paper you are traveling down a path that dozens, sometimes hundreds, of students have already traveled and the topic has been examined and reexamined hundreds of times. When you are writing a term paper you are simply restating the information that you were given in a class to show your professor what you learned. While the mechanics of the paper may seem simple, the usefulness of the paper should not be understated. Without the ability to write at least a passable term paper many people would never make it to the point where they can actually research and write an academic paper. Colleges are the gatekeepers to writers of new entries in the academic canon.

Term papers are most commonly used in college classes near the end of a term. These papers are generally the main assessment tool for the course, or a supporting assessment tool that allows a professor to know that you know the information. Generally there are only two reasons that authors should be writing a term paper. The first is if they are in a class where a term paper is required for your professor to assess their understanding of the course and their ability to write as a student. The second is if you are creating a sample term paper for students to use as a point of reference in your class. If you are falling into the second category, I would suggest teaching your students how to write a simple QMS paper looking at the data that was covered in class. In this way you will allow you students to learn the proper procedure for doing a research paper and still have them cover the material that is needed to show they learned what was taught in class.

This chapter quickly covers the basic elements of a regular college term paper. **The number one rule of any term paper is to give your professors what they ask for.** Simply because you are trained to complete a term paper in a given fashion does not really work as an argument when a professor gives you a failing grade on a paper. While the format covered in this chapter covers most term papers, there are professors out there who have their own method that they defend religiously. In the first section this chapter we talk about the wonderful art of regurgitation. Most professors are looking for the data that they covered in class and that you show the ability to collect some (not much) data outside of those boundaries. If you can follow their basic instructions and regurgitate the data they want you can usually do quite well on a term paper. In the second section we look at how you can parlay the data you collect in your term paper process into other papers. Even if you are doing a simple term paper, you will still be collecting data. If you take the data collection process seriously and treat it like you would the data collection process in any other paper, then you can begin building a repository of data that you may use in later papers. In the third section we return to the golden rule of term papers—that is, give your professors what they want. Your professors are the gatekeepers; they are the ones who give you the grades and they are the arbiters of whether you pass or fail.

REGURGITATION

One of the key issues that students must realize about most term papers is that the professor does not expect you to come up with a totally new idea. If every professor required every student in every class to come up with a new idea, then society would have solved all of our major problems and we would have ushered in a golden age. This is not the case, of course. Most professors simply require that each student turn in a grammatically sound term paper that demonstrates that he or she understands the basic concepts of the class. Students that go beyond this simple rubric tend to find themselves missing some of the basic data, thus they are punished for trying to do more than is required.

Unless your professor requests otherwise, you should be parroting back to the professor what was learned in class with your own personal spin on it. If you are assigned a topic from a basic sociology class and asked to write a paper on rational choice theory, you should use as much information from the course as is relevant to the paper. If you relate the material that you learned in class to the topics covered by the professor, then you should be able to turn in a paper that meets or exceeds the paper topic. Remember, the key source for most term papers is the course itself.

Exceptional term papers go beyond the simple parroting of a professor's lessons and build a research topic around the general information of the class. Students who truly want to excel in writing term papers should use the same format that is used in a transcendental phenomenology.[1] If you use the course materials as a focal point, you can then expand from the focal point with book research. The format of the paper should be a simple report on the data; however, if you take the time to collect good data during your data collection phase you will be able to present a much more robust paper. Good data will result in a better paper.

Many of you will look at a term paper as a means to an end. If this is the case, then make sure that the papers you turn in lead you to the best end possible. Too often students do their term papers late in the evening before they are due, which leads to a lackluster effort that shows when the professor grades the paper. The more effort you put into the paper the better product you can put out. You should always attempt to present the best possible product when you are turning in a written work because whatever you turn in is becoming part of your personal brand. This means that even the basic term papers that you turn into your professors may be what some editor remembers you by purely by happenstance.

DATA FOR USE IN OTHER PAPERS

If you are a truly adventurous student, or a person who is OCD about keeping notes, then you have the option of treating a term paper as a data collection practice for another paper. Good authors expand their archive of usable data for future papers, thus shortening the amount of research time each paper consumes. If you are going to take the time to collect rich data for a term paper, then why would you not save that data to write an academic paper? Every project that you complete throughout your college career should build toward your successful career. If you are going to take the time to research a topic, save that data and keep it in mind for future projects that may intersect that topic.

If you are truly ambitious, or just hate to see good data not used, create a QMS paper from the data that you collect for your term paper. Just because you used a given dataset to create a paper for a specific class does not mean that you cannot augment that research and build a QMS paper for publication.[2] Even if you are in an undergraduate class, taking the time to write a well-designed QMS paper for an undergraduate journal can give your college career a boost. Regardless of wheth-

1. *See* Chapter 21: Phenomenology.
2. *See* Chapter 22: Qualitative Meta-Synthesis.

er you are an undergraduate, a graduate student, or a professional in a given field, a publication on your resume can give your career that much needed push to move you to the next level.

If you follow this philosophy that no work should go unused, then you will find during your time in college—whether four years, six years, seven years, or even fourteen years—you will be able to compile a rather robust archive of data. If you concentrate your term papers on a single ideological thread of data across all of your courses, you can tie your archive to a specific topic. This will give you excellent data and a robust starting point for future professional papers after you get out of college. Time and time again you can return to your archive for new ideas and new data for evolving projects. A datum that is not useful in this year's research project could be the centerpiece of next year's project. Your personal database, if properly maintained, can be your starting point for the majority of your major projects.

GIVE PROFESSORS WHAT THEY WANT

Professors are king of their castle, lord of their fief, and final arbiter of your grade in any given class. When they give you the guidelines for your term paper, pay attention; knowing what they are looking for is the first step in securing a good grade in that class. Even if the requests that they are making for your paper seem pointless, always take the time to ensure that each and every element of what they requested is in your paper. Treat them as you would the editor of a major academic journal, their word is law (at least for the course of this assignment).

A course is like a professor's own private little world, you are a guest in this world and you should follow its laws. The guidelines for a course term paper are an immutable law of the land, so do not challenge it. Unless the professor is asking you to do something morally reprehensible, simply complete the paper as required and move on to the next class. The most vicious term papers tend to be in classes that are not even essential to your major. Complete the paper, then return back to your own major, leaving these professors and their odd paper styles in your wake. You are not building a home in the class; you are simply trying to finish the class with an A.

The syllabus for a course can be a goldmine of information on what you should do to get the best grade possible on your term paper. First, if the professor is doing a good job, the requirements of the paper should be included in the term paper. This should give you a rubric of what you should do and what is needed of you to complete the project with a complete grade. Next, the syllabus should contain the information that is highlighted in the class. The topics that professors give most often tend to be the topics that they will give the most credit for among their papers. Always take the time to look at the learning goals and the topics of information in the class so you can have the best chance of getting a good grade. Finally, look at the assignment deadlines. No matter how much work you put into writing a good paper, if you forget to turn the paper in on time your grade could suffer significantly. Always mark the due date on your calendar.

If there is one theme in this chapter it is, give the professor/lecturer/teachers what they want. Your goal in any class should be to get the best grade possible in that class, bar none. Don't let your opinions or your pride kill your GPA because you know how to write a paper better than your professor. This is a surefire way to destroy your GPA. As a student your job is to get in, get a good grade, learn the materials, and get out. Writing your term paper the way your teacher wants is the best way for you to do this. Don't be that student who knows better than the professor and fails. Take the time, follow the rubric, and get your A.

CHECKLIST

- ❑ Read the syllabus.
- ❑ Find the topics.
- ❑ Give professors the information they want.
- ❑ Get your A.

chapter 32
White Pages

INTRODUCTION

A white page is a business paper, published by a company or group of companies, that provides a semi-academic explanation of a new product, structure, or idea that is being introduced onto the market to entice investors or buyers. Many people who work in business fields will need to write a white page at some time during their business careers. White pages are advertisements in the form of a semi-academic paper, which means that they need to be written professionally to be effective. The more effective you are at presenting your data in a clear, concise, and convincing manner, the more effective you will be at creating white pages for your company.

White pages are an effective tool to broadcast information about your company or product to your buyers, investors, or the public in general. Unlike an academic paper where you are just looking to present the information in support of a hypothesis or theory, in a white page you are looking to convince a person that the product or service that you are promoting in your paper is the best and there is a reason that your reader should be buying or using it. This is one of the key differences between an informative academic paper and a persuasive professional paper. When a person is writing a white page the entire goal of the process is to ensure that your reader buys into the idea of your new product.

A question that many people ask is, "Why would you write a white page if you are a professional writer or an aspiring writer?" The answer is, because you have a product or service that you need to promote on behalf of your own self or your company. Like any other paper, white pages are a tool. As long as your white page is written to fulfill this need you will find that it basically writes itself if you have a good product. If you do not have a good product, then do you want to have a while page selling that product associated with your name? White pages are your statement why a product should be bought and a testament that you believe that the topic of the white page is a good topic. Never write a white page if you feel that it will damage your brand.

Most white pages, however, are going to be written on products or ideas that you have some vested interest in seeing succeed. For these papers, you should set a clear set of goals for your white papers. In the first section of the chapter we cover the first goal, to get the data out. All white papers have a set goal of getting information out into the market. When planning your project, make sure that the document is in a format where the people that you want to target as a readership will read. If no one reads the document then you did not get the information out. In the second section we cover how a white page is a chance to showcase your information. White pages are a sales pitch in document form to your investors and buyers. A good white page can save you millions of dollars in advertising expense later in the product's life. Finally, in the third section we review the need for your white page to read like a report. Readers expect that your white page will be a report that tells them what they need to know to make their life better. As you begin your journey to write your paper, if you are writing a white page make sure there is only once place where your journey should end, with someone investing or buying your product. Every page, every word you write, should move your project to that end.

GET YOUR DATA OUT

Generally, the reason businesses create white pages is because they have a need to get a specific set of data out to a specific group of people. The more focused the data and the more limited the group of target readers, the more you will be able to customize your document to their needs. As a white page is a sales pitch, you should always take into account as much of your readers' interest as possible. A white page can be blasted across the internet to generate interest from every person who reads it, but it is more effectively used as a precision tool to target specific investors or buyers whom you know will be looking for specific data.

Taking a step back from writing unbiased reports and focused academic work, a white page is a report published by a business. This report is meant to be biased and support your businesses image in a specific field. While the constraints of ethics should never be voided and the truth should always be told, you should be writing your white page for a specific purpose. The best white pages are not papers that are written equally and supportive of all players in an industry; rather they are papers with a specific slant that furthers a business's specific interest. Thus when you are writing a white page you are not trying to get all data out, only your data out.[1]

A well-written white page is an excellent tool to get data out to the public. If you need to get your data out, white papers are the method that gives you the most control over what your readership has access to. As long as you have followed the ethical rules and your data is true, then your goal should be to provide your readers with the most persuasive argument about why they should buy your service or product. Your goal should be to give them as much of your data as possible, not just any data. Your ability to control what your readers get is your golden ticket to knowing that they are getting all the information that you want them to have about your product. If they have your information, and it seems like enough, you are well on your way to getting their attention.

LET INVESTORS KNOW YOU ARE PROFESSIONAL

White pages are also a tool that helps you create an image of professionalism in the field. Even though everyone knows that white pages are a persuasive tool for most companies, they are still looked upon as a source of information in the field. If your white page is well written and on the cutting edge of the field, then you may have something that will become a work that is looked upon as an anchor of a new field. As new products enter into the field, investors look to white pages to see the abilities of the company that put out the white page. If a company puts out a bad white page, then investors will look poorly on that product introduction. If the company puts out a good white page, then the product looks better.

White pages allow you to establish yourself as an expert in the field. Investors and buyers are more likely to feel comfortable working with an expert than they are with some Joe Schmoe off the street. This means that white pages are worth putting the time and effort into them to make sure that they are the best product possible. As a professional, white pages become part of your personal brand. It is very important to establish that you are as professional as possible in your writing. If you are unsure of your writing ability, pay an editor. Even if the editor does not make significant changes, it is still better to know that there are no typos or minor problems when you enter into a project. Professionalism can be established or destroyed by something as simple as a misspelled word or a misplaced comma.

---

1. A good mix is two parts general data and one part "sales" data; the other style that is effective in a white paper is to identify the problem then write the solution in a way that makes it common sense for the reader to come to your company for the solution.

Another use that is less common for white pages is to combat rivals white pages. Sometimes your opposition will get a white page out before you have a chance to get one out on your product. In this case, you job is the same—to make your product look as good as possible. However, in these "counter-white pages" you will find that you have the double task of discrediting data presented by your rivals that is incorrect, then presenting your own data to inform your readership. White page battles can get nasty in fields where many people are pushing many innovations at the same time; however, if you are the author that writes professional white pages without negative name calling that marks a bad white page, you can make your brand look better as other brands fall.[2]

READS LIKE A REPORT

The ultimate mastery of a white page is ensuring that it reads like a report. The more professional and formal the document seems the better it will be received by the industry.[3] The first thing that you must remember as you write a white page is that it is a report. It should have the five-part format that makes reports standard the world over. There should be an introduction, at least three main points, then a summary stating why the report is relevant to your readers. If you follow this format, it will be standard enough for readers to assimilate into their business.

As you are writing your report, every sentence and every word should support your position on the data. If something in your report does not support your position in some way, then you should not put it into your report—it is that simple. A white page is like a short story in the idea that there is not room for anything other than the data you need in your report. Always take at least one read-through to determine if any of the information you present in your report is unplanned, neutral, or even harmful to your report. This type of information may be useful in other types of academic or professional papers, but in a white page every single word should further your goals.

The final thing that you want to address when preparing a white page is whether your white page is efficient. Efficiency is what gets white pages read. Without checking and rechecking your white page for efficiency, you run the risk of putting out a product that will not put your goal in a good light. Do not make this mistake. As with all writing, an ounce of prevention is worth a pound of the cure.[4] Sending out a broad or unwieldy white page can do irreparable harm to your image or the image of your company that can make the white page do more harm than good.

---

2. This is reminiscent of the Edison/Tesla battle over electricity.
3. The goal is to make your white page seem unbiased even though it is biased.
4. Ben Franklin (1772).

CHECKLIST

❑ Is your white page about the same length as other white pages in your field (or shorter)?
❑ Does it follow a five-part report structure?
❑ Does each word, phrase, and sentence support your position?
❑ Have someone else look over it before you put it out on the market.

RECOMMENDED READING

Mehring, Jessica (2014). *Content that Sells Without Selling*. New York: Amazon Digital Publishing.

Stelzner, Michael (2006). *Writing White Papers: How to Capture Readers and Keep Them Engaged*. N/A: White Paper Source Publishing.

chapter 33
Reports and Case Reports

INTRODUCTION

A report is a data file where information is supplied without opinion and without major academic analysis. Reports are used constantly in many fields because they are an effective way to build data archives for business, research, and other areas. Even if you are going to be a writer within a specific style of academic writing, learning how to write reports can be good for your career. The better your reports are, the more easily that you and your peers will be able to find data that is already collected. If you can form a good archive of reports on the main subject matter that you write on, then you will have a plethora of developed data and will be able to focus your research on new material in the field rather than searching through old data that you have already harvested.

Case reports are similar to regular reports but they focus on more specific subject matters. Case reports are often used in the same fashion as gists and briefs, as a tool that allows another research-er to build upon your data without having to review all of the sources that you used in compiling it. Well-written case reports will allow you to have a detailed explanation of a given phenomenon or instance without analysis to cloud the objectivity. This can be useful as a primer on a specific phenomenon or instance, or it can be used as a research source for future research that involves a given area.

Reports and case reports have many uses in business and academia, too many to cover in this chapter. The key use of reports and case reports is to keep a record of events that are not important enough that an individual study will be done on them. Most major companies have someone that files reports on various topics throughout the year. These reports are then used for their data in other reports at a later time. Case reports are most often used to catalogue an event. Unlike a normal report, case reports tend to look at an individual event rather than report on all events that are going on during a period of time. This adds a specificity to case reports that is not apparent in normal operational reports. Reports and case studies should be used as a tool to archive data for when it is needed in the future.

This chapter covers the basic elements that should be contained in a report or a case report. As these are not types of major academic papers, the chapter will be necessarily short. Further, each company/firm generally has its own format to write a report or case report. Therefore, if your company tells you that you should write a report in a method that differs from this book, by all means write it the way your employer wants it. In the first section of this chapter we discuss how to write a report as an exercise in condensing data with minimal analysis. This is vital for reports as those reading the reports generally want to know the data, not your findings or opinions. In the second section we reference writing a case report as a case study without the analysis tool. This can be an effective method to build up your writing portfolio because if you rewrite a good case report with an analysis section then you have a case study. In the third section we discuss why you write a case report, as many of you may already be feeling that if all you need to do is write an analysis section, why not write a complete academic paper. We will also discuss why some businesses, colleges, and law firms want reports to be just the data. We conclude in the fourth section with a discussion of how you can turn a report or a case report into a source of rich data for another project. Many times companies will have several people writing reports, so if possible you can use those reports as a data source for your next academic or professional project.

DATA WITHOUT ANALYSIS

First and foremost a report (or a case report) is simply an academic or professional paper without the analysis section. You will still provide your readers with a basic introduction, to inform them about your writing. You will provide them with a brief methodology section so that they know how you procured the data. The data section (rather than the analysis) will be the heart and soul of the report. Then you will provide your opinions or findings (in a very limited way) in a conclusion where you wrap up the topic of the report or case report. If you follow this format, your report will read like a regular academic paper, albeit one that is missing the analysis.

The reason that you often write reports as papers without an analysis section is because you are collecting data for someone else to analyze. While you can input small measures of findings to help your reader come to the same conclusions as you, you must realize that this is their project and you are just a contributor. This can be tough for many young writers (or even veterans) to swallow. However, if you insist on writing complete academic papers, with the analysis included, it can come across as arrogant and that you are doing work above your position. Even worse you could come across as trying to "one up" your boss. This can be devastation for your career. Thus this is an area where you must achieve balance; you must write enough that your boss can tell you are interested in this area at your work, but leave the work brief enough that those in charge of the project can still do their own analysis.

While you are writing a report or a case report, you must always remember that even though this is not your project, it is still your data. You are putting your name on it when you send it to the project leader; thus, this report becomes part of your brand. As it is part of your brand, you should put the same diligence and effort into collecting good rich data as you would for one of your own papers. Anything less could tarnish your reputation in the eyes of the project leader or your company at large. Even if you feel that a job you have been assigned is inconsequential, you should still give it your best effort to ensure that you are putting your best foot forward.

There is an old saying "The devil is in the details."[1] I do not know if the devil is in the details, but I do know that your promotions and your superior's opinions of you are in the details. A good report should be full of the type of data that you would like to have if you were doing a full academic or professional paper on your topic. People who turn in "half-assed" reports end up in the same position, year after year. It is the people who turn in good reports with high-quality data that are noticed by the project managers. It is more like the biblical saying, "Those that can be trusted in small matters can be trusted in great matters."[2] You should create data for others as you would want people to create data for you.

CASE STUDY WITHOUT ANALYSIS

Case reports can be even harder to swallow as a type of report to submit, especially when the conclusion or findings are obvious. While large-scale reports (from the first section) can cover vast amounts of data that require a certain expertise to analyze, cases are generally a fairly simple matter to analyze; thus many young lawyers and writers want to make their findings known in the case

1. Anonymous.
2. Luke 16:10.

report before they are vetted. This can lead a person to look overanxious, or worse if you make a mistake incompetent. Thus when you are doing a case report you should stick to reporting on just the facts.

The first step in a good case report is to look at the case in detail, then look at those details again. This is where legal recursive frame analysis (LRFA) can come in handy. LRFA can help you break down cases into manageable pieces of data, even if it is not a legal case. As a writer you should get into the habit of using the same coding and analysis tools for all your projects where they are the right tool. Even if you are not going to complete the analysis, if you give your project manager a case report where the data is coded and categorized, then it shows that you have initiative but still have enough respect not to take the project too far. If you know the specifics of how the data should be coded, then use those. If not, then you can always code thematically or topically. Just be careful not to take the step between coding and analysis.

Your case report should take great care to present what happened to the readers of your project. The more details you can provide in a brief report, the better your readers will be able to backtrack the data for the information that they need. This is another area where coding can be very useful. If you are able to turn in a good case report, following a logical coding methodology, and your superior needs more data to build a project then you can provide your coded notes and the data will be in the same format throughout. This will let you turn in a brief report and still be able to provide the project leader with addition details if needed.

After you have completed all of this work, it may seem self-defeating to stop short of the analysis. Do not give into the temptation to take your writing process one step too far and write a full paper. This can ruin all the good work that you have put in. While we might like it to be different, humans are emotional beings. If you push too hard and offend your project manager, no matter how good your data is the manager may still find reason to reject it. As you are moving up through the ranks this is something that should be avoided at all costs. Take the time to give your project manager a good report—you can even write the analysis if you want in another file—just do not force it into the report that you turn in. If you are asked for the information, then by all means turn in that extra file (after waiting a short period of time to make it seem like you were not ahead of the game). It is a good career move to show initiative but still give exactly what you are asked for, because going too far can make you seem like a gunner.

CASE STUDY THAT MAY BE NEEDED FOR A JOB OR ARCHIVE

Sometimes it is difficult to do as you are told. Analysis is the fun part of writing a paper (unless the data collection process is in a very cool location); which is why project managers like to do the analysis rather than the data collection. Though it is tempting, do not force your analysis into a report. However, there may be other reasons that they do not want you to do analysis. Many times companies create archives of data for long-term longitudinal projects (which you may not even know about). In these cases the data you collect may be "incomplete." The word incomplete is in quotes because even though you collected the most complete data you were capable of collecting, there may be variances over the course of time that you did not or could not assimilate. This may be why the company wants a report not a paper, because you are collecting data for a project that may not be analyzed for 20 years. By that time, if you do a good job you may be the project manager that is permitted to analyze the data.

Regardless of the purpose for the data you are collecting, it is essential for your career that you produce good reports. Even if someone else "steals" the spotlight for your work, if you turn in bad work for the thief, the buck will simply pass back to you. A good work ethic is essential to most careers and for a writer it is one of the most important elements of your personality. Good writing shows that you have the wherewithal to manage your own project load. When you turn in a good project within a proper time frame your supervisors will be able to see that you are capable of self-management. This is one of the key criteria for managing others. Thus, in every project you do, even if very few people are going to see it, you should make sure that you do the best possible work.

As with anything you do in the writing world, the main goal is likely going to be career related. If you do good jobs with the data collection needed for reports then it is likely that some day you will earn the right to be the person doing the analysis of the data. Good data collection and attention to detail can show those who make the decisions that you have the skills needed to do your own analysis. As with anything in our hegemonic corporate and academic structure we see that patience and good work will pay off. Do not rush to take on work that is not yours to do. Take your time and do the tasks that are assigned to you to ensure that you have set the foundation for promotion.

USE YOUR DATA AS DATA COLLECTION FOR MAJOR PAPERS

If you are permitted to do so, collecting data for others in a report form does not have to be a death sentence for your work on the project. Always check with your supervisors and find out if you can create a public report on the data that you have collected (with proprietary secrets protected). If you are permitted, and most companies will allow this with proper hiding of the company names and practices, you can build your hard work collecting data into an academic paper and/or case report. This will allow you to demonstrate your analytical skills, get a publication, and possibly feed the ego that you had to swallow when you turned your data over to another person.

When working on major projects, good reports can be a good source of data, even if they are not a source you compiled. As long as you have legitimate access to a data source and properly cite it, then you can academically use the data in an academic paper. For the sake of politeness, you should contact the compiler of the data and make sure that this person is not using the data along the same strain as you are, but you will find that most data compilers are putting in time at their job and have no interest in academic writing. Once you find a collection of reports, whether it be in a library or a corporate archive, you have found a rich source of data that can be used in future projects (this is doubly true for business papers, for which collecting data can be quite difficult at times).

Overall, many academics and professionals see writing a good report as drone work that should be regulated to interns or graduate assistants, but it is a good skill builder that can help you get noticed whether in the private sector or in academia. Good reporting is good data collection, and anytime that you can improve your data collection skills you are improving your overall profile as a writer. When asked (or told) to create a report on something, take the task on with relish. These are often tests of trust to see how you do with real research in a corporate or academic setting. Good reports can be a stepping stone to bigger and better jobs, but only if they are done correctly.

CHECKLIST

- ❏ What is your boss looking for?
- ❏ Have you collected all reasonable data on the subject?
- ❏ Have you selected a methodology to organize it?
- ❏ Is it well organized that anyone who is knowledgeable with the topic can understand it?
- ❏ If you are doing a case report, is all data in the report related to the case that you are discussing?
- ❏ If there are any tangents, are they absolutely necessary to the integrity of the report?

chapter 34
Legal Briefs

INTRODUCTION

Of all the miscellaneous techniques, briefs are most commonly used in the professional environment. The interesting element with briefs is that they are not commonly used in the format that they are designed to be used as. While paralegals, interns, and young attorneys tend to write detailed briefs in the IRAC, CREAC, FIRAC, or whatever format their firm/law school taught them to write in, as attorneys develop a particular style about them, the briefs become shorter and shorter and the data becomes more and more condensed. What was needed for a case brief to be efficient when you started doing your own cases becomes redundant when you have done several hundred cases. This chapter looks at the elements that you need to have a good case brief when you get started, and as your personal style evolves you will develop your own strategy and skills.

To begin with a brief (in the legal sense) is a concise document that explains the basic elements of a case, whether for your personal use, your firm's use, or the general or appeals courts' use. This is a writing tool that many lawyers cannot live without. A case brief allows a lawyer, intern, or paralegal to give someone the details of a specific case in a single-page document that allows the recipient of the brief to understand the legal issues used and established in that case. An appellate brief is a concise written argument used for appeals that presents the relevant law and cases to a specific issue in a manner that allows a judge to make a ruling on that matter. More commonly, the patterns and tools used in an appellate brief are used to argue motions before a judge in general common court.

If you learn how to write briefs correctly, they can be an incredibly useful tools to promote your practice and your career. If you write them poorly, they can be the rope that hangs your career in the end. Briefs are a form of data collection and organization that allows lawyers and legal scholars to analyze the legal environment in a specific area and create cases and arguments based on that existing environment. They enable a law firm or group of lawyers to avoid the necessity of reading each and every part of each and every case before entering into the creation of legal theory. This allows the group to act as a semi-hive mind where some of the workers create briefs that can be quickly assimilated by the trial lawyers for use in a case. The method limits the use of higher-ups' more "valuable" time, regulating the majority of the reading to the interns, paralegals, and lower-ranking attorneys.

If you are a legal scholar or a lawyer, you should write a case brief for each and every case you read. These one-page documents can be filed and quickly accessed if you need them later. (Before you write a new brief make sure you do not already have one on the case). Even small firms can use this method to build an excellent archive of data on cases related to matters they normally are involved with. Large firms can build tremendous archives as they have their paralegals constantly looking for new data in any of their practice areas. Briefs are an essential tool to allow a lawyer to work efficiently in the legal sphere.

This chapter covers the basic steps to create an efficient legal brief. Those of you who are legal scholars or lawyers, or want to become legal scholars of lawyers, will eventually form your own methodologies for briefing cases. The methods listed in this chapter are the basic elements designed to give you the framework for developing your own skill set. In the first section we look at the most common methodologies for building a case brief, the IRAC family of organization. This grouping of methodologies has several different acronyms used to organize legal data, and we will look at three in detail. Next, we look specifically at case briefs and how to format them within the FIRAC system. We recommend this system, as the added element of the facts helps the reader associate with the case. In the third section we discuss the methodologies for writing an appellate brief. Once again this is a style that will (1) be highly dictated by the court you are writing to, and (2) develop along the lines of your personal style. This section is foundational and should not be looked at as the "be all and end all" of appellate brief writing. In the fourth section we look at the process of shepardizing the cases you mention in your appellate brief (or motion brief). Shepardizing is the process of checking to make sure that all of the rules and issues in a case you are citing are still valid in the courts in which they were ruled upon. We conclude this chapter with a discussion of how the legal mindset can be useful for writers in other fields.

IRAC FAMILY

The IRAC format of case analysis is one of the most common formats for briefing cases in the American legal system. It stands for:

I: Issue—At the heart of most legal cases is the issue that the case looks at. The issue section in a legal brief should be a one- or two-sentence part that discusses the issue that the case is looking at and whether that issue is relevant to the matter at hand.

R: Rule—The rule section should look at the rule that the case uses in its analysis or the rule that the case creates. This section should generally be very short, just covering what was used by the case or what was created by the case.

A: Analysis—The analysis section of a case brief is its heart and soul. It does not look at your analysis of the case, rather the specific reasoning the judge used to form an opinion in the source case. The analysis section can also have one or two sentences explaining how the case relates to your case, if the relationship is not obvious to the potential reader.[1]

C: Conclusion—The conclusion of your case brief summarizes what the case says, the usefulness of the case, and whether the case should be used in your current matter.

The goal of each of these sections is to provide readers with sufficient information on the topic case so they do not have to read the entire case to know if the case is relevant. This does not replace reading the entirety of relevant cases that an attorney hopes to use, it simply provides an expedited means to sort through which cases are useful and which cases appear to be less useful. As the process became more common in the United States over the last few hundred years, different variations of this format have cropped up from time to time that some of you may find useful.

Another commonly used case briefing format is the CRIAC format. These letters in their new alignment mean the same thing as they do in the IRAC format. The moving of the Conclusion, the Rule, and the Issue are to suit specific needs of the writer. If the conclusion is at the beginning of the brief, those who are using the case can quickly see if the case is useful for their own legal analysis.[2] This allows readers to quickly discard cases that are not going to be useful. Moving the Rule before the Issue, some argue, allows readers to understand the relevance of the issue better in the context of the Rule. Both the IRAC and the CRIAC formats are useful in briefing cases, and you should review your corporate culture to see which format you will be called upon to use.

---

1. Better for personal/single use briefs rather than archival briefs.
2. Very effective as an archival technique.

The preferred format of this book is the FIRAC format. FIRAC allows the writer to do a brief, one-paragraph summarization of the facts related to the case in brief. This format is more useful for those who are arguing appellate cases or arguing motions before a judge as it gives the reader the ability to use the base facts of the case to distinguish or liken the current issue they are arguing to the source case. The "F" in FIRAC stands for the *facts* of the case. There is a tradeoff, however, in including the facts of a case in your case briefs. If you include the facts, then either the length of the document becomes longer (thus lowering the efficiency) or you must take space in the document away from another part (likely the analysis).[3] The latter is the recommended method. This is why FIRAC is suggested as an "argumentative" brief, because you are taking away from what a previous judge said to include facts that support your interpretation of the case.

Any of these case briefing formats can help you in your legal case preparation, but they can also help you in your data collection. If you are working as part of a group, "briefing" articles that you are reviewing can provide a quick resource for your group to determine which articles that they are going to use. Well-briefed articles look at the facts of the research (F section), the Issue of the article (the hypothesis), the Rule of the article (the rindings), the Analysis, and the Conclusion (your conclusion on the usefulness of the article, not the article's conclusion). Briefed articles can also allow you to build a personal archive of Cliffs notes for articles in your field that you may use in a future paper on a related subject.

CASE BRIEFS

If you are in a legal field, or a discipline that shares many boarders with the legal field (criminal justice, criminology, political science, business), learning to brief cases can be a useful tool in your tool box that will save you a lot of time as you do research in your field. A case brief allows you to access data at a more efficient method. With the advent of the digital age, your personal archive of case briefs can be made to be searchable so that when you are looking for a case on a specific topic you can review your archive of cases before moving on to one of the larger case archives (WestLaw or LexisNexis). This provides you with a useful pre-research tool that can allow you to develop your theory (whether legal or academic) before you embark on the bitter journey of reviewing dozens of new cases.

The first rule of good case briefing is that the brief should be one page long, single sided. This rule is commonly broken, however, because people believe that they can get more information if they use another page or the back of the page. While this is true, the problem with expanding the length

---

3. This technique is better for case briefing for use than case briefing for archives.

of a case brief is that it is no longer brief, it is a bastard child of something between a case report and a case brief. When writing your own archive of case briefs, you should resist the temptation to lengthen the brief. If you feel that more data is needed, then you can easily create a case report on the case of interest, then attach (or hyperlink) the report to the brief. The brief can be part of a catalogue of your archive; the report can be part of the more data-intensive section. This will help you make your archive more robust and keep your briefs as useful as possible to you and to others who you may allow to use your archive.

The second rule of writing a good case brief is that it should include as much detail as possible in the limited space that you have. Your brief should provide you with an information-dense, one-page look at a case that is related (or in some cases not related) to the issue that you are dealing with at the present moment. Many people who begin writing case briefs keep them simple, glossing over the more complex concepts so that they can use flowery prose to impress the reader. If you are writing for yourself, then you should not have to impress yourself. If you are writing for others, then they will likely be more impressed with an information-rich document than a poor attempt to write legal Shakespeare. Keep your sentence structures simple with as much factual details as possible. Adjectives should be regulated to provable information that was submitted or accepted in the case.

This easily connects to rule three of writing a good case brief—that is, make it easy to read. While the information may be complex, you should use simple sentence structures. Unless you are using a linked sentence bonded by a semicolon, you should not be using many sentences that are over 10 words long. Simple sentences that are limited in their adjective use will allow you to provide your readers with more data than adjective-laden compound sentences. If you keep the brief easy to read, then readers (whether it be you or other people) will be able to consume the data much more quickly. This will allow the brief to function in its capacity as an archival piece that allows readers to find the data that they need quickly and eliminate time wasted in a known area. This will make your data collection procedure more efficient and will allow you to find the cases that you need much more quickly.

Finally, the fourth rule of a good case brief is to make sure that the rule is written clearly in relation to the matter at hand. The ruling is the key element that you are looking for in most case briefs. While the analysis section will be an important part of how you formulate your arguments in your motion or case, the ruling tells you whether the present case will be used for or against you. If you have the ruling clearly displayed in a brief, then you have already made the brief a useful archival tool in your quest to streamline your case review process.

APPELLATE BRIEFS

One of the elements of briefing that confuses many students (and some young lawyers) is that the term "brief" is used to describe both a case brief and an appellate brief. While both serve the same purpose, an appellate brief is more complex than a case brief. One of the reasons that an appellate brief is more complex is because of its argumentative nature. The appellate brief is written for the benefit of a judge (sometimes the other party if you are trying to settle). This means that you need not only inform the judge of the relevant law in a case, but you also need to inform the judge of why it is relevant and why it supports your case. The second complication is that you need to make the argument why case law that negatively affects your case is not relevant to the matter at hand by distinguishing the negative case law from the matter at hand. Writing a good appellate case brief is an art form that fits volumes of data into the 15-page format required by most courts.

The first goal of an appellate (or motion) brief is to provide as much legal data on the subject at hand as possible that supports your case, while keeping the document within the guidelines required by the court. The term *guidelines* is a misuse of the term as the "guidelines" are very specific requirements set by judges. Some judges will go so far as to force attorneys to rip out excess pages from their briefs if they go beyond the page limit. This makes presenting data as efficiently and concisely as possible imperative in any good appellate brief. As with case briefs, keep your sentence structure simple and avoid flowery prose. Impress the judge with your argument not your literary talent.

In a good appellate brief, you should cover and mention why your opponent's argument is the lesser of the two arguments. It should be obvious that this process should be as professional as possible—name calling will likely not win over a judge. One method that can be used is to place your opponents' arguments between 60% and 75% of the way through the brief, at the point where the human mind starts to slow down while reading. To improve the appearance of your argument in relation to your opponent's argument, put your opponents' arguments in the passive voice and your arguments in the active voice. This creates a "conversational" paradigm where it looks like your opponent is using bad grammar. Even if the judge notices the passive voice, he or she will associate the passive sentences with your opponents' arguments. It is a psychological game, but a game that has won many arguments.

While your opponents' arguments should be mentioned, never let them distract you from the heart of your brief, which is of course your argument. Most of your brief (85%) should be presenting why your argument is the argument that the judge should accept. This can be done by pointing out cases and laws that support the position you have taken. A well-written brief will leave little doubt in the judge's mind that the author of this brief had a better case than the author of the other brief. Unfortunately, this is not just a battle of literary skills, but the basis of our legal system.

SHEPARDIZING

One vital element of writing a good appellate brief is to ensure that you shepardize your case. As mentioned, shepardizing is the process of reviewing all of the cases that you reference in your brief to ensure that the elements within those cases that you are using have not been overturned. Nothing is worse for a lawyer than making a brilliant argument in the brief, only to have it pointed out to the judge that one of the key cases cited has an element overturned that changes the meaning of the case. This can be a blow to an otherwise well-written argument that can be difficult to overcome.

Luckily for those of you reading this, we live in the digital age. Cases can be shepardized quite quickly with one of the major archival systems. All you have to do is enter the cases that you are using in your argument and the system will give you a list of other cases that mention or affect your cases (some will even tell you how they are affected by each other case). Then all you have to do is look at the cases that modify your cases to see if your cases are still valid. This process, which used to take weeks, can now be performed efficiently in a couple of hours by an attorney or a group of paralegals.

Another use of shepardizing that can help a researcher is to "forward-track" the history of a case that you have found. Shepardizing will mention all of the cases that reference your case. If you like, you can use the data presented in each of these new cases in the manner that it supports or discredits the case you originally selected. Many researchers have found that shepardizing allows them to find new cases that are more relevant to their research than the first case that they looked at. With the advent of the digital age, the searching of legal cases (and legal case reviews) has become simple enough that those in the academic sphere without legal training are still able to do proficient legal research.

LEGAL MINDSET (CONCLUSION)

The legal mindset is an efficient way to organize data, whether you are creating a case or creating a paper. Learning some of the legal writing elements used by lawyers can be a boon to an academic in any field. While incorporating the legal mindset into the academic mindset makes the academy more efficient, one who is in the legal field may want to consider incorporating some of the academic mindset into the legal field. In many ways the legal field was a superior field for many years, but as it isolated itself from the other disciplines it stagnated and the rest of academia has caught up with it. If you are in the legal field and want to find a way that you can "get an edge" on your opposition, you may want to look at the LRFA chapter of this book. Using Chenail and Keeney's methodology, lawyers can create coded data for a case that will allow them to link elements of different charges or different claims through common data.[4] While the current process does do this, the current methodology is inefficient as it uses archaic steps that have been replaced with more efficient methodologies. Therefore, this chapter should be a challenge to any of you who are so set in your ways that you refuse to look at new methods and a warning to those of you who are learning the "old ways" of legal writing that are causing the field to stumble and fall behind other fields.

CHECKLIST

Case Brief
- ❏ Is your brief one page in length?
- ❏ Did you read the source case thoroughly?
- ❏ Did you use a specific format (IRAC, FIRAC, CRIAC)?
- ❏ What format does your firm/school use?

Appellate Brief
- ❏ Did you fully research the case?
- ❏ Did you follow the format requirements from the court?
- ❏ Did you discuss why your opponent's argument is the lesser argument?
- ❏ Did you use the formatting suggestions in the chapter?

RECOMMENDED READING

Block, Gertrude (1999). *Effective Legal Writing for Law Students and Lawyers*. New York: Foundation Press

Garner, Bryan A. (2002). *The Redbook: A Manual on Legal Style*. New York: West.

LeClercq, Terri (2004). *The Guide to Legal Writing Style*. New York: Aspen.

---

4. Invivo can be good, too, to "nest" briefs so that similar information can be coded by search term within a personal/firm database.

chapter 35
Grants

INTRODUCTION

A grant is a set amount of funds given to a researcher to complete a project; grants cover the costs of the project, time spent, and equipment needed. Grant writing is the process of applying for grants for your project. Grants are the lifeblood that keeps many research projects, especially in non-profit areas going strong. The more data you have on how your project is going to unfold, the more developed your grant proposal will be. While a good grant writing proposal will not guarantee you a grant for your project, it will increase the likelihood that your project will be selected to be awarded funds.

The reason most academics use grants is simple: as a group we are poor. Academia is not the career path that you select if you want to be a multibillionaire. The way society is currently set up does not pay academics what they are worth, let alone what they want.[1] This means that an academic self-funding a major research project is basically unheard of, and in order for research to progress in our country, we need grants. Grants come in a variety of forms, but the main types are public grants, private grants, and non-profit grants. A public grant is a grant paid for by taxpayer money and given out by the government. A private grant is a grant funded by a corporation and given out by the corporation or a private trust. A non-profit grant is a grant that is funded by a non-profit agency and is given out by that agency. Each type of grant has project types that they predominantly fund, and most donations support the mission of each grant writing group in general.

---

1. I do have to admit that both of my colleges that I work for pay quite well in comparison to other schools.

Authors should apply for grants any time they find a grant that meets with their current research goals. The ability to bring in grant money is one of the most highly sought after skills sets in the academic marketplace today. If you bring in grants to fund your research (thus alleviating pressure from the university), then you will find that you have an easier time moving through the university ranks. Faculty that do not publish, do not move. Those who do not get money coming in tend to have a harder time publishing. Therefore, those who do not have some grant writing methodology tend to fall by the wayside on the tenure track. Building a good academic career requires that you have a good publishing record, and for most of us that record requires grants to fund our research and our projects.

This chapter is brief in that it is the shortest major chapter in the book. In the first section we look at the need that you should have before you apply for a grant. Most of us will find our careers in a constant state of need, but if you do not have a project to which to apply any grant-given funds, then you should not apply just because you can. In the second section we look at the relationship between a grant-giving agency and the people they fund. Grant agencies do not just give out money; they give out money to support a mission. If you know what the mission is that they are supporting, then it is more likely that you will be able to frame your appeal for money in language that they will support. Then we conclude the chapter by looking at how to write a good grant. While there are dozens of opinions out there on what makes a good grant application, there are two things that every grant application should do. It should state a clear message of the need and how the money will be used, and it should meet the requirements of the grant writing agency. If your grants meet these two requirements, then you are already ahead of the game.

PROJECT NEED

The first step in applying for a grant is to make a list of things that you need for your project, then list the things that you want for your project. Grant agencies have a limited amount of money that they can give out to projects, and your application will likely not be the only application that they receive. If you frame your application as a request for funding for things that you need rather than a wish list of things that you want then the people who make the choices at the grant writing agency will see that and be more likely to support the frugal academic rather than the pie-in-the-sky request. Exercising frugality will help make your application more appealing to the grant writers.

That being said, if you cut every cent you can out of your budget and the grant agency gives you less than you ask for, then you will still come up short of your need. This means that you have to build a cushion into your budget. At this point writing the grant becomes a balancing act between how much extra you should put in to make a cushion and how much you should keep out to make the application appealing. This requires an in-depth look at the grant writing agency, the history of grants they have given, and if available some applications that have been rejected (usually from your own attempts or from the attempts of peers). Looking at this data can give you a good idea of what the grant agency is looking for.

The final element of a good grant proposal in regard to need is to explain why you need the money. In a recent proposal, I made sure to mention that the proposal would be for students to have inflatable life vests for snorkeling the Great Barrier Reef in Australia.[2] I noted the reason that we needed them is that they were not included in the price of the dive boat because they are not a requirement in Australia. The dive boat will provide life vests, but they are the foam vests that are used in emergencies, not vests that allow the students to actually dive into the water. The reason we requested the funds for these vests is because we want students who are unsure of their swimming ability to have the same opportunity to explore as those who are expert swimmers. These vests provide the students with this ability. Had I not explained this, they would have simply received a request for $1,500 for 30 inflatable dive vests. The extra information provides the grant agency with a reason for the money to be given out, and safety is generally a good reason. You are more likely to be given a grant if there is need, and the need is better able to be understood if there is a reason for that need.

MISSION OF A GRANT AGENCY

Grant agencies have missions to accomplish. Cancer-related grants are attempting to fund research that helps cancer patients and survivors. Environmental grants fund projects that protect or explore the environment. Corporate grants support the mission of the company that created them. The mission of the grant writing agency can be more important that the type of grant that you are applying for, so if your project aligns with the mission of the grant writing agency you have the ability to form a partnership between your institution and the grant agency. This can create a direct pipeline of funding for your current project and future projects. Keeping an active list of grants in your area, specifically from grant writing agencies that support your interest area, can help you find the right grant for you each time you write a paper.

Knowing the mission of the grant writing agency can also be vital for protecting your brand. Accepting grants from places with an interest in your research coming out a specific way can be dev-

---

2. Unfortunately after this chapter was written, this grant was denied, sometimes something as important as safety will even not be enough to get a grant writer's attention.

astating for the career of a young author. If you wrote in the 1980s that tobacco had no harmful effects and that it helped you lose weight, then you would have lost credibility if your grant was from big tobacco. There are still companies today that buy research, and there are starving authors out there who accept those dirty grants. If you want to be taken seriously as an author, be careful who you take money from. Research money should not come with strings (accept maybe to share all research with the sponsor); it should never force you to have findings decided before you even start the project.

On the other side of the coin are the organizations that have an excellent reputation for giving money to deserving causes. Medical research groups, conflict resolution groups, and others that are just good by their very nature can be an amazing boon to your brand if you can secure a grant from them. These grants are challenging to procure because many people are vying for them; however, it is worth the time to apply for them if you believe your project suits their mission. These grants can not only fund your project but also expand your network in a way that allows you to help even more people.

If you build a good reputation for accepting grants from only good sources and fulfilling your obligations to their missions, you will find that as your career goes on you have more and more opportunities to secure good grants. This is where your personal brand comes into play. Good grant agencies want researchers with good reputations. Always be careful who you accept money from, because it could be the indicator of who funds your future projects.

CLARITY AND REQUIREMENTS

As a concluding note, the two key elements of a grant proposal are clarity and a scope that aligns with the grant agency. These are the two factors that will make your grant application stand out above other applicants. When writing your grant be clear about how much you need, if there is any additional that will make your research more effective, and how you are going to use the money. These are major factors that help a grant writing agency decide if your project fits their mission and has the genuine need that is required for their grant. The second major step is to make sure that your request fits the requirements of the grant writing agency. If you apply for a grant from an agency that gives out billions, but your project has nothing to do with their operation, then not only have you wasted your time writing a grant that was destined to be denied but you have also shown them that you are not willing to play by their rules. This can damage your reputation for future grants.

When writing grants, if you focus on these two key elements (including formatting requirements), then you are already ahead of the pack in your applications. Many faculty at major universities do not follow the guidelines of grant writing agencies, but then they cannot figure out why they did not get money. Meanwhile others are simply following the instructions and getting funds to do seemingly minor projects. It all comes down to following the rules and being clear in your request, because grant agencies are charities that rely on their internal bureaucracies.

CHECKLIST

- ❏ Is your proposal clear?
- ❏ Have you stated what you need?
- ❏ Have you stated additional things that would make your trip more productive?
- ❏ Have you built in a little extra to cover reductions or possible shipping costs?
- ❏ Does your project meet the requirements of the grant writing agency?
- ❏ Have you followed all of the formatting guidelines of the grant writing agency?

RECOMMENDED READING

Browning, Beverly (2014). *Grant Writing for Dummies*. New York: For Dummies.

Karsh, Ellen & Fox, Arlen Sue (2014). *The Only Grant Writing Book You Will Ever Need*. New York: Basic Books.

chapter 36
Gists

INTRODUCTION

A gist is a brief summary of a given topic, often written in outline form. Gists are one of the most basic professional papers that you may be called upon to write by an employer. Gists are an anomaly in this book as they are not generally considered an academic paper, rather they are a tool that most often is used in the professional fields. The academic equivalent would be an annotated bibliography, but there are significant differences that distinguish the two. Whether or not you learn to write good gists should be dependent on whether or not you work in a field that uses them. Odds are if you have no idea what a gist is, then you will not have need of this chapter and can spend your time reading about other methodologies.

Gists are most commonly used by professionals who have to convey large amounts of complex data in a simple format to a superior. This means that they have a limited amount of time or space with which they can present the data that they deem important. As a result those who are effective gist writers will have the ability to condense their important points into a number of bullet points that their superior can use. The goal of a gist is to make readers aware of a topic; if they are interested in the topic they can follow up with you or conduct their own research. Gists bring brevity to an art form as many of the people who will be reading your gists are people whom you would not normally get the time to talk to unless the data had been requested.

As a general rule, gists should only be used when they are requested. Because of their dense nature, they tend to be too complex for a simple report. Likewise the brevity of the document tends to limit its usefulness as an archival document, such as a brief. Gists are used to provide information to a reader, often a single reader, in as condensed a format as possible. This means that unless a gist is requested the data is too dense and too brief to be useful for anyone but the person who requested it. Gists shine as a data/informational methodology when you are presenting volumes of data as a single page to management executives who need to make a selection on what data they will be using to develop further decisions.

There are four key areas of gists that you should take into account when you are writing a gist for another person. In the first section of this chapter we look at the process of condensing data. As with other data-condensing methodologies, case reports, reports, and briefs, putting as much information as possible into a limited space is one of the key ingredients to a good gist. Next we look at keeping the meaning clear and concise. Your reader will be looking for quality information on the topic you are presenting, so the more clearly you state it in your limited space the easier it will be for your reader to assimilate the data. In the third section we look at the reading level of the readers. Most of your gists will be designated for people who are higher up the professional food chain than you; what this means is that they generally have more power, but this does not mean that they have a better reading level. Always be careful to ensure that you do not write above the head of your reader. We conclude this chapter by looking how good gists can lead to a good career. Being able to convey information quickly and efficiently is one of the best tools that you can have in your tool bag as your career progresses. This is why gists are included in this book even though they are not an academic paper.

CONDENSING DATA

When you are in a situation where you will be writing a gist, you are going to find that there is a plethora of data, but a minimal amount of time. This is the genesis of a gist, it is a tool that gives massive amounts of data to a reader in a short amount of space. If you put yourself in the shoes of a corporate CEO who has a thousand decisions to make each day, which gist would you see as the better gist, the one that is only a page long but presents all the data that is needed or a gist that is 10 pages long and still lacking for data? You would select the first one, because it gives you the data you need to make decisions without wasting valuable time and space. Writing a gist is an exercise in discipline as you must keep your writing focused and only use the data that is absolutely needed for the decision maker.

Gists should never be more than a page long, unless the topic that you are covering requires a collection of appendixes to explain the data in the gist or to catalogue items that the gist is about. Gists of this nature should have a single cover page with all the main points of the data on it, then allow that data to be cross-referenced to the appendixes. Any time you allow a gist to be over one page long, you are risking that your reader will not have time to read the whole thing; this could lead to a bad decision that could be bad for your career. Gists require you to be concise in your writing, which can be a good exercise to develop control in your other writing formats.

Gists should be built around an outline format. The main points that you are trying to present should be covered as the main elements of the outline. The supporting information should be integrated into those main points to expand the outline. This will allow your reader to find like material within your document. If you are seeking to build a better gist, always keep the document in a format that your reader can understand. The reader that is able to find data more quickly will be the reader that is more impressed with your skills in writing gists.

If you are a person who is going to be writing a gist for a person making decisions, then it behooves you to know the situation about which you are writing. Knowing what you are writing for will be just as important as knowing what you are writing about. In some situations this will not be possible because your rank within the company may not allow you to be privy to specific data. If this is the situation, then you will have to do the best with what you do know. However, if you can find out more about the situation then you should take the time to know specifically what your readers will want to know so that you can cater your gist to them.

CLEAR AND CONCISE

One of your first goals when writing a gist is to ensure that the data you are providing is clear to your reader. As a gist writer, your readers rely on you to ensure that the data they have to make a decision can be understood by those who will implement the decision. If decision A is based on your gist, then the data that supports decision A must be as valid and easy to understand as possible. Some beginning gist writers find that they are compromising the readability of the data by condensing that data too much. Overly condensed data that is not understood by the reader will not be useful for your reader, nor will it be useful for your career. Take the time to carefully ensure that your data is clear and understandable by your reader.

This creates one of the conundrums of a gist writer's career, which is more important: length or content? Generally, both should be given consideration in equal measure. The one-page rule for a gist should be a hard and fast rule, unless the one-page format will damage the integrity of the data. Generally, when you find that you have too much data for one page, you are trying to put too much into one gist. If this is the case, then take the time to look through each section of the gist and see if every fact and/or sentence is needed to answer the question that was put to you. If you find that everything in the gist is needed to cover your topic, then you can extend the gist, but only as far as is needed for the current data (not new data).

Your gist should be a tool that the reader can use to make a good decision on whatever the topic is or should be able to find the data to make the decision. Sometimes writing a good gist is simply providing a set of summary sentences that are linked to articles or reports that the decision maker can look at if they feel your data is useful. Trying to make the decision with your data can lead you to complex arguments, and these have no place in a gist. Your goal is to provide your readers with the data that they will need to make the best decision that they can make.

READING LEVEL OF READER

As with any good writing, you need to know your audience to write a good gist. That being said, knowing your audience in gist writing involves knowing what reading level you can expect of your reader. If you know the CEO of your company that is reading your gist does not do well with computers and has trouble with technical matters, a gist laced with jargon and computer shorthand will not be a useful report. Rather, you should spend a little more time building a gist around normal language that your reader will understand. Knowing the personality and the skill set of your readers should be a task that you can do by looking through the corporate culture of your profession. If they are important enough to have someone writing gists for them, there will be information on them somewhere.

Never enter into the gist writing process assuming that your readers are geniuses. Many people who have risen to the top of the corporate food chain are not the smartest people in the world. Hard work and cunning behavior are two of the most important traits for leaders in the modern corporate environment. This means that your readers may not be the "brightest light bulb in the tool box." You may have to spell things out to a person who is known not to have a skill set in a specific area. Always be careful not to talk down to your readers, but if you take the time to use language your readers will understand it will be appreciated.

As your readers will likely be the only person to read your gist, writing to their level is essential to writing a good gist. Even if you write the best case report on a subject possible, it will not matter if you were asked to write a simple gist for your readers. Any writing depends on you writing to the audience, and if the audience does not have use for your writing or does not like your writing then you may find that you are in trouble with your boss. Make sure that you take the time to write a gist that is informative but also pitches to your reader, because with a gist only your readers' opinion is going to matter.

GOOD GISTS CAN LEAD TO A GOOD CAREER

If you are an academic who has read through this chapter, then you may be looking for some small way that you can apply the methods in this chapter to the advancement of your career. While you will not be called upon often to write gists for academic work, you may find some of the processes useful for your academic work. First of all, you may find that putting gists into work can help you communicate with your teammates more effectively when you are working as part of a group. By putting that data you feel is relevant in a simple context with bullet points you find that you will be able to discuss information with your peers without them reading all of the data that you have read. Much like a brief in this context, a gist can be used as a data simplification tool.

The use of bullet points can also be helpful in academic work, though many of you will have realized this by now. If you are building a project with academic peers, then you will want your data communication process to be as simple as possible. Bullet points with incomplete thoughts can be a good way to transmit raw data to your peers without converting it to analyzed data. While the use of prose is more effective for transferring complex topics, bullet points are useful for small quantities of raw data. Presenting your basic data as a gist can sometimes be more effective than filing a full report.

Overall, your goal with a gist (whether academic or professional) is to present a quick and clean collection of data to your reader. Always keep the data as condensed as possible so your reader can read through the data as quickly as possible. Although you want your data to be as condensed as possible, do not make the mistake of condensing the data to the point that it is no longer clear. Clarity and brevity should be balanced for a good gist. The final major element of a good gist is to ensure that your gist is within the reading level of your audience. No matter how good you believe your gist to be, if your readers cannot understand what you are writing then you've wasted your effort. Take the time to ensure you know about your audience, because this will enable you to write the best gist possible.

CHECKLIST

❏ Is your gist more than one page? (If it is, why?)

❏ Is your data presented clearly?

❏ Is your gist presented in a way that your readers can understand?

❏ If you are using it for data sharing, have you written it in a way that your readers can follow up on what you have written?

chapter 37
Hybrid Papers

INTRODUCTION

A hybrid paper is any paper that mixes two or more methodologies to meet the needs of a given project. The complexity of a hybrid paper is that you need to have a working knowledge of all the methodologies that you are hybridizing to create your paper's unique methodology. If you are building a predictive case study model based on data collected from a series of hermeneutical and transcendental phenomenologies then you need to know the processes for a predictive statistical paper, a general case study paper, and both hermeneutical and transcendental phenomenologies, their limits and their strengths. This makes hybrid papers the most complex of research projects to enter into outside of the theoretical realm, but if you follow the strategy outlined herein you will have a roadmap for the joining of your methodologies.

As you enter into this chapter, the first thing that you need to know is that we will not be covering every possible combination of research methodologies out there. The family of hybrid research methodologies is infinite in the number of combinations and modifications that you can make out of the two macro- and seven sub-macro-level methodological families. This does not even include the individual types of methodologies under theses sub-macro categories or boutique methodologies created by a specific researcher or specific discipline. Therefore, we look at the three combinations that can be made with the two macro-level research methodologies, quantitative and qualitative.

In the world of research, hybrid methodologies are a specialized tool that can help you on your journey to write a paper. Like any other specialized tool, they require you to know how to use them. The genius of hybrid methodologies is that generally you could do multiple studies with a standard research methodology, then use a QMS technique to combine them into the same product that you would have if you had done a hybrid methodology in the first place. The standard methods are easier to use, but it takes you more work to get to the same place. Similar to using a carpenter's hammer to tear out a floor when you need a sledge hammer, you can chip away at the concrete slowly but what you really need is a specialized tool. Hybrid methodologies are the specialized tools that you create for the specific projects at hand.

Hybrid methodologies should not be used for every paper. Most research projects can be completed quite well with the big seven methodologies (Descriptive Statistics, Predictive Statistics, Ethnography, Phenomenology, Case Study, QMS, Grounded Theory [GT is a theoretical method but still falls within this rubric]). If your research project can be completed with the big seven, then you do not have to go through the complex process of hybridizing a new method for your project. Hybrid methods should be used specifically when the prospective data draws from areas that need multiple methodologies to collect or analyze the data. Specific methodologies have specific areas in which they are most useful; if you cross into multiple areas with the category then you should think about using a hybrid methodology.

In this chapter we look at the basic elements of how to combine two methodologies together. The goal is to optimize the strengths of each methodology and minimize the weaknesses. In the first section we look at how to combine a methodology from the quantitative macro-methodology with a methodology from the qualitative macro-methodology. These hybridizations can be highly complex because many of the data collection, analysis, or reporting methods have different terminology and different data types (qualitative and quantitative). This is by far the most difficult section of the chapter. In the second section we look at how to hybridize a statistical process, using both descriptive and predictive methodologies. This type of hybrid will depend on what specific types of statistical data you are trying to draw from each sub-macro methodology. Next we look at the basic process for combining two qualitative methodologies. (This is made much easier if you follow the advice from Chapter 41 and use RFA as your analytical tool. Using RFA allows you to conceptualize different types of data into thematic groups, thus allowing them to be compared to other like data.) The chapter concludes with a look at how you can fit your methodology to your prospective data. You should never force a hybrid methodology, this specialized tool should only be used in specialized situations.

QUANTITATIVE AND QUALITATIVE METHODOLOGY

Combining a quantitative methodology with a qualitative methodology is one of the more complex methodological hybridizations in academia. Quantitative data and qualitative data are two very different types of data, and their collection and analysis methodologies have been built around the specific elements that make their data unique. We have all read a paper, seen a conference report, or heard a speaker who forced qualitative data into a quantitative rubric or vice versa. This creates complex data schemes and difficult prose, and often leaves the reader/watcher/listener confused as to why the researcher elected to go the chosen route. The general rule of researchers is to let the data you are going to collect lead you to the methodology that you are going to use. When researchers force one data into another category, they are breaking the system.

Misusing data is even more common when people attempt to do a hybrid quantitative/qualitative paper. It is a challenge to turn qualitative data into something that can be analyzed by a quantitative analytical tool. Doing the reverse is even more difficult. Quantitative data is generally very objective and devoid of descriptive adjectives—the numbers themselves are the descriptive tool. Qualitative data is generally rich in observational adjectives and allows a greater latitude of subjective data. Either of these data groups are going to lose some of their essence if they are forcefully converted into the other data collection and analysis methodology. This is where the misunderstanding in quantitative/qualitative hybridization arises; you should not be forcing data into methodology, you should be allowing the data to assist you in creating a methodology that displays the strengths of all data in your study.

A well-done quant/qual study focuses on highlighting the different characteristics of two very different types of data. The quantitative data should not be subject to the qualitative, nor should the qualitative data be subject to the quantitative, both should have a co-equal role in building a rich data environment through which your paper will lead your reader on a journey. This means that you as the researcher have the duty to build a new methodology that highlights the data-rich environment of the qualitative research methodology that you are using, all the while creating a numerical matrix that can allow you to describe/predict the situation that your data comes from. Neither type of data should be mutilated into something that it is not, rather you should coax the vivid description out of the qualitative data while reinforcing the hypothesis with the quantitative data.

Choosing to do a quantitative/qualitative hybrid paper is a labor of love. You need to take the time to not only separate the qualitative data from the quantitative data, but to nurture that data through the analytical process, then reassimilate the two families of data into an environment for your reader, so rich that it goes beyond what either qualitative or quantitative data could do on its own. This type of hybrid is a difficult but rewarding journey for both the writer and the reader, but if mishandled it can become a forest of nightmares for the author to write, and an even worse journey for any reader who dares enter into this morass of mixed methods. If it is done correctly, however, it can be a virtual Xanadu for the reader.

QUANTITATIVE FAMILY OF METHODOLOGY

Building upon quantitative data with more quantitative data may sound like a nightmare for many of you reading this from the social sciences and humanities disciplines. Many academics and professionals avoid statistics like the plague, and the idea of a double dose of statistics work can strike fear into the hearts of many researchers. However, when it comes to combining multiple forms of statistical analysis into one paper, it is actually the simplest hybridization available. The truth is, numbers will always combine with each other; that is the purpose for which they are made. If we take the time to properly do all of the data collection and analysis in a multiple quantitative methods paper, then the writing or the paper should be simple and to the point.

The easiest form of a hybrid quantitative paper is multiple forms of descriptive statistics. Descriptive statistics are used to describe a single population of people, animals, plants, rocks, etc. If you put additional populations of one of these categories in the same paper, then you are doing a hybrid quantitative paper without even knowing. If you look at the number of roses that grow in a specific type of soil based on the number of phosphates in the soil, then you are looking at describing two specific populations—the roses and the soil. The manner of integrating these two studies is simply providing a rich numerical description of each population then comparing the relationship between both populations. Many statistical books present this hybrid methodology as a standard methodology, which it is not, thus adding to the confusion of new statisticians.

Hybrid predictive quantitative studies are more complex, but only slightly so. In a predictive statistical model you are looking at what is going to happen in the future based on the past reactions to factors and the current factors available. While you are only presenting a prediction of what will happen (or a probability) you are still using the data to predict the future. There are two ways that this model can be hybridized. First you could look at what will happen with two different sets of stimuli. Some of you who do statistics quite regularly may have been doing hybrid statistics and not even known it. Each time that there is another research question you implement another research methodology, even if it is the same method. When this occurs you have a hybrid paper. The second case where you have a hybrid predictive statistical paper is similar to the combined descriptive method, when you have two populations. When you are predicting two different populations, then you have two research questions (or questions within questions) and thus two methodologies that are hybridized into one paper.

The final hybridization of statistical methods is when you combine descriptive statistics and predictive statistics. To make it simple, this is every case of predictive statistics out there. If you do not have a descriptive data set for a predictive model then the model is incomplete. Therefore, all predictive statistics (inferential statistics) are a hybrid model. First you apply the descriptive methodology that you are going to use, then you run it through the predictive model. Allowing your statistical models to build upon each other in this way allows for a better understanding of the process. Looking at the predictive family of statistics as a standalone methodology devalues the contribution of the predictive family of statistics to its more complex sister methodology. When entering into any of these hybrid models, take the time to break the model down to its component parts, complete each part in turn, then reassemble the compiled data. This will allow you to go through simple steps and can take away some of the supernaturalism of statistics.

QUALITATIVE FAMILY OF METHODOLOGY

Generally, if you are mixing qualitative methodologies they are complementary. The qualitative family of methodology (along with grounded theory) uses systematic data collection approaches that are designed to build an archive of rich data that the researcher can then use for analysis. Ethnography complements case study. Case study complements phenomenology. Phenomenology compliments ethnography. QMS relies on all three of these methodologies for a data archive. Therefore, the qualitative methodologies form a tight-knit family that works well together.

The danger in using a qualitative/qualitative hybrid is that each methodology is designed to be good at data collection in one specific area. Ethnography shines in the area of observational data, case studies are an excellent etic study methodology, phenomenology builds an emic perspective into the etic system. QMS collects discourse and archived data, even grounded theory draws from a select set of data. As each methodology has its own area of expertise, the temptation of hybridizing two methodologies together in a standard dataset will only lead the researcher to a more complex project that results in the same data. It is similar to going out and buying a $100 hammer when you have a dozen workable hammers at home. Avoid the temptation to reinvent the wheel; use the methodology that is most suited for your project.

That being said, there are projects where qualitative hybrids are a good methodological choice. When you have a project where you are onsight for a significant event, then you can build an ethnographic case study or an ethnographic genetic case study. When you have a person who has archived data for years based on observations of an event happening in a given area, you may have a dataset for a phenomenological transcendental ethnography. The opportunities for these hybridizations are rare, which is why these are advanced methods rather than standard methods, but if you are presented with an opportunity (and the data dictates a hybrid method), then hybrid qualitative methodologies have the potential to give your reader an unparalleled immersive experience.

YOUR METHOD SHOULD FIT YOUR PROSPECTIVE DATA

When you are considering a hybrid paper, always ask yourself whether you need to be creating a hybrid process for your project. While the creative process of developing a new methodological hybrid can be invigorating, it can also take up a large part of your time, which can add to the expense of your project. The reason that the standard methodologies are standard is because they fit the needs of most researchers. That being said there are times when you will need to put on the hat of a methodological explorer and blaze a new methodological hybrid to collect the richest data for your analysis and your readers; just be aware that you need to check the rest of your field before you create a new methodology because if you do not check first you may find that the methodology you need has already been created and the trail that you just blazed is right beside a highway that thousands have traveled.

The first step in creating a new methodology, as we have mentioned, is to check if there is not a boutique methodology already created that meets your needs. While it looks good on a CV if you created a new methodology, it looks very bad on your brand if you claim to have just invented something that has already existed for many years. Take the time to research authors who have studied a topic that requires data similar to yours. It is not a problem to use a methodology that someone else created, because all the standard methods were created by someone else and many of the popular subvariants were likewise. I can name on one hand the people I know who have created new methodologies, and most of them were simple modifications on advancements that others had made. Do not be ashamed to look for boutique methodologies rather than expending time and resources creating something that already exists.

The next step is, let your data guide you. Hybridization is an ala carte method for developing research methodology. If your study will have lots of numbers, then take something from the quantitative family. If your study requires you to observe a group for a period of time, draw a method from an ethnographic or phenomenological methodology. Only take the pieces you need for your method to be valid and reliable. You want your new method to be as streamlined as possible, because the more complex it is the more chance you have of making a mistake.

The third step that you must take to be a good researcher who discovers a new methodology is to make sure that your path is replicable. If others cannot do the same thing that you did (basically) and get similar data then you have not created a new methodology, you have simply "colored outside the lines." As we have established as a mantra in this book, writing is like being a jungle explorer/ guide, and if others cannot follow in your footsteps then all you are doing is a personal exercise. Log each step you conduct in your research to set a new path for others to follow. This is how researchers build the academy; this is how researchers build new methods.

CHECKLIST

- ❑ Have you exhausted all standard methods?
- ❑ Have you looked at similar research to see if someone else has created a boutique method that meets your needs?
- ❑ What type of data are you collecting?
- ❑ Which quantitative elements do you need?
- ❑ Which qualitative elements do you need?
- ❑ Have you kept your process simple?
- ❑ Have you catalogued the steps of your process so others can follow?

RECOMMENDED READING

Anderson, Sweeny, & Williams (1999). STATISTICS FOR BUSINESS AND ECONOMICS, 17TH ED. New York: International Thompson.

Block, Gertrude (1999). EFFECTIVE LEGAL WRITING: FOR LAW STUDENTS AND LAWYERS, 5th ed. New York: Foundation Press.

Druckman, Daniel (2005). DOING RESEARCH: METHODS OF INQUIRY IN CONFLICT ANALYSIS. Thousand Oaks, CA: Sage.

Gibbs, Graham (2007). ANALYZING QUALITATIVE DATA. Thousand Oaks, CA: Sage.

Riessman, Catherine Kohler (2008). NARRATIVE METHODS FOR THE HUMAN SCIENCES. Thousand Oaks, CA: Sage.

Weiss, Neil (2002). INTRODUCTORY STATISTICS, 6TH ED. Boston: Addison-Wesley.

Willis, Jerry (2007). FOUNDATIONS OF QUALITATIVE RESEARCH: INTERPRETIVE AND CRITICAL APPROACHES. Thousand Oaks, CA: Sage.

chapter 38
Newspapers and Magazines

INTRODUCTION

Newspaper and magazine articles are not academic articles, but they are forms of writing that you may be called upon to write at one time or another. Therefore, it can be a useful exercise for a writer to learn how to write in either or both of these formats. There are many key differences between newspaper articles, magazine articles, and academic articles, such as content, review, and length; however, the key elements that we look at in this chapter are the ways in which these tools can be used to advance your career and your notoriety as a writer. Those of you who are considering writing a newspaper or magazine article should realize that even if you are an expert at academic writing you are entering the fields of newspapers and magazines as a novice or a journeyman, thus you will have to prove yourself once again.

A newspaper article is a short, to-the-point article that provides readers (generally a large-scale readership) with easily digestible information about a given topic. This differs from an op-ed piece, which is your opinion as censored by the newspaper. In a newspaper article you are trying to present a single major point about a given topic to a broad readership with minimal tangential offerings or counterpoints. Newspaper articles are to academic articles as short stories are to novels. They focus on one specific area, provide information on that specific area quickly and in detail, and they appeal to a broader readership. Newspaper articles require you to tune back your detail and provide the people with just the information that is necessary for them to have introductory information on the topic.

Magazines are in the same vein as newspaper articles. While they are often longer than a newspaper article (three to five pages rather than a single column) they are still more narrowly formatted than your normal article. Even magazine articles for professional magazines (such as *Popular Science* or *Popular Mechanics*) limit your submission to a single topic or a single story. The advantage of magazines over newspapers is that you can include more detail (or explain complex terms) more easily. The disadvantage is that magazines tend to have a lower readership than newspapers of the same level. This tradeoff does allow you access to a more specific audience.

The choice for an academic writer to use a newspaper or magazine as a medium for expression is an interesting choice. Academics tend to hold both of these mediums in a lesser regard because they are not peer reviewed. That being said, these mediums are read by a much larger segment of the population than academic articles; therefore, your information reaches more people. This becomes the classic argument that academia constantly attacks the Church of the Middle Ages for keeping knowledge safe but away from the people; the academy has become a repository that few know about and even fewer still have access to. They preserve knowledge by denying knowledge to those who are "not worthy." As academics and writers most of us want information to be accessible to all people, and newspapers and magazines provide that open source mentality that many academic journals do not.[1]

In this chapter we first look at the notoriety that can be gained by publishing with a newspaper or a magazine (or a television magazine). This can be a boost for a beginning author's career or a reminder of a great author, but only if these mediums are carefully managed. In the second section we look at how newspapers and magazines can be used to raise awareness of a specific topic to people who are not in the academy. While academics like to think that movements begin in academic journals, true social change begins with the general population. The third section remains in the same vein by discussing how you can start a cause with a newspaper or magazine article, even if you do not intend to. Sometimes as educated people we are called upon to use what we know to help others. In the fourth section we look at how magazines and newspaper articles can be used to correct false information that is already out there in the market. Sometimes experts will duel over competing theories to win over the minds of the public (Edison vs. Tesla for example). The fifth section is advisory not to challenge editors of major papers in their own paper. The general rule is that the paper will always get the last word in, which means that even if you think you win the argument or get a retraction you will still be a target for future reports from a vindictive editor that you may have crossed. They have more ink than you do, and their publications tend to go out to

---

1. This is not to say that there are no enlightened journals allowing open source information to the public. These seem to be part of the new movement of academic writing.

SO YOU WANT TO WRITE A PAPER

a larger readership.[2] The chapter concludes with an advisement not to do fluff pieces. Academics who use fluff pieces to start their career tend to stay in that forum for most of their careers. Fluff pieces are human interest pieces that walk away from the hard science and simply appeal to the lowest common denominator. If you avoid the pitfalls of newspapers and magazines, they can be an excellent tool in your skill kit; however, avoiding the pitfalls requires that you stay disciplined, constantly do brand reviews, and take the time to read any replies that are published to your work. If you can do all of these things then newspapers and magazines can help you advance your academic writing career.

NOTORIETY

One of the key aspects of academic life is getting your name out there so that people associate you with your field. Thus one of the main reasons that many authors write is to gain notoriety for their work. This is the "soft" income that you get from writing academic articles. Soft income is anything that you do to increase your earning potential that does not actually earn you instant money. For most of us who write academic work, we realize that even though we are not getting paid when we submit our articles or when they are printed, we are opening the door to a higher paying job in the future. Building notoriety is part of the soft income of the academic trade.

When we look at notoriety as a part of publishing in a newspaper or magazine, we must first look at how we are entering into the field. When we write as academic authors we are expected to be masters of both the subject matter to which we are writing and the methodology. This is not the case when we write in newspapers or magazines. In these mediums we are expected to be subject matter experts alone, because journalists are the experts within the field of magazines and newspapers. This gives us more wiggle room to turn in "about" what is needed to be submitted. We also should not fashion ourselves as journalists, as this is another field to be covered by another book. When we submit to a newspaper or a magazine we are simply academics trying to contribute to another field in a positive manner.

To gain notoriety as we contribute to the journalistic fields, we need to make sure that the public image that we present is working in unison with the brand that we present in our academic writing. People may read more of your newspaper articles or magazine pieces if they are "fun" and "trendy," but all it takes is one editor of a serious journal reading a fluff piece in a newspaper to put your name on the blacklist for a particular journal. All notoriety that you put out there should build

---

2. This does not mean that you cannot win a war of words with a newspaper, just that it will be a war of attrition that will generally destroy your career more than you destroy theirs. If you challenge a newspaper do it in the court room.

the brand that you are presenting to the academic world. If you want to be taken seriously as an academic, your writing should be of a serious nature. Any time you submit a piece to a newspaper or a magazine (or a journal for that matter) ask yourself whether that piece is advancing your brand.

You must also realize that when you publish in a newspaper or magazine that you are effectively publishing as an expert in an area populated by lay experts. These are people who are not trained but will try to earn their stripes by challenging what you post. While these threats to your brand are nothing in comparison to actual academics who attack your work in journals, these "media trolls" can be an annoyance as you have to deal with false information or fallacious arguments that they put forward. This becomes a balancing act, and you do not want to give them too much attention as to legitimize them, nor do you want to ignore them and allow people to think that they are correct. Generally, a single sentence reply (written as a letter to the editor as a correction) will be enough to correct their misconceptions and be a short enough answer that they do not gain any notoriety from your response.

As a side note, blogging is becoming an important part of an academics social media presence. While it is a bastard form of opinions beside real research where a self-proclaimed expert on neuroscience can mingle their "findings" with pictures of their beloved cat Boots, people are beginning to use more blogs as a source of information as the quality of the media in the United States declines at an ever more rapid pace. A blog can be a great way to get your name out there, but the temptations to mix opinion with fact are rampant. If you decide to take the low road of blogging, please have discipline.

A last area that can be even more dangerous to use as a notoriety tool is TV magazines or journals. There once was a day when the History Channel, the Learning Channel, and the Discovery Channel actually had informative programming like PBS, where all of their experts were actual experts in the field and not futurists or cryptozoologists (the Bigfoot kind, not the extinct animal kind). But those days have gone the way of when MTV, CMT, and VH1 were actually about the music. TV magazine shows will get your name out into society, but as they only use clips of interviews they can be devastating as they only show what they feel is "interesting." While some of these shows still strive to be informative, others are just a platform for failed academics to speculate on conspiracy theories. Do not get trapped into one of these environments. If you do go on one of these shows, then make sure to have a contract that gives you a review of what quotes they show from you. Do not let them "clip and choose" pieces of your interviews to make you look like a wackadoo.[3]

---

3. There are still some good research shows on these channels, *River Monsters*, for instance.

INCREASE AWARENESS

Beyond increasing your notoriety, newspapers and magazines can be an excellent way for a researcher to raise awareness of an existing cause. Many of us have pet causes that we attempt to advance with our research, and sometimes opinions become a stronger part of the work than the actual research. In these cases it can be useful to utilize newspapers and magazines as a tool for this unique mix of fact and opinion. Opinion pieces, when submitted to journals, tend to draw a vicious backlash. The reason for this is that they are easy targets for critics who attack the opinion but leave out the supporting facts that you presented. Newspapers and magazines give you a venue to provide this information to the general public, which is something journals do not do, with limited threat of serious criticism from peers or rivals (though they may take shots at you for publishing in a nonacademic medium).

One reason that newspapers and magazines are useful for pet projects is because more people read these documents on a daily basis. Movements live and die with the public's opinion of them. Journals just do not have the reach to get your information to Joe and Jane America. Newspapers and magazines do. Utilizing newspapers and magazines opens your words up to a whole new group of people compared to traditional academic avenues. There is more freedom in writing style and that alone can allow you to make a more persuasive case to the reader. The more facts that you put in your piece the more likely that it will be in some sort of a column, rather than in the op-ed section.

Some newspapers also allow experts to make a more impassioned argument about their cause. Whether you believe in it or not, newspapers made global warming a phrase that everyone in the United States has some recognition of (even though newspapers cut down a lot of trees, which "contributes" to greenhouse gasses). Academic articles do not allow the emotion of a cause to show through for the reader; newspapers give more latitude in this regard. They want their stories to be true and to keep readers reading, and impassioned arguments bring this in. Arguments can also allow you to give facts to regular readers that would not otherwise be covered by other mediums that they partake of; this alone can be a reason to write a newspaper or magazine article.

One of the hardest elements of writing a newspaper or magazine article is that most of the readership will be reading at about the eighth-grade level. Newspapers and magazines are not the locations for a complicated, in-depth treatise on a dynamic subject. You have neither the space nor the readership to engage in that type of writing. Rather, your goal in a newspaper or magazine article is to present a clear and concise case for your argument in the simplest terms possible, using vivid examples where possible. This will be easier for the readership to consume and will spread your message must faster.

STARTING A CASE

Newspapers and magazines can also be a medium for starting awareness rather than just raising awareness. Some of you who are reading this may someday discover something new that is beneficial to mankind (hopefully). If you are the first one to discover something new, traditionally that new idea would take decades to filter down to the general public. Now with the advent of the internet, you can be your own spokesperson for your work. By publishing in academic journals, newspapers, magazines, and on social media you can build your own case for your research. This can allow people to keep up with your research as it develops and creates an army of personally invested lay experts.

Building a following for your work from the beginning can give you greater access to your readership. Following the traditional pathways to get research out into the field can take decades, and by that time you may not have the time (both professionally and naturally) to deal with the questions that arise around your work. If you get your message into the general public quickly, you will see more response (both positive and negative) but you will also have more time to respond to critics and cooperate with other experts who support your work. The added notoriety is a double-edged sword; however, if you learn to use it properly you will be able to make your research stand out in your field of academia.

It is also key that you know the readership who is responding to your work. Another danger of using mass media such as newspapers or magazines is that you are opening yourself up to a world (literally) of opinions. Separating those opinions from actual substantive challenges to your new idea can be difficult. First of all, it is easier to respond to opinion-based attacks with facts. Opinions are not the best tool to use in an argument, thus those who use them in arguments are generally less of a danger to your research. Critics who actually point out facts that you have overlooked are a more serious threat and the discussion with them is more complex. Some writers choose to fight against the opinions and simply ignore the legitimate questions, which can spill over into your academic writing and cripple a good idea before it ever starts. Secondly, the sheer volume of critiques that can come forward when a new idea is put in the light can overwhelm a writer. Be prepared for a strong backlash if your idea challenges the status quo.

Newspapers and magazines can also be an excellent tool for mobilizing your followers. Properly done, a social media campaign with just a few academic, newspaper, or magazine articles can start a minor trend on the internet. If you have a select group of followers, whether it be students or classmates, who can publicize your article and do targeted mailings to major news outlets, then your newspaper article/journal article combination could hit the mainstream. This will not work for every article; however, if you learn to leverage social media in cooperation with traditional and nontraditional publication sources you can quickly build an army of people who believe in your research and believe in your research's ability to change the world. Use self=promotion with caution, however, for the faster you go up the faster you can come down.

REBUTTALS

Using newspapers and magazines as a tool to rebut other authors who challenge your work or publish work that you find offensive is an excellent way to keep a "beef" from interfering with your professional brand. Any time you respond to something in a magazine or newspaper that you believe to be wrong, concentrate on why you are correct, not what makes you correct. People tend to be impressed with titles and the letters after your name, so use those to make your argument in the short space you have. Once you have established your credentials as a person who can talk knowledgably on the subject, then start presenting facts that discredit your opponents' arguments. Only present the number of facts needed to disprove your opponent (overkill will turn the reader off). Further, do not go into complex arguments of why you are right, present why you should be believed and the evidence that proves your opponent wrong then leave it at that. The more clinical and professional that you come across the more people are likely to believe your side of the argument.

When you point out the error in the other author's work, point it out as a simple mistake. Do not belabor the point that your opponent is wrong, this will only make it look like you are bullying the other author. Your goal is to come across as an expert or a teacher who is correcting an incorrect student, not as a heavyweight fighter beating up on a regular guy. Never put the black hat on yourself, always portray yourself as a good guy in writing. This will cause people to relate with you and see that the other author simply made a mistake.

Regardless of what your opinions are of the other authors' work, do not let yourself write a manifesto to counter their mistakes. The longer your response is the more credence you give to your rival. In the best cases supplying your credentials and a simple one-paragraph response shows you care enough to correct the mistake but not enough to go into a voluminous argument. Keeping your argument short and sweet will allow you to gain credibility with the reader, keep the reader's attention, and avoid giving too much notice to the offending author.

Another reason that you may want to put forward a short rebuttal is because the less information you supply, the less information you give your opponent to build a surrebuttal. A surrebuttal is a rebuttal to a rebuttal. Most people are inclined to attack either the opinion that opposes theirs or the facts. When you present an argument that is based on one or two facts and you leave your opinion out of the argument, this limits the elements that your opponent can reply to. Further, if you limit your reply to one or two facts, and you make sure that these facts are correct, your opponent will have nothing to do but argue points outside of the rebuttal (which most newspapers will not publish) or attack you personally (which makes them the bad guy). Either way you have your readers' attention and can guide them to your side of the argument.

THE EDITOR HAS MORE INK THAN YOU

One thing that you will find if you publish with newspapers or magazines is that they always have the last word. If you write a stunning piece about how one of the staff writers or the editor is wrong, then you can expect that there will be a rebuttal published in the paper and your surrebuttal will never even get looked at. The sad fact of the matter is that the newspaper is going to have more of a publishing presence than you do. This does not mean that you should not correct misinformation, just that you should be prepared for the one-sided argument that will follow.

Editors specifically control the newspaper. They are the king of their castle. To tell a short story, I had two friends in the political sphere in southern Florida. One was a party politico and the other was the owner of a small digital newspaper. To begin the story, they did not get along. He would attack her policies in his paper, she would attack his paper from the podium. From the beginning it was a losing battle for her. She was speaking to 500 people, he was publishing to 10,000 people a week. Do not let yourself get into this type of debate with an editor. Unless you are willing to start your own paper, you may find that you are fighting a battle that you cannot win.

To flip the script, you can eviscerate a newspaper in an academic journal. Few people understand that academic journals are published by major academic presses, which give them an economy of scale only major newspapers can compete with. If you fight your battle in an academic journal, then the editor loses all advantage. You can present your facts, in detail, and all they can do is present a short column in their newspaper that directs readers to your work. You win either way. Further, if there are unrequited attacks against you that become personal, then peers in the field may join in and push the paper to consider replacing the offending editor. To paraphrase Sun Tzu, if you are going to go to battle always pick the ground on which the battle is to be fought.[4]

---

4. Sun Tzu (2001). *The Art of War*. New York: Modern Press.

DO NOT FLUFF

The last temptation of magazines and newspapers (more in magazines) is to present "fluff" research. Fluff research is any research that has no or limited scientific value that focus on human interest pieces and is designed just to gain attention. This style of article includes "10 Ways to Make Your Man Hot" and "Is Your Dog Happy with Your TV Selections?" While they may be based in some form of science, they are being published for their entertainment value. When you enter into these kinds of articles, you are making yourself part of the newspapers product, thus you are no longer part of your own brand but are a punchline to their brand.

Silly articles can haunt you through your whole career. They tend to be the articles that float to the top of Google searches because they are human interest pieces so people read them for the laugh and to feel good. When you are applying for a new job or for tenure, these types of articles can make you look like you do not take your career seriously. I have known several people who have published articles that they wish they had not published. Once articles are in a library they do not go away; once they are on the internet anyone can find them. If you are at all concerned about your brand image then you have to be sure that you do not allow fluff pieces to destroy your career.

The choice whether to publish in a newspaper or a magazine can be difficult for an author. In the beginning of your career the allure can be almost too much to resist. Before you publish with a newspaper always ask yourself why they are looking at you. If you cannot find other places to publish your work, then why are they eager to give you a chance? Newspapers and magazines are in the game for the money. If they think that they can make money off of you they will. This is not inherently bad, but you should always look at how they are going to use your work. Will you be the scholar or the clown?

CHECKLIST

- ❑ Why are you writing this piece?
- ❑ Does it advance your brand?
- ❑ Are you in control of the work?
- ❑ Is it a good publication?

Part VI

DATA COLLECTION

chapter 39
Introduction to Data Collection

INTRODUCTION

Data collection is the bread and butter of most research projects. The concept, the method, the analysis, and the discussion are nothing without data entered into the academic project. How you collect your data can be a major indicator of how well your project is going to be received. The better the data you collect, the better you will be able to perform the analysis and develop your project. Further, your reputation as a researcher will determine how you are perceived when others read your work; if you are known for doing excellent research in your projects your reputation will become your brand and your brand will precede you in your articles.

Your method of data collection can also become part of your "image" that your readers see when they read your paper. Whether you are a jungle-climbing anthropologist, a desert-dwelling archeologist, an urban sociologist, or even a simple book researcher in a library, your data collection method will help your readers picture you as you explain to them your findings in your paper. Therefore, your research methodology has two elements to it. The first element is the data that you provide. Above all else the data that you provide has to be the most accurate, most up to date, and most truthful data possible to ensure that you build a good reputation in your field. Second, your image should have some excitement to it. Whether you vest your book research in the discovery of lost truths or you describe a quest for data in some exotic or domestic local, couching your data in an exciting way can help keep the reader interested in your work, but be careful not to overdo it and make your research project seem surreal. If you are interested in your research, then you can help your readers become interested as well.

The data that you collect should also be valid and reliable. Valid data is data that was collected by an understood and accepted collection methodology. Ethnographic observation is an accepted strategy for collecting data, tarot cards are not. Reliable data is data that can be found again if someone retraces your steps and observes or researches the same topic as you. Even in the instances where you observe a once in a lifetime event, another researcher should be able to follow the same analytical steps that you followed with your data and come to a similar conclusion. Data that is valid and reliable gives a stability to your project that allows readers and other authors to see the legitimacy of your work. Each legitimate byline under your name on your resume is another building block in the success of your brand.

This chapter strives to introduce you to the process of data collecting for an academic paper. This is a preparatory chapter to make the chapters that follow more easy to digest. In the first section of this chapter we look at how data collection is a window from your office into the world. The more vivid you make your data collection techniques the more easily your readers can see into the world you are revealing to them. Rich data not only allows your readers to see your research in more detail, but also for a higher level of analysis as you prepare your project. Each datum can add to your analytical methodology, thus securing a more robust defense of your position. We next look at the principles of good data collection. If you keep your research model in line with good data collection techniques you can help ensure that people will take your project more seriously (at least in your field). Finally, this chapter ends with a discussion of the format for Part VI of this book. We will briefly give an overview of each of the chapters looking at a specific data collection method to prepare you for what is coming.

DATA COLLECTION IS A RESEARCHERS' WINDOW INTO THE WORLD

Most of us live our lives in a very small part of the world. We do not get to see everything that we want to see so we turn to movies, television, and magazines to let us see those things that are beyond our reach. In the academic world, we turn to journal articles to look at things that we do not have access to in our lives. As a researcher, your work becomes your window to the outside world, a portal through which you can draw your reader into the small corner of the world that you are familiar with. The more clearly you create your window, the more effective you can be at describing what you have seen to others. Likewise, the more clearly you can convey your data to your reader, the more informational and entertaining your article can be. The better you make your window of data collection, the better your article will be.

Your data collection method is also your window into your own past. As you are doing your analysis, you are going to be required to recall as much of the data that you have observed, read, or acquired as possible. Your ability to understand this data is predicated on your ability to remember it. Your data collection technique, and to a lesser extent your coding technique, becomes part of the window that allows you to look back into the process to the point where you began collecting your data. The more detail you put into your collected data, the more accurately you are going to be able to remember that data. Additionally, quality of your collected data will dictate the detail of your analysis. As you want to have a very accurate and detailed analysis, it becomes imperative that you create a dataset that is as detailed as possible. This dataset becomes your window into the world where you have been just as much as it becomes your reader's window into your experience.

As you are building your dataset, you must realize that good data collection does not create, it discovers. The world is out there, whether we realize that fact or not. The world has been out there since the beginning of human existence, and it will be there likely long after we have died off or evolved into something else; therefore, unless we are researching ourselves it is arrogant to believe that we are creating data. Realistically, we are simply discovering what is out there in the world around us. When we are doing research, we must take the time and also accept that we are building upon the work of others to discover what exists and what has existed.

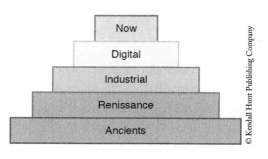

As you are building your window into the world, how and what you view can dictate how and what you research. If you build your research window so that it is looking at a brick wall, whether real or theoretical, then you will not be able to convey your story well to your readers. Likewise, if your window looks into the stacks of the library with no direction or guidance, then it will be at best boring and at worst confusing. Being a skilled researcher and writer requires you to be able to convey your data in a way that is interesting to the reader. The oblique theoretical wall that is blocking new discoveries in your field becomes a "Berlinian" wall that must be scaled or broken through. The stacks of the library become a maze of clues, one factoid leading you to the next until you discover new insight into the topic that you are researching. Framing your data collection in this way (by describing it with energy, not submersing it in creative fiction), allows your research to come to life and your data to have purpose in the eyes of the reader even before you begin the analysis. Good planning of your data collection allows you to build a good window, and that window makes good writing easy.

GOOD DATA COLLECTION = GOOD ANALYSIS

Data is your raw material for writing, and the better the raw material the better you have the capability of making the writing. Good data will not guarantee that you will do a good job with the analysis; however, if you do not start with good data it makes it much harder for your analysis to be thorough and well done. This means that your data collection methods should be as robust as possible. A good rule to remember is that while you can discard data you collected that is not needed for your analysis, you cannot create new data when it is needed if you did not collect it during your data collection period. Thus, you should keep any data that you can see any possible use for when you are doing your data collection stage. This enables you to build a robust dataset that you will be cutting data away from rather than a weak dataset where you have to retrace your steps to find data you missed the first time through.

Detailed data during your data collection phase can serve a second purpose when you are working on your project. Rich, well-collected data can jog your memory as you embark on the writing process. A detailed description of a smell or a color can help you recall what you hear or what you felt at a given time. The sound of a song playing in the background can inspire you to remember the heat of the room or the taste of a food you were eating at the time. Each detail that you write down can help you remember even more details; which in turn can help you build up your dataset to improve the quality of your material. This is why, even in book research, you should always try to collect as much data as possible. As noted above, it is much easier to erase a note off of a page if you do not need it than it is to create new data from your research project when you are miles away and already into the analysis.

Good data collection techniques can also allow your data collection process to build off of itself. If you are doing an observation of a group of teens and how they interact at a local fast-food restaurant, and notice each has a particular symbol on their shirts, then this can inspire you to do book research on the symbol to see what it means or even interview one of the teens to ask. Your data can become much richer if you find that your research and your interview come back with different results. This can lead you down another research path to understand why the accepted meaning of the symbol is different from your subjects' meaning of the symbol. This can lead you to new understandings of your research topics. Good technique can also encourage you to use multiple methods of triangulation to increase the volume of related topics in your dataset. Each supporting datum that you find can increase the quality of your dataset and support the analytical claims that you will make as you develop your project.

Good discipline in your data collection technique can help you build good discipline in other parts of your research strategy. Training your mind to follow a set path to the collection of data will allow you to create a pattern that you can follow each time you do a research project. Get into the habit of good pre-research, taking the time to look through journals and the library to ensure that your topic is new. Establishing a pattern of collecting data, observation/book research → surveys → interviews → the additional book research can allow you to find data, confirm data, then support your confirmed data with multiple sources. Each time you follow this pattern, you will become more familiar with it and it will become second nature to you. Further, having a strong data collection pattern will give you a uniform audit tail for your projects, which will help you get your projects through your local IRB.

PRINCIPLES OF DATA COLLECTION

Some people love lists, and I must confess that I am one of them. I find that it is easier in life if I have a list of steps that I can follow to complete a given project. Luckily, ensuring your quality in data collection can be assisted by following a set of principles that will help you find better data for your project. These principles of good data collection are:

1. **Collect truthful data.** First and foremost you should ensure that the data you collect is truthful to the best of your knowledge and try your best to confirm the truthfulness of your data. If your data is shown to be untruthful, then your entire project can be called into question.
2. **Collect accurate data.** Accurate data uses accepted methods of data collection to build your dataset. The more well respected the data collection methodology you choose to use, the more likely other researchers will accept your data and your findings. If your data is not accurate then you may find that your analysis misses the mark.
3. **Collect data from the best sources possible.** Data that comes from good sources tends to be more reliable than data that comes from other sources. Your data collection techniques will also be seen by your readers as much more reliable. This means that you should stick to academic journals, university reports, government reports, non-profit reports, business reports, newspapers and magazines, and then down the list of online sites like blogs, wikis, YouTube, and personal rant pages. The earlier something appears on the list the more reliable it is generally.
4. **Try to reach a point of data saturation.** This is the point where all new data you are collecting is similar or matches data that you have previously collected.

5. **Triangulate your data if possible.** Triangulation is the process of confirming data collected from one source by finding one or two additional sources. Each additional source that you find for your data can add to the reliability. Generally three sources are good enough for academic papers; however, if you are discussing something extremely contentious you may want to have upwards of six confirming sources (generally supported in a footnote).

6. **Do not data flood, only use data that is related to your topic.** Data flooding is the process of putting extra data in your paper that is not related to your topic for the sake of adding length to your paper. Data flooding is a bad practice to get into because it dilutes the quality of your project.

If you follow these simple steps you will increase the reliability of your data for your paper. Each step that you take to ensure the validity and reliability of your data will help you avoid the attacks of critics if you publish your paper.

FORMAT OF PART VI

Part VI is designed to give you an overview of some of the common data collection practices that you may use in your career as a writer. While I have tried to be as thorough as possible, there are limitations on the number of collection techniques available and the depth for which we can cover each technique. Extremely technical methods and hybrid techniques are not covered because of the extreme breadth and depth of hybrid techniques. The first method that we look at is journal/book research. This is the most common form of research that most people will face in their college careers or even in their professional careers. Book research is the process of harvesting data from books and journals that are already accepted in your discipline. At the very least a researcher should be using book research as a method to pre-research a topic to ensure that someone else has not already researched the same thing. Book research can also be quite useful in meta-summaries or meta-synthesis papers, both qualitative and quantitative.

The second set of collection techniques are recursive frame analysis (RFA) and legal recursive frame analysis (LRFA). While most people will use RFA as a coding methodology, the origin of RFA was in the analysis of data harvested from discourses. RFA is a process of taking contextual elements of data and categorizing that data into thematic and topical groupings that can be interrelated with other data from other sources. LRFA is a variant of RFA that allows the researcher to analyze legal data in the same way that a person would analyze normal qualitative data. LRFA is a break from normal legal discourse as it provides a structured format for developing arguments that parallel the IRAC method.

Interviews and surveys are covered next and they are a more direct data collection technique. Book research and RFA constrain the researcher to the data that has been collected by other researchers; however, interviews and surveys give researchers access to a method that allows them to select the questions that they want to ask and how they ask them. Interviews are conversations with your subject that allow you to probe for data that is needed for your study. Surveys are a method that allow you to ask direct questions of your subjects; however, you do not have the ability to follow up on questions and must rely on the data that your subjects provide. In both interviews and surveys you must ensure that your questions are direct and focused to ensure that you have the best responses possible.

Focus groups are an excellent way to collect data, especially for business groups. A focus group is a small group of subjects who allow you to ask them questions. Functioning like a group interview the emotions of the focus group can play off of one another and allow the group to go into more detail about an experience or a new product. Focus groups also allow the questions of the subject to play upon one another, which can allow the subjects to build the discussion off of their responses as well as yours. Focus groups can also be done by a secondary researcher to ensure that you do not taint the data by expressing your opinions in the group.

Observation is one of the key methodologies that many researchers use in different fields. The technique between observations in a laboratory setting and a field setting are quite different, but the rules are generally the same. When doing an observation, you want to collect as much rich data as possible for later analysis. Whether you are researching the rituals of an Amazon social group or the boiling point of a metallic alloy, collecting as much data as possible as you observe what is going on is vital to a good observational study.

Anecdotal research is similar to observational research to the point that it almost did not get its own chapter. Where observational research requires you to split your attention between all five of your senses, in anecdotal research you concentrate on getting stories from people who have lived through the experience. A combination of phenomenological interviewing and ethnographic observation, anecdotal research can help you gain a deep understanding of past events that you did not have the opportunity to observe. Be careful with anecdotal research, because the transition between the *emic* and the *etic* can be difficult to determine as many people put themselves in their stories, or take themselves out of stories where they are the bad guy.

Chapter 48 wraps up this part of the book with a look at doing research in magazines and news-papers. While this data collection methodology is very similar to book research, there are some marked differences. Newspapers and magazines tend to come out more often than journals, and they are also not subject to the same peer review process that journals go through. This can allow false data to slip into the system and weaken the reliability of the data. Additionally, newspapers and magazines are known to have specific ideological slants, which they do not attempt to hide (some journals have the same problems but they are better able to cover up their bias). While they are not ideal sources, newspapers and magazines can be your best tools to research events that have happened very recently.

CHECKLIST

- ❏ Have you taken the time to do your pre-research?
- ❏ Have you created a research plan?
- ❏ Do you have multiple methodologies available to triangulate your data?
- ❏ What level of repetition do you feel is saturation?

RECOMMENDED READING

Druckman, Daniel (2005). DOING RESEARCH: METHODS OF INQUIRY FOR CONFLICT ANALYSIS. Thousand Oaks, CA: Sage.

Riessman, Catherine K. (2008). NARRATIVE METHODS FOR THE HUMAN SCIENCES. Thousand Oaks, CA: Sage.

Rubin, Herbert J. & Rubin, Irene S. (2005). QUALITATIVE INTERVIEWING: THE ART OF HEARING DATA, 2nd ed. Thousand Oaks, CA: Sage.

chapter 40
Journal and Book Research

INTRODUCTION

Journal and book research is the most common type of research that is done all over the world. Before you start any project, you should do book research. When you want to see if someone else has already answered your question, then you should do book research. When you have a new finding you want to confirm, you should do book research. When you need to know the meaning of a symbol you discover in a society, then you should do book research. Returning to the books is a staple of the academic process. If you are doing a research paper and you are not looking to any books at all, then you should be going back to look at your research procedure because you likely missed something. Book research should be your first inclination when you start a new project and it should be your last level of quality control when you are coming to the end of any writing project.

As book and journal research is the most common form of data collection in the academic setting, one must ask why there is a stigma around meta-studies, meta-summaries, and meta-syntheses. The answer is because these methodologies are done improperly so often that people have become skeptical of the value of these methodologies to a research. In this chapter we look at the reasons why book and journal research should have its rightful place among the pantheon of data collection methods as a primary research methodology. When done correctly a week of book research can save a year of field research by preventing you from making mistakes that have already been made and stopping you from collecting data that has already been collected. Book research is one of your best tools to keep the journey of writing a paper as efficient as possible.

There are three common types of book research that are used in most academic settings. They are so common, in fact, that many people in academic settings do not even know what they are called. These methods are meta-study, meta-summary, and meta-synthesis. Meta-study is the simplest of these methodologies, and it is often the cause of the other two getting a bad rap. Meta-studies are generally a statistical method for garnering data from a collection of other studies to be used in a future study. Meta-studies sometimes approach a research question and at other times avoid research questions entirely and compile data for the sake of having good databases. Meta-studies can be used in qualitative fields, but a database can become unwieldy rather quickly as the sheer volume of data that can be extracted from qualitative studies is immense. That being said, there are people who compile meta-study databases of qualitative data. The bad name comes from when people make assessments from these databases without doing the proper analytical groundwork and hypothesis testing.

Meta-summary is the second level of book research in the academic field. Meta-summary allows the researcher to summarize the data collected from multiple sources on the same topic. Although meta-summaries do not create new synthesis and answer new research questions they do allow researchers to have access to the findings of many authors in the space of a single article. If you can find someone in your discipline that writes and publishes good meta-summaries (also called annotated bibliographies), then you may have found a goldmine that can considerably shorten your writing process. To return to the jungle analogy, when you find someone who writes good meta-summaries it is like finding a bridge on your trek through the jungle, as it can cut days or weeks off your research time. Just be careful, as you would be trusting the builder of the bridge in the jungle with your life, you are trusting the writer of the meta-summary with the validity of your project.

The most aggressive form of book research is research on a new question using the data collected by others. This process is called meta-synthesis. If you are reading this book straight through, then you already have a good idea of what meta-synthesis is (the process of collecting data from other journal articles then using that data to synthesize an answer to your research question). A properly done meta-synthesis can be just as in-depth as a traditional observational or statistical study but can present even more quality control if you select good articles that have gone through the peer review process. Meta-synthesis data can compress and explain the vast volumes of data that are being created in many academic fields today and can allow people to become experts amid the "data explosion."[1]

When doing book or journal research realize that good papers come from good research. If you spend a little extra time working your way through the volumes of books, journals, magazines, newspapers,

1. Howell-Major, Claire & Savin-Baden, Maggi (2010). AN INTRODUCTION TO QUALITATIVE RESEARCH SYNTHESIS: MANAGING THE INFORMATION EXPLOSION IN SOCIAL SCIENCE RESEARCH. New York: Routledge.

and historical records you will find that you will save yourself the time and the headache of someone challenging your work after it is published. As with anything in life, you get out of something what you put into it. Book research can be as effective and as cutting edge as any other form of research; true, it is not as exciting as camping for a week in the Outback or in the Serengeti, but it can make the same impressive contributions to your field or discipline. Do not write off book research as a methodology for a major paper, as the wealth of knowledge is not belied by the savings in costs.

This chapter looks at a few of the elements that will help you make your book research projects more effective. This chapter should be a boon to college students looking to separate themselves from the pack In the first section you will learn how to review the literature to see what it says. You do not have to blaze a new path on your journey to write a paper. You can follow the path someone else wrote and simply make changes to clarify your position against the original author's points. In the second section we look at what the literature does not cover. To merit being called a real researcher, you will eventually have to leave the shadow of others' wings and blaze new research of your own; reviewing the literature will tell you where there are gaps in research that you can fill with your studies.

The third section looks at the specifics of how to do journal research. If you have the opportunity, and you are at a university, take the time to schedule a meeting with a reference librarian; most of them have detailed trainings on how to use the resources that they oversee. Next we review the practices that you should follow when you are using books, anthologies, compellations, and compendiums for your research. Quality control begins with the quality of the sources. The fifth section extends this line of thinking by looking at how to ensure that you are using a recognized source. A recognized source is a publication that comes from a credible organization that has been acknowledged as being authoritative on the subject. In the final section we look at quality control. Quality control in writing is the time you take to make sure that your interpretation of the data you are recording is correct, valid, and reliable. An author can have the best sources in the world, but if their work is nothing but opinions about the works they are citing then the quality of their work is low indeed. Book research can be a valuable tool in your tool pack as you journey to write a paper—like any tool use it for what it was intended for.

WHAT DOES THE LITERATURE SAY?

One of the primary goals of book research is to find out what is already known in the field. There are vast volumes of data out there in the world, so before you go and do a study you should be careful that someone has not beaten you to the subject. Even if you are working in a topic that has been covered by others, there may be a way that you can look at it through a new lens, create an add-on, or critique a specific part of the idea so that you are creating something new. Doing a good literature review will allow you to see what is out there.

A huge reason of why you should look at the work of others is so that you do not reinvent the wheel. While the topic that you are studying may be open and have room to be studied, the methodology for studying in that area may already be established. If you do not have to create a new methodology for studying the parenting habits of primates, then why would you? Let us assume for a moment that you are studying how capuchin monkeys raise their children and you do your book research to find out that no one else has ever looked into this topic in detail. This does not mean you should stop your research there. Finding a person who has looked at the parenting habits of macaw monkeys may give you a methodology for getting close enough to actually do your study. Reinventing the wheel will only force you to do more work than is required for your project.

Book research also allows you to work within the trends that are going on in the field you are working with, not to work against them. Research fields can form cliques, which means that if you are on the outside of a clique you may be fighting against the others in your field. While you should not change your research "just to fit in," if your research already fits into the research you should use examples from the field to support your research position. Each datum that you find in support of your data will allow your research to gain more reliability in the field; therefore you should take advantage of every supporting study that furthers your goal.

Another benefit of book research is that it allows you to consult with the experts in your field, whether they are living or dead. Entering into a book research session with a specific set of questions to answer about your subject can allow you to have your questions answered without having to ever speak to a real person. Many of the questions that support your hypothesis may be answered already, you may simply be required to synthesize the data so that it meets the form of your questions. Taking the time to create a panel of questions on your subject can enable you to answer your hypothesis without ever entering the field.

One way that people set up their book research is to set up a "panel" of experts that they can research each time they are working on a new project. This process is simple. First, select a finite field of data that you are researching. Let's use Marxist economics as an example. Next, find five authors who are known to speak either for or against the subject—we will use Lucacs, Engels, Smith, Weber, and Marx himself. Next, build a catalog of books and articles written by these authors on your subject matter. This is your panel. Each time you have a new research question, take the time to go through the research forwarded by these authors in relation to questions you have about your topic.

As you develop an expertise in your field, add more and more authors to your panel so that you have a large catalog of materials to review each time you start a new project.

Book research is so valuable because most new contributions to a field are not entirely new areas of study, they are specific clarifications within already developed fields. Good research practices allow for you to develop a systematic approach to doing book research. The more comfortable you become with your approach, the easier your book research will be. After a few dozen papers within a given topic area you may find that you will know the page numbers of articles that you cite often. This can streamline the research process and allow you to find data more quickly. Additionally, having a pool of research resources to work with can allow you to backtrack through their research to find even more data on a given subject. Book research allows you to know what has already happened in your field, which tells you what must happen in your research.

WHAT LITERATURE DOES NOT SAY

Just as important as what the literature does say is what the literature does not say. The "gaps" in the literature are the topic areas that have not been covered by other authors. Gaps can be huge, as in the genome of a newly discovered species, or they can be incredibly small, as in the lifestyle choices of roadies for Metallica from June to July 1987. The size of the gap dictates the ease of the study, but more importantly it tells you that you have found an area that is still open for exploration. This is one of the key goals for book research, to find unexplored literary territory and begin your journey to write a paper about that topic.

The holes in the literature are where the jobs are in academia, not the teaching jobs but the research jobs. Each field decides how important the holes in the literature are to the field, but especially in the hard sciences—if you can find a question that has not been answered (or better yet a question that has not been asked) you may have found yourself a niche that you can turn into a job. If you find areas that are not explored, always take the time to write yourself a little note about them. It may be the situation that you are not ready to explore that specific topic yet; however, you may never know if it is something that you or a colleague may want to study in the future. Keeping a jar of "unripe" ideas may save you hours of time in the future when you are looking for a new topic of research.

As academics, most of our work is filling in holes of the literature. If we find a hole we are expected to fill it, or at least point out that there is a hole. This is the main drive with dissertations, theses, and papers. A dissertation looks for a complex hole in the literature to fill, then fills it. A thesis finds a hole in the literature and then talks about how it could be filled. An academic research paper does all three elements—the writer finds a hole, creates (or finds) a methodology to fill the hole, then takes the time to do the work to fill it. Each time new papers are published into the academic world, another hole is filled. Don't be distraught if you think this will limit the topics that you can write about, because each time researchers fill a hole they have to dig somewhere else to find the material with which to fill the hole.

The best papers out there solve a problem that people actually care about; this is why book research is so difficult. Few people in the world know enough people to have a valid survey of whether a problem affects a cross section of the population. This means that we have to find another place to learn if we are researching a salient topic. As researchers we can learn if our topic is a valid topic through book research, which is the cheapest and most effective way to find if there are gaps in the literature.

JOURNALS

Journals are the primary academic source that you will be using during book research. An academic journal is a collection of research papers, written by experts/practitioners in the field, that are peer reviewed and edited to ensure the validity of the research. Journals are often more effective than books for "book research" because journals are published on a monthly basis; books are published every few years with new editions. This allows journals to have a much faster response to new developments in the field. Journals also have the ability to be more adaptive on new "vogue" subjects. If a new topic within a field becomes rapidly popular, then journals can build a monthly edition or a series to revolve around the selected topic. Journals should be your first source in most book research projects.

Legal journals are similar to academic journals except that their focus is exclusively on the legal field. A legal journal is a collection of articles of a legal nature, written by practitioners or academics in the field, which are reviewed by the journal and by peers in the field. Legal journals also have notes, which are articles written by law students, which hold the same validity as a legal article but are generally held in lower esteem. Legal journals are more highly regarded in the legal field, but they are also victim to academic chauvinism, which is the fallacious belief that one professional doctorate is better than the other. Legal journals can be a valuable source of data on many subjects as new journals have a rigorous process to ensure that the author did proper book research before printing the article.

Online journals are academic journals that are published exclusively online. Print journals have a physical printed out format. Most print journals have an online footprint too, so many universities are no longer buying the physical copy of the journal for the school. Print journals tend to be held in higher esteem than online journals, but those gaps are quickly closing as online journals have the ability to respond to the market faster and print weekly supplements to keep up with changes in the culture. In fields that change quickly, such as political science and journalism, online journals may be the future of the field.

With the advent of the internet there have been some factors that can cause you trouble when you are doing journal research. One of these problems is bad sources. All journals are not created equal. The best journals in any given field generally have the best articles; even mediocre journals still get their share of good articles. There are journals out there that are being produced to promote a specific viewpoint, and these journals are little more than magazines that feature academic work. Any time that you are doing book research, always check to see that the journal you find an article in is respectable and accepted in the field. Sometimes all you need to do to give a critic a reason to attack your article is to cite a bad source.

Beyond avoiding bad sources, you should make an effort to ensure that you are using and attempting to publish in the top journals. When you begin a project, take the time to see what the top journals are in the field in which you are working. If you are in the hard sciences, then *Science* is a good journal. If you are in biology or ecology, *Nature* is a good journal. Each field will have a journal that is respected, and if you find that journal using applicable articles, then it can augment your paper. An article from *The Golden Gate Law Review* in environmental law will be much more respected than an article put out by a private company that is a known environmental law offender. If you take the time to find the top journals, then you can build your book research around those articles and the articles that those articles cite.

Another strategy to build the credibility of your book research is to take the time to find out who the top researchers in your field are. Knowing who the best people are and who the best people cite can help build your "network" out from their work to find other authors related to your topic. If you look at who the top authors are citing, then you can build a catalogue of credible sources for your book research project. This is not to say that the top authors do not make mistakes, but if they do make mistakes the authors that cite them should note their mistakes so that you do not fall into the same trap.

BOOKS

Books are the next major source of information for book research. While there are many types of books, only a few types of books are valid to use for research projects. In this section we look at several types of books that may be of use in research. This list of books is not exhaustive, but it should give you an idea of what books to use and not to use in your research.

1. Fiction books are generally not recommended to use as sources in a book research project. There are a limited number of reasons when a fiction book could be useful.

2. Poetry is also not a generally recognized source of book research data, but that being said, old poems can be a useful source for finding information about the time in which the poem was written.

3. Treatises are academic writings on a subject by an expert. These usually follow a standard form of research and are among the best book sources for information.

4. Anthologies are a collected set of works by a selected author. The validity of the anthology is largely dependent on the validity of the author. Good academic authors tend to have good anthologies, whereas an anthology of fiction short stories has limited use in research papers.

5. Encyclopedias can be used as a starting point for research projects. They are not a valid source for serious research projects, because their topics are too broad to be used as an academic source. The exception to this rule is when an encyclopedia is written specifically for a given discipline.

6. Law books are a collection of options of judges on cases. They are an excellent primary source for legal papers. Legal seconds are also excellent sources for research, which are legal experts' analyses of the legal cases as they stand at the time of their writing.

7. Histories are books written by scholars. They are valid sources though they should be taken with note to when they were written. History books are one of the first sources co-opted by propaganda agencies.

8. Yearbooks are descriptions of what has been done in a given topics during a year. These books are useful for starting points but are secondary, not primary, sources.

9. Opinion books have limited use as data sources. The best opinion books use facts to support their opinions, and these facts can be used in meta-synthesis. Most opinion books are not good books to use because they are simply opinions.

10. Diaries and journals are useful when doing research on a specific subject. People tend to lie less to themselves when they write than when they are writing to other people.

11. Memoirs are the opposite of journals and diaries. These are the stories of people's lives that they want others to know about. These are heavily edited to make the person meet the expectation that that person set.

The above list of what books are "good" books and what books are "bad" books is a general list. There are instances when certain types of "bad" books may be usable for specific projects and there are times when "good" books may not apply. Common sense is a great tool to use when you do not know if a book should be used. If you have further questions talk to a reference librarian about whether a source would be respected for your specific field. The higher the quality of your sources the better the quality of your final product.

FINDING RECOGNIZED SOURCES

Good sources are a vital part of doing book research; however, finding good sources can be difficult as there are so many books, websites, and other sources out there used to misdirect people in their research and writing. Therefore, finding good sources can be a challenge. The following list describes some of the sources that you may find in your research and whether or not they are valid.

1. University presses and journals are generally the best sources for data. They have the most rigorous process for fact checking and generally will retract bad information.
2. Government agencies are trustworthy for most government reports, to an extent. If it is a benign subject, then you can generally trust them. If it is a national security issue, then they tend to fake the number a little.
3. Nongovernmental organizations (NGOs) are often a good source for data. Most of the time they rely on a good name to get funding for their projects. When using NGO data always check to see what their reputation is.
4. Non-profits, like NGOs, are often good sources of data. That being said, they often have an agenda. Always check the reputation of a non-profit to find if they are a good source.
5. Private companies put out reports and books all the time. The quality of the data should be judged on why the company is putting the information out.
6. Print mediums (newspapers, magazines, etc.) tend to have good people working for them; however, the 24/7 news cycle has taken away a lot of the quality control. To that effect you should be very careful how you take any information that you receive from a print medium source.
7. Private authors are a crapshoot because of the variety of quality you will find. If you use a private author who is not peer reviewed then you should take the time to check out his or her reputation as a researcher.

8. Blogs, wikis, and other crowd-sourced options are unreliable, even though you will occasionally find sources who actually do their research. These sources require extensive background checking, though, so use them at your own risk.

9. Nonsourced options should be avoided. If you cannot find who is putting out an article, then you should avoid using the article because it may be spreading misinformation and rumors. There are very few instances when a nonsourced article should be used.

If you take the time to look at where your sources are coming from, then you may be able to use common sense to determine whether the source is a valid source or not. A study by tobacco company X stating that smoking will make you more attractive to everyone should be taken with a grain of salt. A study by Y University on the problems that arise from overeating may be a more valid study.

QUALITY CONTROL

Writing based on other writing is like sex, you are trusting everyone that you are with (writing with) and you are trusting everyone that they have been using, too. But unlike sex, ugly researchers use just as many ugly sources as good researchers use good sources. If you cite a source, then you are basing your findings on their information (only do this when necessary). Yes a large bibliography looks good in a paper, but if it is filled with bad sources, the people in your field will know and you will get a reputation. Always take the time to make sure that researchers use good methods when they are doing their work. The people with the best reputations are generally the best authors to cite. It is like sex, if your friends and co-workers tell you someone is bad news, trust them.

The moral of this chapter is to always check your sources, then check out their sources. This can be time consuming but it can save your reputation in the long run. Luckily, most of your work is done for you if you use university presses and academic journals, because they hire people to check out the reliability and validity of the articles they publish. The farther you get from the academy, the more work you will have to do on your own to vet the sources. This is an important part of the research process, and every time you cite someone else positively, then you are saying that you trust their work and their source as a foundation of your paper.

An additional danger that you may find in some fields is when an author is highly regarded, then does something stupid to lose face. but then builds him or herself back up again. This can happen in any field and you need to make sure you are not taking a good author and using work from one of his or her stupid phases. You can check this out by looking for people who are citing your author and see how they talk about the article that you are citing. If it is in high regard, then you should be able to use it. If the article seems to be mocked and lampooned then find out why it is in disgrace and avoid that part of the topic.

Good book research should be used to augment other forms of research. Observations can be augmented by book research to help you understand symbols. Interviews can be augmented by book research to establish context for the topic of your interview. Surveys can be augmented by book research because you can look at the way to form your sentences so that they are not offensive to your research subjects. But beyond that, book research can stand alone as its own form of research that can contribute valuable information to the academy. A good meta-synthesis paper can stand toe to toe with the best ethnography, phenomenology, statistics paper or even a strong theory paper, but to do this you must ensure that you go through all the steps of writing a good paper.

CHECKLIST

- ❑ Did you research your topic before you started?
- ❑ Did you find the gaps in the literature?
- ❑ Did you check to see that your source is well recognized?
- ❑ Did you check to see that the author you are using is a good author?
- ❑ Did you check the source of your source?
- ❑ Did you take the time to do quality control on the source of your source?

RECOMMENDED READING

Major, Claire Howell, and Savin-Baden, Maggi (2010). *An Introduction to Qualitative Research Synthesis: Managing the Information Explosion in Social Science Research.* New York: Routledge.

Sandelowski, Margarete, and Barroso, Julie (2007). *Handbook for Synthesizing Qualitative Research.* New York: Springer.

Sandelowski, Margarete, and Barroso, Julie (2003). "Creating Meta-summaries of Qualitative Findings." *Nursing Research* 52:4 at 4.

Sandelowski, Margarete, and Barroso, Julie (2002). "Finding the Findings in Qualitative Research." *Journal of Nursing Scholarship* 34:3.

chapter 41
Recursive Frame Analysis

INTRODUCTION

Data management is one of the core areas of data collection. As such, recursive frame analysis (RFA) is a useful tool to maintain the organization of your data during your projects. RFA is an integrated data collection/analysis methodology that permits the researcher to organize data based on contextual elements then reintegrate data from multiple sources along thematic or topical lines. A properly conducted RFA study can build an empirical study from collections of transcripts, texts, and video or audio files. When combined with qualitative meta-synthesis, it can be an excellent methodology for college or professional academic writing projects at any level.

RFA is very useful as a coding and analysis technique. Generally, you will combine your RFA methodology with one form or another of book research. While RFA is a standalone methodology, there still should be a data collection strategy added to your audit trail to reinforce the "how" of your data collection. Otherwise, RFA becomes a methodology where you perform interviews to create transcripts then use the analytical methodology to build a dataset.[1] More robust datasets can be created through hybrid processes where you use one of the other data collection methodologies listed in this part in concert with your RFA technique.

---

1. Chenail, Ronald J. (1995). Recursive Frame Analysis. *The Qualitative Report*, Volume 2, Number 2, at http://www.nova.edu/ssss/QR/QR2-2/rfa.html.

RFA is predominantly used in the family therapy and medical fields, which is where the process developed. This technique is effective in these fields because a large portion of the qualitative data generated is in the form of transcripts and discourses. This does not resign RFA to the medical fields, however, because there are many occasions where RFA can be used in connection with other data collection methodologies in the social sciences or the humanities. There is potential for RFA to make inroads into the economic, historical, and legal fields. If you are in another field and feel that it will be an effective methodology then by all means contact your journal or professor and see whether this is a methodology that you can use for data coding and analysis. By and large they will accept it without question.

One of the main reasons that people choose to use RFA for their research projects is because of the structured method that it gives to coding and organization of data. Chenail and Keeney designed RFA around the concept of a museum.[2] As most people are aware of how a museum is set up, it becomes an easily relatable methodology for people of any field. Frames go inside of galleries; galleries make up wings, which in turn make up museums. This simple system of mental imagery can help people focus their meta-data into meta-physical locations along a predetermined design structure. This organization makes accessing the data easier, and allows the researcher efficient access to his or her data.

This chapter walks you through the process of developing your RFA model beginning with your frames. A frame is a contextual element of a discourse, a transcript, a text, or an audio/visual media item. Once you have developed your frames, we then walk through the process of developing galleries of ideas. Galleries are topical organizations of your compiled frames. Galleries open the door to building wings of your data, which are thematic groupings. Then the cycle begins anew with the creation of museums, which are topical groupings of the themes. This process can be repeated until you have condensed your data into an organized dataset based around the thematic or topical groupings.

ORIGINS OF RFA

Before we explore the process of building frames into museums, we should look at the root of RFA. RFA was developed in the family therapy field, thus a large amount of the data is created by the process of interviews and conversational transcripts. This leads to a large amount of the field's data being buried in transcripts. Transcripts can be a difficult form of data to analyze based on the wide

---

2. *Id.*

variety of people who could be speaking in the transcript. RFA grew out of the need to bring order to the massive amounts of data being generated on a daily basis by even the smallest hospital or care center. To this end, it created a systematic approach to minimize the vertical assimilation of the data allowing for large-scale horizontal data assimilation.

Though it began in the family therapy field, RFA soon found acceptance in other areas of the medical and social fields. As it expanded to other fields, the source of the data expanded beyond the normal transcript analysis, beginning to incorporate video and audio data from different data collections. This broadened the usefulness of RFA, but it also expanded the fields that had taken an interest in the methodology. A key breakthrough in the development of RFA, especially in the social fields, was when it was realized that contextual elements can be found in written text as well as in transcripts and interviews.

The element of RFA that links all of these data sources together is that it looks for the building blocks of any good dataset, the most basic datum that can be used as an anchor for other data in the set. Once you have found your anchor data—the first thematic datum that can be linked to other data by its contextual relevance—the rest of the system falls in around this first datum very quickly. Additional anchor datum are generally found quite quickly by distinguishing between the new data and the anchor data that has already been accumulated. Once this occurs the entire process of RFA is associating new datum to the data that has already been collected.

FRAMES

Frames are the basic element of an RFA study. A frame is a sole contextual unit of data that stands alone within its individual source. The simplicity of the frame allows RFA to be translated into so many fields and allows it to work in tandem with other data collection methodologies. Intrinsically, a frame is the smallest contextual unit of data that can be distilled from the source. For instance, you are working with a general text on economics that reads:

> "The [fuel for the {system}] is the workers [ambition] to [{improve} their stake in life]. Each time a [{worker realizes} that they need to work harder] to [{improve} their station]; [they increase their {ability} to build upon] what [they have already developed at their position]. Thus, once [{they have made} the realization] that [hard work will {enable them greater profits}], [they are one step {closer to actually} achieving those greater profits]."

Then this simple random paragraph (created for this example) has several basic contextual elements in it (marked by brackets and braces). For the moment you can ignore the braces, they will be used later in this chapter when we are discussing strokes.

As you can see, we have identified 10 individual contextual elements within this short three-sentence paragraph. Each contextual element has a specific function that it serves in the paragraph to which it is a part:

1. [Fuel for the system]-
2. [Ambition]
3. [Improve their stake in life]
4. [Worker realizes they need to work harder]
5. [Improve their station]
6. [Increase their ability to build upon]
7. [They have already developed a position]
8. [They have made the realization]
9. [Hard work will enable them greater profits]
10. [They are one step closer to actually achieving those greater profits]

Once you have found these frames you can begin to combine them into thematic groups. This allows you to move on to the next stage of RFA development.

GALLERIES

In a museum, galleries are a collection of frames or exhibits. In RFA, a gallery is a collection of frames or contextual elements. In both cases the curator is putting like objects near each other so that they can be examined more easily. In the process of RFA, you are the curator of the project. The more skill you demonstrate as you thematically categorize your frames, the easier your project will be when you begin to analyze your data. Your galleries become the first step in building a qualitative matrix for easy organization of your data.

To continue with the example from above we can create four galleries from our collected data. Now some people would create more galleries and some people would create fewer galleries (the number of galleries depends on the opinions of the researcher) but for this example we will have four galleries. These galleries are:

1. "Goals"
   a. [Ambition]
   b. [Improve their stake in life]
   c. [Improve their station]
2. "Abilities"
   a. [Increasing their abilities]
3. "Understanding"
   a. [Workers realize that they need to work harder]
   b. [They have made a realization]
   c. [Hard work will enable greater profits]
4. "The system"
   a. [Fuel for the system]
   b. [They have developed a system]
   c. [They are one step closer to achieving those profits]

As you can see, it is not uniform how the frames fit into the galleries. Some galleries, even from our brief one paragraph, are populated with three frames. Gallery 2 "People's Abilities" is limited to one frame. This is not a problem, in fact the differences in numbers may enable the researcher to more easily distinguish between data elements in the analysis section of their paper.

WINGS AND MUSEUMS

As we move through our organizational matrix for this dataset, we see that the galleries can be linked together by topic. Abilities (gallery 1) and Goals (gallery 2) are related as physically measurable ideas. On the other hand, "Understanding" (gallery 3) and "The System" (gallery 4) are ethereal concepts that cannot be measured by objective criteria. This takes the four galleries that we had and reduces them to two wings. If in the future we need to find any of the data that we have compiled, we can look into the wing, then look for the gallery, then ultimately find the frame.

The final step in most RFA projects is to build a museum, which is your overarching topic in your project. The museum is a collection of wings (there may be more than one museum in large projects) that gives a topical categorization. Museums are generally your paper's topic. All data that comes within the purview of your paper should fall into one museum; however, some large papers, compiled papers, or books may have multiple museums which allow for a broader organization of the data. Having data organized in this way allows you to put your hands on any one unit of contextual data quickly by filtering it through your newly created data matrix.

STROKES AND DISTRICTS

In some projects, the frame may be too broad of a starting point for your project. Sometimes the meaning that the author puts into the words can be an element of the culture rather than an element of the context. This can cause some confusion as to how the contextual element is to be taken within the matrix. Strokes are a remedy to this problem. Your stroke is the meaning that the author may or may not have put into the words within the culture to which the data is created. The stroke would represent the brush strokes in the museum analogy, returning to our example paragraph:

> "The [fuel for the {system}] is the workers [ambition] to [{improve} their stake in life]. Each time a [{worker realizes} that they need to work harder] to [{improve} their station]; [they increase their {ability} to build upon] what [they have already developed at their position]. Thus, once [{they have made} the realization] that [hard work will {enable them greater profits}], [they are one step {closer to actually} achieving those greater profits]."

The braces demarcate strokes in the data. Individual braces within brackets can indicate some of the cultural meaning that can be implied in a simple statement.

On the other end of the spectrum are the districts. Districts are a catch-all group for when you have multiple museums in a research project. You should still limit your paper to one museum, but if you are writing a book chapter or a collection of articles on one topic then having several districts in which to store museums can be quite useful. In extremely broad fields you may elect to take this one step farther and build cities or even nations of data, but at this point you may be refining your data too broadly and your project may be larger than one person can complete over the course of a lifetime. If you are part of a research organization, large sets of districts and cities may enable many of your researchers to discuss wholly different topics within a uniform conceptual subset.

ORGANIZING YOUR DATA

While RFA is not the only way to organize collected data, it is one of the more efficient methodologies for creating a data structure. If you are diligent in building your qualitative data matrix, then you should be able to put any related data into the matrix at the museum level or lower. However, this can largely be determined by the size of the project. The larger the project the more classifications of data you may have to create. Generally, however, you will find that most data can be categorized at the wing level or lower. For most projects this is a good standard to follow.

The more clearly you mark your frames, galleries, and wings, the easier they will be to retrieve in your analysis phase. Having easily accessible data not only will make your analysis easier, but it will also increase your ability to increase the depth of your data and to triangulate sources. Each additional datum from a gallery should be related closely enough to other data that it allows you to augment any other datum in that set. As we have noted before, the more sources and the more support that you give any assertion in your paper, the more the academic community will set that assertion as valid within the field.

By way of a final note, if you find that your data is becoming to unwieldy for you to navigate within your matrix, you are free to create notes within your matrix to remind you of what you were thinking when you created that specific gallery or wing. Over the course of a project your understanding of the data or your feelings about a specific relationship between data elements can change. If this is the case, then having notes that tell you what you were thinking as you created the matrix can make your life much easier. Take the time to take notes while you are creating your matrix, because you never know when those notes can help lead you to the data you seek.[3]

CHECKLIST

- ❑ Are your frames the most basic contextual elements of your data?
- ❑ When you create a gallery, are all of the frames closely related or do you need more galleries?
- ❑ Are your wings comprised of closely related galleries or are you "cheating" by putting non-related galleries into the same wing?
- ❑ Do all of your wings fit within the same museum or is your project becoming bigger than a single paper?
- ❑ If you create districts or cities, are they really needed for the current project?
- ❑ Are there cultural elements that you need to explore in strokes so that your reader can understand the data in the way that it was meant by its creator?

---

3. Nvivo is an excellent software package that can use its existing structure to build RFA museums. The nodes can be set as frames (or strokes) and can be nested into galleries, wings, and museums.

RECOMMENDED READING

Chenail, Ronald J. (1995). Recursive Frame Analysis. *The Qualitative Report*, Volume 2, Number 2, at http://www.nova.edu/ssss/QR/QR2-2/rfa.html.

Chenail, Ronald (2013). Recursive Frame Analysis for MFT Practice and Research. AAMFT.org at http://www.aamft.org/handouts/107.pdf.

Keeney, Hillary & Keeney, Bradford (2012, March). "Recursive Frame Analysis: Reflections on the Development of a Qualitative Method." *THE QUALITATIVE REPORT*, Volume 17 Number 2, 514-52-4 at http://www.nova.edu/ssss/QR/QR17-2/keeney.pdf.

chapter 42
Legal Recursive Frame Analysis

INTRODUCTION

As you move through this book and see how different elements of the academic system are linked both philosophically and technically, you may have seen how some of the other researcher methodologies or data collection strategies that are used in fields other than your own could be implemented in your own field. While any data collection methodology can transcend the boundaries of academic fields, perhaps no methodology merges into another field as well as RFA. Coming from the therapy/medical field, RFA has many advantages over traditional legal case studies in the way that it handles data. Since laws are and criminal cases are at their most basic level simply discourses, literally RFA was made to be the methodology to collect data from them.

To use RFA as an effective method for compiling legal data, one must first shift his or her view of the legal paradigm. If you cannot accept that evidence is data, then you may want to pursue the more traditional method of legal analysis (see Chapter 34: Legal Briefs). However, if you can see the connection between evidence and data, then you are well on your way to being able to use RFA as an organizational strategy in your personal cases. Basically there are two kinds of data that you look at as evidence, physical evidence and verbal testimony (depositions, testimony, interviews, affidavits, interrogatories). The verbal testimony transitions directly into LRFA because it is discourse and that is what RFA was designed to deal with. The physical evidence can be converted and categorized for the sorting process by simply creating a rich text description of the object(s) for the categorization process. Once you have your data prepared, all you have to do is contextualize it into frames and begin RFA.

Some of you who are in the legal field may be asking, "since IRAC (or its variants) have been used for years, why would I want to learn a new system?" It is a valid question. The legal game is now controlled by those who have the most efficient access to organized data and those who can convey that data to the judge/jury/other party most effectively. IRAC is a briefing system that allows you to understand your own notes for future use; however, it was not designed to be an information organization strategy. RFA was designed to do just that. Further, you do not even have to remove IRAC from your toolbox to implement RFA. In large cases the briefs may be the contextual elements that you are looking for (especially if you use this method in appellate cases). Nothing in this book is designed to replace the tools that you already have in your literary toolbox, these methodologies are merely suggestions to augment what you already know.

As there is already a chapter on RFA in this book (Chapter 41), we are not going to cover the specific methodology of RFA again. Rather, this chapter looks at how the data that you are collecting fits into the RFA strategy and how the terminology of the legal system has direct parallels in the RFA world. In the first section we look at how your frames are individual facts—that is, pieces of data. If you begin looking at your facts as pieces of data that can be converted to frames, your analytical model is already beginning to take shape. Next, we look at how data supports the elements of a crime/civil claim. If you organize your galleries by the charge you are looking to support (or defend), then you build up and triangulate the data that you need for your elements. Elements, of course, are portions of the crime/civil claim/defense, which is the parallel to wings in this system and also the topic of the third section. In the fourth section we explain how this can be related to the entire case (all charges, claims, or defenses) as a museum in LRFA. This chapter concludes with an analysis of IRAC versus LRFA and how IRAC can be integrated into LRFA if it is already in your skill set.

LRFA has the potential to be an effective force in the legal world; the only question is whether you will use it to make your life easier. Effective organization leads to efficient access to your data. The more efficient your data, the more effectively you can augment your case theory with multiple sources for each fact that you offer into evidence. While this should not replace your IRAC format for case briefing, it should augment your system enough that if you want to find a specific fact or piece of evidence within your theory and correlate or juxtapose that fact/evidence to another point, you should be able to do it in mere moments. Effective organization can lead to better case theory.

FRAMES (AS FACTS)

Facts are the basis of any good case theory. While a case can be argued with limited facts, each fact that you have in your favor increases the odds that you will be able to create a good case. Knowing facts that are not in your favor also can be a benefit for you as you try to undermine the validity and reliability of those facts. In this way, a legal case is much like an academic paper in the way that it is designed. Over the years the art of legal case creation has been replaced with the science of theory development. While the system resists this change as much as possible, those who practice in the legal, criminal, dispute resolution, or policing field understand that facts are merely pieces of the evidence that must be collected and analyzed to build your theory of the case.

Dismantling evidence into its contextual parts may seem like you are making more work for yourself; however, when you allow the contextual elements to stand alone oftentimes you can see how they interrelate with other contextual elements beyond the "sum of all parts." This interrelation can allow you to link pieces of evidence that may not be clearly linked on the surface. The first and easiest type of evidence to deconstruct is the verbal evidence (previous testimony, depositions, affidavits, interviews, and interrogatories). These forms of evidence are in discourse format already and can be "run" through the RFA process as they stand. The difference in LRFA (with the exception of policing in some circumstances) is that the framework of your project is already defined before you enter into your analysis. You know the crime/claim you are trying to prove so the museums, wings, and galleries are already known to you. All you need to do is find the facts that will support them.

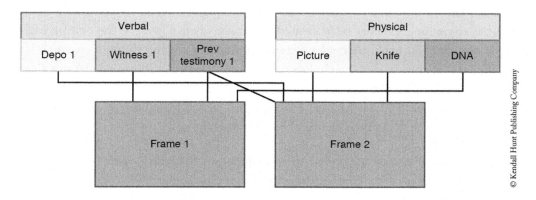

The second type of evidence that you will use to build your case theory in LRFA is physical evidence. Physical evidence is simply "real world" evidence that needs to be contextualized to be integrated into a case theory. While the jury will want to see the evidence, you need the evidence to be verbal to process the data through logic. This means that you should have rich descriptions of the evidence (for more on rich descriptions see Chapters 19 and 46). Each detail becomes a fact and each relevant fact allows you to make your case theory more robust.

The third type of evidence that you will look at is circumstantial evidence. This is not hard evidence and the factoids that you distill out of this type of evidence should be marked with an asterisk. Circumstantial evidence should either be used to augment current data that you have or should be used in conjunction with other data that makes the circumstances more likely. Circumstantial evidence, like verbal evidence, should be translated into prose and then that prose should be broken down into contextual elements (marked with an asterisk) that can then be run through the normal RFA process. The asterisk shows you where you need additional data to triangulate the validity of your data.

Frame level facts are the basic building blocks of case theory. Many times you will have a plethora of facts that do not fit into your case theory; this is completely normal and can help you in the long run. When you are categorizing your data, categorize all data, even that data that does not fit into your case. The external data, which is data that is not directly related to your case, is useful if it is categorized and the opposition uses it in some way that you did not expect. If this is the case, then you will have it categorized and allow your response to be more efficient.

GALLERIES (AS ELEMENTS OF CRIME/CLAIM)

Galleries are the first preformed categorization technique of LRFA. A preformed categorization technique is something that has been created by scholars before you. In the case of LRFA the elements of all crimes and civil claims have been legislated or created through common law and are thus established. If you are doing a civil case, then the elements of the legal claim will be outlined by the law and by case law. If you are doing a criminal case then the elements of the crime will be outlined by the law and by case law. As a theorist in a case, all you have to do is take your factoids of data and match them up to the element that you are hoping to support.

When you are creating your structure, you may find in cases with multiple crimes or claims that are there are elements that cross over between the different crimes and claims. This is perfectly normal and actually makes your job easier. Just like a single frame can fit into multiple galleries, multiple galleries can fit into multiple wings. Each repeat gallery should be analyzed in detail, and the more robust you can make these repeat galleries the better. If your opponent can disrupt the gallery in one crime/claim, then they will have disrupted the gallery in all crimes/claims (that is, if they figure out your theorization strategy).

Using this format allows you to triangulate data in a way that traditional legal models did not enable. Traditionally, providing augmenting data from multiple sources would be seen as repetitious and could draw an objection, but if the data is simply extracted from the evidence in the normal flow of the testimony/presentation and reassembled for the jury in the closing (not to mention your charts will be very useful in defending motions), then it is easily "accepted" because you are only asking the jury to understand data that they previously "knew."

WINGS (AS CRIMES/CLAIMS)

Wings are the second preformed element in LRFA. Your wings are your crimes/claims that you are alleging or your defenses. Once you know what you are claiming or what you are defending, the models are basically already created for you. There are some people who will stretch the models, which is fine. But the vast majority of people will use crimes, claims, and defenses the same way that they have been used since the beginning of the American legal system.

Defenses differ slightly in this regard from crimes and claims as defenses are distinct to individual cases. While your defenses will still be preformed, you will have the additional onerous of figuring out which defenses you are going to claim. This can be done by looking at the defenses that seem to make sense in the case and then taking the frames to see what elements you can support. While this takes slightly more time in the defensive stance, it can be quite an effective strategy.

Once you reach the crime/claim/defense level of your case analysis in LRFA, you have the duty to ensure that all elements of your crime/claim/defense are met. The galleries only provide you with the organizational structure; you have to ensure that the data populates each category before you move on with the case. For instance if you are trying to prove battery, the elements are (1) intent to cause harm (intentional, reckless, or negligent); (2) contact with person or chattels in contact with person; and (3) contact was unwanted.[1] These three elements are the galleries or wings (batteries). As you are populating the wing, if one of the galleries does not have any frames in it (such as that the contact was unwanted), then you need to look for more data that supports your position. Otherwise, you could be subject to a motion to dismiss.

Fully populated galleries and wings lead to good case theory. After the first piece of data that supports a claim, all additional frames that are in support of that same point augment the position of that claim and triangulate the data to protect it from counterarguments. Ideally, you will have at least four supporting frames in each gallery of your case theory; however, we all know that most of

---

1. This is a loose common law version of battery.

the time things in this world are less than ideal; therefore, you should always strive to have at least two frames to support each gallery, as this will insulate you somewhat from counterarguments or human error.

MUSEUMS (AS ENTIRE CASE THEORY)

Your museum is your entire case. If you are pursuing a criminal case revolving around domestic violence you could have three counts of aggravated assault, two counts of aggravated battery, two counts of assault and battery, and a case of attempted homicide in the second degree. If you are looking at a civil case you could have seven counts of fraud, a count of predatory lending, and four counts of breach of contract. These are the cases where LRFA can truly shine. In these types of cases, you can use the gallery level work for one charge/claim to build the same gallery in another charge/claim. As long as a single gallery of each crime is different, or a single gallery of each claim is different, then you have an additional charge/claim. This enables you to build the most efficient case against the other side and allows you to use the full force of the law.

Once you reach the museum level, your LRFA design has become a legal matrix for the case. If you are good at Excel, or any variety of database software, you can create a digital matrix that others in your firm can use to work on the case in conjunction with you. The easy categorization of data allows operators in different areas of the country (or even the world) to input data into the system through a unified case analysis medium. This creates a human computer for analyzing the qualitative data of any legal case, so all you need is someone to build a simple five-page database or spreadsheet.

This organizational matrix can be very useful as you attempt to file motions or present your argument to the jury. Any opposition by your opponents should be manageable by a well-populated matrix. If your opponent counters with, "but if fact A is wrong then the whole case is wrong…" then you can counter with "Fact A is important but Facts B, C, and D show the same intent as fact A, thus even if you have doubts about Fact A, which you should not, you can still see how Facts B, C, and D fulfill the requirements of the case. LRFA helps you build redundancies for redundancies within your case easily and efficiently so that in the amount of time you would normally spend on a case you can build a much more well-developed case with much less effort.

ORGANIZATIONAL ELEMENTS

Some of you who are reading this, who have been trained in the traditional methods of case study, may be too set in your ways to accept a new model. You may have too much sweat equity invested in learning the IRAC method to replace it with LRFA. The good news is that you do not have to replace it. IRAC and LRFA can work hand in hand to increase your legal case study efficiency without dismissing the format that you have been using for years. IRAC can be used as a contextual element of a frame. While this will result in large frames, it will allow you to use IRAC as part of your methodology. As you become more comfortable with the process, you can begin to break your IRAC into multiple frames, thus allowing you ease into the process while maintaining the skills you worked so hard to achieve.

The integration of IRAC and LRFA also allow you to bridge the gaps between two or more fields. The world is becoming more diversified; therefore, it is not too far off when we will see a world where being a subject matter expert in an area of the law will not be enough to be a "go-to guy." People are going to start looking for lawyers to merge their legal talents with academic talents. Lawyers who are publishing on the cutting edge of their subject matter in legal and scholarly journals are going to have a leg up on their competition. Even now, a lay person looking for a lawyer can find data on potential attorneys. Who would you select, Joe A who claims to be an expert on a subject matter or Julian B who literally wrote the book on the topic that you are looking for? Whether or not Julian is the better attorney, for the lay person he will look better. As with any other field, the more tools that you have in your tool box, the more efficient you can be. LRFA is a tool that can help you expand your practice and expand your publishing to areas that were too complicated in the past.

CHECKLIST

- ❑ Have you defined your claim/count/defense (C/C/D)?
- ❑ What are the elements (galleries) of your C/C/D?
- ❑ Did you break your data down into frames?
- ❑ How do your frames fit into different galleries?
- ❑ If a frame fits into multiple galleries it is OK, just be careful to protect that frame.
- ❑ If a gallery fits into multiple wings it is OK, just be careful to protect that gallery.

RECOMMENDED READING

Block, Gertrude (1999). Effective Legal Writing: For Law Students and Lawyers. New York: Foundation Press.

Chenail, Ronald J. (1995). Recursive Frame Analysis. *The Qualitative Report*, Volume 2, Number 2, at http://www.nova.edu/ssss/QR/QR2-2/rfa.html.

Chenail, Ronald (2013). Recursive Frame Analysis for MFT Practice and Research. AAMFT. org at http://www.aamft.org/handouts/107.pdf.

Garner, Bryan A. (2002). The Redbook: A Manual on Legal Style. New York: Thompson West.

Keeney, Hillary & Keeney, Bradford (2012, March). "Recursive Frame Analysis: Reflections on the Development of a Qualitative Method." *The Qualitative Report*, Volume 17 Number 2, 514-52-4 at http://www.nova.edu/ssss/QR/QR17-2/keeney.pdf.

chapter 43
Interviews

INTRODUCTION

Interviews are one of the fundamental tools within the arts, the social sconces, the humanities, and the medical and legal fields. An interview is a conversation with your subject where you allow your subject the opportunity to explain, in detail, the answers to your questions. Interviews can also allow your subjects to explain their answers to your questions in a narrative form, which can give you even more data. Interviews are one of the basic building blocks for good research methodology. If you take the time to learn how to prepare a good interview then you can use that information as a primary source for your paper or allow the information to be triangulation material for other data that you have discovered.

Interviews are useful for both new and developed researchers because they allow the researcher the option of asking follow-up questions. Follow-up questions are questions that a researcher asks to clarify or expound on data that the subject has already given you. Interviews can also give you the opportunity to conduct reflective listening, which can help you build trust with your subjects. Other methods do not enable the same level of interaction (except participatory observation) with your subjects as interviews allow. By exploiting this higher level of interaction a researcher has the ability to build a trove of rich data for a research project. The interaction does not alleviate the researcher of the duty to prepare for the interview. When you are preparing to do an interview or multiple interviews, you should take the time to prepare a list of questions that will keep your subject on task.

The best interviews allow your subjects to tell their story, but still keep enough control that you get the information you need.

Interviews are used in nearly every field to some extent. Whether you are interviewing a researcher who conducted a specific experiment in the "hard sciences" or interviewing a witness of a current event, the interview process throughout the academic community has some basic elements that you must acknowledge. In each field the terminology may be slightly different, but the general process for interviewing involves asking specific open, direct questions that guide your subject toward the information that you are looking for; these questions are followed up by direct closed questions to clarify information. The open questions are used to develop the broad information; the closed questions are used to get specific details that are relevant to your study.

Interviews can be done by anyone, but who does the interview can determine the quality of an interview. The more your subjects consider you an outsider, the more reserved they are going to be about the information that they give you. Likewise, if your subjects can relate with you in some way, or if you have developed some level of trust with your subjects then you can expect that they will give you more information based on this trust. When doing group research, choosing who the correct person to do an interview is can determine whether the interview is a resounding success or a dismal failure. The fact that anyone can do an interview does not mean that anyone should do an interview.

In this chapter we will look at some of the basic procedural elements revolving around an interview, and the basic level of competence needed in designing an interview. If interviewing is to be your primary medium of data collection you may want to invest in additional books and courses on qualitative and quantitative interviewing. This book provides the framework for many fields, but it becomes your responsibility to fill in the framework with discipline-specific tactics. In the first section of this chapter we look at how an interview is a conversation with a subject. Treating an interview as an interrogation will result in sloppy data collection and less cooperation from your subjects. This leads us on to the second section, where we look at how you can allow your subject to talk and have some control over the process of the interview.

In most cases, subjects want to tell you their story, and the key word of this is "their" story. Even if they give you more information than what you need, you can always clean up the story when you are coding the data. In both the second and third sections of this chapter we look at the proper ways to word your questions and when you should ask specific types of questions. Coming from a legal background, the typology of questions is a very important subject in most interviews. In the third section we look at the difference between closed and open questions, both of which are valuable tools in your interviewing repertoire.

In the next section we look at the difference between direct questions and leading questions, which can determine whether your interviews are successful data collection exercises or simply a way for you to interrogate subjects to find out what you already "believe." In the final section we examine the ethical concerns of a researcher doing interviews, specifically whether or not you should push hard for information that your witness is uncomfortable sharing. The ethical considerations are relevant here, as well as the question of whether your subject may be willing to do a follow-up interview if you need more data.

If you follow this basic framework, and acknowledge the ethical considerations laid out in the last section, you should be able to have a reasonably successful interview in most circumstances. This chapter is designed for normal interviews with people who are willing to share their information. This chapter is not designed to create interrogation techniques for people who are less cooperative, such as prisoners who are discussing how they committed a crime that they are still on trial for. Specialized interviews require specialized techniques, and those techniques are beyond the scope of this book. However, if you do research those techniques, they should plug easily into the framework we discuss in this chapter.

CONVERSATION WITH THE SUBJECT

The first thing that any good researcher must realize is that an interview is a conversation between two people where one or both of them are taking notes. As with any other conversation, this requires at least two people. If the subject does not want to talk, then the interviewer will not have much of a conversation to take notes on. Likewise, if the interviewer contributes nothing to the conversation, then it is more of a monologue by the subject that can flow in any direction that it wants. Good interviews require you to treat subjects with the same respect and patience that you would show in a conversation with a friend. There are times where interruptions are appropriate and there are times where it is inappropriate to interrupt. This will largely be dictated by the cultural environment that you are in and your relationship with your subject.

One of the key problems that I see in many of the interviews that I have observed or in interviews that I have read is where a researcher tries to manage an interview. While there is more of an allowance for this in quantitative interviewing, it should be avoided in qualitative interviewing. You are a privileged participant in interviews, and your subjects are allowing you access to their lives and experiences for the good of your project (whether you are paying them or not), which means that you should respect the conversation like you would a conversation with a boss or a teacher. While you should have a goal in the conversation, you are not in complete control of the situation. If you try to grasp the interview too tightly, then you may find that you are choking the usefulness out of the process.

Beginning interviewers also tend to have a problem with their egos. You cannot enter into the interview believing that you are more important than the person that you are interviewing. If you notice the great television interviewers on the major networks and how they do their craft, you will see that they are self-effacing, defer to the subject when the subject stays on track, and generally attempt to impose themselves as minimally into the interview as possible. Beginning interviewers tend to take the opposite approach, ambushing the subject with a flurry of questions that leaves the interviewer frustrated with a lack of answers and the subject confused about what is going on. Realize that you are there because there is something special about the person that you are interviewing, and realize that your research is not all about you.

Above all else, your subject should feel safe in the interview with you. If there is a danger to them for speaking to you, take proper steps to hide their identity. If they have a special need, then try to meet that need. If they cannot travel to you, then you should travel to them or set up a phone/internet meeting. As a researcher you should do everything you can to make the interview as pleasant of an experience for your subject as possible. Good researchers are good handlers of their subjects, because you never know when a subject will be useful again for another interview.

LETTING THEM TALK

Have you ever watched or read an interview where most of the talking was done by the person conducting the interview and the subject said relatively little? Did you get much out of that interview? I am imagining that very few of you are nodding your heads right now for two reasons. First, interviews where the interviewer does most of the talking are not good interviews because all the interviewer collects is data that supports what he or she has already decided about the research project. Not only is this bad interviewing technique, it is also bad research methodology. The second reason I envision that you are not shaking your head is because you are reading a book, and you would look silly responding to a book!

Good interview data comes from the subject, not from the interviewer. If you are going to be a good interviewer in whatever field you have chosen, then you need to swallow your pride and realize that the subjects should be doing most of the talking. The reason for this is that the data needs to come from some source other than the researcher; if it comes from you then it is an opinion piece, not a research document. You are the filter of the information, not the source. Even though an interview is a conversation, it should be a conversation where you do most of the listening and little talking. During the best interviews, the researcher talks about 25% of the time and the subject contributes about 75% of the content. This means that most of what you record or take notes on will come from the subject, which is one of the hallmarks of a good interview.

The more your subject talks, the more data you can accumulate in your study. Talkative subjects can be a good thing, but only if they are talking about things that are related to your study. This is where you come in as part of the conversation. If the witness's narrative begins to stray away from the subject of the interview, then you can use questions to guide the conversation back to the topic. Further, if subjects give you a large block of data (a large period of time where they talk without your input), you can show that you are being attentive by asking follow-up questions to focus their attention on specific points. Not only does this show that you are listening, but it can allow you to make the data richer by getting more information in certain areas.

When you are letting the other person talk, you should also have clarified how you are going to be using the data. An interview that is "on the record" is an interview where you are allowed to use the name and position of the subject in your report and the data that the subject provides can be attributed to that person. An "off the record" interview is an interview in which you receive information from your source, but you can only use that data to find other data sources and you are not permitted to use your source's name or position in your project. The third type of interview is an anonymous interview, in which you can use the information that you gained from the interview but you cannot use your subject's name or position in your project. Knowing what type of interview you are conducting and how you can use the data from that interview can help you build a good reputation in your field as an interviewer. Additionally, if you have an anonymous or "off the record" interview and you expose your subject, you will gain a reputation as an untrustworthy researcher. That is something that you want to avoid at all cost.

OPEN VERSUS CLOSED QUESTIONS

Some researchers will tell you that you should never ask a closed question when you are conducting an interview. As a rule, this is not true. However, to be a good interviewer, you should know the difference between a closed and an open question. Most of your questions in any interview should be open questions; however, closed questions can have their uses. An open question is a question that allows subjects to give their own accounting of what happened in an event, what the cause/effect of a phenomenon was, or their knowledge/opinion about an object. Open questions are useful when you are looking for new data and want subjects to be able to tell their story with limited interruptions. Open questions work well in the humanities and social sciences because the individual details and the *emic* point of view are useful for analysis. When in doubt, the question "What happened next" is always a good follow up.

Open questions are the tools used for broad strokes in your interview, which means that closed questions are the tools used for the detailed work. A closed question is a question where the researcher is directing the subject toward a specific bit of information or a specific topic. Closed questions serve two purposes in an interview. First, closed questions can be used to direct the attention of your subjects back to the topic of the interview. When you are using open questions and allowing subjects to tell their story, sometimes they are so happy that someone is listening to them that they allow their story to wander. If this happens in your interviews, then you can use a closed question to refocus their attention and bring them back to the topic. Be careful using this topic, however, if you have subjects who tend to take the long way to get to a point.

The second way that you can use a closed question in interviews is to allow your subjects to focus on a specific point. Sometimes subjects will not see the importance of a bit of information in their story that may be central to the subject that you are researching. Using a closed follow-up question to dig for more information can not only provide you with a tool to help you get more information but it can also show your subjects that you are paying close attention to what they are saying. This can help you build a trust or a report with your subjects, which may in the long run open them up to giving you more information.

The balance between open and closed questions is largely dependant on your style as a researcher and how cooperative your subjects are. There have been interviews where the interviewer asks subjects one question and their narrative gives the researcher all the information that he or she needs. These types of interviews are very rare, however, and you should expect at least a few follow-up questions. Generally you will use open questions to keep the flow of the interview going and closed questions will help you redirect the flow if it gets out of control. The more interviews you conduct, the better you will be able to judge your question typology and thus you will be able to keep the flow of the interview going more smoothly.

DIRECT VERSUS LEADING QUESTIONS

The dichotomy between direct and leading questions is quite different between the dynamic of open and closed questions. Whereas the dynamic interaction between open and closed questions can help a researcher build an effective interview, the interplay between direct and leading questions can be the difference between a good interview and a poor interrogation. A direct question is a clearly worded query relating to a specific topic that the subject does not feel compelled to answer in a specific way as indicated by the questioner. This can be understood better in context with a leading question. A leading question is a query where the answer is suggested or implied by the questioner. In a good interview, generally only one or two leading questions will be asked, and they will only be asked to remind a subject of something said earlier in that or a previous interview. Leading questions are dangerous because they can taint the interview with the researcher's opinions.

Direct questions should make up 99% of all of your interviews. Direct questions allow subjects the latitude to answer questions in the best way that they can and allow them to provide you with as much "raw" data as possible. Either open or closed questions can be direct questions, because either type of question can be asked without suggesting the answer to the subject. If you do ask one or two leading questions in your interview, it is not the end of the world; however, if you desire to be a good interviewer, you should always take care to avoid getting in the habit of asking leading questions.

DO NOT FORCE ISSUES

As this chapter comes to an end, we need to review one of the cardinal rules of giving a good academic interview—that is, do not force subjects to answer your questions. Interviews are conversations with subjects, not a time for an ambush. Academic research is not reality TV; you are interviewing subjects by their consent and nothing more. If your subjects feel that you are pushing them too hard, then they are able to end the interview and you are left without data. Treat subjects like friends, but during the interview, avoid getting too close to your subjects. Signs of mutual respect will help you build a rapport with them, which should give you access to more information. The fastest way to destroy rapport is by compelling people to discuss something that they do not want to discuss.

Subject participation is not the only reason you do not want to force an issue. If subjects have gone through a traumatic event, then it is unethical to force them to talk about it just because of your research project. A psychologist or a doctor may need them to talk about what happened for treatment, or a lawyer or police officer may need answers to protect others; however, if your only reason for asking the question is to get data for a project (even if it may help others) you should not force subjects to relive a tragic event. If you find that your subjects become uncomfortable talking about something then remind them that they do not have to talk about it. This may cause you to get less information, but it will protect their sanity and may even help them reach the point where they trust you enough to talk about whatever is bothering them.

Your interviews are conversations between you and your subjects, where you are regulated to a secondary role. Always remember that you have the privilege of interviewing your subjects, no matter what their station in life. Interviews are at the discretion of the subjects and you need to respect that to be a good interviewer. You also must realize that you are not the most important person in the room; your subjects have data that you need and they are giving you this information voluntarily. Respect that and you can build a report that will help you procure more data. Use open, direct questions for most of your interview to allow your witnesses to talk most of the time. You can use closed questions to bring them back to topic if they start to wander. Only use leading questions to confirm what they have already said or to help remind them of something that they were talking about earlier. While you can control an interview, the more stress that you put on your subjects, the less useful data they will be willing to give you. However, if you guide your subjects through the interview process and treat it like a conversation between peers or friends, you will find that you can still direct the conversation and the lack of control can lead you to data that you otherwise may never have known.

CHECKLIST

- ❑ What type of interview are you conducting (on the record, off the record, anonymous)?
- ❑ Have you done everything you can reasonably do to make your subject safe?
- ❑ Have you done everything reasonable to make your subject comfortable?
- ❑ Do you have a prepared list of open questions to keep the flow moving?
- ❑ Have you asked if you can record the interview (video or audio, or both)?
- ❑ Do you have a few closed questions to bring your witness back on track?
- ❑ Keep in mind during the interview that if your witnesses get uncomfortable you should tell them they can take a break or stop the interview.

RECOMMENDED READING

Druckman, Daniel (2005). DOING RESEARCH: METHODS OF INQUIRY FOR CONFLICT ANALYSIS. Thousand Oaks, CA: Sage.

Riessman, Catherine K. (2008). NARRATIVE METHODS FOR THE HUMAN SCIENCES. Thousand Oaks, CA: Sage.

Rubin, Herbert J., and Rubin, Irene S. (2005). QUALITATIVE INTERVIEWING: THE ART OF HEARING DATA 2nd ed. Thousand Oaks, CA: Sage.

chapter 44
Surveys

INTRODUCTION

A survey is a limited interview, conducted by using written questions. Surveys provide researchers with a tool allowing them access to large numbers of people within a finite amount of time. Clearly written surveys are one of the greatest tools that researchers have in their toolbox, because they can be adapted to distill specific data from a heterogeneous group without committing to the countless hours it would take to interview entire populations. As researchers, either in the qualitative field or a quantitative field, you should always consider surveys as a possible tool that can help enrich your data.

Surveys give a researcher access to a larger group of people, but they also provide a tool that allows researchers to concentrate the data throughout the course of the research project. Oftentimes, large volumes of collected data must be organized before they can be coded by the researcher or associates. A well-written survey can overcome this problem, however, because it can be written that the data is coded based on the answers, especially for quantitative studies. This allows researchers to assign associates to code the data so that they can focus on the analysis of the data. While this is not an excuse for "sloppy" research it can be a way for researchers to do multiple things at once in their study.

Survey's are extremely effective when you want to sample information from a large population, but it does not matter which members of the population that they sample. For focused studies, such as ethnographies and phenomenologies, the use of surveys may need to be very selective as individuals within society may have more bearing on your research than others. Further, an individual may have the explanation for a specific observation or focus group question. Conversely, in broader approaches such as case studies and grounded theories, more general surveys can be used to capture a more representative sample. Surveys can be difficult to use in situations where the data is increasingly qualitative, because if you need to follow up on the answer of one of your subjects you may find that you are unable to.

This chapter gives you basic information on how to prepare a survey for a research study. If you follow the steps in this chapter you will find that you have a well-written basic survey. There are multiple books on the market that can help you build your survey from a basic level to a more advanced survey. While we will not go into the process for how to do complicated or long surveys, the tools provided in this chapter will help you extract quality data from your subjects. In the first section of this chapter we look at the way that you form a set of questions for your surveys. Having a set of direct open questions will provide your participants the opportunity to give you rich data. If you are collecting data for a quantitative survey, then you should build it around closed or scaled questions. In the next section we look at the differences between open and closed questions. This discussion is followed by a comparison of direct versus leading questions, then we move to a discussion on the differences between qualitative questions, single answer questions, and scaled questions, focusing on how they are used for a research project. In the fifth section we discuss the way that you can create an effective survey to go through the IRB process. Writing a strong survey opens up your options as a researcher because a good survey should be able to pass an IRB easily. Lastly, we break down the concepts of numbers, sample size, and anonymity, and see how they relate to the people who receive your survey.

AN EASY SET OF QUESTIONS

The main element of a good survey is a set of questions that are easy for the subject to understand and answer. Without a set of clear and concise questions your survey will do little to expand your data. As you are writing questions for your survey you should ensure that every question serves the purpose of collecting data that is specific to your topic. Ancillary questions that do not build up on your data collection model should be culled, ether to keep the length of the survey short or to make room for other more relevant questions. The more focused you make your survey, the richer your data will be for later use.

Unless you are researching a hyper-technical field, short surveys tend to be more useful as a tool.[1] People who are filling out your surveys are doing you a service; therefore, you should not demand more from them than necessary. Time is one of the things that your people are sacrificing to fill out your survey. This means that you should keep your survey as short as possible so that your subjects can complete their contribution to your work as quickly as possible. Another reason that you should keep your survey short is because people are more likely to fill it out. Look at your personal life as an example—are you more likely to fill out a three-question survey or a twenty-page survey? Most of you are going to fill out the shorter survey because it costs you less time. This is generally how it is with most other people. While individuals whom you custom design a survey for are more likely willing to fill out a long survey, if you are using your survey to sample a large random population then short surveys are the way to go.

Another key area of survey creation is that your surveys should be easy to read and understand. If you people a survey and they do not understand the first question, then it is extremely likely that they will throw it in the first garbage bin that they pass. Surveys that people understand are more likely to get a response, but the reason you want them to be clear goes much deeper than that. The more clear your surveys are, the easier it will be for your readers to fill them out. Since we know that survey takers are volunteering their valuable time to take the survey, it makes sense to make the survey as easy as possible for them so that they do not have to waste any of their time.

One major flaw that some researchers find themselves stymied by is not making their surveys easy to return. People's goodwill will only take them so far, and they have already volunteered to talk to a stranger and reveal their opinions or facts about their lives. Now you are asking them to return this data, so the least you can do is make it easy for them. One way to do this is to use prepaid envelopes. Although this method is expensive, subjects can simply drop their message in the mail. The internet also makes it easy to return a survey, because the subject simply hits "Send" at the bottom of the page. When handing out copies in the mall, or any area with a low return rate, you should find a place to put a drop box for the people to drop off their completed survey. Drop boxes eliminate the cost of prepaid envelopes while still giving the subject the opportunity to return the survey anonymously.

OPEN QUESTIONS VERSUS CLOSED QUESTIONS

Surveys, like interviews, live or die on the quality of the questions that you present to your subjects. Good questions can open the door to rich data, which will allow you to guide your readers on their

---

1. This can be a problem with good surveys, they tend to be very long so few people fill them out.

journey through your research. What kind of questions you ask depends on what kind of research you are doing. If you are entering into a qualitative research study, then broad, open-ended questions may allow your readers to provide you with rich narrative data that will expand your data pool and deepen your readers' understanding of your topic. Conversely, if you are conducting a quantitative study, then you may want closed or scaled questions to ensure that your subjects' response will fit into your dataset. In this section we define what open and closed questions are and explain how they can be used to collect rich data regardless of your study type.

An open question is a question where respondents have the opportunity to answer the question and explain their answer. This type of question is extremely effective when you are performing a qualitative survey as it provides subjects with the opportunity to explain the underlying meaning of their response. In many types of study, the meaning is just as important as the answer. In a phenomenology, an ethnography, or a case study, the "why" of an answer will often be more important than the actual answer.[2] Open-ended questions give you the opportunity to collect this data and also give the respondent the freedom to explain what they like and simply give an answer if they do not want to go into great detail.

Open questions can present a problem when you have respondents who do not stay on topic. Unlike interviews where you can use closed questions to bring your subjects back on topic, surveys rely totally on your subjects staying on topic. This means that if they start a narrative on topic, the topic could quickly switch to a topic that they want to talk about. This can invalidate major parts of your survey; however, this can also be a benefit to a researcher. While it will not happen often, these times when subjects break away from the topic of the paper can lead them to giving you very rich data that is tangential but related to the subject. When this happens you can code this data to give you deeper insight into the "why" of their answer.

The other end of the spectrum in surveying is closed-ended questions. A closed question has a finite number of answers that respondents can give and the responses are known by the researcher. Closed questions are an excellent tool for collecting quantitative data, or data that you intend to quantify. As the spectrum of answers within a closed dataset are generally able to be converted to numbers, closed questions tend to be used more in the quantitative field than the qualitative field; however, like open questions they can be used in either field.

The danger of closed questions is that an answer is an answer and that is all that it can be. You receive the answer, but do not receive the underlying reason for the answer. This can leave a researcher with more questions than answers. This is a key criticism of closed questions and anonymous surveys in

---

2. This is doubly true in "why" theoretical papers (*see* Chapter 25: "Why" Papers).

general, because you may discover the gem of knowledge that you are looking for exists, only to find that you have no way to track down the person who has access to that knowledge. This can be maddening and may tempt a researcher to violate ethical norms. If you do elect to go with closed questions in a survey, realize that sometimes you will have to let answers get away; "winning" the report is not worth an ethical violation tracking down someone who you told would be anonymous.

DIRECT VERSUS LEADING QUESTIONS

Surveys are vulnerable to the dichotomy between direct and leading questions to a greater extent than other data collection methodologies. A direct question is one that asks a respondent for specific information but does not suggest an answer. This definition comes from the legal concept of direct questioning where you allow witnesses to answer without telling them the answer. In a direct question you make every effort not to suggest the answer that you are looking for to your subjects, so you focus the readers' attention on your subjects rather than on you as a researcher. Direct questions help prevent researcher bias from tainting your survey and leading to bad data.

Conversely, there are leading questions. A leading question is a question where you imply the answer that you are looking for in the delivery of the question. This is a common legal term from cross examinations where the lawyer "leads" the hostile witness to the answer he or she desires. Leading questions lead to a bad survey. If you are going to tell witnesses what you want them to say, then what is the point of giving them a survey? While intentional leading questions are dangerous to a research project, unintentional leading questions can be even more dangerous. If a researcher does not know that the questions are leading questions, then generally the researcher does not know how to write good questions. In such cases, the researcher may be telling the subjects what to answer without even knowing it.

When writing your surveys, seek help to ensure that you are not leading your subjects. If you have a short survey, then ask a friend or co-worker to look over the questions to see if any answers are suggestive. This can be an additional test for your survey, because if it is too long for a friend or co-worker to look at then it will likely be too long for your subjects. The more experience you have writing surveys, the better you will be at writing direct, non-leading questions.[3] When in doubt, review any question to see if there is any hint of the answer you want in the text. If so, then there is a danger of the question being biased. (If you are asking a closed question and all possibilities are suggested equally in the text then this can be an exception to the rule.)

---

3. As long as you avoid building bad habits.

QUALITATIVE, SINGLE, AND SCALE ANSWERS

When coding your answers, the type of answers can dictate how you code them for your analysis. The three types of answers that we will look at in this section are qualitative, single, and scale answers. We are not going to look in detail at numerical answers or false answers because the way that you deal with either is simple. Numerical answers you enter into your calculation matrix and false answers (answers you know to be false) you omit from the study (e.g., When were you born? 49 B.C.). We will briefly look at how each of the other types of answers can be used, but for more detailed instructions on coding look to Chapters 41 and 42, which describe RFA, the preferred method of this book.

Qualitative answers are the type of answers you want for, you guessed it, qualitative research papers. These types of answers tend to come in the narrative form, but can be related in other ways. When you receive a qualitative answer, you should always probe the answer for as much rich data as possible. Every detail should be coded in some way. Even information that does not seem related to your topic when you are coding can be useful further down the road when you are analyzing the data. If you code all the data in any given answer, then you will know where you can find the data later if it is needed. While this is not often needed, if you find one time in your career that you can put your hands on a bit of obscure data quickly rather than searching for it for hours, then the coding of all the data will pay off.

Single-answer questions are much easier to code, as generally they fit into a chart. The most common single-answer questions require a yes or no. Single-answer questions can be coded in many different ways. Qualitative researchers will code them in relation to contextual data to help focus rich data. Quantitative researchers will usually turn the single answer into a number which can then be entered into a matrix. Theoretical researchers may turn a single answer into a whole new research project asking "why?" When writing your survey, find areas where you want your subjects to be very focused when they answer your question (most of these questions will be demographic questions); then write your questions to support this type of answer.

Scale questions are the intermediate type of question between qualitative answers and single-answer questions. In a scale question you will allow your reader to answer the question on a predestinated scale—for instance, "How old are you?" (Most people will fall on a scale of between 0 and 118 years.) This allows you to know something about the answer before you receive it and this allows you to build your research design around these questions. Scale answers can be used in both qualitative and quantitative research and can be a valuable tool in the development of a project.

When writing your survey, take into account what type of data you want to receive. If you are doing an ethnography and desire rich detailed data, then asking a series of single-answer questions will not be very beneficial to you. Further, if you are attempting a predictive statistical study, a question that is designed to provoke a narrative answer from the subject is going to be less useful than a scaled answer. Knowing what you are looking for can help you decide how to approach the task of writing your questions. Once again, good questions come down to good preparation.

INSTITUTIONAL REVIEW BOARDS

As a researcher who looks at macro-economic effects of change on sociocultural norms and conflict through history, generally I do not have to deal with the Institutional Review Board (IRB) at my university. Most of the subjects that I am talking about have been dead for hundreds if not thousands of years and the theories and hypotheses that I propose are at such a macro level that they would have to go through dozens of bureaucratic agencies if anyone ever wanted to implement them (assuming anyone reads them). This field somewhat isolates me from the IRB, but the IRB can be a valuable tool for a researcher when preparing a project.

Too often researchers look at an IRB as a gatekeeper that prevents them from doing the research that they want. The IRB is also seen as a nitpicker who sends back research proposals with supposedly miniscule changes that need to be made for the proposal to pass. If you are just getting started in academia or have been involved and need a new perspective, the IRB is one of the most useful tools that a university researcher (undergrad, graduate, or professional) has available. The IRB is a group of people who have been selected because of their expertise on the subject of good ethical research; since we are all looking to do good ethical research, we should be looking to the IRB for guidance when building projects.

Having a good relationship with your institution's IRB is one of the best relationships that a researcher can build (other than secretaries, who make the world go round). Keep the IRB involved in your research design from the very beginning. The more you involve them, the earlier they can cut off mistakes. Further, the IRB experts can give you advice on how to word your surveys. If they say a question is wrong, ask them why. Do not argue with them but allow them to guide you and help you develop the best surveying instrument that you can possibly make. Not only will this help you put out a good product, but it will also help you in your relationship with the IRB for future projects (do not abuse this relationship, however).

NUMBER AND SAMPLE SIZE

We have reserved this topic for last because it is a simple topic to end the chapter on, "How big should I make my sample?" The answer "big enough." The size of a sample for surveys is based on what you are researching and what population you are looking at. A nationwide survey requires more people than a local survey, but a nationwide survey has more people who may be willing to take your survey. The sample size comes down to (1) what methodology you are using, (2) how many people are in the population, and (3) whether you want your findings to be transferable. If you are doing a case study, then a sample size of one may be workable; however, if you are doing a statistical study of the nationwide effects of drinking on persons between the ages of 18 and 44, then you will need a much bigger survey to be relevant. This is because the case study does not try to say that its research is transferable to a general population, but a statistical study is done for the specific purpose of describing/predicting the actions of a large population using a sample.

When creating survey samples, you must also look to whether the sample should be anonymous or not. If you are doing a detailed case study of a specific person with unique characteristics, then it is difficult to completely hide this person's identity. In these cases you should review if the identity getting out would put the person in danger. If so, then talk to the subject about masking his or her identity. The choice of anonymity should always be in the hands of the subjects. It is their life that you are looking at, therefore it is their right to choose if they want their name exposed. You can also let them choose the level of anonymity that you give them. Some people may be okay with experts or other people knowing that it is them, but not wanting their name to be exposed to the public.

The anonymity of large groups of people is a different story. The way you ensure this is by keeping the respondents anonymous by having them omit their name on the survey. This can be frustrating if you want to ask follow-up questions, but when looking at something controversial (teen marijuana use) you want to take all precautions to safeguard your subjects. At times the ethical researcher must take into consideration the privacy of the subjects before entering into a research project. If privacy is of the highest importance, then sometimes you will have to accept that not all data will be accessible to you. When in doubt, error on the side of ethics.

Surveys are a tool that can open worlds of data to a researcher, if they are used properly. In this chapter we looked at ways that you can create an excellent basic survey; however, if you want to be an expert at taking surveys you should look at more advanced methods that cover sentence context, population selection, randomization, and general format. The ability to give a basic survey is a tool that every researcher should have in his or her tool belt, and after reading this chapter you should have a basic idea of how to conduct one. The two key rules of surveying are (1) do not lead your subjects, keep the facts honest and submitted by them; and (2) protect the identity of vulnerable populations. All other considerations should be secondary to these ethical axioms. Good surveys will yield good research, when combined with other data collection tools they can yield excellent research.

CHECKLIST

- ❏ What methodology are you using?
- ❏ What type of answers are you looking for?
- ❏ Is your survey short?
- ❏ Are your questions clear?
- ❏ Are your questions direct?
- ❏ Are you using open or closed questions?
- ❏ Have you avoided using leading questions?
- ❏ Are you protecting the identity of your subjects? Why or why not?
- ❏ How many surveys do you need?
- ❏ Are you spreading them throughout the population?
- ❏ Has the IRB approved your survey?

RECOMMENDED READING

Blair, Johnny, and Czaja, Ronald (2013). *Designing Surveys: A Guide to Decisions and Procedures.* Thousand Oaks, CA: Sage.

Harris, David (2014). *The Complete Guide to Writing Questionnaires: How to Get Better Decisions.* New York: I & M Press.

chapter 45
Focus Groups

INTRODUCTION

A focus group is a data collection methodology that is commonly used in the business and psychology fields. Focus groups give researchers access to data by conducting group interviews and looking at how the group manifests itself as an intellectual unit in relation to one another and in relation to the topic of the group. A well-preformed focus group can give you excellent data about new ideas, general topics, and new products; however, focus groups increase the difficulty to maintain order among your subjects by about the number of subject you have in the group. Properly done focus groups can open you up to a wealth of data in both the academic and scholarly communities.

The basic use of a focus group is quite simple. A facilitator convenes a group, usually 6 to 12 people, and asks them questions about a product, event, topic, or design. The people in the group answer a series of questions, with no particular question being given to any particular person. Multiple people could answer each question or no one may choose to answer a question. Focus groups combine the ability of the researcher to ask follow-up questions with the group dynamic of an oral history project. Focus groups are commonly used in product design and marketing as they allow a "groupthink" mentality to form within the subgroup, which if it is a representative sample of the population can simulate the mob mentality of society.

Focus groups are effective when you are looking at a specific topic or product. This is not the tool that will allow you to take a broad survey of multiple data sources and topics, because focus groups require the topic of the research to be focused. That being said, focus groups can give researchers access to rich data on their specific topic while still allowing the interplay between multiple subjects at the same time. Group reaction to a product or an idea can be just as important as individual reactions. One person's opinion can cause a herd effect, if the leader loves it you have a group that loves the idea but if the leader hates the idea, then you could have an idea that is doomed to fail before it even starts. Businesses have used focus groups as a tool to preview their products for years, but you can use them as an effective tool to collect data for your research.

In this chapter we look at the use of focus groups as a research tool. The coverage in this chapter will straddle the uses of focus groups from academic use to business use. This dichotomy is because of the versatility of focus groups in multiple fields. In the first section we look at focus groups as a means of opinion collection. Good focus groups can quickly fill up a researcher's need for specific types of data. In the next section we examine the need of a focus group to look at a specific point in the group session. All too often a researcher will attempt to bring too many topics into the focus group, which dilutes the results and confuses the participants. In the third section we look at how focus groups allow a researcher to ask follow-up questions. Like an interview, the follow-up questions in a facilitation can allow you to access even deeper issues within the data. This chapter concludes with a section on allowing discussion among the group. While this may seem like a dangerous methodology that could lead to losing control of the group, it can also allow the group discussion to become rich data for later analysis.

OPINION COLLECTION

When you have a well-designed focus group, you have access to all the minds that are in the group. This means that you have the ability to tap into all their opinions. Focus groups are unique in the fact that they encourage you to look for opinions about products and ideas rather than the facts that other data collection techniques require. Opinions have their place in academic research, but it requires a different type of research question to address them. In an opinion-based research question you are looking for what the people think, not how the people are.

Focus groups give you access to people's ideas, which is one of the most intimate parts of a person's psyche. A focus group also gives you access to the group-think effect that is caused by people who have different individual ideas and allow those ideas to interact with one another. This interplay of ideas can create new understandings between people and allow their opinions to evolve as new ideas are mentioned. One of the most beneficial aspects of a focus group is how the process allows the facilitator to see the evolution of ideas from the introduction to the conclusion of the session. While the opinions of the group may not change how the product or idea develops, it can provide new insight into what the potential of the product is over the long run.

If you are facilitating a focus group, always take the time to allow the interplay of ideas to develop. If you are overly constrictive in the focus group you can actually stymie your research. Good focus groups allow the opinions and ideas of the group to develop over the course of time, which sometimes means allowing the group to get off topic for a period of time. While a good facilitator never allows the group to completely lose control, the organized chaos that is developed by a focus group can give the researcher more data than a series of carefully scripted questions. As a researcher, your goal in a focus group should be to distill as much data from the group as possible, not to exercise your ability to control the group. Adapting your style to allow your group the free reign it needs to give you a full profile of your product/idea is one of the keys of a good facilitation.

During the process of opinion collection, you are looking for what the public wants as a group. This means that a focus group is not constantly looking at the individual goals or opinions but rather at the group goals and opinions. Sometimes this means that you need to watch the film (or listen to the audio) of a focus group several times before you are able to get every bit of information out of it. Transcripts of the focus group are exceptionally useful, but they are by no means a replacement for the ability to see the look on people's faces when they make an impassioned argument or the tone of their voice when they state a position. A good researcher will watch the tape of the focus group several times, each time focusing on the words and actions of a specific person, to glean all possible data from the session.

FOCUS ON A SINGLE POINT OR PRODUCT

As the name implies, a focus group should be focused on a specific topic for it to be effective. As a researcher thinking about using a focus group, you need to take the time to identify the specific topic or product that you are looking to review in a focus group. Even looking at a specific aspect of a topic or product is not too focused. Many researchers when they conduct their first focus group are overeager and allow their group's topic to manifest itself too broadly. This can result in the group being asked too many questions about too many different topics. The result will be a lot of data for the researcher to comb through, but not all of the data will be related to the topic that the researcher needs information on. Keeping your topic focused will make your life easier and will make the experience more enjoyable for your focus group.

In most focus groups you will want to focus on a single aspect of a product or an idea. The more focused the idea that you are working on, the more beneficial your data will be in relation to your topic. If you have the resources, do multiple focus groups to look at multiple aspects of a specific target. Each time you do a focus, use a different focus group. This will allow you to collect very specific data on your product/topic, while still having the ability to look at different aspects from different points of view. Though it may be more work, it will allow you to collect more data in the long run, which for you should pay off with a better research paper.

If you ignore this concept and allow your group to address a broadly worded topic, then you are setting yourself up for a group that will basically waste your time. If your topic is too broad, you will end up with surface data that could have been collected with an interview. By keeping your topic focused, you allow for the interplay of ideas between participants and can delve deeply into specific aspects of the topic. This will augment any data that you have already collected and thus make your dataset a rich source of data. Broad study groups give lean data that will not be as useful as you enter into your analysis phase.

ALLOW FOLLOW-UP QUESTIONS

Focus groups are more like interviews than surveys. In a survey a researcher does not have the ability to ask follow-up questions of the subjects. This can mean that even though a researcher asked all the correct questions at the time, if new information comes up the researcher may not be able to pursue it because an anonymous survey prevents accessing the data anew. Interviews and focus groups allow the researcher the ability to follow up on ideas that develop during the course of the data collection. This allows the research process to evolve over the course of the program and can lead you to information sources that you had not previously thought about.

In a focus group you should always begin with direct open questions. A direct question is a question that does not suggest the answer that you are looking for to your participant. If the subject feels that you want a specific answer they may be inclined to give you that answer just because of your position of authority. Open questions are questions that allow subjects to explain their answer. If you are writing a good direct open question you will find that your subjects have the ability to give you a five-minute answer and still stay on topic. If you can achieve this level of skill in your focus groups you will find that you do not have to talk much at all during the process.

Like interviews, you will find that you are the least important person in the room during a focus group. While the group may defer to you during the meeting, it is their opinions that you want to extract, not your own. This means that during a focus group you should only be talking when it is time to ask a new question or if you need to bring the group back to the topic of the focus group. Generally, less is more. The less you talk the more you give your group the opportunity to contribute to the focus group and the more data that you have to analyze in your analysis phase. Good focus group leaders tend to ask two or three questions during the course of the focus group and then simply direct the group for whose turn it is to answer.

At some points in a focus group, you may have a situation where you need to ask a closed question. As we've discussed, a closed question is a question where there are few answers the subject can give you. Generally, closed questions will result in a simple yes or no answer. More complex closed questions may allow for a discrete set of answers to the question (such as a color or a number between 1 and 10). Closed questions should only be used for very specific circumstances in your focus group, because they tend to break up the flow of the group and can cause group members to quiet down and thus you will have less rich data to analyze.

Follow-up questions can go both ways. Some groups will want to ask you questions. If this is the case let them, as long as they are staying on topic. Their questions can help them keep their focus on the topic, as odd as that seems. Some groups will want to give you the information that you want, but they will not know for sure what you are looking for. The only way that they can find out is to ask you. If a member of your group asks you a relevant question, then answer it as quickly and directly as possible. The "more is less" rule applies here, too; the less time you eat up answering their questions the more time you have for them to give you data on your questions.

ALLOW DISCUSSION

In some focus groups, individuals will begin discussions about your topic/idea. As long as these discussions are not disruptive, allow them to proceed. The less control you exert over normative evolution of the discussion, the better. This is often a fine line to walk in a focus group, because you do not want to let individuals' talking interrupt people who are giving an answer. Only allow discussions that develop naturally and politely to continue. If need be, you can facilitate the discussion by keeping track of whose turn it is to speak. This can allow the discussion to evolve naturally and will give you excellent rich data to analyze when you are watching the tape.

Flowing discussions are one of the key reasons that you should invest in a room with two-way glass. Even though you should always ask the participants if they consent to being recorded, the presence of a camera can disturb some people and cause them to quiet down during the course of the focus group. Two-way glass allows the entire session to be recorded, ideally from multiple angles, while still keeping the camera out of sight and out of mind. Without the natural inhibition that occurs when people are constantly reminded that they are being filmed you may find that your group is more open and thus you get richer data.

Focus groups are useful because they have an excellent potential to give you rich data on whatever topic you are discussing, but only if they are done properly. Your focus group topic should be as specific as possible when you enter into the focus group room. The more focused your topic, the more focused your focus group will be. This means that you have to take the time to identify a specific aspect of your topic or product that you want to look at in this focus group. If you have additional elements or aspects that you want to discuss, then you may want to set up additional focus groups.

CHECKLIST

- ❏ Is your group representative?
- ❏ Do you have permission to record?
- ❏ Is your group a manageable size (varies by topic and researcher)?
- ❏ Are your written questions direct and open?
- ❏ Do you have multiple cameras/voice recorders set up?
- ❏ Are you prepared to field follow-up questions?

RECOMMENDED READING

Krueger, Richard, and Casey, Mary Anne (2014). *Focus Groups: A Practical Guide for Applied Research.* Thousand Oaks, CA: Sage.

Morgan, David (1996). *Focus Groups as Qualitative Research.* Thousand Oaks, CA: Sage.

Stewart, David, and Shamdasani, Prem N. (2014). *Focus Groups: Theory and Practice (Applied Social Research Method).* Thousand Oaks, CA: Sage.

chapter 46
Observations

INTRODUCTION

Of all the methods of data collection, observation should be the most natural to any researcher. As human beings we are literally built to observe the world around us. We have eyes, mounted by nature in a predatory stance to allow us to see into the world with depth and color. We have ears that allow us to understand part of the spectrum of sound. We have senses of smell and taste that help us understand what food is high in the nutritional elements that we need and we have skin covering 99% of our body, which allows us to touch and experience the world through touch. Finally, we have a developed a brain that can compute and understand the data that is coming into our system; this gives us a sixth sense, a feel of a situation that we may not otherwise be able to explain.

Observation allows us to see into the world without many of the filters that other research forms impose on researchers. When we observe we see with our own eyes, feel with our hands, smell with our own nose, taste with our tongues, and hear with our own ears. We do not have to rely on the senses or opinions of others when we ourselves are observing data as it naturally occurs. This gives us a substantial advantage in research, as we know our own shortcomings and we know the biases that we bring to a research project. Observation puts research in our own hands, and that makes it one of the most useful research tools that we have at our disposal. As you are considering observation as your research methodology, you set yourself as your own filter. If you want to write about something that you observe, that is your choice; likewise if you want to censor yourself you also have that option. The breadth of ability that observation provides separates it from many of the other data collection methodologies.

Observation is the key data collection method used in some research methodologies, such as ethnography.[1] In method specific techniques such as this you will find that your chosen research methodology will dictate what form of data collection you use. Some other research methodologies, such as descriptive statistics, allow you a broader choice of what type of data collection procedure you will use. Observation truly shines when it is used in collaboration with other methodologies, such as interviewing and/or surveys.[2] By hybridizing and integrating the observational methodologies, you will find that you can procure much more detailed data, which can then be used for analysis.

Observation also allows you more immersion into a study than many other data collection methodologies. Whereas in surveys, interviews, RFA, or journal research you simply cherry pick the data from a pool that you have selected; in observation you are immersed in your research area, thus you have the opportunity to draw in data with all five senses. This immersion gives you more options on the type of data that you can collect, so you are not limited by other people's choices as in the other methodologies. If you want to see what a culture is doing, then you put yourself in a situation to see what they are doing; if you want to hear the mating calls of some animal, then you place yourself in a position to hear it. If you properly design an observational study you will find that as long as you can ethically and legally put yourself in a position to observe the data then you do not have to rely on the opinions or memories of other people.

In this chapter we look at the processes and principles of doing a well thought out observation. You taking the time to think out the process is a key part of the process. As a researcher, you need to have the discipline to make yourself plan each detail of your observation site, your observation time, your observation subjects, and your observation goals. Then and only then will you be able to optimally use observation as a data collection technique for your project. In the first section of this chapter we look at the actual process of observation. As an observer, you are a sponge. Your goal is to soak up as much data about your subjects or site as you are capable. In the second section we look at the process of taking good field notes. It is a fact that the mental image of what you see, hear, smell, taste, and touch deteriorates the farther away from the event you get, which means that the sooner you take detailed notes the richer your data will be for analysis. In the next section we look at the basic tools that you will use when you are doing an observation. These will be your tools in the field, so selecting the proper tools is essential for your project. Then in the fourth section we examine the difficult question of whether you should write your observations down as you see

---

1. Emerson, Robert (2011). *Writing Ethnographic Fieldnotes*. Chicago: University of Chicago Press.
2. Fetterman, David (2009). *Ethnography: Step by Step (Applied Social Research Method)*. Thousand Oaks, CA: Sage.

them or wait until a later point to begin working on your documentation. In the fifth section we look at the use of recording devices to give you even more data to analyze during later stages of your project. Finally, we discuss details as being the goal and the purpose of using observation as your research methodology.

Observation can be a valuable tool in your research skill set. Observation is the most hands-on data collection methodology (besides participation) available. Good observation enables you to develop your understanding of a subject area that you are well versed in, but also allows you to explore a subject matter that you currently know nothing about. Either way, observation allows you to open your own eyes to a subject that you have an interest in and if done properly can allow you to have the data to transport your reader to your site.

SEEING WHAT IS THERE, NOT WHAT YOU WANT TO SEE

Any time you are entering into a data collection situation, your bias can be a blinder. As a researcher you need to know and understand this limitation to be as efficient as possible in your research situation. As you are doing observational research the problem of bias can be doubly dangerous as your bias can cause you to ignore things that may be relevant to your study. Depending on what you are observing (and depending whether you are in a high-context or low-context culture), missing key elements of what is going on because of your bias can mean that your research study misses the elements that you actually came to observe. This means that in any study where you are doing observational research you need to take the time to do a proper epoche of yourself before you engage in your observation.

As an observational researcher, you must also realize that your goals can control the reality that you are observing. If you are doing a study where you are looking at the eating habits of people of southern Italian decent, then you need to take the time to specifically look at the actual eating habits of your subject group. This can be as narrow as looking at what hand the people in your group eat with or as complicated as looking at the rituals that go along with a specific meal. As an observational researcher, you need to define the parameters of your study before you begin observing or else you will not know what you are looking for. Your goals control what you are looking for, thus you must be aware that your goals control the reality that you see.[3]

---

3. As human beings we tend to see what we are looking for. Have you ever went food shopping when you were hungry and noticed that you buy more food. That is because your brain is looking for food. When doing research we need to program our brains to look for the data we need for our projects.

While you should always keep your goals in mind as you are recording your data, you sometimes may have to let your focus wander slightly. This is one of the benefits of observational research, when something comes up beyond the scope of your research you can take the time to document it, thus allowing it to be tied back to your research should it later become relevant. Especially when you are researching a high-context culture that is not your own you should take the time to document every datum you can to ensure you have the most detailed picture of your subject area possible.[4] In observational research, no element of what you observe is too small to write down if you have the time. You should try to create as detailed a picture of your subject area as possible, using all five senses, so that when you analyze your data you have as much relevant information as possible.

If you are going to become an observational researcher, then you should realize that some things that you believe are going to be insignificant are actually going to be a major part of what you are studying. Most observational research is exploratory, which means that you may not know as much as you would like to know about a subject area before you start to study that area; that being the case, you may not know what information about your research area is important at the beginning of your observations. Take for instance a study of the cultivation of rice patties in sub-Saharan Africa as an experimental carbon sink. Before you enter into the study, you decide that you are going to do five observations of planting techniques over a period of two weeks (approximately one session every three days). If you know very little about this subject area, then some things that you observe on the first day that you do not know are important, may be important parts of the data after you realize what is important and what is not. Thus you will find that all data should be collected if possible, and if all data collection is not possible you should collect as much data as time and physical constraints allow.

When doing observations, you are trying to make the data as rich as possible to ensure that you can augment your report with rich descriptions. This means that when you are in doubt as to whether you should write something down, then that is the time that you definitely should write the data down. No research ever complained that they had an extra datum that they wrote down, and most of us complain that we did not write down enough information when we were doing our fieldwork.[5] If you have the time, write down every possible detail you can. The more you have the more you can draw from. You can always weed out data you do not want later in the process; therefore, there is no drawback to collecting extremely rich data.

---

4. All cultures are high context; those deemed low context tend to be cultures similar to a researcher's own culture where the researcher does not notice the interesting elements of the society. Bad research glosses over the "mundane" details.
5. Emmerson, *Supra.*

GOOD FIELD NOTES

Field notes are your key tool in developing good observational practice. If you keep notes, then you enable yourself to "jog" your memory when you are doing your analytics and data coding.[6] If you have observed extensive data, it can be difficult to keep all of your data clear in your memory. This is why field notes are so useful, because they allow you to have a written record of what you observed during your field sessions. In my writing classes I like to do an experiment where I have someone come into the classroom, then ten minutes later I ask the students to tell me what that person looked like, what the person was wearing, and identify anything about that person that may be of interest in an observation. The more time you place between the observation and the recording the less accurate the data becomes.[7] Shirts change color, accessories are added and removed, and even sex or case can change in the mind of the observer. The lesson of this experiment is that even if you have a good memory, nothing is as useful to an observational researcher as having a good set of field notes so you do not have to rely on your memory.

When you are taking fieldnotes your goals is to write down as detailed an experience as possible. You want to have as many details as you can write down in your time period that you can use for analysis later. Each detail that you write down is something that you may or may not need later; the problem is that if you do not write it down and do need it then you will have to rely on your memory to recall the details. Your mind will tend to fill in the gaps of what you do not remember with information that makes sense to it (most of the time, sometimes it fills in data that does not make sense). This means that the "reality" that you are reporting on may not be reality at all. This is one of the key reasons that good field notes are so important.

Now there is a large difference between your actual fieldnotes and what you will actually analyze as field notes. Your notes from the field will be quick and dirty sets of details, written on a page in a way that will likely only make sense to you. Your notes may say "Large man in green shorts walks into bar and talks to squirrelly guy sitting at corner booth, both look like they are up to no good." This is a good note for the field, then when you go back to your research area you can fill in the details that you remember. For instance, you could write "A large black American man, who appeared to be in his late 50s walked through the side door of the bar. He was wearing an oversized shirt and a pair of jeans. He must have been 400 pounds, some of it fat but he looked like one of those guys who used to be completely ripped. The shirt was red with a stain of some sort on it, I think it was mustard. The man that he went to talk to was a squirrelly white guy, he looked like he should have been the bad guy off of one of those 1980s B movies. He was wearing a Hawaiian shirt that had

6. *Id.*
7. Fetterman, *Supra.*

dancing girls on it and a panama jack hat that was a size or two too big for him. He sat in one of the corner booths flashing a roll of $50 bills so the whole bar could see. Who even gets $50 bills any more? That gave me the feeling that he was up to no good. When the large man made his way over to the small man, they lost their larger than life personas and quietly discussed something before the large man gave the small man something, I could not tell what it was." This type of description is useful, but is difficult to write down in the heat of the moment; therefore, you need notes to help you remember what is going on so you can write your detailed data later.[8]

A distinction that needs to be made when you are writing your field notes is whether you are writing to yourself or whether you are writing to others. When you are writing to yourself you can use your own personal version of shorthand, which will allow you to record more data more quickly; however, if you are writing down observational data for others to follow, then you either have to restrain yourself to write in complete thoughts as you are taking down your notes or you can translate your shorthand into detailed field notes for other researchers. Personally, I feel that the later method is more efficient because it allows you to take down as much information as possible during the observation session, which can then be used to "jog" your memory when you are writing the translated field notes for the other researchers.

As a matter of personal style, you may want to look at using bullet points rather than a narrative method. Bullet points give you the freedom to write down fragments while narrative methods require you to write down complete thoughts. Personally, I have always struggled to write down bullet points because I tend to think in the narrative, but I admit that this is a flaw in my training and method. Bullet points allow you to jot down brief bits of information that you will expand upon as detailed observational data later at your convenience. People, like me, who write in the narrative, tend to spend too much time looking down at their paper and not enough time looking at the subject matter that they are expected to be observing. Therefore, if you are capable, try to learn to write your notes in the field in bullet points, because it will make your life easier when you are doing analysis.

Good field notes go beyond simply taking notes about the who, what, where, when, and why of a situation. Good field notes also try to convey the feelings of importance to the subject. The way a person treats an object or another person can be indicative of reverence or distain. This can help you determine rituals and symbols within your study group, but only if you include it in your field-notes. Always look for deeper meanings in actions—do not look just at what people are doing but also how they are doing it. This can give you more detailed data that can make your observational data more detailed, thus when you begin to do your analysis in whatever methodology you have

---

8. Notes act as a stimulus/catalyst for memories.

SO YOU WANT TO WRITE A PAPER

chosen you will have additional elements that may better explain your hypothesis to your readers.

Some researchers are OCD to the point that they insist upon categorizing and organizing data as they go. While this is a noble trait with book research or with surveys, it can be a fundamental problem for people doing observational data. When you stop to organize your data in the field, you are taking your senses off of the subject matter that you are supposed to be studying. This means that you are missing out on valuable data that you could organize later. When observing, get as much information as you can during your time as an observer. There will be other times to organize the data, but you will never be able to organize the data that you miss. Even if you are doing a long-term study, you should wait until the end of the day before you go to bed to organize your data; if you pull yourself out of the data stream during a time when you should be observing, you may find that you do not have all the data needed to do a proper analysis.

As a final note for this section, one problem that beginning observers face is their reliance on their own memory. This is, in part, evidence of a problem within our school system. We train people that they have to memorize wrought data rather than contextualize it and assimilate it. Thus people try to store lots of information in their short-term memory, which is only useful for a few minutes at a time. We do not train our minds to retain short-term information for a period of time sufficient do proper analysis; therefore, we have to write down our data (or start training our minds to hold more short-term data). While all observational researchers have to trust their memory to some extent, when possible take down notes. If you can write down notes that jog your memory, then do it. If you are like me and resigned to write down narrative data as your observing, do it as well as you can. If you are one of those people who record their data in pictures with descriptions floating around the picture, do that. Find out how your brain is wired and work to your strengths, and do not let anyone else tell you how your mind works.

THE TOOLS

Every data collection methodology has a set of tools that its practitioners use to make the process more efficient, and observation is no different. Since observation is one of the most basic data collection methodologies (and one that we are genetically predisposed to do) there are many tools out there that augment our abilities to collect and write down data for our research. The first and most basic set of data collection tools are the simple pen/pencil and paper. The pen and paper approach allows you to take data in areas where some of the other data collection methodologies are not allowed. You are not allowed to take pictures in high security area (such as an airport) but they generally will not stop you from taking notes. Voice recorders can cause quite a stir in some situations, but people tend to ignore the person with a pen and paper. Pen and paper give you the opportunity to jot down notes so that when you get back to your desk you have a wealth of information to jog your memory so you can write rich detailed data.

The voice recorder has achieved its place of fame as a tool for the observational researcher. Whether it is digital or tape based, a voice recorder allows researchers to keep their notes straight in their head by having their own voice to listen to. The only drawback of a voice recorder is that for the most part it is difficult to use with human subjects. Most people will see that you are talking into a recorder and start to act different because they do not know what you are doing. Further, if they hear what you are saying about them they may elect to change your actions or even tell you to stop watching them. You can use a recorder to record conversations, but if you do so be sure to check local regulations because recording people without their consent is illegal in some areas.

Another excellent tool that allows you to take notes without raising the suspicion of others is your phone or personal digital assistant (PDA). In the modern world, every other person is walking around with their face buried in some type of electronic device. When other see you walking around with your phone or PDA in your hand, they assume you are watching a video or texting. This can be an excellent "undercover" way to take down data during your observational session. Further, many phones and PDAs have a record function which can allow them to operate as a voice recorder.

A laptop can be a useful tool if you are working in a place where you can set your laptop down and simply type on it. In many places in the world you now see people working on their laptops as a completely normal daily occurrence. In appendix one, I sat and typed while observing people for over a half an hour with only one person noticing, and I cannot be sure that she noticed. Further, many people can now type faster than they can jot down notes on a piece of paper, which means that if you are observing with a laptop you may be able to write down more data than you would be able to with a pen and paper.

Two tools that are highly useful in recording data for observation are cameras and digital camcorders. These two mediums for recording data allow you to record visual and auditory data at an unprecedented level. As long as you can get the camera on your subject you can create a permanent record that you can review at your convenience for more details. Further, while a person can argue with your memory as a source of data it is difficult for a person to argue with a photograph or a digital video recording. There are drawbacks of cameras and video cameras, but as a tool cameras are highly detailed and overcome their limited drawbacks.

Selecting the right tools for your project can be as simple as selecting the right tools for yourself. If you like using paper and pen to write down your notes and are comfortable using them, then it is your project and you should use them. If you want to try to use a voice recorder, use it until someone tells you not to; any paper you write is your research project. An important thing to remember is that any permanent record that you create of an observation session should be stored in a safe place so that any data that is personal or identifying to your subject does not get out. For more details on the proper handling of data look to your company or university's Institutional Review Board.

TO WRITE OR NOT TO WRITE

There is a debate as to whether a researcher should be writing down their data as they go through the process of observation. One school of thought is that writing down your data allows you to have a more vivid memory of what happened, thus you are able to have better data to analyze. The other school argues that if your subjects see you writing down your data they will act differently and if you are hiding your recording process from your subjects you may be violating their rights to privacy. Both schools of thought have valid points, and both schools of thought have ardent supporters. It is the responsibility of the researcher to decide what they should and should not do when it comes to research, so we cover the arguments of both schools in this section; however, you should keep in mind that if you elect not to record your data as it happens, then you should record it as soon as possible after you leave your recording area because as time passes so does the reliability of your memory.[9]

The sooner you write down what you observe, the more likely it is that you will be able to recall details. Even if you are of the school of thought that you do not want to "taint" the observations you make by having a pen and paper handy when you are observing, you should still try to get to a location where you can write down your observations as soon as possible after you make them. Each hour, each minute that you wait can allow valuable details to slip away from your memory. If you are against having pen and paper handy while you work, always consider using the note-taking app on your smartphone. This can allow to unobtrusively take notes in most situations.

One area where the school of thought that is against recording while you are observing is spot-on is when a researcher will miss some of the data while looking down and writing. This is inevitable; however, it is a trade-off for more detailed notes, less detailed observations. If you decide to write down your observations later then you have less detailed notes and more detailed observations, so it

---

9. Generally let yourself be guided by your school's IRB.

really comes down to which area of the trade you are more willing to give up—the quality of your notes or the quality of your observation. There is middle ground in taking very quick notes while you are observing, which gives you loose notes but it also allows you to watch people with more detail.

Whichever school of thought you choose, make sure that you do not scare off your subjects with your observational techniques. If you are writing your notes down, you can distract your subjects or tip them off that you are recording details about their lives. They may ask you to stop or leave, they may themselves leave, or they may just change their activities enough to taint your data. If you are not writing your notes down you can still tip off your subjects by the way you are acting. If you are not fitting in with the group you are studying, they may see that you are watching them in detail and thus make them uncomfortable. Be careful to try to fit in as well as possible, because the better you fit in the more likely it is that your subjects will not notice you and will go about their normal routines.

The one major exception to the entire debate is in the hard sciences. In the hard sciences you should always record your notes as you are working, or as soon as possible after your experiment is done if recording during the experiment is not possible. Generally, the hard sciences are not observing how people react in the way that business, social sciences, and humanities do. If you are doing a geological survey then you should be taking down as much information as you can from your observations, and the same can be said about a biological survey of a rainforest. Each detail that you have written down while you are in the field will allow you to augment the data you have from other means.

RECORDING DEVICES

Recording devices can be a valuable tool when you are working in the field; however, when you are using a recording device you need to be aware of the drawbacks of each device. Recording devices give you an unprecedented ability to build a pool of extremely rich data that can be used for data, but if you are using a recording device you must realize that you may make your subjects aware of your presence as a researcher. If you are looking at elements of a biker gang in southern Florida, you should probably not enter into the bar with a camcorder on your shoulder and a set of voice recorders in your pocket. This could cause a negative reaction from your subjects, and in this case a negative reaction that you likely do not want to deal with.

Another problem that you may face is with legal issues. There are places where you are not allowed to record data without special permission. If this is the case, then you are going to be regulated to pen and paper anyway. The very grey area that troubles many researchers is when you are in a situation where the ethics of recording people is questionable. Public spaces will generally not get a researcher in trouble for recording people, if it is obvious that you are recording someone; however, there are public areas where people do have an expectation of privacy. If you are in one of these areas you need to examine the local laws on the subject before you get yourself in trouble.

If you are going to be recording living people, then you should be running your research proposal through an IRB. This process should give you the guidance that you need to be sure you are doing something that is legal. Since this book is designed to speak to a broad cross section of writers, we do not have enough space to cover every single issue that may arise in relation to recording devices; however, if you submit your proposal to an IRB, they should be able to guide you through any ethical or legal quandaries you may face.

THE MORE DETAILED THE BETTER

When you are using observation as a methodology for research, there is a simple fact of life: more details equal the resources for a better analysis. While analytical skills are generally based on the research methodology, the quality of your analysis is largely dependant on the quality of the data you bring to analyze. This means that the more rich data you collect while you are observing your research subjects, the more material that you will have when you begin your analysis. If you choose observation as a data collection method, do not simply show up, look, and then move on to something else. Take the time to properly do your research and you will be able to transport your reader to your site just with the words in your project.

Sight is one of the key factors that we use to relay information about a research subject or research site. Vision is one of the key aspects that human beings are built for, as our bodies store visual data and our lives become dependant on sight. People who have lost their sight have said that the other senses get stronger to make up for the lack of sight; this is because most people are so dependant on our sight. This is not only true as you observe, but also true as you relate information to your readers. The more "visual" cues you give them to think about the site you studied, the more they will be able to use their imagination to visualize what you are explaining to them. Take the time to detail small visual things when you are recording your data and you will be able to relate those images to your readers to increase their ability to "see" what you are saying. This will make your writing more interesting, thus more readable for your readers.

Oddly enough, scent is the mental cue that brings the next most lucid memories or visualizations to the human mind. People can recall where they were, what they were doing, and what they were learning by scent very quickly, sometimes even more quickly than when they are being given visual cues. This means that, if relevant, you should make sure to take down as many olfactory details as you can about your sight. The fact that you smell jambalaya cooking as you study the cultural rituals of Cajuns, or that you smell the acrid smell of sweat as you study prisoners in their cells, can relate a cue that will transport your reader to your site. Just combining visual data with olfactory data can make your paper that much more interesting to your readers because they can actually immerse themselves in your description.

Sound is the next most relatable detail that will help your readers put themselves in your shoes as they read your work. After sight, auditory input is the next most common sense we use in our daily lives. If you tell your readers what you are hearing, rather than just telling them what you think about what you are hearing, you are giving your reader the opportunity to "experience" what you experienced. This should make it easier for you to immerse your readers in the subject matter you are studying. For instance, "The cool wind of the clipper system was blowing across the Jacksonville harbor, while I watched the longshoremen unload their packages from the ships…" is much less immersive than "The humming of the longshoreman seemed to harmonize with the sound of the clipper wind howling across the Jacksonville harbor, the creaking of the cranes and the groaning of the ships seemed to join with the humming and howling to form a symphony of economic progress." As you can see, just adding the words to explain the sound draws you that much farther into the image that the writer is trying to convey.[10]

Touch can be one of the most immersive details that you can convey in descriptive writing because it is a sense that you feel with your whole body. Telling people about the tactile sensations that you are feeling during an experience can take them one step closer to full immersion in your writing. For instance, "The titanium of the cage bobbing in the water was slick from the salt water spray that stung my face as the waves broke against the hull of the ship. I looked into the water swirling around the cage, it had become my own personal abyss. Even in the 25 degree air my heart was pumping rapidly enough that I felt warm in the wetsuit. I took the leap. As I submerged into the water, seeing the titanium of the cage was the only thing separating me from the two ton beast feeding on the scraps of fish we had thrown into the water to lure him in. To the great white I was little more than another piece of meat in an oddly wrapped container, a curiosity that with one errant move could be the next course on his menu. The shock of the dunking was prolonged as the water seeped into the body suit, forming the insulating barrier that would keep me warm from the Antarctic waters. Soon I felt my body heating the water up, at least I hope it was my body heating

---

10. Do not go overboard with the prose to the point you lose the message of the passage.

the suit up and not my fear of the shark." In this example, there is limited visual data, no auditory data, not even any olfactory data, all the information was based on tactile data and the feelings that it caused. This type of writing can be a useful tool that separates your work from the work of other authors, especially when combined with the other senses.

Taste is the final of the normal five senses. It is also the most difficult to use in normative research. Unless you are researching food you are going to find that putting taste in your descriptive writing can be difficult. That being said, a single taste word in a description can be a catalyst for a total immersion of the reader. By way of example, "I looked across the plains of the Outback desert. The heat at 35 degrees centigrade was beating down on me like a steal hammer. I knew I was dehydrated because the sweat that was running down my face and slipping into the corners of my mouth had none of the salt taste it had had but a half hour before, in this heat if I didn't find water soon I would be another casualty of the desert. Then I heard her voice and turned to see my partner and the search party calling out to me in the desert."[11] It does not take much taste to convey a message. In this case the taste was conveying desperation as the researcher's body was dehydrating. If used properly, taste words can add an additional layer of depth to your research and writing.

The final "sense" that you should consider when writing about a location is your sense of "feeling." In this case it is different from your tactile sense as you feel scared or the place feels safe. This can be useful to convey the overall environment of a site. For instance "It felt safe walking into the old church, even though the gangs outside were shooting at one another. The old adobe bricks muffled the sounds of the gunshots as the sounds of a practicing choir drown the sound out completely. It was evening, so other than the electric lights near the piano, the rest of the church was lit by the dim flicker of candle light. It was cool in the church, a sharp contrast to the sticky warmth of the Mexican summer outside. It was not a modern church by any means, this little town could afford no more than a simple mission church that had been built when Spain first invaded. It felt as if I had been taken back in time and the fighting outside the door was not two rival drug gangs fighting each other, but the conquistadors attacking the indigenous people. In either case, this old adobe church with its wooden pews and the scent of incense hanging in the air was a safe haven."[12] Notice the two times that the "feeling" words were used they conveyed a sense of how the site felt. The first time we see that the person felt safe, which lets the readers know that when outside, the observer did not feel safe. The second mention reinforces the feeling of safety, but also layers on a feeling that the readers had gone back in time. Using simple feelings that readers can understand can set the stage for you to fill in details with the other senses. Once you had the feeling of safety you could add visual, auditory, olfactory, and tactile details that bring the site to life.

---

11. This is a made-up example, While I have been to the Outback, I have never been lost there.
12. Also just an example created for this book.

Each detail you add to your observation brings your readers one step deeper into the reality that you have recreated in your writing. Could you visualize the desert or the church from the above examples? It is the details that make observation data so relatable to readers and when they can relate then they are more likely to understand. When you are taking down your notes for an observation, try to get as many details written down from all five senses and the "feel." Each person remembers differently, so find out which senses you tend to forget most quickly and write them down first. Observation is an intense process, but it is the process that has helped humanity grow in its scientific and cultural knowledge for thousands of years.

CHECKLIST

- ❑ Pre-Observation
  - Have you chosen your topic?
  - Have you chosen your research methodology?
  - Is observation something that this research methodology uses commonly?
  - If not, do you have a methodological reason that you have chosen to use it?
  - Where is your site?
  - When will you examine your site?
  - For how long will you examine your site?
  - What equipment are you taking?
  - Does this equipment make sense where you are going?
- ❑ Observation
  - Are you taking notes or not?
  - Did you collect data on sight?
  - Did you collect data on scent?
  - Did you collect data on sound?
  - Did you collect data on touch?
  - Did you collect data on taste?
  - Did you note the feel?
  - Did you use descriptive language?
  - Will you be able to recall more from your notes?

RECOMMENDED READING

Atkinson, Paul, Coffey, Amanda, Delamont, Sara, Lofland, John, and Lofland, Lyn (Eds.) (2001). HANDBOOK OF ETHNOGRAPHY. Thousand Oaks, CA: Sage.

Charmaz, Kathy (2014). CONSTRUCTING GROUNDED THEORY, 2ND ED. Thousand Oaks, CA: Sage.

Druckman, Daniel (2005). DOING RESEARCH: METHODS OF INQUIRY FOR CONFLICT ANALYSIS. Thousand Oaks, CA: Sage.

Emerson, Robert M., Fretz, Rachel I., and Shaw, Linda L. (2011). *Writing Ethnographic Fieldnotes*, 2nd ed. Chicago: University of Chicago Press.

Fetterman, David M. (2010). ETHNOGRAPHY: STEP-BY-STEP, 3RD ED. Thousand Oaks, CA: Sage.

George, Alexander L., and Bennett, Andrew (2005). CASE STUDIES AND THEORY DEVELOPMENT IN THE SOCIAL SCIENCE. Cambridge, MA: Harvard University Press.

Glasser, Barney G., and Strauss, Anselm L. (2008). THE DISCOVERY OF GROUNDED THEORY: STRATEGIES FOR QUALITATIVE RESEARCH. New Brunswick, NJ: Aldine Transaction.

chapter 47
Anecdotal Research

INTRODUCTION

In a world where much of our researcher is derived from direct observations that we have made and the peer-reviewed work of other authors in our field, anecdotal research stands in stark contrast to other research forms. Anecdotal research is research based on the stories people tell about their lived experiences. This research form goes beyond the research that is collected through interviews as it concentrates on the stories that are told by a person, without direct control of the researcher. Anecdotes, more than any other research method, allow researchers direct insight into the lives and thoughts of the research subjects.

Anecdotal evidence has many uses in qualitative research, though it is markedly less useful in the world of statistics. Anecdotal research allows the researcher a deeper *emic* view; even though the report is *etic* in nature, the researcher is given data as it is understood by the subject. As such, researchers should focus on allowing the subjects to tell their story as much in their own time and way as possible, interjecting themselves into the process only when the subjects need assistance in keeping the story going or remembering where they needed to return to after a tangent.

Anecdotal evidence is useful for researchers when they are trying to make something that happened in the past seem real. Whether they collect the data themselves through listening and recording the stories, or collect the data from compellations of stories that have been collected from another time, the stories of those who lived through actual events are a much richer source of data than the secondhand accounts or statistics that most histories present to us. Anecdotal data is the true embodiment of raw data, almost to the point that it rivals observation in its outright purity.

In this chapter we look at the uses of anecdotal evidence in academic research papers. We first look at one of the most common methods for creating anecdotal databases, oral history projects. Oral history projects are an effective tool to preserve the accumulated stories of a generation as it comes nearer and nearer to the common age of mortality. Once people die, the stories that they did not tell to others are lost from the world forever. Next, we look at people's memories as a tool for research. While memories are some of the most direct forms of secondhand data that we can collect, they can be problematic as people tend to remember the very good and the very bad but forget or gloss over the rest. We conclude this brief chapter with a discussion of reliability of anecdotal data by looking at methods you can use to ensure that your subjects give you the most up to date, accurate data according to their memory.

ORAL HISTORIES

One method for collecting anecdotal evidence is oral history projects. An oral history project is a collection of lived experiences related by those who lived them for the purpose of creating a historical archive. Many of the most popular oral history projects focus on some of the major events in human history, such as the Holocaust or the Great Depression. However, even the less exciting (or tragic) history of a nation or a community can be a valuable tool for academic analysis. Researchers have created careers by getting grants and collecting the spoken history of underserved communities so that a record of their history can be collected from a first person point of view.

Oral history projects are a repository of information about the lives of people who lived within a common dynamic. For instance, people who lived in central Pennsylvania all of their lives could be interviewed for their life stories. The reason this differs from a common interview is because there is no direction of the oral history project other than a broad topic, every person's story is their own story and can follow the path that they want it to take. This opens the record up to containing data that no one would think to collect because no one ever knew it existed! Oral history projects expand your access to completely unknown topics or simply let you have access to a better angle of a story.

The more obscure your group, the more useful oral history projects are. This should not be taken to extremes, but if you are researching something that has not been done to death you may find that you have more readers looking for your work. What you collect is often as important as how you collect it, thus if you are looking at a group that others have not looked at then their stories are less likely to have made it into the historical record. Oral history projects are a quest that the learned experience of humanity is not lost to history because those without loud voices are ignored. As a historiographer, you become the voice of those who are unknown and your work becomes a record of what may have been lost without your effort.

Creating an oral history project is a daunting task, as it requires interviewing as many members of a given population as possible. Oftentimes this is not the undertaking of one person, but of a group of people who want to preserve the history of their community, or of the community that witnessed an event. Next, you need to define your population. The more specifically you define your population, the more reasonable you will find the size of your population. The majority of the work in oral history projects is collecting the stories of all the people within the population, thus the more narrowly you define your population the lower the number of people that you need to interview. Next, you want to define what area of their experience you want to collect. The more specific you are about your topic, the easier it will be for your subjects to relate their stories related to that topic. With most oral history projects the majority of your subjects will be older, thus you will want to make the process as convenient as possible for them. Thus, a well-explained topic request will make your subjects' lives easier. The third step is to find a repository for your research. Collecting your data for its own sake can be fun, but it will not be used by other researchers if it is just collecting mold in your basement. As such, you should be sure that you have a university, historical society, government, or a library that will house your research. Finally, you want to find subjects within your population who are willing to do an interview. Even the most well designed oral history project will fail quickly if it has no subjects to interview.

If you have the time and the resources to compile an oral history project, you are creating an excellent resource for the academic community. However, once you have collected the data you should have some use for it. Oral history projects can provide you vast qualitative datasets that allow you access to rich data that you would not otherwise have access to. Even if you have not collected the data yourself, open oral history projects can provide you with rich data for a research project. When you are looking at cultural, historical, or even sociological matters from the past, having secondhand access to people who were really there can be an immense benefit for any researcher.

PEOPLE'S MEMORIES

The memories of people can be one of the greatest assets that a researcher has in their quest for a writing project; however, they can also be a immense liability. As humans, we have the ability to be very selective about our memories. This means that some things that we "remember" as having happened did not happen in exactly the way that we remember them. This is not just a problem for observational researchers that cannot remember exactly what happened during their research project, but can also be a problem for people who use anecdotal research. The failures of other people's memories can be devastating if they do not remember an event or phenomenon correctly. Generally, people's memories are better the closer they are to the event that they are remembering. The data that is stored in our short-term memory is gradually eliminated as time passes between the event and a person's recollection.

Memory tends to be better the more important the event was to that person. This adds a dimension of relativity to people's memories about specific events. Whereas I feel that one event is very important, another person may feel that the event is not very important. Thus I may remember the event more vividly than that other person. Further, one person may remember a specific detail of an event more clearly because of the belief that a specific detail of the event is more important. This can lead to different people's accounts focusing on different aspects of a given event. This is one of the reasons why oral history projects are so effective—that is, multiple people can give you a more complete story of what happened because each person can contribute a new element to your research.

Group recollection can be an interesting element of oral history projects. Many times when you do research about a specific event, couples or families want to be together because of the nature of the event that you are researching. Group mentality can be helpful but it can also be harmful. When people are interviewed in a group for an oral history project, each person's memories may inspire memories in other people. This means that you may have access to data that you otherwise may not have had access to because the subject forgot about it until another subject reminded them. Conversely, if one person remembers something improperly, then the other members of the group may agree with that improper assessment because of a manifestation of groupthink mentality.

People's memories tools that evolve for their survival, not for wrought data storage; therefore, we see that some types of data are remembered more vividly than others. If you find that your research subject is partial to a specific type of data, then you should encourage them to be as vivid as possible when they are recounting their story in that kind of data. Whether you are collecting an oral history to protect the history of a community, or simply collecting anecdotal evidence for a single journal article, the way you inspire, protect, and record a person's memories should be treated with the utmost respect, for you are essentially distilling that person down into their stories for posterity.

RELIABILITY

With the current Brian Williams stories in the news as this chapter is being written, reliability has become an even more important issue in research and writing. If your data is not reliable, then your report may not be reliable. This can cause your career to falter before it even begins (or if you are established it can ruin what you have already developed). This means that when dealing with anecdotal evidence it falls on the researcher to ensure, for the reader, that the data collected is as truthful as possible. This can be difficult, but it can establish you as a person who can be trusted because they make sure the people that they get their information from can be trusted.

If you are relying on a person to recount for you the story of a specific historical event, then the first thing that you should examine is whether that person was actually there for the event that they want to describe. History has been rife with people who want to claim that they were there for a given event because of the fame associated with it, when they were nowhere near the event when it happened. Sometimes these charlatans go a lifetime without ever being discovered. However, when you are collecting anecdotal evidence, you have the burden of ensuring that people were where they said they were for a given event. Most of the time people will be truthful, but sometimes you may see red flags that a subject's story doesn't seem to match up with what you know about the event. If the story seems too far from the other stories, then there may be something there that is another research topic.

Another consideration that you should take into account is where the person was in relation to the event being studied. People are going to be much more interested in the stories of a person who was in the World Trade Center when the planes hit the towers in September 2001, than one who was across the street or in another nearby building. This second observer may also have a story that is historically significant, however. Be careful not to exclude people who have stories that are related to your subject just because they were not in perfect position at the moment your event happened. A person who saw what happened immediately before or after the event can have insight that those who were there may not be privy to.

If people seem to remember the events that you are speaking to them about vividly, then ask them how they have such a good memory of it. This is not a challenge to their story, but it can give you access to other information that they use to remember. They may have a collection of artifacts that they look at from time to time to recall their experience at the event. For instance, a solider may have photos or medals to commemorate an event, others may have an heirloom from the event that they keep to remind them of what happened; or a photo album (which can be copied with the subject's permission) can give your report a greater depth by showing people what happened as well as telling them what happened.

Often, anecdotal evidence is treated as if it is less reliable than evidence that we collected in another way. Even though book research is peer reviewed, it is still secondhand. Interviews and surveys are just extremely focused anecdotal evidence, and by their very format they make themselves secondhand. Only observations give you the access to firsthand data that anecdotes give you, and your observations are subject to the same shortcomings that can affect the recollection of your anecdotal subjects. While anecdotes should be supported by other forms of data, they are a valuable tool in the hands of a dedicated researcher. The details that some people will bring to their stories will allow you access to rich data that may not be available in other forms, or you may not even know exists.

CHECKLIST

- ❑ Have you carefully defined your population?
- ❑ Have you carefully screened your subjects?
- ❑ Have you carefully focused your topic?
- ❑ Were your subjects at the event?
- ❑ Were they peripheral to the event?
- ❑ Have you checked to see if they have any artifacts that they would allow you to see that may provide more rich data?

chapter 48
Newspapers and Magazines

INTRODUCTION

Few methods of data collection have been as flashy and as interesting to the public as the printed word of newspapers and magazines. Hundreds of movies, books, and TV shows have been created depicting the drama, corruption, and diligence of the people who create these mediums. In the modern digital world, the internet is flooded with different digital newspapers and magazines on every topic. These newspapers range from stalwarts of the field such as *The New York Times* and *The Washington Post*, to minor papers such as *The Huffington Post*, to even satirical papers such as *The Onion* or *The Chive*. Magazines have followed a similar course, gracefully accepting the new medium of the internet as a way to reach viewers. With the news cycle going from daily, then to hourly, and now to minute by minute, the world of newspapers and magazines can provide the researcher with access to vast amounts of data; however, this new world is wrought with dangers that can snare an unwary researcher into using data that is less than credible.

Newspapers and magazines writers are required to have up to date information on their beat hourly each and every day. If a department is slow on getting a story posted to its webpage by even a half of an hour, then the story may have already been scooped by someone else. This troubled life of a newspaper worker is made doubly hard by their sister organizations in the magazine world and their cousins in the blogosphere. Whereas newspapers had a rigorous fact checking process, magazines are generally content with minor retractions and blogs have no control over them whatsoever (other than the owner being sued). This has led to the advent of print first, check later media, which has greatly diminished the reliability of what was once a great source of data for researchers in many fields.

Newspaper research is not book research, nor is it journal research. The peer review process that keeps journals and books moving at a snail's pace is nonexistent in the modern world of newspapers and magazines. While each publication will have its own quality control department, this over-worked department has to balance speed with quality in a world where quality has lost much of its meaning. Some papers, such as *The Wall Street Journal*, or magazines, such as *Newsweek*, still strive for the highest level of quality. Other newspapers whose reputations have been tarnished or who never had a strong reputation anyway are more likely to strive for the thrill of being the first outlet to break the story, sometimes at the cost of accuracy. This means that the researcher has the added onerous of checking to ensure that the paper or magazine that they are using is a trusted source of information and not simply a tabloid rag with a nice name on it.

One advantage of newspaper and magazine articles is that they are brief and easy to read for the researcher. Most article lengths range from one to five pages, which means that a researcher can review large amounts of newspaper data over a short period of time. The ease and accessibility of the data also allows a researcher to triangulate the data among different sources. Triangulation is the process of confirming data from one source by finding similar data from other source. On specific occasions a researcher can offset the lack of peer review in newspapers and journals by triangulating the information from multiple outlets. Even with triangulation, however, researchers must still ensure that the source they are using is a serious source. Even the best stories from *Weekly World News* are satire and can destroy the credibility of an article.

Newspapers, and to a lesser extent magazines, have the added advantage of being closer to the story at the time it occurs than most academics. The newspapers are closer to the story in both the location and the time. In the time that it takes for a researcher to get grants to study a specific topic, a newspaper can have five reporters there talking to the people who actually witnessed and lived through an event. This gives them access to people while the event is still fresh in their mind, which can lead to rich data with a higher degree of accuracy. Further, local newspapers tend to be parts of larger conglomerates now, so there is a good chance that even if an event happens in a small town there is a local newspaper with people on the ground.

In this chapter we look at some of the advantages and pitfalls of using newspapers or magazines as primary sources in your research paper. In the first section we look at how newspapers are not an academic source and discusses how the lack of a peer review process can be problematic with this source of data. Next we focus on newspapers, and look at the different types of newspapers that may serve as a data source. In the third section we repeat the process, but with magazines. Then we return to the distinction between quality control and peer review in the fourth section, giving you in-depth data that you need to make a decision whether the quality control is robust enough to validate the information. This chapter and this part conclude with a discussion of data collection methods and how you can effectively integrate them into your writing toolbox.

NONACADEMIC RESEARCH

Newspapers and magazines are without the peer review process, but the very thing that makes them seem like a lesser form of research material is also what makes them useful as a tool that is close to the event. If you think about it, observation is not peer reviewed until an article is written about it. Interviews and surveys are only briefly reviewed by the IRB before they are used and collected. Even a majority of books on the market today are not peer reviewed. If we treat a newspaper as a qualitative data source, not as an authoritative discourse on a subject, then it becomes a much more useful tool for data collection. Just as our other methods require the author to use his or her judgment when using them, so too newspapers and magazines should be judged as to the usability of their content.

There was a time when newspapers were the documents of record for a community (some of them still are); however, with the boom in the internet news system, the blogosphere has become as much a circulating area for opinions (radical or otherwise) as a source of information (some would argue that this was its purpose from the beginning). Newspaper and magazine research, therefore, has the same obligations to a researcher as any other type of data collection; we must separate the facts from the opinions. When you collect a survey, you separate the facts from opinions. When you perform an interview, you separate the facts from the opinions. Even in an observational study you separate the facts from your opinions. Newspapers and magazines should be treated like raw data, because even though they go through a quality control process they have not gone through your quality control process yet.[1]

This returns us to the idea that triangulation is very important to people who are doing newspaper or magazine based research. The more credible sources that you can find for data, the more reliable it will be. Forty years ago, this would have been difficult; however, since the Associated Press has homogenized most of the major newspapers and the online world tends to play off of itself, finding confirming sources is relatively easy. Unfortunately, this has led to a world where if you were tricked

---

1. Flick, Uwe (2007). MANAGING QUALITY IN QUALITATIVE RESEARCH. Thousand Oaks, CA: Sage.

by a spoof site or by a site with bad reporting, then you can slink away into the shadows with everyone else that was tricked with little consequence to your career. Preventing this embarrassment is important, so take the time to triangulate your data and confirm your sources.

NEWSPAPERS

Newspapers come in many varieties. There are the great national giants that are still producing millions of papers each day, despite the decline in readership of print media. Major cities tend to still have a newspaper that is the main source of news for most of the population over age 40. Some small towns keep their local newspapers alive through loyalty, but many of these newspapers are becoming local outlets for the Associated Press's stories. Colleges have newspapers as do some high schools, but even though they have some of the best investigative journalism in the country, they are often looked at as childish or immature. There are even those free local papers sponsored by private classifieds that you find in every gas station around the country, that may have opinion pieces or op-eds from community scions who "need" to have their voice heard. Each of these types of newspaper has a place in society, but what is their place in academic research?

Giant national newspapers have thousands of people working for them, but few of these people are reporters. It is the people who work behind the scenes of a major newspaper that give it an edge as a source of research over the smaller newspapers. Giant newspapers have the funding to hire a multitude of fact checkers to ensure that each and every story that they publish in their paper carries a level of validity that the paper is comfortable with. These fact checking departments work hard and work quickly to ensure that everything published as fact in the paper is valid and that the material comes out quickly. They have the advantage of the giant newspapers being established and in little danger of their market share being overtaken by smaller newspapers. This means that they do not always have to be the first to the story, just the first giant newspaper to publish on the issue.

Major city papers can also be a valuable resource for a researcher looking at an event that was a local new story but that received little attention on the national stage. Major city newspapers have that unique combination of small town interest with big city power that allows them to fact check all their stories while still covering stories of local interest. Major city newspapers do not have the fact checking departments that the giant newspapers have, but they still have a robust staff checking to ensure that each factoid that the newspaper prints lives up to its quality standard. This may differ from paper to paper, but generally a major city newspaper is a safe place to collect data for research (you still have to do your triangulation and your own quality control).

Local newspapers can be a treasure trove of obscure data, especially historical data on a subject. Local newspapers tend to print a majority of their material off of the national line from the AP, but there is still a portion of its content that is focused on events going on in the area. These local newspapers are not blessed with the same fact checking departments that giant and major city newspapers have. In some small towns the paper editor is the entire fact checking department. This eliminates such repetition that catches most of the mistakes, but it replaces it with a sense of pride that cannot be measured. Local newspapers are generally a safe source for a researcher to harvest local data.

College and high school newspapers tend to be good places to harvest data when they make the national news. While their fact checking is limited to the individual reporter who is submitting the case, these types of newspapers tend to have the least censorship of any printed data source. If you can get copies of a college or high school newspaper during a scandal that the paper broke (before the scandalized person takes them down), you can often have data that will be striped from the historical record. You can read through millions of pages of low-quality work before you find that gem that can make your career, so generally using high school or college papers should only be done when you know there is data that will support your case.

The free newspapers that are at gas stations can be a minefield filled with useful data and well, mines. The reason that these papers are free is because they are generally trying to get a specific opinion out into the market. The more obscure the opinion the more the owner of the paper will have to self-fund it. The more moderate papers will have a plethora of paid-for classifieds to fund the cost of the papers. Some of the more established ones will charge a token amount such as a dime or a quarter for their publication. The truly radical papers will be housed by only a few gas stations who support their message, and these can give you great insight into the minds of local movements, outsider groups, and conspiracy theorists. Fact checking in this field is generally nonexistent, but the investigative journalism can be monumental. If you elect to use these types of papers for your research, be careful not to be caught up in the message and lose your objective data collection methods. These papers tend to be highly persuasive because they manage all of the data you are reading in them and ensure that it comes from one ideological standpoint.

The final area of newspapers that are most dangerous to cite are unaffiliated internet newspapers. These newspapers, like *The Huffington Post*, can be a goldmine of information because they have the low overhead and wide readership that allows them to send their reporters quickly to places other newspapers are slower to get to; however, you need to watch the fact checking of these organizations, too. Major online publications like *Huffington Post* or *Drudge Report* are reliable for the most part and their data is good. But there are dozens upon dozens of internet newspapers that are right some of the time and unabashedly wrong the rest of the time. These papers can be a disaster for a researcher. Always be careful to check and recheck your sources when you use an online newspaper.

Some joke sites like to buy domain names that are one letter off of popular sites so that people will think they are real. If a story seems too good to be true, check the spelling in the URL, it probably is.

MAGAZINES

Magazines run much the same gamut of size and reliability that newspapers run. There are the iconic pop culture giants like *Rolling Stone* and *Vogue* that have cult followings to the smaller more trade-specific magazines like *The National Gardener*. More magazines are written for entertainment purposes, so it can be more difficult to distinguish from fiction. This can make magazine research a dangerous exercise for a researcher but there are some general rules that you can follow to ensure that your research will be credible.

Magazines of record, such as *Popular Mechanics* or *Popular Science*, can generally be looked at as reliable in their field. These icons of the industry have relatively well sized fact checking departments along with a multitude of experts and interested lay people who will point out every error made in the magazine. If you use an article from one of these magazines as a source always take the time to peruse the following few months' retraction sections to ensure that there are no changes to the article that you are citing. Magazines of record are a good source for data, but like newspapers you should treat the data as raw data with a formal citation.

Pop culture magazines have a more dubious record for reporting the truth. These magazines look for what is trendy in society and try to publish on that topic before the trend changes. The major publications in the industry are generally well respected for their information, but there are marked examples of them having horrifically wrong data (like the *Rolling Stone*'s rape/fraternity case). Pop culture reporters tend to create the story, then go out looking for data to support it. This is a poor methodology in research and it follows suit that it is a poor methodology in journalism. There are a world of cases out there, so journalists should not go out creating stories to meet personal jihads. Actions such as *Rolling Stone*'s rape/fraternity issue set back the quest to eliminate sexual abuse on college campuses years.

Propaganda magazines out there to create a "record" of a specific viewpoint. These are incredibly dangerous for researchers to use because they use a general formula of two parts truth to one part opinion or speculation. Stories in these types of magazines tend to have the allure of rich data and interesting storylines, but if 33% of that rich data is false or opinion based, then it can be difficult for the researcher to use the truth without having the fiction attached to the work. Generally it is best to steer clear from these sources of data, unless you are researching the group that is putting out the propaganda. Rarely do they contribute anything that another source does not have.

At first glance, humor blogs would seem to be one of the most dangerous places in the world for a researcher to collect data, but even this area of mixed fact and fiction can be useful. Humor shows like "The Daily Show" tend to have a vested goal in reporting the truth, albeit with a humorous spin. If you watch these shows you can collect cutting-edge information about what is going on in the world and triangulate it with other data. This is dangerous, but it can be an effective method for collecting data. Remember if you are using one of these sources, their goal is comedy, not information, so be careful that you do not become the joke.

QUALITY CONTROL VERSUS PEER REVIEW

By this point, I am sure that you are tired of the peer review/quality control comparison; however, understanding the difference between these two methods of data control is vital to ensuring that you collect good data for your project. The peer review process in academia is designed to ensure that publications that have the title "academic" attached to them have a modicum of decorum and correctness as they are part of academic canon when they are printed. This is a high standard of care that many articles written by experienced researchers do not meet. There are thousands of unpublished manuscripts that are discarded for every one paper that is published by a respected journal. This system was created to protect the integrity of the academic process and even though some people may hate it and call it a form of censorship, it does provide us with the peace of mind that we need when we cite the work of another as authoritative in our research and writing lives. Peer review is your protection against poor research, and while it fails from time to time, the vast majority of peer reviewed articles are full of correct data.

Quality control is a different story. Many quality control departments have a budget that an academic journal would love to have for its own operation. Large newspapers and magazines spend millions of dollars a year to ensure that their publication has a certain level of quality. However, the reason is slightly different. While academic publications need the peer review process to protect the integrity of the academic canon, large publishers want people to trust them enough to buy their publication and to ensure that they do not get sued. If a paper publishes a story that is wrong, people collect the bad paper. It is only where there are a series of bad papers that the newspaper needs to worry. The same can be said about magazines; a misprint is a novelty and as long as it happens rarely it can be accepted. Quality control is about protecting the bottom line of the company and ensuring that the customers stay at the newsstands and the newspaper stays out of the courtroom.

When you are performing research with a newspaper or magazine, remember that you should be treating this data as raw data from a source. If you make the mistake of treating the article as if it is a peer reviewed article and it proves to be false, then it can destroy your whole project. If you treat it as a source of raw data then the triangulation process should help you find mistakes and eliminate them before you send your article off to be published. Researching your paper should be a process that is difficult, but it should also be a project that is rewarding. Newspapers and magazines can be valuable sources of data, you just need to know how to use them on your journey to write a paper.

CONCLUSION PART VI: DATA COLLECTION

Data collection is hard work, but all adventures are. When you are writing a paper, you are beginning a literary journey to a place where no one else has been before. If going to these places was easy, then everyone would be doing it. However, just because it can be a difficult process does not mean that it should not be an adventure. Who has ever heard of an adventure without some hardships? Sure, some of your data sources are going to lead to dead ends. Sure, some of your data is going to challenge your hypothesis, but it falls on you as the author to overcome these hardships and put out a good product that you are proud to put your name on.

In your journey to write your paper, your book and journal research is going to be the path that you follow most of the time. You will not stay on this path all of the time because you will want to strike out and blaze your own trail; however, your book and journal research will be the path that gets you close to where you want to go. When doing book and journal research always look for the best sources and seminal works. These sources will be the most well traveled paths and the dangers that other researchers have overcome will be clearly marked and you will be able to avoid making the mistakes that others have made before you. Books and journals should be the first place that you start to pre-research and the last place that you come to validate your research.

As you go through your journey to write a paper, you need a good map to follow to keep what you discover organized. The methods that we recommend in this book for this process are RFA and LRFA. These methods will allow you to contextually, thematically, and topically arrange your data so you are able to find what you have already entered and enter new similar data in the same section. RFA and LRFA also provide you with a tangible research trail that an IRB or a researcher that wants to follow in your footsteps can follow. It also provides you with a clear audit trail so you can go back and revisit data if you need to. Having a good map in your journey to write a paper is vital and while there are other methods, RFA and LRFA will serve you well.

Interviews, surveys, and anecdotes are your chance to interview the locals on your journey of paper writing. Any journey where you do not interact with the locals can be sterile and will lead to less rich data. Meeting the people and collecting their stories and opinions is one of the best ways to make your research more relatable to your readers. You are their guide and they are following you to learn as much as possible about your topic. If the local people are part of your topic and you ignore them, it becomes a warning sign to your readers that you are not giving them the full story. You then become more of a tour guide through a tourist trap than a jungle guide leading your readers to something new.

Observations are your tool to really draw your reader into your journey with you. Your observations can fill in the sights, the scents, the sounds, the tastes, and the feelings that raw data cannot provide to readers. Each detail that you give readers is another step as you guide them through your journey to new knowledge. Each tacit element that you tell them about where you were, what you saw, and what happened at your event will bring them closer to the understanding that you are striving for in any good paper. As you begin your journey to write an excellent paper, always keep in mind that if you are the only one who ever makes this journey, it is an empty exercise. Academia grows through the process of one researcher leading many readers down the path less traveled into new knowledge.

CHECKLIST

- ❑ Do you have a good reason for using newspapers or magazines?
- ❑ What type of paper are you using?
- ❑ Is it a recognized source?
- ❑ What type of magazine are you using?
- ❑ What is the main goal of the magazine?
- ❑ Have you triangulated the data you are using?

RECOMMENDED READING

Arco (2002). *How to Write Articles for News/Mags*, 2nd ed. New York: Arco.
Ricketson, Matthew (2004). *Writing Feature Stories: How to Research and Write Newspaper and Magazine Articles*. New York: Allen & Unwin.

Part VIII

STYLE

chapter 49
Introduction to Part VII

THE EDITORIAL PROCESS AND YOU

Now your draft is done and you are ready to add the bells and whistles that will make your paper a paper that someone will want to read. Good editing is what separates a well-written paper from a great paper, and a great paper is what you will need to get that A in class or get your paper published. The editorial process is an important part of writing any paper. Each time the paper is edited you will scrape away some of the mistakes and grammatical errors that can cause concern in the eyes of an editor. If writers do not take the time to clean up their papers, did they really take the time to do their research properly? Do not leave questions like this hanging on the minds of your readers; take the time to edit your academic works.

There are three phases to writing a paper, just like there are three phases to a journey. In Part I of the book, you began to prepare for your journey. You started to focus on where you wanted to go, what you wanted to do, and even gave some thought to how you were going to do it. This preparation should have made the later stages easier and more efficient. Next, in the intermediary parts of this book, we walked through the process of selecting a methodology and actually writing the paper. This process should have been facilitated by your preparation work. Now we are entering into the editorial phase, the transition phase between you completing the journey of writing and you beginning the journey of turning in your paper (admittedly a boring journey) or your journey of getting your paper published. All academic writing should be cyclic—that is, work you do to finish one project should lead you to the beginning of another project. In this brief chapter we look at what Part VII teaches about writing and style.

A key element to keep in mind as you write is that good papers will take time. Anyone can knock out a term paper in a little over two hours. An academic paper that you are going to build your career on should take more time—a lot more. By focusing on the elements that we have focused on during the course of this book, you should have an exceptional paper already, and now in this part of the paper we are going to work on those finishing touches that will take your exceptional paper to a great paper. One of these elements is taking the time to go through the editing process.

Editing a paper is not a sign of weakness as a writer. True, there are those savants who can write a paper in a day or two with no errors and send it off to a publisher. I am not one of them and if you have read this far in this book I am guessing that neither are you. I take hours to edit my papers to ensure that they are the best product that I can produce before I send them off to my publisher. This little bit of extra care has gotten me dozens of reviews and journal articles considered and published in academic journals. Taking the time to edit is the opposite of weakness in writing, it is the strength to admit when you have made a mistake and the fortitude to change those mistakes before they become a problem for your project or your career.

Overall, good writing habits are part of a good writing style. Good writers take the time to look over what they have written to ensure it is of good quality. Would you trust a chef that does not taste his or her own faire, or an architect who will not walk across a bridge that he or she designed? Of course not, and we should not trust writers who will not read their own work. In your journey of writing, the editing process is you looking back at what you have done and deciding if you could have done better or what you could do better next time. Take the time to edit; take the time to be great.

YOU AS THE FIRST EDITOR

Something that can be difficult for most writers to accept is that you are the first editor when you create a paper, book, or any type of writing. Some feel that their writing is good enough that they do not have to look over their work before they send it in; it is not. Some people feel that others will correct their problems and they can just skid by; they will not. Your job as a writer is to catch as many of the mistakes as possible before you pass on your paper to its next reader. All your first (and sometimes second) rounds of editing are quality assurance, not so much in the paper as in your personal brand. If the editor(s) fixes all of your mistakes, but knows that you turn in a sloppy product, then you still have one or more people who know that your work is not as pristine as it should be. Unfortunately it is these people who you want to think that you are a hard worker who will know the flaws in your brand. By taking the time to do a once over or a twice over, you can cure many of the mistakes that weaken your papers so your "brand" remains intact.

One of the methods that I have found extremely useful when doing self-editing is reading your paper backwards, sentence by sentence or paragraph by paragraph. The key problem with self-editing is that you know what you wanted to say. Thus, your brain may "auto-correct" what you are reading as you read it so that you will not realize the problems in what you have written. Another, problem that many authors face is their interest in the subject. If you are like me and take a week off between writing and editing, then you may have forgotten some of the things that you have written. As a result, when you read through your document you are looking at the theoretical sides of your arguments rather than just doing grammar and structure editing. By reading the paper/article backwards, you break up the flow of the article so that it is hard to focus on the content. This allows your mind to focus on the grammatical editing that is so important to your success.

After your grammatical editing session, you should take a read-through to make sure that your paper is succinct and focused. To draw a comparison, papers are to books like short stories are to novels. Books and novels can have multiple topics that are varied and intertwined; however, short stories and papers should have one topic, one story line that informs or entertains the reader. When editing your paper, let one read-through be solely for the purpose of comparing each sentence to the topic of your paper. If you cannot justify each statement within three degrees of separation, then it is too far from your topic. The only exception to this is when you have future discussion topics, which can be connected by four degrees of separation. If you find yourself constantly justifying why a sentence is related to the paper, is your paper really as focused as you thought it was?

Editing is important because the more mistakes that you catch before you send the paper off to the editor the better your product looks when the editor receives it. Editors, just like every one else, have other things to do with their time. If you make their lives easier by eliminating as many mistakes as possible before you send the paper off to be published (or off to a professor, where you have no editor), you can make the reader's job easier. People will naturally gravitate toward things that allow them to save time and avoid unnecessary work. Help your editor by eliminating as many problems as you can when you do your read-through, and the person you will really be helping is yourself.

FORMAT OF PART VII

This part of the book focuses on the things you can do after your paper is written to ensure that your readers will have the best product from which to learn about the topic you have chosen. By having a good product you can assure yourself more of the market share in a competitive discipline than you would be able to garner with a poor product. Chapter 50 looks at length and style of writing in your academic papers. Length is important because, let's face it, people are lazy. You may have the best 130-page treatise on the ideal growing conditions for blueberries in the world, but most readers are simply going to read the 10- or 20-page primer, and your paper will gather dust on the shelf. Style becomes important because your style should be identified with the publication in which you are writing. Journals have personalities, and your paper should fit the personality of the journal you select.

In Chapters 51 and 52 we look at an important part of writing that we touched on in Part I, voice. Voice is an important part of writing just like voice is an important part of speaking. If you were in a conversation where the person continued to speak about him or herself in the third person, would that not be annoying? Yes, it would. However, many academic papers have authors who refer to themselves as "the researcher did this" or "the researcher did that." Further, there are some authors who jump back and forth with their temporal language, which can be annoying. If one sentence speaks about the paper in the past tense and another sentence speaks about the paper in future tense, it can make the paper difficult to follow and cause the readers disinterest. Keeping the voice of your paper even is just as important as keeping the keel of your voice even as you have a conversation.

In Chapter 53 we turn our attention to coauthors. Some of you who are reading this book are likely writing papers with other people. Whether it is part of a group assignment or a collaboration across universities, writing with other authors is an important way to increase the diversity of the paper while still keeping the topic focused. Additional authors allows the differing biases to be drowned out by the academic process, thus harmonizing your research. Additional authors also increase the writing: time ratio as the workload and research load are shared between the two authors. There are some problems that you may face working with another author, such as personality problems, disagreements in theory, and even interpersonal problems. Here we will help you deal with the benefits and detriments that you may face in a cool and professional way.

Chapter 54 looks at your editors. Pleasing your editors is one of the best ways to ensure that your papers continue to get published in the same journal or even in journals that are affiliated with one another. There are a limited number of editors in the United States, and they do talk to each other from time to time. If you get a bad name with one editor because you are difficult to deal with, then you may find that you have a reputation of being difficult to deal with at other journals as well. Editors talk shop at conferences, just like anyone else. Always try to keep your editor happy, but do not give up on important issues within your paper. If your editors tell you that something is offensive or not researched well enough, then you should at least look at taking their advice. Editors have a brand that will be linked to your brand, and when they are giving you advice they are generally just trying to help you improve your brand.

This part and this book finish with a brief conclusion looking at what we have covered over the course of this book. Rather than summarize what you have read over the course of these pages, in the conclusion of the book we will focus on ways that you can use this book to help your writing after you have already read through it once. Many of you will have read the section that you needed and ignored the rest of the book, and you have every right because you bought the book and can use it however you like. However, if you use all of the resources that this book provides in tandem, then you should be able to increase the efficiency of your writing and become a better writer as you practice time and time again.

chapter 50
Length and Style

INTRODUCTION

Nothing says more about your brand than the dimensions and style that go along with it. Does anyone believe that Nike shoes would be nearly as popular as they are now if they looked like crocks and only came in sizes up to a 6 Medium? Of course not. Product worth is directly related to style and purpose. Papers are no different. Length and style of a paper will be determining factors in whether you get that A or whether the publisher decides that your paper should be published. Taking time to consider the length and style of your paper is a vital part of the writing process, and without considerations your Cadillac of papers may turn out to look like Yugo.

With academic papers, a difficult question is, "How long should it be?" This question has many different answers by many different people, but the best answer may be, "Just as long as it needs to be." There is no hard and fast rule how long any particular type of paper should be. Some papers require 60 to 80 pages (if it's any longer you may want to start thinking about a book) and some papers can be as short as 3 pages. It just comes down to how much space is needed to get the information you are trying to present to your readers across to them. Having a paper that is too long is often more dangerous than having a paper that is too short. With a short paper you can always "leave them wanting more"; however, when your paper is too long you may risk tiring your readers or even worse turning off your readers' interest. As a writer you should always ask yourself, "Is this paper the right length for what I am trying to say?" If you are not good at setting the correct length you can always impose on your friends to tell you if your paper is too long.

Generally in academic writing brevity is your ally. People are more likely to read a reasonably long paper for research than to commit to an exceptionally long treatise on the subject. By having a shorter article you can passively encourage competing readerships to look at your article instead of others. This being said, making your paper too short can be dangerous, too. If you are writing on an important topic, then you should not shorten the paper too much just for the sake of brevity. Make sure that all the data you need to have in your paper is present. This is a difficult line to walk, but the more papers you write the easier it will get. When in doubt always error on the side of focus and brevity.

Style is another issue that many authors never even consider, and if they do they just assume that their style is what it should be. Think about this: Most of your readers will never meet you in person. All that these readers will know about you is information that they have gleaned from the style of your papers. What does your writing say about you? Have you ever picked up an old paper you wrote and read it? What image of yourself did your paper give you? This is what your readers see when they read your papers, the image that your paper creates. If you do not like this image, then you have to carefully edit the style of your paper to match who you really are. Any time you write a paper, your writing becomes part of your personal brand. If you were going to publish art under your name, would you let someone else pick the topic and paint it for you? If you do not edit your work for style, this is exactly what you are doing; you are letting your subconscious tell people who you are. If you want to be a successful writer, concentrate on the image that you present to the world by taking a read through your paper and seeing how you portray yourself to the world.

Another consideration of style is whether your paper fits into the place where it is being sent. If you have a class of people who are submitting timid, tentative papers on an open topic, your paper in which you take a strong stance on topic "X" may draw too much attention and your professor may hold you to a higher standard. If you submit a paper that is critical of global warming to a journal that has staked its reputation on the existence of global warming, you may not stand out in the way you wanted to and may find every aspect of your paper being torn to shreds by the zealots of the other side. Style not only defines who you are as a writer, but it also determines where your paper should be. If you want your paper to be published in a good journal, take the time to see what other kinds of papers that journal is publishing. If you want a good grade on a paper, look at what kinds of papers the professor has graded well in the past.

In this chapter we look at some of the methods that you can use to control the style and length of your paper. The rules outlined herein are general rules and should not be taken as unbreakable. Your style is your style, I would not dream of changing that. If everyone that read this book started doing their style the same way as me, then my style would not be me, it would be the style of a subculture. In the first section we address a method that you can use to ensure brevity of your paper, the Rule of ¼. The Rule of ¼ helps you cut things from your paper that are not central to the topic and thus take away from the focus of your paper. In the second section we ask the question of whether your paper follows a pattern. The human mind likes patterns and while great research may come out of chaos, great writing is seldom ever chaotic. Having a pattern will make your paper that much easer for your readership to follow. In the next three sections we discuss some of the patterns that you can use to make your paper easier for your readership to read. In this part we also look at starting your paper with a wide focus and then narrowing it down through your research. It is the opposite of norm, which shows you how to start your paper with a very narrow scope, then gradually layer on ever widening ideas to make your topic more generalized. In the fifth section we take a wholly different approach by looking at the chronological or narrative format; this format can be useful in ethnographies, phenomenologies, and some grounded theory papers.

This chapter should help you tighten your control over your writing both as an editor and as a writer in future papers. Your paper is a journey to understand who you are, but it can also be a tool to help you change things about yourself and your writing style that you do not like. Once the paper is written, it becomes an avatar of your journey through the process, an avatar that you have created. By taking the time to look at length and style you can be assured that your avatar represents you in a way that you are proud of and you can also control the writing process rather than let the writing process control you.

RULE OF ¼

I learned about the Rule of ¼ during my undergraduate studies at Penn State University. My mentor taught me that my writing had too many tangents and that I needed to shorten it and keep it more focused. Of course as a headstrong young man, I resisted and did not learn that my writing needed to be pruned from time to time until I was in my second doctoral program. Do not repeat my mistakes. Take the time to concentrate your writing down to a focused paper that discusses the topic that you are interested in and nothing more. An academic paper can change the world, but it cannot change the whole world all at once. You may have many good ideas, but they may need to be topics of other papers.

The Rule of ¼ is aptly named because in most papers the author can cut 25% of the paper, or 1/4 , and still keep the paper relevant and detailed. When cutting the chaff from the wheat in your paper, you cannot simply cut the last ¼ of each sentence and hope that your paper makes sense. First you read each paragraph and ask whether it is on topic. Then when you look at a paragraph, you have to take the time to ask whether each sentence needs to be there for the paragraph to be useful. Then you need to take it one step farther and look at each word in each sentence (you can generally do this by groupings) and see whether the word strengthens or weakens your sentence. This process is tedious, but when you are done you will have an excellent paper that nearly anyone can follow.

Going paragraph by paragraph, sentence by sentence, and word by word can be a tedious process. How deeply you delve into the process is always up to you. Generally, I go sentence by sentence when I am editing, but some people do less; I probably should do more. The more often you write, the less you will need to remove pieces from your paper. However, until you become proficient at the process, you should start at the end of your paper and go backwards. Just like the general editing process, starting at the back will keep you from getting caught up in the flow and allow you to do a more thorough job of editing your work. The tedium is worth it, however, when you know you are turning in the best product you are capable of turning it.

Your main target when you are eliminating parts of your paper is the tangents. Even the most highly trained writer still goes off on tangents from time to time, quite often more tangents the more you write. Tangents are any theme or anecdote that drifts away from the central topic of the paper. For example, if you are writing a paper about why cats always land on their feet, a short story about why dogs do not land on their feet may or may not be a tangent. To decide if it is a tangent you should see how far removed it is from your topic. If there is one intermediary topic or less you should be fine. More than one intermediary topic and you may be getting off on a tangent. As you begin to edit you may find that the elimination of tangents gets you down the ¼ you need very quickly.

When you are eliminating tangents, do not just delete them from your paper. Always keep a record of tangents because they can be valuable topics for future papers. By keeping your tangents and the sentences and paragraphs that support them, you can have a strong primer for your next paper. Keeping a log or a journal of these tangents can be a very effective way for you to build a collection of future paper topics that you can have on hand when you receive a request for a paper proposal or when you take another class in the same area. Exploring these tangents in other papers can allow you to become an expert in the general area in which your main topic and tangents fit.

If you follow the Rule of ¼, you will find that your papers are more succinct and require less editing after your reader has reviewed them. Often the editorial problems that you have in your writing are caused by trying to fit too much into your paper. Most grammar is designed to provide as much information as possible in as little space as possible. It is bad grammar that causes long papers, so when you shorten your paper you are killing two birds with one stone. (Another item to keep an eye out for is clichés). The Rule of ¼ will help you get your papers published and can even help with good grades.

DOES YOUR PAPER FOLLOW A PATTERN?

The human mind tends to follow patterns; seemingly this is why human beings like music. The interesting thing with patterns is that we like to see them but we do not like when something is so repetitious that it bores us. Here lies one of a writer's quandaries, how much of a pattern to put into a writing. If you are writing within the system that this book recommends, we suggest that you have a set pattern (title, abstract, intro, method, data, analysis, discussion, works cited) and another level of pattern within that. Then once inside the second pattern you begin to explain the data that you have gathered and introduce your reader to your topic. This allows you to write with enough of a pattern for people to follow, but still leave yourself enough room that you can introduce new data.

There are three basic patterns that we suggest in this chapter as a form of secondary patterns, which are covered in the following section. The wide to narrow pattern is the format that most writers will use when they prepare their papers. In this pattern you start with a survey of the data you collected then narrow the analysis down to the focus of your hypothesis. The second format is the narrow to wide pattern, in which you take your focus of the hypothesis and expand from it to show how it is relevant in the world at large. Finally, there is the chronological or narrative format, which allows the author to tell the story of what happened during the research, which works well for story-based methodologies.

It is important that in a paper you do not mix formats. Once you choose a format you should stay with that format throughout the course of your paper. If you use a narrow to wide format, then switch to a wide to narrow format, you tend to cover some of the same data over and over again and your paper reads like an accordion. If you mix the chronological method with either of the other two, then you find yourself with areas of your paper that do not flow and distract from the timeline you are creating. As you are editing your paper, make sure that you selected one of these styles and kept it throughout. It will make your paper easier to read and it will make it easier for your reader to say "yes" to your paper.

WIDE TO NARROW FORMAT

The wide to narrow format is the most common style of paper most of us will see as we do book research and it is the most common style that we will use when we are writing. There is a good reason for this: Wide to narrow is how most human minds work. We see the forest before we see the trees when we view them from a distance; the human mind likes to separate the individual elements from the group element. When readers are viewing a topic in a research paper that they are not familiar with, they are viewing it from a distance. To them sociology or geography is a forest filled with little areas of its own design. Trying to start your paper with an ultra-specific area of your field, filled with jargon and trade terms, may drive your potential readers away; this is why a good paper will ease your readers into what you are talking about. Analysis such as:

> "To look at this data, we wanted to have a sociological theory that explained what is going on with our findings. Sociology is a very broad field and there are many ways to look at a subject, so we selected a criminological perspective as the best way to explain criminal problems in social systems. This philosophy.... However, we wanted to be more specific than a general criminological approach so we chose gang formation theory as a lens through which to examine our data."

This introductory paragraph to an analysis section shows how a writer can narrow down a discipline to a field and a field to a theory rather quickly. Now as this was an example, it is graceless as a two by four, but it shows you the basic technique.

In introducing your wide pattern, you start with the general and lead the reader toward specifics. In the example above, we chose to start with a broad, discipline-wide area and then build toward a more specific theory near the end. This is not the only way to do this. An author can begin with a broad survey of the data, then slowly narrow the data down to the specific data to support the hypothesis. This can be very useful as it can show the reader the greater context of the data being utilized. You can also look at the effect of your data in a broad sense, then narrow it down to look at the specific effects that what you are studying has on individuals within the system. Any of these methods allow you to introduce your reader to a topic very broadly, then slowly educate them to the specifics of your topic.

A wide to narrow approach lets authors demonstrate that they have a general knowledge beyond the specific topic of the paper. Our nation has become hyper-specialized in the academic fields. Too many students are being forced to select specific elements of their field to be professionals in. Criminologists must choose between policing or criminalistics, business majors much choose between supply chain management and operational efficiency, geologists must select a specific era they intend to study, and this is all happening at the undergraduate level (sometimes high school). As a result, some people are left speculative of whether a researcher is capable of applying narrowly tailored data to a broader scope, or even whether there should be a general interest in the data. The wide to narrow approach allows authors to show that they have an understanding of how their data affects the world beyond their little niche. This demonstration of understanding can make the writing appeal to a much broader audience.

The wide to narrow approach also prevents a writer from trying to cover the entire discipline in one academic paper. If you start out wide with general business principles in the United States and work your way through the system, then you realize that you have narrowed down your scope at least once during the process. Writers tend to be an ambitious lot; we tend to believe that the more we cover the better it will be for our readers. Guess what, we are correct. However, the way that most of us approach the problem is incorrect. While we should write as much as we can to help the world, we should not try to jam it all into one paper. When we do this it makes a paper broad and unwieldy. If you want to cover a macro-topic, write a book, but that is a discipline for another time. Wide to narrow is a common approach that we recommend because this is how human brains are generally wired, thus it can make it easier for your readers to understand your work.

NARROW TO WIDE FORMAT

Some authors choose to come at writing from an opposite angle. They elect to start with a very specific point and work their way outward from that point. This can be a very effective way to write a paper if you can keep control of yourself; however, it is not a technique for novice writers as they can fall into the infinity trap. When going from narrow to wide in a paper you must set specific boundaries for yourself, and these boundaries will keep your paper within a reasonable scope. A writer using this method begins with the building blocks of an element, then the principles of an element, then finally looks at how the element applies to the world in the broader scope of things. If done correctly, narrow to wide can be done very effectively and show the same grasp of general topics as wide to narrow, thus making your reading accessible to a wider group of readers.

Before we explain the pattern of writing a narrow to wide paper, we should first look at the key danger that writers face in this pattern, the infinity trap. The infinity trap is extending writing farther and farther away from your paper's topic, trying to explain every question and every eventuality that can come up in regard to your topic. This trap is caused by forgetting one of the key principles of the methodology that this book is teaching you—that is, you only have to answer your research question (save other questions for other papers). The infinity trap is a continuous stream of "what ifs" that drags your writing away from your research question and hypotheses toward trying to explain an entire discipline or the world in one paper. If you achieve it, wonderful, but throughout history many have tried and all have failed. To ensure your paper gets published, stick to the finite realities of the writing world.

The first level of writing a paper in the narrow to wide format is to start with the building blocks of your research. If you read the chapter on recursive frame analysis (RFA) then you are ahead of the game here. By starting with the contextual elements of your data, you can start the reader at the same point that you started, with mismatched sets of data within a data pool. As you write your analysis, you can build your way out of the data pool toward your research question by selecting specific bits of data (frame) and combining them, thus separating them from the pool. This allows you to separate specific data from general data in the data pool. The more you bring the data together the more the data congeals into something that the reader can relate to your research question.

The next step to building your paper from narrow to wide is applying the contextual clusters of data to a theoretical lens. The application of the theoretical lens moves your writing from just your research into your field in the broad sense. This allows your reader to see that you are not just doing a report on your topic, but you are applying what is known or believed in your field to the data you have collected. This synthesis of data and theory begins to show the relevant points of your project and should start to disprove the null hypothesis and thus support the hypothesis of your paper.

The final element of narrow to wide writing is to show how the synthesis you developed to answer your research question applies to the real world. This is an area where novice writers tend to take the process too far. If your statistics are limited to the greater Des Moines region of Iowa and you have good data on blight in the corn crops there, be proud of the data you have and do not try to speculate beyond like regions in the Midwest (unless you have supporting data, then you must decide if you should write an additional paper on the topic). If you have lived experience data on a gang culture in Las Vegas, know that the phenomenological paper you are writing should not speculate beyond that specific culture. Know the limits of your methodology and you will have a succinct paper that opens the door for other research projects in the area.

Narrow to wide writing patterns are excellent for collecting data that will be used by other authors in meta-summaries and meta-syntheses. This is a more difficult approach to writing, but a rewarding approach if done correctly. When using this style, writing an outline is imperative. The outline is your lifeline to keep you within the spectrum of your topic and research question. If ever you feel that you are getting too far away from your topic, then take a moment to look at your topic and research question, asking yourself whether where you are is where you are supposed to be.

CHRONOLOGICAL/NARRATIVE FORMAT

If you are a qualitative writer, then you may have already written a paper in a chronological or narrative (C/N) format. Ethnography, phenomenology, grounded theory, and even case studies can be written very effectively in the chronological or narrative style. If this is the style of writing you choose to use and you are comfortable writing in it, then it can be one of the most interesting styles for your readers to read. However, chronological/narrative papers require a level of comfort with descriptive language that many people do not have. C/N boarders on creative writing in that your descriptions should take your readers to the research site, thus allowing them to make the discoveries that you have made with you. It is an effective, yet difficult type of writing to complete.

The key advantage of C/N is that it allows the reader to follow along with the development of your research. The narrative story line is generally easy to follow and can increase the interest of your readers by being similar to a short story or novel. This can make reading a C/N article more enjoyable than reading a wide to narrow or narrow to wide article. C/N articles also immerse your readers in the field that they are reading about. This can help them visualize the data that they are trying to assimilate, thus you are educating them as you are explaining your findings. Overall, I prefer to read C/N articles, but they are harder for most people to write.

One of the hallmarks of a C/N article is detailed descriptions. Where a sentence such as, "We discovered the bones of the [Animal] in the jungles outside of Ochoa Rios" is acceptable in wide to narrow or narrow to wide format, you would want something more detailed in a C/N paper: "It was hot the day we discovered the bones of the [Animal] in the sub-tropical rainforest outside of the Jamaican capital. The morning sun was filtering through the palm fronds, casting jagged shadows onto the rich island soil. Then the wind picked up, just slightly, and one of the shadows gave way to the sun-bleached white of the [Animal] bone. At this point, we knew we had found our site." As you can see, the second example draws the reader into the story with more detail than the first statement. That being said, either format is useful in the right type of paper. Wide to narrow and narrow to wide are more function driven, while C/N is more narrative driven.

One of the best parts of writing in the C/N style is that the conclusion/discussion of your paper should write itself. Your process is your conclusion, thus all you have to do is write your discovery. Conclusions can be difficult to write, because often the topics we write about have room to continue and be further developed. In the C/N style, your conclusion is the catharsis to your story. What happened has happened. If you want to continue your study into new areas of your topic, then this begins a new story and a new paper. The conclusion of a C/N paper is your capstone in your story that lets the reader close your paper and say, "So that is what happened."

CHECKLIST

- ❑ How long should your paper be?
- ❑ Have you checked the style of your publisher/professor?
- ❑ Have you edited your paper trying to remove ¼?
- ❑ What pattern does your paper follow?
  - Did you stick with wide to narrow?
  - Did you stick with narrow to wide?
  - Did you follow the chronological/narrative pattern?
- ❑ Did you stick to one pattern?
- ❑ Does the pattern seem to fit your paper?

RECOMMENDED READING

Block, Gertrude (1999). EFFECTIVE LEGAL WRITING: FOR LAW STUDENTS AND LAWYERS, 5th ed. New York: Foundation Press.

Druckman, Daniel (2005). DOING RESEARCH: METHODS OF INQUIRY IN CONFLICT ANALYSIS. Thousand Oaks, CA: Sage.

Gibbs, Graham (2007). ANALYZING QUALITATIVE DATA. Thousand Oaks, CA: Sage.

Riessman, Catherine Kohler (2008). NARRATIVE METHODS FOR THE HUMAN SCIENCES. Thousand Oaks, CA: Sage.

Sabin, William A. (2005). THE GREGG REFERENCE MANUAL, 10th ed. Boston: McGraw-Hill, Irvin.

Troyka, Lynn Quitman (1990). SIMON & SCHUSTER HANDBOOK FOR WRITERS. Upper Saddle River, NJ: Prentice Hall.

Willis, Jerry (2007). FOUNDATIONS OF QUALITATIVE RESEARCH: INTERPRETIVE AND CRITICAL APPROACHES. Thousand Oaks, CA: Sage.

chapter 51
Voice-Person

INTRODUCTION (CLEAN WRITING PART I)

Clean writing can be one of the most beneficial elements of your writing style. The cleaner your drafts are the easier your editing process will be. While some elements of clean writing can take time to develop, one area of clean writing that anyone can do quite quickly is ensure that the voice that they use in their writing is consistent throughout the course of the paper. Your voice in your paper is who you are to the people who are reading your work. Some people choose to be less formal and use the informal "I" in their writing. Others tend to be more formal and use the "we" when the write, still keeping their writing personal but removing their individual ego from their writing. Still others believe that academic writing should be sterile and faceless, and that it is more professional to remove the researcher's persona from the writing entirely. These people do not refer to themselves in the text and when they are forced to they use the neutral term "researcher" or a similar term. Whichever pattern you choose for your writing, it is important that you stick with one pattern. This will make your writing flow better and will allow you to use your writing to create your own personal brand.

The inability to maintain one voice through the entirety of a paper is an easy sign that the writer is a novice writer. That being said, maintaining the same voice throughout should not be confused with an author who dictates ownership of different parts of the paper (or book). In this book, things that pertain specifically to me, I use the term "I" to denote; when an element pertains to both myself and you, the reader, I use the term "we" to denote common ownership; and when something that

I am writing about pertains exclusively to you, then I will use the term "you." This is not mixing voice, rather it is denoting ownership of specific actions. When authors mix the "I," the "we," and the neutral throughout their work, it shows that they did not take the time to edit their project and have allowed the work to be mixed in voice.

This chapter looks at some of the problems that people face when they are writing a paper in regard to personal voice. We are also going to look at some of the "easy" ways to fix these problems. In the first section one of this chapter we look at what voice you should use when you are writing a paper. Personal style becomes a major part of this choice; however, different disciplines have different opinions on what is acceptable in academic writing; when in doubt, always err on the side of your discipline. Next, we study ways to look at voice in your paper; sometimes it is not as simple as the "I," the "we," and the neutral, because there are other terms that can interfere with the flow of your prose. In the third section we present some of the basic reasons why some authors chose to use "I" and "we" in their writing, and while you may agree or disagree with these reason, you should always follow the recommendations of your discipline. In the fifth section we look at the arguments why people support neutrality in writing. This too is a matter of personal preference, but also something that you should compare with your discipline before you send your paper to your professor or off to your publisher. Though I generally do not include conclusions in most chapters, this chapter has a conclusion summarizing the fixes that you can use to improve your writing.

Maintaining voice in your writing is an important part of showing that you are developed as a writer. Novice writers give themselves away when they use multiple voices in the same project. Over the course of your writing career, you will begin to be more comfortable with specific writing voices and eventually choose which one will be your primary vehicle for writing. This voice will become part of your personal brand, so when choosing look at how you want readers to see you each time they read one of your papers. Changing voice in between papers is like a professional football player changing teams between seasons—some of your followers will stick with you through the change, but many who were used to who "you" were in your old voice may have trouble making the adjustment.

DO YOU USE I, WE, OR NEUTRAL?

Before we go on to whether you have used the same voice throughout your project, we are first going to look at what voice you should be using. The position on whether an author should use "I," "we," or neutral varies widely among the different academic professions. Many who are in the traditional social sciences or in the hard sciences are firmly in the camp that using "I" or "we" is too informal for academic writing. These disciplines often insist that authors keep their articles neutral for the sanctity of the science. Other fields, such as the arts or the younger social sciences, tend to feel that academia has become too impersonal, thus they feel that using "I" brings some of the humanity back to the humanities and the human sciences. What voice you use is highly dependant on what fields you are in.

As a general rule, you should use "I" when you are doing solo research in a field that allows the use of "I" and your input to your research is part of your participation. Observational research has a strong argument why "I" should be used rather than "we" or a neutral stance. In an observational setting the observer is the person who is doing the observation, thus his or her perception of the situation may be different than another person who would have seen the same thing. This means that the "I" is being properly used because it is relevant that the observer is the same person as the writer. The converse is also true; if the observer is a different person than the writer then this should be demarcated in the text.

The use of "we" should be used when there are multiple researchers, in which case you would use the same general rules as for "I," but it can also be used when the researcher is relying heavily on the work of others. Too often we forget that we are building our research on the research of others who have come before us, which means that the use of "I" is improper in these situations. A key example of this can be seen in a meta-synthesis paper where the author has drawn data from a collection of sources. "We" gathered the data, the author synthesized it. This distinction is simply giving credit where credit is due. There are instances where a paper can still be proper when "we" is used in the data section and "I" is used in the analysis section—this is where there are multiple actors in the collection phase but one person does the analysis and writes for the group.

In the hard sciences and some of the older social sciences it is proper for the researcher to remove reference of themselves from the research all together (except for the byline of course). The reason for this is that the hard sciences and the older social sciences have accepted that they are part of a progression of human understanding. This goes beyond the research of one person, or the ego of one person. The progression of the field may be reliant on your work, but your work will be reliant on work done by those who came before you. In this case you are writing for the field, not simply a collection of authors. In this case it is proper to keep reference to yourself out of the paper, because those who are interested will know that you were the contributor of this work.

DO YOU KEEP THE SAME VOICE?

From the reason why we use specific voices, now it is time to explain how we ensure that our voice is proper throughout the course of the paper. As we have noted, changing voice throughout the paper should only be done in very specific circumstances, like in a handbook for writers where you are distinguishing between yourself, the group, and the reader. In cases other than this, it becomes an instance of dirty writing, which is writing that is only acceptable in drafts. Thus, if you change voices during the course of your paper, you have a need to edit those changes out and ensure that one voice carries throughout the whole of your paper.

The first step of this editing process is the same as the first step of the others—that is, you should go paragraph by paragraph, sentence by sentence, and word by word to ensure that you do not have multiple voices throughout your paper. As this method is only looking for specific words (*I*, *we*, *you*, *us*, *me*, *our*, etc.) you generally can look at the paragraphs, sentences, and words together. If you are a person who prints out your drafts to review them, then you can go through your draft and circle each instance of the voice words. Then as you go through, if they are not all the same you can go back and make the minor changes to bring them all back in line. If you are a person who does your review digitally on your computer screen you can hotkey a color change and highlight each instance of a voice word. When you have corrected all of the examples of multiple voice, you can select all the document and remove the highlighting.

The next step of examining your paper for multiple voice is to have someone else do it. It can be difficult to look over your paper for specific words, especially if you have followed the advice of this book and done two rounds of editing before this. This is when having friends is a good thing. A friend is a person who will help you, a friend is not a person who you abuse by having this person read every paper you ever write. Do not take advantage of your friends. Simply ask your friend to go through your paper and highlight every example of "I" or "we" and the other voice words. Once your friend does this, you can go back through the document and align the voice with the voice that you have selected for your paper. Then you should probably do something nice for your friend.

Small things make good papers and taking the time to check your voice helps give a continuity to your paper that will set it apart from other papers. While this is one of the more monotonous editing processes that you will go through, it is one that will set your paper apart from novice writers who are still learning the craft. Changing the voice of your paper is like copyediting the brochure for those who want to follow you on your journey—you tell them what you did or you tell them what you and others have done, or maybe you leave yourself out of the story completely and simply tell them about the wonders of the journey.

ARGUMENTS FOR I/WE

As those of you who are reading this are likely in diverse fields, there are some arguments for what voice you choose. Just because your discipline has a preferred voice does not mean that you are locked into that voice. It is recommended, but not required. This section of Chapter 51 looks at some of the arguments that you can make for using either "I" or "we" in a field that does not traditionally use these terms. Remember, when in doubt go with what your field sees as normal, because you will get more papers published if you fit the format than if you argue with the editors.

One reason some people like to write in the first person is because it comes across as more personal. If you are writing about domestic violence to a group of domestic violence survivors, they do not want to be treated as if they are academics in lab coats waiting for the newest treatise on the subject; they want to know that you are a real person who wants to help them with their problems. This can be said about many of the niche topics in the hard sciences and traditional social sciences. This argument should only be applied when you need to be more personable to your reader. The odds of you needing to be personable to the nuclear regulatory commission are slim, so in fully bureaucratic reports, when your discipline says shed the personality, you should probably do it.

Another reason that you may want to use "I" or "we" is when you want to convey a sense of honesty and caring about the subjects or the subject matter. Some subjects are on the cutting edge because people tend to distrust them. Columbus was allowed to have an expedition to the New World because he was willing to put his name and reputation on the line; sometimes you have to link yourself personally to an article to show people how much you believe in the subject. Once again, this comes down to the topic and what field you are in. If you have a new theorem that you want people to take seriously, and you are established enough for your reputation to matter, then it may be necessary to buck the trend and use "I" or "we." However, if you are writing about something common place with extensive evidence that people are likely to believe, fighting against tradition and insisting on using the first person may just be stroking your own ego.

Finally, you may be using the first person to link your research to you and not your institutional affiliation. Sometimes institutions want you to separate yourself from them in your research. It is rare, but your research may be unpopular and the university believes that the research is valid; they are just not ready to have their name attached to it yet. This means that you have to distinguish yourself from your institution; "I" and "we" can sometimes be the way to do this. If this is the case, you should look at whether your research is "ripe" for use. Sometimes research topics are not accepted because they were published at the wrong time. Copernicus spent time in jail because his theories flew in the face of everything that the people "knew" to be true. The church had him recant not only to protect themselves but to protect Copernicus from being burned by the peasantry as a warlock or a heretic. While you are not likely to be burned at the stake for an unpopular position, you may want to question whether your research is ready for the world if your institution asks you to distance yourself from them before you publish it. You never want to put the black hat on yourself.

ARGUMENTS FOR NEUTRAL

Neutral papers are more formal, at least in the eyes of the academy. I have seen many papers that were written in the neutral style that were horrible, tactless, and a disgrace to the academy. I have also seen papers that were written using "I" or "we" whose formality rivaled that of a royal ball. The question therefore becomes whether a paper needs neutrality to be formal or whether it needs neutrality to *appear* formal. Sometimes in academic writing formality is a state of mind and an editor will pass over a paper that does not appear to be formal with excellent content, but will accept a less formal, less well written paper because it has the keynotes of a formal paper (i.e., neutral language).

Another reason that you may want to consider writing your paper in the neutral style is because some academic journals require you to write in that style. It can be a simple rule that if you do not follow the format that they recommend you will not be published in their journal. Game, set, and match. This is one of the hard truths of academic writing, no matter how good your work is, there are those who will not even consider it unless you go through the formalities that have been established for decades if not hundreds of years. This is a reminder that you need to look at the submission guidelines of the journal with whom you want to publish before you finish editing your paper. Something as simple as the wrong voice can remove your paper from consideration completely.

Finally, some people see a neutral writing voice as a sign that you have taken the time to remove your bias from your paper. While this is largely an assumption on the part of the reader, it is an assumption that can dictate whether the reader values your research or not. Bias is a problem in modern academic writing. In old time writing we knew the biases of the writers because of the biases of the age they were writing in. Modern writing's biases have not yet become an established part of the academy and what we know as facts. This means that the appearance of bias, especially in this politically correct culture, can be a death sentence for a very well written paper. Therefore, if you have a paper that is without bias, but is about a topic where people are constantly looking for bias (i.e., race relations, gender studies, global warming), you may want to consider writing your paper in a neutral voice to help distance yourself from the appearance of bias.[1]

---

1. In papers written in the neutral voice it is generally necessary to omit the written epoche because you would not be able to write your personal biases in the neutral.

CONCLUSION

When it comes to style you need to pitch to what your readership wants. No matter how good your style is, if you are not fulfilling the needs of your professor/publisher, then you are writing a paper just as an academic exercise. While maintaining your personal brand is important, you need to know who you are writing for. If a journal has stylistic issues that you simply do not want to deal with, then maybe you should select a different journal. The same can be said for a professor, if you feel strongly that the style the professor wants is not for you then you can look for another professor. One thing will remain the same, your readership will always have some control on how your write a paper because if no one reads your work, then there is no reason to write it.

In Part I of this book, we looked in detail at how to make your work appealing to your reader. As a writer, your reader is your customer. No matter how much we hate to admit it we need our readers. That being said, make sure that you are writing what you need to write for your readers, or else pick new readers. Your brand is part of you, so if one readership will not accept your work you can look for other readers. There are 7 billion people out in the world, so it may take a little work but you can keep your personal brand and still find readers, just maybe not your first choice of readers.

All and all it comes down to the fact that writers who write clean papers and follow the guidelines of their publishers are the writers who get their papers published. Those writers who fight against the system because they do not want to do the work or because they think that they are smarter than everyone else are the authors whose books never get published and whose work never sees the light of day. Writing is an individual event, but getting published is a team sport.

CHECKLIST

- ❑ Have you taken the previous editing steps?
- ❑ Read through your paper and highlight/circle all voice words.
- ❑ Do they all match?
- ❑ If they do, good for you.
- ❑ If they do not, take the time to use the same voice throughout your paper.
- ❑ Reread the publisher's guidelines, because they are there to help you get published.

chapter 52
Voice-Temporal

INTRODUCTION (CLEAN WRITING PART II)

The second type of dirty writing that some people fall into is bad temporal writing. As human beings, we move in a continuous line through time and space, and this timeline becomes part of our character and it becomes something that we expect to follow a reasonable course. Good writing sticks to a workable timeline, whether through research format or through a story, thus it is easy for a reader to follow. Bad writing jumps around a timeline and makes the research difficult to follow. Some authors feel that it is trendy to mask their findings by holding them until the end to surprise the reader, but readers do not read academic writing for the surprise, they read it for the information. Making your paper follow a logical timeline allows your readers to find what they are looking for quickly and painlessly. This makes your paper more useful and helps identify you as a good writer.

There is another group of writers who simply ignore the timeline when they are writing. They simply write the ideas down on the paper as they come to them, check for grammar (sometimes), then turn the paper into the publisher or professor. While these papers may have excellent content, they are difficult to read because they are so chaotic. The human mind seeks order, especially when it is searching for something. At all times when you are writing you must realize that the purpose of your academic writing is to give information to other people. If your writing is chaotic, then it will be difficult for your readers to follow and thus less useful. Therefore, always check your chaos in your writing by preparing an outline.

Good writing will go beyond simply following a structured timeline, and put up "signposts" for readers to follow throughout the paper. A signpost is a term or sentence that tells readers what part of the paper they are in, or what part of an individual section that are in. Signposts can also demarcate the order that operations were done during the research. Novice writers will omit the signposts because they do not feel they are necessary; however, each signpost that allows your readers to find what they are looking for can help your paper immensely. The main kind of signpost is a section heading. "Introduction," "Method," "Data," "Analysis," and "Discussion" are all words that let readers know exactly what they are looking at. Researchers who are doing meta-synthesis research are looking for your data, your analysis is secondary to them; thus, if you have your data section clearly marked they can go directly to the section they want. Further, within sections you can build a timeline such as:

> "First, Smith looked at the correlation between..... The second major research on the area was Karl Marx who said .... Next, Sumner built upon a synthesis of Marx and Smith to come to the conclusion.... This line of economic thought was rounded out by Weber when he stated...."

As you can see, even without the data the flow of the above sentences is easy to follow because it has signposts and follows one temporal voice. This pattern should be repeated in each section of your paper.

One way to keep papers flowing in the same direction is to look at time as an anchor. No matter what the topic, all things that I am writing about have some sort of time stamp. If there are multiple timelines, they cannot be mixed (unless you are synthesizing them); therefore, you can have a new subsection for each different timeline. If you anchor your paper with a first, second, third approach (or firstly, secondly, thirdly for timelines within timelines) you can anchor the temporal aspect of your paper so that it is easy for your readers to follow and find what they are looking for. This will be much appreciated by your readers, even if they do not notice it.

In this chapter we look at the normal way that most people will anchor their paper temporally. This is only one system of writing temporally, there are others. If you choose another method just remember to keep the temporal voices straight throughout the paper. In the first section we discuss how to use past tense temporal voice in an academic paper. Past tense should be regulated to things that have happened in the past, such as previous research. In the second section we look at the present tense. Even though your research was done previous to you writing about it, it is the current topic of your paper and thus all research is in the present tense. The exception to this rule is chronological data presentation, where the story should be in the past tense. In the third section we look at the future tense and how it should be used. If you are using a discussion section rather than a conclusion, then the discussion should be in a future tense as you are talking about what researchers in the future can do to further the subject.

The temporal voice of your paper is one of the small details that separate good writers from exceptional writers and exceptional writers from great writers. If you take the time to practice writing in the proper temporal voice you will eventually begin writing in the proper voice by course of habit and thus you will greatly reduce your editing time. Using proper voice can distinguish you from your competition and your colleagues, showing that you respect readers enough to make your paper as easy as possible for them to read. Voice is important, just like when you speak.

PAST (WHAT OTHERS HAVE SHOWN)

Writing in the past tense should be regulated to when you are talking about the work that has been done in the past on your given topic. This is the work upon which you are building your work. If you are going to build upon the work of others, then it means that the work of the other authors should be already completed or at least some portion of it published. You should also write about this work in the past tense. The reason for this is simple—naturally the human mind is going to realize that you cannot be building something upon something that does not exist yet, though we see academics in ivory towers we do not believe that they can build castles in the air. You anchor your paper to the ground when you speak about the work of other authors in the past tense.

Another reason that you should write about the work of other authors in the past tense is because your work is the current state of the field, their work was building up toward your work. While you never come out and say this, this is what the context of your writing should say. For instance:

> "Adam Smith says that production, focused in the hands of the industrious, is part of building the wealth of nations."

Or

> "Adam Smith said that production, focused in the hands of the industrious, is part of building the wealth of nations."

While the changes between the first example and the second example are minor, the second example puts the arguments of Adam Smith in the past (foundation) while the first example puts them in the present (contemporary). If Smith were your contemporary and he is the expert on the subject, why would your reader not look to his work rather than yours. By putting him in the past tense you are letting readers know that your work is an evolution of Smith's work and therefore should be given more note because it is more current.

One way that you can help teach yourself to keep past research in the past is that when you mention the name of another author, always put it in the past. Whether this author wrote what she said yesterday or a thousand years ago, the writing is still outdated because your writing is an evolution of that thought. Never say this in your paper but keep it firmly in your mind. Know also that someday (hopefully) your research will be one of the building blocks of some other researchers' work. If you have complementary work, sometimes authors who you talk about will talk about you in their work (this can also be true for critical work). When this happens, you each take turns adding on to the subject, moving your discipline ever further into the future by standing upon the work of the past.

PRESENT (WHAT YOU ARE DOING)

When you are writing, what you do is always current. Your research should be in the present tense, your data (except narrative data) should be in the present tense, and your analysis should be in the present tense. Your research should be the focus of your research paper; if this is not the case then why are you writing it? You must believe that what you are writing is important; thus, it should always be the current topic of discussion during your paper. Some schools of thought put their research in the past tense, but the research you have done for this project is part of the digital timestamp of your current work. A digital timestamp is a concept that from start to finish (except narrative work) your paper is a single moment in time, what came before it came before it, what comes in the future will come in the future, and all that is part of your study is in the present and is what the reader should focus on.

As with the idea that while you are writing your paper you should keep your mind focused on the topic, when you are editing your paper you should keep your paper focused on the present. Do not glorify the work of past writers; you can respect them but your work is the substance of the moment. Always keep the focus on the present work and do not let yourself drift into temporal tangents. A temporal tangent is when you shift the focus of your research paper from itself onto another researcher's work. The focus of your study should be your research, other researcher's works should be handled with respect but not focal language.

My trick for keeping my temporal voice in the correct field is to keep a note card near my writing area that says, "They did it, you are doing it, someone else will do more." Creating a note card like this with your topic on it should help you keep your focus on where your temporal voice should be. While the past and the future are arguable whether they are needed in a paper, you should always keep your own research current. Other disciplines can bicker over whether it is proper to put other researchers in the past, or whether you should have a conclusion or a discussion section, but when everything is boiled down you are writing your paper and your paper should be your main focus during your project.

FUTURE (WHAT CAN STILL BE DONE)

It is the height of academic arrogance to believe that your work on a subject is the pinnacle of research in that field. If you ever find yourself saying, "I solved sociology" or "I solved the humanities," then you may want to check yourself into a hospital or see a psychologist. Your work will always be part of the human discovery process. Even if you make a quantum leap forward in particle physics, you are still only leaping down an infinitely long path to better understanding. Like in religion you can never hope to be perfect on your own, only to get a little better each day. Your research will never be the end of a process, it will only further the process down the road.

I like to compare this with the old question, "If you start on the 50 yard line of a football pitch and move half way to the goal each time you move, how long will it take you to cross the end line?" The answer, of course, is that you will never cross the end line. Each time you move forward you are moving a smaller and smaller distance. Some people see this as the glass half-empty, that you will never reach your goal; however, you can also see it as a glass half-full in that you are always moving forward. This is how it is with research—fields will continue to become more and more specific as the mysteries of society and the universe are discovered one by one; however, there will always be new things out there to discover for those who have the vision and the creativity to see new questions.

This is the essence of the future tense, to realize that you are part of a process that has been going on for thousands of years and that will continue to go on for thousands more. Once we know our part in the process, we can contribute to the process as much as our natural talents allow. This means that after we have presented our research in the analysis section of our paper (or the beginning of the discussion depending on your format), we can move on to talking about what others that follow us can research. While writing on a topic you have become apt in the topic, if not an expert, this means that you should be able to ask some of the questions that will be at the forefront of the field you are researching. While you are doing this, do not give away the topic of your next paper so that someone else will be competing with your research, but you can ask the research questions that you do not have the time or the expertise to ask. In this way, you can doubly contribute to the field; first as an author answering your research question and second as a teacher guiding future researchers with new questions. This should all be done in the future tense as these questions and their answers have not been written yet.

BAD VOICE (TIME JUMPS)

One of the key signs of a novice academic writer is jumping around in time. When authors write a paper where they start in the present, then in the same paragraph move through the past to the future, readers are often left wondering where they will go next. These are time jumps, and good writers should avoid them at all cost. The best rule of thumb is, no paragraph should have more than one tense in it. If you are writing a past tense paragraph, then keep it in the past. If you are writing a present tense paragraph, keep it in the present. The same goes for future paragraphs, keep them constant in the time stream. This can even be done at a larger level by keeping your book research in the past, the data you garnered from others in the past, the data you collected in the present, your analysis in the present, and your discussion in the future. This will allow you to keep your paper focused on the proper timeline.

When I am grading papers, one of the key signs of a novice writer (or a writer who does not care) is time jumps. Your temporal voice is another area of a research paper that should be easy to edit. Go through each section and look for past tense verbs and verbs in the future tense, circle them, then bring them in line with one another. It may be tedious, but it is an easy fix to do. Many people do not want to take the time to make these simple fixes, so this is an area where you can distinguish your writing from your competition. Simply keep the voice correct and you can impress editors because you make their job easier for the next time they review one of your papers.

CONSTANT VOICE

Because one of the major writing styles calls for constant voice throughout the paper, it is important that we take a moment to acknowledge this style. Constant voice is when you keep the same voice throughout the paper. The voice can be either past or present, but it should never be future (because you cannot know what research will be done in the future for data collection). Disciplines that require the voice to be constant want to keep the format simple for their writers, which is understandable, but it can cause some confusion as past and present interplay with how people read a paper. If this is something that your discipline calls for, find out if it is required; if not, use the past, present, future format we have covered in this chapter.

Keeping your voice constant section by section is another story, but is something that you need to do to ensure that your paper will be exceptional, at least when it comes to format. When in doubt have one of your friends read over your paper to make sure that you caught all the time jumps. Time jumps are common with new writers, and even some veteran writers still allow a few temporal mistakes to appear in their work when they are trying to complete a project too quickly or if they are writing chapters of a book out of sequence. Do not be embarrassed if you have time jumps in your paper. Just make sure that you take the time to correct them and put each section in temporal alignment. This will save you a lot of time when you send the paper off to a professor or editor, if you have already corrected the problems then they will not have to send the paper back for you to correct. Think of this as checking your journey as you finish so that when you lead others down the same path you do not have to retrace your steps and embarrass yourself.

CHECKLIST

- ❑ Did you complete the previous editing steps?
- ❑ Go through your paper and circle all verbs.
- ❑ Going paragraph by paragraph do they all match in tense?
- ❑ Is your book research in past tense?
- ❑ Is your data from others in past tense?
- ❑ Is your data you collected in present tense (except narrative data)?
- ❑ Is your analysis in present tense?
- ❑ Is your discussion in future tense?
- ❑ Is there a smooth flow to your paper as you read it?

chapter 53
Co-authors

INTRODUCTION (NOT GOING IT ALONE)

Academia is a world where research projects can become intertwined with the works of other authors, some of these are complementary and some are contradictory. When the work two people (or more) are doing is complementary, then it can be in the best interests of the authors to think about writing papers together as coauthors. The arrangements between authors can vary based on the status of each author, but collaboration is becoming more and more common as the detail and cost of individual projects rise. In this chapter we will look at some of the benefits and drawbacks of working with another author for your project.

One of the key reasons that authors tend to work together is because they want to take on a project that is too big for one person to do on their own. This can be because the volume of research is too large, one person cannot get solo funding in the amount needed for the project, or the topic covers too many disciplines. Big projects are needed from time to time to get a field moving forward. Imagine that during your journey to write a paper you are going down a path to find specific information on a topic, but the path is blocked because the research you need has not been done yet. You think about setting aside your current project and removing the blockage by doing this research, but you realize that this project is too big for you. As you are looking at the gap in the literature, you find that others in the field have come up against this problem, too. All the "low hanging fruit" in the area has been picked (i.e., researched) so the blockage is all that remains. This is a time where you may need help on your journey to write a paper.

There are several ways that you can approach a problem such as this. The most common is to find someone in your own discipline that you can work with who will help you work through the literature gap. The two (or more) of you can work through the gap much faster than you could by yourself, thus allowing you to work on both projects at once. The other option is to find someone in a conjoining field, a field that this path seems to lead toward to see if there is a gap in the literature from this side also. If so, then you can work with that person to fill the gap from both sides, either through solo projects or by collaboration. You will find that when one discipline reaches a block on a certain subject that other disciplines also are having the same problem, and by linking the disciplines the overall data from the research may be usable by more people and thus your research project may enjoy more acclaim.

One of the first steps of being successful in academia is knowing when you need help. Some projects are too big for you, and it is alright for you to admit that. The smartest person in the world is not the person who knows everything but is the person who knows where to find things.[1] This is true for academic research also. If you know who to talk to, or who to work with for a project, you can develop your catalogue of work in areas that you are not an expert in but where you know enough to contribute to or collaborate with an expert in the field. Admitting you need help means that you know your limitations, and if you know your limitations you are well on the way to conquering them.

Our last major reason why people collaborate on a project is because they want the feeling of working with someone else. Academics who are friends may be chatting one night and come across a topic that they are both interested in. Other academics may find each other at conferences or in chat rooms and discover that they have a research goal in common. The old notion that two heads are better than one can still be true in academic circles, so do not be afraid to collaborate with a friend just because that is your only reason.

In this chapter we cover some of the issues that cause problems when working with other people on research projects. With large projects, like books, there is the profit and limited fame that can drive people to work together; with a research paper it is generally the love of the topic that binds people together. In the first section we look at the benefits of working with another researcher on a large project. The other researcher can complete the brand that is needed for a specific research project to be considered reliable. In the second section we look at the drawbacks of working with another person. These can be difficult, but if you know them going in to the project you can overcome them. In the third section we look at the time when you enter a project as partners, which differs from the fourth section where we look at projects in which you are the lead researcher and

---

1. Einstein.

you have assistants. The demographic between you and your coauthors can dictate the way that the relationship between you and your coauthors develops. In the fifth section we discuss how sharing credit works and some of the considerations that you should take into account when you are working with someone else. Sometimes two or more people have a hard time agreeing on things other than the actual research.

Coauthors can be life savers or they can be a nightmare depending on how much time you put into choosing your coauthors and defining your relationships. They say familiarity breeds contempt, and nowhere is this more true than the creative process. If you and your collogues look at the possible problems before you enter into your research, you can better prepare for disagreements that could shatter your relationship. Perpetration is key in writing, and that preparation should extend to making sure your coauthor is right for you.

BENEFITS

The benefits of multiple authors can be many, depending on the type of project that you are working on. First and foremost, more authors allow you to spread the work of your project around. It may be cliché but many hands lighten the load. When working with another author to spread the load, you need to agree on a division of labor when you begin the project. Nothing will derail a project faster than two researchers who cannot agree of who has to or who gets to do a specific area of the research. By dividing the workload in your initial agreement to do the project you can help yourself by having a developed plan of who does what (if you are really ambitious you can include when). This can stem future arguments and make the entire process run more smoothly.

A second mind working on the same research question can create more ideas. This is another advantage of working with another researcher or as part of a group. Different people bring different theoretical paradigms and different ideas into the research process. Sometimes when you reach a block in the road that you cannot think your way around you can turn to your coauthors and their different perspectives can allow you to keep going with your research. The coauthors' perspectives can also be valuable when you are marketing your project to a journal or publisher because they may be more in tune with the publisher than you are.

A second set of eyes can also be useful for the practical aspect of a research project, not just the theoretical aspect. Sometimes when you are doing observations or interviews your coauthors will see something that you do not see or vice versa. This can help you make your data collection process more efficient, the less data that you miss can mean that your data is richer for analysis. Further, you can have each researcher concentrate on a specific aspect of what you are researching. Researcher 1 can observe the conversational habits of female persons in the area of observation while Researcher 2 watches the conversational habits of male persons in the area. By dividing the research goals of the two researchers, each researcher is thus able to focus more directly on the research that each is expected to do.

One of the biggest advantages of having a second researcher working on your project is that it may allow you to cross into other disciplines. You do not have to select your coauthor from your own discipline; you can select your coauthor from another discipline. This can double your book research data, double your theoretical perspectives, and double your potential audience. Further, the synthesis of two different disciplines can open up research areas that have not been studied before because they were beyond the realm of any individual discipline. When you are having trouble coming up with a new research project, it is sometimes helpful to go talk to someone in a completely different discipline than your own, and the conflict or synthesis between the disciplines may be the catalyst that you need to come up with a new idea to research.

A less exciting benefit of working with another author is that you can edit each other's work. As we have discussed in the previous chapters, editing your own work can be difficult because your mind knows what you wanted to say. When you look at another person's work this assumption does not seem to crop up as much. You and your coauthor can read each other's work, giving you the advantage of an interim editor before your end of the work goes off to the publisher or journal. Every extra editorial step that you can add to the process can make your paper stronger and improve the writing style, which is one of the key benefits of having a second author working with you.

DRAWBACKS

When you are working with someone else, you need to keep in mind that it will not always be exciting and fun. You are two (or more) different people who may have different views on the subject that you are researching. Sometimes these views do not mesh together well, thus the project can have problems at the conceptual or theoretical level. Generally, these problems can be worked through by two adults who truly believe that the project that they are working on is worthwhile, but sometimes they cannot. When this situation occurs, it may be in the best interest of both authors to take the work that you have and use it toward the creation of two new projects. In this way each person can use the work that you have done together but can work toward their own concept or their own theory. This can allow both authors to keep their "brand" safe, while still allowing for a more limited form of collaboration. When you do this, be sure to give your collaborator credit. If you do this, it can prevent these disagreements from destroying a working relationship or even a friendship.

You may also find that when you are writing with another author that your two styles do not go together. One person may want to use "we" while the other person wants to write in the neutral. There may also be some disagreement on temporal voice. These problems are generally not as severe as the previous problems, but if they are left to fester can seriously derail a project. If you find that you are having stylistic differences with your partner, discuss them together. Sometimes the partner sees the same problems; sometimes the partner sees no problems at all. If you take the time to open up lines of communication, you may be able to save the project and the relationship before the problems become too big for either of you to address. Personal style is part of your personal brand; remember that the coauthor also has a brand. If you cannot reach an agreement on which style to use, then perhaps you should use neither; since it is your synthesis of ideas that makes this project unique, maybe a synthesis of styles will add to the uniqueness of the project.

Another more practical problem that you may face when working with another author is finding the time to collaborate. In the world of modern academics, where teachers are teaching 4x4x4 course load and have families and side projects running at the same time, finding the hours that it takes to do proper research and collaboration together can be challenging. This will come down to how important the project is to you; if the project is important then you will have to make time to ensure that the research is done. One way to do this is to schedule time for consultation, either live or digital, each week the way that you would schedule a class. Block off the time in your calendar and let people know that this is part of your weekly schedule. This may be difficult for the first few weeks that you set this up, but once you get into the routine you will find that the people in your life accept that this is "work time" and you will be able to commit the amount to time you need to make your project work.

PARTNERS

There are two different ways that you can enter into a research project with another person. The first is as partners. Partners in a research project equally share the work, meaning that each person does half. Now how you break the project down into halves (or other fractions if you have more people) is entirely up to you. Each of you can do half the research, half the writing and half the editing, or one of you can do the research, the other the writing and the first can do the editing. The important factor is that you agree on this division of labor at the beginning of the process so that no one can accuse the other of doing less work. As partners you have to enter the project looking at each other as equals; if the arrangement is something other than this, then you should look at the next section.

Another factor of working with a partner is that both partners have equal credit in the work. While we will cover credit in more detail in the fifth section of this chapter, it is important to note that equal credit means equal control of the work. Sometimes papers are written just to be published, other times one of the authors may want to present the data at a conference or symposium. The important factor is that you discuss this at the beginning of the process. What are your goals and what are your partner's goals? If you both understand the goals of your project then you will be better able to allocate resources when these opportunities/commitments come up later.

Partners can also provide the opportunity for long-term collaboration. If you are working with another researcher on a longitudinal study that is going to take 10 years of research, you may have intermediary ideas that can benefit the both of you. If any part of your new idea involves the data that you have already worked on with your partner, then you are ethically required to discuss the idea together. If the partner wants to work with you on the new idea, too, then find a way that you can work together either as partners, associates, or even as your assistant. If the person does not want to be part of the secondary project have him or her sign a release form to ensure that the legality of the situation is covered. Talking with your partner can be beneficial in that it allows you to discuss where you are going with the data and it can help keep your relationship working smoothly for future projects.

ASSISTANTS/ASSOCIATES

Assistants and associates are two different forms of collaboration where you are not sharing an equal part of the workload. If you are the main author on a project where you have associates or assistants then you should be doing the majority of the writing and a large part of the research. The qualifications of these terms differ among fields, but if you are listed as the lead researcher on a project you should be doing most of the work. The additional responsibility also means that you have the liability for the work, meaning you are overseeing those who are working under you. While at the end, you may get the glory, during the project you are the boss and you are the person who gets in trouble if someone steps out of line.

An associate is someone you ask to help you with a part of the project. You may be qualified to do 90% of the project, but there is 10% that you are not comfortable working with. In this situation, you can ask a colleague who is qualified in the 10% to help you out with the project. Although you are "in charge" of the project, you do have to be accepting of the associate's schedule and other commitments. The associate has other projects going too, and no doubt a busy life. This may prevent the associate from working at the speed you desire, but this is a trade-off since most of the time the only payment that the associate will get for doing research for free is a secondary byline on your project. Be understanding of your associate's time constraints, but if it becomes evident that the associate cannot finish the project on time, you may need to find someone else.

Assistants are different in that they are part of the project from the beginning, but they are there to make your job easier. Assistants are generally young professionals or graduate assistants who want to work with you to "learn the ropes" of the field. These are people whom you cannot expect to do hard theoretical reasoning or plan the experiments. Rather, assistants are people who carry out your instructions to complete the data collection practice. Rarely, you can allow an assistant to write some of a research paper, but you should write the majority of the paper if your name is going to be top name on the project. It is unethical to allow assistants to write a paper for you, or for you to use research that was designed and performed by your assistants for a paper where you do not give them proper credit for it. If they do most of the work, then they should get most of the credit (most people in this situation act as a partner as they are using your reputation and their work). Treat your assistants well because someday they could be the new face of the field.

Part of working with associates and assistants is being a good leader. If you understand and get to know your associates and assistants then you can know what type of work to expect out of them. If your assistant is a single father of three children under the age of 10, expecting him to come in each night at 8 p.m. and work until 2 a.m. is expecting a lot of him. Likewise if your assistant has a job and is working for you for free, you cannot expect her to sacrifice time from her paying job to do work for you. You have to understand who is working for you and be fair to them to ensure that you have a good reputation, because let's face it, graduate students talk and if you are treating your assistants poorly, you will have a harder time getting new assistants when the current ones graduate.

When working with assistants, and sometimes eager associates, you are working as a teacher as well as a researcher. You need to take time to teach them the trade rather than simply commanding them to do tasks that you do not want to do. Being a good leader is underscored by being a good teacher, if you can do both then you will be able to get the best assistants each year when the new group comes out. Also, help your assistants build for their future. If you have ancillary data that you are not using, then you may be able to have them use it for a thesis or a dissertation. This can help them move on with their career and allow you to trade an assistant for a colleague.

CREDIT

When you have a coauthor, both of you are likely going to want credit for your own part of the project. Make sure that you spread the credit around properly. If you are the lead author, your name gets to go first; if someone else did most of the writing then this person should be listed first. If you both did an equal amount of writing, then you should find some other way of deciding (how it sounds, alphabetical, who wins a game of Hungry Hungry Hippos). Sometimes who gets the first name in the credit line can cause severe problems in your project, so take the time to discuss it early on so it is not a problem later.

If your name does appear second on the title page, then make sure to get permission from your coauthor to present the paper (if you intend to present at conferences). Some conferences will not allow you to present, or even submit a paper, unless you are the first listed author. All it takes to get beyond this problem is for your coauthor to sign a paper stating that you are equal coauthors and that you have permission to present this paper. You should also give permission to your coauthor as some conventions are requiring all authors to sign off on the paper before it can be presented.

When you give proper credit to one another in your paper, you can also find that it allows you more opportunities for marketing. Assuming that you both have good names in your fields, you can travel together to conferences in each field. This can help you get more publicity, get more people reading your paper, and even begin to create a potential readership for any books that you may author on the subject. But this all comes down to giving proper credit on your paper. Do not fight with your co-author, because there is enough limelight for everyone.

CHECKLIST

- ❏ What type of relationship do you have with your coauthor?
    - With your partner?
    - With your associate?
    - With your assistant?
- ❏ Did you take time to discuss order of names on the title page?
- ❏ Did you break down your responsibilities so that both people know what their jobs are?
- ❏ If you have multiple people working on the project is everyone on the same page?
- ❏ If you have teaching assistants, have you designed the project so that they learn their respective roles?

chapter 54
Editors

INTRODUCTION (LIFESAVERS/GATEKEEPERS)

This chapter was added after the outline for the book was done, but that does not mean that it is an afterthought. Some of you who are reading this book will have the means to hire a professional editor to help you with your work. A professional editor differs from a journal editor in several ways; whereas a journal editor has the interest of the journal in mind, a good professional editor will be solely committed to helping you make your paper the best paper it can be. Secondly, a good professional editor expects that there will be some grammatical errors or occasional spelling errors in your work; this is why you hire an editor. If you have the wherewithal to hire a professional editor, when you send your paper into the journal or other publication where you want it published it should be in near pristine condition.

Before you hire an editor realize that you are paying this person to tell you what you need to hear, not what you want to hear. If you have major problems in your paper, the editor will tell you that it is not ready to be sent in yet. Further, the editor will tell you what you need to fix prior to the editorial process. The editor's job is not to allow you to skip the last five chapters of this book that tell you how to edit, but to take a fully edited manuscript and turn it into something even better. Therefore, when you are shopping around to find a good editor for your work, look for someone who will tell you what you need to hear to make your writing what it needs to be. Hiring an editor that will just tell you what you want to hear will do nothing for your paper and will simply be a waste of money.

If you hire an editor, do not be obstinate. Editors are there to help you, so let them do their job. Many authors push back anytime that an editor asks them for changes. Generally, editors are not going to ask you to change your theoretical construct or your research question. They are there to help you improve the flow of your article. Do not argue with them on grammar—they likely know it better than you do because it is their job to know it. If they want a change, it is in your best interest to make it. However, some newer editors can become overzealous and attempt to change your findings to fit their worldview. If this is the case with an editor that you hire, then fire this person. Editors should help you with the voice of your article, your grammar, and perhaps your spelling, but they are not coauthors so they should not be changing the substance. That being said, editors will tell you when your writing does not make sense, which is a grammatical issue so you should listen to them on this.

In this chapter we will go over some of the things that you want to make sure you have in an editor. This is not a book on how to find a good editor, so the information will be basic. If you want to find a good editor that you can work with for several projects, take the time to research editors and read some of the work that they have edited during their career. Editors, like writers, tend to find a niche and stick with it. If you can find an editor who works in your niche, then you may have found one who can tell you when you are on the wrong track within the field. In the first section we look at building trust with your editor. To work efficiently with editors, you need to be able to trust their grammar decisions, because if you cross check every one of their decisions you are reducing their role to a proofreader. In the second section we look at your style and your editor. You generally want to have the same style in all of your work, so that your readers are comfortable with you as a provider of knowledge; in this case it is best to have the same editor who can add continuity to your style. In the third section we look at the need for you to help your editor help you. You are not the only author that your editor works for (hopefully), which means that you need to make your editor's life easier by taking the steps that we recommend in this book before you send your paper off to be edited. In this way, your editor can get back to you faster and will likely make your writing a top priority.

TRUST

When selecting an editor, select someone that you believe you will be able to trust. The trust between an author and editor is something that you must build over the course of time. Unless you are into trusting people blindly, you will need time for the trust with your editor to develop. To begin the trusting process, you should select an editor with the skills to edit in the field that you have chosen. Anyone can say they are an editor, so you must look at their body of work to see if they actually can live up to the hype that they surround themselves with. You must also be aware that the best editors in the country may not be willing to work with new authors, because their workload may be full with clients they have had for years; thus, you may have to look for editors with some experience but also some room to grow.

Researching your editor can take a significant amount of time. There are many good editors out there, but there are also many poor editors you may not want to hire for your project. If you are going to spend the money to hire an editor, then you should also take the time to find a good editor who can work in your area. There are several sites that will help you find an editor and if you are having trouble you can always call the nearest university and see who they recommend. Spending the time can save you the time and embarrassment of choosing a bad editor.

The reason that trust is so important is that you are paying an editor to make your life easier and your product better. If you do not trust editors and force yourself to review every inch of their work, then you are paying to create more work for yourself. If you are not a trusting person, then it may be in your interest to simply do the editing yourself and roll the die with the publication you are shooting for. Most people do not pay editors for academic papers, only a few people have that luxury. Do not try to force yourself into something that you are not comfortable with. If you can trust an editor and can afford it, then by all means do it. If you are a person who cannot trust an editor with your work, or cannot afford the prices that some editors charge, then you may have to be like the rest of us and do the work yourself.

STYLE OF EDITOR

Once you find an editor, try to stick with this person. Jumping from one editor to another without a good reason can gain you a reputation of being difficult to work with in the editorial community. Editors are a small community, thus news travels fast. Another reason that it is a bad policy to jump back and forth between editors is because once you have a style you need to keep that style, and your editor is part of your style. If you switch back and forth between several editors, each one will have an effect on your style and your brand will be broad and unwieldy. Conversely, if you have one editor then your style will be familiar; thus you will be able to keep a constant style and build your brand.

HELP THEM HELP YOU

When you find a good editor and stick with this person, you will find that your editor's goal becomes to assure your success in your academic project. This is what you are paying for, and if you have a good one, your editor will do everything possible to help you be successful. One of the key obstacles in the editor's job is you. You can hurt the success of your project by constantly second guessing your editor and challenging every comment. If you are a professional grammarian, then why are you hiring an editor? Most of us are limited to the English that we learned in high school or college. One class at the 100 level does not make a person an expert in grammar; thus an editor has an advantage that most of us do not have. Take advantage of this advantage and make sure that you use all the information that your editor has given you.

You must also realize that if you look good in a paper, then you make your editor look good. If your paper receives acclaim, then he or she will be listed as the editor of a famous piece. Conversely, if your work is sloppy and slipshod, then your editor will have that black mark, too. Note also, authors can dump their editors if they do not follow directions, just as editors can dump authors if they fail to fix their writing problems. If a paper is rife with errors, then it makes the editor look bad; and editors have their own brand to worry about so they may dump their authors as clients rather than have a bad article in their catalogue.

Above all remember why you are hiring your editor. You pay editors for their advice and for their skill. You pay them to take what you see as a finished project and polish it to near perfection. You do not hire editors because you are too lazy to do basic editing. If you want to avoid the basic editing, then hire a graduate student to do basic copyediting and grammar checking. The goal of your editor is to take your best work and make it better. For you to truly help your editor, you need to make sure that you give your editor your best work. In your journey to write your paper, your editor becomes the first person to review whether anyone else should make the same journey as you.

CHECKLIST

- ❑ Did you take the time to find an editor who does good work?
- ❑ Did you look for an editor in your field?
- ❑ Did you take your editor's advice?
- ❑ If not, then why are you paying for an editor?

CONCLUSION

At this point, your journey to write your paper is coming to an end. If you have followed all the steps listed in this book, then you should have a paper that is as near to perfect as you can make it. You should have taken the time to go over each element of your paper, editing it thrice and making sure that your style in this paper represents what you want your academic brand to be. You should have ensured that you length is ideal for the type of journal in which you want to publish. You should have checked to make sure that your personal voice is consistent throughout the paper and that the proper temporal voice is used for each section. If you have coauthors or editors, then you should have a basic idea of how to treat them. Your paper should be the best that it can be at this moment, but the more you write the closer to perfection your best will become.

Each time you write, walk yourself through the journey that we have taken together in this book. Make sure that you prepare for your paper just like you would prepare for a journey through the forest. Know where you want to go and how you want to get there. Identify pitfalls that may trip you up and minimize the risk of encountering them. Look for those who may stand in your way, or those who may be willing to help you. Each few moments that you take to prepare for your journey into writing can result in hours that you will save when you are editing or trying to get your paper published. As in real life, the preparation for your journey may be the most important part.

Remember that your method is the vehicle that you will use to get from the beginning of your paper (the concept) to the end (the finished product). Taking care to follow all the steps of your method is akin to checking your vehicle before you leave on a long voyage. The longer the voyage the more you want to be assured that your vehicle is in good working order. The more important your study is the more time you want to dedicate to making sure that your methodology is well developed. There are people who will be critical of your work, no matter how good it is. One of the easiest things for them to attack is your methodology. If you take the time to do a good job on your methodology, you can frustrate critics' attempts to defame you and make sure that your work is taken seriously.

Editing is the third step of the good paper writing trifecta. You are the first editor of your paper, you cannot avoid that. Any attempts to avoid being your own first editor are simply going to make your writing style less effective. You are your own guide in your journey of paper writing. Although this book tells you how to guide yourself through the process, you are the one who will actually make the choices. I believe you can do it, as anyone can write. What it will come down to in the end is whether you have the patience and the interest in your topics to edit your paper until it is ready to be submitted to a publication.

Writing a good paper takes time. Anyone who tells you that you can instantly create an expert paper is probably working for a newspaper, not an academic journal. A course term paper can be completed in about 1 hour 30 minutes start to finish, but an academic paper will take an actual time commitment. Writing your paper is a journey, so do not try to rush it. Getting to the end is half the battle, but learning during the course of your journey is half of the pleasure. Why walk in the forest if you are not going to look at the trees and enjoy the time you are working on this project? Do not rush through your project and let it become something that you hate. Writing a paper is work, but it should be work you enjoy. Now that your journey is complete, take a moment and look back at the process; this is something that you created—now you can see if it stands the test of time.

final discussion

A mentor of mine who is a publisher told me he hates to get papers with conclusions. He told me that the word *conclusion* has such a ring of finality to it, that a project is done and the last word in the paper is the final word on the subject. He said that anyone who believes that they have solved a mystery of the universe totally and unequivocally is fooling themselves, and when they assert that their conclusion is the end of the project they are not only fooling themselves but also fooling their readers. Human knowledge is always progressing, so today's conclusion will be the next generation's starting point. Therefore even though this book is completed and your journey to write a paper done, the future holds for you and I much more writing and many more opportunities to build our skills. Therefore, we end not with a conclusion, but with a final discussion of where we shall go from here.

In this text, we have covered many aspects of the writing process. We began our journey to a better understanding of writing, and I dare say a better understanding of ourselves, with a sojourn into the process of basic writing. We began by looking at the concept, the greater level idea, that would be our context for our paper. Like an explorer entering into the jungle, we then made our plans and began to prepare for our trip. We looked at what type of paper would best accomplish our goal, what hypotheses we were testing (or even what hypotheses), we looked at the format, the approach, and our readership. Then we took the time to look at ourselves to see if we were ready to make this voyage of paper writing, whether we were up to the challenge of tackling this journey. We found that we were ready and it was time to begin writing a paper.

The next four parts of the book looked at the tool kits that we decided to take with us on our journey. As we looked at quantitative research, we saw that many of the problems that made quantitative research so scary were just in our heads; that rather than a math-based methodology, quantitative research was simply a computer science field that relied on good data collection. We saw that the mathematics was secondary to ensuring a good research plan and system of data collection. The specter of "fear" in quantitative research can be dispelled by understanding that the "scary parts" are really secondary to the process. Next, we looked at the qualitative family of methodologies. Whereas our quantitative system was developed around the idea of numbering the times that we study, we found that the qualitative system is based around building rich descriptions and immersing your readers in the research. We found that each quantitative tool was fitted for use in a particular situation, and if we used these tools properly that most of the work is already done for us. The third choice for tool kits was the theoretical approach. This approach, we found out, was both the pinnacle and the foundation of human knowledge. Each discovery that someone makes is the foundation for the next generation of researchers. Finally, we looked at the miscellaneous methods for writing papers. These papers are not academic papers, per se; however, they are useful tools that can help raise our personal brand and make our journey toward writing a paper easier and more convenient. Once we chose our methodology, then it was time to move on to the data collection.

Data collection is the actual exploration of our journey to write a paper. It is the data that truly draws the reader into the project. Many times, especially in college, authors simply dredge up the minimum number of sources for a project then start writing. This is akin to going to Yellowstone and looking at pictures of Old Faithful while inside the car or going to Brazil and reading a book about the Amazon. True research and true discovery relies on leaving no stone unturned and no question unanswered. As a researcher, you should be using every tool at your disposal (book research, observations, surveys, interviews, focus groups, oral history projects, and even newspapers and magazines) to ensure that your research is as in-depth as possible. This will allow you to provide rich data to your readers and draw them into your research project.

The final major section of this book is about style. After you have explored your topic of research, then it is time for you to guide others through what you have discovered. This means that you put a piece of yourself in everything that you write. Dry clinical reports are favored by some fields, but not (I think) by the readers. Readers want to be immersed in the research, they want to "see" what you have seen, "hear" what you have heard, "smell" what you have smelled, "feel" what you have touched, and "taste" what you have tasted. Even in qualitative research, your reader wants to be immersed in what you have discovered. We learned that by putting a little of your personal style into your work, you enable your readers to better understand what you have discovered and give them the vicarious experience of learning something anew.

Once you have written a paper, whether published or not, you have become an author. The next step is evolving to be a published author, then a multi-published author. During this process you must remember that you need to stay yourself as you write (or at least the character you create). The more you write, the more you will have people who follow your writing and expect each project to be in the same voice, the same tone, and the same personality. If you keep the "you" in each project you create, this process will be much easier. Every time you write you are taking a journey to discover something new and present it to the world of the academy, but you also take an internal journey and discover more about yourself. This can be the greatest reward of writing, so as you journey take the time to learn about yourself.

Christopher W. Smithmyer
2015

SAMPLE ETHNOGRAPHY OUTLINE

I.   Title Page
    a. Title
    b. Name
    c. University Affiliation
    d. Year
II.   Abstract
III. Introduction
    a. Hook
        i.   Observation can be a tricky skill to acquire.
        ii.   Fear can be increased by the fact you are doing an ethnography.
        iii. If you allow fear to rule you, it will hold you back.
        iv.   Fear kills legends.
        v.   Building a good study revolves around good observation skills.
    b. Reason for Study
        i.   This study is to show you a sample of an ethnography based on a 30-minute observation.
        ii.   This enables you to see what you should be doing.
        iii. Each step will be walked through for your benefit.
        iv.   Do not push yourself beyond your current skill level.
        v.   We are working together to build up your skill set.
    c. Reason Study Is Relevant
        i.   You are still learning writing skills.
        ii.   This study shows how the skills you have been taught the last two weeks can be used in a paper.
        iii. You should read this study to reinforce your skills.
        iv.   Building skill sets is a progressive process.
        v.   Starting at one point and working toward your goal will take you far.
        vi.   Football analogy and skills.
IV.   Method
    a. What Is Ethnography?
        i.   An ethnography is…
        ii.   There are different types of ethnographies.
        iii. Each has a specific use.
        iv.   The type we learned in class is…
        v.   This is the type of ethnography I chose.
    b. Why I Chose Ethnography
        i.   I chose ethnography because it was required by Dr. Smithmyer.
        ii.   That guy is awesome.
        iii. I think he may be a ninja.
    c. How I Did My Ethnography
        i.   For this ethnography I reviewed the guidelines from the class.

      ii.   Then I read the Fetterman and Emerson texts and some of the additional recommended reading.

     iii.   I found a location and chose a time for my study.

     iv.   I chose this location because...

      v.   When I got to the location I did...

     vi.   I did ... to code.

V. Data

  a. Sight

      i.   Room description (brief)

     ii.   Furniture

    iii.   People

    iv.   Events

  b. Hearing

      i.   Quiet room

     ii.   Girl coughing

    iii.   Earphone girl

    iv.   Sound of my typing

  c. Scent

      i.   Garbage cans

     ii.   Perfume

    iii.   Relatively sound free

  d. Feel

      i.   Couch

     ii.   Wall

    iii.   Temperature

  e. Feeling

      i.   Cave feel

     ii.   Cultural norms

    iii.   Ugly floors

    iv.   Sad girl

     v.   People seemed to be working

VI. Analysis (Theory General Marxism)/Broken Window Theory

  a. Sights Related to Class Conflict

      i.   Utilitarian space

     ii.   Utilitarian furniture

    iii.   Blues, whites, and grays seemed to be uniforms.

    iv.   Some seemed to buck trend (upper classes).

  b. Hearing Related to Class Conflict

      i.   No professors coughed.

     ii.   Poor students more susceptible to sickness

    iii.   Money protects

    iv.   Music as an opiate for the masses

  c. Scent Related to Class Conflict

        i.   Scent of dirty garbage in student area

       ii.   Perfume to cover up unwashed masses

     iii.   Poor students struggling by scent

  d.   Feeling Related to Class Conflict

        i.   The utilitarian feel builds the class conflict.

       ii.   Students used "shared" space.

     iii.   Faculty has "private" offices.

     iv.   Clear sign of conflict between classes.

  e.   Feeling of the Room and General Class Conflict

        i.   Faculty has higher status.

       ii.   Students are oppressed masses.

     iii.   Please tell me that if you are still reading this you are not buying into Marx's theory.

     iv.   No really, the guy was wrong.

      v.   Class conflict is bad viva le revolution (wait, his revolution was Russian).

VII.   Discussion

  a.   What My Findings Are

        i.   Students are oppressed.

       ii.   The faculty have an upper status.

     iii.   There is an overarching bureaucracy which is above the faculty.

     iv.   They have all the power.

      v.   Once again this is a sample paper, I do not believe this Marxist nonsense.

  b.   Why They Are Relevant

        i.   Class ethnographies are relevant because they teach you the status of different people in society.

       ii.   Ethnographies in this class are relevant because they are part of your grade.

     iii.   By doing this paper I have shown you

          1.   how ethnographies can be done.

          2.   and that an ethnography can be done in under the 1 hr 27 min time frame.

  c.   What Further Studies Can Be Completed?

        i.   Further research on this area could look at management and their relationship with students. (You guys are lucky to have a chancellor like Dr. Bechtal.)

       ii.   You could also look at the oppression of student loans on students.

     iii.   This can be related to indentured servitude or slavery since Congress took away your right to bankruptcy.

     iv.   This is actually an important topic.

VIII.   Works Cited

  a.   Cite Fetterman

  b.   Cite Emerson

  c.   Cite anyone else you used

appendix 1
Observational Field Notes
(Example)

The site that I selected for this example is the second floor sitting area at the Hawthorn Building, Penn State Altoona. I chose to do these observations between 3 PM and 3:30 PM on Wednesday January 21st, 2015. I selected this site because of the convenience and because it warrants me the opportunity to watch a number of people move through a relatively small space.

The space where I am sitting is a triangle space, the side of the room with the window, which looks out onto a small hill leading up to the reflecting pond, is longer than the other side of the room, which has a hallway leading to tech support and the stairway leading down to the first floor of the building. The furniture is sparse, common furniture for an academic setting. There is the couch, upon which I am sitting and an ottoman which I have taken to prop up my feel. To my back is a wall, which separates this space from the offices. To my right are two more chairs both of which are occupied by two persons, who I will describe later, typing away. Directly across from me is another chair, also occupied by a young woman typing on her cell phone. To my left are three tables, lined up along the window. Each of the tables has one person sitting at it, though there are three chairs at each table. The center table is higher than the others and is flanked by higher chairs. Along the wall opposite me are four blue recycling containers and a single brown trashcan. The only other furniture is a TV, which is turned off, and a wall mounted flyer unit with information on study abroad classes. That was weird the guy at one of the tables just took off his shirt and put it back on.

The physical aspects of the room are normal for a college building anywhere in the country. The ceiling is those white drop down tiles with recessed lighting. It gives the room the field of a cave that had the lighting added as an afterthought. Most of the light comes in through the window on

529

the long side of the room, which starts about 14 inches off of the floor and runs to the ceiling. The girl to my left is coughing, I hope she is not sick. Two types of tile adorn the floor, the mismatched style seems to play into the mid-2000's style that ugly flooring stimulates the minds of college students. I honestly wonder how many college students actual look at the floor. A woman just walked from the faculty offices directly across from me toward the tech support offices. From the way she was walking she seemed to be a professor. A man jus walked past walking the same way, either he has a feminine gate or the woman's gate was masculine, I can never tell in this PC culture we live in now which is more proper to say, so I will just say that they both walked the same.

There have been six other people in the room since I started typing. The young lady to my left who has been coughing since she arrived, she is sitting laid back at one of the smaller tables, she looks as if she is waiting for something since she has not taken out any extra work to do. I do not want to look to directly at people as it would not be good in this setting and may make people realize what I am doing. The man with the that walked through a few minutes again just walked past again, as did the woman who I compared his walk to. She has on ugg books, a white shirt that is boarder line in appropriate for a professor and black pants. At the second table along the window is sitting the guy who took his shirt off. He now has it back on again, He is within my field of vision and has close cropped black hair, a blue shirt (guy jst walked through with flattop hair and Penn state jacket), oh he is coming back out). Shirtless guy is also wearing grey nike sweatpants. (A girl just walked through, she looked very sad, she was wearing a black fleece jacket and bluejeans. She is about 5'7 with long curly black hair). Back to shirtless guy, he seems to be working quite diligently on something, I cannot see what it is, but he had pulled it out of his backpack. The girl at the end of the row of tables has penn state sweatpants on and a grey sweatshirt. She also has black hair. (the girl who was sitting to my right just got up and left, I thin she was reading my screen and notice that I was writing down information and did not want to be lampooned in an observational report. She is wearing a white shirt with a matching pull over hat and a boho haircut.) Back to the girl at the end of the row of tables. She also seems to be working on something, she is working at her laptop.

The girl in the chair directly across from me is still typing on her phone. She has earbuds in, I thought it was her with the loud music, but it was the boho girl that left. The girl directly across seems to be waiting for something, if I was doing interviews I would ask her. Now she has put her phone away and is staring off into space. The only other Person in the room is a young woman who appears to be Asian American, she is also working on her cell phone. She seems to be more involved with it. She is on the far end of my field of vision so I cant really describe her without staring at her. The other people in the room are different varieties of Caucasian. One seems to be from southern Europe the other seem to have central European features.

This is a half hour of notes, I did not even get to scents (one of the women has on strong perfume, rose based I think).

APPENDIX 1: OBSERVATIONAL FIELD NOTES (EXAMPLE)

The site that I selected for this example is the second floor sitting area at the Hawthorn Building, Penn State Altoona. I chose to do these observations between 3 PM and 3:30 PM on Wednesday January 21st, 2015. I selected this site because of the convenience and because it warrants me the opportunity to watch a number of people move through a relatively small space.

The space where I am sitting is a triangle space, the side of the room with the window, which looks out onto a small hill leading up to the reflecting pond, is longer than the other side of the room, which has a hallway leading to tech support and the stairway leading down to the first floor of the building. The furniture is sparse, common furniture for an academic setting. There is the couch, upon which I am sitting and an ottoman which I have taken to prop up my feet. To my back is a wall, which separates this space from the offices. To my right are two more chairs both of which are occupied by two persons, who I will describe later, typing away. Directly across from me is another chair, also occupied by a young woman typing on her cell phone. To my left are three tables, lined up along the window. Each of the tables has one person sitting at it, though there are three chairs at each table. The center table is higher than the others and is flanked by higher chairs. Along the wall opposite me are four blue recycling containers and a single brown trashcan. The only other furniture is a TV, which is turned off, and a wall mounted flyer unit with information on study abroad classes. That was weird the guy at one of the tables just took off his shirt and put it back on.

> **Chris_Smithmyer 7/9/2015 9:37 AM**
> **Comment [5]:** Later I remembered that her phone was pink.

> **Chris_Smithmyer 7/9/2015 9:37 AM**
> **Comment [6]:** I remember that when I walked past these smelled bad.

The physical aspects of the room are normal for a college building anywhere in the country. The ceiling is those white drop down tiles with recessed lighting. It gives the room the feel of a cave that had the lighting added as an afterthought. Most of the light comes in through the window on the long side of the room, which starts about 14 inches off of the floor and runs to the ceiling. The girl to my left is coughing, I hope she is not sick. Two types of tile adorn the floor, the mismatched style seems to play into the mid-2000's style that ugly flooring stimulates the minds of college students. I honestly wonder how many college students actual look at the floor. A woman just walked from the faculty offices directly across from me toward the tech support offices. From the way she was walking she seemed to be a professor. A man jus walked past walking the same way, either he has a feminine gate or the woman's gate was masculine, I can never tell in this PC culture we live in now which is more proper to say, so I will just say that they both walked the same.

> **Chris_Smithmyer 7/9/2015 9:37 AM**
> **Comment [7]:** This reminded me when I was on a tour of my law schools new location and they taught us about human psyche and decorations.

> **Chris_Smithmyer 7/9/2015 9:37 AM**
> **Comment [8]:** This is a note to show my state of mind at the time, realizing that you would be reading this I spoke about why I was writing this way.

There have been six other people in the room since I started typing. The young lady to my left who has been coughing since she arrived, she is sitting laid back at one of the smaller tables, she looks as if she is waiting for something since she has not taken out any extra work to do. I do not want to look to directly at people as it would not be good in this setting and may make people realize what I am doing. The man with the gate that walked through a few minutes again just walked past again, as did the woman who I compared his walk to. She has on ugg boots, a white shirt that is boarder line inappropriate for a professor and black pants. At the second table along the window is sitting the guy who took his shirt off. He

> **Chris_Smithmyer 7/9/2015 9:37 AM**
> **Comment [9]:** This is an assumption, you should note the difference between assumptions and facts.

CONTENTS

now has it back on again. He is within my field of vision and has close cropped black hair, a blue shirt (guy jst walked through with flattop hair and Penn state jacket), oh he is coming back out). Shirtless guy is also wearing grey nike sweatpants. (A girl just walked through, she looked very sad, she was wearing a black fleece jacket and bluejeans. She is about 5'7 with long curly black hair). Back to shirtless guy, he seems to be working quite diligently on something, I cannot see what it is, but he had pulled it out of his backpack. The girl at the end of the row of tables has penn state sweatpants on and a grey sweatshirt. She also has black hair. (the girl who was sitting to my right just got up and left, I thin she was reading my screen and notice that I was writing down information and did not want to be lampooned in an observational report. She is wearing a white shirt with a matching pull over hat and a boho haircut.) Back to the girl at the end of the row of tables. She also seems to be working on something, she is working at her laptop.

The girl in the chair directly across from me is still typing on her phone. She has earbuds in, I thought it was her with the loud music, but it was the boho girl that left. The girl directly across seems to be waiting for something, if I was doing interviews I would ask her. Now she has put her phone away and is staring off into space. The only other Person in the room is a young Asian woman, she is also working on her cell phone. She seems to be more involved with it. She is on the far end of my field of vision so I cant really describe her without staring at her. The other people in the room are different varieties of Caucasian. One seems to be from southern Europe the other seem to have central European features.

This is a half hour of notes, I did not even get to scents (one of the women has on strong perfume, rose based I think).

Chris_Smithmyer 7/9/2015 9:37 AM
Comment [10]: I put some assumptions with feelings to because it was a feeling.

Chris_Smithmyer 7/9/2015 9:37 AM
Comment [11]: My observation in this instance was mainly visual as there was not a lot of other senses I was using.

Chris_Smithmyer 7/9/2015 9:37 AM
Comment [12]: Another assumption based on stimuli.

Chris_Smithmyer 7/9/2015 9:37 AM
Comment [13]: I remembered here that it was not very warm here.

SO YOU WANT TO WRITE A PAPER

glossary

ABA Bluebook—Common style of legal citation.

Abstract—An academic summary of the contents of a paper or article that gives a researcher ample information about what the article contains to determine whether the article may or may not be useful in the research.

Abstract Search—The process of using a library database to look through abstracts that meet the requirements of your bullion search.

Academic Bias—The belief that only theories and hypotheses discovered or supported in an academic setting are of any use to a given field.

Academic Chauvinism—Mindset of believing that your academic discipline has the only valid theories and skills.

Academic Discipline—The overarching discipline of your major or department (e.g., political science is a subset of the social sciences).

Accurate Data—Data that is truthful at the time that it is collected and is not tainted with excessive bias. Accurate data should also be as specific as possible to identify the minutia of the subject covered.

APA, American Psychological Association—The creator of one of the most common citation styles.

Appeal—Asking a court to overturn a lower court's ruling.

Appellate Brief—A concise written argument used for appeals that presents the relevant law and cases to a specific issue in a manner that allows a judge to make a ruling on that matter.

Area of Concept—Your disciplinary breakdown of your general concept. Ideally your area of writing will bring the macro-level concept into something that is related to your academic discipline.

Argumentative Research—Research that presents an argument.

Assimilating Data—The process of internalizing data, either within oneself or within a project.

Assistant—Someone you direct on what research needs to be done.

Associate—A co-equal researcher on a project who acknowledges that you are the leader of the group.

Audit Trail—A collection of notes demarcating the procedures that a researcher has used during the development and implementation of a research project.

Average—A catch-all term that can be used to describe the mean, the mode, or the median of a number set.

Bar Graph—A graphical representation of data that demonstrates the value of a specific group with a bar.

Basic Theory—The concept level theory that you choose to be the core theoretical lens for your paper.

Bell-Shaped Curve—A graphical representation of the normal distribution of data within a dataset.

Blackhat—A person who is the bad guy in an article, news report, or other form of media, or a researcher who has earned the scorn of his or her peers. This term comes from the idea that all cowboys with black hats in the spaghetti westerns were bad guys.

Book Research—The process of using books as a library resource to build a dataset or pre-research and area that you intend to study.

Brief—A concise document that explains the basic elements of a case, whether for your personal use, your firm's use, general court, or appeals court.

Business Paper—Any paper that is related to a business, whether an academic paper or a company record.

Case—A specific instance or legal matter that is being researched.

Case Brief—A brief that allows a lawyer, intern, or paralegal to give someone the details of a specific case in a single-page document that allows the recipient of the brief to understand the legal issues used and established in that case.

Case Report—A report the focuses on a specific case.

Case Study—An academic approach to analyzing a specific case with an eye to support or disprove a hypothesis.

Case Study, Collective—A case study that uses the work of multiple authors to show the differences between given cases in an effort to support or discredit a hypothesis or hypotheses.

Case Study, Comparative—A case study that looks at two specific topics and compares them to support or discredit a hypothesis.

Case Study, Corrective—A case study that is done to prove another representation wrong in order to correct the historical record.

Case Study, Explanative—A case study that is used to explain a given situation in an effort to support a hypotheses.

Case Study, Exploratory—A case study designed to seek out information about a given hypotheses without knowing specifically what you will find.

Case Study, Historical—A case study that looks at data from a past time to support a valid hypothesis about the data.

Case Study, Intrinsic—A case study where the main focus of the case is the matter of the case itself.

Case Study, Multiple—A case study that looks at multiple hypotheses to show a comparison or contrast between them.

Causal Relationship—A relationship between two things, where one causes the other.

Chart—A set of rows and columns that places information into an easily understandable array.

Chicago Style Citation—Common style of citation in anthropology and some social sciences.

Chronological/Narrative Writing—This style of writing allows the author to "tell a story" and allows the events to flow in a chronological order that the reader can follow.

Closed-Ended Questions (Closed Questions) —A question that has a finite number of answers that the respondent can give and the responses are known by the researcher.

Coding—The process of organizing data so it is easily accessible for analysis.

Concept—A macro-level idea, a basic starting point for your creation of a literary project.

Conflict of Interest—A time when your professional judgment may be affected by a previous relationship with a subject.

Continuous Random Variable—A variable where the value may fall anywhere within an infinite spectrum.

Correlation—A positive or negative relationship between two topics.

Court Brief—A type of case brief that is submitted to a court for an appeal or a motion.

Cross-Referencing—The process of linking one point of data to another or one subject to another. This process can be effective in research projects that go between academic disciplines.

Culture—Big "C" culture is the arts, crafts, and relics of a society that they leave behind.
Small "c" culture is the non-measurable elements of a society on the aggregate, such as traditions, mores, opinions, and rituals.

Data Archive—*See* Data Pool.

Data Flooding—The process of presenting excessive volumes of data on a given subject to cover up a lack of data on another subject within the same paper.

Data Pool—The entirety of data that is collected for a research project.

Data, Visual—Data that is displayed in a method other than text (graphs, pictures, video).

Datum—A single unit of data, the singular of data.

Dependent Variable—The variable in an experiment that is changed by the independent variable.

Descriptive Grammar—Text where the author uses multiple adjectives to provide as detailed a description of a subject as possible. The description should include factors of sight, smell, touch, taste, sound, and "feeling."

Descriptive Methodology—Any methodology that has descriptive methods as its primary data collection methods.

Descriptive Statistics—The family of statistics that is designed to describe a given population.

Digital Timestamp—The temporal boundaries that an author sets for his or her project. These boundaries act as markers for where the primary research should fall. Having good temporal boundaries will help keep the project from becoming too large and unwieldy.

Direct Question—A question that asks a respondent for specific information but does not suggest an answer; this definition comes from the legal concept of direct questioning where you allow your witnesses to answer without telling them the answer.

Dirty Writing—Writing that does not follow basic grammatical rules or is not following a methodological process.

Discipline—The academic grouping in which a writer finds a home or associates.

Discipline, Writing—*See* Writing, Discipline.

Discrete Random Variable—A variable that has a finite number of values that can be given specific probabilities of occurring.

Dot-Plot—A graphical representation of data where each point of data appears as a dot on the graph.

Dumb Bullion Search—The process of entering search terms into a search engine with no procedural modifiers.

Element of Area—Your element of area is a theoretical breakdown of your area of concept. Ideally, your area of concept will take the disciplinary meaning of your conceptual macro-level concept and apply a disciplinary theory to area.

Emic—A position that is from within a group.

Epoche—The process of identifying pre-judgments that can affect research and guarding against negative effects throughout the writing process.

Established Theory—Any theory that is widely held throughout a given discipline.

Estimation—A rough calculation of a number, a value, a quantity, or the outcome of an event.

Ethnography—A type of research methodology, depending heavily on observation, where a researcher attempts to support or disprove a hypothesis based on the understanding of a group, phenomenon, or situation. Ethnographies can be either etic or emic.

Etic—Research from outside of a given group.

Exploratory Research—Research where you have no idea what you will find; research where the hypothesis is that something is out there waiting to be discovered.

External Data—Data that is not directly related to your case.

Field Excursions—Any trip that you leave your office or home to go to a site for research.

Field Notes—The process of writing down data in short "notes" that allow you to write down a more detailed account when you are in a private setting where it will not disrupt your research subject(s).

Field Research—Any research that is conducted outside of your home office or the library. (Caveat: Field research could be carried out in your home, office, or library if you are collecting interactive data in one of these setting or on the internet.)

Flashpoint, Phenomenon—An event or series of events that an outside person thinks of when a phenomenon is mentioned

Fluff Research—Any research that has no or limited scientific value that focuses on human interest pieces and is designed just to gain attention.

Focus Groups—Groups that give researchers access to data by conducting group interviews and looking at how the group manifests itself as an intellectual unit in relation to one another and in relation to the topic of the group.

Follow-up Question—A question that is asked after a speaker has given a statement that is used to clarify the content of the speaker's original statement (type of reflective listening).

Forecasting—The process of using predictive/inferential statistics to predict a future event.

Foundational Hypothesis—Core hypothesis within a theory, if the foundational hypothesis is discredited then the theory is unable to stand.

Freedom of Information Act—A U.S. law that entitles the people of the United States to any data that has not been classified for a just reason.

Freedom of Information Request—A request for data under the Freedom of Information Act that allows the requestor access to government information that was previously unavailable.

Gaps in Literature—Any area of a discipline that has not been studied yet, or points of interest within a subject that have not been explored.

Gatekeeper—Any person who controls whether a paper is published or not.

Gatekeeper Class—An academic class that is designed to test students to see if they are ready to move on to a higher level.

General Data—Data that is collected but has not been sorted to find the relevant data for the project.

General Theory—Overarching theories that cover data that is used in multiple disciplines.

Gist—A concise document that informs someone in a leadership position of the details of a specific case in as brief of a document as possible.

Grant—A set amount of funds that are given to a researcher to complete a project; grants cover the costs of the project, time spent, and equipment needed.

Grant Writing—The process of applying for grants for your project.

Grey Hat—A person who moves back and forth between being a good researcher and a poor researcher. Grey hats tend to pursue personal glory rather than the academic process. The name comes from spaghetti westerns where a person in a grey hat was not a bad guy but could not be trusted.

Grounded Theory—A systematic testing of multiple hypotheses for the purpose of showing an interwoven web of data and hypotheses that support a perspective that is broader than any single hypothesis can support on its own.

Group Formation (External)—When a group identity is imposed on a group from an outside source.

Group Formation (Internal Active)—When a group actively attempts to create a group image for itself by a set of predetermined actions.

Group Formation (Internal Inactive)—When individuals, through traditions, mores, and societal norms, begin to form a group without the active intent to form a group.

Group Lived Experience (GLE)—The experience of a subject within a group that he/she relates to and self-identifies with.

Hard Science—The STEM fields such as math, natural sciences, physical sciences, biology, etc.

Heterogeneous Population—Any population where the members are all the same in relation to a specific variable.

High Context Cultures—A relativistic myth where non-western cultures have greater implied meaning in actions. This myth is created by the lack of epoche for researchers who fail to notice the context that is in actions within their own cultures.

Historogram—A representation of a frequency distribution by means of rectangles whose widths represent class intervals and whose areas are proportional to the corresponding frequencies (Webster).

Homogeneous Population—Any population where the members are different based on a specific variable.

Hybrid Paper—Any paper that mixes two or more methodologies to meet the needs of a given project.

Hypothesis—An assertion that you will try to support or disprove during the course of your research.

Idea (of Element) —A further breakdown of the Element of Area; in your idea you are looking for a part of the element that you can test through a methodological process to support or disprove part of the theory that you have selected.

Independent Variable—The variable in an experiment that is "varied' or changed by the researcher.

Indirect Questions—A question style to be avoided where the person being interviewed or the person who is being surveyed does not understand the point of the question.

Individual Lived Experience (ILE)—The experience of a given subject from his or her perspective without a contextual element beyond the subject's own rationale.

Inferential Statistics—*See* Predictive Statistics.

Infinity Trap—The process of allowing the boundaries of your project to expand to the point that the project is unwieldy and difficult to complete.

Informational Argument—An argument presented on a set of facts that establishes the point being made.

Information Posting—The process of putting up flyers or an announcement on social media that an experiment/project needs participants.

Institutional Review Board (IRB)—An academic body that determines the ethical suitability of a specific study to be done under the university's auspices.

Intent of Meaning—What we are trying to confer when we speak to another person.

Intermediary Topic—A topic that is required to build the foundation of the main topic that a researcher wishes to investigate.

Interrogatories—A set of questions sent out by an attorney to request data, similar to a legal survey.

Interviews—The process of asking questions about/discussing a matter with an individual or group to derive information about a specific event or phenomenon.

Interviews, Group—Allow a researcher to gain the collective understanding of a situation from a group. This differs from focus groups because the interviewed people do not have the opportunity to discuss their answers.

Journal—An academic publication, often peer reviewed, where authors can publish new work on a given subject. Most journals are topic specific.

Journal, Online—A journal that exists primarily in a digital state.

Journal, Print—A journal that is mostly created for a hard copy, but may also have a digital presence.

Language—The social consensus of what words mean as they are used.

Law—A theory which there is no known way that it can be disproved.

Leading Question—A question where you imply the answer that you are looking for in the delivery of the question. This is a common legal term from cross-examinations where the lawyer "leads" the hostile witness to the answer he or she desires.

Legal Journal—The law field's version of an academic journal.

Lens—The theoretical paradigm that you are viewing an event/topic through.

Lived Experiences—The experience that someone who lived through an event or phenomenon has as a memory of it.

Longitudinal Study—A study that takes place over a period of time watching the development of a subject.

Loose Methodologies—A researcher who is practicing loose methodologies when he or she pulls aspects from several different types of research methodology but does not take the time to set the parameters of a hybrid methodology.

Low Context Cultures—A relativistic myth where western cultures have less implied meaning in actions. This myth is created by the lack of epoche for researchers who fail to notice the context that is in actions within their own cultures.

Low Hanging Fruit—Data that is easy to acquire.

Macro-Disciplines—Fields such as Social Sciences which cover multiple disciplines (Conflict, Political Science, Sociology, Criminology, Criminal Justice, Psychology etc.).

Macro-Level Theories—Theories that affect an entire population or subject.

Margin of Error—The amount of variance in your confidence about an answer.

Mean—The numerical representation of the sum of the numbers in a dataset being divided by the number of numbers in a dataset.

Median—If all numbers in the dataset are lined up in ascending value, the median is the lowest number that no less than half of are not greater than, including itself.

Meta-Study—A report on a given topic using the collective work of many authors as sources.

Meta-Summary—A report that summarizes a topic using the collective work of many authors as sources.

Meta-Synthesis—An academic paper that takes the collective work of multiple authors and uses that work as data to prove a new and unique hypothesis.

Meso-Level Theories—Theories that cover a large portion of a population or subject but do not cover the entire thing.

Micro-Level Theories—Theories that deal with a specific event or subject, looking at why, where, when, and how it will happen (or any mix of these).

MLA, Modern Language Association—Common citation style in the arts and humanities.

Mode—The most common number in a dataset.

Multi-Point Saturation—A measurement that not only looks to see that you have reached a saturation point in your research on all relevant hypotheses but also requires that you seek a level of saturation on the interconnected nature of the data.

Narrative Writing—*See* Chronological/Narrative Writing.

Narrow to Wide Writing Style—In this style the author starts with a very narrow aspect of a topic and builds upon the data to widen the scope of the project. This can be effective when you are studying an event with an epicenter, then explaining the conditions that led up to this event.

Negative Correlation—A situation where the relationship between subjects is that as one increases the other decreases or vice versa.

Networking Authors—The process of linking authors in a given subject area together.

Neutral Voice—A writing voice where the author does not put additional emphasis on any of the data, allowing readers to reach their own conclusion.

Newness—The distinct elements of your research concept, area, element, or topic that separates it from others in the field. A topic must be new to contribute to the academic knowledge on the subject.

Noema—The physical object that is the focal point of a thought, judgment, or perception.

Noesis—The exercise of reason as a function of the intellect.

Non-profit Grant—A grant that is funded by a non-profit agency and is given out by that agency.

Note, Legal—A legal article written by a law student.

Note, Observational—A jotting of data that you use to remember rich data for your analysis later. Notes are used not to disrupt the integrity of the investigational scene.

Null Correlation—When there is no active relationship between two topics.

Null Hypothesis—The inverse of your hypothesis, you will try to disprove the null hypothesis to add credibility to your hypothesis.

Objective Data—Data that is void of subjective elements; data that is measured without subjective leeway.

Off the Record—An interview where you receive information from your source, but you can only use that data to find other data sources and you are not permitted to use your source's name or position in your project.

On the Record—An interview where you are allowed to use the name and position of the subjects in your report and the data that they provide can be attributed to them.

Open-Ended Question (Open Question)—A question where the respondent has the opportunity to answer the question and explain the answer.

Oral History Project—A collection of lived experiences related by those who lived them for the purpose of collecting a historical archive.

Outline—A bullet pointed and nested document that acts as a roadmap when you are researching/ writing your project.

Outlier—An event that falls outside the normal distribution of data in your dataset.

Percentile—A relationship between one subject and other subjects in a dataset noting where the primary subject falls as a representation of the percentage that the primary subject is rated higher than.

Personal Brand—The quality of work that people expect from a document with your name on it. Good research will improve your personal brand and poor research can severely weaken it.

Persuasive Argument—An argument based on facts supporting your position, but with room for another opinion to the point that the reader must be persuaded to accept your position.

Phenomenology—The reporting of the lived experiences of an individual or group who shared an experience or common experience of a phenomenon.

Phenomenology, Constitutive— A type of phenomenology that "suspends pregiven status of conscious life as something that exists in the world and is performed in order to secure the ultimate intersubjective grounding for the world and the positive sciences…" (see Citation in text, Chapter 21).

Phenomenology, Existential—A type of phenomenology that strives to go beyond the physical realities of the world and examines the meta-physical and existential elements of culture and society.

Phenomenology, Generative—A type of phenomenology that looks at the new developments within a given society based around a specific event or phenomenon that changed the way the people lived or perceived the world around them.

Phenomenology, Genetic (Auto)—An autobiographical methodology for looking at something that has occurred in your life or something that has occurred in your culture that has changed the way that you view the world.

Phenomenology, Hermeneutical—A type of phenomenology that looks at the world as you would if you were the reflection in the mirror; your reality is not important, only the reality of those on the other side of the looking glass.

Phenomenology, Naturalistic—A type of phenomenology that looks at how natural events and phenomenon are perceived in nature, assuming that the phenomenon and the consciousness of the phenomenon are part of the natural setting.

Phenomenology, Realistic—A type of phenomenology that approaches a research project looking for information that crosses cultural and sociological boundaries and is common within all human socioeconomic groups.

Phenomenology, Transcendental—A philosophical type of phenomenology that looks at events in the world without the constricting influence of morality or reason.

Population—A group of subjects, whether human, animal, or inanimate, that you are trying to discern information about through a representative sample.

Positive Correlation—A relationship where if one variable increases, the other variable(s) also increase.

Postulate—A suggestion or assumption about the existence of the truth, fact, or basis used as a framework for reasoning, discussion, or belief.

Pre-formed Categorization Technique—Something that has been created by scholars before you.

Predicting—The process of generating an educated guess based on previous data and current stimuli.

Predictive Statistics—Statistics that attempt to discern a future event based on patterns of past events and current variables that affect the event.

Principle Research—Primary research for a project.

Private Grant—A grant funded by a corporation and given out by the corporation or a private trust.

Probability—The likelihood that an event will occur within a given parameter as classified as a percentile number between 0 and 1.

Public Grant—A grant paid for by taxpayer money and given out by the government.

Pursekeeper—Any person who controls whether or not money is given to a project.

Qualitative Meta-Synthesis—The methodological approach of collecting rich data from published works to apply that data to a new hypothesis.

Qualitative Research—Research that is based on thick description and an understanding that goes beyond the information that can be provided by numbers. The qualitative family of research is generally not transferable to other populations but provides a very in-depth analysis of the research subjects.

Quantitative Data—Data that is based on numbers; data that is able to be quantified.

Quantitative Research—Research that is based on quantitative data.

Quartile—Similar to a percentile, but tells the primary subjects what quarter of the percentile they are in.

Quotes, Air—The process of putting objects in quotes, without citation, that are to appear to the reader to be sarcastic or sardonic.

Quotes, Ethnographic—Passages of conversation that are taken verbatim the way that they were said by the original speaker.

Radar Graph—A graph where the lines extending from the center represent variables and the bisecting lines represent values for those variables.

Random Numbers—Numbers that are generated with no pattern or rationale to allow for samples to be taken without bias; this is one method to randomize a survey.

Random Sampling—The process of selecting a sample from a population using some method of randomization.

Recognized Source—A source that is accepted by a given field.

Recursive Frame Analysis (RFA)—The process of breaking data down into contextual elements to be coded, topically and thematically, through a process based on a museum analogy. Data is coded contextually (frames), topically (galleries), thematically (wings), then topically again (museums). This process was designed by Chenail and Keeney.

Reflective Listening—The process of rewording and repeating parts of a conversation to allow the other speakers to know that you are listening to what they say.

Regression Models—Charts that allow a researcher to make a prediction based on historic data that has been measured for regression.

Regression, Statistical—A method of estimating the relationship between variables.

Relative Difference—The difference in data that is collected based on the relative observations of different researchers; this is a "soft" researcher error.

Relative Experience—The difference in experience during data collection experienced by different researchers; this can lead to relative differences in the data and "soft" researcher error.

Reliability—The ability of a finding to be repeated if the researcher puts the same data through the same analytical model.

Reliable Data—*See* Reliability.

Report—A collection of data without a major synthesis that proves or disproves a hypothesis.

Representative Sample—A portion of the population that accurately represents the larger population.

Research Trail—A process of keeping a record of your research so that others can follow your research to test reliability.

Reviewer—Any person who reviews your project for content, data, or typographical content.

Rich Data—Data that contains details and relevant data on all five senses or any other subject salient to the research project.

Ripe Subject—A subject that is ready to be a researcher. For example: The psychological effects of a volcano erupting on a village that sites on the edge of the volcano would not be a ripe subject until the volcano erupted, as the effects would not exist until such a time.

Sample—Any group within a population that is less than the entire group, of which you want to use the portion of the group to support or disprove your hypothesis.

Saturation—Researching a subject until the data you are newly collecting is redundant to the data you have already collected.

Second Harvest—In research the practice of collecting data from existing reports to use in a new report. This is based in the primitive practice of searching through waste to find undigested foods that can be reassimilated into the food chain.

Secondary source—A source other than a primary source where the data has already been sorted and analyzed.

Shepardizing—The process of checking to make sure that all of the rules and issues in a case you are citing are still valid in the courts in which they were ruled upon..

Sign Posts—A writing tool to let your reader know where you are going in your paper. The most common of these are transitions and section headings.

Skewing—When data is more heavily situated toward one end of a graph. One can also skew data by targeting specific answers.

Specific Data—An applied point of data relevant to your project.

Specific Topic—A topical idea in the area that has not been researched previously.

Spurious Correlation—A correlation that seems to be valid but actually correlates two dependent variables when the independent variable is a mystery.

Standing in the Mall—A phrase that indicates you are going to a location and giving surveys to random people as they walk past, hoping that enough people will fill out your survey to give you a decent sample size.

Statistical Surveying—A process of sampling a random part of a population with a survey instrument to collect quantitative data.

Subjective Data—Data that is open to interpretation; non-objective data.

Successful Readership—Readership who understands what you are writing about.

Supportive Research—Projects are designed to support an already accepted theory with more modern data.

Surrebuttal—A rebuttal to a rebuttal.

Survey—A limited amount of interviews, conducted by using written questions.

Survey Medium—The tool that you use to complete a survey.

Tangents—A line of inquiry that is not directly related to the main subject that is being researched.

Temporal Bigotry—Assessing cultures from the past by the same moral standard that we use today, or assessing one group of people from the past by our modern moral standards but excusing another culture because they are not from the same subset.

Temporal Nostalgia—Remembering the past as the "good old days."

Temporal Tangents—A line of data that is related to the main topic but is chronologically out of order for the flow of the paper.

Term Paper—A paper written as a requirement for a class to show the professor or lecturer that you know the material that was presented.

Thematic Cluster—A grouping of data that has the same theme.

Thematic Coding—Coding data based on a perceived theme.

Theory—An unproven axiom or a collection of hypotheses that have yet to be disproved. Theories are the base element of the academic process.

Time Jumps—Events that occur when authors move from one point in the story to another in a different time frame without filling in why they are moving to a different time frame.

Timeframe—A specific segment of time clearly defined with a starting point and an endpoint.

Timestamp—A specific moment in time that is documented so the reader can find that time.

Topic (Part of Idea)—The micro-level application of your idea to the element when viewed in regard to the methodology that you are going to use. The topic is the final stage before you break your concept into a hypothesis or new theory.

Topical Cluster—A grouping of data that has the same topic.

Topical Coding—Coding data based on a perceived topic.

Trade Journals—Professional journals in any given field, generally reviewed by an editor as a lesser form of peer review.

Trends—Periods where data seems to flow in the same direction.

Triangulation—The process of looking for complementary data from different sources that confirms (or sometimes denies) information gained in the primary research source.

Truthful Data—Data that is true.

Unripe Idea—An idea that is not ready to be proven yet, something where the data is not yet "ripe" to be examined.

Valid Data—*See* Validity

Validity—The relationship between the methodologies used by researchers and the scientific or research method used in the collection and analysis of data.

Variance—Simply how far numbers tend to spread out in a dataset or study.

Vivid Descriptions—*See* Descriptive Grammar.

Voice—The way that a paper is written, generally refers to first person, second person, or third person.

White Hat—A good researcher who follows the proper procedures and attempts to protect the integrity of the academic research process. The name comes from spaghetti westerns where all the good guys wore white cowboy hats.

White Pages—A business paper, published by a company or group of companies, that provides a semi-academic explanation of a new product, structure, or idea that is being introduced onto the market to entice investors or buyers.

Wide to Narrow Writing—When an author starts with a larger topic then slowly reduces the topic down to a more manageable subject of discourse.

Writing Discipline—The type of writing the author is striving for (i.e., fiction, non-fiction, informative, descriptive, exploratory).

Yale Bluebook—*See* ABA Bluebook.

CPSIA information can be obtained
at www.ICGtesting.com
Printed in the USA
LVOW02s1140201115

462839LV00002B/13/P